SECOND CANADIAN EDITION

Building Interpersonal

messages

Communication Skills

SECOND CANADIAN EDITION

Building Interpersonal

messages

Communication Skills

JOSEPH A. DEVITO
*Hunter College of the
City University of New York*

RENA SHIMONI
Bow Valley College

DAWNE CLARK
Mount Royal College

PEARSON

Toronto

National Library of Canada Cataloguing in Publication

DeVito, Joseph A., 1938–
    Messages : building interpersonal communication skills / Joseph A. DeVito, Rena Shimoni,
Dawne E. Clark. — 2nd Canadian ed.

Includes bibliographical references and index.
ISBN 0-205-42676-X

1. Interpersonal communication. I. Shimoni, Rena, 1948- II. Clark, Dawne, 1952– III. Title.

BF637.C45D48 2005   158.2   C2004-900975-3

Vice-President, Editorial Director: Michael J. Young
Executive Editor: Dave Ward
Marketing Manager: Toivo Pajo
Supervising Developmental Editor: Suzanne Schaan
Production Editor: Charlotte Morrison-Reed
Copy Editor: Karen Alliston
Proofreader: Deborah Viets
Production Manager: Wendy Moran
Page Layout: Carolyn E. Sebestyen
Photo and Permissions Research: Terri Rothman
Art Director: Mary Opper
Cover and Interior Design: Gail Ferreira Ng-A-kien
Cover photograph: Romilly Lockyer/Getty Images

Statistics Canada information is used with the permission of the Minister of Industry, as Minister responsible
for Statistics Canada. Information on the availability of the wide range of data from Statistics Canada can be
obtained from Statistics Canada's Regional Offices, its World Wide Web site at http://www.statcan.ca, and its
toll-free access number 1-800-263-1136.

2 3 4 5   09 08 07 06 05

Printed and bound in the United States of America.

BRIEF *Contents*

TABLE OF *Contents*

SPECIALIZED Contents

Preface

This book was written in response to the need for a text that emphasizes **critical thinking** by integrating it into all aspects of interpersonal communication, encourages the development of **interpersonal skills** (the practical skills for personal, social, and professional success), explains the influence of **culture and gender** on just about every aspect of interpersonal communication, and stresses **listening** as an essential (but too often neglected) part of interpersonal communication.

Messages answers these needs by providing thorough coverage of each of these major elements. Chapter 1 discusses critical thinking, interpersonal skills, culture and gender, and listening as integral components of interpersonal competence. Material presented throughout the book reinforces this discussion and creates a foundation for students to understand these concepts and then apply what they have learned through real-life examples and exercises.

This edition of *Messages* also responds to the specific needs of Canadian students. Although there are many similarities between Canadians and Americans, there are also clear demographic differences in our countries that affect communication. Canada is a bilingual country with two first languages: French and English. Canada's multicultural policies are different than those of the United States. But sometimes, Canadian students just want to see themselves as an entity in their own right, not as an adjunct to the United States. They want to see their flag, their heroes, and their scenery depicted on the pages of the textbooks they read. They want to feel "at home" as they enter a book, and not as a guest in another country.

Therefore, we have included Canadian examples, told Canadian stories, and where possible, quoted Canadian research. Our students need to be aware of the fact that Canadians haven't been as prolific in communication research. If they want more Canadian research, we encourage them to go on to graduate studies, and add more original Canadian research to the existing knowledge bank.

New to This Edition

In addition to the changes noted above, numerous improvements were made throughout the text. Here are some of the major changes.

Ethics is now a major component of the text. Talking Ethics boxes in each chapter call attention to the ethical dimensions of topics considered throughout the text.

Chapter 3, "Interpersonal Perception," has been reconstructed. It now presents the process of perception in five stages so as to incorporate new insights into the ways in which perceptions are organized—by rules, by schemata, and by scripts.

Chapter 10, "Interpersonal Communication and Relationships," has been restructured in this edition to emphasize the types of relationships. The chapter gives prominence to the various kinds of relationships—friendship, romantic ties (including workplace romances), and family—and offers a new conceptualization of ways to improve relationship communication. The material on theories of relationships has been incorporated not only into the text discussion but also into the interactive photo captions.

Practical skills of interpersonal communication continue to be emphasized in this as in all previous editions. Here, however, the application of these skills to the workplace is a special feature. This is seen in the text discussion; in the Skills Toolbox discussions, which are all workplace focused; and in the reprinted articles, all of which highlight work-related applications of interpersonal skills.

New Skill Building Exercises are included at the ends of the chapters. These new exercises deal with giving effective feedback, judging the appropriate time for self-disclosure, analyzing perceptual differences, making decisions about active listening, identifying "must lie" situations, understanding facial expressions, giving emotional advice, opening and closing conversations, analyzing the sources of your cultural beliefs, giving relationship repair advice, and empowering others.

The reprinted articles, all of which focus on interpersonal communication in the workplace, include many that are new to this edition. These new articles deal with topics such as telephone communication, reducing reticence among patients, using vocal qualities to communicate on the job, talking to people with disabilities, how to fight fair, and ways to develop effective working relationships.

Themes

This edition contains a number of themes that highlight the skills of interpersonal communication and that—taken together—define the unique perspective of this text:

- an emphasis on **skill building,** with guidelines and experiences to help students master crucial skills and an emphasis on these skills as they operate in the workplace

- an integration of **listening** skills with the various topics of interpersonal communication

- a consideration of **critical thinking** principles and techniques to help students think more logically about interpersonal communication (or about anything else)

- an emphasis on **culture** and cultural sensitivity as it influences all forms of interpersonal interaction

- a focus on **ethical issues** as they relate to a wide range of interpersonal communication situations

- **power and empowerment** skills for increasing interpersonal effectiveness

- an **interactive presentation** to make learning about interpersonal communication more exciting and more personal

Skill Building

This text emphasizes the development of **interpersonal communication skills** such as accuracy in interpersonal perception, the use of active listening skills, and constructive approaches to interpersonal conflict. These skills are written into the text discussions and appear in all chapters.

In addition, each chapter contains **Skill Building Exercises** that apply the material in the chapter to specific situations. Some of these exercises are designed to increase awareness of the ways in which interpersonal communication actually works so that messages will be more effective. These "awareness" exercises include those focusing on the role of ethics in interpersonal communication, explaining interpersonal difficulties, exploring the sources of cultural beliefs, and analyzing the listening behaviours of men and women.

Other exercises are more clearly in the nature of practice experiences aimed at increasing the ability to formulate more effective messages. These exercises focus on skills such as using performance visualization to reduce apprehension, paraphrasing to ensure understanding, formulating excuses, confronting intercultural difficulties, and generating win–win solutions in interpersonal conflict.

New to this edition is an emphasis on **workplace interpersonal skills**. Although this is not a textbook on business communication, the role of interpersonal communication in the workplace is highlighted in two ways in this edition. First, reprinted articles (one per chapter) provide a different perspective on the skills of interpersonal communication in the workplace. Topics include telephone communication in the workplace, the fear patients have when communicating with physicians, listening on the job, expressing emotion in the workplace, and how health care workers can more effectively talk to people with disabilities. As you can see from this abbreviated list, the skills will prove useful in a wide variety of interpersonal communication situations and are certainly not limited to the workplace. But the workplace context gives the presentation of skills a concreteness and a specificity that will help you understand and apply those skills in any situation. A complete list of these articles appears in the Specialized Contents on page xiv.

Second, a series of **Skills Toolboxes** (one per chapter) are presented throughout the text. These boxes identify a specific skill relevant to the chapter and apply it to the workplace, for example, "6 Ways to Empower Apprehensives in the Workplace," "4 Ways to Network Effectively," "5 Ways to Deal with Workplace Complaints," and "7 Ways to Effective Intercultural Communication." Again, the intention here is not to limit the skill's application to the workplace but to give it a specific context. For example, the ways to empower apprehensives at work are the same techniques that could be used for empowering apprehensives in the classroom or at social gatherings; the same techniques used to deal with workplace complaints can be applied to complaints among friends, lovers, and family members. Each of these Toolboxes ends with a section entitled "Then and Now" that asks students to recall a previous situation and the way they communicated in it and to consider how they would communicate in that same situation now, ideally on the basis of the insights in the chapter and in the Skills Toolbox. A complete list of these Skills Toolboxes appears in the Specialized Contents on page xiv.

Listening

This edition covers listening in two ways. First, Chapter 4 focuses exclusively on listening: It covers the listening process from receiving to responding, examines the role of culture and gender in listening, and provides guidelines for increasing listening effectiveness.

In addition, each chapter includes a **Listen to This** box. These boxes discuss listening skills as they relate to the chapter content—for example, listening to gender differences is presented in the chapter on verbal messages (Chapter 5); listening to the emotions of others is presented in the chapter on emotions (Chapter 7); and sexist, heterosexist, and racist listening is presented in the chapter on culture (Chapter 9). In this way, students can appreciate listening as a fundamental skill that is crucial at each stage in the interpersonal communication experience and in all interpersonal contexts. At the end of each Listen to This box is a case for analysis that asks students to offer listening suggestions in a variety of situations. A complete list of these boxes is given in the Specialized Contents on page xiii.

Critical Thinking

Messages emphasizes critical thinking (thinking logically about interpersonal communication or about anything else) in numerous sections throughout the text, asking students to analyze and evaluate a variety of interpersonal messages, techniques, and conclusions.

Critical thinking is also emphasized in two unique features. First, **Critical Thinking** boxes appear throughout the text. Some of these boxes explain the nature of critical thinking or discuss general concepts that are applicable to all types of thinking and to all areas of communication; for example, the importance of formulating and testing hypotheses before drawing conclusions, the process of using analysis and synthesis to understand complex processes, and ways to assess reliability and validity. Other boxes are more clearly linked to the content of the chapters and discuss specific applications of critical thinking to the chapter topic; for example, they explore thinking critically about listening, attitudes, conclusions, biases, and flexibility. To stimulate students to interact with and personalize the critical thinking concept, each of these boxes concludes with a brief section that asks them to recall specific examples of the types of issues raised in the boxes.

Second, **Critical Thinking Questions** appear in the margins. These questions encourage students to question what they read and to apply the insights to other areas of communication. These questions may be discussed as they come up in the text or reviewed after completing the chapter.

Culture and Intercultural Communication

The text presents interpersonal communication as taking place in a context that is becoming increasingly intercultural. Chapter 9, "Interpersonal Communication and Culture," covers intercultural communication in depth, focusing on the nature of culture and of intercultural communication, the ways in which cultures differ (for example, in individualism and collectivism, high and low context, and masculinity and femininity), and the ways to improve intercultural communication.

In addition, integrated discussions of culture appear throughout the text. These discussions include:

- culture and human communication, including cultural awareness, the relevance of culture, and the aim of a cultural perspective (Chapter 1)
- culture's influence on self-disclosure and on apprehension (Chapter 2)
- stereotypes versus cultural awareness in perceptual accuracy (Chapter 3)
- listening, culture, and gender (Chapter 4)
- gender and cultural differences in verbal directness; language as a cultural institution and cultural maxims; sexism, heterosexism, and racism in language; and cultural identifiers (Chapter 5)
- culture and nonverbal communication; for example, in touching, time, and colour perception (Chapter 6)
- the influence of culture on emotions; societal rules and customs (Chapter 7)
- conversational taboos; cultural sensitivity as a metaskill (Chapter 8)
- interpersonal communication and culture: culture and intercultural communication, how cultures differ, and ways to improve intercultural communication (Chapter 9)
- culture and gender differences in relationships (Chapter 10)
- conflict and culture (Chapter 11)
- cultural power distances; the cultural dimension of power (Chapter 12)

Ethics

New to this edition, a series of **Talking Ethics** boxes highlight a variety of ethical issues in interpersonal communication; for example, the legitimacy of censoring messages and interpersonal interactions, outing, emotional appeals, lying, gossiping, and silence. These boxes will serve as frequent reminders that ethical considerations are an integral part of every interpersonal communication decision. At the end of each box, students are asked, "What would you do?" in response to a real-life situation. In this way, they are encouraged to interact with the material contained in the box and to apply it to ethical questions they will encounter every day.

Power and Empowerment

Because power permeates all forms of interpersonal communication, the themes of **personal empowerment** and **empowering others** are integral to this text. The aim of *Messages* is to provide you with the skills and experiences to become a more effective, more empowered, and more empowering individual. This orientation underlies the book's emphasis on building skills useful at home and at work, and it comes into sharp focus in the final chapter, Chapter 12, "Interpersonal Communication and Power." Here, issues such as increasing personal power through self-esteem, speaking with power, and communicating with greater assertiveness are discussed.

Interactive Pedagogy

The text is written in a highly interactive format that asks you to respond to and get personally involved with the material presented. It seeks to accomplish this goal with a variety of features:

- Nineteen **self-tests** encourage students to assess themselves on a wide variety of interpersonal issues discussed throughout the text; for example, their cultural awareness and beliefs, their willingness to self-disclose, their style of loving, their conversational satisfaction, their flexibility in conversation, and their tendency to be aggressive and argumentative in conflict situations. At the end of each self-test—and new to this edition—are two types of questions. The first asks, "How did you do?" and contains scoring instructions so that students can compute their own score for the self-test. The second asks, "What will you do?" and invites them to consider the changes (if any) they might make in your interpersonal communication behaviour in light of their responses on the test. A complete list of these self-tests appears in the Specialized Contents on page xiii.

- **Skill Building Exercises** appear at the end of the chapters. These exercises are designed to encourage students to interact with and personalize the concepts discussed in the text.

- **Vocabulary Quizzes**, to highlight key terms and make learning new terms easier and more enjoyable, appear at the end of each chapter.

- **Summaries of Concepts and Skills** discussed in each chapter appear at the end of the chapter as checklists, allowing students to review their own mastery of the relevant skills covered in each chapter.

- **Critical Thinking Questions** and provocative **Quotations** in the margins invite active involvement and analysis.

Instructor's Resources

The Instructor's Resource CD-ROM includes the following resources:

Instructor's Manual.

The Instructor's Manual provides chapter overviews and learning and skill objectives for each chapter. It also offers ideas to activate class discussions and contains exercises to illustrate the concepts, principles, and skills of interpersonal communication. The Instructor's Manual can also be downloaded from Pearson Education Canada's protected Instructor Central site at www.pearsoned.ca/instructor; see your local sales representative for an access code.

Test Item File.

The Test Item File contains about 600 multiple choice, true/false, short answer, and essay test questions. The questions are available in both Microsoft Word and TestGen formats.

Pearson TestGen.

The Pearson TestGen is a special computerized version of the Test Item File that enables instructors to view and edit the existing questions, add questions, generate tests, and print the tests in a variety of formats. Powerful search and sort functions make it easy to locate questions and arrange them in any order desired. TestGen also enables instructors to administer tests on a local area network, have the tests graded electronically, and have the results prepared in electronic or printed reports. TestGen is compatible with IBM or Macintosh systems.

Student Resources

Companion Website with Online Practice Tests.

Accessed at www.ablongman.com/devito, this site for the U.S. edition provides web links and Internet activities to enrich the course. The site also contains self-tests and skill development exercises designed exclusively for the Web.

Allyn & Bacon Communication Studies Website.

This site includes modules on interpersonal and small group communication and public speaking and includes web links, enrichment materials, and interactive activities to enhance students' understanding of key concepts. Access this site at www.ablongman.com/commstudies.

Acknowledgments

We want to thank the people who contributed to the second Canadian edition by reviewing material:

Elizabeth Skitmore, Algonqin College
Linda Murdoch, Mohawk College
Frank Daley, Seneca College
Jan Humphrey, Douglas College

We would also like to thank the following reviewers whose feedback was helpful for the first Canadian edition:

Jean Brown, Cambrian College
Vic Parliament, Saint Mary's University
Connie Winder, Humber College of Applied Arts and Technology

CHAPTER TOPICS

This chapter introduces the nature and principles of interpersonal communication and the role of culture.

- What Is Interpersonal Communication?
- Principles of Interpersonal Communication
- Culture and Interpersonal Communication

CHAPTER SKILLS

After completing this chapter, you should be able to:

- interact interpersonally with a recognition of all significant elements.
- engage in interpersonal communication with a clear recognition of its essential principles.
- interact interpersonally with an understanding of cultural differences.

Grace and Mark have been dating for the last three years. Although they're deeply in love, there are some problems facing their relationship. Grace wants to continue her education and become an accountant; Mark wants to continue working at the local gas station. Grace wants to wait to have children; Mark wants lots of children as soon as possible. Grace wants to have her mother live with them; Mark is opposed. Whenever one of them brings up one of these problems, they get into an argument and often stay angry for days at a time. Both Grace and Mark feel that once they get married, they will work out these and any other problems that arise. Love, they feel, will conquer all.

Reno has five children, two preteens, and three teenagers. For most of his life, Reno has worked as a maintenance worker for the Saskatoon School Board. Although he's deeply interested in the lives of his wife and children, he feels he's often ignored. His children rarely confide in him; and whenever there is important news, they go to their mother. Reno feels left out of the family. He feels his only function is to earn money, and he has seriously considered leaving his family and starting a new life in another city.

For the last 14 years, Karla has worked in a toy factory in Vancouver that was recently purchased by a Hong Kong investment firm. The production department, which Karla had headed for the last four years, has been reorganized and is now run by three people—two managers from Hong Kong and Karla. Although production is up, morale is down. Karla used to handle most problems informally by talking with the crew over lunch or at company parties. Now, however, the managers handle all problems at formal business meetings. Karla feels that the new owners have virtually eliminated her job and that she is being kept on just because the union contract protects her. She's thinking of asking for a transfer or seeking a position with another company.

These situations all revolve around problems in interpersonal communication. All these people would profit from learning the principles and skills of interpersonal communication. Whether in a romantic or friendship relationship, a long-established family, or a work environment, the principles of interpersonal communication are powerful tools for dealing with problems such as these. Mark and Grace, for example, don't seem to know how to resolve their differences, and the ways in which they talk about them only aggravate the situation. Their belief that love will conquer all prevents them from seeing the difficulties that confront their relationship now and that will not go away with marriage. The guidelines for conflict resolution discussed in Chapter 11 would help Mark and Grace considerably.

Reno feels left out and doesn't know how to facilitate the self-disclosures of his children or his wife. Nor does he know how to communicate his own feelings. So it's not surprising that his children have learned that their father is not the parent to go to with feelings. Reno wants involvement, but he doesn't know how to get it. The suggestions for facilitating self-disclosure and for communicating empathy and support discussed in Chapters 2 and 8 would prove helpful to Reno.

Karla is having trouble communicating in this new intercultural setting. Morale is down throughout the plant, but the new owners are unaware of this fact—largely because no one has voiced concern. Karla's self-esteem has been damaged; she feels she's lost her importance and doesn't know how to deal with the new situation. Karla would profit from the material on self-esteem in Chapter 12 as well as from the discussions of culture throughout this text, especially Chapter 9's suggestions for improving intercultural communication.

In every realm of life, people can understand and improve these situations and many like them by mastering the skills of interpersonal communication. And that is what this book is about. So important have these skills become that the Conference Board of Canada (2003) has identified interpersonal communication skills, and the ability to work effectively with others, as critical to successful employment. Many recent college graduates, however, lack these skills (Robbins & Hunsaker, 2003). In an attempt to address this deficit, a number of Canadian colleges are now listing good written and oral communication skills as required learning outcomes for all students.

This book, then, is about improving your interpersonal skills so that you'll be more effective in a wide variety of interpersonal communication situations in your personal and professional life. (A website devoted specifically to this textbook and offering lots of useful information on a wide variety of interpersonal communication issues—including the connection between interpersonal communication and the media—is available at www.ablongman.com/devito.)

Before you begin studying this exciting and practical area, examine your own beliefs about interpersonal communication by taking the self-test below.

What other problems might Grace and Mark, Reno, and Karla be experiencing? What suggestions might you make to help them deal with their communication problems?

TEST YOURSELF

What Do You Believe About Interpersonal Communication?

Instructions: Respond to each of the following statements with T (true) if you think the statement is always or usually true and F (false) if you believe the statement is always or usually false.

_____ **1.** Good communicators are born, not made.

_____ **2.** The more you communicate, the better your communication will be.

_____ **3.** Unlike effective speaking, effective listening really cannot be taught.

_____ **4.** Opening lines such as "Hello, how are you?" or "Fine weather today" serve no useful communication purpose.

_____ **5.** The best way to communicate with someone from a different culture is exactly as you would with someone from your own culture.

_____ **6.** When verbal and nonverbal messages contradict each other, people believe the verbal message.

_____ **7.** Complete openness should be the goal of any meaningful interpersonal relationship.

_____ **8.** Interpersonal conflict is a reliable sign that your relationship is in trouble.

_____ **9.** Like good communicators, small-group leaders are born, not made.

_____ **10.** Fear of speaking is detrimental, and the effective speaker must learn to eliminate it.

(continued)

What Is Interpersonal Communication?

If your lips would keep from slips,
Five things observe with care;
To whom you speak, of whom you
    speak,
And how, and when, and where.

—**W. E. Norris**

Interpersonal communication is communication that occurs between two persons who have a relationship between them. **Communication** occurs when you send or receive messages and when you assign meaning to such messages. Interpersonal communication is always distorted by "noise," occurs within a context, and involves some opportunity for feedback.

Interpersonal communicators are conscious of one another and of their connection with one another. They're interdependent; what one person thinks and says impacts on what the other thinks and says. Interpersonal communication includes the conversations that take place between an interviewer and a potential employee, between a son and his father, between two sisters, between a teacher and a student, or between two lovers or two friends. Even the stranger asking for directions from a local resident has a relationship with that person.

Some early theories saw the communication process as linear. In this *linear* view of communication, the speaker spoke and the listener listened; after the speaker finished speaking, the listener would speak. Communication was seen as proceeding in a relatively straight line. Speaking and listening were seen as taking place at different times— when you spoke, you didn't listen; and when you listened, you didn't speak (Figure 1.1).

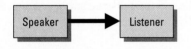

FIGURE 1.1 The Linear View of Human Communication

Communication researchers Judy Pearson and Paul Nelson (2000) suggest that you think of the speaker as passing a ball to the listener, who either catches the ball or fumbles it. Can you think of another analogy or metaphor for this linear view of communication?

This linear **model**, or representation of the process, was soon replaced with an *interactional* view in which the speaker and the listener were seen as exchanging turns at speaking and listening. For example, A spoke while B listened and then B (exchanging the listener's role for the speaker's role) spoke in response to what A said and A listened (Figure 1.2 on page 5). Speaking and listening were still viewed as separate acts that did not overlap and that were not performed at the same time by the same person.

A more satisfying view, and the one currently held, sees communication as a *transactional* process in which each person serves simultaneously as speaker and listener. According to the **transactional view**, at the same time that you send messages, you're also receiving messages from your own communications and from the reactions of the other person (Figure 1.3). And at the same time that you're listening, you're also sending messages. In a transactional view, each person is seen as both speaker and listener, as simultaneously communicating and receiving messages (Watzlawick, Beavin, & Jackson, 1967; Watzlawick, 1977, 1978; Barnlund, 1970; Harris, 2002).

Also, in a transactional view the elements of communication are seen as *inter*dependent (never *in*dependent). Each exists in relation to the others. A change in any one element of this **process** produces changes in the other elements. For example, suppose you're talking with a group of your friends and your mother enters the group. This change in "audience" will lead to other changes; perhaps you'll change what you say or how you say it. Regardless of what change is introduced, other changes will be produced as a result.

Often, of course, interpersonal communication takes place face-to-face; and this is the type of interaction that probably comes to mind when you think of conversation. But, especially today, much conversation takes place online. Online communications are becoming a part of people's experience throughout the world. Such communications are important personally, socially, and professionally. Three major online types of conversation and the ways in which they differ from one another and from face-to-face interaction may be noted here: email, the mailing list group, and the chat group.

In *email,* you usually type your letter in an email program and send it (along with other documents you may wish to attach) from your computer via modem to your server (the computer at your school or at some commercial organization like Sympatico), which relays your message through a series of computer hookups and eventually to the server of the person you're addressing. Unlike face-to-face communication, email does not take place in real time. You may send your message today, but the receiver may not read it for a week and may take another week to respond. Much of the spontaneity created by real time communication is lost here. You may, for example, be very enthusiastic about a topic when you send your email but practically forget it by the time someone responds.

Email is more like a postcard than a letter—it can be read by others along the route. It's also virtually unerasable. Especially in large organizations, employees' emails are stored on hard disk or on backup tapes and may be retrieved for a variety of reasons. Currently, for example, large corporations are being sued because of sexist and racist email that their employees wrote and that plaintiffs' lawyers have retrieved from archives long thought destroyed. Also, your email can easily be forwarded to other people by anyone who has access to your

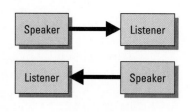

FIGURE 1.2 The Interactional View

In this view, continuing with the ball-throwing analogy, the speaker would pass the ball to the listener, who would then pass the ball back or fumble it (Pearson & Nelson, 2000). What other analogy would work here?

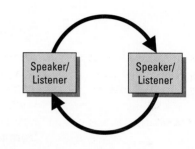

FIGURE 1.3 The Transactional View

In this view, a complex ball game is underway in which each player could send and receive any number of balls at any time. Players would be able to throw and catch balls at the very same time (Pearson & Nelson, 2000). Can you think of any other analogies for this transactional view of communication?

files. And although this practice is considered unethical, it's relatively common.

The *mailing list group* (or listserv) consists of a group of people interested in a particular topic who communicate with one another through email. Generally, you subscribe to a list and communicate with all other members by addressing your mail to the group email address. Any message you send to this address will be sent to each member who subscribes to the list. Your message is sent to all members at the same time; there are no asides to the person sitting next to you, as in face-to-face groups.

Chat groups have proliferated across the internet. These groups enable members to converse in real time in discussion groups called channels. At any one time there are thousands of channels, so your chances of finding a topic you're interested in is high.

Unlike mailing lists, chat communication takes place in real time. You see a member's message as it's being sent; there's virtually no delay. As with both mailing lists and face-to-face conversation, the purposes of chat groups vary from communication that simply maintains connection with others (what many would call "idle chatter" or "phatic communication") to extremely significant discussions in science, education, health, politics, and just about any field you can name.

Communication in a chat group resembles the conversation you'd observe at a large party. The guests divide into small groups varying from two people on up, and each group discusses its own topic or version of a general topic. For example, in a group about travel, five people may be discussing the difficulties of travelling to Communist countries, three people may be discussing airport security systems, and two people may be discussing bargain rates for cruises to Mexico—all on this one channel. Chat groups also allow you to "whisper": to communicate with one other person without giving access to your message to other participants. So, although you may be communicating in one primary group (say, dealing with airport security), you also have your eye trained to pick up something particularly interesting in another group, much as you do at a party. Such groups also notify you when someone new comes into the group and when someone leaves. Like mailing lists, chat groups enable you to communicate with people you would never meet and interact with otherwise. Because such groups are international, they provide excellent exposure to other cultures, other ideas, and other ways of communicating.

In face-to-face conversation you're expected to contribute to the ongoing discussion. In chat groups you can simply observe; in fact, you're encouraged to "lurk"—to observe the participants' interaction before you say anything yourself. In this way, you'll be able to learn the cultural rules and norms of the group.

Another obvious difference between face-to-face and computer communication is that in face-to-face interaction the individuals are clearly identified—at least usually. In computer-mediated communication, however, you may remain anonymous. You may also pose as someone you're not: as a person of another sex or race, for example, or even as someone who is significantly older or younger than you really are, or of significantly different status (Saunders, Robey, & Vaverek, 1994). (An unusual example of this kind of impersonation appeared in the *Calgary Herald* [2003]. The newspaper reported that a Lethbridge alderwoman was accused by police of using computer communication to send herself letters she claimed were being written by a stalker.) In face-to-face communication your physical self—the way you look, the way you're dressed—greatly influences the way your messages will be interpreted. In computer-mediated communication you reveal your physical self through your own descriptions. Although you may send photos of yourself via computer, you can also send photos of others and claim they're of yourself. There is, in short, much greater opportunity for presenting yourself as you want to present yourself when communicating via computer.

Given the basic definition of interpersonal communication, the transactional perspective, and an understanding that interpersonal communication occurs in many different forms, let's expand our model as in Figure 1.4 and look at each of the essential elements in interpersonal communication: source–receiver, competence, messages, feedback, feedforward, channel, noise, and context. (Along with this discussion you may wish to visit www.acc-cca.ca, the website of the Canadian Communication Association. This national organization brings together members of academic, government, and business communities to promote the investigation of communication issues.)

"I loved your E-mail, but I thought you'd be older."

Source–Receiver

Interpersonal communication involves at least two persons. Each functions as a **source** (formulates and sends messages) and operates as a **receiver** (receives and understands messages). The linked term *source–receiver* emphasizes that each person is both source and receiver. (A useful exercise to help you see yourself and others in your class as sources and receivers, "I'd Prefer to Be," is available at www.ablongman.com/devito.)

By putting your meanings into sound waves (or gestures, facial expressions, or postural adjustments) you're putting your thoughts and feelings into a **code**, or a set of symbols—a process called *en*coding. By translating sound (and light) waves into ideas, you're taking them out of the code they're in, a process called *de*coding. So we can call speakers (or, more generally, senders) **encoders**: those who put their meanings *into* a code. And we can call listeners (or, more generally, receivers) **decoders**: those who take meanings *out of* a code. Since encoding and decoding activities are combined in each person, the term *encoding–decoding* is used to emphasize this inevitable dual function.

Usually you encode an idea into a code that the other person understands; for example, you use words and

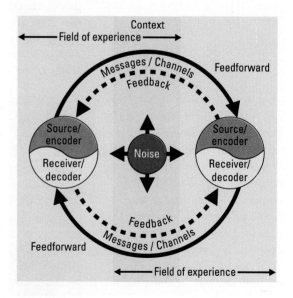

FIGURE 1.4 The Process of Interpersonal Communication

This model puts into visual form the various elements of the interpersonal communication process. How would you diagram the interpersonal communication process?

gestures for which both you and the other person have similar meanings. At times, however, you may want to exclude others; so, for example, you might speak in a language that only one of your listeners knows or use jargon to prevent others from understanding. At other times, you may assume incorrectly that the other person knows your code and, for example, unknowingly use words or gestures the other person simply doesn't understand.

For interpersonal communication to occur, then, meanings must be encoded and decoded. If Jamie has his eyes closed and is wearing stereo headphones as his dad is speaking to him, interpersonal communication is not taking place—simply because the messages, both verbal and nonverbal, are not being received.

Interpersonal Competence

Your ability to communicate effectively is your **interpersonal competence** (Spitzberg & Cupach, 1989). For example, your **competence** includes the knowledge that in certain contexts and with certain listeners one topic is appropriate and another is not. It includes your understanding of the rules of nonverbal communication—such as the appropriateness of touching, vocal volume, and physical closeness.

A major goal of this text (and your course) is to expand and enlarge your competence so that you'll have a greater arsenal of communication choices at your disposal. It's much like learning vocabulary: The more words you know, the more ways you'll have to express yourself. The greater your interpersonal competence, the more options you'll have for communicating with friends, lovers, and family; with colleagues on the job; and in just about any situation where you'll talk with another person. The greater your competence, the greater your own power to accomplish successfully what you want to accomplish—to ask for a raise or a date; establish temporary work relationships, long-term friendships, or romantic relationships; communicate empathy and support; or

Adults, when speaking of things they don't want a child to understand, often spell out key words—speaking in a code that young children can't yet break. Computer communication enables you to do a similar thing. For example, when sending your credit card number to a vendor, you might send it in encrypted form, coded into a symbol system that others will not be able to understand (decode). Similarly, in chat groups you might write in a language that only certain of your readers will understand. In what other types of situations would you use a code that certain others cannot understand?

gain compliance or resist the compliance tactics of others. Whatever your interpersonal goal, increased competence will help you accomplish it more effectively.

In short, interpersonal competence includes knowing how interpersonal communication works and how to best achieve your purposes by adjusting your messages according to the context of the interaction, the person with whom you're interacting, and a host of other factors discussed throughout this text. The process goes like this: Knowledge of interpersonal communication *leads to* greater interpersonal ability, which *leads to* a greater number of available choices or options for interacting, which *leads to* greater likelihood of interpersonal effectiveness.

Interpersonal competence consists largely of understanding the way interpersonal communication works and mastering its *skills* (including the often neglected skills of *listening*). These skills depend on *critical thinking*, are specific to a given *culture*, and rest on an *ethical foundation*. Understanding the nature of these five themes of competence and how they are highlighted in this text will enable you to gain the most from studying and working with this material. (As a complement to the following discussion you may wish to read a paper on communication as it's influenced by biology; see **www.ablongman.com/devito**.)

Competence and Interpersonal Skills   This text explains the theory and research in interpersonal communication in order to provide you with a firm foundation in understanding how interpersonal communication works. (To further explore the role of theory and research, visit **www.ablongman.com/devito** for a self-test, "What do you know about research?" and some useful guidelines for evaluating information found on the internet.) With that understanding as a foundation, you'll be better able to develop and master the very practical skills of interpersonal communication. To help you achieve this goal, this text highlights the skills of interpersonal communication in a variety of ways.

Skills are discussed *throughout the text* along with the relevant theory and research on which they're based.

Skill Building Exercises appear at the end of each chapter, providing you with opportunities to practise some of the skills discussed in the text; for example, reducing apprehension, communicating your emotions (even negative ones), formulating excuses, and confronting intercultural difficulties. A complete list of these Skill Building Exercises appears in the Specialized Contents on page xiii.

This edition gives special emphasis to the skills of interpersonal communication as relevant to a wide variety of workplace environments and tasks. In addition to the skills discussed in the text and the exercises having application to the workplace, two elements of the text further develop this theme:

Reprinted articles present specific skills applied to the workplace. Such articles deal with telephone communication, giving and receiving feedback on the job, reducing fear in doctor–patient communication, listening on the job, and keeping your emotions in check at work. A complete list of these articles appears in the Specialized Contents on page xiii.

If people knew how hard I worked to get my mastery, it wouldn't seem so wonderful after all.

—**Michelangelo**

Skills Toolbox features identify specific interpersonal skills as they are used in the workplace. Such workplace skills include, for example, ways to manage apprehension at work, ways to write more effective business email, ways to network more effectively, and how to deal with workplace complaints. Each of these features ends with a case entitled "Then and Now" that asks you to recall what you did in some past situation and what you would do now (ideally, with your newly mastered skills). A complete list of these Skills Toolbox features appears in the Specialized Contents on page xiii.

Your mastery of interpersonal skills will be greatly enhanced if you engage in self-assessment. No one knows you better than you do, so analyze your own competencies—your strengths as well as your weaknesses. The greater your self-understanding, the better you'll be able to acquire the competencies you need to accomplish your personal and professional goals. Several features in this text will help you in your self-assessment.

First, many of the *critical thinking questions* and *Thinking Critically About boxes* contained throughout the text ask you to reflect on your own attitudes and behaviours—to bring these to conscious awareness and make them available for critical analysis.

Second, the *skill checklists* in the chapter summaries identify the major skills covered in the chapter and ask you to assess your own mastery of them.

Third, the *self-tests* presented throughout the text as well as those on the accompanying website ask you to pause, reflect, and assess your own communication thoughts and behaviours; for example, your level of communication apprehension, your accuracy in perceiving other people, your flexibility and ability to adjust to new and different situations, your touching behaviour, and the kind of lover you are. A complete list of these self-tests appears in the Specialized Contents on page xiii.

Competence and Listening   Competence in interpersonal communication is often viewed as "speaking effectiveness," with little attention paid to listening. But, as demonstrated throughout the text, listening is an integral part of interpersonal communication; you cannot be a competent communicator if you're a poor listener. Both speaking and listening skills are crucial to interpersonal competence. Listening, therefore, is emphasized in this text in two major ways.

First, *an entire chapter (Chapter 4) is devoted to listening.* Discussions cover the nature and importance of listening, the steps you go through in listening, the role of culture and gender in listening, and ways to increase your listening effectiveness.

Second, *Listen to This boxes are positioned throughout the text* to illustrate how listening relates to the topic of the chapter and to provide a variety of specific listening skills. Among the topics these boxes address are: the importance of listening to yourself; the role of gender differences; sexist, heterosexist, and racist listening; ways to listen during conflict; and how to listen to empower others. Each of the listening boxes ends with a case that asks you to offer listening suggestions for a wide variety of interpersonal communication situations. These cases underscore a basic principle of listening: that listening is a process requiring action by the listener; it is not a passive process that simply happens when you open your ears. A complete list of all Listen to This boxes appears in the Specialized Contents on page xiii.

Competence and Critical Thinking   Competence in interpersonal communication depends on **critical thinking**. Without critical thinking there can be no competent exchange of ideas, no competent communication. And these, according to one study of corporate executives, are essential skills for effective management (Robbins & Hunsaker, 2003). Because of the central importance of critical thinking, it is given special prominence in this text.

Throughout the text, Thinking Critically About boxes are presented. In the early chapters these features explain what critical thinking is; in later chapters they identify specific skills that will help you to become a more critical, a more reasoned, and more careful, thinker. Although these critical thinking discussions are couched in the context of interpersonal communication, they are actually relevant to thinking about all forms of communication and in fact all forms of behaviour. A complete list of all critical thinking boxes appears in the Specialized Contents on page xiii.

In addition, frequent questions appear in the margins, asking that you exercise and apply your critical thinking to a wide variety of interpersonal communication issues discussed in the text.

Throughout this text, you'll find numerous recommendations for communicating more effectively. As you read them, keep in mind that the description of these skills are almost always too general; they are rarely specific enough for automatic application to any given situation. So, ask yourself: What is there about your unique and specific situation that you need to take into account in deciding what to do? What are your

LISTEN TO THIS

Listening in Interpersonal Communication

In the popular mind, communication is often taken as synonymous with speaking. Listening is either neglected or regarded as something apart from "real communication." But, as emphasized in the transactional model of communication presented earlier and as stressed throughout this book, listening is integral to all communication; it is a process that is coordinate with speaking.

If you measured importance by the time you spend on an activity, then listening would be your most important communication activity. In one study conducted in 1929 (Rankin), listening occupied 45 percent of people's communication time; speaking was second with 30 percent; reading (10 percent) and writing (9 per-

cent) followed. In another study of college students, conducted in 1980 (Barker, Edwards, Gaines, Gladney, & Holley), listening also occupied the most time—53 percent, compared with reading (17 percent), speaking (16 percent), and writing (14 percent).

SUGGESTIONS?

A group of elementary school teachers who have read these statistics want to incorporate more listening activities in the elementary school classroom to train students to listen more efficiently and more effectively. What kinds of listening activities and experiences would you suggest they focus on?

communication options? Which seem the most promising? Can you play these through in your mind? Also, recognize that although great effort has been made to indicate cultural differences and variation, and to adapt this textbook for a Canadian audience, most of the research on communication available today comes from the United States. So, before using your skills, it's always appropriate to ask if there are cultural differences that might bear on the skill and its successful application.

Competence and Culture   The term *culture* refers to the lifestyle of a group of people. A group's culture consists of their values, beliefs, artifacts, ways of behaving, and ways of communicating. Culture includes all that members of a social group have produced and developed—their language, ways of thinking, art, laws, and religion. Culture is transmitted from one generation to another not through genes but through communication and learning; especially through the teachings of parents, peer groups, schools, religious institutions, and government agencies. Because most cultures teach women and men different attitudes and ways of communicating, many of the gender differences we observe may be considered cultural—although of course the biological differences between men and women also play a part.

THINKING CRITICALLY ABOUT

Critical Thinking

Critical thinking is logical thinking; it's thinking that is well reasoned, unbiased, and clear. It's a way of thinking intelligently, carefully, and with as much clarity as possible. It's the opposite of what you'd call sloppy, illogical, or careless thinking. It's "the process of examining information and reaching a judgment or decision" (Wade & Tavris, 1990).

Critical thinking is always relevant. Regardless of what you're working on, critical thinking will come in handy. It's relevant in your interpersonal relationships and in your professional life, and will prove valuable whether you are solving problems, improving your relationships, or resolving interpersonal conflicts at home or on the job. *Critical thinking is universal across all areas of knowledge and experience.* Although this book focuses on interpersonal communication, probably the most important form of all human behaviour, critical thinking will also prove of value in the arts and humanities, the social sciences, and the sciences, and in just about any situation in which you find yourself.

Critical thinking skills enable you to do a variety of things (Ennis, 1987; Nickerson, 1987; McCarthy, 1991;

Adams & Hamm, 1991; Bransford, Sherwood, & Sturdevant, 1987):

1. To ask and answer questions of clarification or challenge
2. To draw and evaluate conclusions
3. To organize your thoughts and speak or write them coherently
4. To distinguish between logical and illogical inferences
5. To weigh the truth of arguments instead of simply accepting them on faith
6. To make connections between new knowledge and what you already know
7. To obtain relevant and valid information
8. To evaluate the quality and reasonableness of ideas
9. To define a problem precisely
10. To explore and evaluate possible strategies for solving a problem

EXAMPLES?

Can you think of examples of specific interpersonal situations in your personal or professional relationships in which one or more of the above skills would come in handy?

Competence is sometimes culture specific; communications that prove effective in one culture will not necessarily prove effective in another. For example, giving a birthday gift to a close friend would be appreciated by members of many cultures and in some cases would be expected. But it would be frowned upon by Jehovah's Witnesses because they don't celebrate birthdays (Dresser, 1996). Because of the vast range of cultural differences that impact on interpersonal communication, the role of culture is discussed in every chapter. To give you a glimpse of how culture is related to the topics of interpersonal communication, here are a few examples:

- Chapter 1, which introduces interpersonal communication, also introduces and defines culture, discusses its importance, and explains the aim of the cultural perspective taken in this text.

- The chapter on the self (Chapter 2) discusses culture's role in self-concept and self-disclosure and cultural influences on apprehension.

- Chapter 3, on interpersonal perception, covers the role of stereotypes in perception and the importance of cultural sensitivity in perceptual accuracy.

- The listening chapter (4) identifies the cultural and gender differences that influence listening effectiveness.

- Gender and cultural differences in directness; sexism, heterosexism, and racism in language; and cultural identifiers (ways to talk to and about people from different cultures) are discussed in Chapter 5, which deals with verbal messages.

- Chapter 6, which focuses on nonverbal communication, discusses such topics as nonverbal messages that can create problems with members of different cultures, the meanings that different cultures give to colours, and the ways different cultures view time.

- The chapter on emotions (Chapter 7) considers the role that culture and gender play in emotions and the varied societal rules and customs that influence emotional expression.

- Chapter 8, which covers the entire process of conversation, looks at the conversational taboos of different cultures, cultural sensitivity, suggestions for communicating with the deaf, and how the rules of conversation differ on the basis of culture and gender.

- Chapter 9 is devoted entirely to interpersonal communication and culture and discusses the nature of culture and of intercultural communication, how cultures differ, and ways to improve intercultural communication.

- The chapter on interpersonal relationships (Chapter 10) discusses the influence of culture on the way we think about relationships—in the research conducted, in the theories developed, and even in the questions we ask—and the numerous culture and gender differences in friendship and love relationships.

- Chapter 11, on interpersonal conflict, considers the cultural and gender differences in viewing and in managing conflict.

- The final chapter (Chapter 12), on interpersonal power, discusses the cultural dimension of power, particularly the differences between high- and low-power-distance cultures—the degree to which power is unevenly distributed in different societies.

Competence and Ethics   Interpersonal communication also involves questions of **ethics**. There is a moral dimension to any interpersonal communication act (Jaksa & Pritchard, 1994; Bok, 1978). For example, while it might be effective to lie in selling a product, it would not be ethical. The decisions you make concerning communication are guided not only by what you consider effective but also by what you consider right. The relatively recent proliferation of electronic forms of communication, such as the internet, brings with it new moral choices and the need for new frameworks for ethical decision making (Frost, 2003).

Ethical dimensions of interpersonal communication are presented throughout the text in Talking Ethics boxes and include, for example, the ethics of outing, lying, interpersonal silence, motivational appeals, and gossiping about secrets. Each of these ethics boxes presents a case calling for a decision and asks what you would do in the situation described. These cases are designed to illustrate the fact that ethics is not some abstract concept studied in philosophy; ethical principles underlie day-to-day decisions we all have to make. A complete list of all Talking Ethics boxes appears in the Specialized Contents on page xiii.

What Canadian television personalities demonstrate superior interpersonal competence? What personalities demonstrate obvious interpersonal incompetence? How, for example, would you compare Peter Mansbridge from *The National* and "Mike from Canmore" from *This Hour Has 22 Minutes?*

TALKING ETHICS

Approaches to Ethics

In thinking about the ethics of interpersonal communication, you can take the position that ethics is objective or that it's subjective. In an *objective view* you'd argue that the morality of an act is absolute and exists apart from the values or beliefs of any individual or culture. With this view you'd hold that there are standards that apply to all people in all situations at all times. If behaviours such as lying, false advertising, using illegally obtained evidence, or revealing secrets you've promised to keep—to take a few examples—are considered unethical, then, according to the objective view, they are unethical regardless of the circumstances surrounding them or of the values and beliefs of the culture in which they occur.

In a *subjective view* you'd argue that the ethics of a message depends on the culture's values and beliefs as well as the particular circumstances. Thus, a subjective position would claim that lying may be wrong to win votes or sell cigarettes, but that it may be quite ethical if good will result from it; for example, when we try to help friends feel better by telling them that they look great or that they'll get well soon.

WHAT WOULD YOU DO?

You see a student cheating on an examination. After the examination the instructor accuses the student of cheating and asks you if you witnessed the cheating. Although you believe that both cheating and lying are unethical, and although you did witness the cheating, you don't want to make trouble for the student—and probably become instantly unpopular with your classmates. Besides, you feel the examination was grossly unfair. How would a person who held an objective view of ethics respond to the instructor's query? How would a person who held a subjective view? What would you do in this situation?

As you read this text, you'll see that these five themes of competence are not separate and distinct from one another but rather interact and overlap. For example, as already noted, critical thinking pervades the entire interpersonal communication process—but also serves as a foundation for your cultural awareness, listening effectiveness, and skill development. Similarly, an awareness of cultural differences will make you, for example, a more effective listener, a more discerning user of skills, and more conscious of the ethical dimension of interpersonal communication. So, as you read the text and work actively with the concepts, remember that everything in it—the regular text, the boxed features, the material in the margins, the summaries and vocabulary tests at the end of the chapters—is designed to contribute to one overarching aim: to increase your interpersonal communication competence.

Messages

For interpersonal communication to exist, **messages** that express your thoughts and feelings must be sent and received. Interpersonal communication may be verbal or nonverbal, but it's usually a combination of both. You communicate interpersonally with words as well as with gestures and touch, for example. Even the clothes you wear communicate, as do the way you walk and the way you shake hands, comb your hair, sit, smile, or frown. Everything about you has the potential to send interpersonal messages, and every message has an **effect**, or outcome.

In face-to-face communication your messages are both verbal and nonverbal; you supplement your words with facial expressions, body movements, and variations in vocal volume and rate, for example. When you communicate through a keyboard, your message is communicated basically with words. This does not mean that you cannot communicate emotional meanings; in fact, some researchers have argued that diagrams, pictures, and varied typefaces enable you to communicate messages that are rich in emotional meaning (Lea & Spears, 1995). Similarly, you can use emoticons (see the discussion in Chapter 7). But basically a keyboarded or written message is communicated with words. Because of this, sarcasm, for example, is difficult to convey unambiguously—whereas in face-to-face communication you might wink or smile to indicate that your message should not be taken seriously or literally.

Feedback   **Feedback** is a special type of message. When you send a spoken or written message to another person, you get feedback from your own message: You hear what you say, you feel the way you move, you see what you write. On the basis of this information, you may correct yourself, rephrase something, or perhaps smile at a clever turn of phrase. This is self-feedback.

You also get feedback from others. The person with whom you're communicating is constantly sending you messages that indicate how he or she is receiving and responding to your messages. Nods of agreement, smiles, puzzled looks, and questions asking for clarification are all examples of feedback.

Notice that in face-to-face communication you can monitor the feedback of the other person as you're speaking. In computer-mediated

How does feedback work in conversation between persons with impaired hearing? Between a person with impaired hearing and a person with normal hearing? Between persons who are blind? Between a person who is blind and a person who has normal vision?

communication that feedback will come much later and thus is likely to be more clearly thought out and perhaps more closely monitored.

Feedforward   Much as feedback contains information about messages already sent, **feedforward** is information about messages before you send them. Opening comments such as "Wait until you hear this" or "I'm not sure of this, but..." or "Don't get me wrong, but..." are examples of feedforward. These messages tell the listener something about the messages to come or about the way you'd like the listener to respond. Nonverbally, you give feedforward by, for example, your facial expressions, eye contact, and physical posture; with these nonverbal messages you tell the other person something about the messages you'll be sending. A smile may signal a pleasant message; eye avoidance may signal that the message to come is difficult and perhaps uncomfortable to express. A book's table of contents, its preface, and (usually) its first chapter are also examples of feedforward.

Channel

The communication **channel** is the medium through which message signals pass. The channel works like a bridge connecting source and receiver. Normally two, three, or four channels are used simultaneously. Thus, for example, in face-to-face **speech** interactions, you speak and listen, using the vocal–auditory channel. You also, however, make gestures and receive these signals visually, using the visual channel. Similarly, you emit odours and smell those of others (chemical channel). Often you touch one another, and this too communicates (tactile channel).

Another way to classify channels is by the means of communication. Thus, face-to-face contact, telephones, email, movies, television, smoke signals, and telegraph would be types of channels. Of most relevance today, of course, is the difference between face-to-face and computer-mediated interpersonal communication: interaction through email, chat lines, and usenet groups.

Noise

Noise is anything that interferes with your receiving a message someone is sending or with their receiving your message. Noise may be physical (loud talking, honking cars, illegible handwriting, "garbage" on your computer screen), physiological (hearing or visual impairment, articulation disorders), psychological (preconceived ideas, wandering thoughts), or semantic (misunderstood meanings). Technically, noise is anything that distorts or gets in the way of the message.

A useful concept in understanding noise and its importance in communication is **signal-to-noise ratio**. In this phrase the term *signal* refers to information that you'd find useful; *noise* refers to information that is useless (to you). So, for example, a mailing list or newsgroup that contains lots of useful information would be high on signal and low on noise; those that contained lots of useless information would be high on noise and low on signal.

> I am not sure I have learned anything else as important. I have been able to realize what a prime role what I have come to call "feedforward" has in all our doings.
>
> —I. A. Richards

"Do you mind? I happen to be on the phone!"

Because messages may be visual as well as spoken, noise too may be visual. Thus, sunglasses that prevent someone from seeing the nonverbal messages from your eyes would be considered noise, as would blurred type on a printed page. Table 1.1 identifies the four major types of noise in more detail.

All communications contain noise. Noise cannot be totally eliminated, but its effects can be reduced. Making your language more precise, sharpening your skills for sending and receiving nonverbal messages, and improving your listening and feedback skills are some ways to combat the influence of noise.

Context

Communication always takes place within a context: an environment that influences the form and the content of communication. At times this context is so natural that you ignore it, like street noise. At other times the context stands out, and the ways in which it restricts or stimulates your communications are obvious. Think, for example, of the different ways you'd talk at a funeral, in a quiet restaurant, and at a rock concert.

The **context of communication** has at least four dimensions: physical, cultural, social–psychological, and temporal. The room, workplace, or outdoor space in which communication takes place—the tangible or concrete environment—is the *physical dimension*. When you communicate face-to-face you're both in essentially the same physical environment. In computer-mediated communication you may both

TABLE 1.1 Four Types of Noise

One of the most important skills in communication is to recognize the types of noise and to develop ways to combat them. For example, what kinds of noise occur in the classroom? What kinds of noise occur in your family communications? What kinds occur at work? What can you do to combat these kinds of noise?

Type of Noise	Definition	Example
Physical	Interference that is external to both speaker and listener; interferes with the physical transmission of the signal or message	Screeching of passing cars, hum of computer, sunglasses
Physiological	Physical barriers within the speaker or listener	Visual impairments, hearing loss, articulation problems, memory loss
Psychological	Cognitive or mental interference	Biases and prejudices in senders and receivers, closed-mindedness, inaccurate expectations, extreme emotionalism (anger, hate, love, grief)
Semantic	Different meanings assigned by speaker and listener	Language differences, use of jargon or overly complex terms not understood by listener, dialectical differences in meaning

be in drastically different environments; one of you may be on a beach in San Juan while another is in a Bay Street office.

The *cultural dimension* consists of the rules, norms, beliefs, and attitudes of the people communicating that are passed from one generation to another. For example, in some cultures it's considered polite to talk to strangers; in others it's something to be avoided.

The *social–psychological dimension* includes, for example, the status relationships among the participants: distinctions such as who is the employer and who the employee, who is the salesperson and who the store owner. The formality or informality, the friendliness or hostility, the cooperativeness or competitiveness of the interaction are also part of the social–psychological dimension.

The *temporal*, or *time dimension*, has to do with where a particular message fits into a sequence of communication events. For example, if you tell a joke about sickness immediately after your friend tells you she is sick, the joke will be perceived differently from the same joke told as one of a series of similar jokes to your friends in the locker room of the gym.

In face-to-face communication, both people interact in real time. In computer communication this real time interaction occurs only sometimes. In email, "snail mail," and newsgroup communication, for example, the sending and receiving may be separated by several days or much longer. In chat groups, on the other hand, communication takes place in real time; the sending and receiving take place (almost) simultaneously.

Principles of Interpersonal Communication

Another way to define interpersonal communication is to consider its major principles. These principles, although significant in terms of explaining theory, also have very practical applications. These principles will provide insight into such practical issues as:

THINKING CRITICALLY ABOUT
Interpersonal Communication

Think critically about interpersonal communication, recognizing that:

■ The study of interpersonal communication involves both theory and research *and* practical skills for increasing interpersonal effectiveness. A knowledge of theory will help you better understand the skills, and a knowledge of skills will help you better understand theory.

■ The principles discussed throughout this book relate directly to your everyday interactions. To help make this material easier to assimilate, try to recall examples from your own communications to illustrate the ideas considered here.

■ Become willing to change your ways of communicating and even your ways of thinking about interpersonal communication. Carefully assess what you should strengthen or revise and what you should leave as is.

EXAMPLES?

Can you give an example of a situation in which you experimented with ways of communicating different from your usual?

- why disagreements so often centre on trivial issues and yet seem so difficult to resolve
- why you'll never be able to mind read, to know just what another person is thinking
- how communication expresses power relationships
- why you and your partner often see the causes of arguments very differently

A more abbreviated statement of communication principles—principles applied to talking on the telephone but applicable to many forms and functions of communication—is contained in the article on page 20, "Twenty Golden Telephone Rules."

All generalizations are false, including this one.

—Alexander Chase

Interpersonal Communication Is a Package of Signals

Communication behaviours, whether they involve verbal messages, gestures, or some combination thereof, usually occur in "packages" (Pittenger, Hockett, & Danehy, 1960). Usually, verbal and nonverbal behaviours reinforce or support each other. All parts of a message system normally work together to communicate a particular meaning. You don't express fear with words while the rest of your body is relaxed. You don't express anger through your posture while your face smiles. Your entire body works together—verbally and nonverbally—to express your thoughts and feelings.

With any form of communication, whether interpersonal messages, small group communication, public speaking, or mass media, you probably pay little attention to its "packaged" nature. It goes unnoticed. But when there's an incongruity—when the chilly handshake belies the verbal greeting, when the nervous posture belies the focused stare, when the constant preening belies the expressions of being comfortable and at ease—you take notice. Invariably you begin to question the credibility, the sincerity, and the honesty of the individual.

Often contradictory messages are sent over a period of time. Note, for example, that in the following interaction the employee is being given two directives: (1) Use initiative, and (2) Don't use initiative. Regardless of what he or she does, rejection will follow.

Employer: You've got to learn to take more initiative. You never seem to take charge, to take control.

Employee: (Takes the initiative, makes decisions.)

Employer: You've got to learn to follow the chain of command and not do things just because you want to.

Employee: (Goes back to old ways, not taking any initiative.)

Employer: Well, I told you. We expect more initiative from you.

Contradictory messages are particularly damaging when children are involved. Children can neither escape from such situations nor communicate about the communications. They can't talk about the lack of correspondence between one set of messages and another set. They can't ask their parents, for example, why they don't hold them or hug them when they say they love them.

Contradictory messages may be the result of the desire to communicate two different emotions or feelings. For example, you may like a person and want to communicate a positive feeling, but you may also feel resentment toward this person and want to communicate a negative feeling as well. The result is that you communicate both feelings; for example, you say that you're happy to see the person, but your facial

MESSAGES@WORK

Twenty Golden Telephone Rules

Answering the phone is not a difficult physical task, but using it in a businesslike and professional manner is not so straightforward. It is all too easy to believe that other people are causing the problems. Could it be that they are reacting to the way you are dealing with them? Being effective, as well as staying calm and controlled, is quite a demanding task. You might like to appraise your own ability by considering the following questions. How often do you plan your telephone calls, and how effective is your planning? How much time do you waste on the telephone? Are you helpful to callers from overseas? It seems that most of us could do with some help when it comes to using the telephone. A good place to start is with the 20 golden rules.

1. Be prompt, and answer within three or four rings; callers don't like to be kept waiting.
2. If you are going to be away from your telephone for any length of time, remember to forward your calls in order that the caller doesn't have to be repeatedly transferred.
3. Answer with a smile. It comes across in your voice, making you sound friendly and positive.
4. When you answer, give a verbal handshake, announcing the company name and department, as well as your own name.
5. When making a call, make sure it is a convenient time for the other person to receive it.
6. Show empathy to build an instant relationship with your caller by using a warm, friendly tone of voice.
7. Establish the needs of your caller immediately by asking, "How may I help you?"
8. Use open questions to find out facts and information and closed questions to clarify and check understanding.
9. If you can, answer callers' questions promptly and efficiently. If you can't help, tell them what you can do for them.
10. Use continuity sounds to show the caller that you are listening. For example, "Oh yes," "I see," or "That's right."
11. Repeat names, telephone and fax numbers, and dates back to the caller to make sure that you have them right.
12. Make notes, recording all necessary information. It was once said that "a short pencil is far more effective than a long memory."
13. Double check all vital information by reading back, in summary, what you have discussed.
14. Instead of passing callers around from department to department, take the caller's name and telephone number and a brief but comprehensive message, and reassure them that you will pass their message to the appropriate person and have him or her return the call.
15. Give the caller your full attention. Nobody can hold two conversations and retain 100 percent information from both.
16. Keep focused on the subject at hand, and do not interrupt the caller with pointless questions.
17. Remember that both people engaged in a call have the right to know who they are talking to.
18. Agree on any actions that either party will take.
19. End your call on a positive note. Check to see that your caller has asked all the necessary questions and has all the information he or she was asking.
20. "Sign off" properly. Although circumstances vary, this usually means confirming what will happen as a result of the call and thanking the other person for his or her time.

Source: Lin Walker. *Telephone Techniques: The Essential Guide to Thinking and Working Smarter.* New York: American Management Association, 1998.

expression and body posture communicate your negative feelings (Beier, 1974). In this example, and in many similar cases, the socially acceptable message is usually communicated verbally, whereas the less socially acceptable message is communicated nonverbally.

Interpersonal Communication Involves Content and Relationship Messages

Interpersonal messages combine **content and relationship dimensions**. That is, they refer to the real world, to something external to both speaker and listener; and at the same time they also refer to the relationship between the parties. For example, a supervisor may say to a trainee, "See me after the meeting." This simple message has a content message that tells the trainee to see the supervisor after the meeting. It also contains a **relationship message** that says something about the connection between the supervisor and the trainee. Even the use of the simple command shows there is a status difference that allows the supervisor to command the trainee. You can appreciate this most clearly if you visualize this command being made by the trainee to the supervisor. It appears awkward and out of place, because it violates the normal relationship between supervisor and trainee.

Many conflicts arise because people misunderstand relationship messages and cannot clarify them. Other problems arise when people fail to see the difference between content messages and relationship messages. A good example occurred when my mother came to stay for a week at a summer place I had. On the first day she swept the kitchen floor six times. I had repeatedly told her that it did not need sweeping, that I would be tracking in dirt and mud from the outside. She persisted in sweeping, however, saying that the floor was dirty. On the content level, we were talking about the value of sweeping the kitchen floor. On the relationship level, however, we were talking about something quite different. We were each saying, "This is my house." When I realized this, I stopped complaining about the relative usefulness of sweeping a floor that did not need sweeping. Not surprisingly, she stopped sweeping.

Ignoring Relationship Messages   Examine the following interchange and note how relationship considerations are ignored:

MESSAGES	COMMENTS
Paul: I'm going bowling tomorrow. The guys at the plant are starting a team.	He focuses on the content and ignores any relationship implications of the message.
Judy: Why can't we ever do anything together?	She responds primarily on a relationship level, ignoring the content implications of the message and expressing her displeasure at being ignored in his decision.
Paul: We can do something together any time; tomorrow's the day they're organizing the team.	Again, he focuses almost exclusively on the content.

This example reflects research findings that show that men focus more on content messages, whereas women focus more on relationship messages (Wood, 1994). Once you recognize this gender difference, you can increase your sensitivity to the opposite sex.

Acknowledging Relationship Messages   Here is essentially the same situation but with added sensitivity to relationship messages and to gender differences.

MESSAGES	COMMENTS
Paul: The guys at the plant are organizing a bowling team. I'd sure like to be on the team. I'd like to go to the organizational meeting tomorrow. Okay?	Although he focuses on content, he shows awareness of the relationship dimensions by asking if this would be okay and by expressing his desire rather than his decision to attend this meeting.

Judy: That sounds great, but I'd really like to do something together tomorrow.

She focuses on the relationship dimension but also acknowledges his content orientation. Note too that she does not respond defensively, as if she has to defend herself or her emphasis on relationship aspects.

Paul: How about your meeting me at Luigi's and we can have dinner after the organizational meeting?

He responds to the relationship aspect—without abandoning his desire to join the bowling team—and seeks to incorporate it into his communications. He tries to negotiate a solution that will meet both Judy's and his needs.

Judy: That sounds great. I'm dying for spaghetti and meatballs.

She responds to both messages, approving of both his joining the team and their meeting for dinner.

Arguments over the content dimension—such as what happened in a movie—are relatively easy to resolve. You may, for example, simply ask a third person what took place or see the movie again. Arguments on the relationship level, however, are much more difficult to resolve, in part because people seldom recognize that the argument is a relationship one.

In what ways might you misread the meanings of another person by focusing only on the content and neglecting the relationship messages?

Interpersonal Communication Is a Process of Adjustment

The principle of **adjustment** states that interpersonal communication can take place only to the extent that the people talking share the same communication system. We can easily understand this when dealing with speakers of two different languages; much miscommunication is likely to occur. The principle, however, takes on particular relevance when you realize that no two people share identical communication systems. Parents and children, for example, not only have very different vocabularies but, more importantly, have different meanings for some of the terms they have in common. (Consider, for example, the differences between parents' and children's understanding of such terms as *music, success,* and *family.*) Different cultures and social groups, even when they share a common language, also have different nonverbal communication systems. To the extent that these systems differ, communication will be hindered.

Part of the art of interpersonal communication is learning the other person's signals, how they're used, and what they mean. People in close relationships—either as intimate friends or as romantic partners—realize that learning the other person's signals takes a long time and, often, great patience. If you want to understand what another person means—by smiling, by saying "I love you," by arguing about trivial matters, by making self-deprecating comments—you have to learn that person's system of signals. Furthermore, you have to share your own system of

4 Ways to Communicate in the Workplace

You can gain an interesting perspective on interpersonal messages by looking at the way they're treated in an organizational context.

1. **Upward communication** travels from the lower levels of the hierarchy to the upper levels; for example, from line worker to manager, faculty member to dean. These messages give subordinates a sense of belonging to and being a part of the organization and provide management with new ideas from workers. Management can make upward communication more effective by:

   - establishing some nonthreatening system for upward communication, such as anonymous questionnaires, suggestion boxes
   - listening and responding to these messages
   - providing frequent opportunities for worker-to-management communication, such as monthly meetings or chat groups

2. **Downward communication** travels from the higher levels of the hierarchy to the lower levels; for example, orders and explanations of new procedures. Management can make downward messages more effective by:

   - using a vocabulary understood by the workers and keeping technical jargon to a minimum
   - providing workers with sufficient information for them to function effectively
   - avoiding information overload, which can lead to the important information's getting ignored because it's buried with lots of irrelevant notices and memos

3. **Lateral communication** travels between equals—manager to manager, worker to worker—and helps disseminate organizational information and build worker satisfaction. People in an organization can make lateral messages more effective by:

   - being willing to explain the specialized jargon that comes with each specialty
   - being willing to see individual's specialties in perspective rather than as the only important subdivision of the organization

4. Informal or **grapevine messages** follow no formal lines and grow along with the formal communications; the more active the formal communication system, the more active the informal system. You can make informal messages more effective by:

   - using the grapevine as the vital means of information transmission that it is, rather than only for office gossip
   - securing more complete information, given that a message is usually incomplete when it comes through the grapevine
   - not communicating information you do not want sent through the grapevine

THEN AND NOW

Recall a specific workplace communication interaction that did not go as well as it might have. What went wrong? What would you do differently if this same situation occurred today?

signals with others so that they can better understand you. Although some people may know what you mean by your silence or by your avoidance of eye contact, others may not. You cannot expect others to decode your behaviours accurately without help.

This principle is especially important in intercultural communication, largely because people from different cultures use different signals and sometimes the same signals to signify quite different things. In North America, for example, focused eye contact tends to mean honesty and openness. But in Japan and in many Hispanic cultures, that same behaviour may signify arrogance or disrespect if engaged in by, say, a youngster with someone significantly older.

Communication Accommodation   An interesting theory largely revolving around adjustment is communication accommodation theory. This theory holds that speakers will adjust to or accommodate to the speaking style of their listeners so as to gain, for example, social approval and greater communication efficiency (Giles, Mulac, Bradac, & Johnson, 1987). For example, when two people have a similar speech rate, they seem to be attracted to each other more than to those with dissimilar rates (Buller, LePoire, Aune, & Eloy, 1992). Speech rate similarity has also been associated with greater sociability and intimacy (Buller & Aune, 1992). Also, the speaker who uses language intensity similar to that of listeners is judged to have greater credibility than the speaker who uses intensity different from that of listeners (Aune & Kikuchi, 1993). Still another study found that roommates who had similar communication attitudes (both were high in communication competence and willingness to communicate, and low in verbal aggressiveness) were highest in roommate liking and satisfaction (Martin & Anderson, 1995). Although this theory has not been tested on computer communication, it would make the prediction that styles of written communication in email or chat rooms would also evidence accommodation.

As illustrated throughout this text, communication characteristics are influenced greatly by culture (Victor, 2001). Thus, the communication similarities that lead to attraction and more positive perceptions are more likely to be present in *intra*cultural communication than in *inter*cultural encounters. This may present an important (but not insurmountable) obstacle to intercultural communication.

Interpersonal Communication Is Inevitable, Irreversible, and Unrepeatable

Three characteristics often considered together are interpersonal communication's *inevitability, irreversibility,* and *unrepeatability.*

Communication Is Inevitable   Often communication is intentional, purposeful, and consciously motivated. Sometimes, however, you are communicating even though you may not think you are, or may not even want to. Take, for example, the student sitting in the back of the room with an "expressionless" face, perhaps staring out the window. The student may think that she or he is not communicating with the teacher or with the other students. On closer inspection, however, you can see that the student *is* communicating something—perhaps lack of interest or simply anxiety about a private problem. In any event, the student is communicating whether she or he wishes to or not—demonstrating the principle of **inevitability**. You cannot *not* communicate. In the same way, you cannot *not* influence the person you interact with (Watzlawick, 1978). Persuasion, like communication, is also inevitable. (Recent research suggests that the influencing power of communication extends to electronic as well as face-to-face communication. For example, website content is manipulated to draw users to visit particular sites, and to make specific choices during their visit [Knobloch, Hastall, Zillman, & Callison, 2003].) The issue, then, is not whether you will or will not persuade or influence another; rather, it's how you'll exert your influence.

"Careful. He attaches significance to everything you say."

Communication Is Irreversible   Notice that only some processes can be reversed. For example, you can turn water into ice and then reverse the process by turning the ice back into water. Other processes, however, are irreversible. You can, for example, turn grapes into wine, but you cannot reverse the process and turn wine into grapes. Interpersonal communication is an irreversible process. Although you may try to qualify, deny, or somehow reduce the effects of your message, you cannot withdraw the message you have conveyed. Similarly, once you press the send key, your email is in cyberspace and impossible to reverse. Because of **irreversibility**, be careful not to say things you may wish to withdraw later. Similarly, monitor carefully messages of commitment, messages sent in anger, or messages of insult or derision. Otherwise you run the risk of saying something you'll be uncomfortable with later.

Communication Is Unrepeatable   The reason for communication's unrepeatability is simple: Everyone and everything are constantly changing. As a result, you never can recapture the exact same situation, frame of mind, or relationship dynamics that defined a previous interpersonal act. For example, you never can repeat meeting someone for the first time, comforting a grieving friend, or resolving a specific conflict.

You can, of course, try again; you can say, "I'm sorry I came off so pushy, can we try again?" Notice, however, that even when you say this, you have not erased the initial (and perhaps negative) impression. Instead, you try to counteract this impression by going through the motions again. In doing so, you hope to create a more positive impact that will lessen the original negative effect.

Face-to-face communication is evanescent; it fades after you have spoken. There is no trace of your communications outside of the memories of the parties involved or of those who overheard your conversation. In computer-mediated communication, however, the messages are written and may be saved, stored, and printed. Both face-to-face and computer-mediated messages may be kept confidential or revealed publicly. But computer messages can be made public more easily and spread more quickly than face-to-face messages. And, of course, in the case of written messages there is clear evidence of what you said and when you said it.

Interpersonal Communication Serves a Variety of Purposes

Interpersonal communication can be used to accomplish a variety of purposes. Understanding how it serves these purposes will help you more effectively achieve your own interpersonal purposes. Interpersonal communication enables you to *learn,* to better understand the external world—the world of objects, events, and other people. Although a great deal of information comes from the media, you probably discuss and ultimately "learn" or internalize information through interpersonal interactions. In fact, your beliefs, attitudes, and values are probably influenced more by interpersonal encounters than by the media or even by formal education. Through interpersonal communication you also learn about yourself. By talking about yourself with others, you gain valuable feedback on your feelings, thoughts, and behaviours. Through these communications you also learn how you appear to others—who likes you, who dislikes you, and why.

Interpersonal communication helps you *relate*. One of the greatest needs people have is to establish and maintain close relationships. You want to feel loved and liked, and in turn you want to love and like others. Such relationships help to alleviate loneliness and depression, enable you to share and heighten your pleasures, and generally make you feel more positive about yourself.

Very likely, you *influence* the attitudes and behaviours of others in your interpersonal encounters. You may wish another person to vote a particular way, try a new diet, buy a new book, listen to a record, see a movie, take a specific course, think in a particular way, believe that something is true or false, or value some idea—the list is endless. A good deal of your time is probably spent in interpersonal persuasion.

Talking with friends about your weekend activities, discussing sports or dates, telling stories and jokes, and, in general, just passing the time fulfill a *play* function. Far from frivolous, this purpose is an extremely important one. It gives our activities a necessary balance and our mind a needed break from all the seriousness around us. Everyone has an inner child, and that child needs time to play.

Therapists of various kinds serve a helping function professionally by offering guidance through interpersonal interaction. But everyone interacts to *help* in everyday life: You console a friend who has broken off a love affair, counsel another student about courses to take, or offer advice to a colleague about work. Success in accomplishing this helping function, professionally or otherwise, depends on your knowledge and skill in interpersonal communication.

(You may wish to pause and analyze an interaction using the principles just discussed. Visit **www.ablongman.com/devito**.)

The secret of success is constancy to purpose.

—**Benjamin Disraeli**

Culture and Interpersonal Communication

As noted earlier, the word *culture* refers to the **beliefs** (convictions), ways of behaving, and artifacts of a group that are transmitted through communication and learning rather than through genes. Gender is considered a cultural variable, at least in part, because cultures teach men and women different attitudes, beliefs, values, and ways of communicating and relating to one another (MacGregor, Gillihan, Samter, & Clark, 2003). This does not, of course, deny that biological differences also play a role in the differences between male and female behaviour. In fact, recent research continues to uncover biological roots of traits we once thought were entirely learned, such as happiness and shyness (McCroskey, 1998).

Because your interpersonal communications are heavily influenced by the culture in which you were raised (Burleton & Morteson, 2003), culture is given a prominent place in this text. This section explains the relevance of culture to interpersonal communication and the aims and benefits of a cultural perspective.

How relevant do you think cultural differences are to your own current interpersonal interactions? How relevant will cultural differences be to you in the next 10 or 15 years?

A walk through any large city, many small towns, or just about any college or university campus reinforces the fact that Canada is largely a collection of many different cultures. Many cultural groups have been successful in preserving their uniqueness and special traditions while contributing to Canadian society as a whole. In fact, the Canadian identity is considered to be a multicultural mosaic, with the different cultural groups within the mosaic influencing each other in a multitude of ways. The composition of this mosaic is also dynamic, since immigration patterns can change rapidly. Table 1.2 reviews recent patterns.

TABLE 1.2 Recent Immigrants by Country of Last Residence

With immigration patterns changing so rapidly, the portrait illustrated here is likely to look different in the coming years. Do any of these patterns surprise you? What might your own province, city, or town look like 30 years from now, and how might this future cultural landscape affect your own intercultural communication?

	1997–1998	1998–1999	1999–2000	2000–2001	2001–2002
Number of Immigrants					
Total immigrants	**193 452**	**173 198**	**205 666**	**252 271**	**255 272**
Africa	13 443	14 410	16 951	23 118	23 978
Asia	117 089	100 491	126 114	156 722	158 648
India	17 427	15 028	21 214	29 211	31 003
Hong Kong	12 522	2 654	1 115	806	714
Vietnam	1 860	1 473	1 563	1 791	2 628
Philippines	9 467	8 075	9 397	13 328	12 450
Other Asian countries	75 813	73,261	92 825	111 586	111 853
Australasia	1 344	838	878	1 109	1 475
Europe	39 853	37 909	39,976	45 647	42 959
Great Britain	4 228	4 145	4,829	5 208	5 656
France	3 248	3 981	4 096	4 583	4 106
Germany	1 998	2 449	2 933	1 900	1 863
Netherlands	646	769	902	882	784
Greece	267	248	248	368	344
Italy	528	438	451	531	527
Portugal	605	346	383	445	457
Poland	1 545	1 327	1 351	1 236	1 249
Other European countries	26 788	24 206	24 783	30 494	27 973
United States	4 709	5 089	5 761	6 038	6 017
West Indies	7 590	6,203	6 648	8 056	8 532
Other North and Central American countries	3 161	2 628	2 969	3 227	3 523
South America	5 535	5 055	5 967	7 755	9 310
Other countries	728	575	402	599	830

Source: Statistics Canada Internet Site, www.statcan.ca/english/Pgdb/population/demo08.htm, June 20, 2003.

Some of the cultural changes occurring in Canada today can be attributed to changing gender roles. Many Canadian men, for example, are now spending more time performing household duties and caring for their children, particularly if these men are young and well educated (Nelson & Robinson, 2002). More obvious, perhaps, is that women are becoming more visible in fields once occupied exclusively by men—politics, law enforcement, the military, and the clergy are some examples. And, of course, women are increasingly entering corporate executive ranks; the glass ceiling may not have disappeared, but it is cracked.

You may wish to continue this cultural awareness experience by taking the following self-test.

How important is intercultural communication to you? Will its importance change for you in the next 5 or 10 years?

TEST YOURSELF

What Are Your Cultural Beliefs and Values?

Instructions: Here the extremes of 10 cultural differences are identified. For each characteristic indicate your own values:

A. If you feel your values are "very similar" to the extreme statements on the left, select 1; if "very similar" to the extreme statements on the right, select 7.

B. If you feel your values are "quite similar" to the extreme statements on the left, select 2; if "quite similar" to the extreme statements on the right, select 6.

C. If you feel your values are "fairly similar" to the extreme statements on the left, select 3; if "fairly similar" to the extreme statements on the right, select 5.

D. If you feel your values are in the middle of these extreme statements, select 4.

Men and women are equal and are entitled to equality in all areas.	**Gender Equality** 1 2 3 4 5 6 7	Men and women are very different and should stick to the specific roles assigned to them by their culture.
"Success" is measured by your contribution to the group.	**Group and Individual Orientation** 1 2 3 4 5 6 7	"Success" is measured by how far you outperform others.
You should enjoy yourself as much as possible.	**Hedonism** 1 2 3 4 5 6 7	You should work as much as possible.
Religion is the final arbiter of what is right and wrong; your first obligation is to abide by the rules and customs of your religion.	**Religion** 1 2 3 4 5 6 7	Religion is like any other social institution; it's not inherently moral or right just because it's a religion.

(continued)

	Family 1 2 3 4 5 6 7	
Your first obligation is to your family; each person is responsible for the welfare of his or her family.	**Family** 1 2 3 4 5 6 7	Your first obligation is to yourself; each person is responsible for him- or herself.
Work hard now for a better future.	**Time Orientation** 1 2 3 4 5 6 7	Live in the present; the future may never come.
Romantic relationships, once made, are forever.	**Relationship Permanency** 1 2 3 4 5 6 7	Romantic relationships should be maintained as long as they are more rewarding than punishing and dissolved when they are more punishing than rewarding.
People should express their emotions openly and freely.	**Emotional Expression** 1 2 3 4 5 6 7	People should not reveal their emotions, especially those that may reflect negatively on them or others or make others feel uncomfortable.
Money is extremely important and should be a major consideration in just about any decision you make.	**Money** 1 2 3 4 5 6 7	Money is relatively unimportant and should not enter into life's really important decisions, such as what relationship to enter or what career to pursue.
The world is a just place; bad things happen to bad people and good things happen to good people; what goes around comes around.	**Belief in a Just World** 1 2 3 4 5 6 7	The world is random; bad and good things happen to people without any relationship to whether they are good or bad people.

HOW DID YOU DO?

This test was designed to help you explore the possible influence of your cultural beliefs and values on communication. If you visualize communication as involving choices, as already noted in this chapter, these beliefs will influence the choices you make and thus how you communicate and how you listen and respond to the communications of others. For example, your beliefs and values about gender equality will influence the way you communicate with and about the opposite sex. Your group and individual orientation will influence how you perform in work teams and how you deal with your peers at school and at work. Your degree of hedonism will influence the kinds of communications you engage in, the books you read, the television you watch. Your religious beliefs will influence the ethical system you follow in communicating.

WHAT DO YOU DO?

Review the entire list of 10 characteristics and try to identify one *specific* way in which each characteristic influences your communication. As you do this, try to consider what you might do to increase your awareness of how your beliefs influence your communications.

The Importance of Culture

There are lots of reasons for the cultural emphasis you'll find in this book. Most obvious, perhaps, are the vast demographic changes taking place throughout the country. As a result of these changes, Canadians have become increasingly respectful of cultural differences. Rather than wanting everyone to be the same, we are coming to see that diversity enriches our society and that it's possible for a united Canada to embrace a broad range of traditions, beliefs, and ways of living. And with some notable exceptions—hate speech, racism, sexism, homophobia, and classism come quickly to mind—we're more concerned with saying the right thing and ultimately with developing a society in which all cultures can coexist and enrich one another. At the same time, the ability to interact effectively with members of other cultures often translates into financial gain, increased employment opportunities, and better advancement prospects.

Today, most countries are economically dependent on one another. Our economic lives depend on our ability to communicate effectively across cultures. Similarly, our political well-being depends in great part on that of other cultures. Political unrest in any part of the world—in the Middle East or in Eastern Europe, to take just two examples—affects our own security. Intercultural communication and understanding seem now more crucial than ever.

The rapid spread of communication technology has brought foreign and sometimes very different cultures right into your living room. News from foreign countries is commonplace. You see nightly—in vivid colour—what is going on in remote countries. Technology has made intercultural communication easy, practical, and inevitable. Daily the media bombard you with evidence of racial tensions, religious disagreements, sexual bias—in general, of the problems caused when intercultural communication fails. And, of course, the internet has made intercultural communication as easy as writing a note on your computer. You can now communicate by email just as easily with someone in Europe or Asia, for example, as with someone in another city or province.

Still another reason for the importance of cultural awareness is that interpersonal competence is specific to a given culture; what proves effective in one culture may prove ineffective in another. For example, in North America corporate executives get down to business during the first several minutes of a meeting. In Japan, however, business executives interact socially for an extended period and try to find out something about one another. Thus, the communication principle influenced by North American culture would advise participants to tackle the meeting's agenda during the first five minutes. The principle influenced by Japanese culture would advise participants to avoid dealing with business until everyone has socialized sufficiently and feels well enough acquainted to begin negotiations. Neither principle is right and neither is wrong. Each is effective within its own culture, and ineffective outside its own culture.

The Aim of a Cultural Perspective

Because culture permeates all forms of communication, it's necessary to understand its influences if you're to understand how interpersonal communication works and master interpersonal communication skills. As illustrated throughout this text, culture influences communications of all

In the photo on the left, Wayne Gretzky is depicted as a hockey superstar; in the photo on the right he appears with Jean Chrétien and Catriona Le May Doan following Vancouver's successful bid to host the 2010 Winter Olympics. Do you think Gretzky's interpersonal communication style has evolved as his role has grown from that of an athlete to include that of manager and spokesperson? In what ways, if any?

types (Moon, 1996). It influences what you say to yourself and how you talk with friends, lovers, and family in everyday conversation. It influences how you interact in groups and how much importance you place on the group versus the individual. It influences the topics you talk about and the strategies you use in communicating information or in persuading. And it influences how you use the media and the credibility you attribute to them.

A cultural emphasis helps distinguish what is universal (true for all people) from what is relative (true for people in one culture and not true for people in other cultures) (Matsumoto, 1994). The principles for communicating information and for changing listeners' attitudes, for example, will vary from one culture to another. If you're to understand communication, you need to know how its principles vary and how the principles must be qualified and adjusted on the basis of cultural differences.

And of course you need cultural understanding in order to communicate effectively in a wide variety of intercultural situations. Success in interpersonal communication—on your job and in your social life—will depend on your ability to communicate effectively with persons who are culturally different from yourself. Respecting the values and beliefs of others does not necessarily mean that you agree with them. What you are respecting is the right of others to be different from you.

Do you agree that the media and the internet are fostering an Americanization of different cultures? Some people find this an unpleasant prospect and see it as the loss of diversity; others may see it as inevitable and as the result of a democratic process whereby people select the values and customs they wish to adopt. How do you feel about this Americanization?

As demonstrated throughout this text, cultural differences exist across the interpersonal communication spectrum—from the way you use eye contact to the way you develop or dissolve a relationship (Chang & Holt, 1996). But these differences should not blind you to the great number of similarities existing among even the most widely separated cultures. Close interpersonal relationships, for example, are common in all cultures, even though people in different cultures enter into them for very different reasons. Further, remember that differences are usually matters of degree. For example, most cultures value honesty, although not all value it to the same degree. Also, the advances in media and technology and the widespread use of the internet are influencing cultures and cultural change and are perhaps homogenizing different cultures to some degree, lessening differences and increasing similarities. They're also Americanizing different cultures, including Canada's (Tate & Allen, 2003), because the dominant values and customs evidenced in the media and on the internet are in large part American, a product of current U.S. dominance in both media and technology.

SUMMARY OF CONCEPTS AND SKILLS

This chapter explored the nature of interpersonal communication, then looked at several principles of interpersonal communication and last at the centrality of culture.

1. Interpersonal communication is a transactional process that takes place between two people who have a relationship.

2. Essential to an understanding of interpersonal communication are the following elements: source–receiver, encoding–decoding, messages (including feedback and feedforward), channel, noise (physical, physiological, psychological, and semantic), context (physical, cultural, social–psychological, and temporal), and competence.

3. Interpersonal communication is:

   ■ a package of signals that usually reinforce but may also contradict one another
   ■ both content and relationship messages; we communicate about objects and events in the world but simultaneously about the relationship between sources and receivers
   ■ a process by which we each adjust to the specialized communication system of the other
   ■ inevitable (communication will occur whether we want it to or not); irreversible (once something is received, it remains communicated and cannot be erased from a listener's memory); and unrepeatable (no communication act can ever be repeated exactly)
   ■ purposeful; through interpersonal communication we learn, relate, influence, play, and help

4. Interpersonal communication is heavily influenced by culture; by the beliefs, attitudes, and values taught and practised by cultural members.

Several interpersonal skills were also noted in this chapter. Evaluate your own ability to do the following, using this rating scale: 1 = almost always, 2 = often, 3 = sometimes, 4 = rarely, and 5 = almost never.

_____ 1. Interact interpersonally with a recognition that all the elements of communication are in a constant state of transaction, with each element influencing every other element.

_____ 2. Communicate with an understanding that meaning is derived from the entire package of signals, both verbal and nonverbal.

_____ 3. Distinguish between content and relationship messages and respond to both.

_____ 4. Adjust your messages to the unique communication system of the other.

_____ 5. Communicate *after* thinking, especially in light of the inevitability, unrepeatability, and irreversibility of interpersonal communication.

_____ 6. Communicate with a recognition of the variety of purposes that interpersonal interaction may serve.

_____ 7. Use the principles of interpersonal communication with a recognition of its cultural context.

VOCABULARY QUIZ

The Language of Interpersonal Communication

Match the terms of interpersonal communication with their definitions. Record the number of the definition next to the appropriate term.

__7__ interpersonal communication 4

__10__ encoding 7

__1__ feedback 15

__4__ semantic noise 17

__5__ cultural context 18

__3__ feedforward 16

__8__ relationship messages 21

_2_ source–receiver ⌐7

_9_ signal-to-noise ratio 16

_6_ communication as a transactional process 5

1. Messages sent back to the source in response to the source's messages.
2. Each person in the interpersonal communication act.
3. Information about messages that are yet to be sent.
4. Interference that occurs when the receiver does not understand the meanings intended by the sender.
5. The rules and norms, beliefs and attitudes of the people communicating.
6. Communication as an ongoing process in which each part depends on each other part.
7. Communication that takes place between two persons who have a relationship between them.
8. Messages referring to the connection between the two people in communication.
9. A measure of meaningful message compared with interference.
10. The process of sending messages; for example, in speaking or writing.

SKILL BUILDING EXERCISES

1.1 GIVING EFFECTIVE FEEDBACK

How would you give feedback in these varied situations? You may wish to read a bit more about feedback before completing this exercise; if so, see Chapter 8, pages 194–196. Write one or two sentences of feedback for each of these situations:

a friend—whom you like but don't have romantic feelings for—asks you for a date

your instructor asks you to evaluate the course

an interviewer asks if you want a credit card

a homeless person smiles at you on the street

a colleague at work tells a homophobic joke

1.2 EXPLAINING INTERPERSONAL DIFFICULTIES

Using the principles of interpersonal communication discussed in this chapter, try *describing* what is going on in these several cases. These scenarios are extremely brief and are written only as aids to stimulate you to think more concretely about the axioms.

1. Grace feels that her fiancé, Tom, by not defending her proposal at a company where both work, created a negative attitude and encouraged others to reject her ideas. Tom says that he felt he could not defend her proposal because others in the room would have felt his defence was motivated by their relationship. So he felt it was best to say nothing.

2. A couple together for 20 years argues about the seemingly most insignificant things—who takes out the garbage, who does the dishes, who decides where to eat, and on and on. The arguments are so frequent and so unsettling that the two people are seriously considering separating.

3. In the heat of a big argument, Harry said he didn't want to see Peggy's family ever again: "They don't like me and I don't like them." Peggy reciprocated and said she felt the same way about his family. Now, weeks later, there is still a great deal of tension between them, especially when they're with one or both families.

4. Pat and Chris have been online friends for the last two years, communicating with each other at least once a day. Recently, Pat wrote several things that Chris interpreted as insulting and as ridiculing Chris's feelings and dreams. Chris wrote back expressing resentment over these last messages, then stopped writing. Pat has written every day for the last two weeks to try to patch things up, but Chris won't respond.

Thinking Critically About Interpersonal Difficulties.

Although the instructions ask you to describe what is going on in these situations, did you also think of recommendations for reducing the communication problems? What advice would you give these people? What principle would you find especially useful in explaining what is going on to each of the people involved?

1.3 CULTURAL BELIEFS

Review the following cultural maxims. Select any one that seems especially interesting and identify:

a. the meaning of the maxim

b. the cultural value(s) it embodies and speaks to

c. the similarity or difference between it and what your own culture teaches

1. A penny saved is a penny earned.
2. All is not gold that glitters.
3. All things come to those who wait.
4. Blessed are the meek.
5. Blood is thicker than water.
6. Children should be seen and not heard.
7. Do unto others as you would have others do unto you.
8. Don't put off till tomorrow what you can do today.
9. God is just.
10. Honesty is the best policy.
11. If you've got it, flaunt it./Blow your own horn.
12. It's better to light a candle than to curse the darkness.
13. Love thy neighbour.
14. Never give a sucker an even break.
15. No one likes a sore loser.
16. Nothing succeeds like success.
17. Patience is a virtue.
18. Real men don't cry.
19. Respect your elders.
20. Self-praise smells bad.
21. Smile though your heart is breaking.
22. Stick with your own kind.
23. Tell it like it is.
24. The apple doesn't fall far from the tree.
25. There's no defence like a good offence.
26. Throw caution to the wind.
27. Time is money.
28. Time waits for no one.
29. Tomorrow will take care of itself.
30. What goes around comes around.

Thinking Critically About Cultural Maxims.

Have you ever applied your chosen maxim (or any of the maxims listed here) to specific interpersonal situations? What effect did the maxim's application have on the interaction?

Chapter 2

The Self in Interpersonal Communication

CHAPTER TOPICS

This chapter explores the nature and role of the self in interpersonal communication.

- Self-Concept and Self-Awareness
- Self-Disclosure
- Interpersonal Apprehension

CHAPTER SKILLS

After completing this chapter, you should be able to:

- analyze your self-concept and increase self-awareness.
- self-disclose and respond to the disclosures of others appropriately.
- manage your fear of communicating; communicate with confidence in a variety of contexts.

A esop, the great writer of fables, tells the story of Mercury, one of the gods of Ancient Rome. Although only a lesser god, Mercury aspired to be more. So one day, disguised as an ordinary man, he entered a sculptor's studio, where he saw statues of the gods and goddesses for sale. Eyeing a statue of Jupiter, one of the major gods, Mercury asked the price. "A crown," the sculptor said. Mercury laughed, for he thought that was such a low price; maybe Jupiter was not so important after all. Then he asked the price of a statue of Juno, a major goddess. "Half a crown," said the sculptor. This seemed to please Mercury, who thought that surely his likeness would command a much higher price. So, pointing to a statue of himself, he proudly asked its price. "Oh, that; I'll give you that one free if you buy the other two."

Mercury was engaging in **social comparison**, a way of gaining insight into his own self-concept; he was comparing his reputation with the reputations of others. By doing so, Mercury got a good idea of his own relative importance. In this chapter we look at self-concept and self-awareness, and particularly at how you develop your image of yourself and how you can increase your own self-awareness. With this as a foundation, we then look at self-disclosure, the process of revealing yourself to another person; and we consider speaker apprehension and some ways to reduce your own fear of communication.

Self-Concept and Self-Awareness

Central to all forms of interpersonal communication is your self-concept—the image you have of yourself—and how that image is formed. Equally significant is your self-awareness, the degree to which you know yourself. Let's look first at self-concept.

Self-Concept

Your **self-concept** is your image of who you are. It's how you perceive yourself: your feelings and thoughts about your strengths and weaknesses and your abilities and limitations. Self-concept develops from the image that others have of you; the comparisons you draw between yourself and others; your cultural experiences in the realms of race, ethnicity, gender, and gender roles; and your evaluation of your own thoughts and behaviours (Figure 2.1).

Others' Images of You   If you wished to see the way your hair looked, you'd probably look in a mirror. But what would you do if you wanted to see how friendly or how assertive you are? According to the concept of the *looking-glass self* (Cooley, 1922), you would look at the image of yourself that others reveal to you through their behaviours, and especially through the way they treat you and react to you.

What sense of self do members of the Royal Family project? How much of their self-concept do you think comes from the extensive "grooming" they have received for their role as royals? How might a person develop a positive sense of self without such a privileged background?

FIGURE 2.1 The Sources of Self-Concept

This diagram depicts the four sources of self-concept, the four contributors to how you see yourself. As you read about self-concept, consider the influence of each factor throughout your life. Which factor influenced you most as a preteen? Which influences you the most now? Which will influence you the most 25 or 30 years from now?

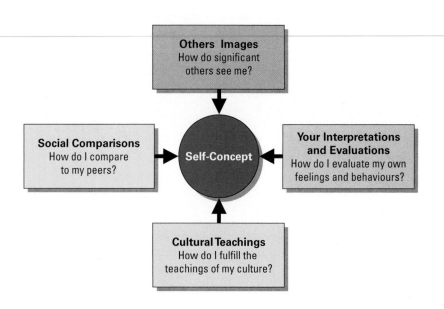

Others Images
How do significant others see me?

Social Comparisons
How do I compare to my peers?

Self-Concept

Your Interpretations and Evaluations
How do I evaluate my own feelings and behaviours?

Cultural Teachings
How do I fulfill the teachings of my culture?

Of course, you would not look to just anyone. Rather, you would look to those who are most significant in your life—to your *significant others.* As a child, for example, you would look to your parents and then to your elementary school teachers. As an adult you might look to your friends and romantic partners. If these significant others think highly of you, you will see a positive self-image reflected in their behaviours; if they think little of you, you will see a more negative image.

Social Comparisons Another way you develop self-concept is to compare yourself with others, to engage in what are called social comparisons (Festinger, 1954; Chin & McConnel, 2003). Again, you don't choose just anyone. Rather, when you want to gain insight into who you are and how effective or competent you are, you look to your peers. For example, after an examination you probably want to know how you performed relative to the other students in your class. This gives you a clearer idea as to how effectively you performed. If you play on a baseball team, it's important to know your batting averages in comparison with the batting averages of others on the team. Your absolute score on the exam or your batting average may be helpful in telling you something about your performance, but you

What kinds of information about yourself do you seek from social comparisons? With whom do you compare yourself?

gain a different perspective when you see your scores in comparison with those of your peers.

Cultural Teachings   Through your parents, teachers, and the media, your culture instills in you a variety of beliefs, values, and attitudes—about matters such as success (how you should define and achieve it); the relevance of religion, race, or nationality; and the ethical principles you should follow in business and in your personal life. These teachings provide benchmarks against which you can measure yourself. For example, your ability to achieve what your culture defines as success will contribute to a positive self-concept. Your failure to achieve what your culture values (for example, not being married by the time you're 30) may contribute to a negative self-concept.

When you demonstrate the qualities that your culture (or organization, because organizations are much like cultures) teaches, you will see yourself as a cultural success and will be rewarded by other members of the culture (or organization). Seeing yourself as culturally successful and getting rewarded by others will contribute positively to your self-concept. When you fail to demonstrate such qualities, you're more likely to see yourself as a cultural failure and to be punished by other members of the culture, contributing to a more negative self-concept.

Your Own Observations, Interpretations, and Evaluations   You also observe, interpret, and evaluate your own behaviour. For example, let's say you believe that lying is wrong. If you lie, you will probably evaluate this behaviour in terms of your internalized beliefs about lying and will react negatively to your own behaviour. You may, for example, experience guilt as a result of your behaviour contradicting your beliefs. On the other hand, let's say that you pull someone out of a burning building at great personal risk. You will probably evaluate this behaviour positively; you will feel good about this behaviour and, as a result, about yourself.

The more you understand why you view yourself as you do, the better you'll understand who you are. You can gain additional insight into yourself by looking more closely at self-awareness—and especially at the Johari model of the self.

Of the four sources of self-concept, which most influences the way you see yourself? Which gives you the most positive feedback? Which gives you the most negative feedback?

Self-Awareness

Because you control your thoughts and behaviours largely to the extent that you understand who you are, it's crucial to increase your self-awareness. **Self-awareness** also helps you identify your strengths and weaknesses so that you can capitalize on your strengths and direct your energies to correcting your weaknesses. The **Johari window**, a model of the four selves, is particularly helpful in explaining the self and in offering suggestions on how to increase self-awareness (Figure 2.2).

Your Four Selves   Assume that the model in Figure 2.2 represents you. The model is divided into quadrants, each of which contains a different self. Visualize the entire model as of constant size but each section as variable: sometimes small, sometimes large. That is, changes in

FIGURE 2.2 The Johari Window

This diagram is a tool commonly used for examining what you know and don't know about yourself. It will also prove an effective way of explaining the nature of self-disclosure, covered later in this chapter. The window gets its name from its inventors, *Joseph Luft* and *Harry* Ingham. When interacting with your peers, which self is your largest? Your smallest?

Source: From *Group Processes: An Introduction to Group Dynamics*, 3rd ed., by Joseph Luft. Copyright © 1984 by Mayfield Publishing. Reprinted by permission.

	Known to self	**Not known to self**
Known to others	**Open Self** Information about yourself that you and others know	**Blind self** Information about yourself that you don't know but that others do know
Not known to others	**Hidden self** Information about yourself that you know but others don't know	**Unknown self** Information about yourself that neither you nor others know

one quadrant will cause changes in the other quadrants. For example, if you enlarge the open self, then another self must get smaller.

The Johari model emphasizes that the several aspects of the self are not separate and distinct pieces. Rather, they're parts of a whole that interact with one another. Like the model of interpersonal communication, this model of the self is transactional: Each part is dependent on each other part.

Your *open self* represents all the information, behaviours, attitudes, feelings, desires, motivations, and ideas that characterize you. The type of information included here might vary, from your name and sex to your age, religious affiliation, and batting average. The size of your open self changes depending on the situation and the individuals you're interacting with. Some people probably make you feel comfortable and support you. To them, you may open yourself wide. To others you might prefer to leave most of yourself closed or unknown.

Your *blind self* represents all the things about yourself that others know but that you do not. These include, for example, your habit of rubbing your nose when you get angry, your defence mechanisms, and your repressed experiences. Interpersonal communication depends on both parties' sharing the same basic information about each other. Where blind areas exist, communication will be more difficult. Yet blind areas always exist. You can shrink your blind area, but you can never totally eliminate it.

Your *hidden self* contains all that you know of yourself but that you keep to yourself. This area includes all your successfully kept secrets. In any interaction, this area includes everything you have not revealed and perhaps seek actively to conceal. When you move information from this area to the open area—as in, say, telling someone a secret—you're self-disclosing, a process examined later in this chapter.

Your *unknown self* represents truths that exist but that neither you nor others know. We infer the existence of this unknown self from dreams, psychological tests, or therapy. For example, through therapy you might become aware of your high need for acceptance and of how this influences the way you allow people to take advantage of you. With this insight, this information moves from the unknown self to the hidden self and perhaps to the open self.

Increasing Self-Awareness   Embedded in the discussion of the Johari window were suggestions on how to increase your own self-awareness, which are discussed more fully below. (Chapter 12 returns to the self and considers the nature of self-esteem and how to increase it.)

Listen to Others.   You can learn a great deal about yourself from *listening to others* and seeing yourself as others do. Conveniently, others are constantly giving you the very feedback you need to increase self-awareness. In every interpersonal interaction, people comment on you in some way—on what you do, what you say, how you look. Sometimes these comments are explicit: "Loosen up," "Don't take things so hard," "You seem angry." Often, however, they're hidden in the way others look at you or in what they talk about. Pay close attention to this kind of in-

LISTEN TO THIS

Listening to Yourself

Very likely you talk to yourself, sometimes silently and perhaps sometimes out loud. This self-talk is important, because it influences your self-concept—the way you feel about yourself. By listening carefully to what you tell yourself, you'll gain in both self-awareness and self-esteem. Listen especially to two types of statements: self-destructive statements and self-affirming statements.

Self-destructive statements damage your self-esteem and prevent you from building meaningful and productive relationships. They may be about yourself ("I'm not creative," "I'm boring"), your world ("The world is an unhappy place," "They'll never offer me this job"), or your relationships ("All the good people are already in relationships," "If I ever fall in love, I know I'll be hurt"). Recognizing that you may have internalized such beliefs is a first step toward eliminating them. A second step involves recognizing that these beliefs are unrealistic and self-defeating and substituting more realistic ones. For example, you might try replacing the unrealistic belief that you always have to please others with the more realistic belief that although it would be nice if others were pleased with you, it certainly isn't essential (Ellis, 1988).

Self-affirming statements, on the other hand, are positive and self-supportive. They remind you of your successes and focus on your good deeds, positive qualities, strengths, and virtues. These statements concentrate on your potential, not your limitations (Brody, 1991). Here is just a small sampling of self-affirmations that you may wish to try saying to yourself—and, most important, listening to:

1. I'm a competent person.
2. I'm worth loving and having as a friend.
3. I'm a good team player.
4. I'm empathic and supportive.
5. I facilitate open communication.
6. I can accept my past but can also let it go.
7. I'm an effective and valuable worker.
8. I'm open-minded and listen fairly to others.
9. I can apologize.
10. I'm flexible and can adjust to different situations.

SUGGESTIONS?

Sindra's 10-year-old son has such low self-esteem that it prevents him from trying to do things that he is probably very capable of doing. For example, he refuses to play baseball because he thinks he can't; he refuses to answer questions in class because he thinks he'll be wrong. What advice would you give Sindra to help her help her son?

formation (both explicit and hidden) and use it to increase your own self-awareness. The discussions of verbal and nonverbal communication (Chapters 5 and 6) offer suggestions and insights for reading these hidden messages.

Increase Your Open Self. Revealing yourself to others will help increase your self-awareness. At the very least, you will bring into focus what you may have buried within. As you discuss yourself, you may see connections that you had previously missed. With feedback from others, you may gain still more insight. Also, by increasing your open self, you increase the chances that others will reveal what they know about you. We must remember that our cultural background will influence our approach to the open, hidden and even blind and unknown self. Canadians tend to be less prone to avid self-disclosure than our American counterparts. Compare, for example, Canadian television talk shows (for example, Vicki Gabereau) with popular American talk shows (for example, Oprah Winfrey, Jerry Springer), whose shows often focus on the disclosure of highly personal and private matters.

Seek Out Information to Reduce Your Blind Self. Encouraging people to reveal what they know about you will further help increase your awareness. You need not be so blatant as to say, "Tell me about myself" or "What do you think of me?" or imitate the egocentric character in the cartoon to the left. You can, however, use some situations that arise every day to gain self-information. "Do you think I came down too hard on the kids today?" "Do you think I was assertive enough when asking for a raise?" But use this route to self-awareness in moderation. If you do it too often, your friends will soon look for someone else to talk with.

Another way to seek out information about yourself is to visualize how you're seen by your parents, teachers, friends, the stranger on the bus, your neighbour's child. Recognize that each of these people sees you differently; to each you're a different person. Yet you're really *all* those persons. The experience will surely give you new and valuable perspectives on yourself. It will convince you that you're actually a different person, depending on the person you're interacting with. For example, my colleagues see me as serious and always doing a hundred things at the same time. My students, however, see me as humorous and laid back.

Self-Disclosure

When you move information from the hidden self into the open self, you're self-disclosing; you're revealing information about yourself to others. You can self-disclose through overt statements as well as through slips of the tongue and unconscious nonverbal movements. **Self-disclosure** may involve information that you tell others freely or information that you normally keep hidden. It may supply information ("I earn $45 000") or reveal feelings

The worst of all deceptions is self-deception.

—Plato

"This isn't about you, Cheryl. In this crazy world your problems don't amount to a hill of beans. This is about me."

("I'm feeling really depressed"). Self-disclosure can vary from the insignificant ("I'm a Sagittarius") to the highly revealing ("I'm currently in an abusive relationship," "I'm always depressed").

Only new knowledge represents "disclosure." To tell someone something about yourself that he or she already knows is not self-disclosure. And self-disclosure involves at least one other individual. It cannot be *intra*personal communication (communication with yourself). Nor may you "disclose" in a way that makes the message impossible for another person to understand. For a communication to be self-disclosure, someone must receive and understand the information.

Factors Influencing Self-Disclosure

Many factors influence whether or not you disclose, what you disclose, and to whom you disclose. Among the most important factors are who you are, your culture, your gender, who your listeners are, and what your topic is.

Who You Are   Highly sociable and extroverted people self-disclose more than those who are less sociable and more introverted. People who are apprehensive about talking in general also self-disclose less than those who are more comfortable in communicating.

People who are viewed in our society as competent communicators tend to engage in self-disclosure more than less competent people (Rubin, Yaung, & Porte, 2000). Perhaps competent people have greater self-confidence and more positive things to reveal. Similarly, their self-confidence may make them more willing to risk possible negative reactions to their disclosures (Crocker, 2002).

Your Culture   Different cultures view self-disclosure differently. People in the United States, for example, disclose more than those in Great Britain, Germany, Japan, or Puerto Rico (Abrams, O'Connor, & Giles, 2002). American students also disclose more than students from most Middle East countries (Jourard, 1971a). Similarly, American students self-disclose more about controversial issues and to different types of people than do Chinese students (Chen, 1992). Chinese Singaporean students consider more topics to be taboo and inappropriate for self-disclosure than their British peers (Goodwin & Lee, 1994). Among the Kabre of Togo, secrecy is a major part of everyday interaction (Piot, 1993).

Would this photo seem strange to you if instead of six women it featured six men? What has your culture taught you about self-disclosure? Does it provide different "rules" for men and for women?

Some cultures view disclosing one's inner feelings as a weakness. Among some groups, for example, it would be considered out of place for a man to cry at a happy occasion like a wedding, whereas that same display of emotion would go unnoticed in some Latin cultures. Similarly, in Japan it's considered undesirable for colleagues to reveal personal information, whereas in much of North America it's expected (Barnlund, 1989; Hall & Hall, 1987).

In some cultures—for example, Mexican—there's a strong emphasis on discussing all matters in a positive mode, and this undoubtedly influences the way Mexicans approach self-disclosure as well. Negative self-disclosures, for example, are usually made only to close intimates and then only after considerable time has elapsed in a relationship. This reluctance to disclose negative information extends to people's HIV-positive status and thus is creating serious problems in Mexico's efforts to prevent and treat HIV infection (Szapocznik, 1995).

These differences aside, there are also important similarities across cultures. For example, people from Great Britain, Germany, the United States, and Puerto Rico are all more apt to disclose certain kinds of personal information—such as details about hobbies, interests, attitudes, and opinions on politics and religion—than to discuss finances, sex, personality, and interpersonal relationships (Jourard, 1971a). Similarly, one study showed self-disclosure patterns between American males to be virtually identical to those between Korean males (Won-Doornink, 1991).

TALKING ETHICS

Outing

An interesting variation on self-disclosure occurs when someone takes information from your hidden self and makes it public. Although this third-party disclosure can concern any aspect of a person's hidden self—for example, an athlete's prison record or drug habit, a movie star's ill health or alcoholism, or a politician's criminal associates or financial dealings—the media have made a special case out of revealing a person's affectional orientation; the process is called **outing** (Gross, 1991; Signorile, 1993; Johansson & Percy, 1994).

Those against outing argue that people have a right to privacy and that no one else should take that right from them. Because outing can lead to severe consequences—for example, loss of job, expulsion from the military, or social and physical harassment—no one but the individual him- or herself has the right to reveal such information. Those in favour of outing argue that it's an expedient political and social weapon to silence those gay men and lesbians who, in an effort to keep their own orientation secret, support or refuse to protest homophobic policies.

WHAT WOULD YOU DO?

An excellent staff reporter and regular contributor to the college newspaper brings the editor a story revealing that a particular professor is a lesbian. This professor has repeatedly voted against adding any courses on gay or lesbian topics to the curriculum. She is also an advisor to an exclusive sorority that has repeatedly refused admission to lesbian students. What would be the ethically responsible thing for this editor to do? What would you do in this situation, if you were the editor and final judge as to whether the article were published?

Your Gender   The popular stereotype of gender differences in self-disclosure emphasizes the male reluctance to speak about himself. For the most part, research supports this view and shows that women disclose more than men. This is especially true in same-sex dyads (two-person groups); women disclose more intimately (and with more emotion) when talking with other women than with men (Dindia, 2000). Men and women, however, make negative disclosures nearly equally (Naifeh & Smith, 1984).

More specifically, women disclose more than men about their previous romantic relationships, their feelings about their closest same-sex friends, their greatest fears, and what they don't like about their partners (Sprecher, 1987). Women also seem to increase the depth of their self-disclosures as the relationship becomes more intimate, while men seem not to change their self-disclosure levels. Men, for example, have more taboo topics that they will not disclose to their friends than do women (Goodwin & Lee, 1994). Finally, women even self-disclose more to members of the extended family than men do (Komarovsky, 1964; Argyle & Henderson, 1985; Moghaddam, Taylor, & Wright, 1993). One notable exception occurs in initial encounters. Here men will disclose more intimately than women, perhaps "in order to control the relationship's development" (Derlega, Winstead, Wong, & Hunter, 1985).

Although to some extent men and women give different reasons for avoiding self-disclosure (Rosenfeld, 1979), both genders share this reason: "If I disclose, I might project an image I do not want to project." In a society in which image is so important—in which a person's image is often the basis for success or failure—this explanation is not surprising. Other reasons for avoiding self-disclosure are unique to men or women. Lawrence Rosenfeld (1979) sums up males' reasons for self-disclosure avoidance: "If I disclose to you, I might project an image I do not want to project, which could make me look bad and cause me to lose control over you. This might go so far as to affect relationships I have with people other than you." In other words, men's principal objective in avoiding self-disclosure is to maintain control. The general reason women avoid self-disclosure, says Rosenfeld, is that "if I disclose to you, I might project an image I do not want to project, such as my being emotionally ill, which you might use against me and which might hurt our relationship." Women's principal objective for avoiding self-disclosure is "to avoid personal hurt and problems with the relationship."

Your Listeners   Self-disclosure occurs more readily in small groups than in large groups. Dyads are the most hospitable setting for self-disclosure. With one listener, you can attend to the responses carefully. You can monitor the disclosures, continuing if there is support from your listener and stopping if there is not. With more than one listener, such monitoring becomes difficult, because the listeners' responses are sure to vary.

Sometimes self-disclosure takes place in group and public speaking situations. In consciousness-raising groups and in meetings like those of Alcoholics Anonymous, members may disclose their most intimate problems to tens or perhaps hundreds of people at one time. In these situations, group members are pledged to be totally supportive.

How might failing to understand cultural or gender differences in self-disclosure distort your evaluation of a person's disclosure messages?

One study suggests that gender differences in self-disclosure may be changing. In this study men and women discussed how their family relationships had changed since they entered college. In this instance men disclosed more than women (Leaper, Carson, Baker, Holliday, et al., 1995). What gender differences in self- disclosure do you observe?

These and similar groups are devoted specifically to encouraging self-disclosure and to providing mutual support for the disclosures.

Because you disclose, generally at least, on the basis of support you receive, you probably disclose to people you like (Derlega, Winstead, Wong, & Greenspan, 1987; Collins & Miller, 1994), to people you trust (Wheeless & Grotz, 1977), to people who show you concern and affection (Roberts & Aruguete, 2000), and to people you feel understand you (Martin, Anderson, & Mottet, 1999). You probably also come to like those to whom you disclose (Berg & Archer, 1983; Collins & Miller, 1994).

Not surprisingly, you're more likely to disclose to people who are close to you in age (Parker & Parrott, 1995). Age also seems to influence your reasons for self-disclosing. For example, younger siblings tend to disclose to older siblings to seek advice and emotional support, whereas older siblings often disclose to teach their younger siblings (Dolgin & Lindsay, 1999).

At times self-disclosure occurs more in temporary than in permanent relationships—for example, between strangers on a train or plane, a kind of "in-flight intimacy" (McGill, 1985). In this kind of situation, two people set up an intimate self-disclosing relationship during a brief travel period, but they don't pursue it beyond that point. In a similar way, you might set up a relationship with one or several people on the internet and engage in significant disclosure. Perhaps knowing that you'll never see these other people and that they will never know where you live or work or what you look like makes it a bit easier. You're also more likely to disclose information you received from a low-level intimate (say a casual acquaintance) to a higher-level intimate (say a best friend) than you are to disclose information you received from a high-level intimate to a low-level intimate. This is a specific instance of the more general principle that you're more likely to communicate important information upward (to those of greater intimacy) than downward (to those of less intimacy) (Yovetich & Drigotas, 1999).

You're more likely to disclose when the person you're with discloses. This **dyadic effect** (what one person does, the other person does likewise) probably leads you to feel more secure and reinforces your own self-disclosing behaviour. Disclosures are also more intimate when they're made in response to the disclosures of others (Berg & Archer, 1983).

Your Topic You're also more likely to disclose about some topics than others. For example, as mentioned earlier, you're probably more likely to self-disclose information about your job or hobbies than about your sex life or financial situation (Jourard, 1968, 1971a). You're also more likely to disclose favourable information than unfavourable information. Generally, the more personal and negative the topic, the less likely people are to self-disclose. However, Canadians seem to be hesitant to share information about their accomplishments and achievements. Considerations of modesty and humility may inhibit disclosures of this nature. (An interesting exercise, "Disclosing Your Hidden Self," will help you explore the types of things people are willing or unwilling to self-disclose; it may be found at www.ablongman.com/devito.)

The self-test on the next page, "How willing to self-disclose are you?" focuses on the influences of the five factors just discussed: you, your culture, your gender, your listeners, and your topic.

As a parent, would you share your financial worries with your children (McLoyd & Wilson, 1992)? Research finds that members of two-parent middle-class families are reluctant to share financial problems with their children, preferring to shelter them from some of life's harsher realities. Low-income single mothers, however, feel that sharing money problems with their children will protect them, because they will know how difficult life is and what they're up against. What would your general advice be to parents?

Instructions: Respond to each statement below by indicating the likelihood that you would disclose such items of information to, say, other members of this class. Use the following scale: 1 = would definitely self-disclose, 2 = would probably self-disclose, 3 = don't know, 4 = would probably not self-disclose, and 5 = would definitely not self-disclose.

_____ 1. My attitudes toward different nationalities and races.

_____ 2. My feelings about my parents.

_____ 3. My sexual fantasies.

_____ 4. My past sexual experiences.

_____ 5. My ideal mate.

_____ 6. My drinking and/or drug-taking behaviour.

_____ 7. My personal goals.

_____ 8. My unfulfilled desires.

_____ 9. My major weaknesses.

_____ 10. My feelings about the people in this group.

HOW DID YOU DO?

There are, of course, no right or wrong answers to this self-test. By considering these topics, however, you may be able to pinpoint more precisely the areas about which you're willing to disclose and the areas about which you aren't willing to disclose. How would your answers have differed if the question asked you to indicate the likelihood of your self-disclosing to your best friend?

WHAT WILL YOU DO?

This test, and ideally talking about it with others who also complete it, should get you started thinking about your own self-disclosing behaviour, and especially about the factors that influence it. What factors most influence your willingness to disclose or not to disclose each of these items of information?

The Rewards and Dangers of Self-Disclosure

Like other forms of interpersonal communication, self-disclosure entails both potential rewards and potential dangers. Let's look first at the rewards.

Rewards of Self-Disclosure   Research shows that self-disclosure helps to increase self-knowledge, communication and relationship effectiveness, and physiological well-being.

Self-Knowledge.   One reward of self-disclosure is that you gain a new perspective on yourself, a deeper understanding of your own behaviour. Through self-disclosure you may bring to consciousness a great deal that you might otherwise keep from conscious analysis. For example, as Tony talks about the difficulties he had living with an alcoholic father, he may remember details of his early life or entertain new feelings.

Even **self-acceptance** is difficult without self-disclosure. You accept yourself largely through the eyes of others. Through self-disclosure and subsequent support, you may be in a better position to see the positive responses to you. And you're more likely to respond by developing a more positive self-concept.

Communication Effectiveness. You understand the messages of another person largely to the extent that you understand the person. For example, you can tell when a friend is serious or joking, when someone you know well is being sarcastic out of fear and when out of resentment. Self-disclosure is an essential condition for getting to know another individual.

Couples who engage in significant self-disclosure are found to remain together longer than couples who do not (Sprecher, 1987). Self-disclosure helps us achieve a closer relationship with the person to whom we self-disclose (Schmidt & Cornelius, 1987). Without self-disclosure, meaningful relationships seem impossible to develop.

Interestingly enough, we also come to increase our affection for our partner when we self-disclose. Think about your own self-disclosures. Have you come to increase your liking for someone after you disclosed to this person? Do others seem to like you more after they disclosed to you?

Physiological Health. People who self-disclose are less vulnerable to illnesses and less likely to feel depressed (Pennebacker, 1991). For example, bereavement over the death of someone very close is linked to physical illness for those who bear this alone and in silence. But it's unrelated to any physical problems for those who share their grief with

THINKING CRITICALLY ABOUT
Building Interpersonal Skills

In learning the skills of interpersonal communication (or any set of skills), you'll probably at first sense an awkwardness and self-consciousness; the new behaviours may not seem to fit comfortably. As you develop more understanding and use the skills more, this awkwardness will gradually fade, and the new behaviours will begin to feel comfortable and natural. You'll facilitate your progression from these early awkward tries to total mastery if you follow a logical system of steps. Here's one possible system, called STEP (Skill, Theory, Example, Practise).

1. Get a clear understanding of what the *skill* is.
2. Understand the *theory;* if you understand the reasons for the suggestions offered, it will help make the skill more logical.
3. Develop *examples,* especially your own; this will help make the material covered here a more integral part of communication behaviour.
4. *Practise* with the Skill Building Exercises alone, then with supportive friends, and then in general.

EXAMPLES?

Give an example of a specific skill, as you would master it using the STEP process described here.

others. Similarly, women who suffer sexual trauma normally experience a variety of illnesses (among them headaches and stomach problems). Women who kept these experiences to themselves, however, suffer these illnesses to a much greater extent than those who talk with others about these traumas. The physiological effort required to keep your burdens to yourself seems to interact with the effects of the trauma to create a combined stress that can lead to physical illness.

Dangers of Self-Disclosure   As is usually the case, when the potential rewards are great, so are the risks. Self-disclosure is no exception; the risks can be considerable and can be personal, relational, and professional.

Personal Risks.   If you self-disclose certain aspects of your life, you may face rejection from even the closest friends and family members. Those who disclose that they have AIDS, for example, may find that their friends and family no longer want to be quite as close as before.

Relationship Risks.   Even in close and long-lasting relationships, self-disclosure can cause problems. Total self-disclosure may prove threatening to a relationship by decreasing trust. Self-disclosures concerning infidelity, romantic fantasies, past indiscretions or crimes, lies, or hidden weaknesses and fears could easily have such negative effects.

Professional Risks.   The extensive media coverage of gays and lesbians in the US military who are coming out in protest of the "don't ask, don't tell" policy illustrates the professional dangers that self-disclosure may entail. Similarly, politicians who disclose they have been in therapy may lose party and voter support. And teachers who disclose former or current drug use, for example, may find themselves denied tenure and may eventually fall victim to "budget cuts."

> Confiding a secret to an unworthy person is like carrying grain in a bag with a hole.
>
> **—Ethiopian proverb**

Guidelines for Self-Disclosure

Because self-disclosure is an important type of interpersonal communication with the potential for great rewards and great dangers, here are some guidelines, first for making self-disclosures and second for responding to the disclosures of others.

Guidelines for Making Self-Disclosures   In trying to answer your first question, "Should I disclose?" consider the following questions.

What Is Your Motivation for Self-Disclosing?   Self-disclose out of a concern for the relationship, for the others involved, and for yourself. Some people self-disclose out of a desire to hurt the listener rather than from a desire to improve the relationship—as when children tell their parents that they never loved them or when a person informs a relationship partner that he or she stifled emo-

How would you describe the dangers of self-disclosing on the job to your subordinates? To your coworkers? To your superiors? What kinds of self-disclosure would be especially dangerous?

tional development. However, let's say that you feel ignored and unimportant because your partner devotes all available time to professional advancement. Instead of letting these feelings smoulder and turn into resentment, it might be helpful to the relationship to disclose them.

> Never reveal all of yourself to other people; hold back something in reserve so that people are never quite sure if they really know you.
>
> —Michael Korda

Is This Self-Disclosure Appropriate? Appropriate self-disclosures include honest expressions of feelings ("I feel uncomfortable when you criticize me in front of my friends"), past behaviours that another has a right to know ("I was married when I was 17; we divorced two years later"), or personal abilities or lack of them that affect others ("I've never hung wallpaper before but I'll do my best"). Self-disclose in an atmosphere in which your listener can give open and honest responses. Don't wait until you're boarding the bus to say to your friend, "I got some really bad news today. I'll tell you about it later."

Is the Other Person Also Disclosing? During your disclosures, give the other person a chance to reciprocate with his or her own disclosures. If the other person does not do so, then reassess your own self-disclosures. The lack of reciprocity may signal that this person, at this time and in this context, does not welcome your disclosures. Therefore, disclose gradually and in small increments so that you can retreat if the responses are not positive enough. Lack of reciprocity may also be due to cultural differences; in some cultures, significant self-disclosure takes place only after an extremely long acquaintanceship or may be considered inappropriate among, say, opposite-sex friends.

(At some point in the relationship, you may feel you have a right to information about your friend or romantic partner. A self-test to help you explore this feeling, "Your right to know," may be found at **www.ablongman.com/devito**.)

Will This Self-Disclosure Impose Burdens? Carefully weigh the potential problems that the self-disclosure may cause. Could you, if you were to disclose your previous prison record, afford to lose your job? If you were to disclose your previous failed romantic relationships, would you be willing to risk discouraging your present relational partner?

Ask yourself whether you're making unreasonable demands on the listener. For example, consider the person who discloses in confidence to his or her own mother-in-law an affair with a neighbour. This type of situation places an unfair burden on the mother-in-law. She is now in a bind: Should she break her promise of secrecy or allow her own child to believe a lie? Parents often place unreasonable burdens on their children by self-disclosing marital problems or infidelities or self-doubts. They fail to realize that the children may be too young or too emotionally involved to deal effectively with this information. Often such disclosures do not make the relationship a better one. Instead they may simply add tension and friction.

In making your choice between disclosing and not disclosing, keep in mind—besides the advantages and dangers already noted—the irreversible nature of communication discussed in Chapter 1. No matter how many times you may try to qualify something or take it back, once you have said something, you cannot withdraw it. You cannot erase the conclusions and inferences listeners have made on the basis of your disclosures. This is not to suggest that you therefore refrain from self-disclosing, but only to suggest that it's especially important here to recognize the irreversible nature of communication.

Guidelines for Responding to Disclosures   When someone discloses to you, it's usually a sign of trust and affection. In serving this most important receiver function, keep the following in mind. ("Tommy's Family," a dialogue that identifies the wrong and then the right way to facilitate self-disclosure, may be found at www.ablongman.com/devito.)

Practise the Skills of Effective and Active Listening.   The skills of effective listening are discussed in detail in Chapter 4. These are especially important when listening to self-disclosures. Listen with empathy. Listen with an open mind. Repeat in your own words what you think the speaker has said so you can be sure you understand both the thoughts and the feelings. Express an understanding of the speaker's feelings to allow the speaker the opportunity to see these through the eyes of another individual. Ask questions to ensure your own understanding and to signal your own interest and attention.

Support the Discloser.   Express support for the person during and after the disclosures. Try to avoid making judgments. Concentrate on **affirmation**—understanding and empathizing with the discloser. Make your supportiveness clear to the discloser through your verbal and nonverbal responses. Nod your head to show you understand and echo the person's feelings and thoughts. Maintain eye contact and otherwise show your positive attitudes toward the discloser and the act of disclosing.

Keep the Disclosures Confidential.   When a person discloses to you, it's because she or he wants you to know these feelings and thoughts. If the discloser wishes others to share these, then it's up to her or him to disclose them. If you reveal these disclosures to others, it will probably inhibit this person's future disclosures. As a result, your relationship will suffer. In addition to keeping the disclosures confidential, avoid using them against the person at some later time. Many self-disclosures expose a vulnerability, a weakness. If you later turn around and use these against the person, you betray the confidence and trust invested in you.

It's interesting to note that one of the netiquette rules of email is that you shouldn't forward mail to third parties without the writer's permission. This rule is a useful one for self-disclosure generally: Maintain confidentiality; don't pass on to others disclosures made to you without the person's permission.

One response that is seldom mentioned in discussions of disclosure is to tell someone that you simply do not want to hear his or her disclosure. Have you ever said this? Has anyone ever responded to your attempted self-disclosure with a refusal to listen? Under what conditions would such refusals be appropriate? Under what conditions would they be inappropriate?

Interpersonal Apprehension

You'll profit most from this discussion if you first take the self-test on page 52. This test measures your **apprehension** (fear or anxiety) in interpersonal communication situations. (Additional self-tests that measure your apprehension in employment interviews, group discussions and meetings, and public speaking may be found at www.ablongman.com/devito. Also on this website is another relevant self-test, "How shy are you?")

The term **communication apprehension** refers to a feeling of fear or anxiety about a situation in which a person must communicate. Some people develop negative feelings about communication and therefore expect the worst of themselves when they're called on to speak. To those who feel high anxiety in such circumstances, it just doesn't seem worthwhile to try. This is not to say that apprehensives are ineffective or unhappy people. Most of them have learned or can learn to deal with their communication anxiety or fear.

TEST YOURSELF

How Apprehensive Are You?

Instructions: This questionnaire consists of six statements concerning your feelings about communication with other people. Please indicate in the space provided the degree to which each statement applies to you by marking whether you (1) strongly agree, (2) agree, (3) are undecided, (4) disagree, or (5) strongly disagree with each statement. There are no right or wrong answers. Work quickly; record your first impression.

_____ **1.** While participating in a conversation with a new acquaintance, I feel very nervous.

_____ **2.** I have no fear of speaking up in conversations.

_____ **3.** Ordinarily I am very tense and nervous in conversations.

_____ **4.** Ordinarily I am very calm and relaxed in conversations.

_____ **5.** While conversing with a new acquaintance, I feel very relaxed.

_____ **6.** I'm afraid to speak up in conversations.

HOW DID YOU DO?

Compute your score as follows:

1. Begin with the number 18; it's used as a base so that you won't wind up with negative numbers.
2. To 18, add your scores for items 2, 4, and 5.
3. Subtract your scores for items 1, 3, and 6 from your step 2 total.
4. The result (which should be somewhere between 6 and 30) is your apprehension score for interpersonal conversations. The higher the score, the greater your apprehension. A score above 18 indicates some degree of apprehension.

WHAT WILL YOU DO?

Try first to identify those interpersonal situations that create the greatest apprehension for you. What factors can you identify that contribute to apprehension? What can you do to reduce the impact of those factors?

Source: From James C. McCroskey, _Introduction to Rhetorical Communication_, 7th ed. (Englewood Cliffs, NJ: Prentice-Hall, 1997).

"Communication apprehension," researchers note, "is probably the most common handicap ... suffered by people in contemporary American society" (McCroskey & Wheeless, 1976). According to surveys of college students, between 10 and 20 percent suffer "severe, debilitating communication apprehension"; another 20 percent suffer from "communication apprehension to a degree substantial enough to interfere to some extent with their normal functioning."

How fearful are you of communicating? In what situations do you have greatest apprehension? How does communication apprehension figure into your social life? Into your professional life? How can it hurt you?

Culture and Apprehension

Interacting with members of cultures different from your own can create uncertainty, fear, and anxiety, all of which contribute to speaker apprehension (Anderson, Hecht, Hoobler, & Smallwood, 2002f).

When you're speaking with people from cultures very different from your own, you're likely to be more uncertain about the situation and

SKILLS TOOLBOX

6 Ways to Empower Apprehensives in the Workplace

As the workplace becomes more and more a place where information is exchanged (rather than, say, where goods are manufactured) and where teams and team interaction dominate the workday, communication apprehension becomes more important. So, at the same time that you want to manage your own apprehension, consider the ways you can help your peers and others you work with to better control their apprehension. Here are some suggestions, based largely on the insights of apprehension researchers (Carducci & Zimbardo, 1996; Richmond & McCroskey, 1996). These suggestions, of course, will apply to all situations, not only to the workplace.

1. Don't overprotect shy people, but don't push them to communicate either. Be supportive (indirectly) and nudge (don't push) such persons to try new communication situations. Most important, don't make decisions for them; apprehensives can communicate if they have to and if they have an extreme desire to do so.

2. Demonstrate your understanding of and empathy for the other person's fear of communicating, but don't assume that the communication apprehensive wants to be like you. Most communication apprehensives are quite happy as they are and don't want to change. At the same time, don't minimize (as people with little apprehension often do) their fear of communication situations.

3. Help the shy person develop self-confidence. Often apprehensives lack self-confidence and may feel inadequate in social situations. Expressing positiveness may help. But don't assume that you can "cure" their apprehension.

4. Give the shy person opportunities to speak; ask his or her opinions, for example. When appropriate, try to steer the conversation in the direction of the shy person's areas of competence. If you're in the position to do so, consider making professional assistance available for those who want to reduce their apprehension.

5. Try to provide alternatives (other than talking) that will allow communication apprehensives to demonstrate their competence; for example, written reports, emails, or chat room discussions.

6. Avoid making shy people the centre of attention. That's exactly what they don't want. Avoid making their fear of communicating the topic of a group conversation. Saying, "Oh, Jane—she has such great ideas but she never talks" only makes it more difficult for Jane to even open her mouth.

THEN AND NOW

Have you ever interacted with a person who was shy or apprehensive about communication? Did you do anything to try to help? What would you do now?

about your hearers' possible responses (Gudykunst & Nishida, 1984; Gudykunst, Yang, & Nishida, 1985). When you're sure of a situation and can predict what will happen, you're more likely to feel comfortable and at ease. But when you cannot predict what will happen, you're likely to become more apprehensive (Gudyykunst, 2002).

Such situations can also engender fear. You might, for example, have a greater fear of saying something that might prove offensive or of revealing your own prejudices. The fear is easily transformed into apprehension. These situations can also create anxiety. For example, if your prior relationships with members of a culturally different group were few or if they were unpleasant, then you're likely to experience greater anxiety when dealing with other members of that group than if your prior experiences were numerous and positive (Stephan & Stephan, 1985, 1992).

Your thoughts and feelings about the other people will also influence your apprehension. For example, if you hold stereotypes and prejudices, or if you feel that you're very different from these other people, you're likely to experience more apprehension than if you saw them as similar to you.

Managing Apprehension

Although most of us suffer from some communication apprehension, we can successfully manage it and control it—at least to some degree. Here are some suggestions (Beatty, 1988; McCroskey, 1997; Richmond & McCroskey, 1996). (An exercise, "Reducing Apprehension with Systematic Desensitization," presents an interesting way to help you manage your apprehension as well as other unrealistic fears. See www.ablongman.com/devito.)

"How will you ever know whether you're a flying squirrel if you don't give it a shot?"

Acquire Communication Skills and Experience   If you lack skills in typing, you can hardly expect to type very well. Yet we rarely assume that a lack of interpersonal skills and experience can cause difficulty with communication and create apprehension. It can. After all, if you had never asked for a date and had no idea how to do it, it would be natural to feel apprehension in doing so. In this course you're gaining the skills of effective interpersonal interaction. Engage in experiences—even if they prove difficult at first—to help you acquire the skills you need most. The more preparation and practice you put into something, the more comfortable you will feel with it.

Focus on Success   The more you perceive a situation as one in which others will evaluate you, the greater your apprehension will be (Beatty, 1988). Employment interviews and asking for a date, for example, are anxiety-provoking largely because they're highly evaluative. Your prior history in similar situations also influences the way you respond to new ones. Prior success generally (though not always) reduces apprehension. Prior failure generally (though not always) increases apprehension. If you see yourself succeeding, you'll stand a good chance of doing just that. So think positively. Visualize others giving you positive evaluations. Concentrate your energies on doing the best job you can in any situation you find yourself in. You now have new skills and new experiences, and these will increase your chances for success. Do be careful, however, that your focus on success does not translate into the need to appear perfect, an attitude that is likely to increase your interpersonal apprehension (Saboonchi, Lundh, & Ost, 1999).

Reduce Unpredictability   The more unpredictable the situation, the greater your apprehension is likely to be. Ambiguous situations and new situations are unpredictable. Therefore, you naturally become anxious. In managing apprehension, therefore, try to reduce any unpredictability. When you're familiar with the situation and with what is expected of you, you're better able to predict what will happen. This will reduce the ambiguity and perceived newness of the situation. So, for example, if you're going to ask the boss for a raise, become familiar with as much of the situation as you can. If possible, sit in the chair you will sit in; then rehearse your statement of the reasons you deserve the raise and the way in which you'll present them.

Put Apprehension in Perspective   Whenever you engage in a communication experience, remember that the world won't end if you don't succeed. Also remember that other people are not able to perceive your apprehension as sharply as you do. You may feel a dryness in your throat and a rapid heartbeat; however, no one knows this but you.

At the same time that you want to manage and perhaps lessen your own apprehension, consider the values and means of empowering others to manage and better control their apprehension. The article on pages 55–57 discusses ways you can help others by identifying the causes of their reticence and helping them communicate. This example is a doctor-patient exchange, but the techniques illustrated can be used to improve communication in other situations.

Some research suggests that people respond more negatively to those they perceive as apprehensive than to those they perceive as more confident and less fearful (Richmond & McCroskey, 1996). Do you respond more negatively to those you see as apprehensive than to those you see as less fearful? Would you prefer to work with one type rather than the other? Would you prefer to date one type rather than the other?

MESSAGES@WORK

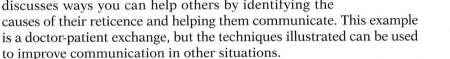

Causes of Reticence

It is first all-important to try to recognize *why* a patient is holding back or having difficulty in expressing himself freely, so that whenever possible something can be done about the inhibiting factor(s). The patient's reticence may be due to the following.

■ The presence of a third party: a nurse, a student, or even an accompanying relative. They should, if necessary, be asked tactfully to leave the room.

■ Sometimes the fact that the doctor is also the family doctor may inhibit an adolescent from speaking freely.

(continued)

- The patient may fear that revealing his complaints will lead to the realization of his worst fears: a diagnosis of serious disease, admission to hospital, an operation.

- A reluctance to take up the doctor's time with concerns that the patient may feel are undeserving of his time and attention: "You are always a very busy man, doctor, and there are several folk still waiting to see you."

- Embarrassment or shame about the nature of the complaint. This might apply to a wide range of disorders, but especially to those with a sexual association: venereal disease; other genital complaints; drinking problems; pregnancy in the unmarried, widowed, or separated; impotence.

- Cultural barriers. For example, many Asian women find it difficult to discuss personal or marital problems with a male doctor or even with a strange female doctor. A youthful or a venerable-looking doctor may be seen as an unsuitable confidant if he or she obviously belongs to a different generation from the patient.

These are some of the more specific obstacles to open communication that should be kept in mind if a patient is holding back. With experience and training, the student will learn to recognize the causes of reticence and be able to overcome them. The communication skills to be employed include non-verbal (body) language, speech, and appropriate use of silences.

WAYS OF FACILITATING COMMUNICATION

Non-verbal

An unhurried manner is a basic essential, conveying the message "I have time to listen." While listening, the doctor can nod attentively (but not nod off!). He should not be afraid to smile, since smiling is often the best way of conveying reassurance, understanding, acceptance, and warmth. If the patient pauses, the doctor may lower his eyes for a moment without looking away and then look back at the patient's face, signaling "Go on." At certain points, it is helpful to discard pen and notes in an obvious way, and push them to one side, perhaps adding "So tell me more about...," referring to a rather sensitive topic that has not yet been ventilated adequately, and about which the doctor feels there is more to be said. If what seems a delicate question has to be posed, it can help to lean forward towards the patient, underlining the intimacy and confidentiality of the conversation.

As the patient talks, the doctor is not just a passive observer, but is "actively" listening—using appropriate body language; hearing not only what the patient says, but how he says it; noting the tone of his voice, his choice of words, expressions, and gestures. Appropriate use of touch can help to convey concern, reassurance, and encouragement, particularly when dealing with the frail, the fearful, or depressed. A brief contact on the back of the hand or forearm (which are the least threatening areas) will often be enough. The gentleness used during clinical touching will also convey a message.

By speech

A variety of simple short responses from the doctor will encourage the patient to continue speaking, especially if accompanied by a brief smile: "Yes, I see," "Go on," "I understand," or sometimes "I don't quite follow you," inviting the patient to give a fuller account.

Reflecting Somewhat similarly, but more positively, the doctor can encourage the patient to continue speaking by repeating, and so *reflecting* back to him, a phrase, idea, or significant word from what the patient has just said. By picking up a word or expression in this way, the patient is prompted to express himself further.

Here is an example of this technique of reflecting.

"Doctor, I can always sense when my husband is building up towards another bout of heavy drinking, but ... well ... I just feel there's absolutely nothing I can do about it. I've given up."

"Nothing?"

"Well ... maybe ... You see, I'm always afraid if I say anything that I'll be to blame for what he's doing. Do you think I should try to talk to him?"

Another example might be the following interchange.

"The period pains are not too bad, but the headaches I get before the period starts make me *desperately* miserable for three or four days every month."

"You feel desperate at that time?"

"Yes, to be honest, I do. Recently there have been several times when I've thought of doing away with myself, because at the time it felt as if there was nothing to live for."

Clarifying This term is used to describe another ploy which helps to make clear to the patient what he is trying to put into words, and also allows the doctor to check on his own tentative deductions:

> "You seem to be saying that, since the pains began, you not only gradually lost your appetite, but also lost interest in all kinds of everyday activities. Is that correct?"

Or, to offer another example:

> "Are you trying to tell me that you're really afraid this is something very serious? Is that what you feel?"

Summarizing It can also be very helpful, particularly when the history is long and complicated, to attempt at some point to summarize all or part of the patient's account of things. This recapitulation must be done tentatively, getting the patient to corroborate the more important details. Otherwise there is the danger that a compliant patient may just accept the doctor's version of the history, which could reflect more the doctor's preconceived ideas than what actually happened:

> "So if we could just go over the main points of what you have told me so far. Your periods were perfectly normal and regular until five months ago. Then you missed two periods completely, and then bled heavily for three weeks. Since that time there has been some scanty loss most days, but no pain at any time. Is that correct?"

> "Could we just recap to be sure I have got it right? You had just finished a huge amount of Chinese take out, when you suddenly began to perspire. When you got up to open the window, the pain behind your breastbone began, and your knees gave way. When you came to on the floor, you felt very nauseated, and were seeing double for a time, and you had this big cut on your forehead."

By appropriate use of silences

One of the nightmarish anxieties of the inexperienced student or doctor is that he will dry up during the interview; that he will run out of questions; and that an embarrassing silence will open up, creating discomfort and disrupting communication. In contrast, an easy interview often seems to flow along in sustained dialogue with barely a pause. The learner can avoid an undesirable hiatus of his own making by having in reserve one or two fill-in questions that cannot be answered very briefly (e.g. a question about the patient's childhood or about other family members) but which have some loose relevance to the presenting symptoms. One of these questions can be thrown in when such a silence threatens; while the patient is answering, the questioner can pick up the threads and poise himself for his next line of enquiry.

It is a mistake to believe that silences must be avoided at all costs. Apart from the nervous silences of the beginner referred to above, other silences can occur, when the patient runs out of words or is unsure about expressing his feelings. In this situation, the doctor must resist the temptation to disarm the silence promptly with a new question on a new topic, and so thereby suppress what the patient may be struggling to say. Rather, he should deliberately let the silence remain unbroken for a little time, while continuing to look at the patient with a facial expression of unhurried interest and concern. Then he can signal "Go on" either verbally or non-verbally.

Source: Philip R. Myerscough & Michael J. Ford et al. *Talking with Patients: Keys to Good Communication,* 3rd ed. New York: Oxford University Press, 1996.

SUMMARY OF CONCEPTS AND SKILLS

This chapter explored the self in interpersonal communication. We looked at the four selves of the Johari model and how to increase self-awareness. Next we looked at self-disclosure, the process of revealing ourselves to others, and at some of its advantages and disadvantages. We then explored apprehension, what causes it, and how it can be managed effectively.

1. The self-concept is the image that you have of yourself and is developed from the images

of you that others have and that they reveal to you, the comparisons you make between yourself and others, and the way you interpret and evaluate your own thoughts and behaviours.

2. The four selves are the open self (what we and others know about us), the blind self (what others know but we do not know), the hidden self (what we know but keep hidden from others), and the unknown self (what neither we nor others know).

3. We may increase self-awareness by asking ourselves about ourselves, listening to others, actively seeking information about ourselves, seeing ourselves from different perspectives, and increasing our open selves.

4. Self-disclosure is a type of communication in which we reveal information about ourselves to others.

5. Self-disclosure is generally reciprocal; the self-disclosures of one person stimulate the self-disclosures of the other person.

6. Both men and women avoid self-disclosure for fear of projecting a negative image. Men also avoid self-disclosure so they can maintain control; women also avoid self-disclosure to avoid personal hurt and problems in relationships.

7. Through self-disclosure you may gain self-knowledge, increase communication effectiveness, enhance the meaningfulness of your interpersonal relationships, and promote physical health.

8. There are also serious dangers in self-disclosing. Your interpersonal, social, and business relationships may be severely damaged if your self-disclosures are not positively received.

9. Communication apprehension is a feeling of fear or anxiety about communication situations.

10. Persons with high apprehension behave differently from persons with low apprehension. High apprehensives communicate less and avoid situations and occupations that demand lots of communication. High apprehensives are less likely than other people to be seen as leaders, have more negative attitudes toward school, and are more likely to drop out of college. High apprehensives are also less satisfied with their jobs and engage more in steady dating.

11. Techniques for managing communication apprehension include acquiring communication skills and experience, focusing on success, reducing unpredictability, and being familiar with the situation.

Check your ability to apply the following skills. You will gain most from this brief exercise if you think carefully about each skill and try to identify instances from your recent communication experiences in which you did or did not act on the basis of the specific skill. Use a rating scale such as the following: 1 = almost always, 2 = often, 3 = sometimes, 4 = rarely, and 5 = almost never.

_____ 1. Analyze your own self-concept and seek to discover the sources that influenced it.

_____ 2. Become aware of your own communication patterns, especially as these relate to self-disclosing messages.

_____ 3. Engage in activities that increase self-awareness.

_____ 4. Regulate self-disclosures on the basis of the topic, listener, purposes, and so on.

_____ 5. Critically weigh the potential rewards and costs of self-disclosure before disclosing.

_____ 6. Self-disclose appropriately.

_____ 7. Respond to the self-disclosures of others as appropriate.

_____ 8. Manage the fear of communicating in interpersonal situations.

_____ 9. Communicate in interpersonal encounters with confidence.

VOCABULARY QUIZ

The Language of the Self

Match the terms listed here with their definitions. Record the number of the definition next to the name of the concept.

_____ Johari model

_____ the open self

_____ the blind self

_____ the hidden self

_____ the unknown self

_____ self-awareness

_____ self-disclosure

_____ the dyadic effect

_____ communication apprehension

_____ gender and culture

1. Fear or anxiety over communicating.

2. The part of the self that contains information about the self that is known to others but unknown to oneself.

3. The tendency for the behaviours of one person to stimulate behaviours in the other person, usually used to refer to the tendency for one person's self-disclosures to stimulate the listener to self-disclose also.

4. The part of the self that contains information about the self that is known to oneself and to others.

5. The part of the self that contains information about the self known to oneself but unknown to (hidden from) others.

6. A diagram of the four selves.

7. A knowledge of oneself.

8. The process of revealing something significant about ourselves to another individual or to a group, something that would not normally be known by them.

9. The part of the self that contains information about the self that is unknown to oneself and to others.

10. Two of the factors that influence self-disclosure.

SKILL BUILDING EXERCISES

2.1 TO DISCLOSE OR NOT TO DISCLOSE?

Whether you should self-disclose is one of the most difficult decisions you have to make in interpersonal communication. Here are several instances of impending self-disclosure. For each, indicate whether you think the self-disclosure would be appropriate and why.

1. A mother of two teenage children (one boy, one girl) has been feeling guilty for the past year over a romantic affair she had with her brother-in-law while her husband was in prison. A few months ago, she and her husband divorced. She wants to self-disclose her affair and her guilt to her children.

2. Tom wants to break up his engagement with Cathy because he has fallen in love with another woman. Tom wants to call Cathy on the phone, break his engagement, and disclose his new relationship.

3. Sam has been living in a romantic relationship with another man for the past several years. Sam wants to tell his parents, with whom he has been very close throughout his life, but can't get up the courage to do so. He decides to tell them in a long letter.

4. Mary and Jim have been married for 12 years. Mary has been honest about most things and has self-disclosed a great deal to Jim—about her past romantic encounters, her fears, her ambitions, and so on. Yet Jim doesn't reciprocate. He almost never shares his feelings and has told Mary almost nothing about his life be-

fore they met. Mary wonders if she should continue her pattern of self-disclosure.

Thinking Critically About Self-Disclosure.

What are your reasons for your judgments? Which self-disclosure do you think will prove most effective? Least effective? Which disclosures seem appropriate to the receiver? Are the intended methods (phone call, letter) likely to prove effective? Will the self-disclosure help accomplish what the person wishes to accomplish?

2.2 TIMES FOR SELF-DISCLOSURE

Self-disclosures occur throughout a relationship, but not always at what you may think is the right time. Some disclosures seem to occur too early and signal an intimacy that is not echoed in the relationship; the disclosures seem prematurely and inappropriately intimate. Some disclosures, on the other hand, occur too late; we feel we should have been told something earlier and may resent learning about it so late in the day. And, of course, some disclosures seem to occur at exactly the right time. This exercise explores the timeliness of self-disclosures.

Another way of looking at this exercise is from an ethical perspective: from the standpoint of your right to know certain information about a person with whom you become relationally involved. At what point in the relationship do you have a right to know this type of information?

Listed below are 10 items of personal information. Next to each item indicate the stage at which you would expect someone with whom you are in a relationship to disclose this type of information. Use X for any item you feel should not be disclosed at any time. Use the following shorthand for the stages appropriate for those items you feel should be disclosed.

Cp = Contact (perceptual)

Ci = Contact (interactional)

It = Involvement (testing)

Ii = Involvement (intensifying)

Iic = Intimacy (interpersonal commitment)

Isb = Intimacy (social bonding)

_____ 1. correct age

_____ 2. history of family mental illness or genetic disorders

_____ 3. relationship history (previous involvements, children)

_____ 4. annual income, assets, and debts

_____ 5. cultural background (race and nationality) and beliefs (for example, prejudices, ethnocentrism)

_____ 6. sexual orientation and inclinations

_____ 7. religion and religious beliefs

_____ 8. HIV status

_____ 9. attitudes toward commitment and fidelity; relationship expectations

_____ 10. political beliefs and attitudes

Thinking Critically About Times for Self-Disclosure.

After you have labelled all 10 items, consider some or all of the following questions; work alone, in groups, or with the class as a whole.

- Does age influence appropriateness? For example, are certain items important at 18 but unimportant at 50? Important at 50 but unimportant at 18?
- Do men and women expect the same level of self-disclosure from their partners? If you have the opportunity, you may wish to compare your responses to the 10 items with those of others in your group or class. Are there noticeable gender differences?
- Do men and women follow different norms or rules in self-disclosing? How would you state these rules?
- In what kinds of relationships would you expect self-disclosure to be highest and lowest? Heterosexual? Gay male? Lesbian? What reasons can you advance to support your prediction? How would you go about testing your prediction?
- Does the future of the relationship (as envisioned by each person) influence the timing of self-disclosures?
- Do cultures vary in the way their members disclose? What implications might these differences have for intercultural communication? For example, can you identify potential problems that different cultural time schedules for self-disclosure might create?

2.3 USING PERFORMANCE VISUALIZATION TO REDUCE APPREHENSION

Performance visualization is a technique designed specifically to reduce the outward manifestations of speaker apprehension and to reduce negative thinking (Ayres & Hopf, 1993, 1995). Try reducing your own communication apprehension by following these two simple suggestions.

1. The first part of performance visualization is to develop a positive attitude and a positive self-perception. So visualize yourself in the role of being an effective speaker. Visualize yourself communicating as a fully and totally confident individual. Look at your listeners and speak. Throughout your conversation see yourself as fully in control of the situation. See your listeners in rapt attention from the time you begin to the time you stop. Throughout this visualization, avoid all negative thoughts. As you visualize yourself an effective speaker, take special note of how you walk, look at your listeners, respond to questions, and especially how you feel about the whole experience.

2. The second part of performance visualization is to model your performance on that of an especially effective speaker. So view a particularly competent speaker and make a mental movie of him or her. Try selecting a presentation that's on video so you can replay it several times. As you review the actual and mental movie, begin to shift yourself into the role of speaker. Become this effective speaker.

Thinking Critically About Performance Visualization.
How did you feel as you were visualizing yourself as a successful and effective speaker? What actions did you see yourself performing? What person did you select to model your performance on? What is there about this person that led you to select him or her as your model? In what ways might you improve your next experience of performance visualization?

Chapter 3

Interpersonal Perception

CHAPTER TOPICS

This chapter introduces interpersonal perception—the ways you see and evaluate other people.

- The Stages of Perception
- The Processes of Perception
- Increasing Accuracy in Interpersonal Perception

CHAPTER SKILLS

After completing this chapter, you should be able to:

- perceive others with the knowledge that perceptions are influenced by who you are and by external stimuli.
- avoid common perceptual barriers while perceiving others.
- perceive others more accurately, using a variety of strategies.

These photographs show two different images of Canadian singer Céline Dion. If you didn't know who she was, what meaning might you assign to each image? For example, would you guess that the photo on the left depicts a popular entertainer? What would you think of the woman shown in the photo on the right?

Appearances are often deceptive, and what you think you see may not be the entire story—a lesson that will prove useful to anyone engaged in perceptions of other people, the topic of this chapter.

What should a popular singer look like?

The Stages of Perception

Perception is the process by which you become aware of objects, events, and especially people through your senses: sight, smell, taste, touch, and hearing. Perception is an active, not a passive process. Your perceptions result from what exists in the outside world *and* from your own experiences, desires, needs and wants, loves and hatreds. One of the reasons why perception is so important in interpersonal communication is that it influences your communication choices. The messages you send and listen to will depend on how you see the world, on how you size up specific situations, on what you think of the people with whom you interact.

Interpersonal perception is a continuous series of processes that blend into one another. *For convenience of discussion* we can separate these processes into five stages: (1) You sense, you pick up some kind of stimulation; (2) you organize the stimuli in some way; (3) you interpret and evaluate what you perceive; (4) you store your perception in memory; and (5) you retrieve it when needed.

> We must always tell what we see. Above all, and this is more difficult, we must always see what we see.
>
> —**Charles Peguy**

Stage One: Stimulation

At this first stage, your sense organs encounter a **stimulus**—you hear a new CD, you see a friend, you smell someone's perfume, you taste an orange, you feel another's sweaty palm. Naturally, you don't perceive everything; rather, you engage in *selective perception*. This general term includes selective attention and selective exposure. In selective attention, you attend to those things that you anticipate will fulfill your needs or will prove enjoyable. For example, when daydreaming in class, you don't hear what the instructor is saying until your name is called. Your selective attention mechanism focuses your senses on your name.

Through **selective exposure** you expose yourself to people or messages that will confirm your existing beliefs, that will contribute to your objectives, or that will prove satisfying in some way. For example, after you buy a car, you're more apt to read and listen to advertisements for the car you just bought, because these messages tell you that you made the right decision. At the same time, you will tend to avoid ads for the cars that you considered but eventually rejected, because these messages would tell you that you made the wrong decision.

You're also more likely to perceive stimuli that are greater in intensity than surrounding stimuli and those that have novelty value (Kagan, 2002). For example, television commercials normally play at a greater intensity than regular programming to ensure that you take special notice. You're also more likely to notice the coworker who dresses in a novel way than you are to notice the one who dresses like everyone else. You will quickly perceive someone who shows up in class wearing a tuxedo or at a formal party in shorts.

Stage Two: Organization

At the second stage, you organize the information your senses pick up. Three interesting ways in which people organize their perceptions are by rules, by schemata, and by scripts. Let's look at each briefly.

Organization by Rules　One frequently used rule is that of *proximity* or physical closeness. The rule, simply stated, would say: Things that are physically close together constitute a unit. Thus, using this rule, you would perceive people who are often together, or messages spoken one immediately after the other, as units—as belonging together. You also assume that verbal and nonverbal signals sent at about the same time are related and constitute a unified whole; you assume they follow a *temporal rule,* which says that things occurring together in time belong together.

Another rule is *similarity:* things that are physically similar, things that look alike, belong together and form a unit. This principle of similarity would lead you to see people who dress alike as belonging together, for example. Or you might assume that people who work at the same jobs, who are of the same religion, who live in the same building, or who talk with the same accent belong together.

You use the principle of *contrast* when you note that some items (people or messages, for example) don't belong together—that they are too different from each other to be part of the same perceptual organization. So, for example, in a conversation or a public speech, listeners will focus their attention on changes in intensity or rate, because these contrast with the rest of the message.

Organization by Schemata　Another way you organize material is by creating **schemata**, mental templates or structures that help you organize the millions of items of information you come into contact with every day as well as those you already have in memory. Schemata may thus be viewed as general ideas about people (about Paulo and Amanda, about Japanese people, about Baptists, about Torontonians), yourself (your qualities, abilities, and even liabilities), or social roles (what's a police officer, professor, or multibillionaire CEO like). (The word *schemata* is the plural of *schema* and is preferred to the alternative plural *schemas.*)

Organization by Scripts　A script is really a type of schema; but because it's a special type, it's given a different name. Like a schema, a

It's not whether you really cry. It's whether the audience thinks you are crying.

— Ingrid Bergman

Attitudes

In addition to mastering specific communication skills, you—as a critical thinker—need to be willing to examine your own **attitudes** about critical thinking and about yourself as a critical thinker.

- Analyze yourself as a critically thinking communicator. Self-analysis is essential if you're to use this material in any meaningful sense. Be open-minded to new ideas, even those that contradict your existing beliefs.

- Observe the behaviours of those around you as well as your own. See in real life what you read about here; it will then have clearer application to your own day-to-day interactions.

- Delay conclusions until you have collected sufficient information. But do realize that eventually you need to make a decision; at some point thinking needs to give way to action.

- Analyze and evaluate ideas instead of accepting them just because they appear in a textbook or are mentioned by an instructor.

EXAMPLES?

Can you find examples of ideas, suggestions, or conclusions discussed in this textbook that you disagree with or that you'd like more evidence for before you accept them? How would you go about investigating the evidence for these ideas, suggestions, or conclusions?

You develop schemata from your own experience—from actual experiences as well as from television, reading, and hearsay. Thus, for example, you might have a schema for college athletes; it might include perceptions that athletes are physically strong, ambitious, academically weak, and egocentric. And, of course, you've probably developed schemata for different religious, racial, and national groups; for men and women; and for people of different affectional orientations. Each group with which you have some familiarity will be represented in your mind in some kind of schema. Schemata help you organize your perceptions by allowing you to classify millions of people into a manageable number of categories or classes. As we'll see below, however, schemata can also create problems—they can lead you to see what is not there or to miss seeing what is there.

---

script is an organized body of information about some action, event, or procedure. It's a general idea of how some event should play out or unfold; it's the rules governing events and their sequence. For example, you probably have a script for eating in a restaurant with the actions organized into a pattern something like this: Enter, take a seat, review the menu, order from the menu, eat your food, ask for the bill, leave a tip, pay the bill, exit the restaurant. Similarly, you probably have scripts for how you do laundry, conduct an interview, introduce someone to someone else, or ask for a date.

What shortcuts do you use in helping yourself to understand, remember, and recall information about people and events? Can you give specific examples of rules, schemata, and scripts that you maintain and that influence your perceptions?

Stage Three: Interpretation–Evaluation

The interpretation–evaluation stage of perception (the two processes cannot be separated) is inevitably subjective and is greatly influenced by your experiences, needs, wants, values, beliefs about the way things are or should be, expectations, physical and emotional state, and so on. Your interpretation–evaluation will be influenced by your rules, schemata, and scripts as well as by your gender; for example, women have been found to view others more positively than men do (Winquist, Mohr, & Kenny, 1998).

How accurate are you at interpersonal perception? What cues do you look for when judging other people after first meeting them?

For example, upon meeting a new person who is introduced to you as a college football player, you will tend to apply your schema to this person and view him as physically strong, ambitious, academically weak, and egocentric. You will, in other words, see this person through the filter of your schema and evaluate him according to your schema for college athletes. Similarly, when viewing someone performing some series of actions (say, eating in a restaurant), you apply your script to this event and view the event through the script. You interpret the actions of the diner as appropriate or inappropriate depending on your script for this behaviour and the ways in which the diner performs the sequence of actions.

In making evaluations of other people, it would seem that we first think about the situation and then make the evaluation. Some research claims, however, that we really don't think before assigning any perception a positive or negative value. This research argues that all perceptions have a positive or negative value attached to them and that these evaluations are most often automatic and involve no conscious thought. Immediately upon perceiving a person, idea, or thing a positive or negative value is attached (*New York Times*, August 8, 1995, C1, C10). What do you think of this claim? One bit of evidence against this position would be to identify three or four or five things, ideas, or people about which you feel *completely* neutral. Can you do it?

Stage Four: Memory

Your perceptions and their interpretations–evaluations are put into memory; they're stored so that you may ultimately retrieve them at some later time. So, for example, you have in memory your schema for college athletes and the fact that Ben Williams is a football player. Ben Williams is then stored in memory with "cognitive tags" that tell you that he's strong, ambitious, academically weak, and egocentric. Now, despite the fact that you've not witnessed Ben's strength or ambitions and have no idea of his academic record or his psychological profile, you still may store your memory of Ben along with the qualities that make up your schema for "college athletes."

Now let's say that at different times you hear that Ben failed Spanish I (normally an A or B course at your school), that Ben got an A in chemistry (normally a tough course), and that Ben is transferring to Queen's University as a theoretical physics major. Schemas act as filters or gatekeepers; they allow certain information to get stored in relatively objective form, much as you heard or read it, but may distort or prevent other information from getting stored. As a result, these three items of information about Ben may get stored very differently in your memory along with your schema for college athletes.

For example, you may readily store the information that Ben failed Spanish, because it's consistent with your schema; it fits neatly into the template you have for college athletes. Information that's consistent with your schema—such as in this example—will strengthen your schema and make it more resistant to change (Aronson, Wilson, & Akert, 1999). Depending on the strength of your schema, you may also store in memory, even though you didn't hear it, a perception that Ben did poorly in other courses as well. The information that Ben got an A in chemistry, because it contradicts your schema (it just doesn't seem right), may easily be distorted or lost. The information that Ben is transferring to

Queen's, however, is a bit different. This information is also inconsistent with your schema; but it is so drastically inconsistent that you may begin to look at this mindfully and may even begin to question your schema, or perhaps to view Ben as an exception to the general rule. In either case, you're going to etch Ben's transferring to Queen's very clearly in your mind.

Stage Five: Recall

At some later date, you may want to recall or access the information you have stored in memory. Let's say you want to retrieve your information about Ben because he's a topic of conversation among you and a few friends. As we'll see in our discussion of listening in Chapter 4, memory isn't reproductive; you don't simply reproduce what you've heard or seen. Rather, you reconstruct what you've heard or seen into a whole that is meaningful to you—depending in great part on your schemata and scripts—and it's this reconstruction that you store in memory. Now, when you want to retrieve this information from memory, you may recall it with a variety of inaccuracies. You're likely to

■ recall information that is consistent with your schema; in fact, you may not even be recalling the specific information (say about Ben) but may actually be recalling your schema (which contains the information about college athletes and, because of this, also about Ben)

■ fail to recall information that is inconsistent with your schema; you have no place to put that information and so you easily lose it or forget it

■ recall information that drastically contradicts your schema, because it forces you to think (and perhaps rethink) about your schema and its accuracy; it may even force you to revise your schema for college athletes in general

Before moving on to the more specific processes involved in interpersonal perception, let's spell out some of the implications of this five-stage model for your own interpersonal perceptions:

1. Everyone relies heavily on shortcuts; rules, schemata, and scripts, for example, are all useful shortcuts that simplify your understanding, remembering, and recalling information about people and events. If you didn't have these shortcuts, then you'd have to treat every person, role, or action differently from each other person, role, or action. This would make every experience a new one totally unrelated to anything you already know. If you didn't use these shortcuts, you'd be unable to generalize, draw connections, or otherwise profit from previously acquired knowledge.

2. Shortcuts, however, may mislead you; they may contribute to your remembering things that are consistent with your schemata even if they didn't occur, and to your distorting or forgetting information that is inconsistent.

3. What you remember about a person or an event isn't an objective recollection but is more likely heavily influenced by your preconceptions or your schemata about what belongs and what doesn't

Tact is the ability to describe others as they see themselves.

—**Eleanor Chaffee**

belong, what fits neatly into the templates in your brain and what doesn't fit. Your reconstruction of an event or person contains a lot of information that was not in the original sensory experience and may omit a lot that was in the experience.

4. Judgments about others are invariably ethnocentric: Because your schemata and scripts are created on the basis of your own cultural experiences, you invariably apply these to members of other cultures. From this it's easy to infer that when members of other cultures do things that conform to your scripts, they're right, and when they do things that contradict your scripts, they're wrong—a classic example of ethnocentric thinking. As you can appreciate, this tendency can easily contribute to intercultural misunderstandings.

5. Memory is especially unreliable when the information is ambiguous—when it can be interpreted in different ways. Thus, for example, consider the statement, "Ben didn't do as well in his other courses as he would have liked." If your schema of Ben was "brilliant" then you might "remember" that Ben got B's. But if, as in our example, your schema was of the academically weak athlete, you might "remember" that Ben got D's. Conveniently, but unreliably, schemata reduce ambiguity.

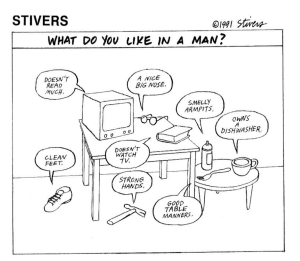

STIVERS ©1991 Stivers

WHAT DO YOU LIKE IN A MAN?

© 1991 Mark Stivers. Reprinted by permission.

The Processes of Perception

Before reading about the specific processes that you use in perceiving other people, examine your own perception strategies by taking the self-test below.

TEST YOURSELF

How Accurate Are You at People Perception?

Instructions: Respond to each of the following statements with T for "true" if the statement is usually or generally accurate in describing your behaviour, and with F for "false" if the statement is usually or generally inaccurate in describing your behaviour. Try to avoid the tendency to give what you feel is the desirable answer; just be truthful.

_____ 1. I base most of my impressions of people on the first few minutes of our meeting.

_____ 2. When I know some things about another person, I can fill in what I don't know.

_____ 3. I make predictions about people's behaviours that generally prove true.

_____ 4. I have clear ideas of what people of different national, racial, and religious groups are really like.

_____ 5. I generally look for lots of cues about a person's attitudes and behaviours, not just their most obvious physical or psychological characteristic.

| | 6. | I avoid making assumptions about what is going on in someone else's head on the basis of their behaviours. |

____ **6.** I avoid making assumptions about what is going on in someone else's head on the basis of their behaviours.

____ **7.** I pay special attention to behaviours of people that might contradict my initial impressions.

____ **8.** On the basis of my observations of people, I formulate guesses about them (which I am willing to revise) rather than firmly held conclusions.

____ **9.** I avoid making judgments about people until I learn a great deal about them and see them in a variety of situations.

____ **10.** After I formulate an initial impression, I check my perceptions by, for example, asking questions or by gathering more evidence.

HOW DID YOU DO?

This brief perception test was designed to raise questions to be considered in this chapter and not to provide you with a specific perception score. The first four questions refer to tendencies to judge others on the basis of first impressions (question 1), implicit personality theories (2), prophecies (3), and stereotypes (4). Ideally you would have answered "false" to these four questions, because they represent sources of distortion. Questions 5 through 10 suggest specific guidelines for increasing accuracy in people perception: looking for a variety of cues (5), avoiding the tendency to mind read (6), being especially alert to contradictory cues (7), formulating hypotheses rather than conclusions (8), recognizing the diversity in people (9), and delaying conclusions until more evidence is in. Ideally you would have answered "true" to these six questions, because they represent suggestions for increased accuracy in perception.

WHAT WILL YOU DO?

As you read this chapter, think about these guidelines and consider how you might use them for more accurate and reasonable people perception. At the same time, recognize that situations vary widely; these suggestions will prove useful most of the time but not all of the time. In fact, you may want to identify situations in which you shouldn't follow these suggestions.

Implicit Personality Theories

Each person has a subconscious or implicit system of rules—an **implicit personality theory**—that says which characteristics of an individual go with other characteristics. Consider, for example, the following brief statements. Note the word in parentheses that you think best completes each sentence:

Carlo is energetic, eager, and (intelligent, stupid).

Kim is bold, defiant, and (extroverted, introverted).

Joe is bright, lively, and (thin, heavy).

Ava is attractive, intelligent, and (likable, unlikable).

Susan is cheerful, positive, and (outgoing, shy).

Angel is handsome, tall, and (friendly, unfriendly).

What makes some of these choices seem right and others wrong is your implicit personality theory. Your theory may, for example, have told you that a person who is energetic and eager is also intelligent, not stupid—even though there is no logical reason why a stupid person could not be energetic and eager.

The widely documented **halo effect** is a function of the implicit personality theory (Riggio, 1987; Beebe, Beebe, Redmond, Geerinck & Milstone, 2000). If you believe a person has some positive qualities, you're likely to infer that she or he also possesses other positive qualities. There is also a *reverse halo effect:* If you know a person possesses several negative qualities, you're more likely to infer that the person also has other negative qualities.

In using implicit personality theories, apply them carefully and critically so as to avoid perceiving qualities in an individual that your theory tells you should be present when they actually are not. For example, you may see goodwill in a friend's "charitable" acts when a tax deduction may have been the real motive.

Similarly, be careful of ignoring or distorting qualities that don't conform to your theory but that are actually present in the individual. For example, you may ignore negative qualities in your friends that you would easily perceive in your enemies.

As might be expected, the implicit personality theories that people hold differ from culture to culture, from group to group, and even from person to person. For example, the Chinese have a concept called *shi gu* that refers to "someone who is worldly, devoted to his or her family, socially skillful, and somewhat reserved" (Aronson, Wilson, & Akert, 1999, p. 117). This concept isn't easily encoded in English, as you can tell by trying to find a general concept that covers this type of person. In English, on the other hand, we have a concept of the "artistic type," a generalization that seems absent in Chinese. Thus, although it is easy for speakers of English or Chinese to refer to specific concepts—as in describing someone as socially skilled or creative—each language creates its own generalized categories. In Chinese the qualities that make up *shi gu* are seen as going together more easily than they might be for an English speaker; they're part of the implicit personality theory of more Chinese speakers than English speakers.

Similarly, consider the different personality theories that graduate students and blue-collar high school dropouts might have for "college students." Likewise, an individual may have had great experiences with doctors and so may have a very positive personality theory of "doctors," whereas another person may have had negative experiences with doctors and may thus have developed a very negative personality theory.

The Self-Fulfilling Prophecy

A **self-fulfilling prophecy** occurs when you make a prediction that comes true because you act on it as if it were true (Merton, 1957; Beebe, Beebe, Redmond, Geerinck & Milstone, 2000). Put differently, a self-fulfilling prophecy occurs when you act on your schema as if it were true and in doing so make it true. There are four basic steps in the self-fulfilling prophecy:

1. You make a prediction or formulate a belief about a person or a situation. For example, you predict that Shafiq is friendly in interpersonal encounters.

It has been argued that the self-fulfilling prophecy may be used in organizations to stimulate higher performance (Eden, 1992; Field, 1989). For example, managers could be given the belief that workers can perform at extremely high levels; managers would then act as if this were true and thus promote this high-level behaviour in the workers. How might self-fulfilling prophecies be used in the college classroom? How might they be used in parenting? Would you consider this behaviour ethical?

2. You act toward that person or situation as if that prediction or belief were true. For example, you act as if Shafiq were a friendly person.

3. Because you act as if the belief were true, it becomes true. For example, because of the way you act toward Shafiq, he becomes comfortable and friendly.

4. You observe *your* effect on the person or the resulting situation, and what you see strengthens your beliefs. For example, you observe Shafiq's friendliness, and this reinforces your belief that he is in fact friendly.

We make self-fulfilling prophecies about ourselves as well as about others. For example, you predict that you'll do poorly in an examination, so you don't read the questions carefully and don't make any great effort to organize your thoughts or support your statements. Or you predict that people won't like you, so you don't extend yourself to others. You can also make positive predictions about yourself, and these too will influence your behaviour. For example, you can assume that others will like you and so approach them with a positive attitude and demeanour. Generally, how do your predictions influence your achieving your personal and professional goals?

A teacher from Calgary tells this story: At the beginning of the year, she was given a list of her students with numbers beside them ranging from 110 to 140. She thought these numbers were the students' IQs and was amazed at the level of intelligence. All year, she treated these students as the bright people she believed them to be and they, of course, responded. At the end of the year, parents and principal were amazed at the progress the students had made. The numbers the teacher had thought were IQs were actually locker numbers, and the students had previously been low achievers.

In one high school study, high school teachers had made the prophecy that boys are more assertive and talked more in class than girls. The teachers then behaved as if this prophecy were true and actually encouraged boys to talk more than girls (Sadker & Sadker, 1994).

The self-fulfilling prophecy can also be seen when you make predictions about yourself and fulfill them. For example, perhaps you enter a group situation convinced that the other members will dislike you. Almost invariably you'll be proved right; the other members will appear to you to dislike you. What you may be doing is acting in a way that encourages the group to respond to you negatively. In this way you fulfill your prophecies about yourself.

Self-fulfilling prophecies can short-circuit critical thinking and influence another person's behaviour (or your own) so that it conforms to your prophecy. As a result, they can lead you to see what you predicted rather than what is really there—for example, to perceive yourself as a failure because you have predicted it rather than because of any actual failures.

Primacy–Recency

Assume for a moment that you're enrolled in a course in which half the classes are extremely dull and half extremely exciting. At the end of the semester, you evaluate the course and the instructor. Will your evaluation be more favourable if the dull classes occurred in the first half of the semester and the exciting classes in the second? Or will it be more favourable if the order were reversed? If what comes first exerts the most influence, you have a *primacy effect*. If what comes last (or most recently) exerts the most influence, you have a *recency effect*.

Manage every second of a first meeting. Do not delude yourself that a bad impression can be easily corrected. Putting things right is a lot harder than getting them right first time.

—David Lewis

I make up my mind about people in the first 10 seconds, and I very rarely change it.

—Margaret Thatcher

In the classic study on the effects of **primacy and recency** in interpersonal perception, college students perceived a person who was described as "intelligent, industrious, impulsive, critical, stubborn, and envious" more positively than a person described as "envious, stubborn, critical, impulsive, industrious, and intelligent" (Asch, 1946). Clearly, there's a tendency to use early information to get a general idea about a person and to use later information to make this impression more specific. The initial information helps you form a schema for the person. Once that schema is formed, you're likely to resist information that contradicts it.

One interesting practical implication of primacy–recency is that the first impression you make on others is likely to be the most important. The reason for this is that the schema that others form of you functions as a filter to admit or block additional information about you. If the initial impression or schema is positive, others are likely to readily remember additional positive information, because it confirms this original positive image or schema—and to forget or distort negative information, because it contradicts this original positive schema; they are also more likely to interpret as positive information that is really ambiguous. If the initial impression is positive, then, you win all three ways.

The tendency to give greater weight to early information and to interpret later information in light of early impressions can lead you to formulate a total picture of an individual on the basis of initial impressions that may not be typical or accurate. For example, if you judge a job applicant as generally nervous when he or she may simply be showing normal nervousness at being interviewed for a much needed job, you will have misperceived this individual.

Similarly, this tendency can lead you to discount or distort subsequent perceptions so as not to disrupt your initial impression or upset your original schema. For example, you may fail to see signs of deceitfulness in someone you like because of your early impression that this person is a good and honest individual.

Consistency

The tendency to maintain balance among perceptions or attitudes is called **consistency** (McBroom & Reed, 1992). You expect certain things to go together and other things not to go together. On a purely intuitive basis, for example, respond to the following sentences by noting your *expected* response:

1. I expect a person I like to (like, dislike) me.
2. I expect a person I dislike to (like, dislike) me.
3. I expect my friend to (like, dislike) my friend.
4. I expect my friend to (like, dislike) my enemy.
5. I expect my enemy to (like, dislike) my friend.
6. I expect my enemy to (like, dislike) my enemy.

How would you describe the first impression that people form of you? What specific cues do you communicate to give them this impression?

According to most consistency theories, your expectations would be as follows: You would expect a person you liked to like you (1) and one you disliked to dislike you (2). You would expect a friend to like a friend (3) and to dislike an enemy (4). You would expect your enemy to dislike your friend (5) and to like your other enemy (6). All these expectations are intuitively satisfying.

Further, you would expect someone you liked to possess characteristics you like or admire. And you would expect your enemies not to possess characteristics you like or admire. Conversely, you would expect people you liked to lack unpleasant characteristics and those you disliked to possess unpleasant characteristics.

Uncritically assuming that an individual is consistent can lead you to ignore or distort your perceptions of behaviours that are inconsistent with your picture of the whole person. For example, you may misinterpret Kim's basic shyness because your image of Kim is "bold, defiant, and extroverted." Consistency can also lead you to see certain behaviours as positive if you interpreted other behaviours positively (the halo effect) or as negative if you interpreted other behaviours negatively (the reverse halo effect).

Stereotyping

One of the most common shortcuts in interpersonal perception is stereotyping. A sociological or psychological **stereotype** is a fixed impression of a group of people; it's a schema. We all have attitudinal stereotypes—of national, religious, sexual, or racial groups, or perhaps of criminals, prostitutes, teachers, or plumbers. If you have these fixed impressions, you will, upon meeting a member of a particular group, often see that person primarily as a member of that group and apply to him or her all the characteristics you assign to that group. If you meet someone who is a prostitute, for example, there is a host of characteristics for prostitutes that you may apply to this one person. To complicate matters further, you will often "see" in this person's behaviour the manifestation of characteristics that you would not "see" if you didn't know that this person was a prostitute. Stereotypes can easily distort accurate perception and prevent you from seeing an individual as an individual rather than as a member of a group.

What stereotypes do you think men entertain about women? What stereotypes do you think women entertain about men? How might these stereotypes influence their interpersonal communication?

MESSAGES@WORK

When You Meet a Blind Person

HOW CAN I OFFER ASSISTANCE TO A BLIND PERSON?

When speaking to blind or visually impaired people, use a normal tone of voice. Let them know you are addressing them by using their name. Remember to let them know when you are leaving.

HOW DO I HELP A BLIND PERSON CROSS THE STREET?

Avoid pulling blind people by the hand or tugging at their sleeves. It is awkward and confusing. Simply offer your assistance and they will tell you the best way to guide them. Let them know when you are

(continued)

coming to a curb and whether you will be stepping up or down.

HOW CAN I HELP A BLIND PERSON FEEL MORE COMFORTABLE IN AN UNFAMILIAR SETTING?

It is very helpful and important to describe the surroundings to blind or visually impaired people. For example, you can describe the layout of a room—whether it is square or narrow, how many tables and chairs there are, and how they are arranged. The same principle applies when travelling with blind or visually impaired people. Describe the landscape, tell them which direction you are travelling (north, south, etc.), and mention the names of towns you pass by. Just remember to give directions clearly and accurately. Pointing or using phrases such as "over there" will be of no assistance.

When you meet a blind or visually impaired person, the key word is "person"—not "blind." Don't hesitate to use the words "see," "look," or "read." Remember that blind and visually impaired people are individuals first. They do the same things as you, but sometimes use different techniques.

The sighted guide technique provides the visually impaired person with a basic travel method using the physical assistance of a sighted person. The visually impaired person learns to interpret the elbow movements of the guide walking with him.

BASIC GUIDE TECHNIQUE

The blind person always holds the sighted guide's arm (not vice versa). The guide puts out her hand or arm to make contact. The blind person then takes her arm just above the elbow. This leaves the guide's hands free (for carrying, opening doors, etc.). With four fingers on the inside and the thumb on the outside of the elbow, the blind person feels the motion of the guide's body.

By flexing his elbow to about 90 degrees, the blind person stays a half-step behind the guide. This allows time to interpret and react to the guide's movements. To minimize his body width and to avoid moving beyond the protection of the guide, the blind person's flexed arm remains close to his body, with his shoulder lined up directly behind the guide's opposite shoulder.

Stairs

The guide alerts the blind person that they are about to go up or down stairs. The guide approaches stairs squarely and pauses at the foot or head. The blind person may or may not wish to switch to the side with the handrail. The blind person brings his foot forward to locate the first step. The guide takes the first step and both proceed. As a cue that they have reached the bottom or top, the guide pauses again at the end.

The process of pausing at tops and bottoms of stairways can be used effectively with street curbs as well.

Narrow Passage Technique

When there is not enough space for the blind person and guide to walk in the usual position (e.g., narrow aisles, doorways, etc.), the narrow passage technique is used. The guide signals a change in position by moving her arm back and to the centre of her back. The blind person then steps behind the guide so the two are in single file. To prevent stepping on the guide's heels, the blind person straightens his arm, thus placing him a full step behind. After leaving the narrow passage, the guide signals by moving her arm back to the side, and normal position is resumed.

WHAT EVERYONE SHOULD KNOW ABOUT GUIDE DOGS

A guide dog is not a pet, but a highly trained animal whose chief responsibility is to guide a blind person from place to place safely and independently.

The guide dog is highly intelligent, but does not possess any unusual powers. Instead, the dog reacts to specific commands given by the owner, such as "Left," "Right," "Forward," and so on. By following these instructions the dog will guide the owner to his/her destination. The dog will also disobey a command which might place the team in a hazardous situation.

All guide dogs, regardless of their breed or school, can be recognized by the leather harness and the U-shaped handle which is held in the owner's left hand.

If a guide dog is wearing a harness, *do not distract or touch the dog without the owner's permission.* Such an action may be dangerous to them both.

Source: Adapted from pamphlets produced by The Canadian National Institute for the Blind.

The tendency to group people and to respond to individuals primarily as members of groups can lead you to perceive an individual as possessing those qualities (usually negative) that you believe characterize his or her group (for example, "All Mexicans are..." or "All Baptists are...")—and therefore to fail to appreciate the multifaceted nature of all individuals and groups. Stereotyping can also lead you to ignore each person's unique characteristics and therefore to fail to benefit from the special contributions each individual can bring to an encounter. You may at this point want to take the self-test below as a way of looking at some of your own stereotypes or as a way of understanding those of others.

What stereotypes, if any, would your family or friends have of the people depicted in this photograph? What stereotypes, if any, do you have?

Attribution

Attribution is the process by which we try to explain the motivation for a person's behaviour. Perhaps the major way we do this is to ask ourselves if the person was in control of the behaviour. If people are in control of their own behaviour, then we feel justified in praising them for positive behaviours and blaming them for negative behaviours. You probably make similar judgments based on controllability in many situations. Consider, for example, how you would respond to situations such as Manju's failing her history exam or Sidney's having his car repossessed because he failed to keep up the payments.

Very likely you would be sympathetic to Manju and Sidney if you feel that they were *not* in control of what happened; for example, if the examination was unfair or if Sidney couldn't make his car payments because he lost his job as a result of discrimination. On the other hand, you probably would not be sympathetic or might blame these people for their problems if you felt that they were in control of what happened; for example, if Manju partied instead of studying or if Sidney gambled his payments away.

Generally, research shows that if we feel people are in control of negative behaviours, we will come to dislike them. If we feel people are not in control of negative behaviours, we will come to feel sorry for them and not blame them for their negative circumstances. (Additional insights into attribution may be found at **www.ablongman.com/devito**.)

Attribution of causality can lead to several major barriers. Three such barriers (the self-serving bias, overattribution, and the fundamental attribution error) are examined in the Skills Toolbox on page 76. (An exercise in applying attribution theory may be found at **www.ablongman.com/devito**.)

> To see ourselves as others see us is a most salutary gift. Hardly less important is the capacity to see others as they see themselves.
>
> —**Aldous Huxley**

Increasing Accuracy in Interpersonal Perception

Successful interpersonal communication depends largely on the accuracy of your interpersonal perception. As we will see, potential barriers that can arise with each of the perceptual processes include the self-serving bias, overattribution, and the fundamental attribution error.

3 Ways to Avoid Attribution Errors

Three major attribution problems can interfere with the accuracy of your interpersonal perceptions whether on the job or off the job.

1. After getting a poor performance evaluation, you're more likely to attribute it to the difficulty of the job or the unfairness of the supervisor (that is, to uncontrollable factors). After getting an extremely positive evaluation, however, you're more likely to attribute it to your ability or hard work (that is, to controllable factors). This tendency is called the **self-serving bias**: our inclination to take credit for the positive and deny responsibility for the negative (Hogg, 2002). To prevent this bias from distorting your attributions, consider the potential influences of both internal and external factors on your positive *and* negative behaviours. Ask yourself to what extent your negative behaviours may be due to internal (controllable) factors and your positive behaviours to external (uncontrollable) factors. Just asking the question will prevent you from mindlessly falling into the self-serving bias trap.

2. If someone you work with had alcoholic parents or is blind or was born into great wealth, there's often a tendency to attribute everything that person does to such factors. For example, "Sally has difficulty working on a team because she grew up in a home of alcoholics," "Alex overeats because he's blind," "Lillian lacks ambition because she always got whatever she wanted without working for it." This is called **overattribution**: the tendency to single out one or two obvious characteristics and attribute everything a person does to these one or two characteristics. To prevent overattribution, recognize that most behaviours result from a lot of factors and that you almost always make a mistake when you select one factor and attribute everything to it. So,

when you make a judgment, ask yourself if other factors might be influencing behaviours that seem at first glance to stem solely from one factor.

3. When Nila is late for a meeting, you're more likely to conclude that she is inconsiderate or irresponsible rather than attributing the lateness to a bus breakdown or to a traffic accident. This tendency to conclude that people do what they do because that's the kind of people they are rather than because of the situation they're in is called the **fundamental attribution error**. When you commit this error, you overvalue the contribution of internal factors and undervalue the influence of external factors. To avoid making this error, ask yourself if you're giving too much emphasis to internal factors and too little emphasis to external factors. Interestingly, this tendency may be culture specific and not universal as previously thought (Goode, 2000). For example, in one study U.S. and Korean students were presented with a speech endorsing a particular position and told that the writer had been instructed to write this and really had no choice. The American students were more likely to conclude that the speaker believed in the position endorsed; they believed that what the speaker said reflected what the speaker believed, not the external circumstances of being forced to write the speech. Korean students, on the other hand, were less likely to believe in the sincerity of the speaker and gave greater weight to the external factor that the speaker was forced to write the speech.

THEN AND NOW

Have you ever fallen into one of these three errors in perceiving another person? What happened? What would you do differently now?

There are, however, additional ways to think more critically about your perceptions and thereby to increase your perceptual accuracy. Some of these are considered in the following discussion. (In addition, a useful exercise that will help identify the common barriers to perceptual accuracy, "Barriers to Accurate Perception," may be found at www.ablongman.com/devito.)

Analyze Your Perceptions

When you become aware of your perceptions, you'll be able to subject them to logical analysis, to critical thinking. Here are a few suggestions.

■ Recognize your own role in perception. Your emotional and physiological state will influence the meaning you give to your perceptions. A movie may seem hysterically funny when you're in a good mood but just plain stupid when you're in a bad mood or when you're preoccupied with family problems. Beware of your own biases. Know when your perceptual evaluations are unduly influenced by your own biases—for example, by a tendency to perceive only the positive in people you like and only the negative in people you don't like.

■ Avoid early conclusions. On the basis of your observations of behaviours, formulate hypotheses to test against additional information and evidence rather than drawing conclusions you then look to confirm. Delay formulating conclusions until you have had a chance to process a wide variety of cues. Similarly, avoid the one-cue conclusion. Look for a variety of cues pointing in the same direction. The more cues pointing to the same conclusion, the more likely your conclusion will be correct. Be especially alert to contradictory cues, ones that refute your initial hypotheses. It's relatively easy to perceive cues that confirm your hypotheses but more difficult to acknowledge contradictory evidence. At the same time, seek validation from others. Do others see things the same way you do? If not, ask yourself if your perceptions may be in some way distorted.

■ Avoid mind reading; that is, don't try to read the thoughts and feelings of other people merely from observing their behaviours.

THINKING CRITICALLY ABOUT
Alternative Visions

Altercasting is a technique that encourages you to put yourself into the frame of mind of someone else and is helpful in providing you with a different perspective, an alternative vision. For example, if you were a real estate sales representative, it would help if you placed yourself in the role of the home buyer and perhaps even went through the process of looking for a home as a would-be buyer. Altercasting is also useful when two people want to understand each other's perspective; each might altercast and play the role of the other. In this *role reversal* you and your romantic partner, for example, might each play the part of the other in a mock argument. The reverse role playing allows you to see how your partner sees you and allows your partner to see how you see him or her.

EXAMPLES?

Give an example of how you might use altercasting in one of the following situations:

■ An advertiser is developing a package for a new cereal, toothpaste, or detergent.

■ A designer for a food store wants to increase sales despite the arrival of two new supermarkets in the area.

■ A new teacher wants to be a great teacher.

■ A company manager supervises 20 culturally diverse men and women.

■ A parent has a child who is often truant.

■ A supervisor's trainees are overly slow.

Regardless of how many behaviours you observe and how carefully you examine them, you can only *guess* what is going on in someone's mind. A person's motives are not open to outside inspection; you can only make assumptions based on overt behaviours.

Check Your Perceptions

Perception checking is another way to reduce uncertainty and to make your perceptions more accurate. The goal of perception checking is not to prove that your initial perception is correct but to explore further the thoughts and feelings of the other person. With this simple technique, you lessen your chances of misinterpreting another's feelings. At the same time, you give the other person an opportunity to elaborate on his or her thoughts and feelings.

In its most basic form, perception checking consists of two steps. First, describe what you see or hear, recognizing that even descriptions are not really objective but are heavily influenced by who you are, your emotional state, and so on. At the same time, you may wish to describe what you think is happening. Again, try to do this as descriptively (not evaluatively) as you can. Sometimes you may wish to offer several possibilities:

Copyright © 1993 Ray Billingsley. Reprinted with special permission of King Features Syndicate.

- You've called me from work a lot this week. You seem concerned that everything is all right at home.

- You've not wanted to talk with me all week. You say that my work is fine, but you don't seem to want to give me the same responsibilities that other editorial assistants have.

Second, ask the other person for confirmation. Do be careful that your request for confirmation doesn't sound as if you already knew the answer, and avoid phrasing your questions defensively. Avoid saying, for example, "You really don't want to go out, do you; I knew you didn't when you turned on that lousy television." Instead, ask for confirmation in as supportive a way as possible: "Would you rather watch TV?" Other examples:

- Are you worried about me or the kids?

- Are you pleased with my work? Is there anything I can do to improve my job performance?

How would you use perception checking in such situations as these: (a) Your friend says he wants to drop out of college; (b) your cousin hasn't called you in several months, though you have called her at least six times; (c) another student seems totally detached from everything that happens in class.

Reduce Your Uncertainty

We all have a tendency to try to reduce uncertainty, a process that enables us to achieve greater accuracy in perception. In large part we learn about uncertainty and how to deal with it from our culture.

Culture and Uncertainty People from different cultures differ greatly in their attitudes toward uncertainty and how to deal with it, and these attitudes have an impact on perceptual accuracy. In some cultures people do little to avoid uncertainty and have little anxiety about not knowing what will happen next. Uncertainty is a normal part of life and is accepted as it comes; members of these cultures don't feel threatened by unknown situations. Examples of such low-anxiety cultures include Singapore, Jamaica, Denmark, Sweden, Hong Kong, Ireland, Great Britain, Malaysia, India, the Philippines, and the United States. Other cultures do much to avoid uncertainty and have a great deal of anxiety about not knowing what will happen next; uncertainty is seen as threatening and something that must be counteracted. Examples of such high-anxiety cultures include Greece, Portugal, Guatemala, Uruguay, Belgium, El Salvador, Japan, Yugoslavia, Peru, France, Chile, Spain, and Costa Rica (Hofstede, 1997).

The potential for communication problems can be great when people come from cultures with different attitudes toward uncertainty. For example, managers from cultures with weak uncertainty avoidance will accept workers who work only when they have to and will not get too upset when workers are late. Managers from cultures with strong uncertainty avoidance will expect workers to be busy at all times and will have little tolerance for lateness.

Because weak uncertainty avoidance cultures have great tolerance for ambiguity and uncertainty, they minimize the rules governing communication and relationships (Hofstede, 1997; Lustig & Koester, 1999). People who don't follow the same rules as the cultural majority are readily tolerated. Different approaches and perspectives may even be en-

Here are three theorems, paraphrased from the theory of uncertainty reduction, a theory concerned with how communication reduces the uncertainty you have about another person (Berger & Calabrese, 1975): (1) The more people communicate, the more they like each other; (2) the more people communicate, the more intimate their communications will be; and (3) the more nonverbally expressive people are, the more they like each other. Do your own experiences support these statements? Can you give a specific example for one of the propositions?

couraged in cultures with weak uncertainty avoidance. In contrast, strong uncertainty avoidance cultures create very clear-cut rules for communication. It's considered unacceptable for people to break these rules.

Students from cultures with weak uncertainty avoidance appreciate freedom in education and prefer vague assignments without specific timetables. These students will want to be rewarded for creativity and will easily accept the instructor's occasional lack of knowledge. Students from strong uncertainty avoidance cultures prefer highly structured experiences where there is little ambiguity; they prefer specific objectives, detailed instructions, and definite timetables. These students expect to be judged on the basis of the right answers and expect the instructor to have all the answers all the time (Hofstede, 1997).

Ways to Reduce Uncertainty A variety of strategies can help reduce uncertainty (Berger & Bradac, 1982; Gudykunst, 1994). Observing another person while he or she is engaged in an active task, preferably interacting with others in more informal social situations, will often reveal a great deal about the person—because in informal situations people are less apt to monitor their behaviours and more likely to reveal their true selves.

You can also manipulate the situation in such a way as to be able to observe the person in more specific and more revealing contexts. Employment interviews, theatrical auditions, and student teaching are some situations people create to observe how a person acts and reacts and hence to reduce uncertainty about the person.

When you log on to an internet chat group for the first time and you lurk, reading exchanges between other group members before saying anything yourself, you're learning about the people in the group and about the group itself and thus reducing uncertainty. When uncertainty is reduced, you're more likely to make contributions that will be appropriate to the group and less likely to violate any of the group's norms; in short, you're more likely to communicate effectively.

Another way to reduce uncertainty is to collect information about a person through asking others. You might inquire of a colleague if a third person finds you interesting and might like to have dinner with you.

And of course you can interact with the individual. For example, you can ask questions: "Do you enjoy sports?" "What did you think of that computer science course?" "What would you do if you got fired?" You also gain knowledge of another by disclosing information about yourself. Your disclosures will help to create an environment that encourages disclosures from the person about whom you wish to learn more.

Increase Your Cultural Sensitivity

Recognizing and being sensitive to cultural differences will help increase your accuracy in perception. For example, Russian or Chinese artists such as ballet dancers will often applaud their audience by clapping, but Canadian audiences seeing this may easily interpret it as egotistical. Similarly, a German man will enter a restaurant before the woman in order to see if the place is respectable enough for the woman to enter. This simple custom can easily be interpreted as rude when viewed by members of cultures in which it's considered courteous for the woman to enter first (Axtell, 1993).

Within every cultural group, of course, there are wide and important differences. Not all Canadians are alike; neither are all Indonesians, Greeks, Mexicans, and so on. When you make assumptions that all people of a certain culture are alike, you're thinking in stereotypes. Recognizing differences between another culture and your own as well as differences among members of a particular culture will help you perceive interpersonal situations more accurately.

SUMMARY OF CONCEPTS AND SKILLS

This chapter discussed the way we receive messages through perception and explained how perception works, the processes that influence it, and how to make your perceptions more accurate.

1. Perception is the process by which you become aware of the many stimuli impinging on your senses. It occurs in five stages: sensory stimulation occurs, sensory stimulation is organized, sensory stimulation is interpreted–evaluated, sensory stimulation is held in memory, and sensory stimulation is recalled.

2. The following processes influence perception: (1) implicit personality theory, (2) self-fulfilling prophecy, (3) primacy–recency, (4) consistency, (5) stereotyping, and (6) attribution.

3. The term *implicit personality theory* refers to the private personality theory that you hold and that influences how you perceive other people.

4. A self-fulfilling prophecy occurs when you make a prediction or formulate a belief that comes true because you have made the prediction and acted as if it were true.

5. Primacy–recency effects have to do with the relative influence of stimuli as a result of their order. If what occurs first exerts greater influence, you have a primacy effect. If what occurs last exerts greater influence, you have a recency effect.

6. Consistency influences you to see what is consistent and not to see what is inconsistent with your expectations.

7. Stereotyping is our tendency to develop and maintain fixed, unchanging perceptions of groups of people and to use these perceptions to evaluate individual members, ignoring their individual, unique characteristics.

8. Attribution is the process through which you try to understand the behaviours of others (and your own, in self-attribution)—particularly the reasons or motivations for these behaviours. Many attributions are made on the basis of controllability. Errors of attribution include the self-serving bias, overattribution, and the fundamental attribution error.

9. You can increase the accuracy of your interpersonal perceptions in several ways. (1) Analyze your perceptions; for example, recognize your role in perception, formulate hypotheses rather than conclusions, look for a variety of cues (especially contradictory ones), avoid mind reading, and beware of your own biases. (2) Check your perceptions, describing what you see or hear and asking for confirmation. (3) Reduce uncertainty by, for example, lurking before joining a group, gathering information about the person or situation, or interacting and observing the interaction. (4) Be culturally sensitive, recognizing the differences between you and others and also the differences among members of any cultural group.

Throughout this discussion of perception, a variety of skills were identified and are presented here in summary. Check your ability to apply these skills: 1 = almost always, 2 = often, 3 = sometimes, 4 = rarely, 5 = hardly ever.

_____ 1. I think mindfully when I use perceptual shortcuts so that they don't mislead and result in inaccurate perceptions.

_____ 2. I guard against ethnocentric thinking by viewing the behaviour and customs of others from a multicultural view rather than from just my cultural view.

_____ 3. I bring to consciousness my implicit personality theories.

_____ 4. To guard against the self-fulfilling prophecy, I take a second look at my perceptions when they conform too closely to my expectations.

_____ 5. Recognizing how primacy–recency works, I actively guard against first impressions that might prevent accurate perceptions of future events; I formulate hypotheses rather than conclusions.

_____ 6. Understanding that assumptions about consistency may lead to inaccurate perceptions, I recognize that people may be inconsistent from one situation to another.

_____ 7. I recognize stereotyping in the messages of others and avoid it in my own.

_____ 8. I am aware of and am careful to avoid the self-serving bias, overattribution, and the fundamental attribution error in trying to account for another person's behaviour.

_____ 9. I think critically about perception, analyzing my perceptions, checking perceptions for accuracy, using uncertainty reduction strategies, and acting with cultural sensitivity.

VOCABULARY QUIZ

The Language of Interpersonal Perception

Match the terms dealing with interpersonal perception listed here with their definitions. Record the number of the definition next to the name of the appropriate concept.

_5_ script 65

_3_ implicit personality theory 69

_6_ stereotype 73

_4_ proximity 64

_1_ the fundamental attribution error 76

_8_ self-fulfilling prophecy 77

_10_ mind reading 70

_2_ perception checking 78

_9_ self-serving bias 76

_7_ schemata 64

1. A process involving overvaluing the contribution of internal factors and undervaluing the influence of external factors in explaining behaviour.

2. A way of increasing accuracy in perception that focuses on describing what you think is going on and then asking for confirmation.

3. A theory of personality that each individual maintains, complete with rules or systems, and through which the individual perceives others.

4. The tendency to see things that are physically close to each other as belonging together, as forming a unit.

5. An organization of information about some action, event, or procedure.

6. A fixed impression of a group of people.

7. The mental templates or structures that help you organize new information as well as the information you already have in memory.

8. The situation in which we make a prediction and then act in a way to make that prediction come true.

9. A tendency that leads us to take credit for positive things and to deny responsibility for negative things.

10. Drawing conclusions about what is going on in the mind of another person, such as the person's motives or intentions.

SKILL BUILDING EXERCISES

3.1 PERSPECTIVE TAKING

Taking the perspective of the other person and looking at the world through this perspective, this point of view, rather than through your own is crucial in achieving mutual understanding. For each of the specific behaviours listed below, identify specific circumstances that would lead to a *positive perception* and specific circumstances that might lead to a *negative perception*. The first one is done for you.

1. A woman gives a homeless person a $20 bill.

> **Positive perception:** *The woman once had to beg to get money for food. She now shares all she has with those who are in that situation.*

> **Negative perception:** *The woman is a first-class snob. She just wants to impress her friends, to show them that she has so much money she can afford to give $20 to a total stranger.*

2. A passerby ignores a homeless person who asks for money.

3. A middle-aged man walks down the street with his arm around a teenage girl.

4. A mother refuses to let her teenage son back into her house.

Thinking Critically About Perspective Taking.

The following should have been clear from this experience: Often, in perceiving a person, you may assume a specific set of circumstances and on this basis evaluate specific behaviours as positive or negative. Also, you may evaluate the very same specific behaviour positively or negatively depending on the circumstances that you infer to be related to the behaviour. Clearly, if you're to understand the perspective of another person, you need to understand the reasons for their behaviours and need to resist defining circumstances from your own perspective.

3.2 PERCEPTUAL DIFFERENCES

Examine each of the following situations, and for each indicate how each of the persons identified might view the situation.

Lily, a single parent, has two small children (ages 7 and 12) who often lack some of the important things children their age should have (e.g., school supplies, sneakers, and toys) because Lily can't afford them. Yet Lily smokes two packs of cigarettes a day.

Lily sees...

The 12-year-old daughter sees...

Lily's parents (who also smoke two packs a day) see...

The children's teacher sees...

Lily has extremely high standards, feels that getting all A's in college is an absolute necessity, and would be devastated with even one B. In fear of earning that first B (after three and a half years of college), Lily cheats on an examination in a Family Communication course and gets caught by the instructor.

Lily sees...

The instructor sees...

The average B– student sees...

Lily, a supervisor in an automobile factory, has been ordered to increase production or be fired. In desperation Lily gives a really tough lecture to the workers—many of whom are greatly insulted and as a result slow down rather than increasing their efforts.

Lily sees...

The average worker sees...

Lily's supervisor sees...

Thinking Critically About Perceptual Differences.

What one principle of perception can you derive from this brief experience? Can you recall a situation in which this principle was ignored or violated? What happened?

Chapter 4
Interpersonal Listening

CHAPTER TOPICS

This chapter introduces the process of listening and offers suggestions for increasing your own listening effectiveness.

- The Stages of Listening
- Listening, Culture, and Gender
- Increasing Listening Effectiveness

CHAPTER SKILLS

After completing this chapter, you should be able to:

- listen more effectively at each of the five stages of listening.
- interact with a clear understanding of cultural and gender listening differences.
- regulate your listening on the basis of empathy, judgment, depth, and active interaction.

EXAMPLE 1

Foreman: Hey, Al, I don't get this production order. We can't handle this run today. What do they think we are?

Supervisor: But that's the order. So get it out as soon as you can. We're under terrific pressure this week.

Foreman: Don't they know we're behind schedule already because of that press breakdown?

Supervisor: Look, Kelly, I don't decide what goes on upstairs. I just have to see that the work gets out and that's what I'm gonna do.

Foreman: The guys aren't gonna like this.

Supervisor: That's something you'll have to work out with them, not me.

EXAMPLE 2

Foreman: Hey, Ross, I don't get this production order. We can't handle this run today. What do they think we are?

Supervisor: Sounds like you're pretty sore about it, Kelly.

Foreman: I sure am. We were just about getting back to schedule after that press breakdown. Now this comes along.

Supervisor: As if you didn't have enough work to do, huh?

Foreman: Yeah. I don't know how I'm gonna tell the guys about this.

Supervisor: Hate to face 'em with it now, is that it?

Foreman: I really do. They're under a real strain today. Seems like everything we do around here is rush, rush.

Supervisor: I guess you feel like it's unfair to load anything more on them.

Foreman: Well, yeah. I know there must be plenty of pressure on everybody up the line, but— well, if that's the way it is... guess I'd better get the word to 'em.

These examples, supplied by Carl Rogers and Richard Farson (1981), reflect an essential difference in listening techniques. In Example 1 the supervisor uses common but ineffective listening. In Example 2 the supervisor uses effective listening techniques. As you read this chapter, think about what the supervisor does in Example 2 but not in Example 1. Why do the supervisor's responses in Example 1 create problems? Why do the supervisor's responses in Example 2 prove more effective?

Although written some 20 years ago, these scenarios are especially relevant today, when companies are coming to recognize listening's importance to their successful and profitable operation. For example, one study concluded that in this era of technological transformation, employees' interpersonal skills will prove especially significant; their advancement will depend on their ability to speak and write effectively, to display proper etiquette, and to listen attentively ("Challenges Facing Workers," 1999). And in a survey of 40 CEOs of Asian and Western multinational companies, a lack of listening skills was cited as the major shortcoming of top executives (Witcher, 1999).

In interpersonal communication, listening is the activity to which we devote most of our time (Janusik, 2002). Throughout this chapter we will explore the differences between ineffective and effective listening. More specifically, this chapter examines the listening process and some of the reasons we listen. It focuses on some of the cultural and gender differences observed in listening and the implications of these differences for effective interpersonal listening. The chapter's major emphasis is

> Big people monopolize the listening. Small people monopolize the talking.
>
> —David Schwartz

Calvin and Hobbes   by Bill Watterson

on the principles of effective listening and on how you can listen more effectively. (You may want to check out the International Listening Association to get an overview of a professional academic organization devoted to listening; visit **www.listen.org**.)

Listening serves a variety of purposes—it helps you to learn, relate, influence, play, and help. Table 4.1 summarizes these purposes along with potential benefits you might derive from accomplishing them.

The Stages of Listening

Listening can be described as a series of five steps: *receiving, understanding, remembering, evaluating,* and *responding.* The process is visualized in Figure 4.1 on page 00. This model, and the suggestions for listening improvement throughout this chapter, draw on theories and models that numerous listening researchers have developed (e.g., Nichols & Stevens, 1957; Nichols, 1961; Barker, 1990; Steil, Barker, & Watson, 1983; Brownell, 1987; Alessandra, 1986; Nichols, 1995). Note that the listening process is a circular one. The responses of Person A serve as the stimuli for Person B, whose responses, in turn, serve as the stimuli for Person A, and so on.

Each of these stages involves dangers or barriers that need to be avoided as you make your way from receiving to responding. (An exercise, "Sequential Listening," will help you identify the various changes that take place as information is passed from one person to another; see **www.ablongman.com/devito**.)

Receiving

Listening is a much more extensive process than hearing. Hearing is essentially the first stage of listening: re-

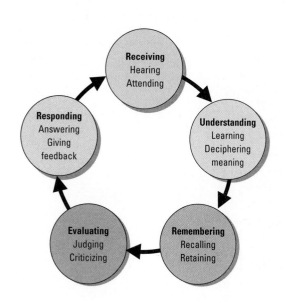

FIGURE 4.1 The Five Stages of Listening

This model depicts the stages involved in listening. Note that receiving or hearing is not the same thing as listening but is in fact only the first step in a five-step process. How would you further distinguish between hearing and listening? Can you identify people you know who "hear" but don't "listen"?

TABLE 4.1 The Purposes and Benefits of Effective Listening

These purposes are, of course, the same as the purposes of interpersonal communication discussed in Chapter 1.

Effective Listening Will Result in Increasing Your Ability to	Because You Will	For Example
learn: to acquire knowledge of others, the world, and yourself, so as to avoid problems and make more reasonable decisions.	profit from the insights of others and acquire more information relevant to decisions you'll be called upon to make in business or in personal life.	Listening to Peter about his travels to Cuba will help you learn more about Peter and about life in another country; listening to the difficulties your sales staff has may help you improve sales training.
relate, to gain social acceptance and popularity.	find that people come to like those who are attentive and supportive.	Others will increase their liking for you once they feel you have genuine concern for them.
influence the attitudes and behaviours of others.	find that people are more likely to respect and follow those they feel have listened to them.	Workers are more likely to follow your advice once they feel you have listened to their insights and concerns.
play.	know when to suspend evaluative thinking and when to engage in supportive and accepting listening.	Listening to your coworkers' anecdotes will enable you to appreciate the relationships between the worlds of work and play.
help others.	hear more, empathize more, and come to understand others more deeply.	Listening to your child's complaints about her teacher will put you in a better position to help your child with school.

ceiving. Listening begins, but does not end, with receiving messages the speaker sends. These messages are both verbal and nonverbal; they consist not only of words but also of gestures, facial expressions, and the like. At this stage you note what is said (verbally and nonverbally) and also what is omitted. For example, you receive not only your friend's request for a loan, but also the omission of any stated intention to pay you back in a reasonable time. The following suggestions should help you receive messages more effectively:

- Focus your attention on the speaker's verbal and nonverbal messages, on what is said and not said.
- Avoid distractions in the environment; if necessary, shut off the stereo or tell your assistant to hold all calls.
- Focus your attention on the speaker, not on what you'll say next.
- Maintain your role as listener; avoid interrupting the speaker until she or he is finished.

Understanding

Understanding occurs when you learn what the speaker means. Understanding includes both the thoughts that are expressed and the emotional tone that accompanies them; for example, the urgency or the joy or sorrow expressed in the message. To achieve understanding:

- Relate the speaker's new information to what you already know. (How will this new proposal change our present health care?)

- See the speaker's messages from the speaker's point of view; avoid judging the message until it's fully understood as the speaker intended it.

- Ask questions for clarification, if necessary; ask for additional details or examples if needed.

- Rephrase (paraphrase) the speaker's ideas to check on your understanding of the speaker's thoughts and feelings.

Remembering

Messages that you receive and understand need to be retained for at least some period of time. In some small group and public speaking situations you can augment your memory by taking notes or by taping the messages. In most interpersonal communication situations, however, such note taking would be considered inappropriate—although you often do write down a phone number or an appointment or directions.

What you remember is not what was actually said, but what you think (or remember) was said. Memory for speech is reconstructive, not reproductive. In other words, you don't simply reproduce in your memory what the speaker said; rather, you reconstruct the messages you hear into a system that makes sense to you—a concept noted in the discussion of perception in Chapter 3. To illustrate this important concept, try to memorize the list of 12 words presented below (Glucksberg & Danks, 1975). Don't worry about the order; only the number remembered counts. Take about 20 seconds to memorize as many words as possible. Don't read any further until you have tried to memorize the list.

Word List

BED	AWAKE
DREAM	NIGHT
COMFORT	SLUMBER
REST	TIRED
WAKE	EAT
SOUND	SNORE

Now close the book and write down as many words from the list as you can remember. Don't read any further until you have tested your own memory. If you're like my students, you not only remembered most of the words, but also added at least one word: *sleep*. Most people recall that *sleep* was on the list; but, as you can see, it wasn't. What happened was that you didn't reproduce the list; you reconstructed it. In this case you gave the list meaning by including the word *sleep*. This happens with all types of messages; they are reconstructed into a meaningful whole—and in the process, a distorted version is often remembered.

Listen to information on subjects you are unacquainted with, instead of always striving to lead the conversation to some favourite one of your own. By the last method you will shine, but will not improve.
—William Hazlitt

To ensure more accurate remembering:

- Identify the central ideas and the major support advanced.
- Summarize the message in an easier-to-retain form, but do not ignore crucial details or qualifications.
- Repeat names and key concepts to yourself silently or, if appropriate, aloud.
- If this is a formal talk with a recognizable organizational structure, identify this structure and use it (see it in your mind) to organize what the speaker is saying.

Evaluating

Evaluating consists of judging the messages. At times you may try to evaluate the speaker's underlying intent, often without much conscious awareness. For example, Elaine tells you she is up for a promotion and is really excited about it. You may then try to judge her intention. Does she want you to use your influence with the company president? Is she preoccupied with the possible promotion, thus telling everyone? Is she looking for a pat on the back? Generally, if you know the person well, you will be able to identify the intention and respond appropriately.

Some people, when they get older, lose some memory ability. But this happens far less than most people's stereotypes would suggest. What are your stereotypes of older people's listening abilities and habits?

In other situations, **evaluation** is more in the nature of a critical analysis. For example, while listening to proposals advanced in a business meeting, you would evaluate them. Are they practical? Will they increase productivity? What is the evidence? Are there more practical alternative proposals? Some suggestions for this stage of listening:

- Resist evaluation until you fully understand the speaker's point of view.
- Assume that the speaker is a person of goodwill, and give the speaker the benefit of any doubt by asking for clarification on issues you object to. (For example, are there any other reasons for accepting this new proposal?)
- Distinguish facts from inferences (see Chapter 5), opinions, and personal interpretations by the speaker.
- Identify any biases, self-interests, or prejudices that may lead the speaker to slant information unfairly.

How can hearing what you expect to hear (a rather natural tendency) prevent you from listening openly about what is being said? Have you ever "heard" what you expected to hear, only to find out later that what you heard was different from what was said?

How does listening work in gossip?

Responding

Responding occurs in two phases: (1) the responses you make while the speaker is talking and (2) the responses you make after the speaker has stopped talking. Responses made while the speaker is talking should be supportive and should acknowledge that you're listening. These in-

THINKING CRITICALLY ABOUT

Listening

Listening critically depends in part on assessing the truth and accuracy of the information and the honesty and motivation of the speaker. Thus, in addition to keeping an open mind and delaying judgments, it's necessary to focus on other issues as well:

- Is what the speaker says the truth as far as you understand it? For example, is this car really that great? Are there any disadvantages to this particular car?

- Has the speaker presented the information in enough detail? Have crucial parts been left out? For example, has the speaker identified all the costs?

- Is the speaker being honest? Is the speaker's motivation merely self-gain? For example, might this speaker be distorting the facts merely to make a sale and earn a commission?

- Does the speaker use fallacious reasoning, such as stating that X causes Y when the evidence merely confirms that X and Y occur together? Are conclusions about "all" or "most" people based on a sample that is both large and representative of the population?

- Does the speaker rely too heavily on emotional appeals? Are these appeals legitimate?

- Has the speaker the credibility you want and expect? For example, is the speaker competent and knowledgeable about the topic?

EXAMPLES?

Can you give an example of a situation in which you got into trouble because you didn't listen critically?

LISTEN TO THIS

Listening Ethically

As a listener you have certain ethical obligations. First, you owe the speaker an *honest hearing*. Avoid prejudging the speaker. Try to put aside prejudices and preconceptions so that you can evaluate the speaker's message fairly. At the same time, try to empathize with the speaker. You don't have to agree with the speaker, but try to understand emotionally as well as intellectually what the speaker means. Then accept or reject the speaker's ideas on the basis of the information offered, not on the basis of some bias or incomplete understanding.

Second, you owe the speaker *honest responses*. Just as you should be honest with the listener when speaking, you should be honest with the speaker when listening. This means giving open and honest feedback. It

also means reflecting honestly on the questions that the speaker raises. Much as the listener has a right to expect an active speaker, the speaker has the right to expect an active listener. The speaker has a right to expect a listener who will actively deal with, rather than just passively hear, the message.

SUGGESTIONS?

Helen, a good friend of yours, has been having difficulty with her friend Sara—who, Helen says, constantly criticizes her and makes her feel inadequate. It's gotten to the point that Helen just tunes Sara out and ignores her. But this, according to Helen, has only made Sara more critical. What advice would you give Helen?

clude what nonverbal researchers call *backchannelling cues:* responses such as "I see," "yes," and "uh-huh," which let the speaker know you're paying attention (more on this in Chapter 8).

Responses after the speaker has stopped talking are generally more elaborate. Examples include expressing empathy ("I know how you must feel"); asking for clarification ("Do you mean this new health plan will replace the old one? Or will it be just a supplement?"); challenging ("I think your evidence is weak"); and agreeing ("You're absolutely right, and I'll support your proposal when it comes up for a vote"). In responding:

- Be supportive of the speaker throughout the talk by using varied backchannelling cues; using only one—for example, saying "uh-huh" throughout—will make it appear that you're not listening but are merely on automatic pilot.

- Express support for the speaker in your final responses.

- Own your own responses; state your thoughts and feelings as your own, using "I" messages. For example, say "I think the new proposal will entail greater expense than you outlined" rather than "everyone will object to the plan's cost."

Before reading about the principles of effective listening, examine your own listening habits and tendencies by taking the self-test "How do you listen?" on this page. The "desirable" answers may seem obvious, but try to give responses that are true for you in most of your listening experiences.

> Listening, not imitation, may be the sincerest form of flattery.
> —Joyce Brothers

TEST YOURSELF

How Do You Listen?

Instructions: Respond to each statement using the following scale: 1 = always, 2 = frequently, 3 = sometimes, 4 = seldom, and 5 = never.

_____ 1. I listen actively, communicate acceptance of the speaker, and prompt the speaker to further explore his or her thoughts.

_____ 2. I listen to what the speaker is saying and feeling; I try to feel what the speaker feels.

_____ 3. I listen without judging the speaker.

_____ 4. I listen to the literal meanings that a speaker communicates; I don't look too deeply into hidden meanings.

_____ 5. I listen without active involvement; I generally remain silent and take in what the other person is saying.

_____ 6. I listen objectively; I focus on the logic of the ideas rather than on the emotional meaning of the message.

_____ 7. I listen critically, evaluating the speaker and what the speaker is saying.

_____ 8. I look for the hidden meanings; the meanings that are revealed by subtle verbal or nonverbal cues.

(continued)

Listening, Culture, and Gender

Listening is difficult in part because of the inevitable differences in communication systems between speaker and listener. To listen effectively, it is important to be aware of both the speaker's communication competence and the listener's expectations (Imhoff, 2002). Because each person has had a unique set of experiences, each person's communication and meaning system is going to be different from the other person's. When speaker and listener come from different cultures or are of different genders, the differences and their effects are naturally so much greater. Let's look first at culture.

Listening and Culture

The culture in which you were raised will influence your listening in a variety of ways. Here we look at some of these: language and speech, direct and indirect styles, nonverbal differences, and feedback.

Even when speaker and listener speak the same language, they speak it with different meanings and different accents. No two speakers speak exactly the same language. Every speaker speaks an *idiolect:* a unique variation of the language (King & DiMichael, 1992). Speakers of the same language will, at the very least, have different meanings for the same terms because they have had different experiences.

Significant differences in expressions and idioms may be found regionally; for example, a Prince Edward Islander will talk about having a "strunt on today" when referring to someone who is sulky or in ill humour. And of course differences in meaning occur between countries: while in Canada the expression "Come to tea" may mean dipping a teabag in a cup of hot water, in Britain it can refer to enjoying a full meal.

Speakers and listeners who have different native languages and who may have learned English as a second language will have even greater differences in meaning. Translations are never precise and never fully capture the meaning in the other language. If you learned your meaning for *house* in a culture in which everyone lived in their own house with lots of land around it, then communicating with someone whose meaning was learned in a neighbourhood of high-rise tenements is going to be difficult. Although each of you will hear the word *house,* the meanings you'll develop will be drastically different. In adjusting your listening—especially when in an intercultural setting—understand that the speaker's meanings may be very different from yours even though you're speaking the same language.

Some cultures—those of Western Europe, Canada, and the United States, for example—favour **direct speech** in communication; they advise us to "say what you mean and mean what you say." This directness is relative. For example, Canadian visitors to Israel would find that a typical Israeli style is even more direct. Many Asian cultures, on the other hand, favour **indirect speech**; they emphasize politeness and maintaining a positive public image rather than literal truth. Listen carefully to persons with different styles of directness. Consider the possibility that the meanings the speaker wishes to communicate with, say, indirectness, may be very different from the meanings you would communicate with indirectness.

Speakers from different cultures also have different *display rules:* cultural rules that govern which nonverbal behaviours are appropriate and which are inappropriate in a public setting. As you listen to other people, you also "listen" to their nonverbals. If these are drastically different from what you expect on the basis of the verbal message, you may perceive a kind of noise or interference or even contradictory messages. Also, of course, different cultures may give very different meanings to the same nonverbal gesture, a topic considered in detail in Chapter 6.

Members of some cultures tend to give direct and honest feedback. Speakers from these cultures expect feedback to be an honest reflection of what their listeners are feeling. In other cultures—Japan and Korea are good examples—it's more important to be positive than to be truthful; listeners may respond with positive feedback (say, in commenting on a business colleague's proposal) even though they don't feel positive. Listen to feedback, as you would all messages, with a full recognition that various cultures view feedback very differently.

Listening and Gender

Deborah Tannen (1990; 2003) illustrates that when men and women talk, men lecture and women listen. The lecturer is positioned as the superior—as the teacher, the expert. The listener is positioned as the inferior—as the student, the nonexpert.

Women, according to Tannen, seek to build rapport and establish a closer relationship and so use a "people-oriented" listening style (Worthington, 2001) to achieve these ends. For example, women use more listening cues that let the other person know they are paying attention and are interested. Men not only use fewer listening cues but interrupt more; and they will often change the topic

> Listen long enough and the person will generally come up with an adequate solution.
>
> —**Mary Kay Ash**

Can you identify the listener in this photograph? In fact, correctional officer Larry Clayton is receiving congratulatory remarks and a medal of bravery from Adrienne Clarkson, Canada's Governor General. Based on your readings in this chapter, how might gender or culture affect the listening in this interaction?

to one they know more about. Their primary goal in a given interaction is to play up their expertise, emphasize it, and use it in dominating the conversation. When doing so, their listening style tends to be more "time-oriented" (Worthington, 2001).

Now you might be tempted to conclude from this that women play fair in conversation and that men don't; for example, that men consistently seek to put themselves in a position superior to women. But that may be too simple an explanation. Research shows that men communicate this way not only with women but also with other men. Men are not showing disrespect for their female conversational partners but are simply communicating as they normally do. Women, too, communicate as they do not only with men but also with other women.

Tannen argues that the goal of a man in conversation is to be accorded respect; so a man seeks to display his knowledge and expertise even if he has to change the topic to one he knows a great deal about. Women, on the other hand, seek to be liked; so a woman expresses interest, rarely interrupts a man to take her turn as speaker, and gives lots of cues (verbally and nonverbally) to indicate that she is listening.

Men and women also show that they are listening in different ways. A woman is more apt to give lots of listening cues, such as interjecting "yeah" or "uh-huh," nodding in agreement, and smiling. A man is more likely to listen quietly without giving lots of listening cues as feedback. Tannen also argues, however, that men do listen less to women than women listen to men. The reason, says Tannen, is that listening places the person in an inferior position, whereas speaking places the person in a superior position.

There is no evidence to show that these differences represent any negative motives—desires on the part of men to prove themselves superior or on the part of women to ingratiate themselves. Rather, these differences in listening are largely the result of the way in which men and women have been socialized. Can men and women change these habitual ways of listening (and speaking)?

SKILLS TOOLBOX

6 Ways to Deal with Difficult Listeners

Walt Whitman once said, "To have great poets, there must be great audiences too." The same is true of interpersonal interaction: To have great interpersonal communication, there must be great listeners as well as great talkers. Here are a few types of difficult listeners and brief suggestions for dealing with them.

1. The *static listener* gives no feedback, remains relatively motionless, reveals no expression. *Ask questions. Pause to allow the person to say something.*

Ask for agreement with your facial expressions.

2. The *monotonous feedback giver* seems responsive, but the responses never vary; regardless of what you say, the response is the same. *Comment on the feedback, saying, for example, "So, you agree?" or "Am I making sense?"*

3. The *overly expressive listener* reacts to just about everything with extreme responses. Even though you're saying nothing provocative, the reaction is

intense. *Some people are just more expressive than others; take pleasure in the fact that you're having such an effect.*

4. The *eye avoider* looks all around the room and at others but never at you. *Maintain eye contact as much as possible, and ask questions; try to involve the other person in what you're saying.*

5. The *preoccupied listener* listens to other things at the same time, perhaps even with headphones turned up so loud that it interferes with your own thinking. *If what you're saying requires total concentration, then ask for it, saying something like "This is really important" or "I really need your total concentration."*

6. The *thought-completing listener* listens a little and then finishes your thought. You wonder if you're really that predictable. *This behaviour often isn't as bad as it seems and may occur simply because the person knows you very well. It does create problems, however, when someone completes your thoughts incorrectly. When this happens, just say so: "No, that's not what I was going to say. Actually, what I was going to say was..."*

THEN AND NOW

Have you ever been confronted by one of these listeners? What did you do to get the person to listen more effectively? What would you do if this happened today?

Increasing Listening Effectiveness

Because you listen for different purposes, the principles of effective listening should vary from one situation to another. The following four dimensions of listening illustrate the appropriateness of different listening modes for different communication situations.

Empathic and Objective Listening

If you want to understand what a person means and what a person is feeling, you need to listen empathically: to feel with them, see the world as they see it, feel what they feel. Yet although empathy is beneficial in most situations, there are also times when you need to go beyond empathy and look at the situation more objectively. It's important to listen to a friend tell you how the entire world hates him or her and to understand how your friend feels and why. But at times you may need to stand back from the situation and perhaps see beyond what your friend sees. Sometimes you have to put your empathic responses aside and listen in a more detached or analytical way.

In adjusting your empathic and objective listening focus, see the sequence of events as punctuated from the speaker's point of view, and see how this can influence what the speaker says and does (Chapter 1). View the speaker as an equal. Seek to understand both thoughts and feelings. Don't consider your listening task finished until you have understood what the speaker is feeling as well as thinking.

To encourage openness and empathy, try to eliminate any physical or psychological barriers to equality; for example, step from behind the large desk separating you from an employee. Avoid interrupting, a sign that you feel what you have to say is more important.

Avoid "offensive listening," the tendency to listen to bits and pieces of information that will help you attack the speaker or find fault with something the speaker has said.

Would it be more difficult to empathize with someone who was overjoyed because of winning $7 million in the lottery or with someone who was overcome with sadness because of the death of a loved one? How easy or difficult would it be for you to empathize with someone who was depressed because an expected raise of $40 000 turned out to be only $25 000? In general, do you find it more difficult to empathize with negative or with positive feelings?

A Question of Choice

Your 90-year-old aunt has been diagnosed with terminal cancer. The physicians tell you that there is no need to tell her about this; it will only depress her and hasten her death. But they leave the decision up to you. If you tell your aunt the truth, you may hurt her emotionally and physically. If you choose not to tell her, you may deny her the option of making choices she might want to make if she knew of her true physical condition. What do you do?

This situation raises the issue of choice in interpersonal communication, an interesting way to look at a person's ethical obligations. The assumption underlying the concept of choice is that people have a right to make their own choices and consequently have a right to hear information bearing on these choices. Thus, interpersonal communications are ethical to the extent that they present a person with this information and thereby facilitate the person's freedom of choice. Communications are unethical to the extent that they prevent the individual's hearing information relevant to the choices he or she will make.

In sum, you have the right to hear information about yourself that others possess and that influences the choices you'll make. For example, you have the right to face your accusers, to know what witnesses will be called to testify against you, to see your credit ratings, and to know what employment insurance payments you'll receive.

At the same time, you also have the obligation to allow others to hear information that you possess that bears on their choices or on choices of society generally. Thus, for example, you have an obligation to identify wrongdoing that you witness, to identify someone in a police lineup, to report criminal activity, and to testify at a trial when you possess pertinent information.

WHAT WOULD YOU DO?

You're heading a five-person team charged with writing your company's annual report. Two of the people on the team do absolutely no work, and this only adds to the burden borne by you and the other two members. Your supervisor has asked how things are going. You feel you have an obligation to the company to report the two negligent workers; yet you've established a friendship with them, and you feel that would violate the friendship—and also make you extremely unpopular with the other workers. You also wonder, if you do tell your supervisor, if you then have the obligation to tell the two members that you told the supervisor that they're not doing their job. Efforts to get the two members to do their share of the work have failed repeatedly. What would you do in this situation?

"It's a cat calendar, so it may not be all that accurate."

© The New Yorker Collection 1995 Jack Ziegler from cartoonbank.com. All Rights Reserved.

Beware, too, of the "friend-or-foe" factor: the risk of distorting messages because of your attitudes toward another person, much like the dog in the cartoon below. For example, if you think Freddy is stupid, then it will take added effort to listen objectively to Freddy's messages and to hear anything that is clear or insightful.

Nonjudgmental and Critical Listening

Effective listening involves both listening nonjudgmentally in order to understand and listening critically in order to make an evaluation or judgment. So listen first with an open mind; this will help you better understand the messages. Then supplement your understanding with critical listening, which will help you better analyze and evaluate the messages. Effective listening requires that you exercise both levels.

Avoid distorting messages through oversimplification, or **levelling**—the tendency to eliminate details and to simplify complex messages so that they're easier to remember. Also avoid filtering out unpleasant or undesirable messages; you may miss the very information you need to change your assumptions or your behaviours.

Recognize your own ethnic, national, or religious biases. Everyone has them, and they can easily interfere with accurate listening. Biases cause you to distort messages by leading you to hear meanings that conform to your own prejudices and expectations. They may lead you to give increased importance to something because it confirms your biases or to minimize it because it contradicts them.

Surface and Depth Listening

In most messages, there is an obvious surface meaning that a literal reading of the words and sentences reveals. But there is often a deeper level of meaning. Sometimes it's the opposite of the expressed literal meaning; sometimes it seems totally unrelated. In reality, few messages have only one level of meaning. Most function on two or three levels at the same time. Consider some frequently heard messages. For example, a friend asks you how you like his new haircut. Another friend asks you how you like her painting. On one level the meaning is clear: Do you like the haircut? Do you like the painting? It's reasonable to assume, however, that on another level your friends are asking you to say something positive—about his appearance, about her artistic ability. The parent who seems at first to be complaining about working hard at the office or in the home may be asking for appreciation. The child who talks about the unfairness of the other children in the playground may be asking for some expression of caring. To appreciate these other meanings, you need to engage in depth listening.

When listening interpersonally, be particularly sensitive to different levels of meaning. If you respond only to the surface-level communication (the literal meaning), you may miss the opportunity to make meaningful contact with the other person's feelings and real needs. For example, if you say to your parent, "You're always complaining. I bet you really love working so hard," you may be failing to answer a very real call for understanding and appreciation.

In regulating your surface and depth listening, focus on both verbal and nonverbal messages. Recognize both consistent and inconsistent "packages" of messages, and take these cues as guides to the meaning the speaker is trying to communicate. Ask questions when in doubt. Listen also to what is omitted.

Listen for both content and relational messages. The student who constantly challenges the teacher is on one level communicating disagreement over content. However, on another level—the relationship level—the student may be voicing objections to the instructor's authority or authoritarianism. If the instructor is to deal effectively with the student, he or she must listen and respond to both types of messages.

In your classroom listening, do you ever tend to filter out unpleasant or difficult messages? What effects might this have?

Which of the suggestions for adjusting your listening between nonjudgmental and critical listening do you regularly follow? What one suggestion do you follow least often?

Can you identify an example from your own experience in which messages were communicated on two different levels but either you or the other person listened to and responded to only one level?

"I can't get off the phone, he won't stop listening!"

Reprinted by permission of Jerry Marcus.

> There is only one cardinal rule: One must always listen to the patient.
>
> —Oliver Sacks

Don't disregard the literal (surface) meaning of interpersonal messages in your attempt to uncover the more hidden (deep) meanings. If you do, you'll quickly find that your listening problems disappear: No one will talk to you any more. Balance your attention between the surface and the underlying meanings. Respond to the various levels of meaning in the messages of others as you would like others to respond to yours—sensitively but not obsessively, readily but not overambitiously.

One listening expert advises that you use your two ears to hear what the person is saying, but use your third ear to listen to why they're saying what they're saying (Rosen, 1998).

Active and Inactive Listening

Active listening is one of the most important communication skills you can learn (Gordon, 1975). Consider the following brief comment and some possible responses:

Aphrodite: That creep gave me a C on the paper. I really worked on that project, and all I get is a lousy C.

Apollo: That's not so bad; most people got around the same grade. I got a C, too.

Athena: So what? This is your last semester. Who cares about grades anyway?

Achilles: You should be pleased with a C. Misha and Michael both failed, and John and Haruki got D's.

Diana: You got a C on that paper you were working on for the last three weeks? You sound really angry and hurt.

All four listeners are probably eager to make Aphrodite feel better, but they go about it in very different ways and, you can be sure, with very different outcomes. The first three listeners give fairly typical responses. Apollo and Athena both try to minimize the significance of a C grade. Minimizing is a common response to someone who has expressed displeasure or disappointment; usually, it's also inappropriate. Although well-intentioned, this response does little to promote meaningful communication and understanding. Achilles tries to give the C grade a more positive meaning. Note, however, that all three listeners also say a great deal more: that Aphrodite should not be feeling unhappy, that her feelings are not legitimate. These responses deny the validity of these feelings and put Aphrodite in the position of having to defend them.

Diana, however, is different. Diana uses **active listening**, a process of sending back to the speaker what the listener thinks the speaker meant, both literally and emotionally. Active listening does not mean simply repeating the speaker's exact words. It's rather a process of putting into some meaningful whole your understanding of the speaker's total message—the verbal and the nonverbal, the content and the feelings.

In Canada, there are cultural differences in the process of active listening. French Canadians, for example, tend to be very expressive, whereas Aboriginal peoples would likely attend to the conversation in a more subdued fashion. It is important to pay attention to the different forms active listening can take.

Purposes of Active Listening   Active listening serves a number of important purposes. First, you *show that you're listening*. Often that is the only thing the speaker really wants—to know that someone cares enough to listen.

Second, it helps you *check how accurately you have understood* what the speaker said and meant. By reflecting back what you perceive to be the speaker's meaning, you give the speaker an opportunity to confirm, clarify, or amend your perceptions. In this way, future messages have a better chance of being relevant and purposeful.

Third, through active listening, you *express acceptance of the speaker's feelings*. Note that in the sample responses given, the first three listeners challenge the speaker; they refuse to give the expressed feelings legitimacy. The active listener accepts the speaker. The speaker's feelings are not challenged; rather, they're echoed in a sympathetic and empathic manner. (Not surprisingly, training in active listening helps to increase a person's empathy [Ikemi & Kubota, 1996].) Note, too, that in the first three responses, the feelings of the speaker are denied without ever actually being identified. Diana, however, not only accepts Aphrodite's feelings but also identifies them explicitly, again allowing the opportunity for correction.

Interestingly enough, when confronted by a person in distress, those listeners who try to solve the person's problem or who veer off the issue by engaging in chitchat come away significantly more depressed than those listeners who show acceptance of the distressed person's problems or who use supportive listening techniques (Notarius & Herrick, 1988).

Fourth, in active listening you *prompt the speaker to further explore his or her feelings and thoughts*. The active listening response gives the speaker a chance to elaborate on these feelings without having to defend them. Active listening sets the stage for meaningful dialogue, a dialogue of mutual understanding. In stimulating this further exploration, active listening also encourages the speaker to resolve his or her own conflicts.

These advantages should not be taken to mean that active listening is always desirable; it isn't. For example, sometimes **passive listening**—listening that is attentive and supportive but less involved—is a better approach. (An exercise, "Making Decisions about Active Listening," will help you separate those situations in which active listening is appropriate from those in which it may not be. See www.ablongman.com/devito.)

Techniques of Active Listening   Three techniques will help you master active listening. At first, these principles may seem awkard and unnatural. With prac-

Do you notice differences in the ways men and women engage in active listening? Can you offer specific examples to bolster your conclusions?

Want to Do Better on the Job?—Listen Up!

When Linda S., an Ohio banking executive, learned she would not be promoted she asked her boss why. He had barely begun to speak when she blurted out, "I know that whatever the reason I can do better!"

Exasperated, he replied, "You always interrupt before you even know what I'm going to say! How can you do better if you never listen?"

"Most people value speaking—which is seen as active—over listening, which is seen as passive," explains Nancy Wyatt, professor of speech communication at Penn State University and co-author with Carol Ashburn of *Successful Listening* (Harper and Row, 1988).

And there are other reasons we might fail to tune in.

We may become so fixed on what WE think that we tune out important information. Or we may react emotionally to a phrase or style the speaker uses and miss the main point. Or we're just too busy to pay attention to what is being said.

Sound familiar? If so, listen up, for changing your ways will pay big dividends.

You'll stop wasting time on misunderstood assignments at work. People will start to see you as a perceptive, smart and sensitive person who understands their needs. And that will open new opportunities on the job, suggests Lyman K. Steil, Ph.D., president of Communication Development Inc., a consulting firm based in St. Paul, Minn.

You can also develop an ear for the crucial but unspoken words in conversation that signal problems in your business relationships.

Here are some suggestions for learning to listen to what is said—and not said—more effectively.

Control distractions: Give a speaker your full attention or you're likely to miss the main point.

Many interruptions cannot be avoided, but you can limit their effect.

If you must take a call while a co-worker is explaining something important, make a choice and devote yourself to one conversation at a time.

Identify the speaker's purpose: Tune into the speaker's agenda. Is he or she there to let off steam, solve a problem, share information or just schmooze?

Once you know, you can respond in the way he or she wants and expects.

Learning to listen may also keep you from inadvertently getting caught in the cross fire of office politics.

Don't finish other people's sentences: Many people have this bad habit. Just observe yourself: Do you cut people off before they finish a thought? Are you so busy thinking about what you want to say that you can't resist breaking in?

"That often happens because the interrupter is bright, thinks she has grasped the point and wants to show off how much she knows," said Dee Soder, Ph.D., president of Endymion, a New York City–based executive consulting firm. "What happens instead is that interrupters are perceived as being arrogant and interested only in themselves."

To break the habit of interrupting, bite your tongue and follow up with your comments only after the other person has had his or her say.

Soder suggests you might even have to literally sit on your hands to keep your gestures from speaking for you.

Finally, if you're not certain that the speaker has finished, ask!

Don't let the speaker's style turn you off: It's easy to tune out when less-than-favorite speakers clear their throats.

One high school teacher confesses that for a long time she found a colleague's slow, deliberate drawl so grating that she simply could not listen to him.

"It was only when I was forced to work with him and had to concentrate on WHAT he was saying rather than HOW that I realized how smart and helpful he was and now we're best friends at work."

Don't be distracted by buzzwords: What springs to mind when you hear the label "feminist" or "right-to-lifer"? If you're like most people emotions take over and you stop paying careful attention to the point a speaker is trying to make.

Listen for what is not being said: Sometimes it's important to "hear between the lines."

"Many people like to avoid conflict and so the person speaking is very reluctant to say anything negative," says Soder.

When you suspect that a delicate or negative subject is being studiously avoided, you have to be prepared to delve deeper and ask the speaker, "Tell me more about that. Could you please explain?"

Show you are listening: Think about what your body language is revealing.

Are you making good eye contact and leaning slightly forward in a way that indicates "I'm open to what you're saying"? Or are you tapping your foot and looking out of the window as if to say, "I have more important things to do than listen to you"?

Make a note of it: Jotting down a word or two can remind you later of the main purpose behind the assignment your boss is giving you.

A brief note can also help you remember the point you would like to raise after the speaker finishes.

Make sure you heard it right: Many misunderstandings could be prevented if we'd just make sure we heard what we thought we heard.

So when in doubt don't be afraid to ask, "Let me make sure I understand what you're saying." It's a hearing test well worth taking.

Source: "Want to do better on the job?—Listen up!" by Diane Cole as appeared in *Working Mother,* March 1991. Copyright © 1991 by Diane Cole. Reprinted by permission of the author.

tice, however, they will flow and blend into a meaningful and effective dialogue.

1. Paraphrase the speaker's meaning.   State in your own words what you think the speaker meant. This paraphrasing helps to ensure understanding because the speaker can correct or modify your restatement. It also communicates your interest and your attention. Everyone wants to feel attended to, especially when angry or depressed. The active listening paraphrase confirms this.

When you paraphrase the speaker's meanings, you give the speaker a kind of green light to go into more detail, to elaborate. Thus, when you echo the thought about the C grade, the speaker can elaborate on why that grade was important. Make your paraphrases objective; be careful not to lead the speaker in the direction you think best. Also, be careful that you don't maximize or minimize the speaker's emotions; try to echo these feelings as accurately as you can.

2. Express understanding of the speaker's feelings.   In addition to paraphrasing the content, echo the feelings you believe the speaker expressed or implied. This enables you to check your perception of the speaker's feelings and provides the speaker with the opportunity to see his or her feelings more objectively.

Expressing understanding is especially helpful when someone is angry, hurt, or depressed. Hearing these feelings objectively and seeing them from a less impassioned perspective will help the person deal effectively with them.

Most of us hold back our feelings until we are certain that others will be accepting. We need to hear statements such as "I understand" and "I see how you feel." When we feel that our emotions are accepted, we then feel free to go into more detail. Active listening provides the speaker with this important opportunity.

3. Ask questions.   Ask questions to make sure that you understand the speaker's thoughts and feelings and to secure additional helpful infor-

Listening is not merely not talking, though even that is beyond most of our powers; it means taking a vigorous, human interest in what is being told us.

—Alice Duer Miller

Do you engage in much active listening? For example, of the four responses given in the dialogue that opened this discussion of active listening, which would you be most likely to give? Do your close friends practise active listening when they listen to you? Can you give a specific example of active listening that you were recently involved in?

mation. Design your questions to provide just enough stimulation and support for the speaker to express the thoughts and feelings he or she wants to express. Avoid questions that pry into irrelevant areas or that challenge the speaker in any way.

Note the active listening techniques used throughout this dialogue:

Petra: That creep demoted me. He told me I wasn't an effective manager. I can't believe he did that, after all I've done for this company.

Saul: I can understand your anger. You've been manager for three or four months now, haven't you?

Petra: A little over three months. I know I was on trial, but I thought I was doing a good job.

Saul: Can you get another trial?

Petra: Yes, he said I could try again in a few months. But I feel like a failure.

Saul: I know what you mean. It's not a pleasant feeling. What else did he say?

Petra: He said I had trouble getting the paperwork done on time.

Saul: You've been late filing the reports?

Petra: A few times.

Saul: Is there a way to delegate the paperwork?

Petra: No, but I think I know now what needs to be done.

Saul: You sound as though you're ready to give that manager's position another try.

Petra: Yes, I think I am, and I'm going to let him know that I intend to apply in the next few months.

Even in this brief interaction, Petra has moved from unproductive anger with the supervisor as well as a feeling of failure to a determination to correct an unpleasant situation. Note, too, that Saul didn't offer solutions but "simply" listened actively.

As stressed throughout this discussion, listening is situational; the type of listening that is appropriate varies with the situation. You can visualize a listening situation as one in which you have to make choices among at least the five dimensions of listening just discussed (Figure 4.2). Each listening situation should call for a somewhat different configuration of listening responses; the art of effective listening is largely one of making appropriate choices along these five dimensions.

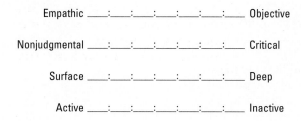

FIGURE 4.2 Listening Choices

Effective listening is largely a matter of adjusting your behaviour along such dimensions as these. Can you identify an interpersonal situation that would call for listening that is empathic, nonjudgmental, surface, and active and another situation that would call for listening that is objective, critical, in-depth, and inactive?

SUMMARY OF CONCEPTS AND SKILLS

This chapter defined listening, explored its five stages, and identified some of the reasons we listen. We looked at the wide cultural and gender differences in listening. Last, we looked at the types of listening and how best to adjust our listening to achieve maximum effectiveness.

1. Listening may be viewed as a five-step process: receiving, understanding, remembering, evaluating, and responding. Listening difficulties and obstacles exist at each of these stages.

2. We listen for a variety of reasons: to learn, to relate, to influence, to play, and to help.

3. Cultural differences in accents, in the directness of people's style of communicating, in nonverbal behaviours, and in the feedback people give and expect may create listening difficulties.

4. Men and women seem to listen with different purposes in mind and with different behaviours.

5. Effective listening depends on varying your listening behaviour appropriately between empathic and objective, nonjudgmental and critical, surface and depth, and active and inactive listening.

Check your ability to apply the skills described below. You will gain most from this brief experience if you think carefully about each skill and try to identify recent instances in which you did or did not act on the basis of the specific skill. Use a rating scale such as the following: 1 = almost always, 2 = often, 3 = sometimes, 4 = rarely, and 5 = almost never.

_____ 1. In receiving messages, focus attention on the speaker's verbal and nonverbal messages, and avoid interrupting.

_____ 2. In understanding messages, relate the new information to what you already know; ask questions and paraphrase to ensure understanding.

_____ 3. In remembering messages, identify the central ideas, summarize the message in an easier to retain form, and use repetition (aloud or to yourself) to help with key terms and names.

_____ 4. In evaluating messages, try first to understand fully what the speaker means; also try to identify any biases and self-interests that may lead to an unfair presentation of material.

_____ 5. In responding to messages, express support and own your own responses.

_____ 6. In listening and in speaking, recognize the cultural differences that can create barriers to mutual understanding.

_____ 7. In listening, recognize that women and men may listen with different purposes in mind and that they may act differently but mean the same thing—or act similarly but mean different things.

_____ 8. Regulate and adjust your listening between empathic and objective, nonjudgmental and critical, surface and depth, and active and inactive listening.

VOCABULARY QUIZ

The Language of Listening

Match these terms about listening with their definitions. Record the number of the definition next to the term.

7 listening 86
6 levelling 97
5 receiving 86

_8_ empathic listening 95

_9_ supportive listening 91

_2_ active listening 98

_1_ memory 88

_4_ paraphrase 101

_3_ evaluating 89

1. A reconstructive not a reproductive process.

2. A process of sending back to the speaker what the listener thinks the speaker meant, literally and emotionally.

3. An essential stage in the listening process in which we make judgments about a message.

4. A restatement of something said in your own words.

5. Only the first stage in listening; similar to hearing.

6. The reduction of the number of details that we remember about something we have heard.

7. A process of receiving, understanding, remembering, evaluating, and responding to messages.

8. Placing ourselves into the position of the speaker so that we feel as the speaker feels.

9. Listening by giving the speaker positive feedback.

SKILL BUILDING EXERCISES

4.1 REDUCING BARRIERS TO LISTENING

Visualize yourself ready to talk with the following people on the topics noted. What barriers to listening (at any stage: receiving, understanding, remembering, evaluating, or responding) might arise in each encounter? What would you do to prevent these barriers from interfering with effective listening?

1. A friend tells you he's HIV positive.

2. An instructor argues that the feminist movement is dead.

3. A coalition of homeless people claims the right to use public spaces.

4. A politician says that relationships between different races will never be better.

5. A Catholic priest argues that people should remain virgins until marriage.

6. A relative argues that abortion, regardless of the circumstances, is murder.

7. A telephone company representative asks that you switch to their new long-distance system.

Thinking Critically About Barriers to Listening.

In thinking about these situations, consider, for example: How would your initial expectations influence your listening? How would you assess the person's credibility (even before you began to talk)? How would this influence your listening? Would you begin listening with a positive, a negative, or a neutral attitude? How might these attitudes influence your listening?

4.2 MAKING DECISIONS ABOUT ACTIVE LISTENING

Here are several situations in which active listening responses seem appropriate. How would you respond to these situations?

1. Your friend Karla has been married for the last three years and has two small children, one two years old and one six months. Recently Karla has been having an affair with a colleague at work. Her husband discovered this and is now suing for divorce. She confides this to you and says, *I really don't know what I'm going to do. I may lose the kids. I could never support myself and live the way we do now. I sure love that BMW. I wish these last two months had never happened and that I had never started up with Taylor.*

2. Your boss, Ruth, has been an especially hard supervisor to work for. She is a perfectionist who doesn't understand that people make mis-

takes. On several occasions she has filed negative evaluation reports on you and other members of your department. This has prevented you and others from getting merit raises in at least three instances. During lunch, Ruth comes over to your table and tells you that she has been fired and has to clean out her desk by 3:00 p.m. She says, *I can't believe they did this to me; I was the best supervisor they had. Our production level was always the highest in the company. They're idiots. Now I don't know what I'm going to do. Where will I get another job?*

3. Your mother has been having a difficult time at work. She was recently passed up for promotion and has received one of the lowest merit raises given in the company. She says, *I'm not sure what I did wrong. I do my work, mind my own business, don't take my sick days like everyone else. How could they give that promotion to Manuela, who's only been with the company for two years? I've given them seven years. Maybe I should just quit and try to find something else.*

Thinking Critically About Active Listening.

What is the single most important value to be achieved through active listening? What is the single most important suggestion to remember when listening actively?

4.3 PARAPHRASING TO ENSURE UNDERSTANDING

One of the most important skills in effective listening is paraphrasing. For each of the following messages, write a paraphrase that you think would be appropriate. After you complete the paraphrases, ask another person if he or she would accept them as objective restatements of the thoughts and feelings expressed. Rework the paraphrases until the other person agrees that they are accurate. A sample paraphrase is provided for number 1.

1. I can't deal with my parents' constant fighting. I've seen it for the last 10 years and I really can't stand it any more.

   Paraphrase: *You have trouble dealing with their fighting. You seem really upset by this last fight.*

2. Did you hear I got engaged to Jerry? Our racial and religious differences are really going to cause difficulties for both of us. But we love each other—we'll work it through.

3. I got a C on that paper. That's the worst grade I've ever received. I just can't believe that I got a C. This is my major. What am I going to do?

4. I can't understand why I didn't get that promotion. I was here longer and did better work than Thompson. Even my two supervisors said I was the next in line for the promotion. And now it looks like another one won't come along for at least a year.

5. That rotten, inconsiderate pig just up and left. He never even said goodbye. We were together for six months and after one small argument he leaves without a word. And he even took my bathrobe—that expensive one he bought for my last birthday.

6. I'm just not sure what to do. I really love Helen. She's the sweetest kid I've ever known. I mean she'd do anything for me. But she really wants to get married. I do too, and yet I don't want to make such a commitment. I mean that's a long-term thing. And, much as I hate to admit it, I don't want the responsibility of a wife, a family, a house. I really don't need that kind of pressure.

Thinking Critically About Paraphrasing.

How might paraphrasing be of value in interpersonal conflict situations? In intercultural communication situations? Can you identify situations where paraphrasing would be inappropriate?

Chapter 5

Verbal Messages

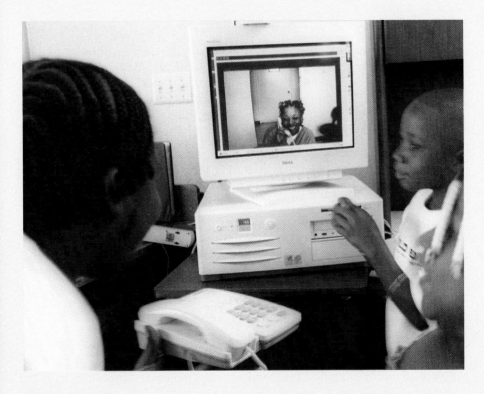

CHAPTER TOPICS

This chapter introduces verbal messages and offers suggestions for making your own messages more effective.

- The Nature of Verbal Messages
- Confirmation and Disconfirmation
- Using Verbal Messages Effectively and Critically

CHAPTER SKILLS

After completing this chapter, you should be able to:

- communicate with a recognition that meanings are in people, are context based, have both denotative and connotative meanings, vary in directness, are culturally based, and vary in abstraction.

- regulate your confirmations as appropriate, especially avoiding sexist, heterosexist, and racist language and, in general, language that puts down other groups.

- identify conceptual distortions in your own and others' language and avoid them in your own messages.

On the second night of their honeymoon, a couple is sitting at a hotel bar. The woman strikes up a conversation with the couple next to her. The husband refuses to communicate with the couple and becomes antagonistic toward his wife and the couple. The wife then grows angry because he has created such an awkward and unpleasant situation. Each becomes increasingly disturbed, and the evening ends in a bitter conflict, each spouse convinced of the other's lack of consideration. Eight years later, the couple analyze this argument.

Apparently the word *honeymoon* had meant different things to each of them. To the husband it meant a golden opportunity to ignore the rest of the world and simply explore each other. He felt his wife's interaction with the other couple implied there was something lacking in him. To the wife her honeymoon meant an opportunity to try out her new role as wife. "I had never had a conversation with another couple as a wife before," she says. "Previous to this I had always been a 'girlfriend' or 'fiancée' or 'daughter' or 'sister.'"

This example—taken from Ronald D. Laing, H. Phillipson, and A. Russell Lee in *Interpersonal Perception* (1966; also Watzlawick, 1977)—illustrates the confusion that can result when you look for meaning in the words and not in the person. This confusion is one of the ways that verbal messages, the topic of this chapter, can fail to communicate their intended meaning.

The Nature of Verbal Messages

In communication you use two major signal systems—the verbal and the nonverbal. This chapter focuses on the *verbal* system: how spoken and written **language** serves as a system for communicating meaning, how it can be used effectively, and how it creates problems when it isn't. It is important to keep in mind that "the world in language is half someone else's" (Salamensky, 2001, p.21). Before words are passed along to the receiver, they exist in the mind of the transmitter. Successful verbal communication, then, will occur if the two sides can arrive at a mutually agreed upon meaning.

Messages Are Denotative and Connotative

Verbal communication is sometimes referred to as symbolic because it uses a learned, socially shared language system in which words or symbols are used to describe reality (Buck & Van Lear, 2002). Within this system, two general types of meaning are essential to identify: denotation and connotation. The term **denotation** refers to the meaning you'd find in a dictionary; it's the meaning that members of the culture assign to a word. **Connotation** is the emotional meaning that specific speakers/listeners give to a word. Take as an example the word *death*. To a doctor this word might mean (denote) the time when the heart stops. This is an objective description of a particular event. On the other hand, to a mother who is informed of her son's death, the word means (connotes) much more. It recalls her son's youth, ambitions, family, illness, and so on. To her *death* is a highly emotional, subjective, and personal word. These emotional, subjective, or personal associations are the word's connotative meaning. The denotation of a word is its objective definition. The connotation of a word is its subjective or emotional meaning.

Messages Vary in Directness

Think about how you'd respond to the following verbal messages:

1a. I'm so bored; I have nothing to do tonight.

2a. I'd like to go to the movies. Would you like to come?

1b. Do you feel like hamburgers tonight?

2b. I'd like hamburgers tonight. How about you?

Statements 1a and 1b are relatively indirect; they're attempts to get the listener to say or do something without committing the speaker. Statements 2a and 2b are more direct—they state more clearly the speaker's preferences and then ask if the listener agrees. Before reading on, you may wish to review the self-test you completed in Chapter 4, which introduced directness and considered some of the cultural and gender differences in directness.

Here we focus on the advantages and disadvantages of directness. For the most part, the advantages of indirect messages are the disadvantages of direct messages, and the disadvantages of indirect messages are the advantages of direct messages.

Advantages of Indirect Messages Indirect messages allow you to express a thought without insulting or offending anyone; they allow you to observe the rules of polite interaction. So instead of saying, "I'm bored with this group," you say, "It's getting late, and I have to get up early tomorrow." Instead of saying, "This food tastes like cardboard," you say, "I just started my diet" or "I just ate." In each instance you're stating a preference indirectly so as to avoid offending someone. Not all direct messages, however, should be considered impolite. In one study of Spanish and English speakers, for example, no evidence was found to support the assumption that politeness and directness were incompatible (Mir, 1993).

Sometimes indirect messages allow you to ask for compliments in a socially acceptable manner. A person who says, "I was thinking of getting a nose job" may hope to get the response, "A nose job? You? Your nose is perfect."

"When you're on their flowers, you're a snail. When they want to eat you, suddenly you're an escargot."

One great use of words is to hide our thoughts.

—**Voltaire**

How would you describe this dinner scene in denotative terms? In connotative terms?

Disadvantages of Indirect Messages   Indirect messages, however, can also create problems. Consider the following dialogue:

Alexis: You wouldn't like to have my parents over for dinner this weekend, would you?

Sam: I really wanted to go to the shore and just relax.

Alexis: Well, if you feel you have to go to the shore, I'll make the dinner myself. You go to the shore. I really hate having them over and doing all the work myself. It's such a drag shopping, cooking, and cleaning all by myself.

Given this situation, Sam has two basic alternatives. One is to stick with the plans to go to the shore and relax. In this case Alexis is going to be upset and Sam is going to be made to feel guilty for not helping with the dinner. A second alternative is to give in to Alexis, help with the dinner, and not go to the shore. In this case Sam is going to have to give up a much desired plan and is likely to resent Alexis's "manipulative" tactics. Regardless of which decision is made, this "win–lose" strategy creates resentment, competition, and often an "I'll get even" attitude. With direct requests, this type of situation is much less likely to develop. Consider:

Alexis: I'd like to have my parents over for dinner this weekend. What do you think?

Sam: Well, I really wanted to go to the shore and just relax.

Regardless of what develops next, both individuals are starting out on relatively equal footing. Each has clearly and directly stated a preference. Although at first these preferences seem mutually exclusive, it may be possible to meet both persons' needs. For example, Sam might say, "How about going to the shore this weekend and having your parents over next weekend? I'm really exhausted; I could use the rest." Here is a direct response to a direct request. Unless there is some pressing need to have Alexis's parents over for dinner this weekend, this response may enable each to meet the other's needs.

The emphasis in internet communication—in email, chat groups, or newsgroups—is on speed (in sending, reading, and responding). For this reason directness, and the brevity it entails, is preferred. This cultural emphasis on speed and directness means that in emailing you can practically eliminate introductory and concluding comments in messages, use abbreviations to express commonly used phrases (BTW for "by the way"), use "signatures" that automatically "sign" your emails, and quote relevant sections of an email you're answering. What role does directness play in other forms of online communication—for example, in chat groups or newsgroups?

Gender and Cultural Differences in Directness   A popular stereotype in much of North America holds that women are indirect in making requests and in giving orders—and that this indirectness communicates powerlessness, a discomfort with authority. Men, the stereotype continues, are direct, sometimes to the point of being blunt or rude. This directness communicates men's power and comfort with their own authority.

Deborah Tannen (1994b) provides an interesting perspective on these stereotypes. Women are, it seems, more indirect in giving orders; they are more likely to say, for example, "It would be great if these letters could go out today" rather than "Have these letters out by three." But Tannen (1994b, p. 84) argues that "issuing orders indirectly can be the prerogative of those in power" and in no way shows powerlessness. Power, to Tannen, is the ability to choose your own style of communication.

Men, however, are also indirect but in different situations (Rundquist, 1992). According to Tannen men are more likely to use indirectness when they express weakness, reveal a problem, or admit an error. Men are more likely to speak indirectly in expressing emotions other than anger. Men are also more indirect when they shrink from expressions of increased romantic intimacy. Men are thus indirect, the theory goes, when they're saying something that goes against the masculine stereotype.

Many Asian and Latin American cultures stress the values of indirectness, largely because indirectness enables a person to avoid appearing criticized or contradicted and thereby losing face (Tae-Seop, 2002). An example of a somewhat different kind of indirectness is the greater use of intermediaries to resolve conflict among the Chinese than among North Americans (Ma, 1992). In most of the United States, however, people are taught that directness is the preferred style. "Be upfront" and "Tell it like it is" are commonly heard communication guidelines. In Canada, while being direct might conflict with the common expectation of "being nice and polite," it is still the preferred mode of communication in many business and personal settings. Contrast this North American preference with the following two Japanese principles of indirectness (Tannen, 1994b):

> *omoiyari*, a concept close to empathy, says that a listener needs to understand the speaker without the speaker's being specific or direct. This style obviously places a much greater demand on the listener than would a direct speaking style.

> *sassuru* advises listeners to anticipate a speaker's meanings and use subtle cues from the speaker to infer his or her total meaning.

In thinking about direct and indirect messages, it's important to be aware of the ease with which misunderstandings can occur. For example, a person who uses an indirect style of speech may be doing so to be polite and may have been taught this style by his or her culture. If you assume, because of your own culture, that the person is using indirectness to be manipulative, then miscommunication is inevitable.

Messages Vary in Abstraction

Consider the following list of terms:

- entertainment
- TV show
- Canadian TV show
- recent Canadian TV
- *Royal Canadian Air Farce*

At the top is the general or abstract word *entertainment*. Note that entertainment includes all the other items on the list plus various other items—films, novels, drama, comics, and so on. *TV show* is more specific and concrete. It includes all of the items below it as well as various

There you have it. The blandest adjective in the English language, and we have claimed it as our own. Canadians are nice.

—**Will Ferguson**

other items such as Indian TV shows or Russian TV shows. It excludes, however, all entertainment that is not TV. *Canadian TV show* is again more specific than TV show and excludes all shows that are not Canadian. *Recent Canadian TV show* further limits Canadian TV shows to a time period. *Royal Canadian Air Farce* specifies concretely the one item to which reference is made.

The most general term—in this case, *entertainment*—conjures up many different images. One person may focus on television, another on music, another on comic books, and still another on radio. To some, *television* may bring to mind documentaries or newscasts. To others, it brings to mind the proliferation of so-called "reality shows." *Royal Canadian Air Farce* guides the listener still further—in this case, to one TV program. But note that even though *the name* identifies one program, different listeners are likely to focus on different aspects of the show: perhaps its theme, perhaps its specific characters, perhaps the political context of a given episode. So, as you get more specific—less abstract—you more effectively guide the images that come to your listeners' minds.

Effective verbal messages include words that range widely in abstractness (Figure 5.1). At times a general term may suit your needs best; at other times a more specific term may serve better. The general suggestion for effective communication is to use abstractions sparingly and to express your meanings specifically with words that are low in

FIGURE 5.1 The Abstraction Ladder

As you go up in abstraction, you get more general; as you go down in abstraction, you get more specific. How would you arrange the following terms in order of abstraction, from most specific to most general: vegetation, tree, elm tree, thing, organic thing, blooming elm tree? (An exercise, "Using the Abstraction Ladder as a Critical Thinking Tool," will help you explore other ways of using this idea of the abstraction ladder; see www.ablongman.com/devito.)

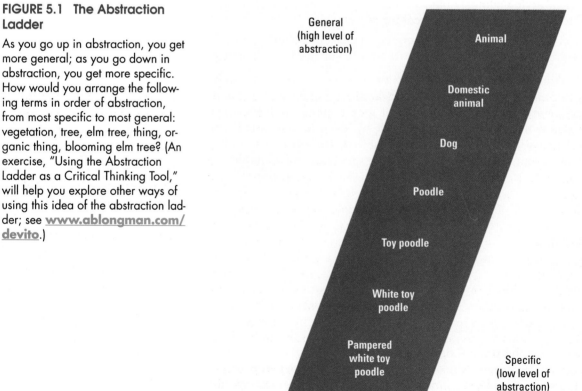

General (high level of abstraction)

Animal

Domestic animal

Dog

Poodle

Toy poodle

White toy poodle

Pampered white toy poodle

Specific (low level of abstraction)

abstraction. However, are there situations when terms high in abstraction would be more effective than specific terms? How would you describe advertisements for cosmetics in terms of high and low abstraction? Advertisements for cereals? Advertisements for cat and dog food? How would you describe political campaign speechs in terms of abstraction?

Message Meanings Are in People

If you wanted to know the meaning of the word *love*, you'd probably turn to a dictionary. There you'd find, according to *Webster's:* "the attraction, desire, or affection felt for a person who arouses delight or admiration or elicits tenderness, sympathetic interest, or benevolence." This is the denotative meaning. (An interesting self-test, "Can you distinguish commonly confused words?" illustrates some of the subtleties of denotative differences; see www.ablongman.com/devito.)

But where would you turn if you wanted to know what Pedro means when he says, "I'm in love"? Of course, you'd turn to Pedro to discover his meaning. It's in this sense that meanings are not in words but in people. Consequently, to uncover meaning, you need to look into people and not merely into words.

Also recognize that as you change, you also change the meanings you created out of past messages. Thus, although the message sent may not have changed, the meanings you created from it yesterday and the meanings you create today may be quite different. Yesterday, when a special someone said, "I love you," you created certain meanings. But today, when you learn that the same "I love you" was said to three other people or when you fall in love with someone else, you drastically change the meanings you draw from those three words.

Message Meanings Depend on Context

Both verbal and nonverbal communications exist in a context, and that context to a large extent determines the meaning of any verbal or nonverbal behaviour. In terms of verbal messages, the same words may have totally different meanings when they occur in different contexts. For example, the greeting "How are you?" means "Hello" to someone you pass regularly on the street but means "Is your health improving?" when said to a friend in the hospital. The Canadian "eh" can be a question or confirmation, depending on the context. Similarly, the meaning of a given message depends on the other behaviour it accompanies or is close to in time. Saying "This stinks to high heaven" in reaction to the behaviour of a politician means something quite different from that same comment in reaction to a piece of overripe cheese. Divorced from the context, it's often impossible to tell what meaning words are intended to convey. Of course, even if you know the context in detail, you still may not be able to decipher the meaning of some messages, because the same words will never have an identical meaning to different people (Harris, 2002).

Especially important is the cultural context, a context emphasized throughout this text. The cultural context will influence not only the meaning assigned to speech but whether your meaning is friendly, of-

"Eh" isn't the only Canadian expression that derives its meaning from its cultural context. If you're unemployed you might be on pogey; if you're going 10 clicks an hour you're probably driving too slow; and if you're cold you might need to put on your toque. And depending on where you are in the country and how old you are, you'll be sitting in either a chesterfield or a couch. Can you think of other expressions that are particular to Canada, or to your region?

Source: The Calgary Herald, June 30, 2003, p. C7.

fensive, lacking in respect, condescending, sensitive, and so on. Some researchers suggest not to focus exclusively on the cultural context, because verbal communication is multidimensional, and in order to decode its meanings, other factors need to be examined as well. (Tzanne, 2000).

Confirmation and Disconfirmation

Before reading about confirmation and disconfirmation, take the self-test below to examine your own communication behaviour.

TEST YOURSELF

How Confirming Are You?

Instructions: In your typical communications, how likely are you to display the following behaviours? Use the following scale in responding to each statement: 5 = always, 4 = often, 3 = sometimes, 2 = rarely, and 1 = never.

_____ **1.** I acknowledge the presence of another person both verbally and nonverbally.

_____ **2.** I acknowledge the contributions of the other person by, for example, supporting or taking issue with what the person says.

_____ **3.** During the conversation, I make nonverbal contact by maintaining direct eye contact, touching, hugging, kissing, and otherwise demonstrating acknowledgment of the other person.

_____ **4.** I communicate as both speaker and listener, with involvement, and with a concern and respect for the other person.

_____ **5.** I signal my understanding of the other person both verbally and nonverbally.

_____ **6.** I reflect back the other person's feelings as a way of showing that I understand these feelings.

_____ **7.** I ask questions as appropriate concerning the other person's thoughts and feelings.

_____ **8.** I respond to the other person's requests, by, for example, returning phone calls and answering letters within a reasonable time.

_____ **9.** I encourage the other person to express his or her thoughts and feelings.

_____ **10.** I respond directly and exclusively to what the other person says.

HOW DID YOU DO?

All 10 statements are phrased so that they express confirming behaviours. Therefore, high scores (say, above 35) reflect a strong tendency to engage in confirmation. Low scores (say, below 25) reflect a strong tendency to engage in disconfirmation. Don't assume, however, that all situations call for confirmation and that only insensitive people are disconfirming. You may wish to consider kinds of situations in which disconfirmation would be, if not an effective response, at least a legitimate one.

A useful way to introduce disconfirmation and its alternatives—confirmation and rejection—is to consider a specific situation: Jessica arrives home late one night. Justin is angry and complains about Jessica's coming home so late. Consider some responses Jessica might make:

1. Stop screaming. I'm not interested in what you're babbling about. I'll do what I want, when I want. I'm going to bed.

2. What are you so angry about? Didn't you get in three hours late last Thursday? When you went to that office party? So knock it off.

3. You have a right to be angry. I should have called when I was going to be late, but I got involved in a serious discussion at work and I couldn't leave until it was resolved.

In response 1, Jessica dismisses Justin's anger and even indicates a dismissal of Justin as a person. In response 2, Jessica rejects the validity of Justin's reasons for being angry but does not dismiss Justin's feelings of anger or Chris as a person. In response 3, Jessica acknowledges Justin's anger and the reasons for being angry. In addition, Jessica provides some kind of explanation and in doing so shows that Justin's feelings matter and that Justin as a person is important and deserves to know what happened. The first response is an example of disconfirmation, the second of rejection, and the third of confirmation.

Psychologist William James once observed that "No more fiendish punishment could be devised, even were such a thing physically possible, than that one should be turned loose in society and remain ab-

The Amish have a practice called "shunning," which involves ignoring a person who has violated one or more of the community's rules. The aim of shunning is to get the individual to repent and to re-enter the community of the faithful. Have you ever practised a form of shunning, perhaps a more modified version?

solutely unnoticed by all the members thereof." In this often quoted observation, James identifies the essence of disconfirmation (Watzlawick, Beavin, & Jackson, 1967; Veenendall & Feinstein, 1995).

Disconfirmation is a communication pattern in which you ignore someone's presence as well as that person's communications. You say, in effect, that this person and what this person has to say are not worth serious attention or effort; that this person and this person's contributions are so unimportant or insignificant that there is no reason to concern yourself with them.

Note that disconfirmation is not the same as **rejection**. In rejection you disagree with the person; you indicate your unwillingness to accept something the other person says or does. In disconfirming someone, however, you deny that person's significance; you claim that what this person says or does simply does not count.

Confirmation is the opposite communication pattern. In confirmation you not only acknowledge the presence of the other person but also indicate your acceptance of this person, of this person's definition of self, and of your relationship as defined or viewed by this other person.

Disconfirmation and confirmation may be communicated in numerous ways. Table 5.1 shows just a few.

TABLE 5.1 Confirmation and Disconfirmation

This table parallels the self-test presented earlier so that you can see clearly not only the confirming but also the opposite, disconfirming behaviours. As you review this table, try to imagine a specific illustration for each of the ways of communicating disconfirmation and confirmation (Pearson, 1993; Galvin & Brommel, 2000).

Confirmation	Disconfirmation
1. Acknowledge the presence and the contributions of the other by either supporting or taking issue with what the other says (self-test items 1 and 2).	1. Ignore the presence and the messages of the other person; express (nonverbally and verbally) indifference to anything the other says.
2. Make nonverbal contact by maintaining direct eye contact, touching, hugging, kissing, and otherwise demonstrating acknowledgment of the other. Engage in dialogue—communication in which both persons are speakers and listeners, both are involved, and both are concerned with each other (items 3 and 4).	2. Make no nonverbal contact; avoid direct eye contact; avoid touching the other person. Engage in monologue—communication in which one person speaks and one person listens, there is no real interaction, and there is no real concern or respect for each other.
3. Demonstrate understanding of what the other says and means and reflect these feelings to demonstrate your understanding (items 5 and 6).	3. Jump to interpretation or evaluation rather than working at understanding what the other means; express your own feelings, ignore feelings of the other, or give abstract intellectualized responses.
4. Ask questions of the other concerning both thoughts and feelings; and acknowledge the questions of the other, return phone calls, answer letters (items 7 and 8).	4. Make statements about yourself; ignore any lack of clarity in the other's remarks; ignore the other's requests; fail to answer questions, return phone calls, or answer letters.
5. Encourage the other to express thoughts and feelings, and respond directly and exclusively to what the other says (items 9 and 10).	5. Interrupt or otherwise make it difficult for the other to express himself or herself; respond only tangentially or by shifting the focus in another direction.

You can gain insight into a wide variety of offensive language practices by viewing them as types of disconfirmation, as language that alienates and separates. Three obvious practices are sexism, heterosexism, and racism.

Sexism

One widespread expression of sexism is **sexist language**: language that puts down someone because of his or her gender (a term usually used to refer to language derogatory toward women). The National Council of Teachers of English (www.ntce.org) has proposed guidelines for nonsexist (gender-free, gender-neutral, or sex-fair) language. These guidelines concern the use of the generic word *man*, the use of generic *he* and *his*, and sex role stereotyping.

Generic *Man*
The word *man* refers most clearly to an adult male. To use the term to refer to both men and women emphasizes maleness at the expense of femaleness. Similarly, the terms *mankind* or *the common man* or even *cavemen* imply a primary focus on adult males. Gender-neutral terms can easily be substituted. Instead of *mankind*, you can say *humanity, people*, or *human beings*. Instead of *the common man*, you can say *the average person* or *ordinary people*. Instead of *cavemen*, you can say *prehistoric people* or *cave dwellers*.

Similarly, the use of terms such as *policeman* or *fireman* and other terms that presume maleness as the norm and femaleness as a deviation from this norm are clear and common examples of sexist language. Consider using nonsexist alternatives for these and similar terms; make these alternatives (for example, *police officer* and *firefighter*) a part of your active vocabulary. Offer alternatives for each of these terms: *man, mankind, countryman, manmade, the common man, manpower, repairman, doorman, fireman, stewardess, waitress, salesman, mailman*, and *actress*.

Generic *He* and *His*
The use of the masculine pronoun to refer to any individual regardless of sex is certainly declining. But it was only as far back as 1975 that all college textbooks, for example, used the masculine pronoun as generic. There seems to be no legitimate reason why the feminine pronoun cannot alternate with the masculine pronoun to refer to hypothetical individuals, or why phrases such as *he and she* or *her and him* cannot be used instead of just *he* or *him*. Alternatively, you can restructure your sentences to eliminate any reference to gender. For example, the NCTE Guidelines suggest that instead of saying, "The average student is worried about his grades," you say, "The average student is worried about grades." Instead of saying, "Ask the student to hand in his work as soon as he is finished," say, "Ask students to hand in their work as soon as they're finished."

Sex Role Stereotyping
The words you use often reflect a sex role bias—the assumption that certain roles or professions belong to men and others belong to women. To eliminate sex role stereotyping from verbal communication, avoid, for example, making the hypothetical elementary

Self-concept is influenced by the way in which you hear yourself talked about. For example, it's been argued that sexist language will influence a woman's self-concept (Tarnove, 1988). Do you find this logical? Do you find it true to your own experiences?

When asked what they would like to change about the communication style of the opposite sex, men said they wanted women to be more direct and women said they wanted men to stop interrupting and offering advice (Noble, 1994). What one change would you like to see in the communication style of the opposite sex? Of your own sex?

school teacher female and the college professor male. Avoid referring to doctors as male and nurses as female. Avoid noting the sex of a professional with terms such as "female doctor" or "male nurse." When you're referring to a specific doctor or nurse, the person's gender will become clear when you use the appropriate pronoun: "Dr. Smith wrote the prescription for her new patient" or "The nurse recorded the patient's temperature himself."

Heterosexism

A close relative of sexism is heterosexism—a relatively new addition to the list of linguistic prejudices. As the term implies, *heterosexism* refers to attitudes, behaviours, and language that disparage gay men and lesbians. As with racist language, **heterosexist language** includes derogatory terms used for lesbians and gay men. For example, recent surveys in the American military show that 80 percent of those surveyed heard "offensive speech, derogatory names, jokes or remarks about gays" and that 85 percent believed that such derogatory speech was "tolerated" (*New York Times*, March 25, 2000, p. A12). You also see heterosexism in more subtle forms of language usage; for example, when you qualify a professional—as in "gay athlete" or "lesbian doctor"—and, in effect, say that athletes and doctors are not normally gay or lesbian. Further, this kind of expression highlights the affectional orientation of the athlete or the doctor in a context where it may have no relevance. This practice, of course, is the same as qualifying by gender, already noted.

In what ways does this photo comment on sex role stereotyping? What interpersonal communication problems (if any) would you anticipate that these firefighters might have?

Still another instance of heterosexism—and perhaps the most difficult to deal with—is the presumption of heterosexuality. Usually, people assume the person they're talking to or about is heterosexual. And usually they're correct, because most people are heterosexual. At the same time, however, note that this presumption denies the lesbian or gay identity a certain legitimacy. The practice is very similar to the presumption of whiteness and maleness that we have made significant inroads in eliminating. Here are a few additional suggestions for avoiding heterosexist, or what some call homophobic, language.

- When talking about gay men and lesbians, avoid offensive nonverbal mannerisms that parody stereotypes.

- Avoid "complimenting" gay men and lesbians by saying that they "don't look it." To gay men and lesbians, this is not a compliment. Similarly, expressing disappointment that a person is gay—often thought to be a compliment, as in comments such as "What a waste!"—is not really a compliment.

- Avoid making the assumption that every gay or lesbian knows what every other gay or lesbian is thinking. It's very similar to asking a Japanese why Sony is investing heavily in Canada or, as one comic put it, asking an African American, "What do you think Jesse Jackson meant by that last speech?"

- Avoid denying individual differences. Saying things like "Lesbians are so loyal" or "Gay men are so open with their feelings," which ignore the reality of wide differences within any group, are potentially insulting to all groups.

- Avoid overattribution, the tendency to attribute just about everything a person does, says, and believes to the fact that the person is gay or lesbian. This tendency helps to recall and perpetuate stereotypes (see Chapter 3).

- Remember that relationship milestones are important to all people. Ignoring anniversaries or birthdays of, say, a relative's partner is resented by everyone.

Racism

According to Andrea Rich (1974), "any language that, through a conscious or unconscious attempt by the user, places a particular racial or ethnic group in an inferior position is racist." **Racist language** expresses racist attitudes. It also, however, contributes to the development of racist attitudes in those who use or hear the language.

Racist terms are used by members of one culture to disparage members of other cultures, their customs, or their accomplishments. Racist language emphasizes differences rather than similarities and separates rather than unites members of different cultures. Generally, racist language is used by the dominant group to establish and maintain power over other groups. The social consequences of racist language in terms of employment, education, housing opportunities, and general community acceptance are well known.

Many people feel that it's permissible for members of a culture to refer to themselves in racist terms. That is, Asians may use the negative terms referring to Asians, Italians may use the negative terms referring to Italians, and so on. This issue is seen clearly in rap music, in which performers use derogatory racial terms (*New York Times*, January 24, 1993, 1, 31). The reasoning seems to be that groups should be able to laugh at themselves.

It's interesting to note that terms denoting some of the major movements in art—for example, *impressionism* and *cubism*—were originally applied negatively. The terms were then adopted by the artists themselves and eventually became positive. A parallel can be seen in the use of the word *queer* by some lesbian and gay organizations. The purpose of these groups in using the term is to cause it to lose its negative connotation.

One possible problem, though, is that such terms may not lose their negative connotations and may simply reinforce the negative stereotypes that society has already assigned to certain groups. By using these terms, members may come to accept the labels with their negative connotations and thus contribute to their own stereotyping.

It has often been pointed out (Ossie Davis, 1973; Bosmajian, 1974) that there are aspects of language that may be inherently racist. For example, one examination of English found 134 synonyms for *white*. Of these, 44 had positive connotations (for example, "clean," "chaste," and

Many interviewers, when they come to talk to me, think they're being progressive by not mentioning in their stories any longer that I'm black. I tell them, 'Don't stop now. If I shot somebody you'd mention it.'

—Colin Powell

Consider this situation: An instructor at your school persists in calling the female students girls, refers to gay men and lesbians as queers, and refers to various racial groups with terms that most people would consider inappropriate. When told that these terms are offensive, the instructor claims the right to free speech and argues that to prevent instructors from using such terms would be a restriction on free speech, which would be a far greater wrong than being culturally or politically incorrect. How would you comment on this argument?

What specialized verbal skills do politicians, such as federal minister Sheila Copps, need to have? Given that so few Canadian women occupy high-level political positions, do you think Copps has changed her verbal communication style to increase her likelihood of success? In what ways?

We have been named; we should now become "namers."

—Lerone Bennett

"unblemished"), and only 10 had negative connotations (for example, "whitewash" and "pale"). The remaining were relatively neutral. Of the 120 synonyms for *black*, 60 had unfavourable connotations ("unclean," "foreboding," and "deadly"), and none had positive connotations.

Cultural Identifiers

Perhaps the best way to avoid sexism, heterosexism, and racism in language is to examine the preferred cultural identifiers to use (and not to use) in talking about members of different cultures. As always, when in doubt, find out. The preferences and many of the specific examples identified here are drawn largely from the findings of the Task Force on Bias-Free Language of the Association of American University Presses (Schwartz, 1995). Do realize that not everyone would agree with these recommendations; they're presented here—in the words of the Task Force—"to encourage sensitivity to usages that may be imprecise, misleading, and needlessly offensive" (Schwartz, 1995, p. ix). They're not presented so that you can "catch" someone being "politically incorrect" or label someone "culturally insensitive."

Generally: The term *girl* should be used only to refer to a very young female and is equivalent to *boy*. Neither term should be used for people older than, say, 13 or 14. *Girl* is never used to refer to a grown woman; nor is *boy* used to refer to persons in blue-collar positions, as it once was. *Lady* is negatively evaluated by many, because it connotes the stereotype of the prim and proper woman. *Woman* or *young woman* is preferred. *Older person* is preferred to *elder, elderly, senior,* or *senior citizen* (technically, someone older than 65).

Generally: *Gay* is the preferred term to refer to a man who has an affectional preference for other men, and *lesbian* is the preferred term for a woman who has an affectional preference for other women. (*Lesbian* means "homosexual woman," so the phrase *lesbian woman* is redundant.) This preference for the term *lesbian* is not universal among homosexual women, however; in one survey, for example, 58 percent preferred *lesbian*, but 34 percent preferred *gay* (Lever, 1995). *Homosexual* refers to both gay men and lesbians but more often merely denotes a sexual orientation to members of one's own sex. *Gay* and *lesbian* refer to a lifestyle and not simply to sexual orientation. *Gay* as a noun, although widely used, may prove offensive in some contexts; for example, "We have two gays on the team." Although used within the gay community in an effort to remove the negative stigma through frequent usage, the term *queer*—as in "queer power"—is often resented when used by outsiders. Because most scientific thinking holds that one's sexuality is genetically determined rather than being a matter of choice, the term *sexual orientation* rather than *sexual preference* or *sexual status* (which is also vague) is preferred.

Generally: Most African Americans prefer *African American* to *black* (Hecht, Collier, & Ribeau, 1993), though *black* is often used with *white* and is used in a variety of other contexts (for example, Department of Black and Puerto Rican Studies, *Journal of Black History,* and Black History Month). In Canada, the term *black* is considered acceptable by members of those communities.

Generally: *White* is used to refer to those whose roots are in European cultures. Some Canadians prefer their national origins to be emphasized, such as *German Canadian* or *Greek Canadian*.

Inuk (plural, *Inuit*) was officially adopted at the Inuit Circumpolar Conference to refer to the indigenous peoples of Alaska, Northern Canada, Greenland, and Eastern Siberia. *Inuk* is preferred to *Eskimo* (a term the U.S. Census Bureau uses), which was applied to the indigenous peoples of Alaska by Europeans and derives from a word that means "raw meat eaters" (Maggio, 1997).

Indian refers only to someone from India and is incorrectly used when applied to members of other Asian countries or to the indigenous peoples of North America. *Aboriginal or First Nations people* are preferred, even though many Native Americans refer to themselves as *Indians* and *Indian people.*

Muslim is the preferred form (rather than the older *Moslem*) to refer to a person who adheres to the religious teachings of Islam. *Quran* (rather than *Koran*) is the preferred term for the scriptures of Islam. The terms "Mohammedan" or "Mohammedanism" are not considered appropriate; they imply worship of Muhammad, the prophet, which is "considered by Muslims to be a blasphemy against the absolute oneness of God" (Maggio, 1997, p. 277).

Although there is no universal agreement, *Jewish people* is thought to be preferable to *Jews;* and *Jewess* (a Jewish female) is considered derogatory. However, this may be due to the fact that successful anti-Jewish propaganda equated the term "Jew" with negative association. In fact, calling someone "a Jew" should be no different than calling someone "a Christian" or "a Muslim."

When history was being written with a European perspective, Europe was taken as the focal point and the rest of the world was defined in terms of its location relative to that continent. Thus, Asia became the East or the Orient, and Asians became *Orientals*—a term that is today considered inappropriate or "Eurocentric." People from Asia are *Asians,* just as people from Africa are *Africans* and people from Europe are *Europeans*.

Using Verbal Messages Effectively and Critically

A chief concern in using verbal messages is to recognize what critical thinking theorists call "conceptual distortions": mental mistakes, misinterpretations, or reasoning fallacies. Avoiding these distortions and substituting a more critical, more realistic analysis is probably the best way to improve your own use of verbal messages. A somewhat different approach to verbal message effectiveness is presented in the article "Using Your Vocal Qualities."

Messages Symbolize Reality (Partially)

Language symbolizes reality; it's not the reality itself. Of course, this is obvious. But consider: Have you ever reacted to the way something was

Visit **www.statcan.ca**. Look up your own city and those cities you've visited or hope to visit, and examine their cultural makeup. What labels are used for the various cultural groups? Are these labels consistent or at variance with the cultural identifiers suggested in this chapter?

What cultural identifiers do you prefer? Have these preferences changed over time? How can you let other people know the designations that you want and those that you don't want to be used to refer to you? An interesting exercise—especially in a large and multicultural class—is for each student to write anonymously his or her preferred cultural identification on an index card and have them all read aloud.

The Active Living Alliance for Canadians with a Disability (**www.ala.ca**) suggests the use of the following principle when referring to a person who has a disability: Describe the person first, then the impairment, but only if it is relevant to the conversation. (When discussing that Aileen has won the lottery, it may not be necessary to indicate that Aileen is a person with a disability.) Instead of *handicapped*, use *person with a disability*; replace *deaf and dumb* with "person with a hearing impairment"; and avoid *retarded or mentally retarded* and substitute *person with an intellectual impairment.* Can you think of other examples?

It is not only true that the language we use puts words in our mouths; it also puts notions in our heads.

—**Wendell Johnson**

6 Ways to Effective Business Email

The rules of netiquette are rules for communicating politely over the internet or over an intranet. Much like the rules of etiquette, which provide guidance for communicating in social situations, the rules of netiquette provide guidance for communicating over the net. These rules, as you'll see, are especially applicable to business email; but they apply generally to all computer-mediated communication.

1. **Don't shout.** WRITING IN CAPS IS PERCEIVED AS SHOUTING. It's okay to use caps occasionally to achieve emphasis. If you wish to give emphasis, underline, _like this_ or *like this*.

2. If your email system has a spellchecker or grammar checker, use it. There's little sense in sending emails that may be read by those making decisions about promotions and work assignments, only to show that you're careless in your spelling or grammar.

3. Respond to emails promptly. Even if you have to look up information or give a more extended response than you now have time for, reply briefly as soon as possible; for example, "Thanks for your email.

I'll need a few days to track down the information you want. I'll be back to you asap." Doing this takes almost no time but goes a long way toward assuring the sender that his or her message reached the right person and will get a response.

4. **Be brief.** Follow the maxim of quantity by communicating only the information that is needed; follow the maxim of manner by communicating clearly, briefly, and in an organized way.

5. When sending email to a group of people, consider the value of not disclosing each person's email address; instead, consider addressing the message to "undisclosed recipients" or to "colleagues."

6. Resist the tendency to clog the email systems of colleagues with baby photos, long drawn-out stories, or attachments that they probably don't want.

THEN AND NOW

Have you ever communicated impolitely over the net? What specifically did you do? What would you do differently now?

Visualize yourself seated with a packet of photographs before you. You're asked to scratch out the eyes in each photograph. You're further told that this is simply an experiment and that the individuals shown (all strangers) will not be aware of anything that has happened here. As you progress through the pictures, scratching out the eyes, you come upon a photograph of your mother. What do you do? Are you able to scratch out the eyes as you have done with the pictures of the strangers? Are you responding intensionally or extensionally?

labelled or described rather than to the actual item? Have you ever bought something because of its name rather than because of the actual object? If so, you were probably responding as if language were reality, a distortion called intensional orientation.

Orientation **Intensional orientation** (the *s* in *intensional* is intentional) refers to our tendency to view people, objects, and events in the way they're talked about—the way they're labelled. For example, if Nila were labelled "uninteresting" you would, responding intensionally, evaluate her as uninteresting even before listening to what she had to say. You'd see Nila through a filter imposed by the label "uninteresting." **Extensional orientation**, on the other hand, is the tendency to look first at the actual people, objects, and events and only afterwards at their labels. In this case, it would mean looking at Nila without any preconceived labels, guided by what she says and does, not by the words used to label her. If the people in the cartoon on page 124 see themselves as "upper-middle-class" because they've been labelled as such, they'll be responding intensionally. If, on the other hand, they realize that their lives won't change just because their label changed, they'll be responding extensionally.

MESSAGES@WORK

Using Your Vocal Qualities

"Don't speak to me in that tone of voice!" is a familiar comment in interpersonal conflict. Your tone of voice often has more impact than your actual words, communicating an important part of you and your personality to others.

Vocal quality is especially important over the telephone. You might find it a worthwhile exercise to tape-record only your half of several phone calls. After each call, replay the tape. How are you coming across to yourself? How does it sound? Are the volume and speed appropriate? What about the rhythm, inflection, resonance, and clarity? Do you feel that you were accurately communicating to the other person the emotions that you meant to communicate to him? By analyzing and constructively critiquing several of these phone calls, you can determine if any of your vocal qualities need improvement. As soon as you can identify these, think about how to improve them so you can start projecting the type of voice you would like to have.

Language can be interpreted in different ways, but through the use of vocal qualities you can clarify the intent of your message and communicate your feelings, likes, and dislikes. By varying tone, you can reinforce what you are saying verbally. For most people who work in an organizational environment, creating a vocal quality that conveys competence and assurance is important. Five aids to developing an assured voice are as follows:

1. Project strong, full, but not overwhelming resonance.
2. Use your mouth and lips to speak clearly and distinctly.
3. Show enthusiasm by using the appropriate pitch, volume, and inflection.
4. Be interesting by varying your vocal qualities—avoid speaking in a monotone voice.
5. Speak naturally and at ease rather than adopting vocal qualities that do not fit who you are.

Your part of the conversation can't be monotonous, or you will be boring. On the other hand, do not vary your intonations in the same manner every time and risk coming across like a machine. A mechanical voice is boring and sounds canned. Both the uninteresting voice and the voice that follows a mechanical pattern are monotonous. You can avoid this monotony by simply varying your vocal qualities as the situation requires.

Speak rapidly when the subject matter permits; then emphasize an important point by speaking more slowly. By watching facial expressions and other nonverbal communications, you can determine the listener's degree of involvement. Emphasize points that apparently interest the listener and then pause to let the idea sink in. As you can see, timing in speech can be highly informative and effective to both you and your listeners.

A study at Yale University showed that the more errors a person made while speaking (errors meaning poor tone, volume, monotony, etc.), the more that speaker's discomfort and anxiety increased. Through practice and awareness, you can reduce these errors. By doing this, you will become much more comfortable with your speaking voice. This in turn will make your listeners more comfortable and they will listen more intently. You will have more credibility with them.

Carelessness in enunciation is likely to be taken as an indication of carelessness in other areas. Poor enunciation is also likely to result in the listener misunderstanding what you are saying. It can easily lead to a breakdown in the communication process. Good enunciation clarifies communication which tends to strengthen and build relationships.

The foregoing vocal suggestions can be effective if they are used appropriately. Overuse or overemphasis of these methods can annoy your listeners and take their attention away from the conversation. Your use of these vocal skills must seem natural and spontaneous, or you will appear insincere. By using the proper vocal intonation, you can draw attention to those areas of your message that impact and benefit your listeners.

Most people know the importance of using effective vocal behavior when speaking to coworkers, employees, upper management, clients, and customers. An awareness of the subtle nuances, feelings, meanings, and emotions of vocal behavior is critical. It allows you to be aware of what you are (nonverbally) communicating to others and what they are (nonverbally) communicating to you. It can make or break working relationships. It can dramatically impact an organiza-

(continued)

tion's productivity as it affects the communication process of people working together. Becoming more aware of and sensitive to your vocal intonations and those of others can help you improve your credibility,

and help you develop stronger working and personal relationships. That payoff seems well worth the effort.

Source: Tony Alessandra and Phil Hunsaker. *Communicating at Work.* New York: Simon & Schuster (Fireside), 1993.

THINKING CRITICALLY ABOUT
Weasel Words

A weasel is a slippery beast; just when you think you're going to catch it, it slips away. Weasel words are words whose meanings are difficult to pin down, words that allow the speaker to weasel out of an implied commitment or agreement (Larson, 1998; Wrighter, 1972). For example, a medicine that claims to work better than Brand X doesn't specify how much better or in what respect it performs better. Is it possible that it is better in one respect and less effective on nine other measures? *Better* is a weasel word. *Like* is another word often used for weaseling, as when a claim is made that "Brand X will make you feel like a new man"—or, with the *like* only implied, that "Brand X makes you feel

young again." Exactly what these claims mean in specific terms would be impossible to pin down. Other weasel words are *helped, virtually, as much as,* and *more economical.* Try looking for weasel words; you'll often find them lurking in the promises of advertisers and politicians.

EXAMPLES?

Choose an example of an advertisement in a recent newspaper or magazine or on the net that uses weasel words. What effect does the advertiser hope these words will have on the reader?

"I now decree you all upper-middle-class."

The way to avoid intensional orientation is to extensionalize. Recognize that language provides labels for things and should never be given greater attention than the actual thing—a truth that the king in the cartoon below seems not to grasp. Give your main attention to the people, things, and events in the world as you see them and not as they're presented in words. For example, when you meet Jack and Jill, observe and interact with them. Then form your impressions. Don't respond to them as "greedy, money-grubbing landlords" simply because Harry labelled them this way. Don't respond to Carmen as "lazy and inconsiderate" because Elaine told you she was.

(An exercise to help you avoid intensional orientation, "Thinking in E-Prime," may be found at **www.ablongman.com/devito**.)

Allness A related distortion is to forget that language symbolizes only a portion of reality, never the whole. When you assume that you can know all or say all about anything, you're into a pattern of behaviour called **allness**. You never see all of anything. You never experience anything fully. You see a part, then conclude what the whole is like. You have to draw conclusions on the basis of insufficient evidence (because you always have insufficient evidence). A useful **extensional device** to help combat the tendency to think that all can or has been said about anything is to end each statement mentally with **et cetera**—a reminder that there is more to learn, more to know, and more to say; that every statement is inevitably incomplete (Korzybski, 1933). Some people overuse "et cetera." They use it not as a mental reminder but as a substitute for being specific. This obviously is to be avoided and merely adds to the distortions in communication.

To avoid allness, recognize that language symbolizes only a part of reality, never the whole. Whatever someone says—regardless of what it is or how extensive it is—is only part of the story.

Messages Express Facts and Inferences

You can construct statements of both facts and inferences without making any linguistic distinction between the two. Similarly, when you articulate or listen to such statements, you often don't make a clear distinction between statements of facts and statements of inference. Yet there are great differences between the two. Barriers to clear thinking can be created when inferences are treated as facts, a tendency called **fact–inference confusion.**

TALKING ETHICS

Lying

Lying occurs when "one person intends to mislead another, doing so deliberately, without prior notification of this purpose, and without having been explicitly asked to do so by the target [the person the liar intends to mislead]" (Ekman, 1985b, p. 28). Although lying usually involves overt statements, it may also be committed by omission; when you omit something relevant, leading others to draw incorrect inferences, you're lying just as surely as if you had stated an untruth. Similarly, although most lies are verbal, some are nonverbal; the innocent facial expression—despite the commission of some wrong—and the knowing nod instead of the honest expression of ignorance are common examples of nonverbal lying (O'Hair, Cody, & McLaughlin, 1981). Lies may range from the "white lie" in which you "just stretch the truth" to lies that form the basis of relationship infidelity, libel, and perjury. And, not surprisingly, lies have ethical implications.

Some lies are considered innocent, acceptable, and generally ethical (for example, lying to a child to protect a fantasy belief in Santa Claus or the Tooth Fairy, telling people who look terrible that they look great, or pub-

licly agreeing with someone just to enable the person to save face). Other lies are considered unacceptable and generally unethical (for example, lying to defraud investors, to falsely accuse someone of a crime, or to get out of paying your fair share of income tax). Still other lies, however, aren't so easy to classify as ethical or unethical. (An interesting self-test, "When is lying unethical?" will help you to further explore the ethical dimensions of lying; visit **www.ablongman.com/ devito**.)

WHAT WOULD YOU DO?

You've been called for jury duty but really don't want to serve. You've served before and have never been empanelled for a trial—because, you suspect, you teach critical thinking courses. So, rather than spend two weeks in a jury room for no reason, you wonder if it would be ethical to lie and say that your invalid mother can't do without you (even though, in fact, your sister could easily fill in for you). Would it be ethical to lie under these circumstances? What would you do in this situation?

For example, you can say, "She's wearing a blue jacket," and you can say, "He's harbouring an illogical hatred." Although the sentences have similar structures, they're different. You can observe the jacket and the blue colour, but how do you observe "illogical hatred"? Obviously, this is not a **factual statement** but an **inferential statement**. It's one you make on the basis not only of what you observe, but of what you infer. For a statement to be considered factual, it must be made by the observer after observation and must be limited to what is observed (Weinberg, 1959).

There is nothing wrong with making inferential statements. You must make them to talk about much that is meaningful to you. The problem arises when you act as if those inferential statements are factual. You may test your ability to distinguish facts from inferences by taking the self-test below (based on tests constructed by Haney, 1973).

TEST YOURSELF

Can You Distinguish Facts from Inferences?

Instructions: Carefully read the following report and the observations based on it. Indicate whether you think, on the basis of the information presented in the report, that the observations are true, false, or doubtful. Write T if the observation is definitely true, F if the observation is definitely false, and ? if the observation may be either true or false. Judge the observations in order. Do not reread the observations after you have indicated your judgment, and do not change any of your answers.

A well-liked college teacher had just completed making up the final examinations and had turned off the lights in the office. Just then a tall, broad figure with dark glasses appeared and demanded the examination. The professor opened the drawer. Everything in the drawer was picked up and the individual ran down the corridor. The dean was notified immediately.

_____ **1.** The thief was tall and broad and wore dark glasses.

_____ **2.** The professor turned off the lights.

_____ **3.** A tall figure demanded the examination.

_____ **4.** The examination was picked up by someone.

_____ **5.** The examination was picked up by the professor.

_____ **6.** A tall, broad figure appeared after the professor turned off the lights in the office.

_____ **7.** The man who opened the drawer was the professor.

_____ **8.** The professor ran down the corridor.

_____ **9.** The drawer was never actually opened.

_____ **10.** Three persons are referred to in this report.

HOW DID YOU DO?

After you answer all 10 questions, form small groups of five or six and discuss the answers. Look at each statement from each member's point of view. For each statement, ask yourself,

To avoid fact–inference confusion, phrase inferential statements not as factual but as tentative. Recognize that they may prove to be wrong. Inferential statements should leave open the possibility of alternatives. If, for example, you treat the statement "Our biology teacher was fired for poor teaching" as factual, you eliminate any alternatives. When making inferential statements, be psychologically prepared to be proved wrong. If you're prepared to be wrong, you will be less hurt if you're shown to be wrong. Be especially sensitive to this distinction when you're listening. Most talk is inferential. Beware of the speaker who presents everything as fact. Analyze closely and you'll uncover a world of inferences.

Messages Are Relatively Static

Language changes only very slowly, especially when compared with the rapid change in people and things. **Static evaluation** is the tendency to retain evaluations without change even if the reality to which they refer is changing. Often a verbal statement you make about an event or person remains static ("That's the way he is; he's always been that way") while the event or person may change enormously. Alfred Korzybski (1933) used an interesting illustration. In a tank you have a large fish and many small fish, the natural food for the large fish. Given freedom in the tank, the large fish will eat the small fish. If you partition the tank, separating the large fish from the small fish by a clear piece of glass, the large fish will continue to attempt to eat the small fish but will fail, knocking instead into the glass partition.

Eventually, the large fish will learn the futility of attempting to eat the small fish. If you now remove the partition, the small fish will swim all around the big fish, but the big fish will not eat them. In fact, the large fish will die of starvation while its natural food swims all around. The large fish has learned a pattern or "map" of behaviour, and even though the actual territory has changed, the map remains static.

While you'd probably agree that everything is in a constant state of flux, do you act as if you know this? Do you act in accordance with the notion of change or just accept it intellectually? Do you realize, for example, that even if you've failed at something once, you need not fail again? Your evaluations of yourself and of others must keep pace with the rapidly changing real world; otherwise your attitudes and beliefs will be about a world that no longer exists.

The mental **date** is an extensional device that helps to keep language (and thinking) up to date and helps guard against static evalua-

A word is not a crystal, transparent and unchanged, it is the skin of a living thought and may vary greatly in color and content according to the circumstances and the time in which it is used.

—Oliver Wendell Holmes

Change is constant.

—Benjamin Disraeli

tion. The procedure is simple: Mentally date your statements and especially your evaluations. Remember that Pat Smith$_{1984}$ is not Pat Smith$_{1996}$; academic abilities$_{1992}$ are not academic abilities$_{1996}$. T. S. Eliot, in *The Cocktail Party*, said, "What we know of other people is only our memory of the moments during which we knew them. And they have changed since then ... at every meeting we are meeting a stranger." In listening, look carefully at messages that claim that what was true still is. It may or may not be. Look for change.

Messages Can Obscure Distinctions

Messages can obscure distinctions, both by generalizing about people or events that are covered by the same label but are really quite different (indiscrimination) and by making it easy to focus on extremes rather than on the vast middle ground (polarization).

Indiscrimination Each word in the language can refer to lots of things; most general terms refer to a wide variety of individuals. Words such as *teacher* or *textbook* or *computer program* refer to lots of specific people and things. When you allow the general term to obscure the specific differences (say, among teachers or among textbooks), you're into a pattern called indiscrimination.

Indiscrimination refers to the failure to distinguish between similar but different people, objects, or events. It occurs when you focus on classes and fail to see that each phenomenon is unique and needs to be looked at individually.

Everything is unlike everything else. Our language, however, provides you with common nouns such as *teacher, student, friend, enemy, war, politician,* and *liberal.* These lead you to focus on similarities—to group together all teachers, all students, all politicians. At the same time, the terms divert attention away from the uniqueness of each person, each object, and each event.

How does indiscrimination operate in intercultural communication? Can you provide specific examples you've witnessed?

THINKING CRITICALLY ABOUT

Snarl and Purr Words

Semanticist S. I. Hayakawa (Hayakawa & Hayakawa, 1989) coined the terms *snarl words* and *purr words* to further clarify the distinction between denotative and connotative meanings. Snarl words are highly negative: "She's an idiot." "He's a pig." "They're a bunch of losers." Sexist, racist, and heterosexist language and hate speech provide lots of other examples. Purr words are highly positive: "She's a real sweetheart." "He's a dream." "They're the greatest."

Snarl and purr words, although they may sometimes seem to have denotative meaning and to refer to the "real world," are actually connotative in meaning. These terms do not describe people or events in the real world but rather the speaker's feelings about these people or events.

EXAMPLES?

Give examples of recent interactions you've had in which someone made snarl or purr statements that were used or interpreted as if they had denotative meaning.

This misevaluation is at the heart of stereotyping on the basis of nationality, race, religion, gender, and affectional orientation. A stereotype, you'll remember from Chapter 3, is a fixed mental picture of a group that is applied to each individual in the group without regard to his or her unique qualities.

Most stereotypes are negative and denigrate the group to which they refer. Some, however, are positive. A particularly glaring example is the popular stereotype of Asian Canadian students as successful, intelligent, and hardworking.

Whether stereotypes are positive or negative, they create the same problem: They provide you with shortcuts that are often inappropriate. For instance, when you meet a particular person, your first reaction may be to pigeonhole him or her into some category—perhaps religious, national, or academic ("She's a typical academic: never thinks of the real world"). Then you assign to this person all the qualities that are part of your stereotype. Regardless of the category you use or the specific qualities you're ready to assign, you fail to give sufficient attention to the individual's unique characteristics. Two people may both be Christian, Asian, and lesbian, for example, but each will be different from the other. Indiscrimination is a denial of another's uniqueness.

A useful antidote to indiscrimination (and stereotyping) is the **index**. This mental subscript identifies each individual as an individual even though both may be covered by the same label. Thus, politician$_1$ is not politician$_2$; teacher$_1$ is not teacher$_2$. The index helps you to discriminate among without discriminating against. Although a label ("politician," for example) covers all politicians, the index makes sure that each politician is thought about as an individual.

Polarization Another way in which language can obscure differences is in its predominance of extreme terms and its relative lack of middle terms, a situation that often leads to **polarization**. You can appreciate the role language plays in fostering polarization by trying to identify the opposites of the following terms: *happy, long, wealth, life, healthy, up, left, legal, heavy, strong.* This should have been relatively easy; you probably identified the opposites very quickly. Now, however, identify the middle terms, the terms referring to the middle ground between the italicized terms and the opposites you supplied. These terms should have been more difficult to come up with and should have taken you more time and effort. Further, if you compare your responses with those of others, you'll find that most people agree on the opposites; most people would have said *unhappy, short, poverty,* and so on. But when it comes to the middle terms, the degree of agreement will be much less. Thus, language makes it easy to focus on opposites and relatively difficult to talk about the middle areas.

Polarization, then, is the tendency to look at the world in terms of opposites and to describe it in extremes—good or bad, positive or negative, healthy or sick, intelligent or stupid. Polarization is often referred to as the fallacy of "either/or" or "black and white." Most of life exists somewhere between the extremes. Yet there's a strong tendency to view only the extremes and to categorize people, objects, and events in terms of these polar opposites.

Problems are created when opposites are used in inappropriate situations. For example, "The politician is either for us or against us." These options do not include all possibilities. The politician may be for us in some things and against us in other things, or may be neutral. During the Vietnam War people were categorized as either hawks or doves. But clearly many people were neither, and many were hawks on certain issues and doves on others.

To correct this polarizing tendency, beware of implying (and believing) that two extreme classes include all possible classes—that an individual must be one or the other, with no alternatives ("Are you pro-choice or pro-life?"). Most people, most events, most qualities exist between polar extremes. When others imply that there are only two sides or two alternatives, look for the middle ground.

SUMMARY OF CONCEPTS AND SKILLS

In this chapter we considered verbal messages. The chapter discussed the nature of language and the ways in which language works; the concept of disconfirmation and how it relates to sexist, heterosexist, and racist language; and the ways in which language can be used more effectively.

1. Language meanings are in people, not in things.

2. Meanings are context based; the same message in a different context will likely mean something different.

3. Language is both denotative (conveying meanings that are objective and generally agreed upon) and connotative (conveying meanings that are subjective and generally highly individual).

4. Language varies in directness; you can use language to state exactly what you mean or to hedge and state your meaning very indirectly.

5. Language is a cultural institution; each culture has its own rules identifying the ways in which language should be used.

6. Language varies in abstraction; words can vary from extremely general to extremely specific.

7. Disconfirmation is the process of ignoring the presence and the communications of others. Confirmation is accepting, supporting, and acknowledging the importance of the other person.

8. Sexist, heterosexist, and racist language puts down and negatively evaluates various cultural groups.

9. Using language effectively involves eliminating conceptual distortions and substituting more accurate assumptions about language, the most important of which are:

- Language symbolizes reality; it's not the reality itself.
- Language can express both facts and inferences, and distinctions need to be made between them.
- Language is relatively static; because reality changes so rapidly, you need to constantly revise the way you talk about people and things.
- Language can obscure distinctions in its use of general terms and in its emphasis on extreme rather than middle terms.

The nature of language, disconfirmation, and popular conceptual distortions have important implications for the skills of effective communication. Check your ability to apply these skills. Use a rating scale such as the following: 1 = almost always, 2 = often, 3 = sometimes, 4 = rarely, and 5 = hardly ever.

_____ 1. I recognize that meaning is in people and not in things and therefore focus on what the person means as well as what the words mean.

_____ 2. I look for both the connotative and the denotative meanings when listening.

_____ 3. I recognize cultural and gender differences in the rules for using language; each culture has its own rules, which must be recognized and taken into consideration if communication is to be effective.

_____ 4. I am generally confirming in my communications and acknowledge others and their contributions.

_____ 5. I avoid disconfirmation through sexist, heterosexist, and racist language.

_____ 6. I avoid responding (intensionally) to labels as if they're objects; instead, I respond extensionally and look first at the reality and only then at the words.

_____ 7. I distinguish facts from inferences and respond to inferences with tentativeness.

_____ 8. I mentally date my statements and thus avoid static evaluation.

_____ 9. I avoid indiscrimination by treating each person and situation as unique.

_____ 10. I avoid using allness statements.

_____ 11. I avoid polarization by using "middle ground" terms and qualifiers in describing the world and especially people.

VOCABULARY QUIZ

The Language of Language

Match these terms about language with their definitions. Record the number of the definition next to the term.

_10_ polarization 121

9 _____ intensional orientation 122

_3_ connotative meaning 108

_1_ fact–inference confusion 125

_4_ confirmation 116

_2_ static evaluation 127

8 _____ indiscrimination 128

___7___ sexist language 117
___6___ level of abstraction 111
___5___ netiquette 122

1. Treating inferences as if they were facts.
2. The denial of change in language and in thinking.
3. The emotional, subjective aspect of meaning.
4. A communication pattern in which we acknowledge the presence of and signal the acceptance of another person.
5. The rules for polite communication on the internet.

6. The degree of generality or specificity of a term.
7. Language derogatory to one sex, generally to women.
8. The failure to see the differences among people or things covered by the same label.
9. A focus on the way things are talked about rather than on the way they exist in the world.
10. An almost exclusive focus on extremes, often to the neglect or omission of the vast middle ground.

SKILL BUILDING EXERCISES

5.1 CLIMBING THE ABSTRACTION LADDER

The "abstraction ladder" is a device to illustrate the different levels of abstraction on which different terms exist. In Figure 5.1 (see page 112), notice that as you go from "animal" to "pampered white toy poodle," you're going down in terms of abstraction; you're getting more and more specific. As you get more specific, you more clearly communicate your own meanings and more easily direct the listener's attention to what you wish. For each of the general terms listed below, provide at least four possible terms that indicate increasing specificity. The first example is done for you.

Level 1	Level 2 *more specific than 1*	Level 3 *more specific than 2*	Level 4 *more specific than 3*	Level 5 *more specific than 4*
house	mansion	brick mansion	large brick mansion	CEO's mansion
desire	_____	_____	_____	_____
car	_____	_____	_____	_____
toy	_____	_____	_____	_____
magazine	_____	_____	_____	_____
sports	_____	_____	_____	_____

Thinking Critically About Abstractions.

The general suggestion for effective communication is to use abstractions sparingly and to express your meanings specifically. However, are there situations in which terms high in abstraction would be more effective than specific terms? How would you describe advertisements for cosmetics in terms of high and low abstraction? Ads for cereals? Ads for cat and dog food? How would you describe political campaign speaking in terms of abstraction?

5.2 CONFIRMING, REJECTING, AND DISCONFIRMING

Classify the various responses to the following scenarios as confirmation, rejection, or disconfirmation. Then develop original scenarios and examples of all three types of responses.

1. Enrique receives this semester's grades in the mail; they're a lot better than previous semesters' grades but are still not great. After opening the letter, Enrique says: "I really tried hard to get my grades up this semester." Enrique's parents respond:

_____ Going out every night hardly seems like trying very hard.

_____ What should we have for dinner?

_____ Keep up the good work.

_____ I can't believe you've really tried your best; how can you study with the stereo blasting in your ears?

_____ I'm sure you've tried really hard.

_____ That's great.

_____ What a rotten day I had at the office.

_____ I can remember when I was in school; I got all B's without ever opening a book.

2. Pat, who has been out of work for the past several weeks, says: "I feel like such a failure; I just can't seem to find a job. I've been pounding the pavement for the last five weeks and still nothing." Pat's friend responds:

_____ I know you've been trying really hard.

_____ You really should get more training so you'd be able to sell yourself more effectively.

_____ I told you a hundred times, you need that college degree.

_____ I've got to go to the dentist on Friday. Boy, do I hate that.

_____ The employment picture is bleak at this time of the year, but your qualifications are really impressive. Something will come up soon.

_____ You're not a failure. You just can't find a job.

_____ What do you need a job for? Stay home and keep house. After all, Chris makes more than enough money for you to live in style.

_____ What's five weeks?

_____ Well, you'll just have to try harder.

Thinking Critically About Confirmation, Rejection, and Disconfirmation.

Generally, communication experts would advise you to be more confirming than disconfirming. Can you identify situations where disconfirmation would be a more effective response than confirmation? Are there situations when confirmation would be inappropriate?

Provide examples of a confirmatory, rejecting, and disconfirmatory response to your friend's statement: "I haven't had a date in the last four months. I'm getting really depressed over this." Another example: Your friend tells you of relationship problems: "Rani and I just can't seem to get along any more. Every day is a hassle. Every day, there's another conflict, another battle. I feel like walking away from the whole mess."

5.3 "MUST LIE" SITUATIONS

In an episode of *Seinfeld*, the group visits a friend who has just had a baby—the ugliest baby anyone has ever seen. But everyone, of course, tells the parents the baby is beautiful, even "breathtaking." It's a "must lie" situation, the group agrees; and anyway, the parents will never know that their baby is not only not beautiful but downright ugly. Can you identify other "must lie" situations—situations in which lying seems the only socially acceptable response? Try recording these, using the following chart:

Liar: Who must lie?	Situation: What is the occasion that prompts the "must lie" situation?	Target: Who is the person who must be lied to?	Pupose: What is the purpose of the lie? What would happen if the truth were told? What does the liar hope to achieve by lying?
1. _____	_____	_____	_____
2. _____	_____	_____	_____
3. _____	_____	_____	_____
4. _____	_____	_____	_____
5. _____	_____	_____	_____

Thinking Critically About "Must Lie" Situations.

What ethical issues are involved in such situations? That is, can any of these lies be considered unethical? Can the failure to lie in any of these situations be considered unethical?

Chapter 6
Nonverbal Messages

CHAPTER TOPICS

This chapter introduces the nonverbal message system, the way you communicate without words.

- The Functions of Nonverbal Messages
- The Channels of Nonverbal Messages
- Culture and Nonverbal Messages

CHAPTER SKILLS

After completing this chapter, you should be able to:

- use nonverbal messages in conjunction with verbal messages to serve a variety of functions.
- use a wide variety of nonverbal communication forms to encode and decode meanings.
- use nonverbal behaviours with an awareness of cultural differences and influences.

In a communication class at the University of Guelph, the instructor asks, "Would anyone like to respond to the question in Chapter 9?" Mohammed, sitting in the front row, energetically puts up his hand. Dana, sitting in the back, slides down in her seat and looks at the floor.

In this example, you see the powerful messages communicated without words. In this chapter we look at these nonverbal messages—the ways they function in interaction with verbal messages, the types or channels of nonverbal messages, and the cultural variations in nonverbal communication.

The Functions of Nonverbal Messages

Nonverbal communication is communication without words. You communicate nonverbally when you gesture, smile or frown, widen your eyes, move your chair closer to someone, wear jewellery, touch someone, raise your vocal volume, or even when you say nothing.

In face-to-face communication you blend verbal and nonverbal messages to best convey your meanings. Here are six ways in which nonverbal messages are used with verbal messages; these will help to highlight this important verbal–nonverbal interaction (Knapp & Hall, 1996).

Nonverbal communication is often used to *accent* or emphasize some part of a verbal message. You might, for example, raise your voice to underscore a particular word or phrase, bang your fist on the desk to stress your commitment, or look longingly into someone's eyes when saying "I love you."

Nonverbal communication may *complement* or add nuances of meaning not communicated by your verbal message. Thus, you might smile when telling a story (to suggest that you find it humorous) or frown and shake your head when recounting someone's deceit (to suggest your disapproval).

When verbal and nonverbal messages contradict each other, do you believe the nonverbal? Under what conditions would you believe the verbal? When would you believe the nonverbal?

THINKING CRITICALLY ABOUT

Nonverbal Messages

Begin your reading of nonverbal communication with the following suggestions in mind:

- Analyze your own nonverbal communication patterns. If you're to use this material in any meaningful way—for example, to change some of your behaviours—then self-analysis is essential.

- Observe. Observe. Observe. Observe both your own behaviours and the behaviours of those around you. See in everyday behaviour what you read about here and discuss in class.

- Resist the temptation to draw conclusions from nonverbal behaviours. Instead, develop hypotheses (educated guesses) about what is going on, and test your hypotheses on the basis of other evidence.

- Connect and relate. Although the channels of nonverbal communication are presented separately in textbooks, in actual communication situations they all work together.

EXAMPLES?

Think of an example of someone you know who uses nonverbal behaviour ineffectively—and an example of someone who uses nonverbal behaviour effectively. What specific nonverbal behaviours do you find effective? Ineffective?

You may deliberately *contradict* your verbal messages with nonverbal movements—for example, by crossing your fingers or winking to indicate that you're lying.

Movements may be used to *regulate*, control, or indicate your desire to control, the flow of verbal messages, as when you purse your lips, lean forward, or make hand gestures to indicate that you want to speak. You might also put up your hand or vocalize your **pauses** (for example, with "um" or "ah") to indicate that you have not finished and are not ready to relinquish the floor to the next speaker.

You can *repeat* or restate the verbal message nonverbally. You can, for example, follow your verbal "Is that all right?" with raised eyebrows and a questioning look, or motion with your head or hand to repeat your verbal "Let's go."

You may also use nonverbal communication to *substitute* or take the place of verbal messages. For instance, you can signal "okay" with a hand gesture. You can nod your head to indicate yes or shake your head to indicate no. Or you can glance at your watch to communicate your concern with time.

The Channels of Nonverbal Messages

Nonverbal communication is probably most easily explained in terms of the various channels through which messages pass. Here we'll survey 10 channels: body, face, eye, space, artifactual, touch, paralanguage, silence, time, and smell.

Body Messages

Two aspects of the body are especially important in communicating messages. First, the movements you make with your body communicate; second, the general appearance of your body communicates.

Body Movements   Nonverbal researchers identify five major types of body movements: emblems, illustrators, affect displays, regulators, and adaptors (Ekman & Friesen, 1969; Knapp & Hall, 1996).

Emblems are body gestures that directly translate into words or phrases, for example, the okay sign, the thumbs-up for "good job," and the V for victory. You use these consciously and purposely to communicate the same meaning as the words. But emblems are culture specific, so be careful when using your culture's emblems in other cultures. For example, when U.S. president Richard Nixon visited Latin America and gestured with the okay sign, intending to communicate something positive, he was quickly informed that this gesture was not universal. In Latin America the gesture has a far more negative meaning. Here are a few cultural differences in the emblems you may commonly use (Axtell, 1993):

- In North America, to say "hello" you wave with your whole hand moving from side to side, but in a large part of Europe that same signal means "no." In Greece such a gesture would be considered insulting to the person to whom you're waving.

- The V for victory is common throughout much of the world; but if you make this gesture in England with the palm facing your face, it's as insulting as the raised middle finger is in North America.

Research shows that women are perceived to be and are in reality more skilled at both encoding and decoding nonverbal messages (Briton & Hall, 1995). Do you notice this in your own interactions?

- In Texas the raised fist with little finger and index finger raised is a positive expression of support, because it represents the Texas longhorn steer. But in Italy it's an insult that means "Your spouse is having an affair." In parts of South America it's a gesture to ward off evil, and in parts of Africa it's a curse: "May you experience bad times."

- In North America and in much of Asia, hugs are rarely exchanged among acquaintances; but among Latins and Southern Europeans hugging is a common greeting gesture, and failing to hug someone may communicate unfriendliness.

> The body says what words cannot.
> —**Martha Graham**

Illustrators enhance (literally "illustrate") the verbal messages they accompany. For example, when referring to something to the left, you might gesture toward the left. Most often you illustrate with your hands, but you can also illustrate with head and general body movements. You might, for example, turn your head or your entire body toward the left. You might also use illustrators to communicate the shape or size of objects you're talking about.

Affect displays include movements of the face (smiling or frowning, for example) as well as of the hands and general body (body tension or relaxation, for example) that communicate emotional meaning. You use affect displays to accompany and reinforce your verbal messages but also as substitutes for words; for example, you might smile while saying how happy you are to see your friend, or you might simply smile. Or you might rush to greet someone with open arms. Because affect displays are centred primarily in the facial area, we'll consider these in more detail in the "Facial Messages" section beginning on page 139. Affect displays are often unconscious; you smile or frown, for example, without awareness. At other times, however, you may smile with awareness, consciously trying to convey pleasure or friendliness.

Regulators are behaviours that monitor, control, coordinate, or maintain the speaking of another individual. When you nod your head, for example, you tell the speaker to keep on speaking; when you lean forward and open your mouth, you tell the speaker that you would like to say something.

Adaptors are gestures that satisfy some personal need. **Self-adaptors** are self-touching movements; for example, rubbing your nose, scratching to relieve an itch, or moving your hair out of your eyes. **Alter-adaptors** are movements directed at the person with whom you're speaking; for example, removing lint from a person's jacket, straightening a person's tie, or folding your arms in front of you to keep others a comfortable distance from you. **Object-adaptors** are gestures focused on objects; for example, doodling on or shredding a Styrofoam coffee cup.

Table 6.1 on page 139 summarizes these five types of body movements.

Body Appearance   Your general body appearance also communicates (Ehrlich, 2000). Height, for example, has been shown to be significant in a wide variety of situations. In the U.S., tall presidential candidates have a much better record of winning the election than do their shorter opponents. Tall people seem to be paid more and are

TABLE 6.1 Five Body Movements

Can you give at least one additional example of each of these five body movements?

	Name and Function	Examples
	EMBLEMS directly translate words or phrases	"Okay" sign, "come here" wave, hitchhiker's sign
	ILLUSTRATORS accompany and literally "illustrate" verbal messages	Circular hand movements when talking of a circle; hands far apart when talking of something large
	AFFECT DISPLAYS communicate emotional meaning	Expressions of happiness, surprise, fear, anger, sadness, disgust/contempt
	REGULATORS monitor, maintain, or control the speaking of another	Facial expressions and hand gestures indicating "keep going," "slow down," or "what else happened?"
	ADAPTORS satisfy some need	Scratching head

favoured by interviewers over shorter applicants (Keyes, 1980; DeVito & Hecht, 1990; Knapp & Hall, 1996; Harris, 2002).

Your body also reveals your race (through skin colour and tone) and may also give clues as to your more specific nationality. Your weight in proportion to your height will also communicate messages to others, as will the length, colour, and style of your hair.

Your general **attractiveness** is also a part of body communication. Attractive people have the advantage in just about every activity you can name (Horton, 2003). They get better grades in school, are more valued as friends and lovers, and are preferred as coworkers (Burgoon, Buller, & Woodall, 1995). Although we normally think that attractiveness is culturally determined—and to some degree it is—recent research seems to show that definitions of attractiveness are becoming universal (Brody, 1994; Chin & McConnel, 2003). A person rated as attractive in one culture is likely to be rated as attractive in other cultures, even in cultures whose people are widely different in appearance.

Facial Messages

Throughout your interpersonal interactions, your face communicates many things, especially your emotions. Facial movements alone seem to communicate the degree of pleasantness, agreement, and sympathy felt; the rest of the body doesn't provide any additional information. But for other emotional messages—for example, the intensity with which an emotion is felt—both facial and bodily cues are used (Graham, Bitti, & Argyle, 1975; Graham & Argyle, 1975).

Some researchers in nonverbal communication claim that facial movements may express at least the following eight emotions: happiness, surprise, fear, anger, sadness, disgust, contempt, and interest (Ekman, Friesen, & Ellsworth, 1972). Others propose that in addition, facial movements may also communicate bewilderment and determination (Leathers, 1997).

Try to express surprise using only facial movements. Do this in front of a mirror and try to describe in as much detail as possible the specific movements of the face that make up a look of surprise. If you signal surprise like most people, you probably use raised and curved eyebrows, long horizontal forehead wrinkles, wide-open eyes, a dropped-open mouth, and lips parted with no tension. Even if there were differences from one person to another—and clearly there would be—you probably could recognize the movements listed here as indicative of surprise.

Of course, some emotions are easier to communicate and to decode than others. For example, in one study, participants judged hap-

LISTEN TO THIS

Listening with Power

Much as you can communicate power and authority with words and nonverbal expression, you also communicate power nonverbally as you listen. Here are some suggestions for communicating power through listening:

- Respond visibly but in moderation; an occasional nod of agreement or a facial expression that says "That's interesting" is usually sufficient. Too little response says you aren't listening, but too much response says you aren't listening critically.

- Avoid adaptors such as playing with your hair or a pencil or drawing pictures on a Styrofoam cup. These signal that you're uncomfortable and hence that you lack power. Such body movements show you to be more concerned with yourself than with the person talking.

- Maintain an open posture. When standing or sitting around a table, resist covering your face, chest, or stomach with your hands. This type of posture is often interpreted as indicating defensiveness and may communicate a feeling of vulnerability and hence powerlessness.

- Avoid interrupting the speaker. The reason is simple: Not interrupting is one of the rules of business communication that powerful people follow and powerless people don't. Completing the speaker's thought (or what you think is the speaker's thought) has a similar effect of connoting powerlessness.

- You can also signal power through "visual dominance behaviour" (Exline, Ellyson, & Long, 1975). For example, the average speaker maintains a high level of eye contact while listening and a lower level while speaking. When you want to signal dominance, you might reverse this pattern—that is, maintain a high level of eye contact while talking but a much lower level while listening.

SUGGESTIONS?

Marco, normally an extremely expressive individual, is a new project director at a conservative advertising company. He wonders if he should curb his natural effusiveness while listening, say, at company meetings, or if he should be his regular self—violating many of the suggestions given above. What listening advice would you give Marco?

piness with 55 to 100 percent accuracy, surprise with 38 to 86 percent accuracy, and sadness with 19 to 88 percent accuracy (Ekman, Friesen, & Ellsworth, 1972). Research finds that women and girls are more accurate judges of facial emotional expression than men and boys (Argyle, 1988; Lewin, & Herlitz, 2002).

Facial Management   As you grew up, you learned your culture's nonverbal system of communication. You also learned certain **facial management techniques**; for example, to hide certain emotions and to emphasize others. Table 6.2 identifies four types of facial management techniques that you will quickly recognize (Malandro, Barker, & Barker, 1989).

We learn these facial management techniques along with display rules that tell us what emotions to express when; they're the rules of appropriateness. For example, when someone gets bad news in which you may secretly take pleasure, the display rule dictates that you frown and otherwise nonverbally signal your displeasure. If you violate these display rules, you will be judged insensitive.

Facial Feedback   The **facial feedback hypothesis** holds that your facial expressions influence physiological arousal (Lanzetta, Cartwright-Smith, & Kleck, 1976; Zuckerman, Klorman, Larrance, & Spiegel, 1981). In one study, for example, participants held a pen in their teeth to simulate a sad expression and then rated a series of photographs. Results showed that mimicking sad expressions actually increased the degree of sadness the participants reported feeling when viewing the photographs (Larsen, Kasimatis, & Frey, 1992).

Further support for this hypothesis comes from a study that compared participants who (1) felt emotions such as happiness and anger with those who (2) both felt and expressed these emotions. In support

> Without wearing any mask we are conscious of, we have a special face for each friend.
> **—Oliver Wendell Holmes**

TABLE 6.2 Facial Management Techniques

Can you identify a specific situation in which you or someone with whom you interacted used one of these techniques?

Technique	Function	Example
Intensifying	To exaggerate a feeling	Exaggerating surprise when friends throw you a party, to make your friends feel better
Deintensifying	To underplay a feeling	Covering up your own joy in the presence of a friend who didn't receive such good news
Neutralizing	To hide a feeling	Covering up your sadness so as not to depress others
Masking	To replace or substitute the expression of one emotion for another	Expressing happiness in order to cover up your disappointment at not receiving the gift you had expected

"Here's the artist's conception of your proposed smile."

of the facial feedback hypothesis, subjects who felt and expressed the emotions became emotionally aroused faster than did those who only felt the emotion (Hess, Kappas, McHugo, Lanzetta, et al., 1992).

Generally, research finds that facial expressions can produce or heighten feelings of sadness, fear, disgust, and anger. But this effect does not occur with all emotions; smiling, for example, doesn't seem to make us feel happier (Burgoon, Buller, & Woodall, 1995). This could be because smiling is not always associated with positive emotions. It is sometimes used in response to perceived social status, with those in power smiling less than their subordinates, and women smiling more than men regardless of their level of power (LaFrance, 2002). Further, it has not been demonstrated that facial expressions can eliminate one feeling and replace it with another. So if you're feeling sad, smiling will not eliminate the sadness and replace it with gladness. A reasonable conclusion seems to be that your facial expressions can influence some feelings but not all (Burgoon, Buller, & Woodall, 1995; Cappella, 1993).

Eye Messages

From Ben Jonson's poetic exhortation "Drink to me only with thine eyes, / And I will pledge with mine" to the scientific observations of modern researchers (Hess, 1975; Marshall, 1983), the eyes have long been regarded as the most important nonverbal message system. Recent research has also highlighted the importance of eyebrows in nonverbal communication, a finding with potential implication for the design of computerized facial recognition systems (Sadr, Jarudi & Sinha, 2003).

Research on communication via the eyes (a study known technically as oculesis) shows that these messages vary depending on the duration, direction, and quality of the eye behaviour. For example, in every culture there are strict, though unstated, rules for the proper duration for eye contact. In mainstream North American culture the average length of gaze is 2.95 seconds. The average length of mutual gaze (two persons gazing at each other) is 1.18 seconds (Argyle & Ingham, 1972; Argyle, 1988). When eye contact falls short of this amount, you may think the person is uninterested, shy, or preoccupied. When the appropriate amount of time is exceeded, you may perceive the person as showing unusually high interest.

The direction of the eye glance also communicates. Among many Canadians, you're expected to glance alternately at the other person's face, then away, then again at the face, and so on. The rule for the public speaker is to scan the entire audience, not focusing for too long on or ignoring any one area of the audience. When you break these directional rules, you communicate different meanings—abnormally high or low interest, self-consciousness, nervousness over the interaction, and so on. The quality of eye behaviour—how wide or how narrow your eyes get during interaction—also communicates meaning, especially interest level and such emotions as surprise, fear, and disgust.

Some intervention programs for children with autism attempt to increase eye contact to a rate of 50 percent of the time or better. However, one study found that while playing with games in small groups, typical 5- to 10-year-olds look at each other's faces, on average, less than 20 percent of the time. This suggests that while some eye contact is important in social interactions ... too much eye contact could make individuals stand out from their peers. During a typical conversation with a friend, what percentage of time do you think *you* spend making eye contact?

Source: **Bridges.** *Bringing Together Albertans on Developmental Disability,* **Spring 2001, p. 13.**

(An exercise, "Eye Contact," will help you explore some of the effects that eye contact and the lack of it have on interpersonal communication. See www.ablongman.com/devito.)

Eye Contact   With eye contact you send a variety of messages. One such message is a request for feedback. In talking with someone, we look at her or him intently, as if to say, "Well, what do you think?" As you might predict, listeners gaze at speakers more than speakers gaze at listeners. In public speaking, you may scan hundreds of people to secure this feedback.

Another type of message informs the other person that the channel of communication is open and that he or she should now speak. You see this regularly in conversation, when one person asks a question or finishes a thought and then looks to you for a response.

Eye contact may also send messages about the nature of the relationship. For example, if you engage in prolonged eye contact coupled with a smile, you'll signal a positive relationship. If you stare or glare at the person while frowning, you'll signal a negative relationship.

Eye contact messages enable you to psychologically lessen the physical distance between yourself and another person. When you catch someone's eye at a party, for example, you become psychologically close though physically far apart.

Eye Avoidance   The eyes are "great intruders," observed sociologist Erving Goffman (1967). When you avoid eye contact or avert your glance, you help others to maintain their privacy. You may do this when you see a couple arguing in public: You turn your eyes away (though your eyes may be wide open) as if to say, "I don't mean to intrude; I respect your privacy." Goffman refers to this behaviour as **civil inattention.**

Eye avoidance can also signal lack of interest—in a person, a conversation, or some visual stimulus. At times you may hide your eyes to block off unpleasant stimuli (a particularly gory or violent scene in a movie, for example) or close your eyes to block out visual stimuli and thus heighten other senses. For example, you may listen to music with your eyes closed. Lovers often close their eyes while kissing, and many prefer to make love in a dark or dimly lit room.

Space Messages

Your use of space to communicate—an area of study known technically as **proxemics**—speaks as surely and as loudly as words and sentences. Speakers who stand close to their listener, with their hands on the listener's shoulders and their eyes focused directly on those of the

In the fifteenth and sixteenth centuries in Italy, women put drops of belladonna (which literally means "beautiful woman") into their eyes to dilate the pupils so that they would look more attractive. Contemporary research supports the logic of these women; people judge dilated pupils as more attractive (Hess, 1975). Your pupils enlarge when you're interested in something or emotionally aroused; perhaps you judge dilated pupils as attractive because you perceive a person's dilated pupils as showing interest in you. More generally, Ekhard Hess (1975) has claimed that pupils dilate in response to positively evaluated attitudes and objects and constrict in response to negatively evaluated attitudes and objects. Do you find this generally true? In what other contexts would pupils dilate? Constrict?

listener, communicate something very different from speakers who stand in a corner with arms folded and eyes downcast. Similarly, for example, **territoriality**—the territory you occupy or own and the way you protect this territory—also communicates. The executive office suite on the top floor with huge windows, private bar, and plush carpeting communicates something totally different from the two-by-two-metre cubicle. There is some evidence that suggests men tend to display firmer boundaries around their territory, yet personalize this space less than women do (Kaya & Weber, 2003).

Spatial Distance Messages   Edward Hall (1959, 1966) distinguishes four distances that define the type of relationship between people and the type of communication in which they're likely to engage (see Table 6.3). In **intimate distance**, ranging from actual touching to 46 centimetres, the presence of the other individual is unmistakable. Each person experiences the sound, smell, and feel of the other's breath. You use intimate distance for lovemaking, comforting, and protecting. This distance is so short that most people do not consider it proper in public.

Personal distance refers to the protective "bubble" that defines your personal space, ranging from 46 centimetres to 1.2 metres. This imaginary bubble keeps you protected and untouched by others. You can still hold or grasp another person at this distance, but only by extending your arms; this allows you to take certain individuals such as loved ones into your protective bubble. At the outer limit of personal distance, you can touch another person only if both of you extend your arms. At this distance you conduct much of your interpersonal interactions; for example, talking with friends and family.

At **social distance**, ranging from 1.2 to 3.7 metres, you lose the visual detail you have at personal distance. You conduct impersonal business and interact at a social gathering at this social distance. The more distance you maintain in your interactions, the more formal they appear. In offices of high officials, the desks are positioned so that the official is assured of at least this distance from clients.

Public distance, from 3.6 to more than 7.6 metres, protects you. At this distance you could take defensive action if threatened. On a public bus or train, for example, you might try to keep at least this distance from a drunken passenger. Although at this distance you lose fine details of the face and eyes, you're still close enough to see what is happening.

Influences on Spatial Distances   Several factors influence the way you relate to and use space in communicating. Here are a few examples of how status, culture, subject matter, gender, and age influence space communication (Burgoon, Buller, & Woodall, 1995).

People of equal *status* maintain shorter distances between themselves than do people of unequal status. When status is unequal, the higher-status person may approach the lower-status person more closely than the lower-status person would approach the higher-status person.

Members of different *cultures* treat space differently. For example, those from northern European cultures and many Americans stand fairly far apart when conversing; those from southern European and Middle Eastern cultures tend to stand much closer. It's easy to see how

In judging whether someone likes you, what nonverbal cues should you look for? List them in the order of their importance, using 1 for the cue that is of most value to you as you make your judgment, 2 for the cue that is next most valuable, and so on down to perhaps 10 or 12. Do you really need two lists? One for judging a woman's liking and one for a man's?

TABLE 6.3 Relationships and Proxemic Distances

Note that these four distances can be further divided into close and far phases and that the far phase of one level (say, personal) blends into the close phase of the next level (social). Do your relationships also blend into one another? Or are, say, your personal relationships totally separated from your social relationships?

Relationship		Distance
	Intimate Relationship	Intimate Distance 0 —————————— 46 centimetres close phase ⠀⠀⠀⠀⠀⠀ far phase
	Personal Relationship	Personal Distance 46 centimetres —————————— 1.2 metres close phase ⠀⠀⠀⠀⠀⠀ far phase
	Social Relationship	Social Distance 1.2 —————————— 3.6 metres close phase ⠀⠀⠀⠀⠀⠀ far phase
	Public Relationship	Public Distance 3.6 —————————— 7.6 + metres close phase ⠀⠀⠀⠀⠀⠀ far phase

those who normally stand far apart may interpret the close distances of others as pushy and overly intimate. It's equally easy to appreciate how those who normally stand close may interpret the far distances of others as cold and unfriendly.

When discussing personal *subjects* you maintain shorter distances than with impersonal subjects. Also, you stand closer to someone who is praising you than to someone criticizing you.

Your *gender* also influences your spatial relationships. Women generally stand closer to each other than men. Similarly, when someone approaches another person, he or she will come closer to a woman than to a man. With increasing *age* there is a tendency for the spaces to become larger. Children stand much closer than do adults. These findings provide some evidence that these distances are learned behaviours.

(You may wish to pursue this topic with the exercise "Interpersonal Interactions and Space," which helps identify some of the factors influencing our spatial behaviour. See www.ablongman.com/devito.)

Territoriality Messages Territoriality, a term from ethology (the study of animals in their natural habitat), is an ownership-like reaction toward a particular space or object. The size and location of human territories also say something about **status**. An apartment or office in midtown Manhattan or downtown Tokyo is extremely high-status territory since the cost restricts it to the wealthy.

Status is also indicated by the unwritten law granting the right of invasion. In some cultures and in some organizations, for example, higher-status individuals have more of a right to invade the territory of others than vice versa. The president of a large company can invade the territory of a junior executive by barging into her or his office, but the reverse would be unthinkable.

Like animals, humans also mark their territory (Hickson & Stacks, 1993). For example, you might place an item of clothing or a book at a table in the cafeteria to claim this seat as your territory. Or you might have initials on your briefcase. Other types of **markers** are used to separate one territory from another; for example, the bar used at the supermarket checkout to separate your groceries from those of the person behind you or the armrest used in a theatre to separate your seat from those next to you.

Artifactual Messages

Artifactual messages are those made by human hands. Thus, colour, clothing, jewellery, and the decoration of space would be considered artifactual. Let's look at each of these briefly.

"Never let her catch you in her garden...
Humans are very territorial."

© 2001. Reprinted courtesy of Bunny Hoest and *Parade* magazine.

Colour   There is some evidence that colours affect us physiologically. For example, respiratory movements increase with red light and decrease with blue light. Similarly, eye blinks increase in frequency when eyes are exposed to red light and decrease when exposed to blue. This seems consistent with our intuitive feelings that blue is more soothing and red more arousing. When a school changed the colour of its walls from orange and white to blue, the blood pressure of the students decreased and their academic performance increased (Malandro, Barker, & Barker, 1989).

Colour communication also influences perceptions and behaviours (Kanner, 1989). People's acceptance of a product, for example, can be largely determined by its packaging, especially its colour. In one study the very same coffee taken from a yellow can was described as weak, from a dark brown can as too strong, from a red can as rich, and from a blue can as mild. Even your acceptance of a person may depend on the colours worn. Consider, for example, the comments of one colour expert (Kanner, 1989): "If you have to pick the wardrobe for your defense lawyer heading into court and choose anything but blue, you deserve to lose the case...." Black is so powerful it could work against the lawyer with the jury. Brown lacks sufficient authority. Green would probably elicit a negative response. Recent research, however, suggests that our responses to colour may be more complex than what was previously thought, and may depend on such factors such as our education and our knowledge about the world (Jacobsen, 2003).

Clothing and Body Adornment   People make inferences about who you are, at least in part, from the way you dress. Whether these inferences are accurate or not, they will influence what people think of you and how they react to you. Your socioeconomic class, your seriousness, your attitudes (for example, whether you're conservative or liberal), your concern for convention, your sense of style, and perhaps even your creativity will all be judged in part by the way you dress (Molloy, 1977; Burgoon, Buller, & Woodall, 1995; Knapp & Hall, 1996). Similarly, college students will perceive an instructor dressed informally as friendly, fair, enthusiastic, and flexible and the same instructor dressed formally as prepared, knowledgeable, and organized (Malandro, Barker, & Barker, 1989).

The way you wear your hair also communicates about aspects of who you are—from a concern about being up to date, to a desire to shock, to perhaps a lack of interest in appearances. Men with long hair will generally be judged as less conservative than those with shorter hair. Your jewellery, too, sends messages about you. Some jewellery is a form of **cultural display**, indicating a particular cultural or religious affiliation. Wedding and engagement rings are obvious examples that communicate specific messages. College rings and political buttons likewise convey specific messages. If you wear a Rolex watch or large precious stones, others are likely to infer that you're rich. Men who wear earrings will be judged differently from men who don't. What judgments are made will depend, of course, on who the receiver is, the communication context, and all the factors identified throughout this text.

Space Decoration   The way you decorate your private spaces speaks about you. The office with mahogany desk and bookcases and oriental rugs communicates your importance and status within the organization, just as a metal desk and bare floor indicate a worker much farther down in the hierarchy.

Similarly, people will make inferences about you based on the way you decorate your home. The expensiveness of the furnishings may communicate your status and wealth; their coordination, your sense of style. The magazines you choose may reflect your interests, and the

A popular tactic of American defence lawyers in sex crimes against women, gay men, and lesbians is to blame the victim by, among other things, implying that the way the victim was dressed provoked the attack. New York and Florida prohibit defence attorneys from referring to the way a sex-crime victim was dressed at the time of the attack (*New York Times*, July 30, 1994, p. 22). What do you think of this?

What inferences would you make about the owner of this home solely on the basis of what appears in this photo?

arrangement of chairs around a television set may reveal how important watching television is to you. The contents of bookcases lining the walls reveal the importance of reading in your life. Even the food and beverages you serve or display in your home can send out messages about your lifestyle and priorities (Bourque, 2001). In fact, there is probably little in your home that would not send messages from which others would draw inferences about you. Computers, widescreen televisions, well-equipped kitchens, and oil paintings of great grandparents, for example, all say something about the people who live in the home.

Similarly, the absence of certain items will communicate something about you. Consider what messages you would get from a home where no television, phone, or books could be seen.

Touch Messages

Touch communication, or **tactile communication**, is perhaps the most primitive form of communication (Montagu, 1971). Touch develops before the other senses; even in the womb the child is stimulated by touch. Soon after birth the child is fondled, caressed, patted, and stroked. In turn, the child explores his or her world through touch and quickly learns to communicate a variety of meanings through touch.

The Meanings of Touch   Researchers in the field of **haptics**—the study of touch—have identified the major meanings of touch (Jones & Yarbrough, 1985; Jones, 1999):

- *Positive emotion.* Touch may communicate such positive feelings as support, appreciation, inclusion, sexual interest or intent, and affection.

- *Playfulness.* Touch often communicates our intention to play, either affectionately or aggressively.

- *Control.* Touch may direct the behaviours, attitudes, or feelings of the other person. To get attention, for example, you may touch a person as if to say, "Look at me" or "Look over here."

- *Ritual.* Ritualistic touching centres on greetings and departures; for example, shaking hands to say hello or goodbye or hugging, kissing, or putting your arm around another's shoulder when greeting or saying farewell.

- *Task-relatedness.* Task-related touching occurs while you're performing some function, such as removing a speck of dust from another person's face or helping someone out of a car.

Do recognize that different cultures will view these types of touching differently. For example, some task-related touching, viewed as acceptable in much of North America, would be viewed negatively in some cultures. Among Koreans, for example, it's considered disrespectful for a storekeeper to touch a customer in, say, handing back change; it's considered too intimate a gesture. But members of other cultures, expecting some touching, may consider the Koreans' behaviour cold and insulting.

"There is a very simple rule about touching," the manager continued. "*When you touch, don't take.* Touch the people you manage only when you are *giving* them something—reassurance, support, encouragement, whatever.

—Kenneth Blanchard and Spencer Johnson

Touch Avoidance   Much as we touch and are touched, we also avoid touch from certain people and in certain circumstances. Researchers in nonverbal communication have found some interesting relationships between **touch avoidance** and other significant communication variables (Andersen & Leibowitz, 1978; Hall, 1996).

Among research findings, for example, is the fact that touch avoidance is positively related to communication apprehension; those who fear oral communication also score high on touch avoidance. Touch avoidance is also high with those who self-disclose little. Both touch and self-disclosure are intimate forms of communication; thus, people who are reluctant to get close to another person by self-disclosing also seem reluctant to get close by touching.

Older people have higher touch-avoidance scores for opposite-sex persons than do younger people. As we get older we're touched less by members of the opposite sex, and this decreased frequency may lead us to avoid touching.

Males score higher on same-sex touch avoidance than do females, a finding that confirms popular stereotypes. Men avoid touching other men, but women may and do touch other women. On the other hand, women have higher touch-avoidance scores for opposite-sex touching than do men.

Today, there is growing recognition in Canada that touching can be highly disrespectful. Employers, for example, are much more careful not to touch their employees, as are college instructors with their students.

Paralanguage Messages

The term **paralanguage** refers to the vocal but nonverbal dimensions of speech. It refers to how you say something, not what you say. A traditional exercise students use to increase their ability to express different emotions, feelings, and attitudes is to repeat a sentence while accenting or stressing different words. One popular sentence is, "Is this the face that launched a thousand ships?" Significant differences in meaning are easily communicated depending on where the speaker places the stress. Consider the following variations:

How would you describe the rules of touch avoidance for passengers on a commuter train? For students at a football stadium? For members of your family at dinner?

1. *Is* this the face that launched a thousand ships?
2. Is *this* the face that launched a thousand ships?
3. Is this *the face* that launched a thousand ships?
4. Is this the face *that launched* a thousand ships?
5. Is this the face that launched *a thousand ships?*

Each sentence communicates something different; in fact, each asks a different question, although the words are the same. All that distinguishes the sentences is stress, one aspect of paralanguage. (An exercise, "Praising and Criticizing," focuses on how the same words may communicate drastically different meanings when the paralanguage features are varied. See www.ablongman.com/devito.)

In addition to stress and **pitch** (highness or lowness), paralanguage includes such **voice qualities** or vocal characteristics as **rate** (speed), **volume** (loudness), and rhythm as well as the vocalizations you make in crying, whispering, moaning, belching, yawning, and yelling (Trager, 1958, 1961; Argyle, 1988). A variation in any of these features communicates. When you speak quickly, for example, you communicate something different from when you speak slowly. Even though the words may be the same, if the speed (or volume, rhythm, or pitch) differs, the meanings people receive will also differ.

Judgments About People   Paralanguage cues are often used as a basis for judgments about people; for example, evaluations of their emotional state or even their personality. A listener can accurately judge the emotional state of a speaker from vocal expression alone, if both speaker and listener speak the same language. Paralanguage cues are not so accurate when used to communicate emotions to those who speak a different language (Albas, McCluskey, & Albas, 1976). In studies in this field, speakers recite the alphabet or numbers while expressing emotions. Some emotions are easier to identify than others; it's easy to distinguish between hate and sympathy but more difficult to distinguish between fear and anxiety. And, of course, listeners vary in their ability to decode, and speakers in their ability to encode emotions (Scherer, 1986).

Less reliable are judgments made about personality. Some people, for example, may conclude that those who speak softly feel inferior, believing that no one wants to listen and nothing they say is significant, or that people who speak loudly have overinflated egos and think everyone in the world wants to hear them.

(An exercise, "Who?" enables the entire class to explore some of the nonverbal cues members used in forming impressions of each other. See www.ablongman.com/devito.)

Silence Messages

Like words and gestures, **silence**, too, communicates important meanings and serves important functions (Johannesen, 1974; Jaworski, 1993; Kim & Markus, 2001). Silence allows the speaker *time to think,* time to formulate and organize his or her verbal communications. Before messages of intense conflict, as well as before those confessing undying love, there is often silence. Again, silence seems to prepare the receiver for the importance of these messages.

Some people use silence as a *weapon* to hurt others. We often speak of giving someone "the silent treatment." After a conflict, for example, one or both individuals may remain silent as a kind of punishment. Silence used to hurt others may also take the form of refusal to acknowledge the presence of another person, as in disconfirmation (see Chapter 5); here silence is a dramatic demonstration of the total indifference one person feels toward the other.

Sometimes silence is used as a *response to personal anxiety,* shyness, or threats. You may feel anxious or shy among new people and prefer to remain silent. By remaining silent you preclude the chance of rejection. Only when you break your silence and make an attempt to communicate with another person do you risk rejection.

Might drawing conclusions (rather than hypotheses) about personality from people's nonverbal behaviours prevent you from seeking further information and hinder you from seeing evidence contrary to your conclusion? Have you ever drawn conclusions about another person and then acted as if these conclusions were accurate when they weren't? Has anyone ever drawn conclusions in this way about you?

Speaking is silver, silence is gold.
—**German proverb**

Silence may be used *to prevent communication* of certain messages. In conflict situations silence is sometimes used to prevent certain topics from surfacing and to prevent one or both parties from saying things they may later regret. In such situations silence often allows us time to cool off before expressing hatred, severe criticism, or personal attacks— which, as we know, are irreversible.

Like the eyes, face, or hands, silence can also be used *to communicate emotional responses* (Ehrenhaus, 1988). Sometimes silence communicates a determination to be uncooperative or defiant; by refusing to engage in verbal communication, you defy the authority or the legitimacy of the other person's position. Silence is often used to communicate annoyance, particularly when accompanied by a pouting expression, arms crossed in front of the chest, and nostrils flared. Silence may express affection or love, especially when coupled with long and longing gazes into each other's eyes.

Of course, you may also use silence when you simply have *nothing to say*, when nothing occurs to you, or when you don't want to say anything. James Russell Lowell expressed this best: "Blessed are they who have nothing to say, and who cannot be persuaded to say it." Silence may also be used to avoid responsibility for wrongdoing (Beach, 1990–1991).

Time Messages

The study of **temporal communication**, known technically as **chronemics**, concerns the use of time—how you organize it, react to it, and communicate messages through it (Bruneau, 1990; Harris, 2002). Consider, for example, **psychological time**: the emphasis you place on the past, pre-

> Seize the day, and put the least possible trust in tomorrow.
>
> **—Horace**

TALKING ETHICS

Interpersonal Silence

Often, but not always, you have the right to remain silent. You have a right to preserve your privacy and to withhold information that has no bearing on the matter at hand. In most job-related situations your previous relationship history, affectional orientation, or religion is usually irrelevant to your ability to function—as, for example, a doctor or police officer—and may thus be kept private. If these issues become relevant—say, if you're about to enter a new relationship—then there *may be* an obligation to reveal information such as your relationship history, affectional orientation, or religion.

In a court, of course, you have the right to refuse to incriminate yourself: to reveal information about yourself that could be used against you. But you don't have the right to refuse to reveal information about the criminal activities of others, although in some situations psychiatrists, clergy, and lawyers may be exempt from this general rule.

WHAT WOULD YOU DO?

As you walk by a house, you witness a mother shaking and hitting her two- or three-year-old child in the backyard. You worry that the mother might harm the child, and your first impulse is to report the incident to the police. At the same time, you don't want to interfere with a mother's right to discipline her child, nor to make trouble for someone who may be an excellent parent generally but is perhaps having a particularly bad time today. What is your ethical obligation in this case? What would you do in this situation?

sent, and future. In a past orientation, you have special reverence for the past. You relive old times and regard the old methods as the best. You see events as circular and recurring, so the wisdom of yesterday is applicable also to today and tomorrow. In a present orientation, however, you live in the present: for now, not tomorrow. In a future orientation, you look toward and live for the future. You save today, work hard in college, and deny yourself luxuries because you're preparing for the future. Before reading more about time, take the self-test below.

TEST YOURSELF

What Time Do You Have?

Instructions: For each statement, indicate whether the statement is true (T) or untrue (F) of your general attitude and behaviour.

_____ 1. Meeting tomorrow's deadlines and doing other necessary work comes before tonight's partying.

_____ 2. I meet my obligations to friends and authorities on time.

_____ 3. I complete projects on time by making steady progress.

_____ 4. I am able to resist temptations when I know there is work to be done.

_____ 5. I keep working at a difficult, uninteresting task if it will help me get ahead.

_____ 6. If things don't get done on time, I don't worry about it.

_____ 7. I think it's useless to plan too far ahead because things hardly ever come out the way you planned anyway.

_____ 8. I try to live one day at a time.

_____ 9. I live to make better what is rather than to be concerned about what will be.

_____ 10. It seems to me that it doesn't make sense to worry about the future, since fate determines that whatever will be, will be.

_____ 11. I believe that getting together with friends to party is one of life's important pleasures.

_____ 12. I do things impulsively, making decisions on the spur of the moment.

_____ 13. I take risks to put excitement in my life.

_____ 14. I get drunk at parties.

_____ 15. It's fun to gamble.

_____ 16. Thinking about the future is pleasant to me.

_____ 17. When I want to achieve something, I set subgoals and consider specific means for reaching those goals.

_____ 18. It seems to me that my career path is pretty well laid out.

_____ 19. It upsets me to be late for appointments.

_____ 20. I meet my obligations to friends and authorities on time.

_____ 21. I get irritated at people who keep me waiting when we've agreed to meet at a given time.

_____ 22. It makes sense to invest a substantial part of my income in insurance premiums.

_____ 23. I believe that "A stitch in time saves nine."

_____ 24. I believe that "A bird in the hand is worth two in the bush."

_____ 25. I believe it is important to save for a rainy day.

_____ 26. I believe a person's day should be planned each morning.

_____ 27. I make lists of things I must do.

_____ 28. When I want to achieve something, I set subgoals and consider specific means for reaching those goals.

HOW DID YOU DO?

This time test measures seven different factors. If you selected true (T) for all or most of the questions within any given factor, you're high on that factor. If you selected untrue (F) for all or most of the questions within any given factor, you're low on that factor.

The first factor, measured by questions 1–5, is a future, work motivation, perseverance orientation. These people have a strong work ethic and are committed to completing a task despite difficulties. The second factor (questions 6–10) is a present, fatalistic, worry-free orientation. High scorers on this factor live one day at a time, not necessarily to enjoy the day but to avoid planning for the next day.

The third factor (questions 11–15) is a present, pleasure-seeking, partying orientation. These people enjoy the present, take risks, and engage in a variety of impulsive actions. The fourth factor (questions 16–18) is a future, goal-seeking, and planning orientation. These people derive pleasure from planning and achieving a variety of goals.

The fifth factor (questions 19–21) is a time-sensitivity orientation. People who score high are especially sensitive to time and its role in social obligations. The sixth factor (questions 22–25) is a future, practical action orientation. These people do what they have to do—take practical actions—to achieve the future they want.

The seventh factor (questions 26–28) is a future, somewhat obsessive daily planning orientation. High scorers make daily "to do" lists and devote great attention to detail.

WHAT WILL YOU DO?

Now that you have some idea of how you treat time, consider how these attitudes and behaviours work for you. For example, will your time orientations help you achieve your social and professional goals? If not, what might you do about changing these attitudes and behaviours?

Source: From "Time in Perspective" by Alexander Gonzalez and Philip G. Zimbardo. Reprinted with permission from _Psychology Today_ magazine. Copyright © 1985 (Sussex Publishers, Inc.).

The time orientation you develop depends to a great extent on your socioeconomic class and your personal experiences. Gonzalez and Zimbardo (1985), who developed the scale in the time self-test and upon whose research the scoring is based, observe: "A child with parents in unskilled and semiskilled occupations is usually socialized in a way that promotes a present-oriented fatalism and hedonism. A child of parents who are managers, teachers, or other professionals learns future-oriented values and strategies designed to promote achievement." In North America, not surprisingly, future income is positively related to future orientation; the more future oriented you are, the greater your income is likely to be.

Different time perspectives also account for much intercultural misunderstanding, as different cultures often teach their members drastically different time orientations. For example, people from some Latin cultures would rather be late for an appointment than end a conversation abruptly or before it has come to a natural end. So the Latin may see lateness as a result of politeness. But others may see this as impolite to the person with whom he or she had the appointment (Hall & Hall, 1987).

Similarly, the future-oriented person who works for tomorrow's goals will frequently look down on the present-oriented person as lazy and poorly motivated for enjoying today and not planning for tomorrow. In turn, the present-oriented person may see those with strong future orientations as obsessed with amassing wealth or rising in status.

(Another time-related topic is the theory of biorhythms: the idea that our bodies operate on physical, intellectual, and emotional time cycles, each of which lasts for different periods of time. An interesting website that enables you to figure out your own biorhythms may be found at **www.kfu.com/~nsayer/compat.html**.)

Those who live to the future must always appear selfish to those who live to the present.

—**Ralph Waldo Emerson**

Smell Messages

Smell communication, or **olfactory communication**, is extremely important in a wide variety of situations and is now big business today (Kleinfeld, 1992). For example, there is some evidence (though clearly not very conclusive evidence) that the smell of lemon contributes to a perception of heath, the smells of lavender and eucalyptus seem to increase alertness, and the smell of rose oil seems to reduce blood pressure. Findings such as these have contributed to the growth of aromatherapy and the profession of aromatherapists (Furlow, 1996). Because humans possess "denser skin concentrations of scent glands than almost any other mammal," it has been argued that it only remains for us to discover how we use scent to communicate a wide variety of messages (Furlow, 1996, p. 41). Here are some of the most important messages scent seems to communicate.

- *Attraction messages.* Humans use perfumes, colognes, aftershave lotions, powders, and the like to enhance their attractiveness to others and to themselves. After all, you also smell yourself. When the smells are pleasant, you feel better about yourself.

- *Taste messages.* Without smell, taste would be severely impaired. For example, without smell it would be extremely difficult to taste the difference between a raw potato and an apple. Street vendors selling hot dogs, sausages, and similar foods are aided greatly by the smells, which stimulate the appetites of passersby.

- *Memory messages.* Smell is a powerful memory aid; you often recall situations from months and even years ago when you happen upon a similar smell.

- *Identification messages.* Smell is often used to create an image or an identity for a product. Advertisers and manufacturers spend millions of dollars each year creating scents for cleaning products and toothpastes, for example. These scents have nothing to do with the products' cleaning power; instead, they function solely to help create an image. There is also evidence that we can identify specific significant others by smell. For example, young children were able to identify the T-shirts of their brothers and sisters solely on the basis of smell (Porter & Moore, 1981). And one researcher goes so far as to advise: "If your man's odor reminds you of Dad or your brother, you may want genetic tests before trying to conceive a child" (Furlow, 1996, p. 41).

Culture and Nonverbal Messages

Not surprisingly, nonverbal communication is heavily influenced by culture. Consider a variety of differences. At the sight of unpleasant pictures, members of some cultures (Canadian and European, for example) will facially express disgust. Members of other cultures (Japanese, for example) will avoid facially expressing disgust (Ekman, 1985b; Matsumoto, 1991).

Although Canadians consider direct eye contact an expression of honesty and forthrightness, the Japanese often view this as a lack of respect. The Japanese will glance at the other person's face rarely and

SKILLS TOOLBOX

6 Ways to Nonverbal Power at Work

Your nonverbal communication skills greatly influence the interpersonal power you're seen to have on the job and just about anywhere else. Here are some suggestions for communicating power nonverbally (Lewis, 1989; Burgoon, Buller, & Woodall, 1995).

1. Other things being equal, dress relatively conservatively if you want to influence others; conservative clothing is associated with power and status. This is doubly true if you're working at a generally conservative office or if you're responsible for meeting clients.

2. Use facial expressions and gestures as appropriate; these help you express your concern for the other person and for the interaction.

3. When you break eye contact, direct your gaze downward; otherwise you'll signal a lack of interest in the other person.

4. Use consistent packaging; that is, be especially careful that your verbal and nonverbal messages don't contradict each other—the principle of congruence.

5. To communicate dominance with your handshake, exert more pressure than usual and hold the grip a bit longer than normal.

6. Walk slowly and deliberately. To appear hurried is to appear to be without power, as if you were rushing to meet the expectations of a supervisor who had power over you.

THEN AND NOW

Have you ever been in a situation where you wanted to communicate power but for some reason failed to do so? Why do you think you failed? What might you do differently now?

then only for very short periods (Axtell, 1990). Among some Latin Americans and American Indians, direct eye contact between, say, a teacher and a student is considered inappropriate, perhaps aggressive; appropriate student behaviour is to avoid eye contact with the teacher. Table 6.4 on this page presents a variety of other nonverbal signals, identified by Axtell (1993), that can get you into trouble if used in certain cultures.

In North America, living next door to someone means that you're expected to be friendly and to interact with that person. This cultural expectation seems so natural that Canadians and members of many other cultures probably don't even consider that it is not shared by all cultures. In Japan, the fact that your house is next to another's does not imply that you should become close or visit each other. Consider, therefore, the situation in which a Japanese person buys a house next to a Canadian. The Japanese may see the Canadian as overly familiar and as taking friendship for granted. The Canadian may see the Japanese as distant, unfriendly, and unneighbourly. Yet each person is merely fulfilling the expectations of his or her own culture (Hall & Hall, 1987).

Different cultures also assign different meanings to colours. Some of these cultural meanings are listed in Table 6.5—but before looking at the table, think about the meanings your own culture gives to such colours as red, green, black, white, blue, yellow, and purple.

Another aspect of artifactual communication that varies greatly from one culture to another is the meaning that gifts have. In some cultures a set of knives for the kitchen would be an appropriate house gift;

A "Pygmalion gift" is a gift that is designed to change the recipient into what the donor wants him or her to become. The parent who gives a child books or science equipment may be asking the child to be a scholar. What messages have you recently communicated in your gift-giving behaviour? What messages do you think others have communicated to you by gifts they gave you?

TABLE 6.4 A Few Nonverbal Behaviours That Can Get You into Trouble

Can you identify other behaviours that can create cultural problems?

Communication Behaviour	May Be Considered
Blinking your eyes	impolite in Taiwan
Folding your arms over your chest	disrespectful in Fiji
Waving your hand	insulting in Nigeria and Greece
Gesturing with the thumb up	rude in Australia
Tapping your two index fingers together	an invitation to sleep together in Egypt
Pointing with the index finger	impolite in many Middle Eastern countries
Bowing to a lesser degree than your host	a statement of superiority in Japan
With a clenched fist, inserting your thumb between your index and middle finger	obscene in some southern European countries
Pointing at someone with your index and third fingers	a wish that evil fall on the person in some African countries
Resting your feet on a table or chair	insulting in some Middle Eastern countries

How many of the cultural differences in nonverbal signals discussed here have you witnessed? Have you seen cultural differences not discussed here?

TABLE 6.5 Some Cultural Meanings of Colour

This table, constructed from research reported by Henry Dreyfuss (1971), Nancy Hoft (1995), and Norine Dresser (1996), illustrates only some of the different meanings that colours may communicate in different cultures. As you read this table, consider the meanings you give to these colours and where your meanings came from.

Colour	Cultural Meanings and Comments
Red	In China, red signifies prosperity and rebirth and is used for festive and joyous occasions; in France and the United Kingdom, it signifies masculinity; in many African countries, blasphemy or death; and in Japan, anger and danger. Koreans, especially Korean Buddhists, use red ink only to write a person's name at the time of death or on the anniversary of the person's death; this creates lots of problems when Canadian teachers use red ink to mark homework.
Green	In North America, green signifies capitalism, "go ahead," and envy; in Ireland, patriotism; among some Native Americans, femininity; to the Egyptians, fertility and strength; and to the Japanese, youth and energy.
Black	In Thailand, black signifies old age, in parts of Malaysia courage, and in much of Europe death.
White	In Thailand, white signifies purity; in many Muslim and Hindu cultures, purity and peace; but in Japan and other Asian countries, death and mourning.
Blue	In Iran, blue signifies something negative, in Egypt truth, and in Ghana joy; among the Cherokee it signifies defeat, and for Egyptians virtue and truth.
Yellow	In China, yellow signifies wealth and authority, in North America caution and cowardice, in Egypt happiness and prosperity; and in many countries throughout the world, femininity.
Purple	In Latin America, purple signifies death, in Europe royalty, in Egypt virtue and faith, in Japan grace and nobility, and in China barbarism.

in other cultures (for example, Chinese) it would be considered inappropriate and offensive. (An exercise, "Artifacts and Culture: The Case of Gifts," will help you explore this aspect of nonverbal communication; it may be found at www.ablongman.com/devito.)

Touching, too, varies greatly across cultures. For example, African Americans touch one another more than do whites. Similarly, touching declines from kindergarten to grade 6 for white but not for African American children (Burgoon, Buller, & Woodall, 1995). Similarly, Japanese touch one another much less than do Anglo-Saxons, who in turn touch one another much less than do southern Europeans (Morris, 1977; Burgoon, Buller, & Woodall, 1995).

Not surprisingly, the role of silence is seen differently in different cultures (Basso, 1972). Among the Apache, for example, mutual friends do not feel the need to introduce strangers who may be working in the same area or on the same project. The strangers may remain silent for several days. During this time the individuals look each other over, trying to determine if the other person is all right. Only after this period do the individuals talk. When courting, especially during the initial stages, the Apache remain silent for hours; if they do talk, they generally talk very little. Only after a couple has been dating for several months will they have lengthy conversations. These periods of silence are generally attributed to shyness or self-consciousness. But the use of silence is explicitly taught to Apache women, who are especially discouraged from engaging in long discussions with their dates. Silence during courtship is a sign of modesty to many Apache.

In Iranian culture there's an expression, *qahr*, which means not being on speaking terms with someone, giving someone the silent treatment. For example, when children disobey their parents, or are disrespectful, or fail to do their chores as they should, they are given this silent treatment. With adults *qahr* may be instituted when one person insults or injures another. After a cooling-off period, *ashti* (making up after *qahr*) may be initiated. *Qahr* lasts for a relatively short time when between parents and children but longer when between adults. *Qahr* is more frequently initiated between two women than between two men, but when men experience *qahr* it lasts much longer and often requires the intercession of a mediator to establish *ashti* (Behzadi, 1994).

Time is another communication channel with great cultural differences. Two types of cultural time are especially important in nonverbal communication: formal and informal. In North American culture, *formal time* is divided into seconds, minutes, hours, days, weeks, months, and years. Other cultures may use seasons or phases of the moon to delineate time periods. In some colleges, courses are divided into 50- or 75-minute periods that meet two or three times a week for 14-week periods called semesters; eight semesters of 15 or 16 50-minute periods per week equal a college education. Other colleges use quarters or trimesters. As these examples illustrate, formal time units are arbitrary. The culture establishes them for convenience.

Informal time terms are more general—for example, expressions such as "forever," "immediately," "soon," "right away," "as soon as possible." Informal time creates the most communication problems, because the terms have different meanings for different people.

Another interesting distinction is that between **monochronic** and **polychronic time orientations** (Hall, 1959, 1976; Hall & Hall, 1987). Monochronic people or cultures (Canada, the United States, Germany, Scandinavia, and Switzerland are good examples) schedule one thing at a time. Time is compartmentalized; there is a time for everything, and everything has its own time. Polychronic people or cultures (Latin Americans, Mediterranean people, and Arabs are good examples), on the other hand, schedule multiple things at the same time. Eating, conducting business with several different people, and taking care of family matters may all be conducted at the same time. No culture is entirely monochronic or polychronic; rather, these are general tendencies that are found across a large part of the culture. Some cultures combine both time orientations; Japanese culture is an example in which both orientations are found. Table 6.6, based on Hall and Hall (1987), identifies some of the distinctions between these two time orientations.

Attitudes toward time vary from one culture to another. One study, for example, measured the accuracy of clocks in six cultures—Japan, Indonesia, Italy, England, Taiwan, and the United States. Japan had the most accurate clocks, Indonesia the least accurate. And a measure of the speed at which people in these six cultures walked found that the Japanese walked the fastest, the Indonesians the slowest (LeVine & Bartlett, 1984).

Another interesting aspect of **cultural time** is your "social clock" (Neugarten, 1979). Your culture, as well as your more specific society, maintains a schedule for the right time to do a variety of important things; for example, the right time to start dating, to finish college, to buy your own home, to have a child. You may well tend to evaluate your own social and professional development on the basis of this social clock. If you're on

This photo was taken at a ceremony celebrating the collaboration between Correctional Services Canada and the Beardy's/Okemasis First Nation in promoting culturally sensitive support for Aboriginal offenders. How do the nonverbal messages depicted here support the themes of collaboration and celebration?

TABLE 6.6 Monochronic and Polychronic Time

Can you identify specific potentials for miscommunication that these differences might create when M-time and P-time people interact?

The Monochronic Person	The Polychronic Person
Does one thing at a time	Does several things at one time
Treats time schedules and plans very seriously; they may be broken only for the most serious of reasons	Treats time schedules and plans as useful, but not sacred; they may be broken for a variety of causes
Considers the job the most important part of life, ahead of even family	Considers the family and interpersonal relationships more important than the job
Considers privacy extremely important; seldom borrows or lends to others; works independently	Is actively involved with others; works in the presence of and with lots of people at the same time

time relative to the rest of your peers—for example, if you all started dating at around the same age or you're all finishing college at around the same age—then you will feel well adjusted, competent, and a part of the group. If you're late, you will probably experience feelings of dissatisfaction. Recent research, however, shows that this social clock is becoming more flexible; people are becoming more willing to tolerate deviations from the established, socially acceptable timetable for accomplishing many of life's transitional events (Peterson, 1996).

SUMMARY OF CONCEPTS AND SKILLS

In this chapter we explored nonverbal communication—communication without words—and considered such areas as body movements, facial and eye movements, spatial and territorial communication, artifactual communication, touch communication, paralanguage, silence, and time communication.

1. The five body movements are emblems (nonverbal behaviours that rather directly translate words or phrases); illustrators (nonverbal behaviours that accompany and literally "illustrate" the verbal messages); affect displays (nonverbal behaviours that communicate emotional meaning); regulators (nonverbal behaviours that coordinate, monitor, maintain, or control the speaking of another individual); and adaptors (nonverbal behaviours that usually serve some kind of need, as in scratching an itch).

2. Facial movements may communicate a variety of emotions. The most frequently studied are happiness, surprise, fear, anger, sadness, and disgust/contempt. Facial management techniques enable you to control revealing the emotions you feel.

3. The facial feedback hypothesis claims that facial display of an emotion can lead to physiological and psychological changes.

4. Eye movements may seek feedback, signal to others to speak, signal the nature of a relationship, and compensate for increased physical distance.

5. Pupil size shows one's interest and level of emotional arousal. Pupils enlarge when one is interested in something or is emotionally aroused in a positive way.

6. Proxemics is the study of the communicative function of space and spatial relationships. Four important proxemic distances are: (1) intimate distance, ranging from actual touching to 46 centimetres; (2) personal distance, ranging from 46 centimetres to 1.2 metres; (3) social distance, ranging from 1.2 to 3.6 metres; and (4) public distance, ranging from 3.6 to more than 7.6 metres.

7. Your treatment of space is influenced by such factors as status, culture, context, subject matter, sex, age, and positive or negative evaluation of the other person.

8. Territoriality has to do with your possessive reaction to an area of space or to particular objects.

9. Artifactual communication consists of messages that are human-made; for example, messages conveyed by colour, clothing and body adornment, or space decoration.

10. Touch (or haptics) may communicate a variety of meanings, the most important being positive affect, playfulness, control, ritual, and task-relatedness. Touch avoidance is the desire to avoid touching and being touched by others.

11. Paralanguage consists of the vocal but nonverbal dimensions of speech. It includes rate, pitch, volume, resonance, and vocal quality as well as pauses and hesitations. Based on paralanguage we make judgments about people and their communication effectiveness.

12. Silence communicates in a variety of ways, from hurting another with the "silent treatment" to communicating deep emotional responses.

13. Time can be used to communicate, and chronemics is the study of the messages communicated by our treatment of time.

14. Smell can communicate messages that enhance attraction, taste, memory, and identification.

15. Cultural variations in nonverbal communication are great. Different cultures, for example, assign different meanings to facial expressions and to colours, have different spatial rules, and treat time very differently.

This chapter has covered a variety of communication skills. Check your ability to apply these skills by indicating how often the following statements apply to you. Use the following rating scale: 1 = almost always, 2 = often, 3 = sometimes, 4 = rarely, and 5 = almost never.

_____ 1. You recognize messages communicated by body gestures and facial and eye movements.

_____ 2. You take into consideration the interaction of emotional feelings and nonverbal expressions of the emotion; each influences the other.

_____ 3. You recognize that what you perceive is only a part of the total nonverbal expression.

_____ 4. You use eye movements to seek feedback, to inform others to speak, to signal the nature of your relationship with others, and to compensate for increased physical distance.

_____ 5. You give others the space they need—for example, giving more space to those who are angry or disturbed.

_____ 6. You use artifacts to communicate the desired messages.

_____ 7. You are sensitive to the touching behaviours of others and distinguish among touches that communicate positive emotion, playfulness, control, ritual, and task-relatedness.

_____ 8. You recognize and respect each person's touch-avoidance tendency; you pay special attention to cultural and gender differences in touching preferences and in touch-avoidance tendencies.

_____ 9. You vary paralinguistic features (such as rate, pausing, pitch, and volume) to communicate intended meanings.

_____ 10. You use silence to communicate intended meanings and are sensitive to the meanings communicated by the silence of others.

_____ 11. You are specific when using normally informal time terms.

_____ 12. You interpret time cues from the cultural perspective of the person with whom you're interacting.

VOCABULARY QUIZ

The Language of Nonverbal Communication

Match the terms of nonverbal communication with their definitions on the next page. Record the number of the appropriate definition next to each term.

_4_ emblems 137

_1_ affect displays 138

_8_ proxemics 143

_9_ territoriality 144

_5_ haptics 148

_10_ paralanguage 149

_2_ chronemics 152

_7_ artifactual communication 146

_3_ social clock 160

_6_ psychological time 151

1. Movements of the facial area that convey emotional meaning—for example, anger, fear, or surprise.

2. The study of the communicative nature of time—how we treat time and how we use it to communicate.

3. The timetable that a culture establishes for appropriately achieving certain milestones.

4. Nonverbal behaviours that directly translate words or phrases—for example, the signs for "okay" and "peace."

5. Touch or tactile communication.

6. One's orientation to the past, present, or future.

7. Communication that takes place through various artifacts—for example, clothing, jewellery, buttons, or the furniture in your house and its arrangement.

8. The study of the communicative function of space; the study of how people unconsciously structure their space—the distance between people in their interactions, the organization of space in homes and offices, and even the design of cities.

9. A possessive or ownership reaction to an area of space or to particular objects.

10. The vocal but nonverbal aspect of speech; for example, the rate, volume, pitch, and stress variations that communicate different meanings.

SKILL BUILDING EXERCISES

6.1 INTEGRATING VERBAL AND NONVERBAL MESSAGES

Think about how you integrate verbal and nonverbal messages in your own everyday communications. Try reading each of the following statements and describing (rather than acting out) the nonverbal messages that you would use in making these statements in normal conversation.

1. I couldn't agree with you more.

2. Absolutely not. I don't agree.

3. Hurry up; we're an hour late already.

4. You look really depressed. What happened?

5. I'm so depressed I can't stand it.

6. Life is great, isn't it? I just got the job of a lifetime.

7. I feel so relaxed and satisfied.

8. I'm feeling sick; I think I have to throw up.

9. You look fantastic; what did you do to yourself?

10. Did you see that accident yesterday?

Thinking Critically About Verbal and Nonverbal Messages.

This experience was probably a lot more difficult than it seemed at first. The reason is that we're generally unaware of the nonverbal movements we make; often they function below the level of conscious awareness. What value might there be in bringing these processes to consciousness? Can you identify any problems with this?

6.2 FACIAL EXPRESSIONS

The objective of this exercise is to gain a greater understanding of the role of facial features in communicating different emotions. Draw faces, depicting only eyebrows, eyes, and mouth, to illustrate the primary emotions: happiness (provided as an example), surprise, fear, anger, sadness, disgust, contempt, and interest. In the space provided, write a verbal description of how one would facially express each of these emotions. Follow the format provided in the happiness example.

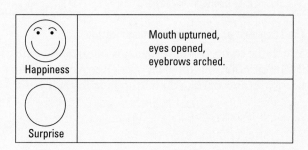

Happiness	Mouth upturned, eyes opened, eyebrows arched.
Surprise	

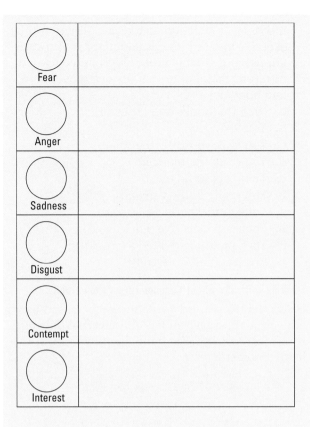

◯ Fear	
◯ Anger	
◯ Sadness	
◯ Disgust	
◯ Contempt	
◯ Interest	

Thinking Critically About Facial Expressions.

Compare your faces and descriptions with those done by others. What do the several faces for each emotion have in common? How do they differ? What do the verbal descriptions have in common? How do they differ?

6.3 COMMUNICATING NONVERBALLY

This exercise has several parts and asks you to explore the various channels of nonverbal communication discussed in this chapter in different ways.

1. The objective of this first exercise is to gain a greater understanding of the role of nonverbal channels in communicating emotions. Using any nonverbal channels you wish, communicate these primary emotions: happiness, surprise, fear, anger, sadness, disgust, contempt, and interest. In a small group discussion, brief talk, email, or brief paper, describe the nonverbals you would use in communicating any one

of these emotions. Consider as many as possible of the 10 channels discussed in this chapter.

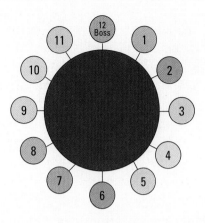

2. **Sitting at the Company Meeting** Where would you sit in each of the four situations identified below? What would be your first choice? Your second choice?
   a. You want to polish the apple and ingratiate yourself with your boss.
   b. You aren't prepared and want to be ignored.
   c. You want to challenge your boss on a certain policy that will come up for a vote.
   d. You want to be accepted as a new (but important) member of the company.

   Why did you make the choices you made? Do you normally make choices based on such factors as these? What interpersonal factors—for example, the desire to talk to or the desire to get a closer look at someone—influence your day-to-day seating behaviour?

3. Consider the meanings colours communicate. The colour spectrum is presented on page 164 with numbers from 1 to 25 to facilitate identifying the colours. Assume that you're working for an advertising agency and that your task is to select colours for the following products: a herbal tea made from basil, a children's candy-flavoured toothpaste, and a low-calorie ice cream. What major colours would you use? What colours would serve as accents?

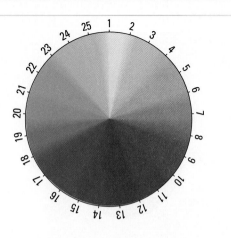

nicate the praise and criticism. Although this exercise focused on paralanguage (vocal variations), did you also read the statements with different facial expressions, eye movements, and body postures?

a. Now that looks good on you.
b. You lost weight.
c. You look younger than that.
d. You're gonna make it.
e. That was some meal.
f. You really know yourself.
g. You're an expert.
h. You're so sensitive. I'm amazed.
i. Your parents are really something.
j. Are you ready? Already?

4. Paralanguage variations can communicate praise and criticism. Read aloud each of the following 10 sentences, first to communicate praise and second, criticism. Then consider which paralanguage cues you used to commu-

Thinking Critically About Communicating Nonverbally.

How effective would you consider yourself as a nonverbal message sender? A nonverbal message receiver? With which channels are you most effective? Least effective?

Chapter 7

Emotional Messages

CHAPTER TOPICS

This chapter explores the nature of emotions, discusses problems in communicating emotions, and offers suggestions for more effective emotional communication.

- Emotions and Emotional Messages
- Obstacles in Communicating Emotions
- Guidelines for Communicating Emotions

CHAPTER SKILLS

After completing this chapter, you should be able to:

- communicate your positive and negative emotions more appropriately.
- combat the common obstacles in communicating emotions.
- communicate emotions and respond to the emotions of others more effectively.

A young wife leaves her house one morning to draw water from the local well; her husband watches from the porch. As she walks back from the well, a stranger stops her and asks for some water. She gives him a cupful, then invites him home to dinner. He accepts. The husband, wife, and guest have a pleasant meal together. The husband, in a gesture of hospitality, invites the guest to spend the night—with his wife. The guest accepts. In the morning the husband leaves early to bring home breakfast. When he returns, he finds his wife again in bed with the visitor.

The question is: At what point in this story does the husband feel angry?

The answer is: It depends on the culture to which you belong (Hupka, 1981). In Canada or the United States, a husband would likely feel angry at a wife who slept with a stranger and a wife would likely feel angry at being offered to a guest as if she were a lamb chop. But these reactions are not universal.

- A Pawnee husband of the nineteenth century would have been enraged at any man who dared ask his wife for water.

- An Ammassalik husband finds it perfectly honourable to offer his wife to a stranger, but only once. He would be angry to find his wife and the guest having a second encounter.

- A Toda husband at the turn of the century in India would not have been angry at all. The Todas allowed both husband and wife to take lovers, and women were even allowed to have several husbands. Both spouses might feel angry, though, if one of them had a *sneaky* affair without announcing it publicly.

This report by Carole Wade and Carol Tavris (1998, p. 400) illustrates that the emotions you feel depend, at least in part, on your culture. In this chapter we look at emotions and especially at the communication of emotions. What are emotions? What makes you experience emotion? Why do you find it difficult to express emotions? How can you learn to better communicate your emotions? How can you better deal with the emotions of others? These are some of the questions we'll consider.

Emotions and Emotional Messages

Communicating emotions is both difficult and important. It's difficult because our thinking often gets confused when we are intensely emotional. It's also difficult because we were not taught how to communicate emotions and we have few effective models we might imitate. Communicating emotions is also most important. Feelings represent a great part of your meanings. If you don't convey your feelings or if you communicate these feelings inadequately, you will fail to communicate a great part of your meaning. Consider what your communications would be like if you left out your feelings when talking about flunking a recent test, winning the lottery, becoming a parent, getting engaged, driving a car for the first time, becoming a citizen, or being promoted to supervisor.

> When dealing with people, remember you are not dealing with creatures of logic, but with creatures of emotion, creatures bristling with prejudice, and motivated by pride and vanity.
>
> —Dale Carnegie

The Body, Mind, and Culture in Emotions

Emotion involves at least three parts: bodily reactions (such as blushing when you're embarrassed); mental evaluations and interpretations (as in calculating the odds of drawing an inside straight at poker); and cultural rules and beliefs (for example, feeling proud when your child graduates from college).

Bodily reactions are the most obvious aspect of our emotional experience, because we can observe them easily. Such reactions span a wide range. They include, for example, the dilated pupils of attraction, the sweating palms that accompany nervousness, and the self-touching that goes with discomfort. When you judge people's emotions, you probably look to these nonverbal behaviours. You conclude that Ramon is happy to see you because of his smile and his open body posture. You conclude that Lisa is nervous from her tense posture, vocal hesitations, and awkward movements.

The mental part of emotional experience involves the evaluations and interpretations you make on the basis of your behaviours. For example, leading psychotherapist Albert Ellis (1988; Ellis & Harper, 1975), whose insights are used throughout this chapter, claims that your evaluations of what happens have a greater influence on your feelings than what actually happens. Let's say, for example, that your best friend, Ling, ignores you in the college cafeteria. The emotions you feel will depend on what you think this behaviour means. You may feel pity if you figure that Ling is depressed because her father died. You may feel anger if you believe that Ling is simply rude and insensitive and snubbed you on purpose. Or you may feel sadness if you believe that Ling is no longer interested in being friends with you.

In an interesting study that illustrates the influence that our interpretations have on the emotions we experience, students were asked how they felt when they failed or did well on a college examination (Weiner, Russell, & Lerman, 1979). Students who did poorly felt *anger* or *hostility* if they believed that others were responsible for their failure—for example, if they felt the instructor gave an unfair examination. Those

Generally speaking, how accurate do you think you are in judging the emotions of others from only their facial expression? What specific facial cues do you use most in making your judgments?

who believed that they themselves were responsible for the failure felt *guilt* or *regret*. Students who did very well felt *pride* and *satisfaction* if they believed their success was due to their own efforts, or felt *gratitude* and *surprise* (or even felt *guilt*) if they believed that their success was due to luck or chance. More recently, Mathews and Mackintosh (2000) reported on five different studies, which showed that the interpretation of personally relevant information can be changed through providing alternative interpretations. In these studies, participants were persuaded to interpret ambiguous information either in a threatening or a benign way. Have your own interpretations ever influenced the emotions you experienced? Have they ever not influenced the emotions you felt?

The culture you were raised in and live in gives you a framework both for interpreting emotions in others and, as we'll see in the section on "Emotional Expression and Culture," for expressing emotions. A colleague gave a lecture in Beijing to a group of Chinese college students. The students listened politely, but they made no comments and asked no questions after her lecture. At first, she concluded that the students were bored and uninterested. Later, she learned that Chinese students show respect by being quiet and seemingly passive. They think that asking questions would imply that she was not clear in her lecture. In other words, the culture—whether Canadian or Chinese—influenced the interpretation of the students' feelings.

Stephan, Stephan, and de Vargas (1996) examined the different ways people expressed their emotions depending upon whether they were from a collectivist or an individualistic culture using participants from Costa Rica and the United States. (See Chapter 9 for descriptions of these types of cultures.) Participants from Costa Rica, a collectivist culture, were careful to express emotions in ways that did not negatively affect others, whereas participants from the United States were more concerned about revealing their true feelings regardless of the impact on others.

Emotions, Arousal, and Expression

How would you feel in each of the following situations?

1. You have just heard that you won the lottery.
2. Your best friend just died.
3. You were just told you got the job you applied for.
4. Your parents just told you they are getting divorced.

You would obviously feel very differently in each of these situations. In fact, each feeling is unique and unrepeatable. Yet amid all these differences there is some similarity. For example, most people would argue that the feelings in situations 1 and 3 are more similar to each other than are 1 and 2. Similarly, 2 and 4 are more similar to each other than are 3 and 4.

Your Basic Emotions   To capture the similarities among emotions, many researchers have tried to identify basic or primary emotions. Robert Plutchik (1980; Havlena, Holbrook, & Lehmann, 1989) developed a most helpful model. In this model, as shown in Figure 7.1, the eight pieces of the pie represent the eight basic emotions: joy, acceptance, fear, surprise, sadness, disgust, anger, and anticipation. Emotions that are close to each other on this wheel are also close to each other in meaning. For example, joy and anticipation are more closely related than are joy and sadness or acceptance and disgust. Emotions that are opposite each other on the wheel are also opposite each other in their meaning. For example, joy is the opposite of sadness; anger is the opposite of fear.

In this model there are also blends. These are emotions that are combinations of the primary emotions. These are noted outside the emotion wheel. For example, according to this model, love is a blend of joy and acceptance. Remorse is a blend of disgust and sadness.

Emotional Arousal
If you were to describe the events leading up to emotional arousal, you would probably describe three stages: (1) An event occurs. (2) You experience an emotion; you feel surprise, joy, anger. (3) You respond physiologically; your heart beats faster, your face flushes, and so on. Figure 7.2 (A) on page 170 depicts this commonsense view of emotions.

Psychologist William James and physiologist Carl Lange offered a different explanation. Their theory places the physiological arousal before the experience of the emotion. The James–Lange sequence is: (1) An event occurs. (2) You respond physiologically. And (3) you experience an emotion; for example, you feel joy or sadness. Figure 7.2 (B) depicts the James–Lange view of emotions.

Psychologist Stanley Schachter (1964) has presented evidence for a **cognitive labelling theory** of emotional arousal. According to Schachter you interpret the physiological arousal and, on the basis of this interpretation, experience the emotions of joy, sadness, or whatever. The sequence of events goes like this: (1) An event occurs. (2) You respond physiologically. (3) *You interpret this arousal—that is, you decide what emotion you're experiencing.* And (4) you experience the emotion. Your interpretation of your arousal will depend on the situation you're in. For example, if you experience an increased pulse rate after someone you've been admiring smiles at you, you may interpret this as joy. You may, however, interpret that same increased heartbeat as fear when three suspicious-looking strangers approach you on a dark street. It's only after you make the interpretation that you experience the emotion; for example, the joy or the fear. This sequence of events is pictured in Figure 7.2 (C).

Emotional Expression
Emotions are the feelings you have—your feelings of anger, sorrow, guilt, depression, happiness, and so on. Emotional expression, on the other hand, is the way you communicate these feelings. Theorists do not agree over whether you can choose the emotions you *feel*. Some argue that you can, others argue that you cannot. You are,

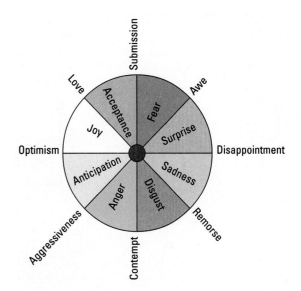

Figure 7.1 A Model of the Emotions

Do you agree with the basic assumptions of this model? For example, do you see love as a combination of joy and acceptance, and optimism as a combination of joy and anticipation?

Source: From Emotion: A Psychoevolutionary Synthesis by Robert Plutchik. Copyright © 1980 by Robert Plutchik. Reprinted by permission of Allyn & Bacon.

A popular belief about relationships is that if a relationship is not characterized by strong emotions and emotional expression, then there must be something wrong with it. Would you agree with this?

One implication of the cognitive labelling theory of emotions is that you and only you can make yourself feel angry or sad or anxious. This view is often phrased popularly as "Other people can only hurt you physically; only you can hurt yourself emotionally." Do you agree with this? What evidence can you advance to support or refute this position?

Figure 7.2 Three Views of Emotion

How would you describe emotional arousal?

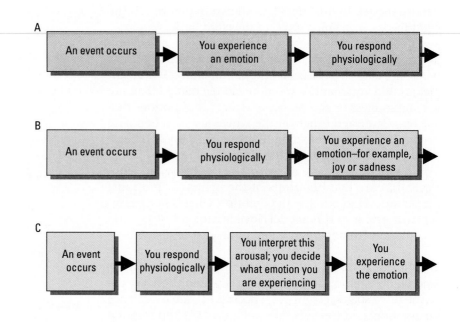

A
An event occurs → You experience an emotion → You respond physiologically →

B
An event occurs → You respond physiologically → You experience an emotion–for example, joy or sadness →

C
An event occurs → You respond physiologically → You interpret this arousal; you decide what emotion you are experiencing → You experience the emotion →

however, clearly in some control of the ways in which you *express* your emotions. You do not have to express what you feel.

Whether or not you choose to express your emotions will depend on your own attitudes about emotional expression, which you may wish to explore by taking the self-test below. For example, if you feel anger, you may choose to express or not to express it. You do not have to express anger just because you feel angry. In fact, you may feel angry but outwardly act calmly, dispassionately, and lovingly. For example, if there are several promotions to be made in your office and you don't get the first one, you may feel anger. But you may decide that to show your anger could hurt your chances for getting one of the other promotions. You may, therefore, decide to respond calmly, on the assumption that this will help your advancement more than will an expression of anger.

TEST YOURSELF

How Do You Feel About Communicating Emotions?

Instructions: Respond to each of the following statements with T if you feel the statement is a generally true description of your attitudes about expressing emotions, or with F if you feel the statement is generally a false description of your attitudes.

_____ 1. Expressing feelings is healthy; it reduces stress and prevents wasting energy on concealment.

_____ 2. Expressing feelings can lead to interpersonal relationship problems.

_____ 3. Expressing feelings can assist others in understanding you.

_____   **4.** Emotional expression is often an effective means of persuading others to do as you wish.

_____   **5.** Expressing emotions may lead others to perceive you negatively.

_____   **6.** Emotional expression can lead to greater and not less stress; expressing anger, for example, may actually increase your feelings of anger.

HOW DID YOU DO?

These statements are arguments that are often made for and against expressing emotions. Statements 1, 3, and 4 are arguments made in favour of expressing emotions; 2, 5, and 6 are arguments made against expressing emotions. You can look at your responses as revealing (in part) your attitude favouring or opposing the expression of feelings. "True" responses to statements 1, 3, and 4 and "False" responses to statements 2, 5, and 6 would indicate a favourable attitude to expressing feelings. "False" responses to statements 1, 3, and 4 and "True" responses to statements 2, 5, and 6 indicate a negative attitude.

WHAT WILL YOU DO?

There is evidence suggesting that expressing emotions can lead to all six outcomes—the positives and the negatives—so general suggestions for increasing your willingness to express your emotions are not offered. These attitudes and their consequences underscore the importance of critically assessing your options for emotional expression. Be flexible, remembering that what will work in one situation will not work in another.

If you decide to communicate your feelings, you need to make several decisions. For example, you have to choose how to do so—face-to-face or by letter, phone, email, or office memo. And you have to choose the specific emotions you will and will not reveal. And third, you have to choose the language in which you express your emotions.

Here is a list of terms for describing your emotions. It's adapted from the model of emotions developed by Plutchik (1980). Notice that the terms included for each basic emotion provide you with lots of choices for expressing the intensity level you're feeling. For example, if you're extremely happy, then *bliss, ecstasy,* or *enchantment* may be an appropriate description. If you're mildly happy, then perhaps *contentment, satisfaction,* or *well-being* would be more descriptive. Look over the list and try grouping the terms into three levels of intensity: high, middle, and low. Before doing that, however, look up the meanings of any words that are unfamiliar to you.

Happiness: bliss, cheer, contentment, delight, ecstasy, enchantment, enjoyment, felicity, joy, rapture, gratification, pleasure, satisfaction, well-being

Surprise: amazement, astonishment, awe, eye-opener, incredulity, jolt, revelation, shock, unexpectedness, wonder, startle, catch off-guard, unforeseen

Fear: anxiety, apprehension, awe, concern, consternation, dread, fright, misgiving, phobia, terror, trepidation, worry, qualm, terror

Anger: acrimony, annoyance, bitterness, displeasure, exasperation, fury, ire, irritation, outrage, rage, resentment, tantrum, umbrage, wrath, hostility

Sadness: dejected, depressed, dismal, distressed, grief, loneliness, melancholy, misery, sorrowful, unhappiness

Disgust: abhorrence, aversion, loathing, repugnance, repulsion, revulsion, sickness, nausea, offensiveness

Contempt: abhorrence, aversion, derision, disdain, disgust, distaste, indignity, insolence, ridicule, scorn, snobbery, revulsion, disrespect

Interest: attention, appeal, concern, curiosity, fascination, notice, spice, zest, absorb, engage, engross

"I've been thinking—it might be good for Andrew if he could see you cry once in a while."

Emotion is not something shameful, subordinate, second-rate; it is a supremely valid phase of humanity at its noblest and most mature.

—**Joshua Loth Liebman**

Emotions, Culture, and Gender The chapter opening vignette provided an excellent example of the influence of culture on emotional expression and illustrated the role of **cultural display rules**. These are cultural teachings that advise members of a society about which emotions are permissible to express as well as the circumstances or contexts in which emotional expression is considered appropriate. For example, in one study Japanese and American students watched a particularly unpleasant film of an operation (Ekman, 1985b). The students were videotaped both in an interview situation about the film and alone while watching the film. When alone, both American and Japanese students showed very similar reactions. But in the interview, American and Japanese students followed different rules for the display of emotions: The American students readily displayed facial expressions indicating displeasure, whereas the Japanese students did not display any great emotion. Similarly, cultural display rules influence what is and what is not considered appropriate emotional expression in a romantic relationship, depending on the stage your relationship is at. You're more likely to inhibit any expression of negative emotions in early stages of a relationship than after you've achieved some level of involvement or intimacy (Aune, Buller, & Aune, 1996).

Cultural differences also exist in decoding the meaning of a facial expression. For example, American and Japanese students were asked to judge the meaning of a smiling and a neutral facial expression. The American rated the smiling face as more attractive, more intelligent, and more sociable than the neutral face. The Japanese, however, rated the smiling face as more sociable but not as more attractive. The Japanese, in fact, rated the neutral face as the more intelligent (Matsumoto & Kudoh, 1993).

Similarly, Japanese women are not supposed to reveal broad smiles and so will hide their smile, sometimes with their hands (Ma, 1996). Women in North America, on the other hand, have no such restrictions and so are more likely to smile openly.

Part of thinking critically about messages involves identifying and analyzing emotional appeals and realizing that these appeals do not constitute logical proof.

One popular emotional appeal is to pity. Organizations use this appeal in seeking support for aid to needy children. You're shown the hungry and sad children and you feel pity. The objective, of course, is to get you to experience so much pity that you'll contribute to finance the aid efforts. People who beg for money often emphasize their difficulties in an effort to evoke pity and donations.

Another popular appeal is to guilt. A person who does something for you may make you feel guilty unless you do something in return. Or someone may present himself or herself as being in desperate need and make you feel guilty for having what you have and not sharing it.

Listen to a message's emotional dimension critically:

- Realize that emotional appeal does not constitute proof. No matter how passionate the speaker is, remember that passion does not prove the case.
- Realize that as a listener you really can't tell with certainty what the speaker is actually feeling. The speaker may, in fact, be using a wide variety of facial management techniques to communicate emotions without actually feeling them.
- Realize that some speakers may use emotional appeals instead of evidence and logical arguments. Some, in fact, may try to use emotional appeals to divert attention away from a lack of evidence.

EXAMPLES?

Give an example of emotional appeals you witnessed or used recently. Were they effective in achieving their aim?

North Americans are also more apt to express negative emotions to their friends and positive emotions to relative strangers. In contrast, Poles and Hungarians are more likely to express negative emotions to strangers and positive emotions to friends (Matsumoto, 1996).

Canadians, by and large, tend to be more reluctant to openly express emotions than are their American neighbours. The popularity of talk shows where people openly cry, yell, and scream in front of millions of viewers suggests the acceptability of emotional expression in American culture. It's interesting, for example, to compare a Canadian drama such as *Anne of Green Gables* with an American one to see if there is a difference in the intensity of emotional expression.

Researchers agree that men and women experience emotions similarly (Oatley & Duncan, 1994; Cherulnik, 1979; Wade & Tavris, 1998). The differences that are observed are differences in emotional expression. Men and women seem to have different **gender display rules**, much as different cultures have different cultural display rules. Gray and Heatherington (2003) examined the effect of social context on the extent to which young men express sadness. They induced sadness in 87 college men and then invited them into a room with two others (either two men or two women) to talk about their feelings. In general, participants expressed significantly more sadness when the others in the room were expressive and accepting. To a lesser extent, the male college students were more able to talk about their feelings of sadness to other men rather than to women.

Some societies permit and even expect men to show strong emotions. They expect men to cry, to show fear, to express anger openly. Other societies—and many groups within general Canadian culture—criticize men for experiencing and expressing such emotions. Plant, Hyde, and Devine (2000) conducted three separate studies to determine the relationship between gender and the interpretation of emotionally expressive behaviour. Participants believed that women experienced and expressed emotions more often than men. What did your culture teach you about gender and the expression of emotions, particularly strongly felt emotions and emotions that show weakness (such as fear, discomfort, or uncertainty)?

What has your experience revealed about the ways men and women express emotions? What similarities and differences have you observed?

Women talk more about feelings and emotions and use communication for emotional expression more than men (Barbato & Perse, 1992). Perhaps because of this, they also express themselves facially more than men. Even junior and senior high school students show this gender difference. Recent research has found that this difference may well be due to differences in the brains of men and women; women's brains have a significantly larger inferior parietal lobe, which seems to account for women's greater awareness of feelings (Barta, 1999).

Women are also more likely to express socially acceptable emotions than are men (Brody, 1985). For example, women smile significantly more often than men. In fact, women smile even when smiling is not appropriate—for example, when reprimanding a subordinate. Men, on the other hand, are more likely than women to express anger and aggression (Fischer, 1993; DePaulo, 1992; Wade & Tavris, 1998). Similarly, women are more effective at communicating happiness and men are more effective at communicating anger (Coats & Feldman, 1996).

Some research has also looked at reactions to emotional expression of men and women. In one study, participants, watching a video of a courtroom trial, rated women most guilty when they displayed extremely high or extremely little emotion. Women were rated least guilty when they expressed moderate levels of emotion. Men, on the other hand, were rated similarly regardless of the level of emotions they displayed (Salekin, Ogloff, McGarland, & Rogers, 1995).

Can you think of a specific instance when failing to appreciate the cultural and gender differences in emotional expression led you to miss another's meaning?

Other research also suggests that women respond well to men who express emotions (Werrbach, Grotevant, & Cooper, 1990). While watching a movie, a confederate of the experimenter in one study displayed a variety of emotions; participants were then asked what they thought of this person. Results showed that men were liked best when they cried, whereas women were liked best when they did not cry (Labott, Martin, Eason, & Berkey, 1991).

Principles of Emotional Communication

Identifying several major principles of **emotional communication** should further explain how emotions work in communication.

Emotions Are Always Important   Although emotions are especially salient in conflict situations and in relationship development and dissolution, they are actually a part of all messages. Emotions are always present—sometimes to a very strong extent, though sometimes only mildly—and they must be recognized as a part of the communication experience. This is not to say that emotions should always be talked about or that all emotions you feel should be expressed. In some instances, as we've already seen, you may want to avoid revealing your emotions; for example, you might not want to show your frustration over a customer's indecision or reveal to your children your doubts about finding a job.

Emotional Feelings and Emotional Expression Are Not the Same
Recall from our earlier discussion of facial management techniques (Chapter 6) that emotions are frequently disguised. Remember that you can intensify, de-intensify, neutralize, and mask your emotions so that others will think you're feeling something different from what you really are feeling. From this simple principle two useful corollaries can be derived:

- You cannot tell what other people are feeling simply from observing them, so don't assume you can. It's far better to ask the person to clarify what he or she is feeling.

- Others cannot always tell what you're feeling from the way you act. So if you want others to know how you feel, it's probably a good idea to tell them.

Emotions Are Communicated Verbally *and* Nonverbally   As with most meanings, emotions are encoded both verbally and nonverbally. Your words, the emphasis you give them, and the gestures and facial expressions that accompany them all help to communicate your feelings. Conversely, emotions are decoded on the basis of both verbal and nonverbal cues. And of course emotions, like all messages, are most effectively communicated when verbal and nonverbal messages reinforce and complement each other.

Emotional Expression Can Be Good *and* Bad   In a relationship, expressing emotions can be cathartic and may even benefit the relationship. Expressing emotions can help you air dissatisfactions and perhaps reduce or even eliminate them. Through emotional expression you can come to understand each other better, which may lead to a closer and more meaningful relationship.

On the other hand, expressing emotions may cause relationship difficulties. Expressing your irritation with a worker's customary way of answering the phone, for example, may generate hostility. Expressing jealousy when your partner spends time with friends may lead your partner to fear being controlled and losing autonomy.

How might confusing emotional expression with feelings lead you to make inferential leaps from, say, a person's facial expression to his or her feelings of depression? Can you recall an instance in which someone confused your emotional expression with your feelings?

There is some evidence that it's actually more difficult to judge when an intimate is lying than when a stranger is lying (Metts, 1989). Do you find this generally true?

Expressing your own feelings is only half of the process of emotional communication; the other half is listening. Sometimes you may feel awkward listening to the feelings of others, almost as if you're eavesdropping and overhearing matters that are really too personal. At other times you may feel awkward because you don't quite know what to say. Here are a few guidelines for making an often difficult process a little easier.

- Don't (as the stereotypical male supposedly does) equate responding to another's feelings with solving the person's problems (Tannen, 1990). It's usually more productive to view your task in more limited terms—as encouraging the person to express and perhaps clarify his or her feelings and as providing a supportive atmosphere.

- Empathize with the person. Try to see the situation from the point of view of the speaker, to put yourself into the position of the other person. Be especially careful to avoid evaluating the other person's feelings. For example, saying "Don't cry; (s)he wasn't worth it" or "You'll get promoted next year" can easily be interpreted as meaning "Your feelings are wrong or inappropriate."

- Focus on the other person. Avoid responding with your own problems. It's very easy, in hearing a friend talk of a broken love affair, to interject with your own similar past situations. And although this can be a useful technique for showing your understanding, it creates problems if it refocuses the conversation on you and away from the person who needs to talk.

- Show your interest by encouraging the person to explore his or her feelings. You might, for example, use simple encouragers like "I see" or "I understand." Or ask questions that let the speaker know that you're listening and that you're interested in hearing more.

SUGGESTIONS?

Your best friend tells you that he suspects his girlfriend is seeing someone else. He's extremely upset and tells you that he wants to confront her with his suspicions but is afraid of what he'll hear. What listening guidelines would you suggest he use if he does confront his girlfriend?

Emotions Are Often Contagious   If you've ever watched an infant and mother interacting, you have seen how quickly the infant mimics the emotional expressions of the mother. If the mother smiles, the infant smiles; if the mother frowns, the infant frowns. As a child gets older, he or she begins to pick up more subtle expressions of emotions. A parent's anxiety or fear or anger, for example, are quickly identified and often mimicked by the child. In a study of college roommates, the depression of one roommate spread to the other over a period of just three weeks (Joiner, 1994). In short, through **emotional contagion** emotions are passed from one person to another. In conversation and in small groups, the strong emotions of one person can easily prove contagious to others present; this can be productive when the emotions are productive or unproductive when the emotions are unproductive.

Obstacles in Communicating Emotions

The expression of feelings is a part of most meaningful relationships. Yet it's often very difficult. For that reason we need to examine the obstacles to effective emotional expression and to consider some guidelines. Three major obstacles stand in the way of effective emotional communication: (1) society's rules and customs, (2) fear, and (3) inadequate interpersonal skills.

Societal Rules and Customs

The "cowboy syndrome" is a pattern of behaviour seen in the old cowboy movies from which it gets its name (Balswick & Peck, 1971) and is still prevalent in rural areas of western Canada. The cowboy syndrome describes the closed and unexpressive male. This man is strong but silent. He never feels any of the softer emotions (such as compassion, love, or contentment). He would never ever cry, experience fear, or feel sorry for himself. And he would never ask—as does our hero in the cartoon—for "a bigger emotional share." Unfortunately, many men grow up trying to live up to this unrealistic image. It's a syndrome that prevents open and honest expression. Researcher Ronald Levant (*Time*, January 20, 1992, p. 44) has argued that men's inability to deal with emotions as effectively as women is a "trained incompetence." Such training begins early in life when boys are taught not to cry and to ignore pain. This is not necessarily to suggest, however, that men should communicate their emotions more openly. Unfortunately, there are many who will negatively evaluate men who express emotions openly and often; such men may be judged ineffective, insecure, or unmanly.

"Rebecca, I'm looking for a bigger emotional share here."

Nor are women exempt from the difficulties of emotional expression. At one time our society permitted and encouraged women to express emotions openly. The tide now is turning, especially for women in executive and managerial positions. Today the executive woman is being forced into the same cowboy syndrome. She is not allowed to cry or to show any of the once acceptable "soft" emotions. She is especially denied these feelings while she is on the job.

For both men and women, the best advice (as with self-disclosure or any of the characteristics of communication effectiveness discussed in this book) is to express your emotions selectively. Carefully weigh the arguments for and against expressing your emotions. Consider the situation, the people you're with, the emotions themselves, and all the elements that make up the communication act. And, most important, consider your options for communicating—not only what you'll say but also how you'll say it.

Fear

A variety of types of fear stand in the way of emotional expression. Emotional expression exposes a part of you that makes you vulnerable to attack. For example, if you ex-

As noted in the text, men have an especially hard time expressing grief. Why do you think this is so?

press your love for another person, you risk being rejected. That is, by exposing a "weakness," you can now easily be hurt by the uncaring and the insensitive. Of course, you may also fear hurting someone else by, say, voicing your feelings about past loves. Or you may be angry and want to say something but fear that you might hurt the person and then feel guilty yourself.

In addition, you may not reveal your emotions for fear of causing a conflict. Expressing your dislike for your partner's friends, for example, may create difficulties for the two of you, and you may not be willing to risk the argument and its aftermath.

Because of fears such as these, you may deny to others and perhaps even to yourself that you have certain feelings. In fact, this kind of **denial** is the way many people were taught to deal with emotions.

Inadequate Interpersonal Skills

Perhaps the most important obstacle to effective emotional communication is lack of interpersonal skills. Many people simply don't know how to express their feelings. Some people, for example, can express anger only through violence or avoidance. Others can deal with anger only by blaming and accusing others. And many people cannot express love. They literally cannot say, "I love you."

Expressing negative feelings is doubly difficult. Many of us suppress or fail to communicate negative feelings for fear of offending the other person or making matters worse. But failing to express negative feelings will probably not help the relationship, especially if these feelings are concealed frequently and over a long time. (Learning to express negative feelings positively and constructively seems the better alternative and is addressed in the exercise, "Expressing Negative Feelings." See www.ablongman.com/devito.)

Guidelines for Communicating Emotions

Communicating your emotions and responding appropriately to the emotional expressions of others are as important as they are difficult. Your first task, or series of tasks, is intrapersonal: understanding your emotions, deciding if you wish to express them, and assessing your communication options should you decide to express your emotions. Let's focus on these tasks first; then we'll consider some guidelines for their actual expression. As a complement to this discussion, the article on pages 179–180, "Keeping Your Cool at Work," offers additional suggestions for communicating and not communicating your emotions in the workplace.

Your first task is to *understand the emotions you're feeling*. For example, consider how you would feel if your best friend just got the promotion that you wanted or if your brother, a police officer, was shot while breaking up a street riot. Think about your emotions as objectively as possible. Think about the bodily reactions you'd be experiencing as well as the interpretations and evaluations you'd be giving to these reactions. Further, identify (in terms as specific as possible) the antecedent conditions that may be influencing your feelings. Try to an-

By starving emotions we become humorless, rigid and stereotyped; by repressing them we become literal, reformatory and holier-than-thou; encouraged, they perform life; discouraged, they poison it.

— Joseph Collins

swer the question, "Why am I feeling this way?" or "What happened to lead me to feel as I do?"

Your second task is to *decide if, in fact, you want to express your emotions*. It will not always be possible to stop and think about whether you wish to express your emotions—at times you may respond almost automatically. More often than not, however, you will have the time and the chance to ask yourself whether you wish to communicate your emotions. When you do have this chance, remember that it isn't always necessary or wise to give vent to every feeling you have. Another issue to consider is whether or not your emotional communication will be a truthful expression of your feelings. When emotional expressions are faked—when, for example, you smile though feeling angry—you may actually be creating emotional and physical stress (Grandey, 2000).

> People *can* change their feelings. No matter what happens to them, they *can* creatively decide to feel one way or another about it. And they have quite a range of possible feelings to choose from!
>
> —Albert Ellis

MESSAGES@WORK

Keeping Your Cool at Work

We all know it's healthier to express our feelings than to keep them bottled up inside. But is a temper tantrum at the office good for your career? Probably not. So where do you find the happy medium between voicing your feelings and safeguarding your job?

Certainly, there's a fine line to be drawn. If you don't verbally air your feelings—or resolve them in some way—you're bound to act them out. That can mean sloppy work, irritability, sarcasm, or procrastination. Your body suffers, too: You may develop tension headaches, neck and back pain, fatigue, even ulcers.

"The truth is you *can* express emotions at work," says Venda Raye-Johnson, a Kansas City, Missouri, career counselor and coauthor of *Staying Up When Your Job Pulls You Down*, "as long as you do it in an acceptable way. But first you've got to get those emotions under control."

1. TAKE A TIME-OUT

Your boss unfairly criticizes a project you've slaved over—in front of others, no less. Your first reaction is to fight back: Yell at her during the meeting and defend your work.

Don't do it! Instead, step back and buy yourself some time—from five minutes to five days, says Duffy Spencer, Ph.D., a management consultant in Long Island, New York, "Take as long as you need to analyze your feelings and switch from a reactive, blinded-by-emotion mind set to a rational, thinking mode." What if

you're being asked to respond? "You can say, 'I'm not sure about that; let me get back to you,'" Spencer notes.

2. ANALYZE YOUR FEELINGS

Once away from the situation, try doing a perception check, says Raye-Johnson. Stand back and ask yourself: What am I really upset about? Is there something about this situation that is "pushing my buttons"?

Sometimes we react strongly, not to the situation at hand but because it revives many old and painful feelings from our childhood. If that is the case, just realizing the parallel can help to calm you down.

Another way to gain some perspective is to ask yourself, Can I see why the other person behaved the way she did? Viewing a situation from another person's perspective allows you to understand that her or his intent may not have been vindictive.

3. EXPRESS YOURSELF

Even though you may now understand why you're feeling the way you do, you still need a positive outlet for your emotions. Tom Miller, Ph.D., a psychologist who lectures nationwide on self-discipline and emotional control, suggests, "Let out your feelings on paper. Unedited. Uncensored. Then review what you've written and destroy the evidence. Whatever you do, don't let your emotions churn around in your head. You need the cathartic release to get back in control and to see if you're overreacting."

(continued)

Sometimes just being heard and having your emotions validated can restore your sense of balance. Try talking with friends, family, and *trusted* co-workers. Besides being a sounding board, they can also offer an objective assessment of the situation and your reaction to it.

If you *are* overreacting, it may stem from flagging self-esteem. "We're typically much harder on ourselves than we are on others and more likely to call ourselves 'zeros' in the face of a problem," says Miller. If you've been chewed out by your boss or passed over for a promotion, try boosting your self-worth with the "best friend test." "Put your best friend in your situation, and ask yourself if you would think she was a zero. Not likely," contends Miller. This test can help you see the error of your interpretations—and help you keep the calamity of the situation in perspective.

Deciding the Best Course of Action

Once you understand what's at the root of your feelings, the next step is to decide what you want to do about them. Surprisingly, one option is to do nothing.

The decision to confront a co-worker would be based on these two key issues:

- What you hope to gain by speaking out (respect, responsibility, and recognition are key goals).

- How likely you are to achieve your goals with the individual involved. If an idea of yours is stolen by an egotistic and credit-needy boss, even if you do speak out it's not likely you'll get far. And it may hurt you in the long run if you antagonize her.

When there is a concrete benefit to speaking up—you'll receive credit for your idea or will correct a damaging work situation—it's probably worth it to confront a colleague. However, plan your discussion carefully. Experts say the following techniques work best:

Be Assertive About Your Beliefs and Responsive to the Other Person's Perspective

"You want to get your needs across without alienating your co-worker," stresses Spencer. The best way to do this, explains Raye-Johnson, is to empathize with that person. "Let her know you understand her viewpoint. But also tell her how you see the situation, and make a statement about how you'd like to proceed."

Start Slow and Small

Even when your emotions are under control it's still possible to be overly confrontational, loud, or forceful.

That's likely to make a co-worker feel as if she's being attacked—and it's likely to turn her off. "The goal of speaking out is to create a willingness in the other person to do what you want," says Miller. So start by calmly explaining your position and feelings. Then, as the conversation progresses and you get a sense of the other person's reactions, you can choose to strengthen your stance and push harder.

Stick to the Issue at Hand

Don't make the mistake of trying to bring up every sore issue from the past in one conversation. If you're telling your boss that you're disappointed you didn't get a recent plum assignment, don't throw in that you're also peeved about not being invited to certain meetings. Stick to one issue. And once you've made your point, stop, and wait for a response. Then go for an agreement or negotiation, advises Spencer.

Use the D.E.S.C. Script

Describe the situation; **E**xpress your feelings; **S**pecify what you want; and talk about the **C**onsequences. If you're upset because you're not receiving memos, tell your boss that you're feeling out of the loop and that if you were privy to memos you would be able to do a better job. Don't point the finger or talk about others. You'll get much further by using "I" statements and by emphasizing how co-workers can help you improve your performance, says Spencer.

Keeping Cool under Pressure

It's an undeniable fact that we bring emotions to work. The key to managing these feelings is to know what drives them and *how* to express them. "You want people to know that you're concerned, annoyed, or upset," Miller explains, "but you don't want them to think you've handled the situation badly."

Politically, it's often probably best *not* to speak up—and certainly you should never confront someone when you're on "react." But keeping silent isn't the same as suppressing feelings, experts say. If it's not in your best interest to let emotions out at work, be sure to vent them at home, with friends, or on paper. At least one person will notice the effort—you—and your mind and body will thank you for it.

Source: "Keeping Your Cool at Work" by Nancy Monson as published in *New Woman*, October 1993, pp. 70, 72. Copyright © 1993 by Nancy Monson. Reprinted by permission of the author.

Remember, too, the irreversibility of communication discussed in Chapter 1; once you communicate something, you cannot take it back. Therefore, consider carefully the arguments for and against expressing your emotions.

If you decide to express your emotions, your third task is to *evaluate your communication options* in terms of both effectiveness (what will work best and help you achieve your goal) and ethics (what is right or morally justified). When thinking in terms of effectiveness, consider, for example, the time and setting, the persons you want to reveal these feelings to, and the available methods of communication. For example, do you arrange a special meeting with your supervisor to discuss your being passed up for promotion? Or do you simply let your anger out immediately after you hear about it? What are the benefits or disadvantages of communicating your feelings of inadequacy to your spouse, your parents, your children, or your best friend? Is it better to ask for a date, confess your love, or ask for a divorce on the telephone, by letter, or face-to-face?

When thinking in terms of ethics, consider the legitimacy of appeals based on emotions. As a parent, for example, is it ethical to use appeals to fear to dissuade your teenage children from engaging in sexual relationships? From smoking? From taking drugs? From associating with people of another race or affectional orientation? Is your motive relevant to the question of whether such appeals are ethical or unethical? Is it ethical to use emotional appeals (say to guilt or fear or sympathy) to get a friend to lend you money? To take a vacation with you? To have sex with you?

Now that you understand your emotions, have decided that you want to express them, and have carefully assessed the effectiveness and ethics of your available options, consider the following guidelines for emotional expression.

> You can handle people more successfully by enlisting their feelings than by convincing their reason.
>
> —Paul P. Parker

TALKING ETHICS

Motivational Appeals

Appeals to motives are commonplace. For example, if you want a friend to take a vacation with you, you're likely to appeal to motives such as the desire for fun and excitement, the financial advantage of taking the trip now rather than at the height of the season, and perhaps the possibility that you or your friend might find romance on the vacation. If you look at the advertisements for cruises and vacation packages, you'll see very similar motives being appealed to. And there can be no doubt that such motivational appeals are effective. But are they ethical? Or would you say they are ethical under certain conditions but unethical under other conditions?

WHAT WOULD YOU DO?

You're a car dealer and your job is to sell cars. A potential customer comes into the showroom. After a brief interview, you know that this person should logically buy a moderately priced car rather than going into debt to buy the higher-priced fancy sports model. Would it be ethical for you to appeal to the customer's desire for status and sexual gratification to ensure the sale of the expensive sports car? Would it be ethical for you to appeal to the same status and sex motives with a customer who could easily afford the most expensive car on the lot? What would you do in each of these situations?

Describe Your Feelings

General and abstract descriptions of emotions are usually ineffective; be as specific as possible. Consider, for example, the frequently heard "I feel bad." Does it mean "I feel guilty" (because I lied to my best friend)? Does it mean "I feel lonely" (because I haven't had a date in the last two months)? Does it mean "I feel depressed" (because I failed that last exam)? Clearly, specificity helps. Describe also the intensity with which you feel the emotion. *I feel so angry I think I could quit this job. I feel so hurt I want to cry.* Although you experience many emotions and feelings, you probably use few terms to describe them. Learn to describe these emotions and feelings in specific and concrete terms.

Identify the Reasons for Your Feelings

The examples used above illustrate the next guideline: Identify the reasons for your feelings. For example, "I'm feeling guilty because I lied to my best friend." "I feel lonely; I haven't had a date for the last two months." "I'm really depressed from failing that last exam." If your feelings were influenced by something the person you're talking to did or said, describe this also. For example, "I felt so angry when you said you wouldn't help me. I felt hurt when you didn't invite me to the party".

Identifying the reasons for your emotions will enable you to accomplish two important goals. First, it will help you to understand *how* you feel and *why* you feel as you do. Second, it will help you tell what you must do to reduce or get rid of these negative feelings. In the examples used, these might include avoiding lying, being more assertive about dating, and studying harder.

Anchor Your Feelings to the Present

In expressing feelings—inwardly or outwardly—try to link your emotions to present circumstances. Be especially careful not to fall into the trap of believing negative things you may say about yourself. Statements such as "I'm a failure" or "I'm foolish" or "I'm stupid" are especially destructive. These statements imply that failure, foolishness, and stupidity are *in* you and will *always* be in you. Instead, include references to the here and now. Coupled with specific description and identification of the reasons for your feelings, such statements might look like this:

> "I feel like a failure right now; I've erased this computer file three times today."
>
> "I felt foolish when I couldn't think of that formula."
>
> "I feel stupid when you point out my grammatical errors."

Own Your Own Feelings

Perhaps the most important guideline for effective emotional communication is this: Own your feelings, take personal responsibility for your feelings (Proctor, 1991). Consider the following statements:

> "You make me angry."
>
> "'You make me feel like a loser."

One of the greatest gifts you can give the people you love is to hear their anger and frustration without judging or contradicting them.

—**Harold H. Bloomfield**

Most examples of how we fail to own our own feelings express negative judgments. But we can also fail to own our own feelings when expressing positive evaluation, as in "The class seemed to enjoy the presentation" (instead of "I gave a really good speech") or "Everyone seems to think I know what I'm doing" (instead of "I finally mastered this business"). Do you own both positive and negative feelings equally?

"You make me feel stupid."

"You make me feel like I don't belong here."

Note that in these statements the speaker is blaming the other person for the way he or she is feeling. Of course, you know—on more sober reflection—that no one can make anyone feel anything. Others may do things or say things to us, but it is we who interpret them. It is we who develop feelings as a result of the interaction between, for example, what people say and our own interpretations. **Owning feelings** means taking responsibility for them. It means acknowledging that our feelings are *our* feelings. The best way to own our statements is to use **I-messages**, rather than **you-messages**. With this acknowledgment of responsibility, the above statements would look like these:

"I get angry when you come home late without calling."

"I begin to think of myself as a loser when you criticize me in front of my friends."

"I feel so stupid when you use medical terms that I don't understand."

"When you ignore me in public, I feel like I don't belong here."

Note that these rephrased statements do not attack the other person and demand that he or she change certain behaviours. They merely identify and describe your feelings about those behaviours. The rephrased statements do not encourage defensiveness. With I-message statements, it's easier for other people to acknowledge their behaviours and to offer to change them.

Also use I-messages to describe what, if anything, you want the listener to do: "I'm feeling sorry for myself right now; just give me some space. I'll give you a call in a few days." Or, more directly: "I'd prefer to be alone right now."

SUMMARY OF CONCEPTS AND SKILLS

In this chapter we explored the nature and role of emotions in interpersonal communication. We examined the role of the body, mind, and culture in defining emotions, and we looked at some basic or primary emotions. More important, we looked at the obstacles to meaningful emotional communication and some guidelines that might help us communicate our feelings more effectively and also respond to the feelings of others.

1. Emotions consist of a physical part (our physiological reactions), a cognitive part (our interpretations of our feelings), and a cultural part (the influence of our cultural traditions on our emotional evaluations and expressions).

2. Our primary emotions, according to Robert Plutchik, are joy, acceptance, fear, surprise, sadness, disgust, anger, and anticipation.

3. Psychologists have proposed different explanations of how emotions are aroused. One reasonable sequence is this: An event occurs, we respond physiologically, we interpret this arousal, we experience the emotion.

4. Emotional expression is largely a matter of choice, though it is heavily influenced by your culture and gender.

5. Useful principles of emotional communication include the following: Emotions are always important; emotional expression and emotional feeling are not the same thing; emotions are communicated both verbally and nonverbally; emotional expression can be both good and bad; and emotions are contagious.

6. Among the obstacles to effective communication of feelings are societal rules and customs, fear of making oneself vulnerable, denial, and inadequate communication skills.

7. The following guidelines should help make your emotional expression more meaningful: Understand your feelings; decide if you wish to express your feelings (not all feelings need be or should be expressed); assess your communication options; describe your feelings as accurately as possible; identify the reasons for your feelings; anchor your feelings and their expression to the present time; and own your own feelings.

8. In responding to the emotions of others, try to see the situation from the perspective of the other person. Avoid refocusing the conversation on yourself. Show interest and provide the speaker with the opportunity to talk and explore his or her feelings. Avoid evaluating the feelings of the other person.

Check your ability to apply the following skills. You will gain most from this brief exercise if you think carefully about each skill and try to identify instances from your recent communication experiences in which you did or did not act on the basis of the specific skill. Use a rating scale such as the following: 1 = almost always, 2 = often, 3 = sometimes, 4 = rarely, and 5 = almost never.

_____ 1. Identify destructive and constructive beliefs about emotions.

_____ 2. Identify and be able to describe emotions (both positive and negative) more clearly.

_____ 3. Use I-messages in communicating your feelings.

_____ 4. Communicate more effectively with the grief stricken.

_____ 5. Communicate emotions more effectively.

_____ 6. Respond to the emotions of others more appropriately by using, for example, active listening skills.

_____ 7. Evaluate the arguments for and against expressing emotions for each specific situation.

VOCABULARY QUIZ

The Language of Emotions

Match the terms concerning the communication of emotions with their definitions. Record the number of the definition next to the appropriate term.

__6__ emotion⁸ 169

__5__ James–Lange theory 169

__9__ cognitive labelling theory 169

__10__ emotional expression 169

__1__ cowboy syndrome 177

__2__ owning feelings 182

__3__ I-messages 183

__8__ emotional appeals 173

__7__ gender display rules 173

__4__ cultural display rules 172

1. The male's lack of ability to reveal the emotions he is feeling because of the belief that men should be strong and silent.

2. The process by which we take responsibility for our own feelings instead of attributing them to others.

3. Messages that explicitly claim responsibility for one's own feelings.

4. Rules for expressing and not expressing various emotions that different cultures teach its members.

5. Definition of the sequence of events in emotions as follows: An event occurs; we respond physiologically; we experience the emotion.

6. The feelings we have; for example, our feelings of guilt, anger, or sorrow.

7. Conventional ideas about what emotional expressions are appropriate for one gender or the other.

8. Nonlogical means of persuasion.

9. Definition of the sequence of events in emotions as follows: An event occurs; we respond physiologically; we interpret this arousal (that is, we decide what emotion we are experiencing); we experience the emotion.

10. The way one chooses to communicate one's feelings.

SKILL BUILDING EXERCISES

7.1 COMMUNICATING YOUR EMOTIONS

Communicating emotions is one of the most difficult of all communication tasks. Here are some situations to practise on. Visualize yourself in each of the following situations, and respond as you think an effective communicator would respond.

1. A colleague at work has revealed some of the things you did while you were in college—many of which you would rather not have others on the job know about. You told your colleague these things in confidence and now just about everyone on the job knows. You're angry and decide to confront your colleague.

2. A close friend comes to your apartment in deep depression, and tells you that his or her spouse of 22 years has fallen in love with another person and wants a divorce. Your friend is at a total loss as to what to do and comes to you for comfort and guidance.

3. A neighbour who has lived next door to you for the last 10 years and who has had many difficult financial times has just won several million dollars in the lottery. You meet in the hallway of your apartment house.

4. Your grandmother is dying and calls you to spend some time with her. She says she knows she is dying and wants you to know how much she has always loved you and that her only regret in dying is not being able to see you any more.

Thinking Critically About Communicating Your Emotions.

If you have the opportunity, compare your responses with those of others. Can you derive two or three general principles for effectively communicating emotions from this experience?

7.2 EMOTIONAL ADVICE

For each of the following situations, identify (1) the nature of the problem—what is going wrong; (2) two or three possible solutions that might correct or at least lessen the problem; and (3) the one solution you would recommend to the parties involved.

1. Joe is extremely honest and open, maybe a bit too honest; he regularly says everything he feels without self-censorship or self-monitoring. Not surprisingly, he often offends people. Joe's entering a new work environment and worries that his total honesty may not be the best way to win friends and influence people.

2. Marie and Tom have been married for several years. Marie is extremely expressive, yelling one minute, crying the next. Tom, on the other hand, is the stereotypical non-expressive male; rarely can you tell what he's thinking or feeling. Recently, this difference has been causing interpersonal problems. Tom feels Marie doesn't think through her feelings but just reacts impulsively; Marie feels that Tom is unwilling to share his inner life with her.

3. Alex and Deirdre have dated steadily for the last four years. Deirdre is extremely unexpressive but believes that because of their long and close relationship, Alex should know how she's feeling without her having to spell it out. When Alex doesn't respond appropriately, Deirdre becomes angry and says that Alex doesn't understand her because he doesn't really love her; if he did, she says, he would know what she's feeling without her being explicit. Alex says this is crazy; he's no mind reader and never claimed to be. If Deirdre wants something, he says, she ought to say so; he doesn't feel he has the obligation to guess what is going on in Deirdre's head.

4. Tobin has recently been put in charge of a group of blue-collar workers at a small printer repair firm. Tobin is extremely reserved and rarely reveals any extreme emotion. He gives instructions, praises the workers, and offers criticisms all with the same tone of voice and facial expressions. This has led the workers to feel he's insincere and isn't really feeling what he says.

5. Shasta always smiles; no matter what she says, she smiles and expresses herself in a lilting tone that leads most people to feel she is pleased. In her work as a high school history teacher, this tendency seems to have created problems. When the students don't do their homework or otherwise violate established rules, her criticism seems to carry no weight. The students never feel Shasta is disturbed or really chastising them. It has gotten to the point where she has lost all control and authority in the classroom.

Thinking Critically About Communicating Your Emotions.

Discuss these situations and your recommended solutions for lessening the problems with others in your class. Do men and women offer different types of advice? Can you identify typical male solutions and typical female solutions?

7.3 COMMUNICATING EMOTIONS EFFECTIVELY

The 10 statements below are all ineffective expressions of feelings. For each statement (1) identify why the statement is ineffective (for example, what problem or distortion the statement creates) and (2) rephrase the statement into a more effective message in which you:

- describe your feelings and their intensity as accurately as possible
- identify the reasons for your feelings and what influenced or stimulated you to feel as you do
- anchor your feelings to the present
- use I-messages to own your own feelings and claim responsibility for these feelings
- use I-messages to describe what (if anything) you want the other person to do because of your feelings

1. Your lack of consideration makes me so angry I can't stand it any more.

2. You hurt me when you ignore me. Don't ever do that again.

3. I'll never forgive that louse. The hatred and resentment will never leave me.

4. I hate you. I'll always hate you. I never want to see you again. Never.

5. Look. I really can't bear to hear about your problems of deciding who to date tomorrow and who to date the next day and the next. Give me a break. It's boring. Boring.

6. You did that just to upset me. You enjoy seeing me get upset, don't you?

7. Don't talk to me in that tone of voice. Don't you dare insult me with that attitude of yours.

8. You make me look like an idiot just so you can act like a know-it-all. You always have to be superior, always the damn teacher.

9. I just can't think straight. That assignment frightens me to death. I know I'll fail.

10. When I left the interview, I let the door slam behind me. I made a fool of myself, a real fool. I'll never get that job. Why can't I ever do anything right? Why must I always make a fool of myself?

Thinking Critically About Communicating Emotions Effectively.

Which of the five guidelines listed above do you see violated most often in these statements? With which guideline do you have the most difficulty? In one sentence, how would you describe the difference between the ineffective and effective communication of feelings?

Chapter 8

Conversation Messages

CHAPTER TOPICS

This chapter discusses the process of conversation, what it is, how it's managed, and how you can make it more effective.

- The Process of Conversation
- Managing Conversation
- Effective Conversation

CHAPTER SKILLS

After completing this chapter, you should be able to:

- follow the basic structure for conversation.
- initiate, maintain, and close conversations more effectively.
- use the principles of conversational effectiveness (openness, empathy, positiveness, immediacy, inter-action management, expressiveness, and other-orientation) with mindfulness, flexibility, cultural sensitivity, and metacommunication.

Dear Ann: Can you stand one more letter about parents who are "boring and repetitious"? I found solutions. May I share them?

Show interest. My father-in-law (74) brings up his World War II service every time we see him. So I ask questions. What part of the South Pacific? What were your duties? Do you still hear from people you served with? I ask him to pull out his maps and show me exactly where he was. It turns into a fascinating story and, of course, he loves it.

Your first Plymouth only cost $800? What colour was it? Was it automatic? How many miles did you get on a gallon of gas? Do you have pictures of it? Where were you living then? I mention the car I'm driving and laugh about the contrasts and comparisons.

When Mom wants to talk about the past, I encourage her to tell us again about how she met Dad. She loves that story. Another favourite topic is the day I was born. Her eyes shine with delight every time she tells us how "babies come when they are ready—doctor or no doctor."

Our parents made room for us in their lives, whether they wanted to or not. So now it's our turn to make room for them.

—————

"Seeing Myself in 40 Years"

This letter to Ann Landers, "Seeing Myself in 40 Years," shows unusual insight into the topic of this chapter—conversational effectiveness. Interpersonal researcher Margaret McLaughlin (1984) defines **conversation** as "relatively informal social interaction in which the roles of speaker and hearer are exchanged in a nonautomatic fashion under the collaborative management of all parties."

In this chapter we look at the conversation process—what the process is; the principles you follow in conversing; how you manage a conversation (for example, opening, maintaining, and closing); and how you try to prevent and repair conversational problems.

Before reading about the process of conversation, think about some of your own conversations—both satisfactory and unsatisfactory interactions. You may find it helpful to think of a specific recent conversation as you respond to the conversation self-test below. This test will also make a great discussion stimulus if you and your conversational partner each complete the test with the same conversation in mind. Taking this test now will help highlight the characteristics of conversational behaviour and the qualities that make some conversations satisfying and others unsatisfying. (A self-test based on this same research but focusing on public speaking appears at www.ablongman.com/devito and may be interesting to take for comparison purposes.)

> Conversation is the socializing instrument par excellence, and in its style one can see reflected the capacities of a race.
>
> —José Ortega y Gasset

TEST YOURSELF

How Satisfying Is Your Conversation?

Instructions: Respond to each of the following statements by recording the number best representing your experience. Use the following scale: 1 = strongly agree, 2 = moderately agree, 3 = slightly agree, 4 = neutral, 5 = slightly disagree, 6 = moderately disagree, and 7 = strongly disagree.

_____   1. The other person let me know that I was communicating effectively.

_____   2. Nothing was accomplished.

(*continued*)

_____ 3. I would like to have another conversation like this one.

_____ 4. The other person genuinely wanted to get to know me.

_____ 5. I was very dissatisfied with the conversation.

_____ 6. I felt that during the conversation I was able to present myself as I wanted the other person to view me.

_____ 7. I was very satisfied with the conversation.

_____ 8. The other person expressed a lot of interest in what I had to say.

_____ 9. I did NOT enjoy the conversation.

_____ 10. The other person did NOT provide support for what he/she was saying.

_____ 11. I felt I could talk about anything with the other person.

_____ 12. We each got to say what we wanted.

_____ 13. I felt that we could laugh easily together.

_____ 14. The conversation flowed smoothly.

_____ 15. The other person frequently said things which added little to the conversation.

_____ 16. We talked about something I was NOT interested in.

HOW DID YOU DO?

To score your test:

1. Add the scores for items 1, 3, 4, 6, 7, 8, 11, 12, 13, and 14. This is your Step 1 total.

2. Reverse the scores for items 2, 5, 9, 10, 15, and 16. For example, if you responded to Question 2 with a 7, reverse this to 1; reverse 6 to 2; reverse 5 to 3; keep 4 as 4; reverse 3 to 5; reverse 2 to 6; and reverse 1 to 7. Add these reversed scores. This is your Step 2 total.

3. Add the totals from Steps 1 and 2 to get your communication satisfaction score.

You may interpret your score along the following scale:

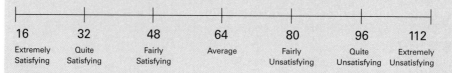

16	32	48	64	80	96	112
Extremely Satisfying	Quite Satisfying	Fairly Satisfying	Average	Fairly Unsatisfying	Quite Unsatisfying	Extremely Unsatisfying

WHAT WILL YOU DO?

More important than locating your score on this continuum is identifying the qualities that make a conversation satisfying for you. How will these qualities vary depending on the type of conversation you're engaged in—say, a business meeting with your supervisor or an intimate talk with a close friend? To increase your conversational satisfaction, as this chapter will explain, the best advice is to try to incorporate qualities of interpersonal effectiveness into your own conversations: Be positive, empathic, other-oriented, and so on.

Source: This test was developed by Michael Hecht. It appeared in Michael Hecht, "The Conceptualization and Measurement of Interpersonal Communication Satisfaction," _Human Communication Research_ 4 (1978):253–264 and is reprinted by permission of the author.

The Process of Conversation

Most often, of course, conversation takes place face-to-face. And this is the type of interaction that probably comes to mind when you think of conversation. But today much conversation also takes place online. Online communication is becoming a part of people's experience worldwide. Such communications are important personally, socially, and professionally. Three major types of online conversation (email; mailing list groups, or listservs; and chat groups) and the ways in which they differ from face-to-face interaction were described in Chapter 1 and should be kept in mind as you think about the conversation process.

With the understanding that conversation can take place in a wide variety of channels, let's look at the way conversation works. Conversation takes place in five steps: opening, feedforward, business, feedback, and closing (Figure 8.1).

Step One: Opening

The first step is to open the conversation, usually with some verbal or non-verbal greeting: "Hi," "How are you?" "Hello, this is Joe," a smile, or a wave.

You can accomplish a great deal in your opening (Krivonos & Knapp, 1975). First, your greeting can tell others that you're accessible, that you're available to them for conversation. You can also reveal important information about the relationship between yourself and the other person. For example, a big smile and a warm "Hi, it's been a long time" may signal that your relationship is still a friendly one, that you aren't angry any longer, or any of numerous other messages. Your greeting also helps maintain the relationship. You see this function served between workers who pass each other frequently. This greeting-in-passing assures both people that even though they don't stop and talk for an extended period, they still have access to each other.

In normal conversation, your greeting is returned by the other person with a greeting that is similar in its formality and intensity. When it isn't—when the other person turns away or responds coldly to your friendly "Good morning"—you know that something is wrong. Similarly, openings are generally consistent in tone with the main part of the conversation; you would not normally follow a cheery "How ya doing today, big guy?" with news of a family death.

Log on to an international Internet Relay Chat channel (for example, #brazil, #finland, #italia, #polska). What can you learn about the conversational practices of other cultures from simply lurking on this channel?

The time has come," the Walrus said,
"To talk of many things:
Of shoes—and ships—and sealing wax—
Of cabbages—and kings—
And why the sea is boiling hot—
And whether pigs have wings.
—**Lewis Carroll**

What other methods seem to work for opening a conversation? Do you use similar or different methods when opening a conversation with a man and with a woman? Would you use similar or different methods depending on whether you wanted to establish a romantic-type or a business-type relationship?

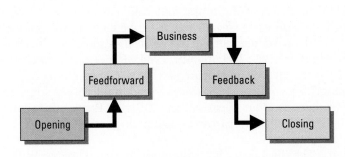

FIGURE 8.1 The Conversation Process

The process is viewed as occurring in five basic steps: opening, feedforward, business, feedback, and closing. Can you break down the conversation process into steps or stages that are significantly different from those identified here?

Step Two: Feedforward

At the second step there is usually some kind of feedforward (see Chapter 1). Here you give the other person a general idea of what the conversation will focus on: "I have to tell you about Jack," "Did you hear what happened in class yesterday?" or "We need to talk about our vacation plans." When feedforwards are misused—for example, when they are overly long or insensitive—they can create conversational problems. Goldsmith (2003) has found that feedforward is an important skill for leaders, primarily because people enjoy receiving feedforward for a variety of reasons. Feedforward allows people to see that while they may not be able to change the past, they can change the future and assumes that people can make positive changes in the future. Feedforward operates on the principle that it is more productive to help people be right than to prove them wrong. In addition, successful people like getting ideas that will help them achieve their goals. Goldsmith (2003) also found that people do not take feedforward as personally as they tend to take feedback.

As with the greeting, you can accomplish a great deal with feedforward. For example, you can (1) open the channels of communication, (2) preview the message, (3) altercast, and (4) disclaim. Let's look at each in more detail.

"I know this sounds like a line, but nice shooting."

Open the Channels of Communication   **Phatic communication** (messages that open the channels of communication) is a perfect example of feedforward. Phatic communication tells us that the normal, expected, and accepted rules of interaction will be in effect. It's information that tells us another person is willing to communicate.

Preview Future Messages   Feedforward messages frequently preview other messages. Feedforward may, for example, preview the content ("I'm afraid I have bad news for you"), the importance ("Listen to this before you make a move"), the form or style ("I'll tell you all the gory details"), and the positive or negative quality ("You're not going to like this, but here's what I heard") of subsequent messages.

Altercast   Feedforward is often used to place the receiver in a specific role and to request that the receiver respond to you in terms of this assumed role. This process, introduced in Chapter 3 and known as *altercasting,* asks the receiver to approach your message from a particular perspective or even as someone else (Weinstein & Deutschberger, 1963; McLaughlin, 1984). For example, you might ask a friend, "As an advertising executive, what would you think of corrective advertising?" This question casts your friend in the role of advertising executive (rather than that of parent, an NDPer, or Baptist, for example). It asks your friend to answer from a particular point of view.

Disclaim   The **disclaimer** is a statement that aims to ensure that your message will be understood and will not reflect negatively on you (Hewitt

& Stokes, 1975; McLaughlin, 1984). Suppose, for example, you fear that your listeners will think your comment is inappropriate, or that they may rush to judge you without hearing your full account, or that they may think you're not in full possession of your faculties. In such cases you may use some form of disclaimer and say, for example, "This may not be the place to say this, but …" or "Just hear me out before you hang up." Five popular disclaimers, along with their definitions and examples, are discussed in the Listen to This box below.

Step Three: Business

The third step in the conversational process is the "business," the substance or focus of the conversation. The business is conducted through exchanges of speaker and listener roles. Usually, brief (rather than long) speaking turns characterize most satisfying conversations.

Business is a good word to use for this stage, because the term emphasizes that most conversations are goal-directed. You converse to fulfill one or several of the purposes of interpersonal communication: to learn, relate, influence, play, or help (Chapter 1). The term is also general enough to include all kinds of interactions. During the business stage you talk about Jack, what happened in class, or your vacation plans. This is obviously the longest part of the conversation and the

LISTEN TO THIS

Listening to Disclaimers

Learn to listen to disclaimers (statements that ask the listener to receive what you're saying in a positive light)—not only disclaimers that others offer but also those you make yourself (Hewitt & Stokes, 1975; McLaughlin, 1984). Listen to the way in which disclaimers are phrased, the functions they serve, and the effects they have on the individuals and on the conversation as a whole. The listening experience will sensitize you to the crucial role that disclaimers play in everyday conversation.

- In *hedging* you disclaim the importance of the message to your own identity; you make it clear that listeners may reject the message without rejecting you: *I didn't read the entire report, but...*

- In *credentialing* you try to prevent listeners' drawing undesirable inferences, so you seek to establish special qualifications: *Don't get the wrong idea; I'm not sexist, but...*

- With *sin licences* you announce that you will violate some social or cultural rule but should be "for-

given" in advance (a "licence to sin"): *I realize that this may not be the time to talk about money, but...*

- With *cognitive disclaimers* you seek to reaffirm your cognitive abilities in anticipation of any listener doubts: *I know you think I'm drunk, but I'm as sober as...*

- With *appeals for the suspension of judgment*, you ask listeners to delay making judgments until you have had a chance to present the complete account: *Don't say anything until I explain the real story...*

SUGGESTIONS?

Jennifer is a supervisor in a large electronics corporation and has been asked to make the final selection for the position of assistant manager and present her decision to the all-male board of directors. Four men and one woman applied for the position, and Jennifer has selected the woman. She wonders if she should use any disclaimers in presenting her selection. What would you advise Jennifer to do?

reason for both the opening and the feedforward. Not surprisingly, each culture has its own conversational **taboos**—topics or language that should be avoided, especially by visitors from other cultures (see Table 8.1 below).

Step Four: Feedback

The feedback step is the reverse of the feedforward step. Here you reflect back on the conversation to signal that the business is completed: "So, you may want to send Jack a get-well card," "Wasn't that the craziest class you ever heard of?" or "I'll call for reservations while you shop for what we need."

In another sense, as described in Chapter 1, feedback takes place throughout the interpersonal communication process. Speakers and listeners constantly exchange feedback—messages sent back to the speaker concerning reactions to what is said (Clement & Frandsen, 1976). Feedback tells the speaker what effect he or she is having on listeners. On

TABLE 8.1 Conversational Taboos Around the World

This table lists several examples of topics that Roger Axtell (in *Do's and Taboos Around the World*, 1993) recommends that visitors from North America avoid when in other countries. These examples are not intended to be exhaustive, but rather should serve as a reminder that each culture defines what is and what is not an appropriate topic of conversation. Can you think of other examples?

Country	Conversational Taboos
Belgium	Politics, language differences between French and Flemish, religion
Norway	Salaries, social status
Spain	Family, religion, jobs, negative comments on bullfighting
Egypt	Middle Eastern politics
Nigeria	Religion
Libya	Politics, religion
Iraq	Religion, Middle Eastern politics
Japan	World War II
Pakistan	Politics
Philippines	Politics, religion, corruption, foreign aid
South Korea	Internal politics, socialism or communism, criticism of the government
Bolivia	Politics, religion
Colombia	Politics, criticism of bullfighting
Mexico	Mexican–American war, illegal aliens
Caribbean nations	Race, local politics, religion

the basis of this feedback, the speaker may adjust, modify, strengthen, de-emphasize, or change the content or form of the messages.

Feedback can take many forms. A frown or a smile, a yea or a nay, a pat on the back or a punch in the mouth are all types of feedback. We can think about feedback in terms of five important dimensions: positive–negative, person focused–message focused, immediate–delayed, low monitoring–high monitoring, and supportive–critical. To use feedback effectively, you need to make educated choices along these dimensions (Figure 8.2).

Positive feedback (applause, smiles, head nods signifying approval) tells the speaker that his or her message is being well received and that essentially the speaker should continue speaking in the same general mode. **Negative feedback** (boos, frowns and puzzled looks, gestures signifying disapproval) tells the speaker that something is wrong and that some adjustment needs to be made. The art of feedback involves giving positive feedback without strings and giving negative feedback positively.

Feedback may be *person focused* ("You're sweet," "You have a great smile") or *message focused* ("Can you repeat that phone number?" "Your argument is a good one"). Especially when you are giving criticism, it's important to make clear that your feedback relates to, say, the organization of the budget report and not to the person himself or herself.

Feedback can be *immediate* or *delayed*. Generally, the most effective feedback is that which is most immediate. In interpersonal situations feedback is most often sent immediately after the message is received. Feedback, like reinforcement, loses its effectiveness with time. The longer you wait to praise or punish, for example, the less effect it will have. In other communication situations, however, the feedback may be delayed. Instructor evaluation questionnaires completed at the end of the course provide feedback long after the class is over. In interview situations the feedback may come weeks afterwards.

Feedback varies from the spontaneous and totally honest reaction (*low-monitored* feedback) to the carefully constructed response designed to serve a specific purpose (*high-monitored* feedback). In most interpersonal situations you probably give feedback spontaneously; you allow your responses to show without any monitoring. At other times,

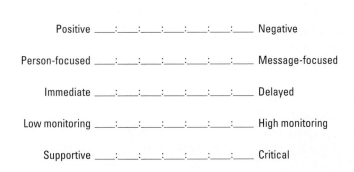

FIGURE 8.2 Five Dimensions of Feedback

Try classifying the last few examples of conversational feedback you encountered along these five dimensions. Can you identify other dimensions of feedback?

however, you may be more guarded, as when your boss asks you how you like your job or when your grandfather asks what you think of his new motorcycle outfit.

Feedback is *supportive* when you console another or when you simply encourage the other to talk or when you affirm another's self-definition. *Critical* feedback, on the other hand, is evaluative. When you give critical feedback, you judge another's performance—as in, for example, evaluating a speech or coaching someone who is learning a new skill.

Step Five: Closing

The fifth and last step in conversation, the opposite of the first step, is the closing, the goodbye (Knapp, Hart, Friedrich, & Shulman, 1973; Knapp & Vangelisti, 2000). Most obviously, this step signals the end of accessibility. Just as the opening signalled access, the closing signals the end of access. The closing may also signal some degree of supportiveness; for example, you might express your pleasure in interacting through a comment such as "Well, it was good talking with you." In some conversations the closing summarizes the interaction. Like the opening, the closing may be verbal or nonverbal but is usually a combination of both. Examples of verbal closings include expressions of appreciation ("Well, I appreciate the time you've given me"), concern for the other's welfare ("Do take care of yourself"), or reinforcement ("It was great seeing you again") as well as leave-taking phrases ("Goodbye," "So long"). Nonverbal closings include breaking eye contact, positioning your legs or feet toward the door and away from the person you're talking with, leaning forward, and placing your hands on your knees or legs (often accompanied by forward leaning) to signal the in-

THINKING CRITICALLY ABOUT
Conclusions

When drawing conclusions about other people, try out these few suggestions:

- *Formulate hypotheses* to test against additional information and evidence—rather than drawing conclusions you then look to confirm.

- *Delay formulating conclusions* until you've had a chance to process a variety of cues. At the same time, seek additional evidence. For example, compare your perceptions with those of others. Do others see things in the same way you do? If not, ask yourself if your perceptions may be in some way distorted.

- *Look for a variety of cues* in making a judgment. For example, in making a judgment about a place to work, you'd logically use a variety of cues—salary, opportunity for advancement, benefits package, the

working environment, and probably lots of other factors as well. After examining these cues, you'd make a judgment about the suitability of this job. In a similar way, it's useful to use a variety of cues when making a judgment about a person.

- *Be especially alert to contradictory cues,* cues that refute your initial hypotheses. It's easy to perceive cues that confirm your hypotheses or conclusions but more difficult to acknowledge contradictory evidence.

EXAMPLES?

Think of an example of a situation in which you formulated a conclusion that proved to be unreliable. Did you ignore any of the suggestions offered here?

tention to stand up. As with openings, usually the verbal and the non-verbal are combined; for example, you might say "It was good seeing you again" while leaning forward with hands on your knees.

Reflections on the Steps of Conversation

Not all conversations will be neatly divided into these five steps. Often the opening and the feedforward are combined—as when you see someone on campus, for example, and say "Hey, listen to this"; or when, in a work situation, someone says, "Well, folks, let's get the meeting going." In a similar way, the feedback and the closing might be combined: "Look, I've got to think more about this commitment, okay?"

As already noted, the business is the longest part of the conversation. The opening and the closing are usually about the same length, and the feedforward and feedback are usually about equal in length. When these relative lengths are severely distorted, you may feel that something is wrong. For example, when someone uses a too-short opening or a long feedforward, you may suspect that what is to follow is extremely serious.

This conversational process model can help us to identify conversational skill deficits and to distinguish effective and satisfying from ineffective and unsatisfying conversations. Consider, for example, how people can damage entire conversations through the following violations:

- using openings that are insensitive; for example, "Wow, you've gained a few pounds"

- using openers that fail to acknowledge the listener; for example, never asking "How are you?"

- using overly long feedforwards that make you wonder if the speaker will ever get to the business

HAGAR THE HORRIBLE © 1993 Chris Browne. Reprinted with special permission of King Features Syndicate.

- omitting feedforward before a truly shocking message (for example, the death or illness of a friend or relative), which leads you to see the other person as insensitive or uncaring

- doing business without the normally expected greeting; as when, for example, your doctor begins the conversation with "Well, what's wrong?"

- omitting feedback, which leads you to wonder if the listener heard what you said or cared

- omitting an appropriate closing, which makes you wonder if the other person is disturbed or angry with you

- not giving clear closure (say, on the phone) so it's not clear if the person wants to hang up or continue talking

Of course, each culture will alter the five basic steps in different ways. In some cultures the openings are especially short; in others the openings are elaborate, lengthy, and sometimes highly ritualized. It's easy in intercultural communication situations to violate another culture's conversational rules. Being overly friendly, too formal, or too forward may easily hinder the remainder of the conversation. The reason why such violations may have significant consequences is that people are not aware of these rules and therefore do not see violations as simply cultural differences. Rather, we see the rule violator as too aggressive, too stuffy, or too pushy—almost immediately we dislike the person and put a negative cast on the future conversation.

(You may wish to experience the conversation process as it applies to giving and responding to directions by conducting the group exercise, "Giving and Taking Directions," at www.ablongman.com/devito.)

In what types of situations do you have the most difficulty communicating? What might you do to make such conversations more effective?

Managing Conversation

Speakers and listeners have to work together to make conversation an effective and satisfying experience. We can look at **conversational management** in terms of opening, maintaining, repairing, and closing conversations. (You may wish to try your hand at conversational analysis either before or after reading this section on conversational management. See the exercise, "Conversational Analysis," at www.ablongman.com/devito.)

Opening Conversations

Opening a conversation is especially difficult. At times you may not be sure of what to say or how to say it. You may fear being rejected or having someone not understand your meaning. One way to develop opening approaches is to focus on the elements of the interpersonal communication process we discussed in Chapter 1. From these we can derive several avenues for opening a conversation:

- *Self-references.* Say something about yourself. Such references may be of the name, rank, and serial number type of statement; for example, "My name is Mike, I'm from Canmore." Or, on the first day of class, students might say, "I'm worried about this class" or "I took a class from this instructor last semester; she was excellent."

- *Other references*. Say something about the other person, or ask a question: "I like that sweater." "Didn't we meet at Charlie's?"

- *Relational references*. Say something about the two of you; for example, "May I buy you a drink?" "Would you like to dance?" or simply "May I join you?"

- *Context references*. Say something about the physical, cultural, social–psychological, or temporal context. The familiar "Do you have the time?" is of this type. But you can be more creative; for example, "This place seems really friendly" or "That painting is just great."

Keep in mind two general rules. First, be positive. Lead off with something positive rather than something negative. Say, for example, "I really enjoy coming here" instead of "Don't you just hate this place?" Second, do not be too revealing; don't self-disclose too much early in an interaction. If you do, people will think it strange.

The Opening Line Another way of looking at the process of initiating conversations is to examine the infamous "opening line." Interpersonal researcher Chris Kleinke (1986), who suggests that opening lines are of three basic types, provides some excellent examples.

Cute–flippant openers are humorous, indirect, and ambiguous about whether the person opening the conversation really wants an extended encounter. Examples: "Is that really your hair?" "Bet I can outdrink you." "I bet the cherry jubilee isn't as sweet as you are."

Innocuous openers are highly ambiguous as to whether they are simple comments that might be made to just anyone or openers designed to initiate an extended encounter. Examples: "What do you think of the band?" "I haven't been here before. What's good on the menu?" "Could you show me how to work this machine?"

Direct openers clearly show the speaker's interest in meeting the other person. Examples: "I feel a little embarrassed about this, but I'd like to meet you." "Would you like to have a drink after dinner?" "Since we're both eating alone, would you like to join me?"

The opening lines most preferred by both men and women are generally those that are direct or innocuous (Kleinke, 1986). The lines least preferred by both men and women are those that are cute–flippant—and women dislike these openers even more than men. Men, who generally underestimate how much women dislike the cute–flippant openers, probably continue to use these lines because they are indirect enough to cushion any rejection. Men also underestimate how much women actually like innocuous openers. Women prefer men to use openers that are modest and avoid coming on too strong. Women, in contrast, tend to also overestimate how much men like innocuous lines. And women generally underestimate how much men like direct openers. Most men prefer openers that are very clear in meaning, which may be because men are not used to having a woman initiate a meeting.

Does your experience agree or disagree with Chris Kleinke's conclusions about how men and women use and respond to opening lines? What evidence can you point to that supports or contradicts Kleinke's findings?

What kinds of openers work best for you? What kinds of openers do you respond to best?

Maintaining Conversations

In maintaining conversations you follow a variety of principles and rules. Let's consider one key general principle and its several maxims; then we'll look at the ways in which the speaker and listener turns are exchanged in conversation.

The Principle of Cooperation   During conversation you probably follow the **principle of cooperation**, agreeing with the other person that you will both cooperate in trying to understand each other (Grice, 1975). If you didn't agree on **cooperation**, then communication would be extremely difficult, if not impossible. You cooperate largely by adhering to four **conversational maxims**—rules that speakers and listeners in Canada and in many other cultures follow in conversation. Although the names for these maxims may be new, the principles themselves will be easily recognized from your own experiences.

You follow the **quantity maxim** when you're only as informative as necessary to communicate the intended meaning. Thus, you include information that makes the meaning clear but omit what does not. The maxim of quantity requires that you give neither too little nor too much information. You see people violate this principle when they try to relate an incident and digress to give unnecessary information. You find yourself thinking, or even saying, "Get to the point; what happened?" This maxim is also violated when necessary information is omitted. In this situation, you find yourself constantly interrupting to ask questions: "Where were they?" "When did this happen?" "Who else was there?"

You follow the **quality maxim** by saying what you know or believe to be true and by not saying what you know to be false. When you're in conversation, you assume that the other person's information is true—at least as far as he or she knows. When you speak with a person who frequently violates the maxim of quality by lying, exaggerating, or minimizing major problems, you come to distrust what the person is saying and wonder what is true and what is fabricated.

You follow the **relation maxim** when you talk about what is relevant to the conversation. Thus, if you're talking about Pat and Chris and say, for example, "Money causes all sorts of relationship problems," it is assumed by others that your comment is somehow related to Pat and Chris. Speakers who digress widely and frequently interject irrelevant comments violate the maxim of relation.

You follow the **manner maxim** by being clear, by avoiding ambiguities, by being relatively brief, and by organizing your thoughts into a meaningful sequence. Thus, you use terms that the listener understands and omit or clarify terms that you suspect the listener will not understand. You see the maxim of manner in action when you adjust your speech on the basis of your listener. For example, when talking to a close friend, you can refer to mutual acquaintances and to experiences you've shared. When talking to a stranger, however, you either omit such references or explain them. Similarly, when talking with a child, you simplify your vocabulary so that the child will understand your meaning.

Conversational Maxims, Culture, and Gender   The four maxims just discussed aptly describe most conversations as they take place in much of Canada. Recognize, however, that these maxims may not apply in all cultures; also, other cultures may have other maxims. Some of these other maxims may contradict the advice generally given to persons communicating in Canada or in other cultures (Keenan, 1976). Here are a few maxims appropriate in countries other than Canada, but also appropriate to some degree throughout Canada.

Researchers on Japanese conversations and group discussions have noted a maxim of preserving peaceful relationships with others (Midooka, 1990). The ways in which such peaceful relationships may be maintained will vary with the person with whom you're interacting. For example, in Japan your status or position in the hierarchy will influence the amount of self-expression you're expected to engage in. Similarly, there is a great distinction made between public and private conversations. The maxim of peaceful relationships is much more important in public than in private conversations, in which the maxim may be and often is violated.

What types of conversation do you find stressful? Can you identify how you might reduce such stress?

The maxim of self-denigration, observed in the conversations of Chinese speakers, may require that you avoid taking credit for some accomplishment or make less of some ability or talent you have (Gu, 1990). To put yourself down in this way is a form of politeness that seeks to elevate the person to whom you're speaking.

The maxim of politeness is probably universal across all cultures (Brown & Levinson, 1987). Cultures differ, however, in how they define politeness and in how important politeness is in comparison with, say, openness or honesty. Cultures also differ in their rules for expressing politeness or impoliteness and in their punishments for violating the accepted rules of politeness (Mao, 1994; Strecker, 1993). You may wish to take the self-test on the next page to help you think about your own level of politeness. (A somewhat more extensive self-test on politeness appears at www.ablongman.com/devito.)

In New York City, to take one example, the low level of politeness between cab drivers and riders has elicited a great deal of criticism. In an attempt to combat this negative attitude, cab drivers have been given 50 polite phrases and are instructed to use these frequently: "May I open (close) the window for you?" "Madam (Sir), is the temperature OK for you?" "I'm sorry, I made a wrong turn. I'll take care of it, and we can deduct it from the fare" (*New York Times*, May 6, 1996, p. B1).

People in Asian cultures, especially the Chinese and Japanese, are often singled out because they emphasize politeness more and mete out harsher social punishments for violations of courtesy norms than

Their remarks and responses were like a Ping-Pong game with each volley clearing the net and flying back to the opposition.

—Maya Angelou

How Polite Is Your Conversation?

Instructions: This is an approach to a conversational politeness scale—a device for measuring politeness in conversation. Try estimating your own level of politeness. For each item below indicate how closely the statement describes your *typical* behaviour in conversations with peers. Avoid giving responses that you feel might be considered "socially acceptable"; instead, give responses that accurately represent your typical conversational behaviours. Use a 10-point scale, with 10 being "very accurate description of my typical communications in conversations" and 1 being "very inaccurate description of my typical communications in conversations."

_____ **1.** I make jokes at the expense of another nationality, race, religion, or affectional orientation.

_____ **2.** I say "please" when asking someone to do something.

_____ **3.** When talking with guests in my home, I leave the television on.

_____ **4.** I make an effort to make sure that other people are not embarrassed.

_____ **5.** I use body adaptors when in conversation—for example, touching my hair or face, playing with a pen or Styrofoam cup, or touching the clothing of the other person.

_____ **6.** I ask people I call if it's a good time to talk.

_____ **7.** I will raise my voice to take charge of the conversation.

_____ **8.** I give the speaker cues to show that I'm listening and interested.

_____ **9.** I avoid using terms that might prove offensive to people with whom I'm talking, such as terms that might be considered sexist, racist, or heterosexist.

_____ **10.** I interrupt the speaker when I think I have something important to say.

HOW DID YOU DO?

This scale was developed to encourage you to consider some of the ways in which politeness is signalled in conversations and to encourage you to examine your own politeness behaviours. Nevertheless, you may want to compile a general politeness score that you can compare with those of others. To compile your politeness score, follow these steps:

- Step 1. Add up your scores for items 2, 4, 6, 8, and 9.

- Step 2. Reverse your scores for items 1, 3, 5, 7, and 10. For example, if you ranked a statement 10, it becomes 1; if you ranked a statement 9, it becomes 2; 8 becomes 3, 7 becomes 4, 6 becomes 5, 5 becomes 6, 4 becomes 7, 3 becomes 8, 2 becomes 9, and 1 becomes 10.

- Step 3. Add the scores for Steps 1 and 2 (using the reversed scores, of course, for the items noted in Step 2).

- Your score should fall somewhere between 10 (extremely impolite) to 100 (extremely polite).

WHAT WILL YOU DO?

Realize that this "scale" is only a pedagogical tool; it's not a scientifically valid research instrument. So use it to stimulate thinking about your own interpersonal politeness behaviours rather than to give yourself a label. Notice that your score indicates your evaluation of your own conversational behaviours, so this score may be very different from the scores others would assign to you. Generally, do you think you see yourself as more (or less) polite than your peers see you? What might you do to increase your level of perceived politeness?

would most people in, say, North America or western Europe. This pattern has led some to propose that a maxim of politeness operates in Asian cultures (Fraser, 1990). When this maxim operates, it may actually conflict with other maxims. For example, the maxim of politeness may require that you not tell the truth—a situation that would violate the maxim of quality.

In internet communication, politeness is covered very specifically by the rules of netiquette, which are very clearly stated in most computer books (see the Skills Toolbox in Chapter 5). For example: Find out what a group is talking about before breaking in with your own comment; be tolerant of newbies (those who are new to newsgroups or chat groups); don't send duplicate messages; don't attack other people.

There are also large gender differences (as well as some similarities) in the expression of politeness (Holmes, 1995). Generally, studies from several different cultures show that women use more polite forms than men (Brown, 1980; Wetzel, 1988; Holmes, 1995). For example, both in informal conversation and in conflict situations, women tend to seek areas of agreement more than do men. Young girls are more apt to try to modify expressions of disagreements, whereas young boys are more apt to express more "bald disagreements" (Holmes, 1995). There are also similarities. For example, both men and women in the United States and New Zealand seem to pay compliments in similar ways (Manes & Wolfson, 1981; Holmes, 1986, 1995), and both men and women use politeness strategies when communicating bad news in an organization (Lee, 1993).

Politeness also varies with the type of relationship. One researcher, for example, has proposed that politeness is considerably greater with friends than with either strangers or intimates (Wolfson, 1988; Holmes, 1995). Wolfson (1998) depicts this relationship as in Figure 8.3.

Conversational Turns   The defining feature of conversation is that the roles of speaker and listener are exchanged throughout the interaction. We use a wide variety of verbal and nonverbal cues to signal **conversational turns**—the changing (or maintaining) of the speaker or listener role during the conversation. Combining the insights of a variety of communication researchers (Burgoon, Buller, & Woodall, 1995; Duncan, 1972; Pearson & Spitzberg, 1990), let's examine conversational turns in terms of speaker cues and listener cues.

Speaker Cues. As a speaker you regulate the conversation through two major types of cues. *Turn-maintaining cues* enable you to maintain the role of speaker. You communicate these cues by, for example, audibly inhaling breath to show that you have more to say, continuing a gesture to show that your thought is not

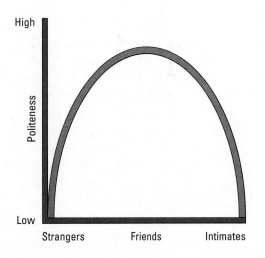

FIGURE 8.3 Wolfson's Bulge Model of Politeness

Do you find this model a generally accurate representation of your own level of politeness in different types of relationships? Can you build a case for an inverted U theory, in which politeness would be high with both strangers and intimates and low with friends?

yet complete, avoiding eye contact with the listener so as not to indicate that you're passing the speaking turn on to the listener, or vocalizing pauses ("er," "umm") to prevent the listener from speaking and to show that you're still talking.

Turn-yielding cues tell the listener that you're finished and wish to exchange the role of speaker for the role of listener. You may communicate these cues by dropping your intonation, by a prolonged silence, by making direct eye contact with a listener, by asking a question, or by nodding in the direction of a particular listener.

Listener Cues. As a listener you can regulate the conversation by using three types of cues. First, *turn-requesting cues* tell the speaker that you would like to take a turn as speaker; you might transmit these cues by using some vocalized "er" or "um" that tells the speaker that you would now like to speak, by opening your eyes and mouth as if to say something, by beginning to gesture with a hand, or by leaning forward.

Second, through *turn-denying cues* you indicate your reluctance to assume the role of speaker by, for example, intoning a slurred "I don't know"; giving the speaker some brief grunt that signals you have nothing to say; avoiding eye contact with the speaker who wishes you now to take on the role of speaker; or engaging in some behaviour that is incompatible with speaking—for example, coughing or blowing your nose.

Third, through *backchannelling cues* you communicate various meanings back to the speaker—but without assuming the role of the speaker. For example, you can indicate your *agreement* or *disagreement* with the speaker through smiles or frowns, nods of approval or disapproval; brief comments such as "right," "exactly," or "never"; or vocalizations such as "uh-huh" or "uh-uh." You convey your *involvement* or *boredom* with the speaker through attentive posture, forward leaning, and focused eye contact, which tell the speaker that you're involved in the conversation—or through an inattentive posture, backward leaning, and avoidance of eye contact, which communicate your lack of involvement. You can also request that the speaker *pace* the conversation differently, perhaps asking the speaker to slow down by raising your hand near your ear and leaning forward, or to speed up by continually nodding your head. Or you can signal the speaker to give you *clarification;* a puzzled facial expression, perhaps coupled with a forward lean, will probably tell most speakers that you need something clarified.

Some backchannelling cues are actually *interruptions.* Backchannelling interruptions, however, are generally confirming rather than disconfirming. They tell the speaker that you're listening and are involved (Kennedy & Camden, 1988). Other interruptions are not as confirming and simply take the speaking turn away from the speaker, either temporarily or permanently. Sometimes the interrupter may apologize for breaking in; at other times the interrupter may not even seem aware of interrupting.

Interruptions can, of course, serve a variety of specific functions. For example, interruptions may be used to change the topic ("I have to tell you this story before I bust"); to correct the speaker ("You mean four months, not years, don't you?"); to seek information or clarification ("Are you talking about Jeff's cousin?"); or to introduce essential information ("Your car's on fire"). And, of course, you can interrupt to end the conversation ("I hate to interrupt, but I really have to get back to the office").

Not surprisingly, research finds that superiors (bosses, supervisors) and those in positions of authority (police officers, interviewers) interrupt those in inferior positions more than the other way around (Ashcraft, 1998; Carroll, 1994;). In fact, it would probably strike you as strange to see a worker repeatedly interrupting a supervisor or a student repeatedly interrupting a professor.

Another and even more often studied aspect of interruption is that of gender difference. Do men or women interrupt more? Research here is conflicting. These few research findings will give you an idea of the differing results (Pearson, West, & Turner, 1995):

- The more male-like the person's gender identity—regardless of the person's biological sex—the more likely it is that the person will interrupt (Drass, 1986).

- There are no significant differences between boys and girls (aged two to five) in interrupting behaviour (Greif, 1980).

- Fathers interrupt their children more than mothers do (Greif, 1980).

- Women judge "simultaneous talk" as being interruptions more than men do (Bresnahan & Cai, 1996).

- Men interrupt more than women do (West & Zimmerman, 1977; Zimmerman & West, 1975).

- Men and women do not differ in their interrupting behaviour (Roger & Nesshoever, 1987).

- No single linguistic feature has been found that definitely identifies a message as an interruption (Coon & Schwanenflugel, 1996).

Figure 8.4 on the next page summarizes the various turn-taking cues and how they correspond to the conversational wants of speaker and listener. (An exercise to help clarify appropriate turn taking in conversation, "Conversational Turns," can be found at www.ablongman.com/devito.)

Repairing Conversations

At times you may say the wrong thing, but you can't erase the message—communication really is irreversible. So you may try to account for it. Perhaps the most common way of doing this is with the excuse (Snyder, 1984; Snyder, Higgins, & Stucky, 1983).

You learn early in life that when you do something that others will view negatively, an **excuse** is in order to justify your performance. You're especially likely to offer an excuse when you say or are accused of saying something that runs counter to what is expected, sanctioned, or considered "right" by your listeners. Ideally, the excuse lessens the negative impact of the message.

Motives for Excuse Making The major motive for excuse making seems to be to maintain self-esteem, to project a positive image to your-

After reviewing the research on the empathic and listening abilities of men and women, Pearson, West, and Turner (1995) conclude: "Men and women do not differ as much as conventional wisdom would have us believe. In many instances, she thinks like a man and he thinks like a woman because they both think alike." Does your experience support or contradict this observation?

FIGURE 8.4 Turn-Taking and Conversational Wants

Quadrant 1 represents the speaker who wishes to continue to speak and uses turn-maintaining cues; quadrant 2, the speaker who wishes to listen and uses turn-yielding cues. Quadrant 3 represents the listener who wishes to speak and uses turn-requesting cues; quadrant 4, the listener who wishes to continue listening and uses turn-denying cues. Backchannelling cues would appear in quadrant 4, as they are cues that listeners use while they continue to listen. Interruptions would appear in quadrant 3, though they are not so much cues that request a turn as actual takeovers of the speaker's position.

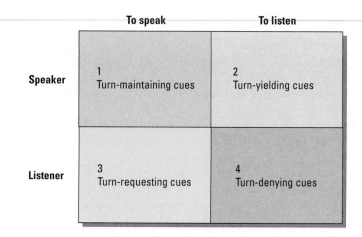

Have you heard (or used) any excuses lately? What functions did these excuses serve? Were they effective? How might they have been made more effective? In what types of situations do you find that excuses only aggravate the problems they were meant to solve? If you were compiling a book on *The World's Worst Excuses,* which one(s) would you include? Which would you include in *The World's Best Excuses?*

To make excuses before they are needed is to blame one's self.

— Spanish proverb

self and to others. You may also offer an excuse to reduce the stress that may be created by a bad performance. You may feel that if you can offer an excuse—especially a good one that is accepted by those around you—it will reduce the negative reaction and the subsequent stress that might accompany your possible poor performance.

Excuses also enable you to maintain effective interpersonal relationships even after some negative behaviour. For example, after criticizing a friend's behaviour and observing the friend's negative reaction to your criticism, you might offer an excuse such as "Please forgive me; I'm really exhausted. I'm just not thinking straight." Excuses place your messages—even your failures—in a more favourable light.

Good and Bad Excuses   The most important question to most people is what makes a good excuse and what makes a bad excuse (Snyder, 1984; Slade, 1995). How can you make good excuses and thus get out of problems—and how can you avoid making bad excuses and thus only making matters worse? Here are some differences between good and bad excuses that may guide your own excuse making:

- Good excuses are used in moderation; bad excuses are used excessively.

- Good excuses avoid blaming others; bad excuses seek to shift to others the blame for your own failures.

- Good excuses incorporate an acknowledgment of responsibility for doing something wrong (although not of a basic lack of competence); bad excuses avoid acknowledgment of any personal responsibility.

- Good excuses ask for forgiveness; bad excuses (because they seldom admit any wrongdoing) do not ask for forgiveness.

- Good excuses promise that things will be better in the future and that this failure will never happen again; bad excuses fail to mention any ways in which the problem will be avoided in the future.

Closing Conversations

Closing a conversation is almost as difficult as opening a conversation. It's frequently an awkward and uncomfortable part of interpersonal interaction. Here are a few **leave-taking cues** you might consider for closing a conversation.

- Reflect back on the conversation and briefly summarize it to bring it to a close. For example, "I'm glad I ran into you and found out what happened at that union meeting. I'll probably be seeing you at the workshops."

- State the desire to end the conversation directly and to get on with other things. For example, "I'd like to continue talking but I really have to run. I'll see you around."

- Refer to future interaction. For example, "Why don't we get together next week sometime and continue this discussion."

- Ask for closure. For example, "Have I covered what you wanted to know?"

- Say that you enjoyed the interaction. For example, "I really enjoyed talking with you."

With any of these closings, it should be clear to the other person that you're attempting to end the conversation. Obviously, you will have to use more direct methods with those who don't take these subtle hints—who don't realize that *both* persons are responsible for the interpersonal interaction and for bringing it to a satisfying closing. (An exercise, "Opening and Closing Conversations," may help clarify some of the appropriate and inappropriate ways of opening and closing a conversation; visit www.ablongman.com/devito.)

Effective Conversation

Because each conversation is unique, the skills of **interpersonal effectiveness** cannot be applied indiscriminately. Shortly we'll consider specific conversational skills, but you'll need to apply these skills selectively. For example, although openness is a generally positive quality in, say, romantic relationships, it may be quite inappropriate with your supervisor or postal worker. Fortunately, there are general skills to help you regulate your more specific skills. (If you have not already done so, visit the Allyn and Bacon communication studies website at www.ablongman.com/commstudies.)

General Conversational Skills

Four general skills will prove especially valuable in helping you decide how to apply your specific skills; these are mindfulness, flexibility, cultural sensitivity, and metalinguistic abilities.

Mindfulness After you have learned a skill or rule, you may have a tendency to apply it without thinking, or "mindlessly"—without, for example, considering the novel aspects of a situation. For instance, after learning the skills of active listening, many people tend to use them in

Courtesy of Mel Yauk.

response to all situations. Some of these responses will be appropriate, but others will prove inappropriate and ineffective. In interpersonal and even in small group situations (Elmes & Gemmill, 1990), choose **mindfulness** over **mindlessness** as you apply conversational skills (Langer, 1989).

Langer (1989) offers several suggestions for increasing mindfulness:

- Create and recreate categories. See an object, event, or person as belonging to a variety of categories. Avoid storing in memory an image of a person, for example, with only one specific label; it will be difficult to recategorize that image later.

- Be open to new information even if it contradicts your most firmly held stereotypes.

- Be willing to see your own and others' behaviours from a variety of perspectives.

- Be careful of relying too heavily on first impressions; treat first impressions as tentative, as hypotheses.

Flexibility   Before reading about flexibility, take the self-test below, "How flexible are you in communication?"

TEST YOURSELF

How Flexible Are You in Communication?

Instructions: Here are some scenarios that illustrate how people sometimes act when communicating with others. The first sentence in each situation asks you to imagine that you are in the situation; the second sentence identifies a course of action. How much would your own behaviour be like the action described in each scenario? If the action is exactly like you, mark a 5; if it is a lot like you, mark a 4; if it is somewhat like you, mark a 3; if it is not much like you, mark a 2; and if it is not at all like you, mark a 1.

_____ 1. Last week, as you were discussing your strained finances with your family, family members came up with several possible solutions. Even though you already decided on one solution, you decided to spend more time considering all the possibilities before making a final decision.

_____ 2. You were invited to a Halloween party, and assuming it was a costume party, you dressed as a pumpkin. When you arrived at the party and found everyone else dressed in formal attire, you laughed and joked about the misunderstanding, and decided to stay and enjoy the party.

_____ 3. You have always enjoyed being with your friend Chris, but don't enjoy Chris's habit of always interrupting you. The last time you met, every time Chris interrupted you, you then interrupted Chris to teach Chris a lesson.

_____ 4. Your daily schedule is very structured and your calendar is full of appointments and commitments. When asked to make a change in your schedule, you replied that changes are impossible before even considering the change.

_____ 5. You went to a party where over 50 people attended. You had a good time, but spent most of the evening talking to one close friend rather than meeting new people.

_____ 6. When discussing a personal problem with a group of friends, you noticed that many different solutions were offered. Although several of the solutions seemed feasible, you already had your opinion and didn't listen to any of the alternative solutions.

_____ 7. You and a friend are planning a fun evening, and you're dressed and ready ahead of time. You find that you're unable to do anything else until your friend arrives.

_____ 8. When you found your seat at the ball game, you realized you didn't know anyone sitting nearby. However, you introduced yourself to the people sitting next to you and attempted to strike up a conversation.

_____ 9. You had lunch with your friend Chris, and Chris told you about a too-personal family problem. You quickly finished your lunch and stated that you had to leave because you had a lot to do that afternoon.

_____ 10. You were involved in a discussion about international politics with a group of acquaintances and you assumed that the members of the group were as knowledgeable as you on the topic; but, as the discussion progressed, you learned that most of the group knew little about the subject. Instead of explaining your point of view, you decided to withdraw from the discussion.

_____ 11. You and a group of friends got into a discussion about gun control and, after a while, it became obvious that your opinions differed greatly from the rest of the group. You explained your position once again, but you agreed to respect the group's opinion also.

_____ 12. You were asked to speak to a group you belong to, so you worked hard preparing a 30-minute presentation; but at the meeting, the organizer asked you to lead a question-and-answer session instead of giving your presentation. You agreed, and answered the group's questions as candidly and fully as possible.

_____ 13. You were offered a managerial position where every day you would face new tasks and challenges and a changing day-to-day routine. You decided to accept this position instead of one that has a stable daily routine.

_____ 14. You were asked to give a speech at a Chamber of Commerce breakfast. Because you didn't know anyone at the breakfast and would feel uncomfortable not knowing anyone in the audience, you declined the invitation.

HOW DID YOU DO?

To compute your score:
1. Reverse the scoring for items 4, 5, 6, 7, 9, 10, and 14. That is, for each of these questions, substitute as follows: If you answered 5, reverse it to 1; if you answered 4, reverse it to 2; if you answered 3, keep it as 3; if you answered 2, reverse it to 4; and if you answered 1, reverse it to 5.

(continued)

2. Add the scores for all 14 items. Be sure to use the reversed scores for items 4, 5, 6, 7, 9, 10, and 14 instead of your original responses. Use your original scores for items 1, 2, 3, 8, 11, 12, and 13. In general, you can interpret your score as follows:

- 65–70 = much more flexible than average
- 57–64 = more flexible than average
- 44–56 = about average
- 37–43 = less flexible than average
- 14–36 = much less flexible than average

WHAT WILL YOU DO?

Are you satisfied with your level of flexibility? What specific steps might you take to cultivate greater flexibility in general and greater interpersonal communication flexibility in particular?

Source: From "Development of a Communication Flexibility Measure" by Matthew M. Martin and Rebecca B. Rubin, *The Southern Communication Journal* 59 (Winter 1994), pp. 171–178. Reprinted by permission of the Southern States Communication Association.

Although this text provides general principles for effective interpersonal communication, conversational **flexibility** means sensitivity to the unique factors in each situation. Self-disclosure, for example, is beneficial sometimes and with some people but dangerous in other situations and with other people (Chapter 2). The same is true with other effectiveness skills to be discussed here. Effective interpersonal communication depends on understanding the principles and applying them flexibly—with a consideration for all the elements in the communication act.

Here are a few suggestions for cultivating flexibility:

- Recall the principle of indiscrimination (Chapter 5)—no two things or situations are exactly alike. Ask yourself, What is different about this situation?

- Realize that communication always takes place in a context (Chapter 1); ask yourself what is unique about this specific context that might alter your communications. Will cultural differences play a role in this communication?

- Remember that everything is in a constant state of change (Chapter 5); therefore, responses that were appropriate yesterday may not be appropriate today. Responding protectively when your child is 5 may be appropriate; at 18 that same response may be inappropriate. Also, recognize that sudden changes may also exert great influence on communication: A breakup with a lover, a new diagnosis of chronic illness, the birth of a child, a promotion at work are just a few examples.

- Recall that everyone is different. Thus, you may need to be frank and spontaneous when talking with a close friend about your feelings, but you may not want to be so open when talking with your grandmother about the dinner she prepared that you disliked.

Cultural Sensitivity What may prove appropriate for a town hall meeting of Saskatchewan farmers may prove inappropriate among a group of Toronto-Dominion bankers. What works in Japan may not work in Mexico. The direct eye contact that signals immediacy in mainstream Canadian cultures may be deemed disrespectful in Aboriginal or other cultures. The extended silences of some may be interpreted as apathy or lack of intelligence.

Metacommunicational Ability   Much talk concerns people, objects, and events in the world. But you also talk about your talk, or meta-communicate. **Metacommunication** is communication about communication. Your interpersonal effectiveness often hinges on this ability to metacommunicate. Let's say that someone says something positive but in a negative way; for example, the person says, "Yes, I think you did... a good job," but without enthusiasm and with an avoidance of eye contact. You are faced with several alternatives. You may, for example, respond to the message as positive or as negative. Another alternative, however, is to talk about the message, saying something like "I'm not sure I understand if you're pleased or displeased with what I did. You said you were pleased, but I detect dissatisfaction in your voice. Am I wrong?" In this way, you may avoid lots of misunderstandings.

   Here are a few suggestions for using metacommunication:

- Give clear feedforward. This will help the other person get a general picture of the message that will follow and make understanding easier.

- Confront contradictory or inconsistent messages. At the same time, explain any message of your own that may appear inconsistent to your listener.

- Explain the feelings that go with your thoughts. Often people communicate only the thinking part of their message, with the result that listeners are not able to appreciate the other parts of their meaning.

What potential barriers (cultural, status, age, etc.) seem to have been overcome in this photograph of a professor and her students?

- Paraphrase your own complex messages. Similarly, to check on your own understanding of another's message, paraphrase what you think the other person means and ask if you are accurate.

- Ask questions. If you have doubts about another's meaning, don't assume; instead, ask.

- When you do talk about talk, do so only to enhance clarity or to gain an understanding of the other person's thoughts and feelings. Avoid substituting talk about talk for talk about a specific problem.

Specific Conversational Skills

The skills of conversational effectiveness we discuss here are (1) openness, (2) empathy, (3) positiveness, (4) immediacy, (5) interaction management, (6) expressiveness, and (7) other-orientation. These qualities are derived from a wide spectrum of ongoing research (Bochner & Kelly, 1974; Cupach, 1984, 1989; Rubin & Graham, 1988; Spitzberg & Hecht, 1984; Spitzberg & Rubin, 1985, 1986; Whalen-Bell, 2003; Wiemann, 1977). As you read about these concepts, keep the general skills in mind.

Openness **Openness** embraces three aspects of interpersonal communication. First, you should be willing to self-disclose—to reveal information about yourself. Of course, these disclosures need to be appropriate to the entire communication act (see Chapter 2). Openness should also prevail when you listen to others; you should be open to the thoughts and feelings of the person with whom you're communicating.

A second aspect of openness is willingness to react honestly to the situations that confront you. We want people to react openly to what we say, and we have a right to expect this. We show openness by responding spontaneously and honestly to the communications and the feedback of others.

Third, as discussed in Chapter 7, openness calls for the owning of feelings and thoughts. To be open in this sense is to acknowledge that the feelings and thoughts you express are yours and that you bear the responsibility for them.

When you own your own messages, you use I-messages instead of you-messages. Instead of saying, "You make me feel so stupid when you ask what everyone else thinks but don't ask my opinion," the person who owns his or her feelings says, "I feel stupid when you ask everyone else what they think but don't ask me." When you own your feelings and thoughts, when you use I-messages, you say in effect, "This is how *I* feel," "This is how *I* see the situation," "This is what *I* think," with the *I* always paramount. Instead of saying, "This discussion is useless," you would say, "*I'm* bored by this discussion" or "*I* want to talk more about the steps we're going to take," or any other such statement that includes a reference to the fact that you're making an evaluation and not describing objective reality.

Empathy To empathize with someone is to feel as that person feels. When you feel **empathy** for another, you're able to understand what the

7 Ways to Avoid Being Conversationally Difficult

At work meetings or at the water cooler, some people make conversation extremely difficult. Here's a brief list of conversationally difficult people and some suggestions to avoid becoming one of them.

1. *The detour taker* begins to talk about a topic; but then a key word or idea suggests another topic, and off this person goes pursuing the new topic. *Follow a logical pattern in conversation; avoid long and/or frequent detours.*

2. *The moralist* seems to have an inside track on what's right and what's wrong. The moralist's business is judgment, and this individual frequently interjects moral judgments into even the most mundane conversations: "You really shouldn't have said that" or "You know, you should..." *Avoid evaluation and judgment; see the world through the eyes of the other person and (perhaps) the other culture.*

3. *The storyteller* has difficulty talking about the here and now and so tells stories. Mention a topic and the storyteller has a ready tale that makes you sorry you ever brought the subject up in the first place. This is especially problematic at company meetings, in which you want to accomplish a certain amount of work in the allotted time. *Talk about yourself in moderation; be other-oriented.*

4. *The interrogator* is a mixture of police officer, lawyer, and teacher and seems to do nothing but ask questions. No sooner have you answered one question than you are peppered with another and another and another. *Ask questions in modera-* *tion—to secure needed information, not to get every detail imaginable.*

5. *The egotist* is interested only in himself or herself and shows this by connecting even the most wide-ranging topics to self-related concerns. Often this gets in the way of effective team conferences, and invariably it wastes everyone's time. *Be other-oriented; focus on the other person as an individual; listen as much as you speak, and speak about the listener at least as much as you speak about yourself.*

6. *The doomsayer* is the ultimate negative thinker. No matter what you say, the doomsayer will read something negative into it. To the doomsayer the past was a problem, the present is unsatisfying, and the future is bleak. *Be positive.*

7. *The advisor* assumes, whenever you express a doubt or mention a decision, that you want advice; this person proceeds to analyze the pros and cons of each alternative and then provides the solution. The idea that you simply wanted to express a doubt never occurs to the conversational advisor. *Avoid giving unsolicited advice. Don't assume that discussing a problem is the same as asking for a solution.*

THEN AND NOW

Have you ever been in a conversation in which you acted the role of one or more of these conversationally difficult people? What specifically did you do to make the conversation difficult? If you were having the same conversation today, what would you do differently?

---

other is experiencing from that person's point of view. Empathy does *not* necessarily mean that you agree with what the other person says or does. You never lose your own identity or your own attitudes and beliefs. To *sympathize,* on the other hand, is to feel *for* the individual—to feel sorry for the person, for example.

Empathy, then, enables you to understand, emotionally and intellectually, what another person is experiencing. Not surprisingly, empathy can have significant effects. For example, a study of physician empathy found that patients with empathic physicians experienced significantly less depression and were less likely to consider euthanasia than those with nonempathic physicians (Emanuel, Fairclough,

Slutsman, & Emanuel, 2000). The article on page 213 may suggest why this would be so. Here are a few suggestions for communicating empathy both verbally and nonverbally:

- Self-disclose. Express the similarities between your experiences and the experiences of the other person. At the same time, however, acknowledge that you're aware of the differences. For example, *I never failed a course, but I got enough D's to understand why you feel so down. I felt it was a kind of rejection from someone I really wanted to impress.*

- Avoid judgmental and evaluative (nonempathic) responses. Avoid *should* and *ought* statements that try to tell the other person how he or she *should* feel. For example, avoid expressions such as *Don't feel so bad, Don't cry, Cheer up, In time you'll forget all about this,* and *You should start dating others; by next month you won't even remember her name.*

- Use reinforcing comments. Let the speaker know that you understand what the speaker is saying, and encourage him or her to continue talking about the issue. For example, use comments such as *I see, I get it, I understand, Yes,* and *Right.*

- Demonstrate interest by maintaining eye contact (avoid scanning the room or focusing on objects or persons other than the person with whom you're interacting); maintaining physical closeness (avoid large spaces between yourself and the other person); leaning toward (not away from) the other person; and showing your attentiveness with your facial expressions, nods, and eye movements.

Positiveness   You can communicate **positiveness** in interpersonal communication in at least two ways: stating positive attitudes and complimenting the person with whom you interact.

Attitudinal positiveness in interpersonal communication is a positive regard for oneself, for the other person, and for the general communication situation. Your feelings (whether positive or negative) become clear during conversation and greatly influence the satisfaction (or dissatisfaction) you derive from the interaction. Negative feelings usually make communication more difficult and can contribute to its eventual breakdown. In fact, in a study of law enforcement personnel (though the principle is no doubt applicable more generally), the failure to express positiveness toward others was found to have negative effects on personnel and on the department as a whole (Leonard, 1997). Whalen-Bell (2003) found that the majority of complaints about noncommunication in the workplace actually resulted from a feeling by employees that there is a lack of courtesy and respect toward them by management. He suggests that, when communicating with others, try to keep the negative comments separate from the positive ones to allow the listener to bask in the glory of receiving positive news. Better yet, rephrasing negative language may further the dialogue on working together to address issues.

"Cheer up, Nicole! What does Princeton know? Say, you got any plans for that last bit of cobbler?"

Positiveness is seen most clearly in the way you phrase statements. Consider these two sets of sentences:

1a. I wish you wouldn't handle me so roughly.

1b. I really enjoy it when you're especially gentle.

2a. You look horrible in stripes.

2b. You look your best, I think, in solid colours.

The "a" sentences are negative; they are critical and will almost surely encourage defensive or angry responses. The "b" sentences, in contrast, express the speaker's thought clearly but are phrased positively and should encourage cooperative responses.

Complimenting—talking about the positive qualities in another person (friendliness, helpfulness, or generosity) or about something he or she did that you evaluate positively (giving time to charitable work, working to correct some injustice, or helping those less fortunate)—is another way to express positiveness. Many people, in fact, structure interpersonal encounters almost solely for the purpose of getting complimented. People may buy new clothes to get complimented, compliment associates so that the associates compliment back, do favours for people in order to receive thanks, associate with certain people because they are generous with their compliments, and so on. Some people even enter relationships because they hold the promise of frequent compliments.

What constitutes an appropriate compliment will naturally vary with the culture (Dresser, 1996). For example, in Canada it would be considered appropriate for a teacher to publicly compliment a student on getting the highest grade in an examination or for a supervisor to compliment a worker for doing an exceptional job on some project. But in other cultures (collectivist cultures, for example) compliments like these would be considered inappropriate, because they single out the individual and separate that person from the group. Similarly, the responses to compliments will vary from one culture to another (Chen, 1993). While many Canadians often have difficulty accepting compliments, a compliment is generally supposed to be accepted graciously; you did a good job and have a right to have that acknowledged. In more collectivist cultures, however, you're expected to deny your right to the compliment and instead to credit the group or the situation—"It was a very easy thing to do," "I didn't do it by myself," "Others deserve the credit," and so on.

Immediacy The term **immediacy** refers to the joining of the speaker and listener, the creation of a sense of togetherness. The communicator who demonstrates immediacy conveys a sense of interest and attention, a liking for and an attraction to the other person. People respond favourably to immediacy.

You can communicate immediacy in several ways:

- Maintain appropriate eye contact and limit looking around at others; smile and otherwise express your interest.

- Maintain a physical closeness, which suggests a psychological closeness; maintain a direct and open body posture.

> There is nothing you can say in answer to a compliment. I have been complimented myself a great many times, and they always embarrass me—I always feel that they have not said enough.
>
> **—Mark Twain**

- Focus on the other person's remarks. Make the speaker know that you heard and understood what was said and will base your feedback on it.

- Reinforce, reward, or compliment the other person. Use expressions such as "I like your new outfit" or "Your comments were really to the point."

Interaction Management   The effective communicator controls the interaction to the satisfaction of both parties. In effective **interaction management** neither person feels ignored or on stage. Each contributes to the total communication interchange. Maintaining your role as speaker or listener and passing back and forth the opportunity to speak are interaction management skills. If one person speaks all the time and the other listens all the time, effective conversation becomes difficult if not impossible. Depending on the situation, one person may speak more than the other person. This, however, should occur because of the situation and not because one person is a "talker" and another a "listener."

Effective interaction managers avoid interrupting the other person. Interruption signals that what you have to say is more important than what the other person is saying and puts the other person in an inferior position. The result is dissatisfaction with the conversation. Similarly, effective interaction management includes keeping the conversation flowing and fluent without long and awkward pauses that make everyone uncomfortable.

Self-monitoring, the manipulation of the image that you present to others in your interpersonal interactions, is integrally related to interpersonal interaction management. High self-monitors carefully adjust their behaviours on the basis of feedback from others so that they produce the most desirable effect. Low self-monitors communicate their thoughts and feelings with no attempt to manipulate the impressions they create. Most of us lie somewhere between the two extremes.

Listening involves more than just hearing words, as the human body sends messages in many ways. Hurston and Wilson (1978) suggest that one way to self-monitor is to train the eyes to "listen" for parts of the message that were either not heard or properly interpreted by monitoring the speaker's eyes, body motion, and posture. This is important for three primary reasons: 1) to hear beyond the verbal message; 2) to understand the effect of one's nonverbal communication on others; and 3) to appreciate the value and competence of nonverbal communicators.

(One of the best ways to look at interaction management is to take the self-test, "How much do you self-monitor?" This test will help you to identify the qualities that make for the effective management of interpersonal communication situations. See www.ablongman.com/devito.)

Expressiveness   **Expressiveness** communicates genuine involvement in the interpersonal interaction. The expressive speaker plays the game instead of just watching it as a spectator. Expressiveness is similar to openness in its emphasis on involvement. It includes taking responsibility for your thoughts and feelings, encouraging expressiveness or openness in others, and providing appropriate feedback. This quality also includes taking responsibility for both talking and listening. In conflict situations, expressiveness involves fighting actively and stating disagreement directly. More specifically, expressiveness may be communicated in a variety of ways. Here are a few guidelines:

- Practise active listening by paraphrasing, expressing understanding of the thoughts and feelings of the other person, and asking relevant questions (as explained in Chapter 4).

- Avoid clichés and trite expressions that signal a lack of personal involvement and originality; they make it appear that there is nothing special in this specific conversation.

- Address messages (verbal or nonverbal) that contradict each other. Also address messages that somehow seem unrealistic to you; for example, statements claiming that the breakup of a long-term relationship is completely forgotten or that failing a course doesn't mean anything.

- Use I-messages to signal personal involvement and a willingness to share your feelings. Instead of saying "You never give me a chance to make any decisions," say, "I'd like to contribute to the decisions that affect both of us."

Nonverbally you can communicate expressiveness by using appropriate variations in vocal rate, pitch, volume, and rhythm to convey involvement and interest and by allowing your facial muscles to reflect and echo this inner involvement. Similarly, the appropriate use of gestures communicates involvement. Too few gestures signal disinterest, while too many may signal discomfort, uneasiness, and awkwardness. The speaker who talks about sex, winning the lottery, and fatal illness all in the same tone of voice, with a static posture and an expressionless face, is the stereotype of the ineffective interaction manager.

Shy people are often at a disadvantage when communicating. Shafer (1993) suggests that shy people learn to keep a conversation going by learning how to listen effectively and to ask appropriate questions. Learning how to self-disclose and to be comfortable doing so is also an important element in managing a conversation effectively.

Other-Orientation   **Other-orientation** shows consideration and respect—as when you ask if it's all right to dump your troubles on someone before doing so, or ask if your phone call comes at an inopportune time before launching into your conversation. Other-orientation also involves acknowledging others' feelings as legitimate: "I can understand why you're so angry; I would be too." Other-orientation is the opposite of self-orientation and is illustrated in the letter to Ann Landers that opened this chapter. It involves the ability to communicate attentiveness to and interest in the other person and in what is being said.

You can communicate other-orientation in a variety of ways:

- Use focused eye contact, smiles, and head nods; lean toward the other person, and display feelings and emotions through appropriate facial expression.

If you can't say anything good about someone, sit right here by me.

—Alice Roosevelt Longworth

Gossiping About Secrets

There can be no doubt that everyone spends a great deal of time in **gossip**. In fact, gossip seems a universal among all cultures (Laing, 1993), and among some it's a commonly accepted ritual (Hall, 1993). Gossip is third-party talk about another person; the word "now embraces both the talker and the talk, the tattler and the tattle, the newsmonger and the newsmongering" (Bremner, 1980, p. 178). Gossip is an inevitable part of daily interactions, and to advise anyone not to gossip would be absurd. Not gossiping would eliminate one of the most frequent and enjoyable forms of communication.

But gossip can be highly damaging; it can, in fact, destroy a person's life.

In *Secrets* (1983), ethicist Sissela Bok identifies three types of situations in which she argues that it is unethical to reveal secrets about another person. First, it's unethical to reveal information that you have promised to keep secret. And when there are significant reasons for not keeping such information confidential, the information should be revealed only to those who must know it, not to the world at large.

Second, it's unethical to pass along gossip about another person when you know the information to be false. Third, it's unethical to invade the privacy to which everyone has a right; for example, when it concerns matters that are properly considered private and when the gossip can hurt the individuals involved. In a study of 133 school executives, board presidents, and superintendents, the majority received communications that violated an employee's right to confidentiality (Wilson & Bishard, 1994). And in a study of elevator rides of medical personnel, 14 percent of these rides included gossip about patients (Ubel, Zell, & Miller, et al., 1995).

WHAT WOULD YOU DO?

As Bok suggests, consider the case of an 18-year-old student with whom you're fairly friendly. He tells you in strict confidence that he intends to commit suicide. Using these three guidelines, how would you evaluate the ethics involved in revealing or not revealing this secret? What ethical justification might be offered for revealing such a secret? What would you do in this situation?

- Ask the other person for suggestions, opinions, and clarification as appropriate. Statements such as "How do you feel about it?" or "What do you think?" will go a long way toward focusing the communication on the other person.

- Express agreement when appropriate. Comments such as "You're right" or "That's interesting" help to focus the interaction on the other person, which encourages greater openness.

- Use backchannelling cues to encourage the other person to express himself or herself. For example, *yes, I see,* or even *aha* or *hmm* will tell the other person that you're interested in his or her continued comments.

What one quality of conversational effectiveness do you think is the most important in establishing a romantic relationship? In dealing effectively with interpersonal conflict? In employer–employee communication? Why?

- Use positive affect statements to refer to the other person and to his or her contributions to the interaction. For example, "I really enjoy talking with you" or "That was a clever way of looking at things" are positive affect statements that are often felt but rarely expressed.

(An exercise, "The Qualities of Effectiveness," will help summarize some of these qualities of effective conversation and of interpersonal communication generally; see www.ablongman.com/devito.)

A Note on Computer Conversation Skills

Research has just begun to focus on the skills of computer communication. There is some research evidence, for example, that small computer-communicating groups function in some ways better than face-to-face groups (Harris, 1995; Kiesler & Sproull, 1992; Olaniran, 1994). Compared with face-to-face groups, computer groups generated a greater number of unique ideas, proposed more unconventional or risky decisions, took longer to reach agreement, engaged in more explicit and outspoken advocacy, and had more equal participation among members.

In many cases, studies found that students preferred computer-mediated communication over face-to-face communication. The reason, it seems, was that in mediated communication the students didn't have to worry about the rules for interpersonal communication, such as those for eye contact and body communication; computer use also lessened their concerns about shyness (Mendoza, 1995). The insights from studies such as these are just beginning to be incorporated into interpersonal communication courses and textbooks (Harris, 1995).

Here are some guidelines for making your own online communication more effective:

- Watch your spelling. If you have a spellchecker, use it.

- Remember that what you write can easily be made public. So, to quote Sidney Biddle Barrows, "Never say anything on the [internet] that you wouldn't want your mother to hear at your trial."

- Follow the rules of netiquette (Chapter 5), and avoid potential sources of conflict such as spamming and flaming (Chapter 11).

THINKING CRITICALLY ABOUT
Communicating with a New Canadian

Lin Chu, originally from Hong Kong, was introduced at a party shortly after her arrival in Vancouver. The hostess, anxious to make her feel welcome, spoke to her in "English Made Easy." Using expressive gestures and speaking in a loud, clearly articulated voice, she asked, "Would you (pointing to Chu) like something to eat (pointing to her mouth and making chewing motions)?" Chu responded, "I'd love a sherry." She had spent the last four years earning her PhD at Oxford University in England.

Our good intentions to assist new Canadians can be insulting if we make assumptions that are unfounded.

Consider the following list of "don'ts."

Don't assume that you have to:

- Speak in elementary English
- Gesture more than normal
- Speak slower than normal
- Speak louder than normal
- Explain everything in great detail

EXAMPLES?

Many new Canadians do need time to develop proficiency in English. Have you had the experience of trying to communicate in an unfamiliar language? What assistance would you have appreciated? What assumptions would you hope others would avoid making?

- Clean up your writing—consider your choices for communicating mindfully.

- Be explicit as to your good intentions; avoid the possibility of being misunderstood. If, for example, you think your sarcasm may not be interpreted as humour, then use the smiling emoticon :-).

- Follow the suggestions and guidelines for interpersonal communication generally; after all, they aren't that different.

SUMMARY OF CONCEPTS AND SKILLS

In this chapter we looked at conversation and identified five stages that are especially important. We looked at conversational management (issues involved in initiating, maintaining, repairing, and closing conversations) and at the skills of conversational effectiveness.

1. Conversation consists of five general stages: opening, feedforward, business, feedback, and closing.

2. The disclaimer (a statement that helps ensure that your message will be understood as you wish and will not reflect negatively on you) is often used to prevent conversational problems. Hedges, credentialing, sin licences, cognitive disclaimers, and appeals for the suspension of judgment are the major types of disclaimers.

3. Initiating conversations can be accomplished in various ways; for example, with self, other, relational, and context references.

4. People maintain conversations by taking turns at speaking and listening. Turn-maintaining and turn-yielding cues are used by the speaker; turn-requesting, turn-denying, and backchannelling cues are used by the listener.

5. You can close a conversation using a variety of methods. For example: Reflect back on conversation as in summarizing, directly state your desire to end the conversation, refer to future interaction, ask for closure, and/or state your pleasure with the interaction.

6. Conversational repair is frequently undertaken through excuses (statements of explanation designed to lessen the negative impact of a speaker's messages). "I didn't do it," "It wasn't so bad," and "Yes, but" are major types of excuses.

7. The skills of conversational effectiveness need to be applied with mindfulness, flexibility, cultural sensitivity, and metacommunication (as appropriate). Among the skills of conversational effectiveness are openness, empathy, positiveness, immediacy, interaction management, expressiveness, and other-orientation.

Check your ability to apply the following skills. You will gain most from this brief exercise if you think carefully about each skill and try to identify instances from your recent communication experiences in which you did or did not act on the basis of the specific skill. Use a rating scale such as the following: 1 = almost always, 2 = often, 3 = sometimes, 4 = rarely, and 5 = almost never.

_____ 1. Follow the basic structure of conversations but deviate with good reason.

_____ 2. Regulate feedback in terms of positiveness, person and message focus, immediacy, self-monitoring, and supportiveness as appropriate to the situation.

_____ 3. Initiate conversations with a variety of people with comfort and relative ease.

_____ 4. Maintain conversations by smoothly passing the speaker turn back and forth.

_____ 5. Recognize when conversational repair is necessary and make the appropriate repairs in a timely fashion.

_____ 6. Close conversations with comfort and relative ease.

_____ 7. Apply the specific skills of interpersonal communication mindfully, flexibly, and with cultural sensitivity, and metacommunicate as appropriate.

_____ 8. Use the skills of conversational effectiveness (openness, empathy, positiveness, immediacy, interaction management, expressiveness, and other-orientation).

VOCABULARY QUIZ

The Language of Conversation

Match the terms listed here with their definitions. Record the number of the definition next to the term.

_2_ excuse

_____ disclaimer

_____ business

_____ turn-yielding cues

_____ feedforward

_8_ backchannelling cues

_____ altercasting

_____ conversation

_10_ immediacy

_____ phatic communication

1. An interaction in which speaker and listener exchange their roles nonautomatically.

2. A form of conversation repair.

3. Information that tells the listener about the messages that will follow.

4. A statement that aims to ensure that your message will be understood and will not reflect negatively on you.

5. A conversation stage during which the major purpose of the interaction is accomplished.

6. Cues that tell the listener that the speaker is finished and wishes to exchange the role of speaker for the role of listener.

7. A kind of feedforward in which you place the listener in a specific role.

8. Cues through which the listener communicates information back to the speaker without assuming the role of speaker.

9. Messages that open the channels of communication.

10. The joining of speaker and listener.

SKILL BUILDING EXERCISES

8.1 GENDER AND THE TOPICS OF CONVERSATION

Below is a chart for recording topics of conversation that you think would be extremely comfortable (and therefore highly likely to occur) and extremely uncomfortable (and therefore highly unlikely to occur) for men talking to men, for women talking to women, and for men and women talking to each other. Fill in each section with at least three topics. After you have completed the chart, you can compare your responses with those of others in a small group or with those of the entire class. One interesting way to do this is for one person to read out a topic (without revealing the particular section he or she put it in) and see if others can identify the "appropriate" section. This experience will give you a general idea of how widely held are our beliefs about the topics that men and women talk about. General discussion may centre on a variety of issues; for example:

1. Why did certain topics seem more appropriately positioned in one section rather than another? For example, what evidence did you use for classifying some topics as comfortable for men or for women?

2. What communication problems might arise because of these differences in the likelihood of certain topics being discussed?

3. How would you go about testing the accuracy of your predictions about which topics go in which sections?

	Man to Man	Woman to Woman	Man to Woman or Woman to Man
Comfortable/highly likely to occur	1.	1.	1.
	2.	2.	2.
	3.	3.	3.
Uncomfortable/highly unlikely to occur	1.	1.	1.
	2.	2.	2.
	3.	3.	3.

Thinking Critically About Gender and Conversation.

Why did certain topics seem more appropriately positioned in one box than in another? What evidence did you use for classifying some topics as comfortable for men or for women, for example? Can you identify potential communication problems that might arise because of these differences in the likelihood of certain topics being discussed? How would you go about testing the accuracy of your predictions for which topics go in which boxes?

8.2 OPENING AND CLOSING A CONVERSATION

Think about how you might open a conversation with the persons described in the following scenarios. What general approaches would meet with a favourable response? What general approaches seem frowned on?

1. On the first day of class, you and another student are the first to come into the classroom and are seated in the room alone.

2. You are a guest at a friend's party. You are one of the first guests to arrive and are now there with several other people to whom you have only just been introduced. Your friend, the host, is busy with other matters.

3. You have just started a new job in a large office where you are one of several computer operators. It seems as if most of the other people know one another.

4. You are in the college cafeteria eating alone. You see another student who is also eating alone and whom you recognize from your English literature class. But you're not sure if this person has noticed you in class.

Now think about how you might go about closing each of the following conversations. What types of closing seem most effective? Which seem least effective?

1. You and a friend have been talking on the phone for the last hour, but not much new is being said. You have a great deal of work to get to and would like to close the conversation. Your friend just doesn't seem to hear your subtle cues.

2. You are at a party and are anxious to meet a person with whom you have exchanged eye contact for the last 10 minutes. The problem is that a friendly and talkative former teacher of yours is demanding all your attention. You don't want to insult the instructor, but at the same time you want to make contact with this other person.

3. You have had a conference with a supervisor and have learned what you needed to know. The supervisor, however, doesn't seem to know how to end the conversation, seems very ill at ease, and continues to go over what has already been said. You have to get back to your desk and must close the conversation.

4. You are at a party and notice a person you would like to get to know. You initiate a conversation, but after a few minutes you realize that this person is not someone with whom you wish to spend any more time. You want to close the conversation as soon as possible.

Thinking Critically About Opening and Concluding Conversations

What kinds of conversational openers and closers do you find particularly ineffective, offensive, or annoying? In what situations do you find these types of openers and closers occur most often?

8.3 FORMULATING EXCUSES

Although excuses are not necessarily appropriate in every situation, there are many instances in which an excuse can help to lessen possible negative effects of a mishap. For each of the five situations listed above, try formulating a suitable excuse and a justification explaining why this excuse will lessen any negative consequences. Three general types of excuses that you might use as starting points are:

- I didn't do what I'm accused of doing, or I did do what I'm accused of not doing ("I didn't say that." "I wasn't even near the place." "I did try to get in touch with you to tell you I'd be late.")
- It wasn't so bad. ("Sure I pushed him, but I didn't kill him.")
- Yes, but. ("It was just my jealousy making those accusations.")

1. Because of an email glitch, colleagues at work all receive a recent personal letter you sent to a friend in which you admitted to having racist feelings. You even gave several examples. As you enter work, you see a group of colleagues discussing your letter. They are not pleased.

2. Your boss accuses you of making lots of long-distance personal phone calls from work, a practice explicitly forbidden.

3. In a discussion with your supervisor, you tell a joke that puts down lesbians and gay men. Your supervisor tells you she finds the joke homophobic and offensive to everyone; and, she adds, she has a gay son and is proud of him. Because you just started the job, you're still on probation, and this supervisor's recommendation will count heavily.

4. Your friend tells you that he thinks you hurt Joe's feelings when you criticized his presentation.

5. Your history instructor is walking behind you and hears you and another student discussing your class. Your instructor clearly hears your comment that "the last lecture was a total waste of time" but says nothing.

Thinking Critically About Excuses.

Can you identify specific situations in which excuses would be inappropriate? What effect does repeated excuse making have on a romantic relationship? Do you have stereotypes of people who consistently make excuses for just about everything they do?

Chapter 9

Interpersonal Communication and Culture

CHAPTER TOPICS

This chapter discusses culture and intercultural communication and offers suggestions for improving your own intercultural communication.

- Culture and Intercultural Communication
- How Cultures Differ
- Improving Intercultural Communication

CHAPTER SKILLS

After completing this chapter, you should be able to:

- send and receive messages with a recognition of the influence of cultural factors.
- communicate with the recognition that cultures differ in important ways and that these differences impact on interpersonal communication.
- follow the guidelines for intercultural communication.

The culture of the Snaidanac is still very poorly understood. They are a North American group living in the territory between the Inuit of the north and the American Plains' Sioux. Little is known of their origin, although tradition states that they came from the east. According to Snaidanac mythology, their nation was founded by the cultural hero Jon-mac, who is otherwise known as the originator of an attempt to connect several tribes by magical iron rods placed end to end. Legend has it that Jon-mac (pronounced yon-mic) was also famous for his extensive use of organic medicines which often made him physically sick.

A great deal of the Snaidanac's day is spent in ritual and ceremony. The centre of this activity involves the human body; its appearance and health is vitally important for these people. While this is not unusual, the ceremony and philosophy concerning the body are unique.

The fundamental belief behind their whole system of living appears to be that the human body is ugly and that its natural tendency is to decay and disease. The only hope to avoid decay and disease is religious ritual and ceremony. Every household has one or more shrines for this ritual and ceremony. Powerful people in the society have several shrines in their houses.

The strange rituals of the shrine are not shared by the family together, but are private and secret. The rituals are normally only discussed with children when they are young and being initiated into these mysteries. I was able, however, to talk with the natives and learn something of their shrines and the rituals done around them.

The most important place in the shrine is a box or chest which is built into the wall. In this chest, the native keeps his important charms and magical potions. These charms are bought from special religious people, something like wizards. The most important of these wizards are the medicine men. They do not provide the magic potions or charms to the everyday native, however. They write down the ingredients in an ancient and secret language. The native must take this to an herbalist, very wise in plants and herbs. It is he who, for a gift, supplies the charm.

Beneath the charm-box is a small font or basin. Each day every member of the family, one after the other, enters the shrine room, bows his head before the charm-box, mixes different sorts of holy water in the font, and then proceeds with a brief rite similar to the Christian baptism. The holy waters come from the Water Temple of the community, where the priests hold elaborate ceremonies to make the liquid ritually pure.

Below the medicine men in prestige are specialists who, translated, could best be called "holy-mouth-men." The Snaidanac have a supernatural horror of and fascination with the mouth. It influences all the social relationships of these natives. Were it not for the rituals of the mouth, they believe their teeth would fall out, their gums bleed, the jaws shrink, their friends desert them, and their lovers reject them.

The daily body ritual performed by everyone includes a mouth-rite. Despite the fact that these people are so careful about care of the mouth, this rite strikes the uninitiated stranger as revolting. It was reported to me that the ritual consists of inserting a small bundle of hog hairs into the mouth, along with certain magical powders, and then moving the bundles in a highly formalized series of gestures....

Source: Snaidanac concept developed by Horace Miner. Reproduced by permission of the American Anthropological Association from *American Anthropologist*, 58:3, June 1956. Not for further reproduction.

> You're a real Canadian if somebody steps on your toe and you say, 'Oh, I'm sorry!'
>
> — **Will Ferguson**

From these observations of anthropologist Horace Miner (1956), you might conclude that the Snaidanac are a truly strange people. Look more carefully, however, and you will see that we are the Snaidanac and the rituals are our own: *Snaidanac* is *Canadians* spelled backwards. This excerpt brings into focus the fact that cultural customs (our own and those of others) are not necessarily logical or natural. Rather, they are better viewed as useful or not useful to the members of that particular culture. The excerpt is an appropriate reminder against ethnocentrism—the tendency to think that your culture's customs are right and the customs of others are wrong. It also awakens our consciousness, our mindful state, to our own customs and values.

Culture and Intercultural Communication

The word *culture,* you'll recall from Chapter 1, refers to the lifestyle of a group of people, their values, beliefs, artifacts, ways of behaving, and ways of communicating. Culture includes all that members of a social group have produced and developed—their language, ways of thinking, art, laws, and religion—and that is transmitted from one generation to another through a process known as **enculturation**. You learn the values of your culture (that is, you become enculturated) through the teachings of your parents, peer groups, schools, religious institutions, government agencies, and media. When discussing the learned nature of culture, Hall (1976, p. 42) explains that everything that people do and are is modified by learning, which gradually sinks below the surface of the mind to appear as innate. Thus, one's own culture appears natural and right and as the only way to act. This can cause people to compare other cultures and to judge them on the basis of their own culture; in other words, to be ethnocentric.

Acculturation refers to the processes by which a person's culture is modified through direct contact with or exposure to another culture, through, say, the mass media (Kim, 1988). For example, when immigrants settle in the host culture, their own culture becomes influenced by the host culture. Gradually, the values, ways of behaving, and beliefs of the host culture become more and more a part of the immigrants' culture. At the same time, of course, the host culture changes, too. Generally, however, the culture of the immigrant changes more.

The acceptance of the new culture depends on several factors (Kim, 1988). Immigrants who come from cultures similar to the host culture will become acculturated more easily. Similarly, those who are younger and better educated become acculturated more quickly than do older and less educated persons. Personality factors are also relevant. Persons who are risk-takers and open-minded, for example, have a greater acculturation potential. Also, persons who are familiar with the host culture before immigration—whether through interpersonal contact or mass media exposure—will be acculturated more readily.

Canada is unique, however, in that it is guided by its focus on multiculturalism—an acceptance and understanding of all the different cultural groups in a community. And yet Canadians seem to have difficulty describing a Canadian culture or a Canadian identity. We can often describe it in terms of what Canadians are not—we are not Americans, for example; and we are not aggressive. Bibby (1990, p. 93) contends that Americans have created a creed that binds, a commitment to ties of church, family, school, and community, and individualism with a pronounced group context. Canadians, on the other hand, don't seem to have an ideology of Canadianism. While Americans have heroes, Canadians often ignore their historical record and almost exclusively adopt the heroes of other nations.

"I am not an Athenian or a Greek, but a citizen of the world."

—Socrates

What part does intercultural communication play in your personal, social, and professional life? Has this changed in the last five years? Is it likely to change in the next five years?

Visit one of the Web sites for Canadian census data (for example, **www.statcan.ca**). What interesting cultural information can you find that would be of value to someone learning the skills of interpersonal communication?

And yet Canadians are generally proud of their "mosaic" concept of society, as opposed to the American "melting pot" version. Bibby (1990, p. 95) maintains that what is holding our country together is not loyalty to anything in particular but rather a tenuous agreement to coexist. As a result, Canadians have become "champions of choice" (Bibby, 1990, p. 97). We seem so interested in and willing to adopt the foods, clothing, books, music, and activities of other countries that we find it hard to remember what might be distinctly Canadian. And maybe this is exactly what is Canadian—the multicultural component of our society.

Intercultural communication, then, refers to communication that takes place between persons of different cultures and will be greatly influenced by both enculturation and acculturation processes. **Barriers to intercultural communication** often exist between persons who have different cultural beliefs, values, or ways of behaving.

Note, too, that you send messages from your specific and unique cultural context. That context influences what you say and how you say it. Culture influences every aspect of your communication experience and, of course, you receive messages through the filters imposed by a unique culture. Cultural filters, like filters on a camera, colour the messages you receive. They influence what you receive and how you receive it. Cultures differ in their tendencies to trust different sources of messages. Some would place their trust in a religious leader, others in an elder, and still others in the television reporter.

The term *intercultural* is used broadly to refer to all forms of communication among persons from different groups as well as to the more narrowly defined area of communication between different cultures. The following types of communication may all be considered "intercultural" and, more important, subject to the same principles of effective communication identified in this chapter.

■ Communication between cultures—for example, between Chinese and Portuguese, or between French and Norwegian.

THINKING CRITICALLY ABOUT

Anecdotal "Evidence"

Often you'll hear people use anecdotes to prove a point: "Women are like that; I know, because I have three sisters." "That's the way Japanese managers are; I have one, I know." These observations are often useful starting points for collecting evidence and systematically studying some aspect of communication. But they are not evidence in any meaningful sense. One reason this type of "evidence" is inadequate is that it usually relies on just one or a few observations; it's usually a clear case of overgeneralizing on the basis of too little evidence. A second reason is that one person's observations may be unduly clouded by his or her own attitudes and beliefs; your attitudes toward women or the Japanese, for example, may cloud accurate perception of their behaviours. A third reason is that there is no way to test the reliability and validity of these observations.

EXAMPLES?

Can you give an example of an interaction in which someone (or perhaps you yourself) used only anecdotal evidence to support a broad generalization?

TABLE 9.1 Intercultural Value Conflict Areas

We generally find that most difficulties revolve around different assumptions concerning the following areas.

North American Values	Contrast to North American Values
I. Individual versus Family	
(a) Individual perceived as a separate entity;	(a) Individual perceived in context of his or her family;
(b) Individual responsibility is most important;	(b) Involvement and dependence on family is encouraged;
(c) Decisions must involve the individual as much as possible.	(c) Decisions must involve the older respected members of the family.
II. Acceptance of Others	
(a) North Americans relate to others in terms of their roles;	(a) Individuals from other cultures react to other people in terms of the whole person, not the role;
(b) North Americans don't need to like or agree with someone to avail themselves of his or her services, e.g., student/teacher.	(b) Individuals from contrast cultures tend to accept or reject others completely and have difficulty working with those who are unacceptable.
III. Social Relations	
(a) Differences in status, etc., are minimized to make others feel comfortable;	(a) Differences in status and hierarchical rank are noted and stressed;
(b) A direct informal style of communicating is also used to achieve the same result.	(b) Communication follows a predictable, formal series of steps which make others feel more comfortable.
IV. Progress versus Fate	
(a) North Americans believe humans are rational and can construct machines and develop techniques to solve problems.	(a) Humans are perceived by many cultures in a fatalistic manner and such things as disease and suffering are accepted more easily.
V. Time	
(a) Time is perceived in terms of clock time (supper is at 5:30 p.m.);	(a) Time is perceived in terms of the right time to do something (supper is when you eat);
(b) Time moves quickly from past to present to future; one must keep up with it, use it to change and master one's environment.	(b) Time moves slowly; humans must integrate themselves with the environment and adapt to it rather than change it.

Source: Adapted from Michael J. Miner and M. Kim Harker, International Briefing Associates. Ottawa, ON.

- Communication between ethnic groups (sometimes called *interethnic communication*)—for example, between Chinese Canadians and indigenous Canadians.
- Communication between religions—for example, between Roman Catholics and Anglicans, or between Muslims and Jews.
- Communication between nations (sometimes called *international communication*)—for example, between Canada and Argentina, or between China and Italy.
- Communication between smaller cultures existing within the larger culture—for example, between doctors and patients, or between research scientists and the general public.

When you have to ask directions, you're confessing, in some way, your ignorance and your inability to control the situation by yourself. Men, according to Deborah Tannen (1990, 1994b), are especially reluctant to ask for directions because they want to maintain control; by asking for directions, they lose it. Do you find that men are more reluctant to ask for directions? Do you agree with Tannen's explanation?

"Because my genetic programming *prevents* me from stopping to ask directions—*that's* why!"

© The New Yorker Collection 1991 Donald Reilly from cartoonbank.com. All Rights Reserved.

- Communication between a smaller culture and the dominant culture—for example, between homosexuals and heterosexuals, or between senior citizens and the not-yet seniors.

- Communication between genders—between men and women. Some researchers would consider intergender communication as a separate area and only a part of intercultural communication when the two people are also from different races or nationalities. But, because gender roles are largely learned through culture, it seems useful to consider male–female communication as intercultural (Tannen, 1994b).

Regardless of your own cultural background, you will surely come into close contact with people from a variety of other cultures—people who speak different languages, eat different foods, practise different religions, and approach work and relationships in very different ways. It doesn't matter whether you're a longtime resident or a newly arrived immigrant. You are or soon will be living, going to school, working with, and forming relationships with people who are from very different cultures. Your day-to-day experiences are sure to become increasingly intercultural.

Visit one of the numerous travel Web sites (for example, **www.lonelyplanet.com** and **www.travel.epicurious.com**). What can you learn about intercultural communication from such sources?

How Cultures Differ

Cultures differ in terms of their (1) orientation (whether individualistic or collectivist), (2) context (whether high or low), and (3) masculinity–femininity. Each of these dimensions of difference has a significant impact on interpersonal communication (Hofstede, 1997; Hall & Hall, 1987; Gudykunst, 1991). Cultures also differ in their characteristic attitude toward uncertainty, a topic discussed in Chapter 3.

Individualist and Collectivist Cultures

Does the individualistic or collectivist nature of one's culture influence success in college? How would you go about researching this question?

Before reading about individualism versus collectivism, take the self-test on page 231, "How individualistic are you?" to see where you and your own culture stand on this concept.

The distinction between **individualistic** and **collectivist** cultures revolves around the extent to which the individual's goals or the group's goals are given greater importance. Individual and collective tendencies are not mutually exclusive; this is not an all-or-none orientation but rather one of emphasis. Thus, you may, for example, compete with other members of your basketball team for most baskets or most valuable player award. At the same time, however, you will—in a game—act in a way that will benefit the group. In actual practice both individualistic and collectivist tendencies will help you and your team each achieve your goals. At times, however, these tendencies may conflict; for example, do you shoot for the basket and try to raise your own individual score or do you pass the ball to another player who is better positioned to score the basket and thus benefit your team?

TEST YOURSELF

How Individualistic Are You?

Instructions: Respond to each of the following statements in terms of how true they are of your behaviour and thinking: 1 = almost always true, 2 = more often true than false, 3 = true about half the time and false about half the time, 4 = more often false than true, 5 = almost always false.

_____ **1.** My own goals rather than the goals of my group (for example, my extended family, my organization) are the more important.

_____ **2.** I feel responsible for myself and to my own conscience rather than for the entire group and to the group's values and rules.

_____ **3.** Success depends on my contribution to the group effort and the group's success rather than my own individual success or surpassing others.

_____ **4.** I make a clear distinction between who is the leader and who are the followers, and similarly make a clear distinction between members of my own cultural group and outsiders.

_____ **5.** In business transactions personal relationships are extremely important, and so I would spend considerable time getting to know people with whom I do business.

_____ **6.** In my communications I prefer a direct and explicit communication style; I believe in "telling it like it is," even if it hurts.

HOW DID YOU DO?

To compute your individualist–collectivist score, follow these steps:

1. Reverse the scores for items 3 and 5. That is, if your response was 1, reverse it to a 5; if your response was 2, reverse it to a 4; 3, keep it as 3; 4, reverse it to a 2; 5, reverse it to 1.

2. Add your scores for all six items, being sure to use the reverse scores for items 3 and 5 in your calculations. Your score should be between 6 (indicating a highly individualist orientation) to 30 (indicating a highly collectivist orientation).

3. Position your score on the following scale:

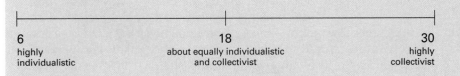

6	18	30
highly individualistic	about equally individualistic and collectivist	highly collectivist

WHAT WILL YOU DO?

Does this scale and score accurately measure the way in which you see yourself on this dimension? Is this orientation going to help you achieve your personal and professional goals? Might it hinder you?

In an individualistic culture, you're responsible for yourself and perhaps your immediate family; in a collectivist culture you're responsible for the entire group. Success, in an individualistic culture, is measured by the extent to which you surpass other members of your group;

What does this photograph tell you about Canadian culture?

you would take pride in standing out from the crowd. And your heroes—in the media, for example—are likely to be those who are unique and who stand apart. In a collectivist culture, success is measured by your contribution to the achievements of the group as a whole; you would take pride in your similarity to other members of your group. Your heroes, in contrast, are more likely to be team players who do not stand out from the rest of the group's members.

In an individualistic culture you're responsible to your own conscience, and responsibility is largely an individual matter. In a collectivist culture you're responsible to the rules of the social group, and responsibility for an accomplishment or a failure is shared by all members. Competition is promoted in individualistic cultures, while cooperation is promoted in collectivist cultures.

Distinctions between in-group members and out-group members are extremely important in collectivist cultures. In individualist cultures, where a person's individuality is prized, the distinction is likely to be less important.

High- and Low-Context Cultures

In a **high-context culture**, much of the information in communication is in the context or in the person—for example, information shared through previous communications, through assumptions about each other, and through shared experiences. The information is not explicitly stated in the verbal message. In a **low-context culture** most information is explicitly stated in verbal messages, or, in formal transactions, in written (contract) form.

To appreciate the distinction between high and low context, consider giving directions ("Where's the post office?") to someone who knows the neighbourhood and to a newcomer to your city. To someone who knows the neighbourhood (a high-context situation), you can assume the person knows the local landmarks. So, you can give directions such as "next to the laundromat on Main Street" or "the corner of Albany and Elm." To the newcomer (a low-context situation), you cannot assume the person shares any information with you. So, you would have to use only those directions that even a stranger would understand, for example, "Make a left at the next stop sign" or "Go two blocks and then turn right."

High-context cultures are also collectivist cultures. These cultures (Japanese, Arabic, Aboriginal, Thai, Korean, and Mexican are examples) place great emphasis on personal relationships and oral agreements (Victor, 1992). Low-context cultures, on the other hand, are individualistic cultures. These cultures (German, Swedish, Norwegian, and Canadian are examples) place less emphasis on personal relationships and more emphasis on the written, explicit explanation, and, for example, on the written contracts in business transactions.

How do you, your family, and your friends view interethnic friendships? Interethnic romantic relationships? Are there certain interethnic relationships that are "approved" and others that are "not approved"?

Members of high-context cultures spend lots of time getting to know each other before any important transactions take place. Because of this prior personal knowledge, a great deal of information is shared and therefore does not have to be explicitly stated. Members of low-context cultures spend less time getting to know each other and therefore do not have that shared knowledge. As a result, everything has to be stated explicitly. High-context societies, for example, rely more on nonverbal cues in reducing uncertainty (Sanders, Wiseman, & Matz, 1991).

When this simple difference is not taken into account, misunderstandings can easily result. For example, the directness and explicitness characteristic of the low-context culture may prove insulting, insensitive, or unnecessary to members of the high-context culture. Conversely, to members of a low-context culture, someone from a high-context culture may appear vague, underhanded, or dishonest in his or her reluctance to be explicit or engage in communication that a low-context member would consider open and direct.

Another frequent difference and source of misunderstanding between high- and low-context cultures is face-saving (Hall & Hall, 1987). People in high-context cultures place a great deal more emphasis on face-saving. For example, they are more likely to avoid argument for fear of causing others to lose face, whereas people in low-context cultures (with their individualistic orientation) will use argument to win a point. Similarly, in high-context cultures criticism should take place only in private so that the person can save face. Low-context cultures may not make this public–private distinction.

Members of high-context cultures are reluctant to say no for fear of offending and causing the person to lose face. And so, for example, it's necessary to understand when the Japanese executive's yes means yes and when it means no. The difference is not in the words themselves but in the way they are used. It's easy to see how the low-context individual may interpret this reluctance to be direct—to say no when you mean no—as a weakness or as an unwillingness to confront reality.

Members of high-context cultures are also reluctant to question the judgments of their superiors. So, for example, if a product was being manufactured with a defect, workers might be reluctant to communicate this back to management (Gross, Turner, & Cederholm, 1987). Similarly, workers may detect problems in procedures proposed by management but never communicate their concerns back to management. A knowledge of this tendency would alert a low-context management to look more deeply into the absence of communication. Table 9.2 presents a summary of these differences as they relate to interpersonal communication.

Masculine and Feminine Cultures

Cultures differ in the extent to which gender roles are distinct or overlap (Hofstede, 1997). A **masculine culture** typically views men as assertive, oriented to material success, and strong; people in such a culture tend to see women as modest, focused on the quality of life, and tender. In a **feminine culture** both men and women are supposed to be modest, oriented to maintaining the quality of life, and tender. On the basis of Hofstede's research on 53 countries, the 10 countries with the highest masculinity score (from the highest) are Japan, Austria, Venezuela, Italy, Switzerland, Mexico, Ireland, Jamaica, Great Britain, and Germany. The 10 countries with the highest femininity score (from the highest) are Sweden, Norway, Netherlands, Denmark, Costa Rica, Yugoslavia, Finland, Chile, Portugal, and Thailand.

TABLE 9.2 Some Individualistic and Collectivist Culture Differences

This table, based on the work of Hofstede (1997), Hall and Hall (1987; Hall, 1983) and on interpretations by Gudykunst (1991) and Victor (1992), parallels the self-test presented earlier. As you read through the table, consider which statements you agree with, which you disagree with, and how these beliefs influence your communications. Can you identify additional differences between individualistic and collectivist cultures?

Individualistic (Low-Context) Cultures	Collectivist (High-Context) Cultures
Your goals are most important	The group's goals are most important
You're responsible for yourself and to your own conscience	You're responsible for the entire group and to the group's values and rules
Success depends on your surpassing others; competition is emphasized	Success depends on your contribution to the group; cooperation is emphasized
Clear distinction is made between leaders and members	Little distinction is made between leaders and members; leadership is normally shared
Personal relationships are less important; hence, little time is spent getting to know each other in meetings	Personal relationships are extremely important; hence, much time is spent getting to know each other in meetings
Directness is valued; face-saving is seldom considered	Indirectness is valued; face-saving is a major consideration

Conceptions of masculinity and femininity change over time and as circumstances change. For example, Haddad and Lam (1988) conducted interviews with over 100 new Canadian fathers from nine different national or ethnic backgrounds. Only a small proportion of these men (17 percent) upheld their traditional view of the role of the father after being in Canada for some time. The other participants in the study adapted their beliefs, either for pragmatic reasons or in order to maximize the well-being of their family.

Improving Intercultural Communication

Here are a variety of principles for increasing intercultural communication effectiveness—in conversation, on the job, in friendship and romantic relationships. These guidelines are based on the intercultural research of a wide variety of researchers (Barna, 1985; Ruben, 1985; Gudykunst, 1991; Hofstede, 1997). (Either before or after reading this section you may want to try your hand at intercultural communication with an exercise, "Random Pairs," at **www.ablongman.com/devito**.)

Recognize and Reduce Your Ethnocentrism

How would you explain the teachings of your culture in terms of masculinity and femininity?

Ethnocentrism, one of the biggest obstacles to intercultural communication, is the tendency to see others and their behaviours through your own cultural filters, often as distortions of your own behaviours. It's the tendency to evaluate the values, beliefs, and behaviours of your own culture as more positive, superior, logical, and natural than those of other cultures. To achieve effective interpersonal communication, you need to see both yourself and others as different but with neither being inferior or superior—not a very easily accomplished task.

Ethnocentrism exists on a continuum. People are not either ethnocentric or not ethnocentric; rather, most are somewhere between these polar opposites (see Table 9.3 on p. 237). Note also that your degree of ethnocentrism will depend on the group on which you're focusing. For example, if you're of Greek origin, you may have a low degree of ethnocentrism when dealing with people of Italian origin but a high degree when dealing with people of Turkish or Japanese origin. Most important for our purposes is that your degree of ethnocentrism (and we are all ethnocentric to at least some degree) will influence your interpersonal (intercultural) communications.

How would you explain ethnocentrism? Can you give an example of your own ethnocentrism? Are your friends and relatives ethnocentric? How does this manifest itself in everyday interpersonal communications?

Be Mindful

Being mindful rather than mindless (a distinction considered in Chapter 8) is generally helpful in intercultural communication situations. When you're in a mindless state, you behave with assumptions that would not normally pass intellectual scrutiny. For example, you know that cancer is not contagious and yet many people will avoid touching cancer patients. You know that people

"I've never trusted cows."

who cannot see do not have hearing problems and yet many people use a louder voice when talking to persons without sight. When the discrepancies between evidence and behaviours are pointed out and your

SKILLS TOOLBOX

7 Ways to Effective Intercultural Communication

The characteristics of conversational effectiveness (discussed in detail in Chapter 8) are especially useful in intercultural communication, though caution needs to be exercised since there are likely to be important cultural differences in the way these characteristics are expected to be used. So, generally:

1. *Be open* to differences among people. Be especially open to the different values, beliefs, and attitudes, as well as ways of behaving. Recognize, too, that a person's willingness to self-disclose or to respond to the openness of others is culturally influenced. Cultural differences may help to explain differences in openness and in responsiveness to openness.

2. *Empathize* with the other person; put yourself into the position of the person from another culture. Try to see the world from this different perspective. Let the person know that you feel as he or she is feeling. Use facial expressions, an attentive and interested body posture, and understanding and agreement responses to communicate your empathy.

3. *Communicate positiveness* to others; it helps put the other person at ease. It tells the other person that you're feeling good about interacting and are enjoying communicating. The appropriateness of positive statements about the self will vary greatly with the culture. For example, some cultures expect speakers to use self-denigrating comments and to minimize their own successes and abilities. Other cultures expect success and ability to be acknowledged openly and without embarrassment.

4. *Use immediacy* to unite yourself with others and to surmount the differences. In intercultural communication this quality takes on special importance because of the great differences between you and the culturally different. Communicate a sense of togetherness to counteract the obvious intercultural differences, but realize that members of some cultures may prefer to maintain greater interpersonal and psychological distance from others.

5. *Engage in effective interaction management*—for example, be especially sensitive to the differences in turn-taking. Many North Americans, especially those from large urban centres, have the habit of interrupting or of completing the other person's sentences. Some cultures consider this especially rude.

6. *Communicate expressiveness.* When differences among people are great, some feel uneasy and unsure of themselves. Counteract this by communicating genuine involvement in the interaction. Let the other person know that you're enjoying the interaction. Smile. Allow your facial muscles to express your interest and concern. Recognize, however, that some cultures may frown on too much expressiveness. So don't assume (necessarily) that the absence of expressiveness shows an unwillingness to participate in conversation; it may indicate just a difference in the way in which members of different cultures reveal their feelings.

7. *Be other-oriented,* by, for example, focusing your attention and the conversation on the other person. See both the content and the relationship issues from the other person's point of view. Use the techniques already considered to show other-orientation, such as active listening, asking questions, and maintaining eye contact (see Chapter 8). Some cultures, however, may find these techniques too intrusive. So, look carefully for feedback that comments on your own degree of other-orientation. Ask, for example, if your focus on the other person makes that person feel uncomfortable.

THEN AND NOW

Recall a recent intercultural interaction that did not go as well as it might have. If you were having the same conversation today, what could you do to make it more effective?

TABLE 9.3 The Ethnocentrism Continuum

Drawing from several researchers (Lukens, 1978; Gudykunst & Kim, 1984; Gudykunst, 1991), this table summarizes some interconnections between ethnocentrism and communication. In this table, five degrees of ethnocentrism are identified; in reality, of course, there are as many degrees as there are people. The "Communication Distances" are simply general terms that highlight the major communication attitude that dominates that level of ethnocentrism. Under "Communications" are some ways people might interact given their particular degree of ethnocentrism. How would you have rated yourself on this scale five years ago? How would you rate yourself today?

Degrees of Ethnocentrism	Communication Distance	Communications
Low	Equality	Treats others as equals; evaluates other ways of doing things as equal to one's own
	Sensitivity	Wants to decrease distance between self and others
	Indifference	Lacks concern for others but is not hostile
	Avoidance	Avoids and limits interpersonal interactions with others; prefers to be with one's own kind
High	Disparagement	Engages in hostile behaviour; belittles others; views one's own culture as superior to other cultures

mindful state is awakened, you quickly realize that these behaviours are not logical or realistic.

When you deal with people from other cultures you're often in a mindless state and therefore function nonrationally in many ways. When your mindful state is awakened, as it is in textbook discussions such as this one, you may then resort to a more critical thinking mode, and recognize, for example, that other people and other cultural systems are different but not inferior or superior. Thus, these suggestions for increasing intercultural communication effectiveness may appear logical (even obvious) to your mindful state but are probably frequently ignored in your mindless state.

Face Fears

Another factor that stands in the way of effective intercultural communication is fear (Stephan & Stephan, 1985; Gudykunst, 1991). For example, you may fear for your self-esteem. You may become anxious about your ability to control the intercultural situation or you may worry about your own level of discomfort. You may fear that you will be taken advantage of by the member of this other culture. Depending upon your own stereotypes, you may fear being lied to, financially duped, or made fun of. You may fear that members of this other group will react to you negatively: They may not like you or may disapprove of your attitudes or beliefs or they may even reject you as a person. Conversely, you may fear negative reactions from members of your own

Do you agree with the assumption that everyone is ethnocentric to some degree? If so, where would you place yourself on the ethnocentric continuum when the "other" is a person of the opposite sex? A member of a different affectional orientation? A member of a different race? A member of a different religion?

group. They might, for example, disapprove of your socializing with someone who is interculturally different.

These fears—coupled with the greater effort that intercultural communication takes and the ease with which you communicate with those who are culturally similar—can easily create sufficient anxiety to make some people give up.

Recognize Differences

"I was raised to believe that excellence is the best deterrent to racism or sexism. And that's how I operate my life."

—Oprah Winfrey

When you assume that all people are similar and ignore the differences between yourself and those who are culturally different from you, your intercultural efforts are likely to fail. This is especially true in the area of values, attitudes, and beliefs. It's easy to see and accept different hairstyles, clothing, and foods. But when it comes to values and beliefs, it's easier to assume (mindlessly) that deep down we're all similar. We aren't. Henry may be a devout Baptist, while Carol may be an atheist, and Jan may be a Muslim. Each, consequently, sees his or her own life as having very different meanings because of the differences in their religious views. When you assume similarities and ignore differences, you may implicitly communicate to others that you feel your ways are the right ways and their ways are the wrong ways. The result is confusion and misunderstanding on both sides.

Also become mindful of the differences within any cultural group. Just as we know that all Canadians are not alike (think of the various groups found in your city or just your own school), so neither are all Jamaicans, Koreans, Mexicans, and so on. Within each culture there are many smaller cultures. These smaller cultures differ from each other and from the majority culture. Further, members of one smaller cul-

THINKING CRITICALLY ABOUT

Exceptions

"Exceptional analysis" is a useful technique when you're confronted by a generalization, a statement of folk wisdom, or a general rule that you want to go beyond (Koberg & Bagnall, 1976a, 1976b; Michalko, 1991). For example, in the face of the enormous number of research findings you'll encounter in college and in your professional career, it may be helpful to take time out and ask about the exceptions. After all, even research results citing "the vast majority of those surveyed" or "95 percent of the subjects"—and few research findings are that conclusive—still don't account for everyone.

In a similar way, each culture maintains its own system of "truths" that are often true but in some cases may not be true. For example, members of many Asian cultures, influenced by Confucian principles, believe that (in the words of Confucius) "the protruding nail gets pounded down" and are therefore not likely to voice disagreement with the majority at a group meeting. North Americans, influenced by the belief that "the squeaky wheel gets the grease," are more likely to voice disagreement or to act differently from other group members. Mindless adherence to either principle is probably not a very good idea, and a search for exceptions might prove helpful. By looking at the exceptions to the rule, you'll often gain a different perspective on an issue. For example, to the statement "No one likes a smart aleck," you might add "unless the smart aleck is a stand-up comic." To the statement "Money has nothing to do with happiness" you might add "unless you're comparing those above and those below the poverty line; in these cases money does make a difference. Those above the poverty line may be happier than those below."

EXAMPLES?

How might you use exceptional analysis to examine generally accepted truisms? Examples: "Absence makes the heart grow fonder." "Admit your mistakes." "Be positive in conversation." "Empathize with your relationship partner." "Honesty is the best policy." "Never betray a confidence." "Work hard." "You can catch more flies with honey than you can with vinegar."

ture may share a great deal with members of that same smaller culture in another part of the world. For example, farmers in Saskatchewan may have more in common with farmers in Borneo than with bankers in Toronto. All will be concerned with and knowledgeable about weather conditions and their effects on crop growth, crop rotation techniques, and soil composition. Of course, in many other things these farmers, so similar when it comes to farming, may be drastically different on such issues as government subsidies, trade regulations, and sales techniques.

Avoid Overattribution

You'll recall from Chapter 3 that overattribution is the tendency to attribute too much of a person's behaviour or attitudes to one of that person's characteristics: "She thinks that way because she's a woman"; "He believes that because he was raised a Catholic." In intercultural communication situations, you see overattribution in two ways. First, it's the tendency to see too much of what a

There are some distinctive groups in this photograph. Has anyone ever assumed something about you (because you were a member of a particular culture) that was not true? Have you ever been asked to speak on behalf of "your" group? Did you find this disturbing?

person believes or does as caused by the person's cultural identification. Second, it's the tendency to see a person as a spokesperson for that particular culture just because she or he is a member. Therefore, be careful not to assume that everyone from India is Hindu and a vegetarian or that all students of Chinese origin are good in math. As demonstrated in the discussion of perception in Chapter 3, people's ways of thinking and ways of behaving are influenced by a wide variety of factors; culture is just one of them.

Recognize Meaning Differences in Verbal and Nonverbal Messages

In Chapter 5 we noted that meaning does not exist in the words we use; rather, it exists in the person using the words. This principle is especially important in intercultural communication. Consider the differences in meaning that might exist for the word *woman* to a Canadian and an Iranian. What about *religion* to a Christian fundamentalist and to an atheist or *lunch* to a Chinese rice farmer and a Bay Street executive? Or think about the meanings of the terms *security, future,* and *family* to a Vancouver college student and a homeless teenager in Toronto.

When it comes to nonverbal messages, the potential differences are even greater. Thus, the over-the-head clasped hands that signify victory

Are such statements as "Columbus discovered America in 1492" and "All Canadians are immigrants" ethnocentric? If so, how would you rephrase them so that they represent a more multicultural perspective?

LISTEN TO THIS

Listening Without Sexist, Racist, or Heterosexist Attitudes

Just as sexist, racist, and heterosexist attitudes will influence your language, they also influence your listening. In biased listening, you hear what the speaker is saying filtered through your stereotypes. You assume unfairly that what the speaker is saying is necessarily influenced by the speaker's gender, ethnicity, or affectional orientation.

Sexist, racist, and heterosexist listening occur in a wide variety of situations. For example, when you dismiss a valid argument or attribute validity to an invalid argument, when you refuse to give someone a fair hearing, or when you give less credibility (or more credibility) to a speaker because the speaker is of a particular ethnicity, gender, or affectional orientation, you're practising sexist, racist, or heterosexist listening. Put differently, sexist, racist, or heterosexist listening occurs when you listen differently to a person because of his or her gender, ethnicity, or affectional orientation, despite the fact that these characteristics are irrelevant to the communication.

But there are many instances where these characteristics are relevant and pertinent to your evaluation of the message. For example, the gender of the speaker talking about pregnancy, fathering a child, birth control, or surrogate fatherhood is, most would agree, probably relevant to the message. On such topics it is not sexist listening to hear the topic through the gender of the speaker. But it is sexist listening to assume that only one gender has anything to say that's worth hearing or that what one gender can be discounted without a fair hearing. The same is true when stereotypes about a person's ethnicity or affectional orientation affect your listening.

SUGGESTIONS?

Chloe, a good friend of yours and a new trainee at the company you work for, has been assigned to a supervisor of a different ethnicity. Chloe confides in you that she just can't get herself to work with this person; she admits she is just too prejudiced to appreciate anything this supervisor says or does. What listening advice would you give Chloe?

A Few Choice Words

Pamela Levi is beautiful. She is nineteen years old and her hair tumbles down her shoulders to waist length. She fidgets, smiles, shrugs. Every now and then she sweeps back her hair and laughs. It makes it hard to conduct an interview. I keep losing my train of thought.

Pamela is a Micmac dancer featured in a musical production called *Spirit of a Nation*.

"How do you feel when you dance? What goes through your mind?"

"I feel proud," she says. "Proud to be an Indian."

I sit smiling at her for a few moments until she says, "I think your tape stopped."

Oh. I hit eject, flip over the mini-cassette and press record. "Sorry. Now then, you were saying that when you dance you feel proud to be a Native Canadian."

But that is not what she said. She gives me a puzzled and slightly annoyed look. "I said, I feel proud to be an *Indian*."

Later, I play the tape back, both sides, and discover that she is right. I also discover that during the entire interview I have twisted and contorted my syntax to avoid using the word Indian at all. I say "Native North American." I say "Aboriginal." I say "People of the First Nations." But nowhere do I say, simply, "Indian."

Words, like ideas, can fall out of fashion. Others become tainted. The error made by the Politically Correct movement was in trying to hurry the process along. It isn't something that can be dictated by committee; it just happens. For a long time, the word *squaw* was used simply to mean any Native woman. Today it has a crude, offensive sound to it.

What of the word *Indian* itself? For one thing, it isn't accurate. Columbus was convinced to his dying day that he had reached Asia and that the people he had encountered were honest-to-God Indians. That doesn't necessarily make the word an insult. After all, the name Canada itself is a case of mistaken identity (derived from a Native word for "village"), but no one would find the term *Canadian* demeaning.

I decided to call Gary Abbott.

I met Gary the same way I met Pamela, through the musical theatre of *Spirit of a Nation*. Gary is a member of the Thompson Nation of British Columbia. He is president of NAPA (the North American Pow-Wow Association) and has been a pow-wow dancer since the age of two. He specializes in the Hoop Dance, an intricate ritual involving twenty-nine separate hoops, which he pulls in and around his body to reveal woven moons, wombs and animal shapes.

Gary is very much aware of the nuance of words. When I referred to the various, spectacular costumes he wears during his dances, he said, "They aren't costumes. The correct term is regalia." I also notice, when I replay my interviews with Gary, that he avoids the word Indian as well. He refers instead to Natives and non-Natives.

Gary Abbott has been active in Native society as a social worker and as a crisis prevention caseworker. He is also the head of his own Vancouver-based software development company, and he is now planning to enter medical school in Vancouver, where his long-term goal is to combine modern medical techniques with older, herbal and meditative treatments. All this, and he is still in his twenties.

No one would ever accuse Gary Abbott of being one-dimensional. He straddles several worlds, from the art of the dance to the competition of the pow-wow to the intricacies of cyberspace.

I once asked Gary, "Who are you? Are you a dancer? A businessman? A computer developer? A social worker? A doctor? A medicine man?"

He shrugged. "I am whatever I am doing—at that moment. If I'm dancing, I'm a dancer. If I'm doing software development, I'm a software developer."

What began as a minor semantic quest had taken a new turn. We were no longer talking about mere labels; we were talking about identity. This is what I had been chasing ever since I returned from Asia, my own definition of self, that tenuous connection between the abstract and the specific, between a concept—*Canadian*—and the concrete—*me*.

We are defined by multiple layers, beginning with Canadian and working our way down, peeling the onion—and at the core?

"Are you an Indian?"

It's a stupid question. Of course Gary is an Indian. I rephrase the question. "Is the word Indian offensive?"

He thinks a moment. "It isn't offensive. But it is outdated. We aren't Indians. We are Native Canadians. The proper term is First Nations."

(continued)

So I called my sister.

Darla is my youngest sister—the Quiet Ferguson, they call her—and she is Cree.

"Is the word Indian offensive?" I ask her.

"No."

I wait, but that's it. "Come on, help me out here. I'm trying to write a book. Give me something pithy and insightful."

She sighs. Darla is a very practical-minded woman and such hairsplitting annoys her.

"Well," she says, "it's like anything. It depends on how it's used. I don't find it offensive, but there are some people who will take offence at anything. I suppose Native sounds better, but most Indians don't really care." Then, as an afterthought. "The volleyball team I play with is called the Hobbema Indians. I helped pick the name."

Words are empty vessels. They take on whatever meaning we give them, good or bad. The single, multi-syllable word *Canadian* carries enough weight and context to fill an entire book. The word *Indian* is even more complex, more ambiguous, more problematic.

Will *Indian* ever become socially taboo? Perhaps. But somehow I doubt it. For one thing, the Politically Correct Wave seems to have peaked. For another, the Indians themselves don't seem overly concerned. But most importantly, Pamela Levi of Big Cove, New Brunswick, is proud. Proud to be a dancer. Proud to be an Indian. But above all, proud of herself.

In the end, words fail us.

Jimmy Cardinal, raconteur and general ne'er-do-well from my home town, put it best. "Personally," he says, "I prefer to call myself a First Nations Aboriginal North American Native Indigenous Canadian Person. But it doesn't fit on the forms."

Source: Will Ferguson. *Why I Hate Canadians* (Vancouver: Douglas and McIntyre), 1997.

to a North American may signify friendship to a Russian. To someone from Britain, holding up two fingers to make a V signifies victory. To certain South Americans, however, it's an obscene gesture that corresponds to our extended middle finger. Tapping the side of your nose will signify that you and the other person are in on a secret—if in England or Scotland—but that the other person is nosy—if in Wales. A friendly wave of the hand will prove insulting in Greece, where the wave of friendship must show the back rather than the front of the hand. (Even icons that you may assume are universal are actually culture specific; for a self-test, "Can you distinguish universal from culture-specific icons?" see www.ablongman.com/devito.)

Avoid Violating Cultural Rules and Customs

> "The first need of a free people is to be able to define their own terms and have those terms recognized by their oppressors."
>
> —Stokely Carmichael

Each culture has its own rules and customs for communicating. **Cultural rules** identify what is appropriate and what is inappropriate. Thus, if you lived in a middle-class community in British Columbia you would follow the rules of the culture and call the person you wish to date three or four days in advance. If you lived in a different culture, you might be expected to call the parents of your future date weeks or even months in advance. In this same British Columbian community, you might say, as a friendly gesture to people you don't ever want to see again, "Let's have coffee sometime." To members of other cultures, this comment is sufficient for them to visit at their convenience.

In some cultures, people show respect by avoiding direct eye contact with the person to whom they are speaking. In other cultures this same eye avoidance would signal lack of interest. In some Mediterranean cultures men walk arm in arm. Other cultures consider this inappropriate.

A good example of a series of rules for an extremely large and important culture that many people do not know appears in Table 9.4.

Avoid Evaluating Differences Negatively

Be careful not to fall into the trap of ethnocentric thinking—evaluating your culture positively and other cultures negatively. For example, many Canadians of Northern European descent evaluate negatively the tendency of many Hispanics and Southern Europeans to use the street for a gathering place, for playing dominos, and for just sitting on a cool evening. Whether you like or dislike using the street in this way, recognize that neither is logically correct and neither is incorrect. This street behaviour is simply adequate or inadequate for *members of the culture.*

Remember that you learned your behaviours from your culture. The behaviours are not natural or innate. Therefore, try viewing these variations nonevaluatively. See these as different but equal.

Recognize That Culture Shock Is Normal

Culture shock is the psychological reaction you experience upon entering a culture very different from your own (Furnham & Bochner,

---

TABLE 9.4 Ten Commandments for Communicating with People with Disabilities

In looking over this list of suggestions, consider if you've seen any violations of these "commandments." Were you explicitly taught any of these principles?

1. Speak directly rather than through a companion or sign language interpreter who may be present.

2. Offer to shake hands when introduced. People with limited hand use or an artificial limb can usually shake hands, and offering the left hand is an acceptable greeting.

3. Always identify yourself and others who may be with you when meeting someone with a visual impairment. When conversing in a group, remember to identify the person to whom you're speaking.

4. If you offer assistance, wait until the offer is accepted. Then listen or ask for instructions.

5. Treat adults as adults. Address people who have disabilities by their first names only when extending that same familiarity to all others. Never patronize people in wheelchairs by patting them on the head or shoulder.

6. Do not lean against or hang on someone's wheelchair. Bear in mind that disabled people treat their chairs as extensions of their bodies.

7. Listen attentively when talking with people who have difficulty speaking and wait for them to finish. If necessary, ask short questions that require short answers, a nod, or shake of the head. Never pretend to understand if you're having difficulty doing so. Instead repeat what you have understood and allow the person to respond.

8. Place yourself at eye level when speaking with someone in a wheelchair or on crutches.

9. Tap a hearing-impaired person on the shoulder or wave your hand to get his or her attention. Look directly at the person and speak clearly, slowly, and expressively to establish if the person can read your lips. If so, try to face the light source and keep hands, cigarettes, and food away from your mouth when speaking.

10. Relax. Don't be embarrassed if you happen to use common expressions such as "See you later," or "Did you hear about this?" that seem to relate to a person's disability.

Source: From *The New York Times,* June 7, 1993. Courtesy of NYT Permissions.

A commonly encountered case of culture shock occurs with international students. If you're an international student, can you describe your culture shock experiences? If you're not an international student, can you visualize the culture shock you might experience if you were to study in another culture?

"Prejudice is a raft onto which the shipwrecked mind clambers and paddles to safety."

—Ben Hecht

1986). Culture shock is normal; most people experience it. Nevertheless, the experience can be unpleasant and frustrating and can sometimes lead to a permanently negative attitude toward the new culture. Understanding the normalcy of culture shock will help lessen any potential negative implications. (One obvious way to prevent at least some culture shock is to learn as much as you can about the different culture before encountering it. Numerous websites provide information on a wide variety of cultures; one useful site is www.worldbiz.com. Or, of course, you can just use your favourite search engine to call up websites on the specific culture you're interested in.)

Part of culture shock results from your feelings of alienation, conspicuousness, and difference from everyone else. When you lack knowledge of the rules and customs of the new society, you cannot communicate effectively. You're apt to blunder frequently and seriously. The person experiencing culture shock may not know some very basic things:

- how to ask someone for a favour or pay someone a compliment
- how to extend or accept an invitation for dinner
- how early or how late to arrive for an appointment or how long to stay
- how to distinguish seriousness from playfulness and politeness from indifference
- how to dress for an informal, formal, or business function
- how to order a meal in a restaurant or how to summon a waiter

Anthropologist Kalervo Oberg (1960), who first used the term *culture shock,* notes that it occurs in stages. These stages are useful for examining many encounters with the new and the different. Going away to college, getting married, or simply moving to a new town or city, for example, can all result in culture shock.

At the first stage, the *honeymoon,* there is fascination, even enchantment, with the new culture and its people. You finally have your own apartment. You're your own boss. Finally, on your own! Among people who are culturally different, the early (and superficial) relationships of this stage are characterized by cordiality and friendship. Many tourists remain at this stage because their stay in foreign countries is so brief.

At stage two, the *crisis stage,* the differences between your own culture and the new one create problems. If you've just moved to your own apartment, for example, no longer do you find dinner ready for you unless you do it yourself. Your clothes aren't washed or ironed unless you do them yourself. Feelings of frustration and inadequacy come to the fore. This is the stage at which you experience the actual shock of the new culture. In one study of foreign students from over 100 different countries and studying in 11 different countries, it was found that 25 percent of the students experienced depression (Klineberg & Hull, 1979).

During the third period, the *recovery,* you gain the skills necessary to function effectively. You learn how to shop, cook, and plan a meal. You find a local laundry and figure you'll learn how to iron later. You learn the language and ways of the new culture. Your feelings of inadequacy subside.

At the final stage, the *adjustment,* you adjust to and come to enjoy the new culture and the new experiences. You may still experience periodic difficulties and strains, but on a whole, the experience is pleasant. Actually, you're now a pretty decent cook. You're even coming to enjoy it. You're making a good salary, so why learn to iron?

Time spent in a foreign country is not in itself sufficient for the development of positive attitudes; in fact, the development of negative attitudes often seem to develop over time. Rather, friendships with nationals are crucial for satisfaction with the new culture. Maintaining contacts only with other expatriates or sojourners is not sufficient (Torbiorn, 1982).

People may also experience culture shock when they return to their original culture after living in a foreign culture—a kind of reverse culture shock (Jandt, 1995). Consider, for example, members of the Canadian Armed Forces who serve overseas for several years. Upon returning to their bases in Cold Lake or Moose Jaw, they too may experience culture shock. Students who live and study abroad and then return to home communities may also experience culture shock. In these cases, however, the recovery period is shorter and the sense of inadequacy and frustration is less.

SUMMARY OF CONCEPTS AND SKILLS

In this chapter we explored culture and intercultural communication, the ways in which cultures differ, and suggestions for improving intercultural communication.

1. A culture is the specialized lifestyle of a group of people. It consists of their values, beliefs, artifacts, ways of behaving, and ways of communicating. Each generation teaches its culture to the next generation. It's transmitted through a process of enculturation. Acculturation is the processes by which your culture is modified through direct contact with or exposure to another culture.

2. Intercultural communication encompasses a broad range of communication. It includes at least the following: communication between cultures, between races, between ethnic groups, between religions, and between nations.

3. Cultures differ in the degree to which they teach individualist or collectivist orientations.

4. High-context cultures are those in which much of the information is in the context or in the person's nonverbals; low-context cultures are those in which most of the information is explicitly stated in the message.

5. Cultures differ in the degree to which gender roles are distinct or overlap. In a masculine culture men are viewed as assertive, oriented to material success, and strong; women are viewed as modest, focused on the quality of life, and tender.

6. Intercultural communication can be made more effective by, for example, reducing ethnocentrism, communicating, mindfully, facing fears, recognizing cultural differences between yourself and others, recognizing cul-

tural differences within any group, recognizing meaning differences, not violating cultural rules and customs, and not evaluating differences negatively.

Check your ability to apply the skills discussed in this chapter, using a rating scale such as the following: 1 = almost always, 2 = often, 3 = sometimes, 4 = rarely, and 5 = almost never.

_____ 1. Communicate with an understanding of the role of culture and how it influences the messages sent and the messages received.

_____ 2. Appreciate the communication differences in individualistic and collectivist cultures and adjust communications accordingly.

_____ 3. Respond to intercultural communications in light of high- and low-context differences.

_____ 4. Respond to intercultural communications in light of differences in masculinity and femininity.

_____ 5. Recognize and try to combat ethnocentric thinking.

_____ 6. Be mindful of the intercultural communication process.

_____ 7. Communicate in intercultural situations with a recognition of potential differences between yourself and the culturally different.

_____ 8. Communicate in intercultural situations with a recognition of the differences within any cultural group.

_____ 9. Communicate in intercultural situations with a recognition of the possible differences within any cultural group.

_____ 10. Communicate in intercultural situations with a recognition of the possible differences in cultural rules and customs.

_____ 11. Communicate in intercultural situations without evaluating differences negatively.

_____ 12. Communicate interculturally with appropriate degrees of openness, empathy, positiveness, immediacy, interaction management, expressiveness, and other-orientation.

VOCABULARY QUIZ

The Language of Intercultural Communication

Match the terms of intercultural communication with their definitions. Record the number of the definition next to the appropriate term.

_____ high-context cultures

_____ acculturation

_____ intercultural communication

_____ low-context cultures

_____ ethnocentrism

_____ culture

_____ mindfulness

_____ enculturation

_____ individual cultures

_____ collectivist cultures

1. A culture in which most information is explicitly stated in the verbal message.

2. The specialized lifestyle of a group of people—consisting of their values, beliefs, artifacts, ways of behaving, and ways of communicating—passed on from one generation to the next.

3. The process by which culture is transmitted from one generation to another by, for example, parents, peer groups, and schools.

4. Communication that takes place between persons of different cultures or who have different cultural beliefs, values, or ways of behaving.

5. The process through which a person's culture is modified through contact with another culture.

6. The tendency to evaluate other cultures negatively and our own culture positively.

7. That mental state in which we are aware of the logic that governs behaviours.

8. Cultures that emphasize competition, individual success, and where your responsibility is largely to yourself.

9. A culture in which much of the information in communication is in the context or the person and is not made explicit in the verbal message.

10. Cultures that emphasize the member's responsibility to the entire group rather than just to himself or herself.

SKILL BUILDING EXERCISES

9.1 THE SOURCE OF YOUR CULTURAL BELIEFS

This exercise is designed to increase your awareness of your cultural beliefs and how you got them. For each of the categories or belief noted below, try to answer these six questions.

What were you taught? Phrase it as specifically as possible; for example, "I was taught to believe that..."

Who taught you? Parents? Teachers? Television? Peers? Coaches?

How were you taught? By example? By explicit teaching?

When were you taught this? As a child? As a high school student? As an adult?

Where were you taught this? In your home? Around the dinner table? At school? On the playground?

Why do you suppose you were taught this? What motives led your parents, teachers, peers, or other sources to teach you this belief?

Beliefs

1. The nature of God (for example, the existence of God, organized religion, atheism, an afterlife).

2. The importance of family (respect for elders, interconnectedness, responsibilities to other family members).

3. The meaning of and means to success (the qualities that make for success, financial and relational "success").

4. The rules for sexual appropriateness (sex outside of committed relationships, same-sex, and opposite-sex relationships).

5. The role of education (the role of education in defining success, the obligation to becoming educated, education as a tool for earning a living).

6. Male–female differences (recognizing differences, feminism).

7. Intercultural interactions (friendship and romance with those of other religions, races, nationalities; importance of in-group versus out-group).

8. The importance of money (amount that's realistic or desirable; acquisition at what price; money and professional goals; relative importance compared with relationships, job satisfaction).

9. The meaning of life (major goal in life, this life versus an afterlife).

10. Time (the importance of being on time; the value of time; wasting time; adherence to the social timetable of your peers—doing what they do at about the same age).

Thinking Critically About Beliefs and Interpersonal Communication.

In which one way did each of your cultural beliefs influence your interpersonal communication style? If you have the opportunity for interaction in small groups, a good way to gain added insight into cultural beliefs is for each person to select one belief, talk about how he or she answered each of the six questions, and comment on how the belief influences the person's way of communicating interpersonally. If the principles for effective interpersonal and intercultural communication (Chapters 8 and 9) are followed, this simple interchange should result in formidable interpersonal and intercultural insight.

9.2 HOW DO YOU TALK? AS A WOMAN? AS A MAN?

Consider how you would respond in each of these situations if you were a typical woman and if you were a typical man.

1. A supervisor criticizes your poorly written report and says that it must be redone.
2. An associate at work tells you she may be HIV-positive and is awaiting results of her blood tests.
3. You see two neighbourhood preteens fighting in your street; no other adults are around, and you worry that the children may get hurt.
4. An elderly member of your family tells you that he has to go into a nursing home.
5. A colleague confides that she was sexually harassed and doesn't know what to do.
6. You're fed up with neighbours who act decidedly unneighbourly—playing the television at extremely high volume, asking you to watch their two young children while they do shopping, and borrowing things they rarely remember to return.

Thinking Critically About Woman and Man Talk.

Using your responses and those of others, compile profiles of the following:

a. the typical woman as seen by women
b. the typical woman as seen by men
c. the typical man as seen by men
d. the typical man as seen by women

Consider the sources of the profiles. For example, were the profiles drawn on the basis of actual experience? Popular stereotypes in the media? Evidence from research studies? How do these perceptions of the way women and men talk influence actual communication between women and men?

9.3 CONFRONTING INTERCULTURAL DIFFICULTIES

How might you deal with the obstacles to intercultural understanding and communication in each of the following scenarios?

1. Your friend makes fun of Radha, who comes to class in her native African dress. You feel you want to object to this.
2. Craig and Louise are an interracial couple. Craig's family treat him fairly well but virtually ignore Louise. They never invite Craig and Louise as a couple to come to dinner or to partake in any of the family affairs. The couple decide that they should confront Craig's family.
3. Malcolm is a close friend and is really an open-minded person. But he has the habit of referring to members of other racial and ethnic groups with the most derogatory language. You decide to tell him that you object to this way of talking.
4. Tom, a good friend of yours, wants to ask Himani out for a date. Both you and Tom know that Himani is a lesbian and will refuse the date, yet Tom says he's going to have some fun and ask her anyway—just to give her a hard time. You think this is wrong and want to tell Tom you think so.
5. Your parents persist in holding stereotypes about other religious, racial, and ethnic groups. These stereotypes come up in all sorts of conversations. You're really embarrassed by these attitudes and feel you must tell your parents how incorrect you think these stereotypes are.
6. Lenny, a colleague at work, recently underwent a religious conversion. He now persists in trying to get everyone else—yourself included—to do the same. Every day he tells you why you should convert, gives you literature to read, and otherwise persists in trying to proselytize you. You decide to tell him that you find this behaviour offensive.

Thinking Critically About Intercultural Difficulties.

Why is it so difficult to call to the attention of friends or family their intercultural communication shortcomings? Of all the intercultural problems discussed in this chapter, with which do you have the greatest difficulty? Are these difficulties the result of attitudes and beliefs you hold? Of habit? Of custom?

Chapter 10
Interpersonal Communication and Relationships

CHAPTER TOPICS

This chapter looks at the nature and stages of interpersonal relationships, the types of relationships you maintain, and how you can communicate more effectively in these relationships.

- Relationships and Relationship Stages
- Relationship Types
- A "POSITIVE" Approach to Improving Relationship Communication

CHAPTER SKILLS

After completing this chapter, you should be able to:

- formulate both verbal and nonverbal messages appropriate to the relationship stage.
- communicate as appropriate and effective in varied types of relationships.
- use the "POSITIVE" approach to relationship improvement.

The story is told that in ancient Greece a young man named Pythias was condemned to death by the tyrant Dionysius for speaking out against the government. Pythias begged Dionysius to delay his execution until he was able to put his family affairs in order. Dionysius agreed but insisted that someone remain in Pythias's place just in case he didn't come back. Damon, Pythias's friend, volunteered and agreed to be executed if Pythias did not return. Damon was then placed in prison while Pythias travelled home. On the day of the scheduled execution, Pythias was nowhere to be found. Without any anger or animosity toward his friend, Damon prepared to die. But just before the execution could be carried out, Pythias arrived and begged the court's forgiveness for his unavoidable delay; he was ready to be executed and asked that his friend be set free. Dionysius was so impressed that he not only freed Damon but pardoned Pythias and asked if he could join the two of them in this extraordinary friendship.

Of course, this is the story of an exceptional relationship. In a way, however, all relationships are exceptional and all tell exceptional stories.

Relationships and Relationship Stages

Relationships come in many forms, as you'll see throughout this chapter. Central to friendships, romantic relationships, family, and in fact to all kinds of relationships is communication. In fact, the term **relationship communication** is almost synonymous with interpersonal communication.

Although most relationships are face-to-face interactions, internet relationships also are widespread in Canada and around the world. As the number of internet users increases, commercial services are adding, expanding, and improving their services for computer relationships. Even television talk shows have focused on computer relationships, especially on bringing together people who have established a relationship online but have never met. Clearly, many people are turning to the internet to find a friend or, perhaps just as often, a romantic partner. Some are using the internet as their only means of interaction; others are using it as a way of beginning a relationship and intend to supplement computer talk later with photographs, phone calls, and face-to-face meetings.

Advantages and Disadvantages of Interpersonal Relationships

Like most things in life, interpersonal relationships have both advantages and disadvantages. Let's look first at the advantages.

People are more frightened of being lonely than of being hungry, or being deprived of sleep, or of having their sexual needs unfulfilled.

—Frieda Fromm Reichman

Advantages of Interpersonal Relationships   Whether face-to-face or online, and for whatever reason, each person develops interpersonal relationships out of a sense that relationships will provide several important advantages over a life without such relationships. For example, interacting with another person helps you lessen loneliness. People who have experienced long periods of isolation seem unanimous in reporting that the major difficulty was the lack of human contact, of someone to talk with. Also, people need the stimulation of the ideas and personalities others provide. This is probably the reason why studies show that elderly people who have few interpersonal relationships are more likely to deteriorate mentally than those with rich relationships (Fratiglioni, Wang, Ericsson, Maytan, & Winblad, 2000).

Largely through contact with others, you learn about yourself. You see yourself in part through the eyes of others. If your friends see you as warm and generous, for example, you will also see yourself as warm and generous.

Relationships also help you enhance your self-esteem, your sense of self-worth. Having a relational partner makes you feel worthy and desirable. When you're fortunate enough to have a supportive partner, your relationship enhances your self-esteem even more. The most general reason for establishing relationships is to maximize your physical, mental, and social pleasures and minimize your pains. You want to share with others both your good fortune and your pain.

Online relationships have a few additional advantages. For example, communicating online is safe in terms of avoiding the potential for physical violence as well as the risk of catching sexually transmitted diseases from someone you really don't know. Unlike relationships established in face-to-face encounters, in which physical appearance tends to outweigh personality, relationships on the net allow the person's inner qualities to be communicated first. Friendship and romantic interaction on the net is a natural boon to shut-ins and to the extremely shy, for whom traditional ways of meeting people can be difficult. Another obvious advantage is that the number of people you can reach online is so vast that it's relatively easy to find someone who matches what you're looking for. The situation is analogous to your chances of finding just the book you need in a library of millions of volumes rather than in a local branch library of several thousands. Still another advantage, for many, is that the socioeconomic and educational status of people on the net is significantly higher than you're likely to find in bars or singles groups.

Some researchers also have argued that computer talk is more empowering for those with "physical disabilities or disfigurements," for whom face-to-face interactions often are superficial and often end with withdrawal (Lea & Spears, 1995; Bull & Rumsey, 1988). By eliminating physical cues, computer talk equalizes the interaction and does not put the disfigured person, for example, at an immediate disadvantage in a society in which physical attractiveness is so highly valued. You're more in control of what you want to reveal of your physical self, and of course you may do it gradually.

Disadvantages of Interpersonal Relationships   Relationships can also, however, involve disadvantages. For example, close relationships put pressure on you to reveal yourself and to expose your vulnerabilities. In the context of a supporting and caring relationship, this vulnerability is generally worthwhile; but it may backfire if the relationship deteriorates and your weaknesses are used against you. Furthermore, many people find no satisfaction in revealing themselves and no advantage in exposing weaknesses.

In close relationships one person's behaviour influences the other person's, sometimes to great extents. Your time is no longer entirely your own. And although you enter a relationship to spend more time with this special person, you also incur time obligations with which you may not be happy. Similarly, if your money is pooled (as it is in many close relationships), then your financial successes have to be shared, as do your partner's losses. On the positive side, of course, your partner shares your losses and you share in your partner's gains. Perhaps the obligations that create the most difficulty are the emotional obligations you incur. To be emotionally responsive and sensitive is not always easy. When one person becomes ill, the pressures of caretaking increase sometimes to the point of breakdown.

Being in a close relationship can result in your abandoning other relationships. Sometimes this issue involves someone you like but your partner can't stand; you may give up this person or see him or her less often. More often, however, it's simply a matter of time and energy; the **intimacy claims** involved in close relationships take a lot of both. You consequently have less to give to other, less intimate relationships.

Once entered into, a relationship may prove difficult to get out of. In some cultures, for example, religious pressures may prevent married couples from separating. Or if children are part of the relationship, it may be emotionally difficult to exit. If lots of money is involved, dissolving a marriage relationship can often mean giving up the fortune you have spent your life accumulating.

And, of course, your partner may break your heart. Your partner may leave you, against all your pleading and promises. Your hurt will be in proportion to how much you care for and need your partner. The person who cares a lot is hurt a lot, the person who cares little is hurt little; it's one of life's little ironies.

Online relationships have their own unique disadvantages. In most online setups, you can't see what the person looks like. Unless you exchange photos or meet face-to-face, you won't know what the person looks like. And even if photos are exchanged, how certain can you be that the photos are of the person or that they were taken recently? In addition, you cannot hear the person's voice—which communicates a great deal of information. Of course, you can always make an occasional phone call. Or you can upgrade your computer setup to enable you to transmit and receive audio and visual messages.

Communicating online lets people present a false self with little chance of detection. For example, minors may present themselves as adults; and adults may present themselves as children for illicit and illegal sexual communications and, perhaps, meetings. Similarly, you can present yourself as rich when you're poor, as mature when you're immature, as serious and committed when you're just enjoying the experience.

Some research claims that in seeking relationships online you may become overly picky, less forgiving of minor imperfections, and less willing to work out differences because the field of available people is so vast. After all, you might figure, there are lots of other people with whom you can correspond just as soon as you return to your computer (Cohen, 2001).

Another potential disadvantage of online relationships—though some might argue it is actually an advantage—is that computer interactions may become too consuming and may substitute for face-to-face interpersonal relationships. Some people argue that those who have relationships online become socially isolated. People get so absorbed in communicating online with people they'll probably never see that they can't find the time or the inclination to interact with others face-to-face. But recent studies seem to show that this may not be true. For example, regular internet users were found to have more offline social interactions than nonusers and reported that they had a significantly larger number of friends and relatives to go to in time of need. Further, only 8 percent of net users studied reported that they felt socially isolated, whereas 18 percent of the nonusers reported feelings of social isolation (Raney, 2000).

All relationships have the potential for bringing rewards and punishments, advantages and disadvantages; in an imperfect world, that's to be expected. The insights and skills of interpersonal communication in relationships, however, should stack the odds in favour of greater and longer-lived advantages and fewer and shorter-lived disadvantages.

You're no doubt attracted to some people and not attracted to others. In a similar way, some people are attracted to you and some people are not. If you're like most people, you're attracted to others on the basis of four major factors: attractiveness (physical appearance and personality); similarity in interests, especially in attitudes; proximity (simple physical closeness, as when you live in the same neighbourhood, attend the same classes, or work together); and reinforcement (the person gives you rewards). Do these factors account for your own attraction to others? If not, what additional factors might influence attraction?

Cultural Influences on Interpersonal Relationships

Cultural factors play important roles in the formation of relationships. In most of North America, interpersonal friendships are drawn from a relatively large pool. Out of all the people you come into regular contact with, you choose relatively few as friends. And with computer chat groups the number of friends you can have has increased enormously, as has the range of people from which you can choose these friends. In rural areas and in small villages throughout the world, however, people have very few choices. The two or three other children your age become your friends; there's no real choice, because these are the only possible friends you could make. In some cultures children's friends are primarily members of their extended family.

Most cultures assume that relationships should be permanent or at least long lasting. Consequently, it's assumed that people want to keep relationships together and will exert considerable energy to maintain relationships. Because of this bias, there is little research that has studied how to move effortlessly from one intimate relationship to another or that advises you how to do this more effectively and efficiently.

Culture influences heterosexual relationships by assigning different roles to men and women. In North America men and women are supposed to be equal; at least, that's the stated ideal. As a result, both men and women can initiate relationships and both can dissolve them. Both men and women are expected to derive satisfaction from their interpersonal relationships; and when that satisfaction isn't present, either

"Please listen carefully to the available options."

partner may seek to exit the relationship. However, in many Middle Eastern countries, for example, only the man has the right to dissolve a marriage without giving reasons.

In some cultures gay and lesbian relationships are accepted, and in others they are condemned. In Canada, same-sex marriage is legal in British Columbia and Ontario, and legislation has been proposed that will extend the right to same-sex marriage across the country. In some parts of the United States, formally registered "domestic partnerships" grant gay men, lesbians, and (in some cases) unmarried heterosexuals rights that were formerly reserved only for married couples—such as health insurance benefits and one partner's right to make decisions when the other is incapacitated. In Norway, Sweden, and Denmark, same-sex relationship partners have the same rights as married partners.

Stages of Interpersonal Relationships

The six-stage model shown in Figure 10.1 describes the significant stages you may go through in developing (and perhaps in dissolving) a relationship as you try to achieve your relationship goals. As a general description of the development of relationships, the stages seem standard: They apply to all relationships, whether friendship or love. The six stages are *contact, involvement, intimacy, deterioration, repair,* and *dissolution.* Each stage can be divided into an initial and a final phase. Because relationships differ so widely, though, it's best to think of any relationship model as a tool for talking about relationships rather than as a specific map that indicates how you move from one relationship position to another.

Contact At the **contact** stage there is first *perceptual contact*—you see what the person looks like, you hear what the person sounds like, you may even smell the person. From this you get a physical picture: sex, approximate age, height, and so on. After this perception there is usually *interactional contact.* Here the interaction is superficial and impersonal. This is the stage of "Hello, my name is Joe"—the stage at which you exchange basic information that needs to come before any more intense involvement. This interactional contact may also be nonverbal, as in, for example, exchanging smiles, concentrating your focus on one person, or decreasing the physical distance between the two of you.

This is the stage at which you initiate interaction ("May I join you?") and engage in invitational communication ("May I buy you a drink?"). According to some researchers, it's at this contact stage—within the first four minutes of initial interaction—that you decide if you want to pursue the relationship or not (Zunin & Zunin, 1972).

Physical appearance is especially important in the initial development of **attraction**, because it's the most readily available to sensory inspection. Yet through both verbal and nonverbal behaviours, quali-

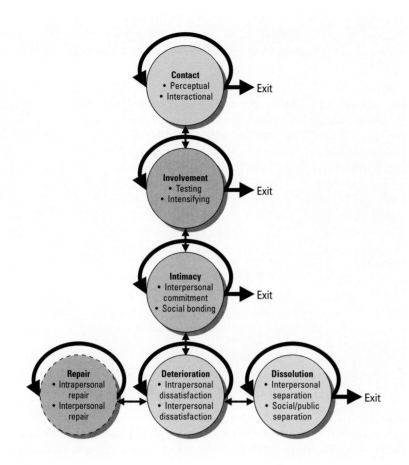

FIGURE 10.1 The Six Stages of Relationships

This is a general model, but are there other stages that you can identify that would further explain what goes on in relationships? Can you provide a specific example, from literature or from your own experience, that would illustrate some or all of these stages?

ties such as friendliness, warmth, openness, and dynamism are also revealed at the contact stage.

Involvement   At the **involvement** stage a sense of mutuality, of being connected, develops. During this stage you experiment and try to learn more about the other person. At the initial phase of involvement a kind of preliminary *testing* goes on. You want to see if your initial judgment—made perhaps at the contact stage—proves reasonable. So you may ask questions—"Where do you work?" "What are you majoring in?"

If you're committed to getting to know the person even better, you continue your involvement by *intensifying* your interaction. Here you not only try to get to know the other person better but also begin to reveal yourself. It's at this stage that you begin to share your feelings and your emotions. If this is to be a romantic relationship, you might date. If it's to be a friendship, you might share in activities related to mutual interests—go to the movies or to some sports event together.

And throughout the relationship process, but especially during the involvement and early stages of intimacy, partners continue testing each other. Each person tests the other; each tries to find out how the other feels about the relationship. For example, you might ask your partner directly how he or she feels; or you might disclose your own feelings on the

> Laughter is not at all a bad beginning for a friendship.
>
> —Oscar Wilde

THINKING CRITICALLY ABOUT

Analyzing and Synthesizing

Analysis and synthesis are two ways you can understand and learn about people, problems, concepts, and so on. In *analysis* you break down a problem or idea into its parts and examine each of these. For example, you might analyze a communication event into sources–receivers, messages, and contexts, much the way we considered communication in the section, "What Is Interpersonal Communication?" in Chapter 1. However, regardless of how thorough your examination of these parts might be, a full understanding would require seeing these pieces as they interact with one another. For example, to understand the appropriateness of self-disclosure in an intercultural situation, you would have to know the relationship between speaker and listener, the context in which they interacted, the cultural backgrounds of the individuals, and how all these factors interacted with each other.

In *synthesis* you combine elements into more meaningful wholes; you arrange and rearrange the elements into different patterns so that you can see the problem from different perspectives. A synthesized explanation of communication would describe it as a set of interacting, interdependent elements—as in the discussion in Chapter 1 of the transactional model and its section on "Principles of Interpersonal Communication."

Both analysis and synthesis help you achieve understanding of a complex process such as communication or culture: analysis to understand the individual parts in detail and synthesis to understand how these parts interact and work together.

EXAMPLES?

Think of an example of how you might apply analysis and synthesis to a problem you've recently encountered. Does each process provide a different perspective?

---

assumption that your partner will also self-disclose; or you might joke about a shared future together, touch more intimately, or hint that you're serious about the relationship; or you might question mutual friends as to your partner's feelings (Bell & Buerkel-Rothfuss, 1990; Baxter & Wilmot, 1984).

Intimacy   At the **intimacy** stage you commit yourself still further to the other person and, in fact, establish a kind of relationship in which this individual becomes your best or closest friend, lover, or companion. Usually the intimacy stage divides itself quite neatly into two phases: an *interpersonal commitment* phase in which you commit yourselves to each other in a kind of private way, and a *social bonding* phase in which the commitment is made public—perhaps to family and friends, perhaps to the public at large through formal marriage. Here the two of you become a unit, a pair. (A self-test, "How committed are you?" will enable you to explore your own level of commitment and offer insight into the types of commitments people make in interpersonal relationships. See www.ablongman.com/devito.)

Commitment may take many forms; it may be an engagement or a marriage, a commitment to help the person or to be with the person, or a commitment to reveal your deepest secrets. It may consist of living together or agreeing to become lovers. The type of commitment varies with the relationship and with the individuals. The important characteristic is that the commitment made is a special one; it's a commitment that you do not make lightly or to everyone. Each of us reserves this

True love comes quietly, without banners or flashing lights. If you hear bells, get your ears checked.
—Erich Segal

MESSAGES@WORK

Developing Effective Working Relationships

The key "relationship skills" of a competent leader can be divided into critical leadership behaviors and social skills. Both are closely linked to "emotional intelligence." The critical leadership behaviors underpin working relationships with the team; the social skills are needed for relationships outside the team.

The skills involve establishing empathy with others, genuinely understanding their viewpoint, and responding in a way that engenders trust. This response takes into account not only each individual's logical attitudes but also their emotions, on which much of their response is based.

EXPERIENCE

As experience and maturity build during your career, you tend to become better at these skills. Perhaps that is because you have learned that your chances of success increase if you take into account the feelings of those on your team, rather than ignoring them.

Also, having a boss who was either very good or very bad at this may help you do a better job of understanding others. Some people naturally have a sense of how others are feeling or thinking. They have an advantage in this area, but those with less sensitivity can develop the skill.

LISTEN

No matter how good or bad you are in this area, one of the best ways to improve is to listen much more than you speak. Try to listen more attentively, don't interrupt or finish other people's sentences. Ask people why they feel as they do. You are then getting information you would not otherwise have had, as well as letting them see your genuine interest.

SHADOWING

Another very effective way to improve is to get someone whose judgment you value and who understands this area to listen in as you work—during meetings, speaking to team members, or talking on the phone.

This person should note how you respond to others and how you could improve the way you do so. He or she will notice many things you would overlook in the way your approach influences your working relationships.

For example, on many occasions, you may not give people the time to finish what they want to say, or you may dismiss an idea without saying why. In the rush of the day-to-day business, you might miss this, but your listener won't.

Two lines that might help are, "good leaders listen," and "always engage brain before opening mouth!"

Source: Chris Roebuck. *Effective Leadership: The Essential Guide to Thinking and Working Smarter.* New York. American Management Association, 1999.

---

level of intimacy for very few people at any given time—sometimes just one person; sometimes two, three, or perhaps four. Rarely do people have more than four intimates, except in a family situation.

Deterioration Although many relationships remain at the intimacy stage, some enter the stage of **deterioration**—the stage that focuses on the weakening of bonds between the parties and that represents the downside of the relationship progression. Relationships deteriorate for many reasons. When the reasons for coming together are no longer present or change drastically, relationships may deteriorate. Thus, for example, when your relationship no longer lessens your loneliness or provides stimulation or self-knowledge, or when it fails to increase your self-esteem or maximize pleasures and minimize pains, it may be in the process of deteriorating. Among the other reasons for deterioration

How important is money to your relationship decisions and relationship happiness? That is, do you make any relationship decisions on the basis of money? To what extent—if any—does your relationship happiness depend on money?

In an interesting study on love, men and women from different cultures were asked the following question: "If a man (woman) had all the other qualities you desired, would you marry this person if you were not in love with him (her)?" How would you answer this question? Results varied greatly from one culture to another (Levine, Sato, Hashimoto, & Verma, 1994). For example, 50.4 percent of the respondents from Pakistan said yes, 49 percent of those from India said yes, and 18.8 percent from Thailand said yes. At the other extreme were those from Japan (only 2.3 percent said yes), the United States (only 3.5 percent said yes), and Brazil (only 4.3 percent said yes).

Having two bathrooms ruined the capacity to cooperate.

—Margaret Mead

How would you distinguish between repair designed to *maintain* a relationship ("preventive maintenance," to keep the relationship satisfying and functioning smoothly) and repair designed to *reverse deterioration* ("corrective maintenance," to fix something that is broken or not functioning properly) (Davis, 1973)? Do these two kinds of repair rely on different strategies?

are third-party relationships, sexual dissatisfaction, dissatisfaction with work, or financial difficulties (Blumstein & Schwartz, 1983).

The first phase of deterioration is usually *intrapersonal dissatisfaction*. You begin to feel that this relationship may not be as important as you had previously thought. You may experience personal dissatisfaction with everyday interactions and begin to view the future together negatively. If this dissatisfaction continues or grows, you may pass to the second phase, *interpersonal deterioration*, in which you discuss these dissatisfactions with your partner.

During the process of deterioration, communication patterns change drastically. These patterns are in part a response to the deterioration; you communicate as you do because of the way you feel your relationship is deteriorating. However, the way you communicate (or fail to communicate) also influences the fate of your relationship. During the deterioration stage you may, for example, increase withdrawal, talk and listen less, and self-disclose less.

Repair   The first phase of **repair** is *intrapersonal repair*, in which you analyze what went wrong and consider ways of solving your relational difficulties. At this stage you may consider changing your behaviours or perhaps changing your expectations of your partner. You may also weigh the rewards of your relationship as it is now against the rewards you could anticipate if your relationship ended.

If you decide that you want to repair your relationship, you may discuss this with your partner at the *interpersonal repair* level. Here you may talk about the problems in the relationship, the corrections you would want to see, and perhaps what you would be willing to do and what you would want the other person to do. This is the stage of negotiating new agreements, new behaviours. You and your partner may try to solve your problems yourselves, seek the advice of friends or family, or perhaps enter professional counselling. (Two exercises—"Relational Repair from Advice Columnists" and "Giving Repair Advice"—will enable you to explore repair advice for a variety of situations. See www.ablongman.com/devito.)

You can look at the strategies for repairing a relationship in terms of the following six suggestions (See Figure 10.2)—which conveniently spell out the word *repair*, a useful reminder that repair is not a one-step but a multistep process: Recognize the problem, Engage in productive conflict resolution, Pose possible solutions, Affirm each other, Integrate solutions into normal behaviour, and Risk.

- *Recognize* the problem. What, in concrete terms, is wrong with your present relationship? What changes would be needed to make it better—again, in specific terms? Create a picture of your relationship as you would want it to be and compare that picture with the way the relationship looks now.

- *Engage* in productive conflict resolution. Interpersonal conflict is an inevitable part of relationship life. It's not so much the conflict that causes relationship difficulties as the way in which the conflict is approached (Chapter 11). If it's confronted through productive strategies, the conflict may be resolved, and the relationship may actually emerge stronger and healthier. If, however, unproductive and destructive strategies are used, the relationship may well deteriorate further.

- *Pose* possible solutions. Ideally, each person will ask, "What can we do to resolve the difficulty that will allow both of us to get what we want?"

- *Affirm* each other. For example, happily married couples engage in greater positive behaviour exchange; that is, they communicate more agreement, approval, and positive affect than do unhappily married couples (Din-dia & Fitzpatrick, 1985).

- *Integrate* solutions into normal behaviour. Make the solutions a part of your normal behaviour.

- *Risk*. Risk giving favours without any certainty of reciprocity. Risk rejection by making the first move to make up or say you're sorry. Be willing to change, to adapt, to take on new tasks and responsibilities.

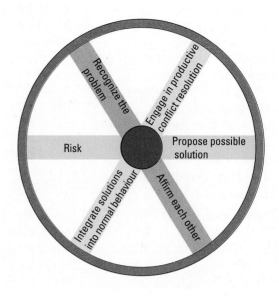

FIGURE 10.2 The Relationship Repair Wheel

The wheel seems an apt metaphor for the repair process: The specific repair strategies—the spokes—all work together in a constant process. The wheel is difficult to get started, but once in motion it becomes easier. And, of course, it's easier to start when two people are pushing. How would you describe the repair process?

Dissolution   The **dissolution** stage, in both friendship and romance, is the cutting of the bonds tying you together. At first it usually takes the form of *interpersonal separation*, in which you may not see each other any more. If you live together, you move into separate apartments and begin to lead lives apart from each other. If this relationship is a marriage, you may seek a legal separation. If this separation period proves workable and if the original relationship is not repaired, you may enter the phase of *social or public separation*. If this is a marriage, this phase corresponds to divorce. Avoidance of each other and a return to being "single" are among the primary identifiable features of dissolution. In some

After all, my erstwhile dear,
My no longer cherished,
Need we say it was not love,
Just because it perished?

—Edna St. Vincent Millay

One way to improve communication during difficult times is to ask your partner to initiate positive behaviours rather than to stop negative behaviours. In keeping with this idea, suggest alternatives to the following comments: (1) I hate it when you ignore me at business functions. (2) I can't stand going to these cheap restaurants; when are you going to start spending a few bucks? (3) Stop being so negative; you criticize everything and everyone.

cases, however, the former partners change the definition of their relationship; for example, ex-lovers become friends, or ex-friends become "just" business partners.

This final, "goodbye," phase of dissolution is the point at which you become an ex-lover or ex-friend. In some cases this is a stage of relief and relaxation; finally it's over. In other cases this is a stage of anxiety and frustration, of guilt and regret, of resentment over time ill spent and now lost. In more materialistic terms, the goodbye phase is the stage when property is divided and when legal battles may ensue over who should get what.

No matter how friendly the breakup, there is likely to be some emotional difficulty. Here are some suggestions for dealing with this.

Break the Loneliness–Depression Cycle. Realize, first, that your feelings of loneliness and depression are not insignificant (Rubenstein & Shaver, 1982). And keep in mind that recent research shows that both men and women get depressed when their relationships deteriorate (Spangler & Burns, 2000) and that men are more likely than women to commit suicide as a result of relationship breakups (Kposow, 2000). Avoid *sad passivity*, a state where you feel sorry for yourself, sit alone, and perhaps cry. This may actually make you feel worse. Instead, try to engage in *active solitude* (exercise, write, study, play computer games) and seek *distraction* (do things to put loneliness out of your mind; for example, take a long drive or shop). The most effective way to deal with loneliness is through *social action*, especially through helping people in need.

Take Time Out. Take some time for yourself. Renew your relationship with yourself. If you were in a long-term relationship, you probably saw yourself as part of a team, as one of a pair. Get to know yourself as a unique individual, standing alone now but fully capable of entering a meaningful relationship in the future.

Bolster Self-Esteem. If your relationship failed, you may experience a lowering of self-esteem. Positive and successful experiences are most helpful in building self-esteem. As in dealing with loneliness, helping others is one of the best ways to raise your own self-esteem. And engage in other activities that you enjoy, that you do well, and that are likely to result in success.

Seek the Support of Others. It's an effective antidote to the discomfort and unhappiness that occurs when a relationship ends. Avail yourself of your friends and family for support. Seek out people who are positive and nurturing; avoid negative individuals who will paint the world in even darker tones. Also, make the distinction between seeking support and seeking advice. If you feel you need advice, seek out a professional.

Avoid Repeating Negative Patterns. Many enter second and third relationships with the same blinders and unrealistic expectations with which they entered earlier relationships. Ask, at the start of a new relationship, if you're entering a relationship modelled on the previous one. If the answer is yes, be especially careful that you do not repeat the problems. At the same time, avoid becoming a prophet of doom. Do not see in every new relationship vestiges of the old. Do not jump at the first conflict and say, "Here it goes again." Treat the new relationship as the unique relationship it is. Use past relationships and experiences as guides, not filters.

Movement Among the Stages   Movement among and within relationship stages is depicted in Figure 10.1 (see p. 255) by the different types of arrows. The *exit* arrows show that each stage offers the opportunity to exit the relationship. After saying hello you can say goodbye and exit. The vertical, or *movement,* arrows going to the next stage and back again represent the fact that you can move to another stage—either to one that is more intense (say, from involvement to intimacy) or to one that is less intense (say, from intimacy to deterioration). The *self-reflexive* arrows—the arrows that return to the beginning of the same level or stage—signify that any relationship may become stabilized at any point. You may, for example, continue to maintain a relationship at the intimate level without its deteriorating or going back to a less intense stage of involvement. Or you may remain at the "Hello, how are you?" stage—the contact stage—without getting further involved.

Within each relationship and within each relationship stage, there are dynamic tensions between opposing desires. The assumption made by **relational dialectics theory** is that all relationships can be defined by a series of opposites. For example, some research has found three such pairs of opposites (Baxter, 1988, 1990; Baxter & Simon, 1993). The ten-

Do any of your relationships involve tension between such opposites as autonomy–connection, novelty–predictability, and closedness–openness? How are these tensions dealt with and reconciled?

LISTEN TO THIS

Listening to Stage Talk

Learning to listen for stage-talk messages—messages expressing a desire to move the relationship in a particular way or to maintain it at a particular stage—will help you understand and manage your own interpersonal relationships, whether business or personal. Over the next few days listen carefully to all stage-talk messages. Listen to messages referring to your own relationships as well as to messages that friends or coworkers disclose about their relationships. Collect these messages and classify them into the following categories.

1. *Contact messages* express a desire for contact: "Hi, my name is Joe."
2. *Closeness messages* express a desire for increased closeness, involvement, or intimacy: "I'd like to see you more often."
3. *Maintenance messages* express a desire to stabilize the relationship at one stage: "Let's stay friends for now. I'm afraid to get more involved at this point in my life."

4. *Distancing messages* express a person's desire to distance himself or herself from a relationship: "I think we should spend a few weeks apart."
5. *Repair messages* express a desire to repair the relationship: "Can we discuss this issue again, this time in a more constructive way? I didn't mean to hurt your feelings."
6. *Dissolution messages* express a desire to break up or dissolve the existing relationship: "Look, it's just not working out as we planned; let's each go our own way."

SUGGESTIONS?

Grace has been dating Thomas for the past few months and admits that she really can't tell if Tom wants the relationship to become more intimate or more distant. And Tom admits that he has difficulty reading Grace's stage talk. What specific advice would you give both Grace and Tom to help them read each other's stage talk?

sion between *autonomy and connection* has to do with your desire to remain an individual but also to be intimately connected to another person and to a relationship. The tension between *novelty and predictability* focuses on your desires for newness and adventure on the one hand, and for sameness and comfortableness on the other. The tension between *closedness and openness* relates to your desires to be in an exclusive relationship and, at the other extreme, to be in a relationship that is open to different people. Research indicates that the closedness–openness tension is more in evidence during the early stages of relationship development. Autonomy–connection and novelty–predictability tensions are more frequent as the relationship progresses (Baxter, 1988, 1990; Baxter & Simon, 1993).

(An exercise, "Analyzing Stage Talk," will enable you to practise identifying the types of messages that are used at each of the various relationship stages. Another exercise, "Changing the Distance Between You," focuses on affinity-seeking and disengagement strategies, the techniques that you use to increase and to decrease intimacy. See **www.ablongman.com/devito**.)

Relationship Types

In this section we look at friendship, love, family, and work relationships and their various types. (An interesting exercise, "Interpersonal Relationships in Songs and Greeting Cards," focuses on the verbal and nonverbal messages that we use to communicate our friendship or love. See **www.ablongman.com/devito**.)

Friendship

Friendship is an interpersonal relationship between two persons that is mutually productive and characterized by mutual positive regard.

Friendship is an interpersonal relationship; communication interactions must have taken place between the people. Further, the interpersonal relationship involves a "personalistic focus" (Wright, 1978, 1984). That is, friends react to each other as complete persons; as unique, genuine, and irreplaceable individuals.

Friendships must be mutually productive; by definition, they cannot be destructive to either person. Once destructiveness enters into a relationship, it can no longer be characterized as friendship. Love relationships, marriage relationships, parent–child relationships, and just about any other possible relationship can be either destructive or productive. But friendship must enhance the potential of each person and can only be productive.

Friendships are characterized by mutual positive regard. Liking people is essential if we are to call them friends. Three major characteristics of friendship—trust, emotional support, and sharing of interests (Blieszner & Adams, 1992)—testify to this positive regard.

The closer friends are, the more *interdependent* they become; that is, when friends are especially close, the actions of one will impact more significantly on the other than they would if the friends were just casual acquaintances. At the same time, however, the closer friends are, the more *independent* they are of, for example, the attitudes and behaviours of others. Also, they're less influenced by the societal rules that govern more casual relationships. In other words, close friends are likely to make up their own rules for interacting with each other; they decide what they will talk about and when, what they can say to each other without offending and what they can't, when and for what reasons one friend can call the other, and so on.

Friends serve a variety of needs; as your needs change, the qualities you look for in friendships also change. In many instances, old friends are dropped from your close circle to be replaced by new friends who better meet new needs. For example, as your own experience is likely to confirm, friendships serve such needs as *utility* (friends may have special talents, skills, or resources that prove useful to you), *affirmation* (friends may affirm your personal values), *ego support* (friends help you to view yourself as a worthy and competent individual), *stimulation* (friends introduce you to new ideas and new ways of seeing the world), and *security* (friends do nothing to hurt you or to emphasize your inadequacies or weaknesses) (Wright, 1978, 1984). (For some of the qualities that research identifies as the most important in friendship, see www.ablongman.com/devito.)

Types of Friendships Not all friendships are the same. But how do they differ? One way of answering this question is by distinguishing among the three major types of friendship: reciprocity, receptivity, and association (Reisman 1979, 1981).

The friendship of *reciprocity* is the ideal type, characterized by loyalty, self-sacrifice, mutual affection, and generosity. A friendship of reciprocity is based on equality: Each individual shares equally in giving and receiving the benefits and rewards of the relationship. In the friendship of *receptivity,* in contrast, there is an imbalance in giving and receiving; one person is the primary giver and one the primary receiver.

Social penetration theory describes relationships in terms of the number of topics that people talk about and the degree of "personalness" of these topics (Altman & Taylor, 1973). The breadth of a relationship has to do with the number of topics you and your partner talk about. The depth of a relationship relates to the degree to which friends penetrate each other's inner personality—the core of each person's individuality—in communication. How would you describe the breadth and depth of your close and your casual friendships?

This imbalance, however, is a positive one, because each person gains something from the relationship. The different needs of both the person who receives and the person who gives are satisfied. This is the friendship that may develop between a teacher and a student or between a doctor and a patient. In fact, a difference in status is essential for the friendship of receptivity to develop.

The friendship of *association* is a transitory one. It might be described as a friendly relationship rather than a true friendship. Associative friendships are the kind we often have with classmates, neighbours, or coworkers. There is no great loyalty, no great trust, no great giving or receiving. The association is cordial but not intense.

(You may wish to examine your own feelings about friendship with the exercise "Friendship Behaviours" at www.ablongman.com/devito.)

Cultural and Gender Differences in Friendship   Your friendships and the way you look at friendships will be influenced by your culture and your gender. In Canada, you can be friends with someone yet never really be expected to go much out of your way for this person. Many Middle Easterners, Asians, and Latin Americans, on the other hand, would consider going significantly out of their way an absolute essential ingredient in friendship; if you're not willing to sacrifice for your friend, then this person is really not your friend (Dresser, 1996).

Generally, friendships are closer in collectivist cultures than in individualistic cultures (see Chapter 9). In their emphasis on the group and on cooperating, collectivist cultures foster the development of close friendship bonds. Members of collectivist cultures are expected to help others in the group. When you help or do things for someone else, you increase your own attraction to—and attractiveness to—the person, and this is certainly a good start for a friendship. And of course the culture continues to reward these close associations. Members of individualistic cultures, on the other hand, are expected to look out for number one. Consequently, they're more likely to compete and to try to do better than one another—conditions that don't support, generally at least, the development of friendships. Do realize that these characteristics are extremes: Most people have both collectivist and individualistic values but have them to different degrees, and that is what we are talking about here—differences in degree of collectivist and individualistic orientations.

Generally, it has been found that women rate higher on the relational functions of friendship than do men (Fritz, 1997). Perhaps the best-documented finding, already noted in our discussion of self-disclosure in Chapter 2, is that women self-disclose more than men do (e.g., Dolgin, Meyer, & Schwartz, 1991). This difference holds throughout male and female friendships: Male friends self-disclose less often and with less intimate details than female friends do. Men generally don't view intimacy as a necessary quality of their friendships (Hart, 1990).

Women engage in significantly more affectional behaviours with their friends than do males (Hays, 1989). This difference, Hays notes, may account for the greater difficulty men experience in beginning and maintaining close friendships. Women engage in more casual communication; they also share greater intimacy and more confidences with

Reliability and Validity

Reliability is a measure of consistency. For example, a test to measure an individual's love style must yield similar scores from one time to another, not fluctuate widely. Intelligence tests are extremely reliable; your score on an intelligence test is likely to remain relatively consistent over the years. When a research study is referred to as having "high reliability," this means that similar findings are highly likely to be found in other studies conducted at other times and with other (but similar) participants. Research is often conducted to test the reliability of earlier research—to see if the original findings and conclusions can be replicated within an acceptable range. So when you read research studies, look at their reliability. Ask yourself if these findings are likely to be found at other times.

Validity is a measure of the extent to which a research effort, say, a test, measures what it claims to measure. Although intelligence tests are extremely reliable,

there's considerable debate about their validity. To be valid, an intelligence test must measure what we normally think of as intelligence and not, for example, knowledge of vocabulary or mathematical formulas. In reading research studies, ask yourself if the study actually measured what it claimed to measure. For example, if you take the self-test, "What Kind of Lover Are You?" (see page 266), ask yourself if the test really measures your own level of romanticism. Look through the self-tests in this text; how would you judge their validity?

EXAMPLES?

Take a look at some of the self-tests in this text that are based on research. Can you give an example of a research instrument whose validity you are not quite willing to accept, even though the test can be shown to be highly reliable?

their friends than do men. Communication, in all its forms and functions, seems a much more important dimension of women's friendships.

Men's friendships are often built around shared activities—attending a ball game, playing cards, working on a project at the office. Women's friendships, on the other hand, are built more around a sharing of feelings, support, and "personalism." One study found that similarity in status, in willingness to protect one's friend in uncomfortable situations, in academic major, and even in proficiency in playing Password were significantly related to the relationship closeness of male–male friends but not of female–female or female–male friends (Griffin & Sparks, 1990). Perhaps similarity is a criterion for male friendships but not for female or mixed-sex friendships.

The ways in which men and women develop and maintain their friendships will undoubtedly change considerably—as will all gender-related variables—in coming years. Perhaps there will be a further differentiation, or perhaps an increase in similarities. In the meantime, given the present state of research in gender differences, we need to be careful not to exaggerate or to treat small differences as if they were highly significant. We need to avoid stereotyping and stressing opposites to the neglect of the huge number of similarities between men and women (Wright, 1988; Deaux & LaFrance, 1998).

How do you see the changes in gender differences? Do you see the differences between men and women increasing or decreasing? What do you see as the major difference between men and women in their attitudes and beliefs about friendship? About romantic relationships? About family relationships?

We love because it's the only true adventure.

—Nikki Giovanni

Love

Although there are many theories about **love**, a model that has long interested interpersonal researchers is Lee's (1976) proposal that not one but six types of love exist. View the following descriptions of the six types as broad characterizations that are generally but not always true. As a preface to this discussion of the types of love, you may wish to respond to the self-test below.

TEST YOURSELF

What Kind of Lover Are You?

Instructions: Respond to each of the following statements with T if you believe the statement to be a generally accurate representation of your attitudes about love, or with F if you believe the statement does not adequately represent your attitudes about love.

_____ 1. My lover and I have the right physical "chemistry" between us.

_____ 2. I feel that my lover and I were meant for each other.

_____ 3. My lover and I really understand each other.

_____ 4. I believe that what my lover doesn't know about me won't hurt him/her.

_____ 5. My lover would get upset if he/she knew of some of the things I've done with other people.

_____ 6. When my lover gets too dependent on me, I want to back off a little.

_____ 7. I expect to always be friends with my lover.

_____ 8. Our love is really a deep friendship, not a mysterious, mystical emotion.

_____ 9. Our love relationship is the most satisfying because it developed from a good friendship.

_____ 10. In choosing my lover, I believed it was best to love someone with a similar background.

_____ 11. An important factor in choosing a partner is whether or not he/she would be a good parent.

_____ 12. One consideration in choosing my lover was how he/she would reflect on my career.

_____ 13. Sometimes I get so excited about being in love with my lover that I can't sleep.

_____ 14. When my lover doesn't pay attention to me, I feel sick all over.

_____ 15. I cannot relax if I suspect that my lover is with someone else.

_____ 16. I would rather suffer myself than let my lover suffer.

_____ 17. When my lover gets angry with me, I still love him/her fully and unconditionally.

_____ 18. I would endure all things for the sake of my lover.

HOW DID YOU DO?

This scale is from Hendrick and Hendrick (1990) and is based on the work of Lee (1976), as is the text's discussion of the six types of love. The statements refer to the six types of love described in the text: eros, ludus, storge, pragma, mania, and agape. For example, statements 1–3 are characteristic of the eros lover. If you answered "true" to these statements, you have a strong eros component to your love style; if you answered "false," you have a weak eros component. Statements

4-6 refer to ludus love, 7-9 to storge love, 10-12 to pragma love, 13-15 to manic love, and 16-18 to agapic love.

WHAT WILL YOU DO?

Are there things you can do to become more aware of the different love styles and to become a more well-rounded lover? Incorporating the qualities of effective interpersonal communication—for example, being more flexible, more polite, and more other-oriented—will go a long way toward making you a more responsive love partner.

Source: Scale from "A Relationship-Specific Version of the Love Attitudes Scale" by Clyde Hendrick and Susan Hendrick, *Journal of Social Behavior and Personality, 5,* 1990. Reprinted by permission of Select Press.

Types of Love The self-test, "What kind of lover are you?" identified six types of love: eros, ludus, storge, pragma, mania, and agape.

Eros: Beauty and Sexuality. Like Narcissus, who fell in love with the beauty of his own image, the *erotic* lover focuses on beauty and physical attractiveness, sometimes to the exclusion of qualities you might consider more important and more lasting. Also like Narcissus, the erotic lover has an idealized image of beauty that is unattainable in reality. Consequently, the erotic lover often feels unfulfilled. Not surprisingly, erotic lovers are particularly sensitive to physical imperfections in the ones they love.

Ludus: Entertainment and Excitement. *Ludus* love is experienced as a game, as fun. The better the lover can play the game, the greater the enjoyment. Love is not to be taken too seriously; emotions are to be held in check lest they get out of hand and make trouble; passions never rise to the point where they get out of control. A ludic lover is self-controlled, always aware of the need to manage love rather than allowing it to be in control. Perhaps because of this need to control love, some researchers have proposed that ludic love tendencies may reveal tendencies to sexual aggression (Sarwer, Kalichman, Johnson, Early, et al., 1993). Not surprisingly, the ludic lover retains a partner only as long as he or she is interesting and amusing. When interest fades, it's time to change partners. Perhaps because love is a game, sexual fidelity is of little importance to ludic lovers. In fact, recent research shows that people who score high on ludic love are more likely to engage in extradyadic (outside-the-couple) dating and sex than those who score low on ludus (Wiederman & Hurd, 1999).

Storge: Peace and Slowness. *Storge* love lacks passion and intensity. Storgic lovers don't set out to find a lover but to establish a companionable relationship with someone they know and with whom they can share interests and activities. Storgic love is a gradual process of unfolding thoughts and feelings; the changes seem to come so slowly and so gradually that it's often difficult to define exactly where the relationship is at any point in time. Sex in storgic relationships comes late, and when it comes it assumes no great importance.

Pragma: Practicality and Tradition. The *pragma* lover is practical and seeks a relationship that will work. Pragma lovers want compatibility and a relationship in which their important needs and desires will be satisfied. They're concerned with the social qualifications of a potential mate even more than with personal qualities; family and background are extremely important to the pragma lover, who relies not so much on feelings as on logic. The pragma lover views love as a useful relationship, one that makes the rest of life easier. So the pragma lover asks such questions of a potential mate as "Will this person earn a good living?" "Can this person cook?" "Will my family get along with this person?" Pragma lovers' relationships rarely deteriorate. This is partly because pragma lovers choose their mates carefully and emphasize similarities. Another reason is that they have realistic romantic expectations.

Mania: Elation and Depression. *Mania* is characterized by extreme highs and extreme lows. The manic lover loves intensely and at the same time worries intensely about the loss of the love. This fear often prevents the manic lover from deriving as much pleasure as possible from the relationship. With little provocation, the manic lover may experience extreme jealousy. Manic love is obsessive; the manic lover has to possess the beloved completely. In return, the manic lover wishes to be possessed, to be loved intensely. The manic lover's poor self-image seems capable of being improved only by being loved; self-worth comes from being loved rather than from any sense of inner satisfaction. Because love is so important, danger signs in a relationship are often ignored; the manic lover believes that if there is love, then nothing else matters.

Agape: Compassion and Selflessness. *Agape* (ah-guh-pay) is a compassionate, egoless, self-giving love. The agapic lover loves even people with whom he or she has no close ties. This lover loves the stranger on the road even though they will probably never meet again. Agape is a spiritual love, offered without concern for personal reward or gain. This lover loves without expecting that the love will be reciprocated. Jesus, Buddha, and Gandhi practised and preached this unqualified love (Lee, 1976). In one sense, agape is more a philosophical kind of love than a love that most people have the strength to achieve.

Cultural and Gender Differences in Love   Although most of the research on the six love styles has been done in North America, some research has been conducted in other cultures. Here is just a sampling of the research findings—just enough to illustrate that culture is an important factor in love. The test and the love styles have been found to have validity among Germans (Bierhoff & Klein, 1991). Asians have been found to be more friendship oriented in their love style than are Europeans (Dion & Dion, 1993b). Members of individualistic cultures (for example, Europeans) are likely to place greater emphasis on romantic love and on individual fulfillment. Members of collectivist cul-

"I myself don't see much hope for an inter-utensil relationship."

tures are likely to spread their love over a large network of relatives (Dion & Dion, 1993a).

One study finds a love style among Mexicans characterized as calm, compassionate, and deliberate (Leon, Philbrick, Parra, Escobedo, et al., 1994). In comparisons between love styles in North America and France, it was found that people in North America scored higher on storge and mania than the French; in contrast, the French scored higher on agape (Murstein, Merighi, & Vyse, 1991). North American Caucasian women scored higher on mania than African American women, whereas African American women scored higher on agape. North American Caucasian and African American men, however, scored very similarly on love styles; no statistically significant differences have been found (Morrow, Clark, & Brock, 1995).

In North America the differences between men and women in love are considered great. In poetry, novels, and the mass media, women and men are depicted as acting very differently when falling in love, being in love, and ending a love relationship. As Lord Byron put it in *Don Juan*, "Man's love is of man's life a thing apart, / 'Tis woman's whole existence." Women are portrayed as emotional, men as logical. Women are supposed to love intensely; men are supposed to love with detachment.

Women and men seem to experience love to a similar degree (Rubin, 1973). However, women indicate greater love for their same-sex friends than men do. This may reflect a real difference between the sexes, or it may be a function of the greater social restrictions on men: A man is not supposed to admit his love for another man. Women are permitted greater freedom to communicate their love for other women.

Men and women also differ in the types of love they prefer (Hendrick, Hendrick, Foote, & Slapion-Foote, 1984). For example, on one version of the love self-test on page 266, men have been found to score higher on erotic and ludic love, whereas women score higher on manic, pragmatic, and storgic love. No difference has been found for agapic love. (Another gender difference frequently noted is that of romanticism. You may wish to take the self-test, "How romantic are you?" And two exercises, "Mate Preferences: I Prefer Someone Who" and "Male and Female," will help you explore your own preferences for romantic partners and the differences between men and women in relationships. See www.ablongman.com/devito.)

The "matching hypothesis" claims that people date and mate people who are very similar to themselves in physical attractiveness (Walster & Walster, 1978). When this does not happen—for example, when a very attractive person dates someone of average attractiveness—the theory suggests that you look for "compensating factors": attributes that compensate or make up for a relative lack of physical attractiveness. What evidence can you find to support or contradict this theory? How would you go about testing this theory?

Family Relationships

If you had to define the word *family*, your first instinct might be to say that a family consists of a husband, a wife, and one or more children. When pressed, you might add that some families also consist of other relatives: brothers and sisters, grandparents, aunts and uncles, in-laws, and so on. But there are other types of relationships that are, to their own members, "families."

One obvious example is the family with one parent. Data from the Government of Canada indicates that an increasing number of children under the age of 18 are living in single-parent families (Government of Canada). Data from 1998/99 indicates that while the overwhelming majority (85.9 percent) of children live in two-parent homes, 13.5 percent of children are being raised in female-headed families while 0.6 percent are being raised in male-headed families. Between 1971 and 1991, lone-parent families increased from 9.4 percent of all families to 13 percent of all families. Almost 25 percent of children born in the late 1980s will have experienced the divorce of their parents before their sixth birthday.

Another obvious example is people who are not married but live together in an exclusive relationship. For the most part, these cohabitants live as if they were married: There is an exclusive sexual commitment; there may be children; there are shared financial responsibilities, shared time, shared space, and so on. These relationships often mirror traditional marriages, except that in marriage the union is recognized by a religious body, the state, or both, whereas in a relationship of cohabitants it generally is not. In Canada, common-law unions have increased steadily since 1981, especially in Quebec, where the rates rose from 8 percent in 1981 to 25 percent in 1996 (Government of Canada). In the rest of Canada, common-law unions have increased at a lesser but still steady rate, from 6 percent in 1981 to 10 percent in 1996. More dramatically, the numbers of common-law unions with children have increased by 47 percent between 1991 and 1996. In 1996, 434 950 common-law families had at least one child living at home; 209 230 of those families were located in Quebec.

Another example is the gay male or lesbian couple who live together and have all the characteristics of a family. Many of these couples have children from previous heterosexual unions, through artificial insemination, or by adoption. Although accurate statistics are difficult to secure, couplehood among gays and lesbians seems more common than the popular media might lead us to believe. Some research has estimated the number of gay and lesbian couples to be between 70 and 80 percent of the gay population (itself estimated variously at between 4 percent and 16 percent of the total population, depending on the definitions used and the studies cited). In summarizing these previous studies and their own research, Blumstein and Schwartz (1983) conclude, "'Couplehood,' either as a reality or as an aspiration, is as strong among gay people as it is among heterosexuals."

The communication principles that apply to the traditional nuclear family (the mother–father–child family) also apply to these varied relationships. In the following discussion, the term **primary relationship** denotes the relationship between the two principal parties—the husband and wife, the lovers, or the domestic partners, for example—and the term **family** denotes the broader constellation that may include children, relatives, and assorted significant others. (A list of definitions of *family* by family communication researchers appears at **www.ablongman.com/devito**.)

All primary relationships and families have several characteristics that further define this relationship type: defined roles, recognition of responsibilities, shared history and future, shared living space, and established rules for communicating.

For example, primary relationship partners have relatively *defined roles* that each person is expected to play in relation to the other and to the relationship as a whole. Each has acquired the rules of the culture and social group; each knows approximately what his or her obligations, duties, privileges, and responsibilities are. The partners' roles might include wage earner, cook, house cleaner, child care giver, social secretary, home decorator, plumber, carpenter, food shopper, money manager, nurturer, philosopher, comedian, organizer, and so on. At times the roles may be shared, but even then it's generally assumed that one person has primary responsibility for certain tasks and the other person for others.

Family members have a *recognition of responsibilities* to one another; for example, responsibilities to help others financially; to offer comfort when family members are distressed; to take pleasure in family members' pleasures, to feel their pain, to raise their spirits.

Primary relationships have *a shared history and the prospect of a shared future.* For a relationship to become a primary one, there must be some history, some significant past interaction. This interaction enables the members to get to know each other, to understand each other a little better, and ideally to like and even love each other. Similarly, the individuals view the relationship as having a potential future.

All families teach *rules for communicating;* for example, never contradict the family in front of outsiders, never talk finances with outsiders.

(You can explore an extremely interesting typology of primary relationships—based on responses from more than 1000 couples to questions concerning their degree of sharing, space needs, conflicts, and time spent together—with an interesting self-test, "What type of relationship do you prefer?" at www.ablongman.com/devito.)

Workplace Relationships

Workplace relationships are becoming more and more important as more of our time is spent in work relationship situations, whether face-to-face in the traditional office or online. Here we look at three kinds of workplace relationships: romantic, mentoring, and networking relationships.

Romantic Relationships in the Workplace   In television depictions, workers always seem to be best friends who would do anything for one another, and characters move in and out of interoffice romances with no difficulties—at least with no difficulties that can't be resolved in 24 minutes. Real life is quite different.

Opinions concerning workplace romances vary widely. Some organizations, on the assumption that romantic relationships are basically detrimental to the success of the workplace, have explicit rules prohibiting such relationships. In some organizations workers can even be fired for getting involved in workplace romances.

On the positive side, the work environment seems a perfect place to meet a potential romantic partner. After all, by virtue of the fact that you're working in the same office,

You can gain an interesting perspective on interpersonal relationships by looking at them in terms of the rules that govern them. The general assumption of rules theory is that friendship, love, family, and work relationships are held together by adherence to certain (often unspoken) rules. When those rules are broken, the relationship may deteriorate and even dissolve. What rules operate in your interpersonal relationships? (You may wish to explore this further with the exercise "The Television Relationship." See www.ablongman.com/devito.)

you both are probably interested in the same field, have similar training and ambitions, and will spend considerable time together—all factors that foster the development of a successful interpersonal relationship.

Similarly, office romances can lead to greater work satisfaction. If you're romantically attracted to another worker, it can make going to work, working together, and even working added hours more enjoyable and more satisfying. If the relationship is good and mutually satisfying, the individuals are likely to develop empathy for each other and act in ways that are supportive, cooperative, and friendly; in short, the workers are more likely to act with all the characteristics of effective communication noted throughout this book.

However, even when the relationship is good for the two individuals, it may not necessarily be a positive factor for other workers. Seeing the loving couple every day in every way may generate destructive office gossip. Or fellow workers may see the lovers as a team that has to be confronted as a pair, feeling that they can't criticize one lover without incurring the wrath of the other.

Similarly, such relationships may cause problems for management when, for example, promotion or relocation decisions are necessary. Can you legitimately ask one lover to move to Winnipeg and the other to move to Vancouver? Will it prove difficult for management to put one lover in the position of supervising the other?

The workplace also puts pressure on the individuals. Most organizations in Canada are highly competitive, and one person's success often means another's failure. In this environment a romantic couple may find, for example, that the self-disclosures that normally accompany increased intimacy (and which often reveal weaknesses, self-doubts, and misgivings), may actually prove a competitive liability.

There's a popular belief that women see office romances as a route to some kind of personal gain. For example, researchers who surveyed 218 male and female business school graduates found that despite a lack of any evidence, people perceived women as entering office romances in order to achieve advancement (Anderson & Fisher, 1991). So the woman who does participate in an office romance may have to deal with the negative reactions of both her male and female colleagues—assumptions that she is in this relationship just to advance her career.

Of course, when an office romance goes bad or when it's one-sided, there are even more disadvantages. One obvious problem is that it can be stressful for the former partners to see each other regularly and perhaps to work together. And other workers may feel they have to take sides, being supportive of one partner and critical of the other. This can easily cause friction throughout the organization. Another and perhaps more serious issue is the potential for charges of workplace sexual harassment, especially if the romance is between a supervisor and a worker. Whether the charges are legitimate or merely the result of an unhappy love affair that has nothing to do with the organization, management will find itself in the middle, facing the expenditure of time and money to investigate and ultimately act on the charges—or, still worse, to defend against lawsuits.

On balance, the generally negative attitude of management toward office love affairs and the problems of dealing with the normal stress of both work and romance seem to outweigh the positive benefits that could be derived from such relationships. Workers are thus generally advised not to romance their colleagues. Friendships seem the much safer course.

Mentoring Relationships   In a **mentoring relationship** an experienced individual helps to train a person who is less experienced. An accomplished teacher, for example, might mentor a young teacher who is newly arrived or who has never taught before. The mentor guides the new person through the ropes, teaches the strategies and techniques for success, and otherwise communicates his or her accumulated knowledge and experience to the "mentee."

The mentoring relationship provides an ideal learning environment. It's usually a supportive and trusting one-on-one relationship between expert and novice. There's a mutual and open sharing of information and thoughts about the job. The relationship enables the novice to try out new skills under the guidance of an expert, to ask questions, and to obtain the feedback so necessary to the acquisition of complex skills. Mentoring is perhaps best characterized as a relationship in which the experienced and powerful mentor empowers the novice, giving the novice the tools and techniques for gaining the same power the mentor now holds. Few mentoring relationships have as much potential for personal growth as the relationship between a manager and an employee (Brown, 2003).

One study found the mentoring relationship to be one of the three primary paths to career achievement among African American men and women (Bridges, 1996). And another study (of middle-level managers) found that people who had mentors and participated in mentoring relationships got more promotions and higher salaries than those who did not have mentors (Scandura, 1992).

At the same time, the mentor benefits from clarifying his or her thoughts, from seeing the job from the perspective of a newcomer, and from considering and formulating answers to a variety of questions. Much as a teacher learns from teaching, a mentor learns from mentoring.

Networking Relationships   In the popular mind, networking is often viewed simply as a technique for securing a job. But it's actually a much broader process. **Networking** can be viewed as using other people to help you solve your problems, or at least to offer insights that bear on your problems—for example, how to publish your manuscript, where to look for low-cost auto insurance, how to find an affordable apartment, or how to defrag your hard drive.

Networking comes in at least two forms: informal and formal. Informal networking is what we do every day when we find ourselves in a new situation or unable to answer questions. Thus, for example, if you're new at a school, you might ask someone in your class what's the best place to eat or shop for clothes or who's the best teacher for interpersonal communication. In the same way, when you enter a new work environment, you might ask more experienced workers how to perform certain tasks or whom to avoid or approach when you have questions.

Formal networking is the same thing, except that it's a lot more systematic and strategic. It's establishing connections with people who can help you—who can answer questions, help you get a job, help you get promoted, help you relocate or accomplish any task you want to accomplish.

A "POSITIVE" Approach to Improving Relationship Communication

There seems little doubt that effective communication is at the heart of effective interpersonal relationships. Without effective communication such relationships are likely to be a lot less meaningful and satisfying than they could be. And friends, lovers, and families can improve and strengthen interpersonal communication by applying the same principles that improve communication in other contexts. The acronym "POSITIVE" stands for general principles of effective communication that

SKILLS TOOLBOX

4 Ways to Network Effectively

Here are a few suggestions for making networking more effective.

1. Begin by networking with people you already know. If you review the list of your friends, relatives, and acquaintances, you'll probably find that you know lots of people with specialized knowledge who can help you in a variety of ways. In some cultures—Brazil is one example—friendships are often established partly for the sake of potential networking connections (Rector & Neiva, 1996). Beginning with people you know, you can then branch out to network with people who know people you know. Thus, you may contact a friend's friend to find out if the firm he or she works for is hiring. Or you may contact people you have no connection with. Perhaps you've read something a person wrote or you've heard the person's name raised in connection with an area in which you're interested. With email addresses readily available, it's now quite common to email individuals who have particular expertise and ask them questions.

2. Try to establish relationships that are mutually beneficial. After all, much as others are useful sources of information for you, you're likely to be a useful source of information for others. And if you can help others, it's more likely that they will be helpful to you.

3. Consider developing files of people you can contact. For example, if you're a freelance artist, come up with a list of persons who might be in positions to offer you work. Authors, editors, art directors, administrative assistants, people in advertising, and a host of others might eventually provide useful leads and can often simplify your search for freelance work.

4. Take an active part in locating and establishing networking connections. Be proactive; initiate contacts rather than waiting for them to come to you. But don't overdo it; you don't want to rely on other people to do work you can easily do yourself. Yet if you're also willing to help others, there's nothing wrong in asking these same people to help you. If you're respectful of their time and expertise, most people will respond positively to your networking attempts. Following up your requests with thank-you notes, for example, will help you establish networks that can be productive ongoing relationships rather than one-shot affairs.

THEN AND NOW

Have you ever needed information that others had but been unable to secure it? What might you have done to get the information? What would you do now if you needed that same information?

enhance all interpersonal relationships: positiveness, openness, supportiveness, interest, truthfulness, involvement, value, and equality.

Positiveness

Positiveness in conversation, as discussed in Chapter 8, entails both a positive attitude toward the communication act and the expression of positiveness toward the other person—as in, say, complimenting. In relationship effectiveness, it includes a positiveness toward the relationship, toward the prospect of continued "couplehood." It includes not only being positive toward your partner but also being positive about your partner when interacting with third parties.

Don't confuse positiveness with perfection. Sometimes, whether influenced by the media, by a self-commitment to have relationships better than their parents', or by a mistaken belief that other relationships are a lot better than their own, people look for and expect perfection. But this quest sets up unrealistic expectations; it is almost sure to result in dissatisfaction and disappointment with existing relationships and, in fact, with any relationship that's likely to come along. Psychologist John DeCecco (1988) puts this in perspective when he argues that relationships should be characterized by reasonableness—"*reasonableness* of need and expectation, avoiding the wasteful pursuit of the extravagant fantasy that *every* desire will be fulfilled, so that the relationship does not consume its partners or leave them chronically dissatisfied."

Openness

Openness entails a variety of attitudes and behaviours. It includes a readiness to listen to the other person—whether you want to or not. It means you're open to listening to the anxieties and worries of your partner, even when you honestly believe these are minor issues and will go away in the morning. And it means you're open to listening even when you really want to watch the ball game or focus on some work-related project.

Openness entails a willingness to empathize with your partner—to experience the feelings of your partner as your partner feels them, to see the world as your partner sees it. It does not mean that you should simply take on the feelings of your partner or even necessarily agree with them, but that you should understand them as your partner experiences them.

Openness recognizes that throughout any significant relationship, there will be numerous changes in each of the individuals and in the relationship itself. Because persons in relationships are interconnected, with each having an impact on the other, changes in one person may demand changes in the other person. Frequently asked-for changes include, for example, giving more attention, complimenting more often, and expressing feelings more openly (Noller, 1982). Your willingness to be responsive to such changes, to be adaptable and flexible, is likely to enhance relationship satisfaction (Noller & Fitzpatrick, 1993). Openness thus entails a willingness to consider new ideas, new ways of seeing your partner and your relationship, and new ways of interacting.

Supportiveness

As will be detailed further in the discussion of conflict in Chapter 11, supportiveness entails a variety of behaviours, such as being descriptive rather than evaluative, focusing on the problem rather than trying to control the other person, acting spontaneously rather than strategically, being empathic, treating the other person as an equal, and recognizing that you don't know everything.

In relationship communication, being supportive also includes encouraging the other person to be the best he or she can be. It entails empowering your partner by raising his or her self-esteem, by sharing the skills you have that your partner needs to control his or her own destiny, and by offering constructive criticism rather than simple but discouraging fault-finding.

Interest

The more interested you are in your partner, the more likely it is that your partner will be interested in you. Learning to appreciate the job your partner does outside the home as well as inside will enable you to share more of your lives with each other and thereby get to know and understand each other a lot better. Developing shared interests—learning new skills or hobbies together, learning to appreciate new music as a couple, or even something as simple as going to the movies once a week to share the experience together—may help two people learn about each other's likes and dislikes, values and interests, emotions and motivations. In the process, each of you is likely to become a more interesting person, which contributes further to communication enhancement. After all, it's a lot easier and more rewarding to communicate with interesting than with uninteresting people.

Children (and even pets) are a good example of a joint interest that partners come to experience as a couple. As parents share child rearing and its accompanying joys and problems, they often grow closer as a couple. Through this experience they come to know each other better because they see each other in a new set of circumstances.

Truthfulness

Honesty and truthfulness does not mean revealing every thought and every desire you have. Nor does it mean that your partner must reveal everything he or she is thinking. After all, everyone has a right to some privacy. At times it may be expedient to omit mentioning, for example, past indiscretions, certain fears, or perceived personal inadequacies if these disclosures might lead to negative perceptions or damage the relationship in some way. As already stressed, in any decision concerning self-disclosure, the possible effects on the relationship should be considered (Chapter 2). Total self-disclosure, in fact, may not always be effective (Noller & Fitzpatrick, 1993). But effectiveness is not the only consideration that needs to be recognized. It's also necessary to consider ethical issues—specifically, the other person's right to know about behaviours and thoughts that might influence the choices he or she will make.

One of the most difficult issues in interpersonal relationships occurs when you're asked a question and there is a tension between your desire to be truthful and your wish to be effective in achieving your communication goal.

WHAT WOULD YOU DO?

Here are a few questions that others might ask you. For each question, however, there are specific circumstances that may make it difficult for you to be completely honest; these are noted as the "Thoughts" you have as you consider your possible answers. What would you do in each of these three situations?

Question [Your 16-year-old twins ask:] Do you smoke dope?

Thoughts I do smoke on occasion, but I don't want to make the practice seem acceptable—and I certainly don't want to influence my children to smoke.

Question [A romantic partner asks:] Do you love me?

Thoughts I don't want to commit myself, but I don't want to end the relationship either. I want to allow the relationship to progress further before making any commitment.

Question [A 15-year-old adopted child asks:] Who are my real parents?

Thoughts I fear that you'll look for your biological parents, and when you find them you'll leave me!

Most relationships would profit from greater self-disclosure of present feelings rather than details of past sexual experiences or past psychological problems. The truthful sharing of present feelings also helps a great deal in enabling each person to empathize with the other; each comes to understand the other's point of view better when these self-disclosures are made.

Truthfulness as a quality of effective relationship communication means that what you do reveal will be an honest reflection of what you feel rather than, say, attempts to manipulate your partner's feelings to achieve a particular and perhaps selfish goal.

Involvement

Involvement means active participation in the relationship. Simply being there or going through the motions is not sufficient. Relationship involvement calls for active sharing in the other person's life (although not to the point of intrusion; after all, most mature people want some independence) and in the other person's goals. It includes active nurturing of the relationship—taking responsibility for its maintenance, satisfaction, and growth. In conflict resolution, as mentioned in Chapter 11, withdrawal and silence are generally unfair conflict strategies. In contrast, actively listening to your partner's complaints, actively searching for solutions to problems and differences, and actively working to incorporate these solutions into your everyday lives are all part of relationship involvement.

Value

When you fall in love or develop a close friendship, you probably do so, in part at least, because you see **value** and worth in the other person.

Equity theory claims that you develop and maintain relationships in which your cost–benefit ratio is approximately equal to your partner's (Walster, Walster, & Berscheid, 1978; Messick & Cook, 1983). An equitable relationship is simply one in which each party derives rewards that are proportional to their costs. If you contribute more to the relationship than your partner, then equity requires that you should get greater rewards. If you each work equally hard, then equity demands that you should each get approximately equal rewards. Conversely, inequity would exist in a relationship if you paid more of the costs (for example, if you did more of the unpleasant tasks) but your partner enjoyed more of the rewards. Inequity would also exist if you and your partner worked equally hard but one of you got more of the rewards. How equitable are your relationships? Are your equitable relationships more satisfying than your inequitable ones?

You're attracted to the person because of some inner qualities you feel this person has. Sometimes this sense of appreciation is lost over the years, and you may eventually come to take the other person for granted—a situation that can seriously damage an interpersonal relationship. So it's often helpful to renew and review your reasons for establishing the relationship in the first place and perhaps to focus on the values that originally brought you together. Very likely these qualities have not changed; what may have changed instead is that they're no longer as salient as they once were. Your task is to bring these values to the forefront again and to learn to appreciate them anew.

Equality

Equality entails a sharing of power and decision making in conflict resolution as well as in any significant relationship undertaking. We can gain an interesting perspective on equality by looking at interpersonal and relationship conflict. Conflict is inevitable; it's an essential part of every meaningful interpersonal relationship. Perhaps the most general rule to follow is to fight fair. Winning at all costs, beating down the other person, and getting one's own way have little value in a primary or family relationship largely because these are unfair and unequal exercises of power. More productive substitutes are cooperation, compromise, and mutual understanding—the strategies of equality. If you enter into conflict with a person you love with the idea that you must win and the other must lose, the conflict has to hurt at least one partner, very often both. However, if you enter a conflict as equal cooperating partners, with the aim of resolving the problem by reaching some kind of mutual understanding, neither party need be hurt; and both parties may benefit from the clash of ideas or desires, from the airing of differences, and from the search for reasonable solutions.

SUMMARY OF CONCEPTS AND SKILLS

In this chapter we explored aspects and major types of interpersonal relationships, and we considered ways to make relationships more effective and more satisfying.

1. Interpersonal relationships have both advantages and disadvantages. Among the advantages are that relationships stimulate you, help you learn about yourself, and generally enhance your self-esteem. Among the disadvantages are that relationships often force you to expose your vulnerabilities, make great demands on your time, and may result in your abandoning other relationships.

2. Typical stages of relationships include contact, involvement, intimacy, deterioration, repair, and dissolution.

3. In contact there is first perceptual contact and then interaction.

4. In involvement there is a testing phase ("Will this be a suitable relationship?") and an intensifying of the interaction; here, often, a sense of mutuality and connectedness begins.

5. In intimacy there is an interpersonal commitment and perhaps a social bonding in which the commitment is made public.

6. Some relationships deteriorate, proceeding through a period of intrapersonal dissatisfaction to interpersonal deterioration.

7. When there are difficulties, repair may be initiated. Generally, an intrapersonal repair comes first ("Should I change my behaviour?"); this may be followed by an interpersonal repair, in which you and your partner discuss your problems and seek remedies.

8. If repair fails, the relationship may dissolve, moving first to interpersonal separation and later, perhaps, to public or social separation.

9. Among the major interpersonal relationships are friendship, love, family, and work relationships.

10. Friendship is an interpersonal relationship between two persons that is mutually productive and characterized by mutual positive regard.

11. Love refers to the romantic relationship existing between two people and comes in a variety of forms. Eros, ludus, storge, pragma, mania, and agape are commonly distinguished types of love.

12. Family relationships are those existing between two or more people who have defined roles, recognize their responsibilities to one another, have a shared history and a prospect of a shared future, and interact with a shared system of communication rules.

13. Among the workplace relationships that need to be considered are romantic relationships (their positives and their negatives), mentoring relationships (in which one experienced worker helps a less experienced one), and networking relationships (in which helping relationships are established either informally or formally).

14. A communication enhancement approach to relationship effectiveness can be spelled out with the acronym "POSITIVE": positiveness, openness, supportiveness, interest, truth, involvement, value, and equality.

Check your ability to apply the skills discussed in this chapter. How often do you do the following? Use a rating scale such as the following: 1 = almost always, 2 = often, 3 = sometimes, 4 = rarely, and 5 = almost never.

_____ 1. See relationships as serving a variety of functions but not necessarily all at the same time.

_____ 2. Formulate both verbal and nonverbal messages that are appropriate to the stage of the relationship.

_____ 3. Establish, maintain, repair, and end a wide variety of relationships with a measure of comfort and control.

_____ 4. Recognize the cultural influences on all interpersonal relationships.

_____ 5. Enhance relationship communication by stressing positiveness, openness, supportiveness, interest, truthfulness, involvement, value, and equality.

VOCABULARY QUIZ

The Language of Interpersonal Relationships

Match the terms dealing with interpersonal relationships with their definitions. Record the number of the definition next to the appropriate term.

_____ friendship

_____ agape

_____ interpersonal repair

_____ mentoring

_____ networking

_____ family

_____ dissolution

_____ reciprocity

_____ supportiveness

_____ equality

1. A type of friendship based on equality.
2. A selfless, compassionate love.
3. A relationship in which there is a shared history and a prospect of a shared future, recognition of mutual responsibilities, defined roles, and rules for communicating.

4. An interpersonal relationship that is mutually productive and characterized by mutual positive regard.
5. An approach to relationship communication that includes empowering your partner by raising his or her self-esteem while avoiding fault-finding.
6. A quality of relationship effectiveness in which each person profits from the relationship and cooperation rather than competition defines interactions.
7. A stage in some relationships in which the partners recognize a problem and engage in productive conflict resolution.
8. A relationship in which an experienced worker helps to train a less-experienced worker.
9. Establishment of connections with people who can help you.
10. A stage of some relationships that consists of interpersonal separation and social or public separation.

SKILL BUILDING EXERCISES

10.1 RESPONDING TO PROBLEMS

On the basis of your reading of this chapter, your prior readings, and your own experiences, how would you respond to each of the following "letters" if you were an advice columnist?

Love and Age Difference I'm in love with an older woman. She's 51 and I'm 22 but very mature; in fact, I'm a lot more mature than she is. I want to get married but she doesn't; she says she doesn't love me, but I know she does. She wants to break up our romance and "become friends." How can I win her over?

22 and Determined

Love and the Best Friend Chris and I have been best friends for the last 10 years. Chris has fallen in love and is moving to Moose Jaw. I became angry and hurt at the idea of losing my best friend and I said things I shouldn't have. Although we still talk, things aren't the same ever since I opened my big mouth. How can I patch things up?

Big Mouth

Love and Sports My relationship of the last 20 years has been great—except for one thing: I can't watch sports on television. If I turn on the game Mariko moans and groans until I turn it off. Mariko wants to talk; I want to watch the game. I work hard during the week and on the weekend I want to watch sports, drink beer, and fall asleep on the couch. This problem has gotten so bad that I'm seriously considering separating. What should I do?

Sports Lover

Love and the Dilemma I'm 49 and have been dating fairly steadily two really great people. Each knows about my relationship with the other, and for a while they went along with it and tolerated what they felt was an unpleasant situation. They now threaten to break up if I don't make a decision. To be perfectly honest, I like both of them a great deal and simply need more time before I can make the decision and choose one as my life mate. How can I get them to stay with the status quo for maybe another year or so?

Simply Undecided

Thinking Critically About Relationship Problems.

What general principles did you follow in offering the advice? What role did communication play in your advice?

10.2 FROM CULTURE TO GENDER

This exercise is designed to help you explore how cultures teach men and women different values and beliefs and how these in turn might influence the ways in which men and women communicate in relationships.

Select one of the areas of belief listed below and indicate what you think the views of the "typical man" and the "typical woman" on this subject would be. For example: *Men believe that women make more effective parents than men do* or *Women believe that men have a higher commitment to career and desire for success than women do.*

Try to identify one way you think these beliefs influence the typical man's behaviour, the typical woman's behaviour, and the typical male–female interpersonal interaction. For example: *Men's belief that women make better parents leads men to leave parenting behaviours up to women* or *Men's belief that women make better parents leads men to avoid making parenting decisions.*

What evidence can you offer for your beliefs about gender differences and about how these cultural beliefs influence interpersonal communication? You may wish to extend this journey by actually locating evidence bearing on your hypotheses. One way to do this is to access the CD-ROM databases that your school library is likely to have; for example, Proquest Direct, ERIC, Psychlit, or Sociofile. Do a find search for "gender" and the

key word of the proposition; for example, gender + friendship or gender + money. Try several variations for each combination, such as gender + finances, men + money, gender differences + finance. Some abstracts you'll find will give you the results of the study. Others will just identify the hypotheses studied; to discover what was found, you'll have to consult the original research study.

Beliefs

1. The three most important qualities necessary for developing a romantic relationship
2. The importance of money in a relationship and in defining one's success or achievement
3. The role of politeness in interpersonal relationships
4. The tendency to nurture others
5. Effectiveness in parenting
6. The tendency to think emotionally rather than logically
7. The likelihood of becoming hysterical—say, during an argument or when placed in a dangerous situation
8. High commitment to career and desire for success
9. The likelihood of becoming depressed because of real or imagined problems
10. The importance of winning—with friends, loved ones, and business associates

Thinking Critically About Culture and Gender.

On the basis of your analysis and research, would you revise your beliefs? State them with even stronger conviction? Urge caution in accepting such beliefs?

10.3 GIVING REPAIR ADVICE

Whether expert or novice, each of us gives relationship repair advice; and probably each of us seeks it from time to time, from friends and sometimes from therapists. Here are a few situations that call for repair. Can you use what you've read here (as well as your own experiences, readings, observations, and so on) to explain what is going on in these situations? What repair advice would you give to each of the people in these situations?

Friends and Colleagues Mike and Abdul, friends for 20 years, had a falling-out over the fact that Mike supported another person for promotion over Abdul. Abdul is resentful and feels that Mike should have stood by him; Mike's support would have secured a promotion and raise for Abdul, which Abdul and his large family could surely use. Mike feels that his first obligation was to the company and that he chose the person he felt would be best for the job. Mike also feels that if Abdul can't understand or appreciate his motives, then he no longer cares to be friends. Assuming that both Mike and Abdul want the friendship to continue or will at some later time, what do you suggest Mike do? What do you suggest Abdul do?

Coming Out Tom, a second-year college student, recently came out as gay to his family. Contrary to his every expectation, they went ballistic. His parents want him out of the house, and his two brothers refuse to talk with him. In fact, they now refer to him only in the third person; and when they do speak of him, they use derogatory hate speech. Assuming that all parties will be sorry at some later time if the relationship is not repaired, what would you suggest Tom's mother and father do? What do you suggest Tom's brothers do? What do you suggest Tom do?

Betraying a Confidence Josh and Tanya have been best friends since elementary school and even now, in their twenties, speak every day and rely on each other for emotional and sometimes financial support. Recently, however, Josh betrayed a confidence and told several mutual friends that Tanya had been having emotional problems and had been considering suicide. Tanya found out and no longer wants to maintain the friendship; in fact, Tanya refuses even to talk with Josh. Assuming that the friendship is more good than bad and that both parties will be sorry if they don't patch things up, what do you suggest Josh do? What do you suggest Tanya do?

Thinking Critically About Giving Repair Advice.

Look over the repair advice you've offered and see if there is anything in that advice that could cause difficulties. That is, is there anything in your suggestions that could delay the repair process, make it more difficult, or actually prevent it? An alternative way of looking at this is to consciously try to propose advice that will aggravate the problems identified here and contrast them with your initial suggestions. How do the "good" suggestions and the "bad" suggestions differ?

Chapter 11

Interpersonal Communication and Conflict

CHAPTER TOPICS

This chapter focuses on interpersonal conflict and how to make your own conflict interactions more productive.

- The Process of Interpersonal Conflict
- A Model for Resolving Conflicts
- Ways to Manage Conflict

CHAPTER SKILLS

After completing this chapter, you should be able to:

- recognize the differences between content and relationship conflicts and respond appropriately to each.
- deal with interpersonal conflicts in a systematic way.
- use more productive conflict strategies and avoid their unproductive counterparts.

In ancient times, the beautiful woman Mi Tzu-hsia was the favourite of the king of Wei. According to the law of Wei, anyone who rode in the king's carriage without permission would be punished by amputation of the foot. When Mi Tzu-hsia's mother fell ill, she took the king's carriage and went out, and the king only praised her for it. "Such filial devotion!" he said. "For her mother's sake she risked the punishment of amputation!"

Another day she was dallying with the king in the fruit garden. She took a peach, which she found so sweet that instead of finishing it she handed it to the king to taste. "How she loves me," said the king, "forgetting the pleasure of her own taste to share with me!"

But when Mi Tzu-hsia's beauty began to fade, the king's affection cooled. And when she offended the king, he said, "Didn't she once take my carriage without permission? And didn't she once give me a peach that she had already chewed on?"

This folktale—taken from *Chinese Fairy Tales and Fantasies* (Roberts, 1979)—captures our common tendency to evaluate the same behaviour in very different ways, depending on how we feel about the person. This tendency is especially clear in interpersonal conflict, the subject of this chapter. More specifically, in this chapter we consider what interpersonal conflict is, how it can go wrong, and how it can be used to improve your interpersonal relationships.

The Process of Interpersonal Conflict

Tranh wants to go to the movies and Sara wants to stay home. Tranh's insistence on going to the movies interferes with Sara's staying home, and Sara's determination to stay home interferes with Tranh's going to the movies. Randy and Grace have been dating. Randy wants to get married; Grace wants to continue dating. The two of them have opposing goals, and each person interferes with the other's attaining his or her goal.

As experience teaches us, **conflict** can arise over numerous types of issues. Some examples:

- goals to be pursued ("We want you to go to college and become a teacher or a doctor, not a dancer")

- allocation of resources such as money or time ("I want to save the tax refund, not spend it on new furniture")

- decisions to be made ("I refuse to have the Jeffersons over for dinner")

- behaviours that are considered appropriate or desirable by one person and inappropriate or undesirable by the other ("I hate it when you get drunk, pinch me, ridicule me in front of others, flirt with others, dress provocatively....")

Interpersonal conflict refers to a disagreement between or among connected individuals: coworkers, close friends, lovers, or family members. The word *connected* in this definition emphasizes the transactional nature of interpersonal conflict, the fact that each person's position

It is seldom the fault of one when two argue.

—**Swedish proverb**

How would you describe interpersonal conflict? How does conflict with a close friend or romantic partner differ from conflict with, say, a stranger on a bus?

affects the other person. That is, the positions in interpersonal conflicts are to some degree interrelated and incompatible.

The Negatives and Positives of Conflict

Interpersonal conflict, because it often occurs between lovers, best friends, siblings, and parent and child, can be especially difficult: We care for, like, even love the individual with whom we are in disagreement. Yet there are both negative and positive aspects or dimensions to interpersonal conflict, and each of these should be noted.

Negative Aspects   Conflict often leads to increased negative regard for the opponent. One reason for this is that many conflicts involve unfair fighting methods and are focused largely on hurting the other person. When one person hurts the other, increased negative feelings are inevitable; even the strongest relationship has limits.

At times, conflict may lead you to close yourself off from the other person. When you hide your true self from an intimate, you prevent meaningful communication from taking place. Because the need for intimacy is so strong, one or both parties may then seek intimacy elsewhere. This often leads to further conflict, mutual hurt, and resentment—qualities that add heavily to the costs carried by the relationship. Meanwhile, rewards may become difficult to exchange. In this situation, the costs increase and the rewards decrease, which often results in relationship deterioration and eventual dissolution.

Positive Aspects   The major value of interpersonal conflict is that it forces you to examine a problem and work toward a potential solution. If productive conflict strategies are used, the relationship may well emerge from the encounter stronger, healthier, and more satisfying than before. And you may emerge stronger, more confident, and better able to stand up for yourself (Bedford, 1996).

Conflict enables each of you to state what you want and—if the conflict is resolved effectively—perhaps to get it. For example, let's say that I want to spend our money on a new car (my old one is unreliable) and you want to spend it on a vacation (you feel the need for a change of pace). By talking about our conflict, we should be able to learn what each really wants—in this case, a reliable car and a break from routine. We may then be able to figure out a way for each of us to get what we want. I might accept a good used car or a less expensive new car, and you might accept a shorter or less expensive vacation. Or we might buy a used car and take an inexpensive motor trip. Each of these solutions will satisfy both of us. They are win–win solutions—each of us gets at least part of what we wanted.

Through conflict and its resolution we also can stop resentment from increasing and let our needs be known. For example, suppose I need lots of attention when I come home from work, but you need to review and get closure on the day's work. If we both can appreciate the legitimacy of these needs, then solutions may be easily identified. Perhaps your important phone call can be made after my attention needs are met, or perhaps I can delay my need for attention until you get closure

Where there is no difference, there is only indifference.

—**Louis Nizer**

about work. Or perhaps I can learn to provide for your closure needs and in doing so get my attention needs met. Again, we have win–win solutions; each of us gets our needs met.

Consider, too, that when you try to resolve conflict within an interpersonal relationship, you're saying in effect that the relationship is worth the effort; otherwise you would walk away from such a conflict. Usually, confronting a conflict indicates commitment and a desire to preserve the relationship.

Conflict, Culture, and Gender

As in other areas of interpersonal communication, it helps to view conflict in light of culture and gender. Both exert powerful influences on how conflict is viewed and how it's resolved.

Conflict and Culture   As with other topics of interpersonal communication, it helps to view conflict in light of culture. Notice how the following three Canadians responded to the question, "What did you learn about culture from your family?"

Anna is a member of the Métis nation. Her father is Cree. "When I was a child, the kids would try to get me to fight, by calling me a half-breed. 'Make them laugh,' said my father. 'Laughing is stronger than punching.'"

Hadassah is an immigrant to Canada from Israel. Her grandparents are Holocaust survivors. "Always keep one step ahead of those who would hurt you. Outsmart them. Use your head, not your fists to deal with conflict."

Dawne's family is of British origin—and has been in Canada for several generations. "Conflict? What is that?" she said. "We don't like to even acknowledge that conflict exists."

The types of conflicts that arise depend on the cultural orientation of the individuals involved. For example, in collectivist cultures, such as those of Ecuador, Indonesia, and Korea, conflicts are more likely to centre on violating collective or group norms and values. Conversely, in individualistic cultures, such as those of Canada, the United States, and western Europe, conflicts are more likely to occur when individual norms are violated (Ting-Toomey, 1985).

When North American and Chinese students were asked to analyze a conflict episode between a mother and her daughter, they saw it quite differently (Goode, 2000). North American students, for example, were more likely to decide in favour of the mother or the daughter—to see one side as right and one side as wrong. The Chinese students, however, were more likely to see the validity of both sides; both mother and daughter were right but both were also wrong. This finding is consistent with the Chinese preference for proverbs that contain a contradiction (for example, "Too modest is half boastful") and North Americans' reactions to these as "irritating."

The ways in which members of different cultures express conflict also differ. In Japan, for example, it's especially important that you not embarrass the person with whom you are in conflict, especially if the disagreement occurs in public. This face-saving principle prohibits the use of such strategies as personal rejection or verbal aggressiveness. In Canada, men and women, ideally at least, are both expected to express their desires and complaints openly and directly. Many Middle Eastern and Pacific Rim cultures, however, would discourage women from such expressions; rather, a more agreeable and submissive posture would be expected.

Even within a given general culture, more specific cultures differ from one another in their methods of conflict management. For example, according to one study, African American men and women and European American men and women engage in conflict in very different ways. The issues that cause conflict and aggravate conflict, the conflict strategies that are expected and accepted, and the entire attitude toward conflict vary from one group to the other. For example, African American men preferred clear arguments and a focus on problem solving. African American women, however, preferred assertiveness and respect (Collier, 1991). Another study found that African American females used more direct controlling strategies (for example, assuming control over the conflict and arguing persistently for their point of view) than did European American females. European American females, on the other hand, used more problem solution–oriented conflict management styles than did African American women. Interestingly, African American and European American men were very similar in their relationship conflict strategies: Both tended to avoid or withdraw from relationship conflict. They preferred to keep quiet about or downplay the significance of differences (Ting-Toomey, 1986).

Among Mexican Americans, studies found that men preferred to achieve mutual understanding by discussing the reasons for the conflict, whereas women focused on being supportive of the relationship. Among Anglo Americans, men preferred direct and rational argument; women preferred flexibility (Collier, 1991). These, of course, are merely examples— but the underlying principle is that techniques for dealing with interpersonal conflict will be viewed differently by different cultures.

Conflict and Gender   Do men and women engage in interpersonal conflict differently? One of the few stereotypes that is supported by research is that of the withdrawing and sometimes aggressive male. Men are more apt to withdraw from a conflict situation than are women. It has been argued that this may happen because men become more psychologically and physiologically aroused during conflict (and retain this heightened level of arousal much longer than do women) and so may try to distance themselves and withdraw from the conflict to prevent further arousal (Gottman & Carrere, 1994; Canary, Cupach, & Messman, 1995; Goleman, 1995). Women, on the other hand, want to get closer to the conflict; they want to talk about it and resolve it. Even adolescents reveal these differences; in a study of boys and girls aged 11 to 17, boys withdrew more than girls but were more aggressive when they didn't withdraw (Lindeman, Harakka, & Keltikangas-Jarvinen, 1997). Similarly, in a study of offensive language, girls were found to be more easily offended by language than were boys; but boys were more apt to fight when they were offended by the words used (Heasley, Babbitt, & Burbach, 1995). In another study, young girls were found to use more prosocial strategies than did boys (Rose & Asher, 1999).

Do you find that men and women are equally likely to argue about relationship issues? Are men and women equally likely to address relationship issues in their attempts at conflict resolution?

Other research has found that women tend to be more emotional and men more logical when they argue (Schaap, Buunk, & Kerkstra, 1988; Canary, Cupach, & Messman, 1995). Women have been defined as conflict "feelers" and men as conflict "thinkers" (Sorenson, Hawkins, & Sorenson, 1995). Another difference is that women are more apt to reveal their negative feelings than are men (Schaap, Buunk, & Kerkstra, 1988; Canary, Cupach, & Messman, 1995).

Nevertheless, from a close examination of the research it would have to be concluded that the differences between men and women in interpersonal conflict are a lot less clear in reality than they are in popular stereotypes. Much research fails to find the differences that cartoons, situation comedies, novels, and films portray so readily. For example, several studies dealing with both college students and men and women in business found no significant differences in the way men and women engage in conflict (Wilkins & Andersen, 1991; Canary & Hause, 1993; Canary, Cupach, & Messman 1995). In an interesting longitudinal study of 2000 Ontario adolescents in grades 5 to 13, researcher Debra Pepler shows that bullying may be related to gender and that children don't grow out of it (as cited in Smyth, 2003). They may begin by bullying children of their own gender but often move to verbal or physical attacks on the opposite sex. Bullying may also lead to sexual harassment and other forms of abuse.

(An exercise, "How Do You Fight? Like a Man? Like a Woman?" will help you explore your beliefs about gender differences in conflict; see www.ablongman.com/devito.)

THINKING CRITICALLY ABOUT

Biases

Let's say you're on a jury. Do you (a) keep an open mind until all the evidence is in and then evaluate the facts and render a judgment, or (b) render a judgment early in the trial and then interpret the evidence in light of your judgment? Although we'd all like to think we would render a judgment only after considering all the evidence, research finds that many people make their judgments early and then interpret the evidence through the filter of this judgment (Edwards & Smith, 1996; Kuhn, Weinstock, & Flaton, 1994).

A natural tendency is to seek out and evaluate and interpret information that supports or confirms your own position, your own bias (a confirmation bias).

Conversely, you may actively avoid or punch holes in any information that would contradict or disconfirm your position or bias (disconfirmation bias). When acquiring and evaluating information, ask yourself if you're being influenced by either of these biases. Bringing this possibility to consciousness will help you think more critically and more fairly about the information.

EXAMPLES?

Think of examples from your own recent experience. Did your biases get in the way of your making accurate judgments about people or ideas?

Content and Relationship Conflicts

Using concepts developed in Chapter 1, we can distinguish between content conflict and relationship conflict. *Content conflict* centres on objects, events, and persons in the world that are usually, though not always, external to the parties involved in the conflict. Content conflicts have to do with the millions of issues that we argue and fight about every day—the merit of a particular movie, what to watch on television, the fairness of the last examination or job promotion, the way to spend our savings.

Relationship conflicts are equally numerous and include such examples as a younger brother who refuses to obey his older brother, two partners who each want an equal say in making vacation plans, and a mother and daughter who each want to have the final word concerning the daughter's lifestyle. Here the conflicts are concerned not so much with some external object as with the relationships between the individuals—with issues like who is in charge, how equal are the members in a primary relationship, or who has the right to set down rules of behaviour.

Of course, content and relationship dimensions are always easier to separate in a textbook than they are in real life, in which many conflicts contain elements of both. Consider, for example, some of the issues that people argue about. In one study, researchers analyzed the conflicts of heterosexual, gay male, and lesbian couples and discovered that all these couples argued about the same six topics with approximately the same level of frequency (Kurdek, 1994):

- intimacy issues such as affection and sex
- power issues such as excessive demands or possessiveness, lack of equality in the relationship, friends, and leisure time
- personal flaws issues such as drinking or smoking, personal grooming, and driving style
- personal distance issues such as frequent absences and school or job commitments
- social issues such as political and social differences, parents, and personal values
- distrust issues such as previous lovers and lying

Another study found that four conditions typically lead up to a couple's "first big fight" (Siegert & Stamp, 1994):

- uncertainty over commitment
- jealousy
- violation of expectations
- personality differences

Online Conflicts

Just as you experience conflict in face-to-face communication, you can experience the same conflicts online. There are, however, a few conflict situations that are unique to online communication.

TALKING ETHICS

Libel, Slander, and More

The Canadian Charter of Rights and Freedoms states that everyone has the following fundamental freedoms:

a) freedom of conscience and religion;

b) freedom of thought, belief, opinion and expression, including freedom of the press and other media of communication;

c) freedom of peaceful assembly; and

d) freedom of association.

But expressions of thought, belief, and opinion are not always free. Some kinds of speech, for example, are unlawful and unethical. It's generally considered unethical (and it's illegal as well) to defame another person—to falsely attack his or her reputation, causing damage to it. When this attack is done in print or in pictures, it's called *libel;* when done through speech, it's called *slander.*

People are becoming increasingly sensitive to and respectful of cultural differences. Whereas a few decades ago it would have been considered quite acceptable to use racist, sexist, or homophobic terms in conversation or to tell jokes at the expense of various cultural groups, today most Canadians consider these forms of speech inappropriate. Today most Canadians disapprove of speech demeaning another person because of that person's sex, age, race, nationality, affectional orientation, or religion, and most people avoid speaking in cultural stereotypes—fixed images of groups that promote generally negative pictures.

Sexual harassment is unethical, and verbal sexual harassment is a form of speech that would not be protected by the Charter of Rights and Freedoms. Also, the courts have ruled that sexual harassment can take place by either sex against either sex.

WHAT WOULD YOU DO?

At the water cooler in the office, you join two of your colleagues only to discover that they're exchanging racist jokes. You don't want to criticize them, for fear that you'll become unpopular and these colleagues will make it harder for you to get ahead. At the same time, you don't want to remain silent, for fear it would imply that you're accepting of this type of talk. What would you do in this situation?

Sending commercial messages to those who didn't request them often creates conflict. Junk mail is junk mail; but on the internet, the receiver has to pay for the time it takes to read and delete these unwanted messages.

Spamming often causes conflict. Spamming is sending someone unsolicited mail, repeatedly sending the same mail, or posting the same message on lots of bulletin boards, even when the message is irrelevant to the focus of the group. One very practical reason why spamming is frowned upon is that it generally costs people money. And even if the email is free, it takes up valuable time and energy to read something you didn't want in the first place. Another reason, of course, is that spam clogs the system, slowing things down for everyone.

Flaming, especially common in newsgroups, is sending messages that personally attack another user. Flaming frequently leads to flame wars; everyone in the group gets into the act and attacks other users. Generally, flaming and flame wars prevent us from achieving our communication goals and so are counterproductive.

In what other ways is face-to-face conflict different from conflict on the net?

Before and After the Conflict

If you're to make conflict truly productive, consider these suggestions for preparing for conflict and for using conflict as a method for relational growth.

Before the Conflict   Try to fight in private. When you air your conflicts in front of others, you create a wide variety of additional problems. You may not be willing to be totally honest when third parties are present; you may feel you have to save face and therefore must win the fight at all costs. This may lead you to use strategies to win the argument rather than to resolve the conflict. Also, you run the risk of embarrassing your partner in front of others, and that may build resentment and hostility.

Make sure you're both relatively free of other problems and ready to deal with the conflict at hand. Confronting your partner when she or he comes home after a hard day of work may not be the right tactic for resolving a conflict.

Know what you're fighting about. Sometimes people in a relationship become so hurt and angry that they lash out at the other person just to vent their own frustration. The immediate trigger for the conflict (for example, the uncapped toothpaste tube) may merely be an excuse to express anger. Instead, it's the underlying hostility, anger, and frustration that need to be addressed.

Fight about problems that can be solved. Fighting about past behaviours or about family members or situations over which you have no control solves nothing; instead, it creates additional difficulties. Any attempt at resolution is doomed to failure, because the problems are incapable of being solved. Often such conflicts are concealed attempts at expressing one or both partners' frustration or dissatisfaction on other fronts.

After the Conflict   Learn from the conflict and from the process you went through in trying to resolve it. For example, can you identify the fight strategies that aggravated the situation? Do you or your

5 Ways to Deal with Workplace Complaints

Because complaints are often preludes to conflict in the workplace, they need to be listened to and responded to appropriately. Here are some suggestions for dealing with complaints.

1. Let the person know that you're open to complaints; you view them as helpful sources of information, and you're listening. Be careful not to fall into the trap of seeing someone who voices a complaint as someone to avoid.

2. Try to understand both the thoughts and the feelings that go with the complaint. For example, listen both to the complaint about the inadequate copying facilities and to the frustration the worker feels when he or she has to turn in work that looks amateurishly prepared. Express not only your concern about the inadequate facilities but also your understanding of the frustration this person is feeling.

3. Respect confidentiality. Let the person know that the complaint will be treated in strict confidence or that it will be revealed only to those he or she wishes.

4. Ask the person what he or she would like you to do. Sometimes all a person wants is for someone to hear the complaint and to appreciate its legitimacy. Other times, the complaint is presented in hopes that you will do something specific. So find out what the person wants you to do.

5. Thank the person for voicing the complaint, and assure him or her of your intention to follow up: "Thanks for bringing this to my attention, Joe. I hear so little about what goes on in the mail room, and I really have to know about these things if we're to raise the quality of our service. We have a section managers' meeting on Monday and I'll bring up your concerns then. And I'll keep you posted on what happens."

THEN AND NOW

Has someone ever voiced to you a complaint that you did not take in the positive spirit advocated here? What happened? If you received the same complaint today, would you handle it any differently?

partner need a cooling-off period? Can you tell when minor issues are going to escalate into major arguments? What issues are particularly disturbing and likely to cause difficulties? How can these be avoided?

Keep the conflict in perspective. Be careful not to blow it out of proportion. In most relationships, conflicts actually occupy a very small percentage of the couple's time, yet in the couple's recollections they often loom extremely large. Don't view yourself, your partner, or your relationship as a failure just because you have conflicts.

Attack your negative feelings. Often such feelings arise because unfair fight strategies such as blame or verbal aggressiveness were used to undermine the other person. Resolve to avoid such unfair tactics in the future; at the same time, let go of guilt or blame for yourself and your partner.

Increase the exchange of rewards and **cherishing behaviours**. These small affectionate gestures will show your positive feelings and demonstrate that you're over the conflict and want the relationship to survive.

(Before reading about the various methods of conflict resolution, you may want to try your hand at analyzing a conflict episode. Go to **www.ablongman.com/devito**.)

Perhaps the most difficult type of listening occurs in the conflict situation; tempers may be running high, and you may find yourself being attacked or at least disagreed with. Here are some suggestions for listening more effectively in the conflict situation.

- Act in the role of the listener. Turn off the television, stereo, or computer; face the other person. And think as a listener: Devote your total attention to what the other person is saying.

- Make sure you understand what the person is saying and feeling. One way to make sure, obviously, is to ask questions. Another way is to paraphrase what the other person is saying and ask for confirmation: "You feel that if we pooled our money and didn't have separate savings accounts, this would be a more equitable relationship. Is that the way you feel?"

- Express your support or empathy for what the other person is saying and feeling: "I can understand how you feel. I know I control the finances and that can create a feeling of inequality."

- If appropriate, indicate your agreement: "You're right to be disturbed."

- State your thoughts and feelings on the issue as objectively as you can; if you disagree with what the other person said, then say so: "My problem is that when we did have equal control over the finances, you ran up so many bills that we still haven't recovered from. And, to be honest with you, I'm worried the same thing will happen again."

- Get ready to listen to the other person's responses to your statement.

SUGGESTIONS?

Your friend is a new teacher at an elementary school, and the parents of a student who has been doing very poorly and has created all sorts of discipline problems in class come to see your friend and complain that their daughter hates school and isn't learning anything. They want her to be transferred to another class with another teacher. What listening guidelines would you suggest that your friend try to follow in talking with these parents?

A Model for Resolving Conflicts

The model in Figure 11.1 (see page 294) helps explain conflict more fully and at the same time provides guidance for dealing with conflicts effectively. This five-step model is based on the problem-solving technique introduced by John Dewey (1910) and used by most contemporary theorists (e.g., Beebe & Masterson, 2000; Patton, Giffin, & Patton, 1989). The assumption made here is that interpersonal conflict is essentially a problem that needs to be solved. This model should not be taken as suggesting that there is only one path to conflict resolution. This is just a general way of envisioning the process. Recall a specific conflict that you had recently and try to trace it through the five stages as you read about them.

Define the Conflict

Your first step is to define the conflict. This is the most essential step in the entire process of managing conflict. *Define both the content and the relationship issues.* Define the obvious content issues (who should do the dishes, who should take the kids to school, who should take out the

FIGURE 11.1 The Stages of Conflict Resolution

This model derives from John Dewey's stages of reflective thinking and is a general pattern for understanding and resolving any type of problem.

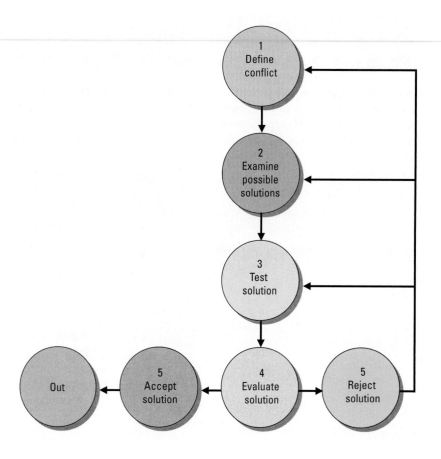

dog) as well as the underlying relational issues (who's been avoiding household responsibilities, who has been neglecting their responsibility toward the kids, whose time is more valuable).

Define the problem in specific terms. Conflict defined in the abstract is difficult to deal with and resolve. It's one thing for the husband to say that his wife is "cold and unfeeling" and quite another to say she doesn't call him at the office or kiss him when he comes home or hold his hand when they're at a party. These behaviours can be agreed upon and dealt with, but the abstract "cold and unfeeling" remains elusive.

Let's select an example: a conflict between a couple named Raul and Julia. Their conflict revolves around Raul's not wanting to socialize with Julia's friends. Julia is devoted to her friends, but Raul actively dislikes them. Julia thinks they're wonderful and exciting; Raul thinks they're unpleasant and boring. Julia says that these friends make her feel important and intelligent. For example, her friends frequently look to her for advice. Let's follow this example through the remaining steps of the conflict-resolution model.

"We only learned to talk yesterday, and now we're not speaking."

THINKING CRITICALLY ABOUT

Problems

Critical thinking pioneer Edward de Bono (1987) suggests that in analyzing problems, you put on six "thinking hats." With each hat you look at the problem from a different perspective. Consider this problem: Julia and Raul are in an exclusive romantic relationship and are relatively happy. The problem is that Julia likes to interact with her friends, all of whom Raul dislikes. Here's how looking at this problem with the six hats might work:

- *The fact hat* focuses attention on the facts and figures that bear on the problem. For example, how can Raul learn more about the rewards that Julia gets from her friends? How can Julia find out why Raul doesn't like her friends?

- *The feeling hat* focuses attention on the emotional responses to the problem. How does Raul feel when Julia goes out with friends? How does Julia feel when Raul refuses to meet them?

- *The negative argument hat* asks you to become the devil's advocate. How might this relationship deteriorate if Julia continues seeing her friends without Raul or if Raul resists interacting with Julia's friends?

- *The positive benefits hat* asks you to look at the upside. What are the opportunities that Julia's seeing friends without Raul might yield? What benefits might Raul and Julia get from this new arrangement?

- *The creative new idea hat* focuses on new ways of looking at the problem. In what other ways can you look at this problem? What other possible solutions might you consider?

- *The control of thinking hat* helps you analyze what you're doing. It asks you to reflect on your own thinking. Have you adequately defined the problem? Are you focusing too much on insignificant issues? Have you given enough attention to possible negative effects?

EXAMPLES?

Recall an example of a problem you had—perhaps a misunderstanding or other interpersonal conflict. Would it have helped if you had analyzed it with each of these six hats?

Examine Possible Solutions

The second step is to look for possible ways of resolving the conflict. Most conflicts can probably be resolved in a variety of ways. At this stage, try to identify as many solutions as possible.

Look for *win–win* solutions. Look for solutions that will enable each party to win—to get something he or she wants. Avoid *win–lose* solutions. These solutions, in which one of you wins and one of you loses, will frequently cause frustration and resentment. In trying to achieve win–win solutions, consider the value of compromise, in which you each willingly give up a part of what you want so that you both can achieve some positive result. In our example, Raul might agree to meet with Julia and her friends *occasionally*. Julia, on the other hand, might agree *occasionally* to give up some meetings with her friends and devote this time only to Raul (Folger, Poole, & Stutman, 1997).

In examining these various potential solutions, carefully weigh the costs and the rewards that each solution will entail. Most solutions will involve costs to one or both parties (after all, someone has to take the dog out). Seek solutions in which the costs will be evenly shared. Similarly, seek solutions in which both parties share equally (or about equally) in the rewards.

Among the solutions that Raul and Julia identify are these:

1. Julia should not interact with her friends any more.
2. Raul should interact with Julia's friends.
3. Julia should see her friends without Raul.

Clearly solutions 1 and 2 are win–lose solutions. In solution 1, Raul wins and Julia loses. In solution 2, Julia wins and Raul loses. Solution 3 has some possibilities. Both might win and neither must necessarily lose. Let's examine this solution more closely by testing it.

Test a Solution

Once you have examined all possible solutions, select one and test it out. First test the solution mentally. How does it feel now? How will it feel tomorrow? Are you comfortable with the solution? Will Raul be comfortable about Julia's socializing with her friends without him? Some of Julia's friends are attractive unmarried men; is this going to make a difference? Will Julia be comfortable socializing with her friends without Raul? Will she give people too much to gossip about? Will she feel guilty? Will she enjoy herself without Raul?

Then test the solution in actual practice. How does it work? Give each solution a fair chance. Perhaps Julia might go out once without Raul to try it out. How was it? Did her friends think there was something wrong with her relationship with Raul? Did she feel guilty? Did she enjoy herself? How did Raul feel? Did he feel jealous? Did he feel lonely or abandoned?

Evaluate the Solution

Did the test solution help resolve the conflict? Is the situation better now than it was before the solution was tentatively put into operation? Share your feelings and evaluations of the solution. Use the skills for expressing emotions covered in Chapter 7.

Raul and Julia now need to share their perceptions of this possible solution. Would they be comfortable with this solution on a monthly basis? Is the solution worth the costs that each will pay? Are the costs and the rewards about evenly distributed? Might other solutions be more effective?

Accept or Reject the Solution

Recall a recent conflict. Did you follow (at least generally) the five stages identified in this model? If not, can you identify the steps you did follow? How effective was the pattern you did use?

If you accept the solution, you're ready to put this solution into more permanent operation. If you decide, on the basis of your evaluation, that this is not the right solution for the conflict, then there are two major alternatives. First, you might test another solution. Perhaps you might now re-examine a runner-up idea or approach. Second, you might go back to the definition of the conflict. As the diagram in Figure 11.1 illustrates, you can re-enter the conflict-resolution process at any of the first three stages.

Let's say that Raul is actually quite happy with the solution. He took the opportunity of his evening alone to visit his brother. The next time

Julia goes out with her friends, Raul intends to go to wrestling. And Julia feels pretty good about seeing her friends without Raul. She simply explained that occasionally she and Raul socialized separately and that both were comfortable with this.

Ways to Manage Conflict

Throughout the process of resolving conflict, try to avoid the common but damaging **unproductive conflict strategies** that can destroy a relationship. At the same time, seek to apply strategies that will help to resolve the conflict and even improve the relationship. The article "Fight Right" offers practical suggestions that will complement the following discussion.

Avoidance and Fighting Actively

Avoidance may involve actual physical flight. You may leave the scene of the conflict (walk out of the apartment or go to another part of the office or shop), fall asleep, or blast the stereo to drown out all conversation. It may also take the form of emotional or intellectual avoidance, in which you may leave the conflict psychologically by not dealing with any of the arguments or problems raised.

Nonnegotiation is a special type of avoidance. Here you refuse to discuss the conflict or to listen to the other person's argument. At times nonnegotiation takes the form of hammering away at one's own point of view until the other person gives in. We call this technique "steamrolling."

Instead of avoiding the issues, take an active role in your interpersonal conflicts. Involve yourself on both sides of the communication exchange. Be an active participant as a speaker and as a listener; voice your own feelings and listen carefully to the voicing of your opponent's feelings. This is not to say that periodic moratoriums aren't helpful; sometimes they are. But in general, be willing to communicate.

Another part of active fighting involves owning your thoughts and feelings. For example, when you disagree with your partner or find fault with her or his behaviour, take responsibility for these feelings. Say, for example, "I disagree with..." or "I don't like it when you...." Avoid statements that deny your responsibility; for example, "Everybody thinks you're wrong about..." or "Chris thinks you shouldn't...."

To gain further ideas for conflict resolution, visit some game sites (for example, **www.gamesdomain.co.uk** or **www.gamepen.com/yellowpages**) and examine the rules of the games. What kinds of conflict strategies do these game rules embody? Do you think these influence people's interpersonal conflict strategies?

Force and Talk

When confronted with conflict, many people prefer not to deal with the issues but rather to force their position on the other person. The **force** may be emotional (for example, compelling a partner to give in by evoking feel-

The aim of an argument or discussion should not be victory, but progress.

—Joseph Joubert

"What ever happened to 'Never go to bed angry'?"

Fight Right

Fight Right identifies 11 conflict-resolution behaviors. In order to be able to practice these behaviors consistently, you need to know how well you do with each of them. Once you know how fully you practice each one, you can focus your energies on those that are weak or lacking in your conflict-resolution repertoire.

STEP 1: TAKE THE "CONFLICT-RESOLUTION SURVEY."

Try to recall the typical interactions you have with a particular person when the two of you disagree. Use the survey below to improve your conflict-resolution skills by indicating how you behave with the person you have identified. The more honest you can be on the survey, the more valuable it will be to you.

Conflict-Resolution Survey 5: Almost always   4: Often
3: Sometimes   2: Infrequently   1: Rarely   0: Never

_____ 1. When I disagree, I am honest about the fact that I disagree, and why.

_____ 2. When proven wrong, I admit it, rather than deny it or try to cover my tracks.

_____ 3. In our oral exchanges I let the other person talk first; I don't have to get in my two cents' worth before he or she speaks.

_____ 4. Before I respond to the other person's assertions, I ask questions or attempt to paraphrase his or her points to make certain I understand what was said.

_____ 5. I stay calm and rational, being careful not to engage in name-calling or to otherwise say anything I'll regret later.

_____ 6. When I do allow myself to get angry, I talk about that anger, rather than what the person did to elicit it.

_____ 7. I am careful to direct my attacks at issues, not personalities. I condemn this person's claims without condemning him or her for making them.

_____ 8. Even as I may disagree with the person's assertions, I recognize the validity of his or her feelings.

_____ 9. I direct our attention to _fixing the future_ rather than rehashing the past.

_____ 10. I keep the focus on our comparative needs, _not our opposing positions_, so we can search for creative ways to meet both sets of needs and reach a common ground.

_____ 11. I use _we, us,_ and _our,_ rather than _I, me,_ and _you,_ when discussing the issue.

STEP 2: CIRCLE ALL SCORES BELOW A 4.

Are these items more a reflection of your relationship with this particular person or more a reflection of your personal conflict-resolution style? One way to answer this question is to complete the survey for other people in your life with whom you have disagreements. Note which items tend to be scored differently—a reflection of the relationship—and which remain unchanged—your conflict-resolution style. What do these scores suggest you do differently the next time you come into conflict with this person or someone else?

STEP 3: CHOOSE THE NEW CONFLICT-RESOLUTION BEHAVIORS YOU WILL ADOPT.

These recommended improvements in problem-solving skills are keyed by number to the items in the survey.

1. **Honesty.** When you disagree with someone, what is the trigger that brings your disagreement into discussion? Is it because you say something like, "We have a problem"? Or does the discussion begin only after the person notices you acting strangely and calls you on it? Do you admit your disagreement, or do you sulk? When you have something to say but choose not to, you engage in a form of passive–aggressive behaviour. You are being unfair to the other person, to your team, and to yourself.

2. **"I was wrong."** Many people foolishly believe that admitting error is a sign of weakness that will compromise their position in a disagreement. Quite the opposite is true. When you admit to having been wrong about something, you are in the best position to ask other people to reciprocate in some way.... Admitting wrong also happens to be the right thing to do.

3. **Speak second.** In an argument it is foolish to go first and smart to go second for at least four reasons. First, letting other people "get it all out" will help to calm them down and defuse their anger. Second, your willingness to wait is a sign of respect that they will appreciate. Third, by listening carefully to their assertions, you will gain clues to what it will take to persuade them over to your way of thinking. (That's why someone once said, "The second lie always wins.") Finally, and most important, only after others have emptied themselves of their ideas, emotions, and anger are they likely to pay much attention to yours.

4. **Make sure you understand.** The single greatest cause of interpersonal conflict is little more than misunderstanding. Don't take a chance that miscommunication is at the root of a disagreement you have with someone. Ask clarifying questions before you put your foot into your mouth. When possible encourage the playing of the "paraphrasing game." The first person starts by stating his or her position. The second person must paraphrase to the first person's satisfaction what he or she just said before earning the right to respond. Continue the entire conversation in this manner with permission to talk always tied to a successful paraphrase. You'll be amazed at the results!

5. **Bite your tongue.** A number of years ago, 100 people aged 95 and older were asked the question. "If you could live your life over again, what would you do differently?" The most frequent response they gave was that they would have thought longer before they did and said to others some of the stupid things they did and said. In other words, they realized that three things in life cannot be recalled: time passed, the spent arrow, and the spoken word....

6. **Talk about your anger.** Much of the advice in the survey is intended to limit your anger. When that advice doesn't work and you lose your temper, start immediately to talk about it. Describe your emotions, your pain, your fear. Only when you have vented completely should you then talk about the incident you got angry about. *Never* talk about what the person did to make you angry, because that would be a lie. People don't have the ability to make you angry without your full cooperation.

7. **Condemn claims, not claimers.** Attack issues with full force, while letting people escape unscathed. Don't accuse others of a dishonest intent. They'll never see it that way and therefore will conclude that you are malicious. Instead, pinpoint the behavior or the issue and state what your needs are in regard to it....

8. **Allow for feelings.** All feelings are valid. They are part of our human nature and are not contrived. We should never say something inappropriate like "You have no right to feel that way." Some people have a powerful need to discuss their feelings as a prelude to resolving the conflict into which those feelings are woven. Give them every opportunity to do that even if you don't share that need. You will increase your chances for a win–win outcome.

9. **Fix the future.** Why do we resolve conflict? To prevent more of the same in the future. The ideal posture to take with regard to your antagonists is best described by the question "What can we do to keep this from happening again?" At some point two people in conflict need to stop talking about the behavior that has contributed to the clash and even stop talking about the feelings that have resulted. One trick for getting the two of you on track to a solution is to invoke the "30-minute rule." It works like this: "Let's agree that for the rest of this discussion neither one of us will talk about anything that happened more than a half hour ago."

10. **Meet needs; don't take positions.** Two people in a disagreement often take opposite positions on an issue. As the debate flares, they harden their stances. This approach leaves little in the way of resolution possibilities other than compromise. A fragile peace is won only after both sides are willing to retreat from their positions to a middle ground that neither side likes, but both realize they must accept. A more satisfying outcome for both parties is possible when they define their differences in terms of needs, not positions. When each person has the opportunity to say, "This is what I want to accomplish by taking this position, or these are the values and beliefs I have that lead me to this conclusion," the two of you can engage in problem solving....

11. **Favor cooperative pronouns.** Pronouns like "I," "me," and "mine" represent the language of a position taker. Pronouns like "we," "our," and "us" encourage collaboration and mutual problem solving.

Source: Sam Deep and Lyle Sussman. *Power Tools: 33 Management Inventions You Can Use Today.* © 1998 by Sam Deep and Lyle Sussman.

ings of guilt or sympathy) or physical. In either case, however, the issues are avoided and the person who "wins" is the one who exerts the most force. This is the technique of warring nations, quarrelling children, and even some normally sensible and mature adults.

Canadian research on family violence tells us the disturbing fact that over 50 percent of Canadian women over the age of 16 have been victims of violence, and 29 percent of married or previously married women have been assaulted by their husband (Lynn, 1996). Moreover, the majority of acts of violence against women are committed by someone they know. The Status of Women Canada conducted a survey in 2000 of 166 police departments representing 53 percent of reported crime. The results of the survey showed that 37 percent of the women were victims of violence by a close friend or acquaintance, 20 percent by a current or past partner, and 11 percent by other family members, including parents. Women were victims of violence by a stranger in 19 percent of reported cases. (Some useful websites to help you explore this topic of relationship violence in more detail may be found at www.ccsd.ca, www.cfc-efc.ca, www.hc-sc.gc.ca, www.statcan.ca, and www.swc-cfc.gc.ca.)

The only real alternative to force is talk. Instead of resorting to force, talk and listen. The qualities of openness, empathy, and positiveness, for example, are suitable starting points (see Chapter 8).

Defensiveness and Supportiveness

Although talk is preferred to force, not all talk is equally productive in conflict resolution. One of the best ways to look at destructive versus productive talk is to look at how the style of your communications can create unproductive **defensiveness** or a productive sense of **supportiveness** (Gibb, 1961). The type of talk that generally proves destructive and sets up defensive reactions in the listener is talk that is evaluative, controlling, strategic, indifferent or neutral, superior, and certain.

Evaluation. When you evaluate or judge another person or what that person has done, that person is likely to become resentful and defensive and is likely to respond with attempts to defend himself or herself and perhaps at the same time to become equally evaluative and judgmental. In contrast, when you describe what happened or what you want, it creates no such defensiveness and is generally seen as supportive. The distinction between evaluation and description can be seen in the differences between you-messages and I-messages.

Evaluative You-Messages	Descriptive I-Messages
You never reveal your feelings.	I sure would like to hear how you feel about this.
You just don't plan ahead.	I need to know what our schedule for the next few days will be.
You never call me.	I'd enjoy hearing from you more often.

If you put yourself in the role of the listener hearing these statements, you probably can feel the resentment or defensiveness that the evaluative messages (you-messages) would create and the supportiveness from the descriptive messages (I-messages).

Control. When you try to control the behaviour of the other person, when you order the other person to do this or that, or when you make decisions without mutual discussion and agreement, defensiveness is a likely response. Control messages deny the legitimacy of the person's contributions and in fact deny his or her importance. They say, in effect, "You don't count; your contributions are meaningless." When, on the other hand, you focus on the problem at hand—and not on controlling the situation or getting your own way—defensiveness is much less likely. This problem orientation invites mutual participation and recognizes the significance of each person's contributions.

One of the most puzzling findings on violence is that many victims interpret it as a sign of love. For some reason, they see being beaten or verbally abused as a sign that their partner is fully in love with them. Many victims, in fact, accept responsibility for contributing to the violence instead of blaming their partners (Gelles & Cornell, 1985). Why do you think this is so?

Strategy. When you use **strategy** and try to get around the other person or the situation through **manipulation**—especially when you conceal your true purposes—that person is likely to resent it and to respond defensively. But when you act openly and with **spontaneity**, you're more likely to create an atmosphere that is equal and honest.

Neutrality. When you demonstrate **neutrality**—in the sense of indifference or a lack of caring for the other person—it's likely to create defensiveness. Neutrality seems to show a lack of interest in the thoughts and feelings of the other person and is especially damaging when intimates are in conflict. This kind of talk says, in effect, "You're not important or deserving of attention and caring." When, on the other hand, you demonstrate empathy, defensiveness is unlikely to occur. Although it can be especially difficult in conflict situations, try to show that you can understand what the other person is going through and that you accept these feelings.

Superiority. When you present yourself as superior to the other person, you're in effect putting the other person in an inferior position, and this is likely to be resented. Such **superiority** messages say in effect that the other person is inadequate or somehow second-class. It's a violation of the implicit contract that people in a close relationship have—namely, that each person is equal. The other person may then begin to attack your superiority; the conflict can easily degenerate into a conflict over who's the boss, with personal attack being the mode of interaction.

Certainty. The person who appears to know it all is likely to be resented, so **certainty** often sets up a defensive climate. After all, there is little room for negotiation or mutual problem solving when one person already has the answer. An attitude of **provisionalism**—"Let's explore this issue together and try to find a solution"—is likely to be much more productive than **closed-mindedness.**

Face-Detracting and Face-Enhancing Strategies

Another dimension of conflict strategies is that of face orientation. Face-detracting or face-attacking strategies involve treating the other person as incompetent or untrustworthy, as unable or bad (Donohue & Kolt, 1992). Such attacks can vary from mildly embarrassing the other person to severely damaging his or her ego or reputation. When such attacks become extreme they may be similar to verbal aggressiveness—a tactic explained below.

Face-enhancing techniques involve helping the other person maintain a positive image—the image of a person who is competent and trustworthy, able and good. There is some evidence to show that even when you get what you want, say, at bargaining, it's wise to help the other person retain positive face. This makes it less likely that future conflicts will arise (Donohue & Kolt, 1992). Not surprisingly, people are more likely to make an effort to support someone's "face" if they like the person than if they don't (Meyer, 1994).

Generally, collectivist cultures like those of Korea and Japan place greater emphasis on face, especially on maintaining a positive image in public. Face is generally less crucial in individualistic cultures such as that of Canada or the United States. And yet there are, of course, many shadings to any such broad generalization. For example, in parts of China, whose highly collectivist culture puts great stress on face-saving, criminals are paraded publicly at rallies and humiliated before being put to death (Tyler, 1996). Perhaps the importance of face-saving in China gives this particular punishment a meaning that it could not have in more individualistic cultures.

Confirming the other person's definition of self (Chapter 5), avoiding attack and blame, and using excuses and apologies as appropriate are some generally useful face-enhancing strategies.

How important is face-saving to you? What did your culture teach you about the importance of face-saving?

Blame and Empathy

Sometimes conflict is caused by the actions of one of the individuals. Sometimes it's caused by clearly identifiable outside forces. Most of the time, however, it's caused by a wide variety of factors. Any attempt to single out one or two factors for **blame** is sure to fail. Yet a frequently used fight strategy is to blame someone for the situation. Consider, for example, a couple who are fighting over their child's getting into trouble with the police. Instead of dealing with the problem itself, the parents may blame each other for the child's troubles. Such blaming, of course, does nothing to resolve the problem or to help the child.

Perhaps the best alternative to blame is empathy. Once you have empathically understood your opponent's feelings, validate those feelings as appropriate. If your partner is hurt or angry and you feel that (from the other person's point of view) such feelings are legitimate and justified, say so; say, "You have a right to be angry; I shouldn't have called your mother a slob. I'm sorry. But I still don't want to go on vacation with her." Once again, in expressing affirmation and validation you are not necessarily expressing agreement on the issue in conflict; you're merely stating that your partner has feelings that are legitimate and that you recognize them as such. This simple strategy has also been found to reduce verbal aggressiveness (Infante, Rancer, & Jordan, 1996).

> I never take my own side in a quarrel.
>
> —**Robert Frost**

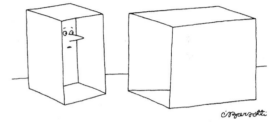

"I do understand, Sabrina. I've been hurt, too."

Silencers and Facilitating Open Expression

Silencers are a wide variety of unproductive fighting techniques that literally silence the other individual. One frequently used silencer is crying. When a person is unable to deal with a conflict or when winning seems unlikely, he or she may cry and thus silence the other person.

Another silencer is to feign extreme emotionalism—to yell and scream and pretend to be losing control. Still another is to develop some "physical" reaction—headaches and shortness of breath are probably the most popular. One of the major problems with such silencers is that we can never be certain that they are mere tactics; they *may* be real physical reactions that we should pay attention to. Regardless of what we do, the conflict remains unexamined and unresolved.

In addition to avoiding silencers, avoid power tactics (raising your voice or threatening physical force) that suppress or inhibit freedom of expression. Such tactics are designed to put the other person down and to subvert real interpersonal equality. Grant other people permission to express themselves freely and openly, to be themselves.

> Never go to bed mad. Stay up and fight.
>
> —**Phyllis Diller**

Gunnysacking and Present Focus

A gunnysack is a large bag, usually made of burlap. As a conflict strategy, **gunnysacking** is the unproductive practice of storing up grievances so as to unload them at another time (Bach & Wyden, 1968). The immediate occasion for unloading may be relatively simple (or so it may seem at first); for example, you come home late one night without calling. Instead of arguing about this, the gunnysacker pours out all past grievances: the birthday you forgot, the time you arrived late for dinner, the hotel reservations you forgot to make. As you probably know from experience, gunnysacking often begets gunnysacking. When one person gunnysacks, the other person gunnysacks. The result is that we have two people dumping their stored-up grievances on each other. Frequently the trigger problem never gets addressed. Instead, resentment and hostility escalate.

Focus on the present, on the here and now, rather than on issues that occurred two months ago. Similarly, focus your conflict on the person with whom you're fighting, not on the person's mother, child, or friends.

Fighting Below and Above the Belt

Like fighters in a ring, each of us has a "belt line." When you hit someone below his or her emotional belt line, a tactic called **beltlining**, you can inflict serious injury (Bach & Wyden, 1968). When you hit above the belt, however, the person is able to absorb the blow. With most interpersonal relationships, especially those of long standing, we know where the belt line is. You know, for example, that to hit Maria with the inability to have children is to hit below the belt. You know that to hit Nadim with the failure to get a permanent job is to hit below the belt. Hitting below the belt line causes all persons involved added problems. Keep blows to areas your opponent can absorb and handle.

Remember that the aim of a relationship conflict is not for you to win and your opponent to lose. Rather, it is to resolve a problem and strengthen the relationship. Keep this ultimate goal always in clear focus, especially when you're angry or hurt.

Verbal Aggressiveness and Argumentativeness

An especially interesting perspective on conflict is emerging from work on verbal aggressiveness and argumentativeness (Infante & Rancer, 1982; Infante & Wigley, 1986; Infante, 1988). Understanding these two concepts will help you understand some of the reasons why things go wrong and some of the ways in which you can use conflict to actually improve your relationships.

Verbal aggressiveness is a method of winning an argument by inflicting psychological pain, by attacking the other person's self-concept. It is a type of disconfirmation (and the opposite of confirmation) in that it seeks to discredit the opponent's view of himself or herself (see Chapter 5). Atkin, Smith, Roberto, Fediuk, and Wagner (2002) suggest that verbal aggression is widespread in North American society. Further, they suggest that committing and experiencing verbal aggression is reciprocal and that there is a strong relationship between verbal and physical aggression. To explore this tendency further, take the self-test on verbal aggressiveness on page 305.

Contrary to popular usage, **argumentativeness** is a quality to be cultivated rather than avoided. Your argumentativeness is your willingness to argue for a point of view, your tendency to speak your mind on significant issues. It's the mode of dealing with disagreements that is

Have you ever used any of these unproductive conflict strategies? Which unproductive conflict strategy, if any, are you most ashamed of using? Why? Which unproductive conflict strategies, if any, have you used in the last two or three months? What effects—both immediate and long-term—did your use of these strategies have?

People generally quarrel because they cannot argue.

—Gilbert Keith Chesterton

Which of the unproductive methods for dealing with conflict discussed here have you experienced? What effects did they have on the conflict and on the relationship? Which unproductive conflict strategy do you think is potentially the most damaging to a relationship? Which would you resent the most?

How Verbally Aggressive Are You?

Instructions: This scale is designed to measure how people try to win arguments through verbal aggression. For each statement, indicate the extent to which you feel it is true for you. Use the following scale: 1 = almost never true, 2 = rarely true, 3 = occasionally true, 4 = often true, and 5 = almost always true.

_____ 1. I am extremely careful to avoid attacking individuals' intelligence when I attack their ideas.

_____ 2. When individuals are very stubborn, I use insults to soften the stubbornness.

_____ 3. I try very hard to avoid having other people feel bad about themselves when I try to influence them.

_____ 4. When people refuse to do a task I know is important, without good reason, I tell them they are unreasonable.

_____ 5. When others do things I regard as stupid, I try to be extremely gentle with them.

_____ 6. If individuals I am trying to influence really deserve it, I attack their character.

_____ 7. When people behave in ways that are really in very poor taste, I insult them in order to shock them into proper behaviour.

_____ 8. I try to make people feel good about themselves even when their ideas are stupid.

_____ 9. When people simply will not budge on a matter of importance, I lose my temper and say rather strong things to them.

_____ 10. When people criticize my shortcomings, I take it in good humour and do not try to get back at them.

_____ 11. When individuals insult me, I get a lot of pleasure out of really telling them off.

_____ 12. When I dislike individuals greatly, I try not to show it in what I say or how I say it.

_____ 13. I like poking fun at people who do things which are very stupid in order to stimulate their intelligence.

_____ 14. When I attack a person's ideas, I try not to damage their self-concepts.

_____ 15. When I try to influence people, I make a great effort not to offend them.

_____ 16. When people do things which are mean or cruel, I attack their character in order to help correct their behaviour.

_____ 17. I refuse to participate in arguments when they involve personal attacks.

_____ 18. When nothing seems to work in trying to influence others, I yell and scream in order to get some movement from them.

_____ 19. When I am not able to refute others' positions, I try to make them feel defensive in order to weaken their positions.

_____ 20. When an argument shifts to personal attacks, I try very hard to change the subject.

(continued)

HOW DID YOU DO?

To compute your verbal aggressiveness score, follow these steps:

1. Add your scores on items 2, 4, 6, 7, 9, 11, 13, 16, 18, and 19.

2. Add your scores on items 1, 3, 5, 8, 10, 12, 14, 15, 17, and 20.

3. Subtract the sum obtained in step 2 from 60.

4. To compute your verbal aggressiveness score, add the total obtained in step 1 to the result obtained in step 3.

If you scored between 59 and 100, you're high in verbal aggressiveness; if you scored between 39 and 58, you're moderate in verbal aggressiveness; and if you scored between 20 and 38, you're low in verbal aggressiveness. In looking over your responses, make special note of the characteristics identified in the 20 statements that indicate a tendency to act verbally aggressive. Note those inappropriate behaviours that you're especially prone to commit. High agreement (4s or 5s) with statements 2, 4, 6, 7, 9, 11, 13, 16, 18, and 19 and low agreement (1s or 2s) with statements 1, 3, 5, 8, 10, 12, 14, 15, 17, and 20 will help you highlight any significant verbal aggressiveness you might have.

WHAT WILL YOU DO?

Because verbal aggressiveness is likely to seriously reduce interpersonal effectiveness, you probably want to reduce your tendencies to respond aggressively. Review the times when you acted verbally aggressive. What effect did such actions have on your subsequent interaction? What effect did they have on your relationship with the other person? What alternative ways of getting your point across might you have used? Might these have proved more effective? Interestingly, perhaps the most general suggestion for reducing verbal aggressiveness is to increase your argumentativeness.

Source: From "Verbal Aggressiveness" by Dominic Infante and C. J. Wigley, *Communication Monographs, 53,* 1986. Copyright © 1986 by the Speech Communication Association. Reprinted by permission of the publisher and authors.

the preferred alternative to verbal aggressiveness. Before reading about ways to increase your argumentativeness, take the self-test on argumentativeness below.

TEST YOURSELF

How Argumentative Are You?

Instructions: This questionnaire contains statements about ways of dealing with controversial issues. Indicate how often each statement is true for you personally according to the following scale: 1 = almost never true, 2 = rarely true, 3 = occasionally true, 4 = often true, and 5 = almost always true.

_____ 1. While in an argument, I worry that the person I am arguing with will form a negative impression of me.

_____ 2. Arguing over controversial issues improves my intelligence.

_____ **3.** I enjoy avoiding arguments.

_____ **4.** I am energetic and enthusiastic when I argue.

_____ **5.** Once I finish an argument, I promise myself that I will not get into another.

_____ **6.** Arguing with a person creates more problems for me than it solves.

_____ **7.** I have a pleasant, good feeling when I win a point in an argument.

_____ **8.** When I finish arguing with someone, I feel nervous and upset.

_____ **9.** I enjoy a good argument over a controversial issue.

_____ **10.** I get an unpleasant feeling when I realize I am about to get into an argument.

_____ **11.** I enjoy defending my point of view on an issue.

_____ **12.** I am happy when I keep an argument from happening.

_____ **13.** I do not like to miss the opportunity to argue a controversial issue.

_____ **14.** I prefer being with people who rarely disagree with me.

_____ **15.** I consider an argument an exciting intellectual challenge.

_____ **16.** I find myself unable to think of effective points during an argument.

_____ **17.** I feel refreshed and satisfied after an argument on a controversial issue.

_____ **18.** I have the ability to do well in an argument.

_____ **19.** I try to avoid getting into arguments.

_____ **20.** I feel excitement when I expect that a conversation I am in is leading to an argument.

HOW DID YOU DO?

To compute your argumentativeness score follow these steps:

1. Add your scores on items 2, 4, 7, 9, 11, 13, 15, 17, 18, and 20.

2. Add 60 to the sum obtained in Step 1.

3. Add your scores on items 1, 3, 5, 6, 8, 10, 12, 14, 16, and 19.

4. To compute your argumentativeness score, subtract the total obtained in step 3 from the total obtained in step 2.

The following guidelines will help you interpret your score:

Scores between 73 and 100 indicate high argumentativeness.

Scores between 56 and 72 indicate moderate argumentativeness.

Scores between 20 and 55 indicate low argumentativeness.

WHAT WILL YOU DO?

Infante and Rancer (1982) note that both high and low argumentatives may experience communication difficulties. The high argumentative, for example, may argue needlessly, too often, and too forcefully. The low argumentative, on the other hand, may avoid taking a stand even when it seems necessary. Persons scoring somewhere in the middle are probably the more interpersonally skilled and adaptable, arguing when it is necessary but avoiding arguments that are needless and repetitive. Does your experience support these observations? What specific actions might you take to improve your argumentativeness?

Source: This scale was developed by Dominic Infante and Andrew Rancer and appears in Dominic Infante and Andrew Rancer, "A Conceptualization and Measure of Argumentativeness," _Journal of Personality Assessment, 46_ (1982): 72–80.

What one principle from this chapter will most influence your own conflict behaviour?

The researchers who developed the argumentativeness test note that those who score high in argumentativeness have a strong tendency to state their position on controversial issues and to argue against the positions of others (Infante & Rancer, 1982). A high scorer sees arguing as exciting, intellectually challenging, and as an opportunity to win a kind of contest. The low scorer sees arguing as unpleasant and unsatisfying. Not surprisingly, this person has little confidence in his or her ability to argue effectively. The person who scores low in argumentativeness tries to prevent arguments. This person derives satisfaction not from arguing but from avoiding arguments. The moderately argumentative individual possesses some of the qualities of the high argumentative and some of the qualities of the low argumentative.

Here are some suggestions for cultivating argumentativeness and for preventing it from degenerating into aggressiveness (Infante, 1988):

- Treat disagreements as objectively as possible; avoid assuming that because someone takes issue with your position or your interpretation, that they are attacking you as a person.

- Avoid attacking the other person (rather than the person's arguments) even if this would give you a tactical advantage; personal attacks will probably backfire at some later time and make your relationship more difficult.

- Avoid interrupting; allow the other person to state her or his position fully before you respond.

- Express interest in the other person's position, attitude, and point of view; reaffirm the other person's sense of competence; compliment the other person as appropriate.

- Avoid presenting your arguments too emotionally; using an overly loud voice or interjecting vulgar expressions will prove offensive and ineffective.

- Allow the other person to save face; never humiliate the other person.

What changes would you like to see your relational partners (friends, family members, romantic partners) make in their own verbal aggressiveness and argumentativeness? What might you do to more effectively regulate your own verbal aggressiveness and argumentativeness?

SUMMARY OF CONCEPTS AND SKILLS

In this chapter we examined interpersonal conflict. We looked at the distinction between content and relationship conflict and at conflict's positive and negative aspects. We considered a model of conflict resolution and surveyed a variety of unproductive conflict strategies and their more productive counterparts.

1. Interpersonal conflict is disagreement between or among connected individuals. The positions in interpersonal conflicts are to some degree interrelated and incompatible.

2. Content conflict centres on objects, events, and persons in the world that are usually, though not always, external to the parties involved in the conflict. Relationship conflicts are concerned more with the relationships between the individuals: with such issues as who is in charge, the equality of a primary relationship, and who has the right to set down rules of behaviour.

3. Recommendations for before the conflict: Try to fight in private, be sure you're each ready to

fight, know what you're fighting about, avoid fighting about problems that cannot be solved. After the conflict: Keep the conflict in perspective, challenge your negative feelings, increase the exchange of rewards.

4. A five-step model is often helpful in resolving conflict: define the conflict, examine possible solutions, test a solution, evaluate the solution, and accept or reject the solution.

5. Unproductive versus productive conflict strategies include avoidance versus fighting actively, force versus talk, face-detracting versus face-enhancing strategies, blame versus empathy, silencers versus facilitating open expression, gunnysacking versus present focus, fighting below versus above the belt, and verbal aggressiveness versus argumentativeness.

6. To cultivate productive argumentativeness, treat disagreements objectively and avoid attacking the other person; reaffirm the other's sense of competence; avoid interrupting; stress equality and similarities; express interest in the other's position; avoid presenting your arguments too emotionally; and allow the other to save face.

Check your ability to apply the following skills. Use a rating scale such as the following: 1 = almost always, 2 = often, 3 = sometimes, 4 = rarely, and 5 = almost never.

_____ 1. Recognize the differences between content and relationship conflicts and respond to each accordingly.

_____ 2. Prepare for conflict and follow it up so that it remains in perspective.

_____ 3. Deal with interpersonal conflicts via systematic steps, such as definition, examination of possible solutions, testing of a solution, evaluation of the solution, and acceptance or rejection of the solution.

_____ 4. View problems and solutions from the perspective of facts, feelings, negative argument, positive benefits, creative new ideas, and control of thinking.

_____ 5. Use productive interpersonal conflict strategies such as active engagement in the conflict, empathy, facilitating open expression, present focus, fighting above the belt, and constructive argumentativeness.

_____ 6. Avoid unproductive conflict strategies such as avoidance, blame, silencers, gunnysacking, beltlining, and verbal aggressiveness.

VOCABULARY QUIZ

The Language of Conflict

Match the terms dealing with interpersonal conflict with their definitions. Record the number of the definition next to the appropriate term.

_____ six hats technique

_____ silencers

_____ argumentativeness

_____ gunnysacking

_____ beltline

_____ verbal aggressiveness

_____ spamming

_____ complaint

_____ interpersonal conflict

_____ conflict resolution model

1. A disagreement between connected individuals.

2. An unproductive conflict strategy of storing up grievances and holding these in readiness to dump on the person with whom one is in conflict.

3. A person's level of tolerance for absorbing a personal attack.

4. A tendency or willingness to argue for a point of view, to speak your mind on significant issues.

5. An expressed dissatisfaction that's a valuable source of feedback.

6. A tendency to try to win arguments by attacking opponents' self-concept.

7. A relatively standard set of procedures for dealing with conflict consisting of five steps: define the conflict, examine possible solutions, test a solution, evaluate the solution, and accept or reject the solution.

8. Varied ways of looking at a particular issue to give you different perspectives.

9. Sending unsolicited e-mail or repeatedly posting the same message.

10. A group of unproductive conflict strategies including crying and pretending to be extremely emotional.

SKILL BUILDING EXERCISES

11.1 DEALING WITH CONFLICT STARTERS

The purpose of this exercise is to give you some practice in responding to potential interpersonal conflicts. Use your own conflict experiences as a guide in this exercise. For each "starter": (1) Write an unproductive response; that is, a response that will aggravate the potential conflict. Why do you believe this response will intensify the conflict? (2) Write a productive response; that is, a response that will lessen the potential conflict. Why do you believe this response will help resolve the conflict?

Conflict "Starters"

1. You're late again. You're always late. Your lateness is very inconsiderate of my time and the time of the entire team.

2. I just can't bear another weekend of sitting home watching cartoon shows with the kids. I'm just not going to do that again.

3. Who forgot to phone for reservations?

4. Well, there goes another anniversary and another anniversary that you forgot.

5. You think I'm fat, don't you?

6. You always complain that I don't participate at meetings, but I do.

7. Did I hear you say your mother knows how to dress?

8. We should have been more available when he needed us. I was always at work.

9. Where's the pepper? Is there no pepper in this house?

10. The Romeros think we should spend our money and start enjoying life.

Thinking Critically About Conflict Starters.

Having read this chapter, ask yourself if your attitudes toward conflict have changed. Will you approach real-life interpersonal conflict with different strategies from now on?

11.2 GENERATING WIN–WIN SOLUTIONS

Often, people involved in interpersonal conflict fail to consider if there are possible win–win solutions and what they might be. To get into the habit of looking for win–win solutions, consider the following conflict situations, either alone or in groups of five or six. For each situation, try generating win–win solutions, as many as possible, that you feel the individuals involved in the conflict could reasonably accept. Give yourself two minutes for each case. Write down all the solutions you (or the group) think of; don't censor yourself or any members of the group.

1. Emily and Connor plan to take a two-week vacation in August. Emily wants to go to the shore and relax by the water. Connor wants to go hiking and camping in the mountains.

2. Emily recently got a totally unexpected $3000 bonus. She wants to buy a new computer and

printer; Connor wants to have the house painted.

3. Connor hangs around the house in nothing but underwear. Emily really hates this, and they argue about it almost daily.

4. Vicky is 17 and pregnant. She wants her parents to accept her decision to keep the child and not to marry the child's father. Her parents refuse to accept this and have said that she must either have an abortion or marry the child's father.

5. Workers at the local bottling plant want a 20 percent raise to bring their salaries into line with the salaries of similar workers at other plants. Management has repeatedly turned down their requests.

Thinking Critically About Win–Win Solutions.

If possible, share your win–win solutions with other individuals or groups. From this experience it should be clear that win–win solutions exist for most conflict situations but not necessarily all. And, of course, some situations will allow for the easy generation of a lot more win–win solutions than others. Not all conflicts are equal. How might you incorporate win–win strategies into your own conflict management behaviour?

11.3 INCREASING PRODUCTIVE CONFLICT MANAGEMENT

The following brief dialogue was written to illustrate unproductive conflict and to provide a stimulus for the consideration of alternative and more productive methods of conflict management. Identify each unproductive strategy and propose more productive alternatives.

Connor: It's me. Just came in to get my papers for the meeting tonight.

Emily: You're not going to another meeting tonight, are you?

Connor: I told you last month that I had to give this lecture to the new managers on how to use some new research methods. What do you think I've been working on for the past two weeks? If you cared about what I do, you'd have known I was working on this lecture and that it was especially important for it to go well.

Emily: What about shopping? We always do the shopping on Friday night.

Connor: The shopping will have to wait; this lecture is important.

Emily: Shopping is important, too, and so are the children and so is my job and so is the leak in the basement that's been driving me crazy since last week and that I've asked you to look at every day since then.

Connor: Get off it. We can do the shopping any time. Your job is fine and the children are fine and we'll get a plumber just as soon as I get his name from the Johnsons.

Emily: You always do that. You always think only you count, only you matter. Even when we were in school, your classes were the important ones, your papers, your tests were the important ones. Remember when I had that chemistry final and you had to have your history paper typed? We stayed up all night typing *your* paper. I failed chemistry, remember? That's not so good when you're premed! I suppose I should thank you that I'm not a doctor? But you got your A in history. It's always been that way. You never give a damn what's important in my life.

Connor: I really don't want to talk about it. I'll only get upset and bomb out with the lecture. Forget it. I don't want to hear any more about it. So just shut up before I do something I should do more often.

Emily: You hit me and I'll call the cops. I'm not putting up with another black eye or another fat lip—never, never again.

Connor: Well, then, just shut up. I just don't want to talk about it any more. Forget it. I have to give the lecture and that's that.

Emily: The children were looking forward to going shopping. Johnny wanted to get a new CD, and Jennifer needed to get a book for school. You promised them.

Connor: I didn't promise anyone anything. You promised them and now you want me to take the blame. You know, you promise too much. You should only promise what you can deliver, like fidelity. Remember you promised to be faithful? Or did you forget that promise? Why don't you tell the kids about that? Or do they already know? Were they here when you had your sordid affair? Did they see their loving parent loving some stranger?

Emily: I thought we agreed not to talk about that. You know how bad I feel about what happened. And anyway, that was six months ago. What has that got to do with tonight?

Connor: You're the one who brought up promises, not me. You're always bringing up the past. You live in the past.

Emily: Well, at least the kids would have seen me enjoying myself—one enjoyable experience in eight years isn't too much, is it?

Connor: I'm leaving. Don't wait up.

Thinking Critically About Productive Conflict Management.

Can you identify one possible effect that might result from using each of the unproductive conflict strategies illustrated here? How do these effects differ from those that might result from using the more productive strategies? As you read this dialogue, what assumptions did you make about the genders of the characters? On what basis?

Chapter 12

Interpersonal Communication and Power

Jackie has been having difficulties in all sorts of interpersonal situations. For example, although a competent worker, she has little confidence in her ability to do the work. She especially shies away from new tasks that may prove challenging and as a result she has been overlooked repeatedly when promotions come around. Interpersonally, she has few friends and is seldom asked out. Although attractive and bright, she acts as if she is grossly unattractive and has little to offer another person.

Pedro is a counsellor at a local boys' club, where his major problem is discipline. None of the younger boys respect him, and consequently none of them will listen to his admonitions. The administration is considering letting him go. He just doesn't seem able to exert the necessary control over the boys.

Clara is employed at the local automobile showroom, where she sells new Pontiacs. Although a competent salesperson, Clara often finds herself used by her coworkers. For example, when the salespeople want coffee they often ask Clara to get it. She doesn't really want to be the showroom gofer, but she doesn't know how to say no. Clara runs into similar problems at home, where her brothers and sisters and even her parents take advantage of her good nature.

All of these interpersonal difficulties revolve around interpersonal **power**. Jackie lacks self-esteem and communicates this to those she works with as well as her friends. Jackie has to raise her self-esteem and become more empowered. Pedro's problem centres on his lack of ability to communicate his authority, his power. He needs to learn the principles for communicating power to others. Clara is a classic example of the nonassertive person. She wants to stand up for her rights but doesn't know how. Clara needs training in assertiveness.

The word *power* conjures up very different associations for different people. For many, it brings forth negative feelings associated with being treated unfairly by someone in a position of authority. Others see power as a trait that is associated with success at work and in personal relationships. We look at power mostly as the ability to influence and/or to have authority. Parents have power over children. Teachers have the power to pass or fail students. And supervisors have the power to hire and fire staff. In all these situations, people with more power have the responsibility and obligation to use this power in an ethical way. Power, however, does not necessarily go with authority. People who have the ability to make themselves heard, and to influence others, have power.

In this final chapter we focus on self-esteem, interpersonal power, and assertiveness. All three topics are held together by their common focus on self-empowerment: on increasing your ability to exert influence with others and control over yourself.

Communication is power. Those who have mastered its effective use can change their own experience of the world, and the world's experience of them.

—Anthony Robbins

Self-Esteem

How much do you like yourself? How valuable a person do you think you are? How competent do you think you are? The answers to these questions will reflect your **self-esteem**, the value that you place on yourself.

Success breeds success. When you feel good about yourself—about who you are and what you're capable of doing—you will perform better. When you think like a success, you're more likely to act like a success.

What symbols of power can you identify in this photo?

When you think you're a failure, you're more likely to act like a failure. Increasing self-esteem will, therefore, help you to function more effectively in school, in interpersonal relationships, and in careers. Here are a few suggestions for increasing self-esteem.

Replace Self-Destructive Beliefs with Self-Affirming Beliefs

Actively challenge those beliefs you have about yourself that you find are unproductive or that make it more difficult for you to achieve your goals. Representative of such unproductive beliefs are the beliefs that you have to succeed in everything you do and that you have to be loved by everyone. Replace these self-destructive beliefs with more productive ones, more self-affirming beliefs; for example, "I succeed in many things; I don't have to succeed in everything" and "It would be nice to be loved by everyone, but it isn't necessary to my well-being or my happiness—and anyway, some pretty important people do love me." (A useful exercise, "Rewriting Unrealistic Beliefs," provides practice in replacing destructive beliefs about yourself with more realistic and productive ones. See www.ablongman.com/devito.)

"So, when he says, 'What a good boy am I,' Jack is really reinforcing his self-esteem."

Drawing by M. Twohy; © 1993 The New Yorker Magazine, Inc.

Seek Out Nourishing People

Psychologist Carl Rogers (1970) drew a distinction between noxious and nourishing people. Noxious people criticize and find fault with just about everything. Nourishing people, on the other hand, are positive and optimistic. Most important, they reward us, they stroke us, they make us feel good about ourselves. Seek out these people. At the same time, avoid noxious others, those who make you feel negatively about yourself.

Work on Projects That Will Result in Success

Some people want to fail, or so it seems. Often, they select projects that will result in failure simply because they are impossible to complete. Instead, they should select projects that will result in success. Each success will help build self-esteem. Each success will make the next success a little easier.

When a project does fail, recognize that this does not mean that you're a failure. Everyone fails somewhere along the line. Failure is something that happens. It's not necessarily something you have created, and it's not something inside you. Further, your failing once does not mean that you'll fail the next time. So, put failure in perspective. Don't make it an excuse for not trying again.

Speaking with Power

Power is a factor in all interpersonal communication. It affects what you do, when, and with whom. It affects the employment you seek and the employment you get. It affects the friends you choose and do not choose and those who choose you and those who do not. It affects your romantic and family relationships—their success, failure, and level of satisfaction or dissatisfaction. Effective interpersonal communication empowers you to influence the behaviour of others.

Power in interpersonal relationships is governed by a few important principles. These principles spell out the basic characteristics of power. They help explain how power works interpersonally and how you may more effectively deal with power. Haddock (2003) writes that communicating a sense of personal power comes from a belief that you

What suggestions for increasing self-esteem do you think are particularly useful? What additional suggestions might you offer?

THINKING CRITICALLY ABOUT

Flexibility

Flexibility is your ability to switch gears and think in different directions. In a well-known flexibility exercise, group members try to come up with varied uses for a common object. Some members tend to think of uses from a wide variety of fields, whereas others focus on one or two narrow fields. For example, for the uses of a toothbrush, if you gave all cleaning uses you would be showing less flexibility than if you gave cleaning uses plus uses in gardening, decorating, and cooking. A good example of flexibility is the thinking that went into identifying the wide uses of a product such as baking soda—it's used in cleaning clothes,

cooking, deodorizing, brushing teeth. Another example is the manufacturer's presentation of widely different foods that can be prepared with a product such as Bisquick. The flexibility with which you can use these products is largely responsible for their enormous success.

EXAMPLES?

How might increased flexibility be of value in your own interpersonal interactions, say with friends, romantic partners, or business associates? How might the lack of flexibility create problems for such relationships?

can reach your goals in your own way. He suggests that you communicate a sense of power by developing authority, accessibility, assertiveness, a positive image, and solid communication skills.

Different Kinds of Power

Some people have "positional power"—that is, power that's integral to the role or position they are in. School principals have power, prime ministers have power, and members of the police force have power. How people in these roles use this power depends very much on their interpersonal skills, motivation, and ethics.

Some people have power by virtue of their wealth. Heads of large corporations often have more success in lobbying politicians than do daycare workers. Some people have authoritative power—that is, they have power because they have knowledge and/or expertise in certain areas. A yoga instructor has power over her class not because of her position or wealth, but because people trust that she knows more than they do about yoga.

But many people who have neither position nor wealth have a great deal of power. They have the ability to influence others and to take control over many of the factors that affect their lives. "Persuasive power" refers to the kind of power that one gains because of his or her personal attributes that make people want to listen or follow. Notice, for example, the child in the schoolyard whom all the other children seem to follow. What are some of the traits exhibited by that child that give her that power? Some people seem to be born with those traits that lead to power. However, it is possible to learn and to practise the kinds of interpersonal skills that will help you become empowered.

Confidence communicates power. One of the clearest ways in which you can communicate power is by demonstrating confidence in your verbal and nonverbal behaviours. Recognizing these messages in the communications of others will help you recognize them in your own interactions and put you in a better position to manage and control them.

Most people have some communication apprehension or **shyness** (see Chapter 2). The confident communicator, however, does not let it interfere with communication. Confidence also enables the speaker to make those who are anxious or shy more comfortable.

The confident communicator is relaxed (rather than rigid), flexible in voice and body (rather than locked into one or two ranges of voice or body movement), and controlled (rather than shaky or awkward). A relaxed posture, researchers find, communicates a sense of control, status, and power. Tenseness, rigidity, and discomfort, on the other hand, signal a lack of self-control (Spitzberg & Hecht, 1984). This, in turn, signals a general inability to control one's environment or fellow workers.

Here are a few additional suggestions for communicating confidence (bear in mind that these suggestions may not be universal):

- Take the initiative in introducing yourself to others and in introducing topics of conversation; try not to wait for others. When you react, rather than act, you're more likely to communicate a lack of confidence and control over the situation.

All animals are equal. But some animals are more equal than others.

—George Orwell

Equality is what does not exist among equals.

—e. e. cummings

How would you describe your own interpersonal power? In what situations are you especially powerful? In what situations do you feel you have significantly less power?

Confidence is that feeling by which the mind embarks on great and honourable courses with a sure hope and trust in itself.

—Cicero

- Use open-ended questions to involve the other person in the inter-action (as opposed to questions that merely ask for a yes or no answer). Follow up these questions with appropriate comments or additional questions.

- Use "you-statements," which refer directly to the other person—not the accusatory kind, but those that signal a direct and personalized focus on the other person, such as "Do you agree?" or "How do you feel about that?" This one feature, incidentally, has been shown to increase men's attractiveness to women.

Calm self-confidence is as far from conceit as the desire to earn a decent living is remote from greed.

—Channing Pollock

- Avoid the various forms of language that are identified in Table 12.1, including statements that express a lack of conviction or that are self-critical.

Another way to communicate power is with compliance-gaining and compliance-resisting strategies. **Compliance-gaining strategies** are the tactics that influence others to do what you want them to do (Table 12.1). **Compliance-resisting strategies** are the tactics that enable you to say no and resist another person's attempts to influence you.

TABLE 12.1 Compliance-Gaining Strategies

These compliance-gaining strategies come from the research of Marwell and Schmitt (1967) and the further developments by Miller and Parks (1982). What other compliance-gaining strategies can you identify?

Strategy	Examples
Pre-giving. Pat rewards Chris and then requests compliance.	Pat: *I'm glad you enjoyed dinner. I used my grandmother's recipe. How about helping with the dishes?*
Liking. Pat is helpful and friendly in order to get Chris in a good mood so that Chris will be more likely to comply with Pat's request.	Pat: [After cleaning up the living room and bedroom] *I'd really like to relax and bowl a few games with Terry. Okay?*
Promise. Pat promises to reward Chris if Chris complies with Pat's request.	Pat: *I'll give you anything you want if you will just give me a divorce. You can have the house; just give me my freedom.*
Positive or negative expertise. Pat promises that Chris will be rewarded for compliance (or punished for not complying) because of "the nature of things."	Pat: *If you don't listen to the doctor, you're going to wind up back in the hospital.*
Positive or negative self-feelings. Pat promises that Chris will feel better if Chris complies (or feel worse if Chris does not comply) with Pat's request.	Pat: *You will feel a lot better if you study for the exam rather than watching TV.*
Positive or negative altercasting. Pat casts Chris in the role of the "good" or "bad" person and argues that Chris should comply because a person with "good" qualities would comply (and a person with "bad" qualities would not).	Pat: *Any intelligent person would grant their partner a divorce when the relationship has died.*

Compliance-resisting strategies also demonstrate power. Let's say that someone you know asks you to do something that you don't want to do, such as lend your term paper so that this person might copy it and turn it in to another teacher. Research with college students shows that there are four major ways of responding (McLaughlin, Cody, & Robey, 1980; O'Hair, Cody, & O'Hair, 1991):

In **identity management** you resist by trying to manipulate the image of the person making the request. You might do this negatively or positively. In negative identity management, you might portray the requesting agent as unreasonable or unfair and say, "That's really unfair of you to ask me to compromise my ethics." Or you might tell the person that it hurts that he or she would even think you would do such a thing. In positive identity management, you resist complying by making the requesting agent feel good about himself or herself. For example, you might say, "You know this material much better than I do; you can easily do a much better paper yourself."

Another way to resist compliance is to use nonnegotiation, a direct refusal to do as requested. You might simply say, "No, I don't lend my papers out." In **negotiation**, you resist compliance by perhaps offering a compromise ("I'll let you read my paper but not copy it") or by offering to help the person in some other way ("If you write a first draft, I'll go over it and try to make some comments"). If the request was a more romantic one—for example, a request to go away for a ski weekend—you might resist by discussing your feelings and proposing an alternative—"Let's double date first."

Another way to resist compliance is through **justification**. Here you justify your refusal by citing possible consequences of compliance or noncompliance. For example, you might cite a negative consequence if you complied ("I'm afraid that I'd get caught and then I'd fail the course") or you might cite a positive consequence of your not complying ("You'll really enjoy writing this paper; it's a lot of fun").

Another aspect of power differences is that some people are more Machiavellian than others. Before reading about this fascinating concept, take the self-test on page 320, "How Machiavellian Are You?" It focuses on your beliefs about how easily people can be manipulated.

The term **Machiavellian** refers to techniques or tactics used to control others. Understanding and recognizing these techniques may empower us to avoid being manipulated or controlled. Niccolo Machiavelli (1469–1527) was a political philosopher and adviser and wrote his theory of political control in *The Prince*. The book took the position (in greatly simplified form) that the prince must do whatever is necessary to rule the people; the ends justified the means. The ruler was in fact obligated to use power to gain more power and thus better achieve the desired goals (Steinfatt, 1987).

Research finds significant differences between those who score high and those who score low on the "Mach" scale. Low Machs yield more readily to social influence; they are more susceptible to **persuasion**. High Machs are more resistant to persuasion. High Machs are most effective at persuading others when the situation allows them to improvise (Christie, 1970). High Machs are also rated higher on job performance when they function within a loosely structured work en-

Note that the compliance-gaining strategies are regarded as generally effective though not necessarily moral or ethical. Which strategies would you consider ethical? Which would you consider unethical?

Do you think men and women use the same compliance-gaining strategies?

TEST YOURSELF

How Machiavellian Are You?

Instructions: For each statement record the number that most closely represents your attitude, using the following scale: 1 = disagree a lot, 2 = disagree a little, 3 = neutral, 4 = agree a bit, 5 = agree a lot.

_____ **1.** The best way to handle people is to tell them what they want to hear.

_____ **2.** When you ask someone to do something for you, it's best to give the real reasons rather than giving reasons that might carry more weight.

_____ **3.** Anyone who completely trusts anyone else is asking for trouble.

_____ **4.** It's hard to get ahead without cutting corners here and there.

_____ **5.** It's safest to assume that all people have a vicious streak and it will come out when they are given a chance.

_____ **6.** One should take action only when sure it's morally right.

_____ **7.** Most people are basically good and kind.

_____ **8.** There is no excuse for lying to someone.

_____ **9.** Most people forget more easily the death of their parents than the loss of their property.

_____ **10.** Generally speaking, people won't work hard unless they're forced to.

HOW DID YOU DO?

To compute your Mach score, follow these steps:

1. Reverse the scores on items 2, 6, 7, and 8 as follows: If you responded with 5, change it to 1; if 4, change it to 2; if 3, keep it as 3; if 2, change it to 4; if 1, change it to 5.

2. Add all 10 scores, being sure to use the reversed numbers for 2, 6, 7, and 8.

Your Mach score is a measure of the degree to which you believe that people in general are manipulable—not necessarily of the degree to which you would or do manipulate others. If you scored somewhere between 35 and 50, you would be considered a high Mach; if you scored between 10 and 15, you would be considered a low Mach. Most of us would score in between these extremes.

WHAT WILL YOU DO?

As you read the text's discussion of Machiavellianism, try to visualize what you would do in the various situations described. See if your score on this test is a generally accurate description of your own Machiavellianism.

Source: From "The Machiavellis Among Us," by Richard Christie, _Psychology Today,_ November 1970. Reprinted with permission from _Psychology Today_ magazine, copyright © 1970 Sussex Publishers, Inc.

vironment that allows them to improvise (Gable, Hollon, & Dangello, 1992). Low Machs are more empathic while high Machs are more logical. Low Machs are more interpersonally oriented and involved with other people; high Machs are more assertive and more controlling.

Business students (especially marketing students) score higher in Machiavellianism than do nonbusiness majors (McLean & Jones, 1992).

You will note a similarity between this concept and self-monitoring (discussed in Chapter 8). Both high self-monitors and high Machs try to manipulate others and get their own way. The difference is that self-monitors change their own behaviours as a way of pleasing and manipulating others; Machiavellians try to change the behaviours of others to get what they want.

Machiavellianism seems, in part at least, to be culturally conditioned. Individualistic orientation, which favours competition and being number one, seems more conducive to the development of Machiavellianism. Collectivist orientation, which favours cooperation and being one of a group, seems a less friendly environment for the development of Machiavellianism in its members. Some evidence of this comes from research showing that Chinese students attending a traditional Chinese (Confucian) school rated lower in Machiavellianism than similar Chinese students attending a Western-style school (Christie, 1970).

Your own beliefs and values, as well as your skills, will influence your use of Machiavellian strategies. (A self-test, "When is persuasion unethical?" will help you to explore further the ethical dimensions of power and influence. See www.ablongman.com/devito.)

Power Dimensions of Interpersonal Messages

Power is a dimension in most interpersonal relationships. Consider your own relationships with friends and relatives. What kind of power do people in these relationships have? The factors that contribute to different kinds of power include age, wealth, gender, knowledge, and position.

People who are powerful communicate their power in a variety of ways. Table 12.2 (see p. 322) summarizes some of the major characteristics of powerless speech—verbal habits to avoid if you want to convey power in the way you talk.

Just as you communicate your power verbally, you also communicate it nonverbally. Nonverbal power is associated with cultural values and contexts. For example, a huge diamond ring may indicate power in some circles but may be meaningless in others. An expensive business suit may suggest power among bankers in Toronto, whereas a strong, muscular body may be more suggestive of power to athletes. Looking old is associated with powerlessness in some cultures but commands respect in others.

Similarly, nonverbal behaviour often betrays a lack of power, as when someone fidgets and engages in lots of self-touching movements (adaptors) at a meeting, indicating discomfort. A powerful person may be bored but will not appear uncomfortable or ill at ease.

The amount and arrangement of space can also suggest power or lack of power. In traditional male-dominated corporate culture, the location and size of the office is often an indicator of a person's power. This view has been challenged

"It's all about power—getting it and keeping it."
Drawing by Brian Savage; © 1996 The New Yorker Magazine, Inc.

TABLE 12.2 Toward More Powerful Speech

Can you identify other examples of powerless and powerful speech?

Suggestions	Examples	Reasons
Avoid hesitations.	"I, er, want to say that, ah, this one is, er, the best, you know."	Hesitations cause you to sound unprepared and uncertain.
Avoid too many intensifiers.	"Really, this was the greatest; it was truly awesome."	Too many intensifiers make speech sound the same and do not allow for intensifying what should be emphasized.
Avoid disqualifiers.	"I didn't read the entire article, but..." "I didn't actually see the accident, but..."	Disqualifiers signal a lack of competence and a feeling of uncertainty.
Avoid tag questions.	"That was a great movie, wasn't it?" "She's brilliant, don't you think?"	Tag questions ask for another's agreement and therefore signal both your need for agreement and your uncertainty.
Avoid simple one-word answers.	"Yes." "No." "Okay." "Sure."	One-word answers may signal a lack of communication skills and a lack of interest and commitment.
Avoid self-critical statements.	"I'm not very good at this." "This is my first public speech."	Self-critical statements signal a lack of confidence and make public one's inadequacies.
Avoid overpoliteness.	"Excuse me, please, sir."	Overpolite forms signal subordinate status.
Avoid vulgar and slang expressions.	"##!!!///****!" "No problem!"	Vulgarity and slang signal low social class and hence little power.

by some women who head large and successful corporations. They believe that hierarchical status symbols are not productive, and purposefully have their offices among those of all the employees. "Bigger is better," in other words, is not a universal truth.

The most important aspect of communicating power is to evidence your knowledge, your preparation, and your organization over whatever you're dealing with. If you can exhibit control over your own responsibilities, it's generally concluded that you can and do also exhibit control over others.

Power Follows the Principle of Less Interest

Power is the great aphrodisiac.
—Henry Kissinger

In any interpersonal relationship, the person who holds the power is the one less interested in and less dependent on the rewards and punishments controlled by the other person. If, for example, you can walk away from whatever rewards your partner has to offer or can handle whatever punishments your partner can mete out, then you control the relationship. If, on the other hand, you need the rewards or are unable or unwilling to suffer the punishments, then your partner has the power and controls the relationship.

Some people believe that the person with less investment in a relationship has more power. So, for example, the partner who cares less about the relationship can make more demands over the person who wants, more than anything else, for the relationship to continue. Certainly this appears to be true in many cases. A deep commitment to a relationship, of course, can be highly empowering as well.

Power Has a Cultural Dimension

In some cultures power is concentrated in the hands of a few, and there is a great difference in the power held by these people and by the ordinary citizen. These are called high-power-distance cultures; examples are Mexico, Brazil, India, and the Philippines (Hofstede, 1997). In low-power-distance cultures, power is more evenly distributed throughout the citizenry; examples include Denmark, New Zealand, Sweden, and, to a lesser extent, Canada. Keep in mind, however, that the differences between high- and low-power-distance cultures are a matter of degree.

In India (a high-power-distance culture), friendships and romantic relationships are expected to take place within your cultural class; in Sweden (a low-power-distance culture), a person is expected to select friends and romantic partners on the basis, not of class or culture, but of individual factors such as personality, appearance, and the like.

Examine one of your relationships—a friendship, a romantic relationship, or a family relationship—for power. What kinds of power exist in this relationship? Who maintains greater power? How is it exercised?

In low-power-distance cultures you're expected to confront a friend, partner, or supervisor assertively; there is in these cultures a general feeling of equality that is consistent with an upfront approach (Borden, 1991). In high-power-distance cultures this kind of direct confrontation and assertiveness may be viewed negatively, especially if directed at a superior.

In high-power-distance cultures you're taught to have great respect for authority, and generally people in these cultures see authority as desirable and beneficial; challenges to authority are generally not welcomed (Westwood, Tang, & Kirkbride, 1992; also see Bochner & Hesketh, 1994). Low-power-distance cultures often share a certain distrust of authority; it's seen as a kind of necessary evil that should be limited as much as possible. This difference in attitudes toward authority can be seen right in the classroom. In high-power-distance cultures there is a great power distance between students and teachers; students are expected to be modest, polite, and respectful. In low-power-distance cultures such as Canada's, students are expected to demonstrate their knowledge and command of the subject matter, participate in discussions with the teacher, and even challenge the teacher—something many high-power-distance culture members wouldn't even think of doing.

The same differences can be seen in patient–doctor communication. Patients from high-power-distance cultures are less likely to chal-

We cannot live by power, and a culture that seeks to live by it becomes brutal and sterile.

—**Max Lerner**

Think about your own culture and how power is distributed. Would you consider it a high- or a low-power-distance culture?

lenge their doctor or admit that they don't understand the medical terminology than are patients in low-power-distance cultures.

High-power-distance cultures rely more on symbols of power. For example, titles (Doctor, Professor, Chef, Inspector) are more important in high-power-distance cultures. Failure to include these in forms of address is a serious breach of etiquette. Low-power-distance cultures rely less on symbols of power, and less of a problem is created if you fail to use a respectful title (Victor, 1992). But even in low-power-distance cultures you may create problems if, for example, you call a medical doctor, police captain, military officer, or professor Ms. or Mr.

In North America, many people quickly move from title plus last name (Mr. Smith) to first name (Joe). In low-power-distance cultures in general, it is not a problem if you're too informal or if you presume to exchange first names before sufficient interaction has taken place. Again, however, in even the lowest-power-distance culture you may still create problems if you call your English professor by his or her first name. And in high-power-distance cultures too great an informality—especially between those differing in power—would violate important cultural rules.

In many Asian, African, and Arab cultures (as well as in many European cultures such as Italian and Greek), there is a great power distance between men and women. Men have the greater power, and women are expected to recognize this and abide by its implications. Men, for example, make the important decisions and have the final word in any difference of opinion (Hatfield & Rapson, 1996). Yet clear role differentiation, some would argue, does not necessarily imply a power differential. For example, in some Latin American and East Asian cultures many women may have absolute control over child-rearing and household decisions, which may be viewed as equally or more important than financial decisions.

In North America, the male–female power structure is undergoing considerable changes. And yet many women still feel they don't have equal power to men. If income is an indicator, they are correct. Canadian women are over-represented in the lowest paying jobs: while they hold 47 percent of all jobs in the market, 61 percent of these jobs are the lowest paid (Lochhead, 1997, p. 137). It is still the case that in places of employment, at community functions, and in private settings, men are often more influential. Perhaps they are more socialized to communicate powerfully than are women. In fact, many professional women struggle with the following dilemma: They can adopt the mannerisms of speech, body language, and style that have traditionally been associated with power, or they can strive to change the norms so that communication styles more traditionally associated with women (for example, soft-spokenness) come to be considered equally persuasive.

> All human beings are born free and equal in dignity and rights.
> —UN Declaration of Human Rights, Article I

> All possibility of understanding is rooted in the ability to say no.
> —Susan Sontag

What has your culture taught you about power? Have these teachings helped you get where you want to get, achieve what you want to achieve?

Abuse of Power

Although it would be nice to believe that power is wielded for the good of all, it's often abused.

Harassment   Harassment can be defined as "unwanted, unsolicited remarks, behaviours or communications in any form directed toward an individual or group which has the effect on that individual or group of a) causing feelings of being demeaned, intimidated or humiliated, or b) preventing or impairing full enjoyment of employment/educational services, benefits, or opportunities" ("Policy: Personal Harassment," Mount Royal College, 1999).

According to the Criminal Code of Canada, some kinds of harassment are not only abusive but illegal. These include behaviours that may cause another person to fear for their safety or for the safety of anyone known to them (Criminal Code, R.S.C. 1993, c. 45, subsection 264[2]). Even less extreme forms of harassment cause grief and emotional damage. These include remarks, jokes, or actions that demean or humiliate another person and deny individuals dignity and respect. While these actions may not be illegal according to the Criminal Code, many institutions are developing policies to protect individuals (Calgary's Mount Royal College's policy, outlined in the box on this page and on the next one, is one example).

One form of harassment, most commonly associated with children, is bullying. Bullying can take both active and passive forms. Active bullying ranges from jokes, name calling, and teasing to pushing, hitting, and other physical interactions. Passive bullying includes exclusion from the group, ignoring, or deliberately leaving another until last when choosing playmates. These practices often leave invisible scars. It is, therefore, the responsibility of adults to prevent bullying behaviours by teaching children to communicate effectively.

MESSAGES@WORK

Discrimination and Harassment Are Not New ... But Can Be Illegal

WHAT IS THE LAW?

Discrimination and harassment based on discrimination are prohibited in Alberta by the Alberta Human Rights, Citizenship and Multiculturalism Act.

WHAT IS THE COLLEGE POLICY?

In keeping with efforts to establish and maintain an environment in which the dignity and worth of all members of the College community are respected, it is the policy of Mount Royal College that discrimination/harassment of students and employees is unacceptable and will not be tolerated.

WHAT ARE THE PROHIBITED GROUNDS?

At Mount Royal College the prohibited grounds of discrimination are:

- race
- ancestry
- religious beliefs
- physical disability
- age
- family status
- marital status
- colour
- place of origin
- gender
- mental disability
- sexual orientation
- source of income

(continued)

WHAT IS DISCRIMINATION?

Discrimination is behaviour which is usually rooted in prejudicial attitude. Discrimination results in unequal treatment of an individual as a member of a group or of the group itself, which can either favour or disadvantage the individual or group. Discrimination often excludes an individual from a right to which he/she would otherwise be entitled.

WHAT IS HARASSMENT?

Harassment is behaviour that is known or ought to be known as unwelcome. Harassment can include remarks, jokes, or actions which demean or humiliate another person and which deny individuals their dignity and respect.

WHAT CAN YOU DO?

- Know your rights
- Identify your feelings
- Deal with the situation immediately
- Tell the person to stop, or write a letter to the person
- Tell someone you trust
- Document the behaviour

WHO CAN HELP?

- Advisor for Individual Rights
- Your instructor or department chair
- Your supervisor
- Deans and Directors
- Human Resources personnel
- An executive member of the Students' Association of Mount Royal College, Mount Royal Support Staff Association or Mount Royal Faculty Association

CAN DISCRIMINATION AND HARASSMENT BE STOPPED?

YES. We can stop it together. Speak out. Support others who are victims. Encourage them to seek help. This campus does not tolerate discrimination or harassment.

What Are the Procedures?

Informal
- Talk or write to the person
- Consult with someone you trust
- Meet with the Advisor or Assistant to discuss options
- Request mediation

Formal Meet with the Advisor for Individual Rights to determine whether an informal route will work. If not, the Advisor will explain the formal complaint process. If necessary, the Advisor will assist you in filling out a formal complaint form, which will lead to a formal hearing before an investigatory committee.

What Services Are Provided by the Advisor?
- Confidential consultation
- An explanation of informal and formal procedures
- Assistance with informal procedures
- Guidance through the formal complaint process
- Educational presentations for departments, groups or classes

Source: Discrimination and Harassment brochure, 1999. Individual Rights Services of Mount Royal College.

Sexual Harassment   According to Memorial University's Sexual Harassment Policy, sexual harassment is defined as follows:

Conduct of a sexual nature, directed at an individual or individuals by a person who knows or ought reasonably to know that such attention is unwanted, constitutes sexual harassment when:

a) submission to such conduct is made either explicitly or implicitly a term or condition of an individual's employment, academic status or academic accreditation, or

b) submission to or rejection of such conduct by an individual is used as the basis for employment, or for academic performance, status or accreditation decisions affecting such individual, or

c) such conduct interferes with an individual's work or academic performance, or

d) such conduct creates an intimidating, hostile, or offensive work or academic environment.

Such conduct includes, but is not limited to:

- unwelcome sexual invitations or requests
- demands for sexual favours
- unnecessary touching or patting, leering at a person's body
- unwelcome and repeated innuendos or taunting about a person's body, appearance or sexual orientation
- suggestive remarks or other verbal abuse of a sexual nature
- visual displays of degrading or offensive sexual images
- threats of a sexual nature, sexual assault, and any other verbal or physical conduct of a sexual nature.

People often have difficulty deciding whether an offending behaviour is sexual harassment or simply flirting. Sexual harassment, however, is not flirting nor is it a normal way of expressing attraction. The chart below illustrates that sexual harassment and flirting are experienced very differently.

SEXUAL HARASSMENT	FLIRTING
Feels bad	Feels good
One-sided	Reciprocal
Feels unattractive	Feels attractive
Is degrading	Is a compliment
Feels powerless	In control
Power-based	Equality
Negative touching	Positive touching
Unwanted	Wanted
Illegal	Legal
Invading	Open
Demeaning	Flattering
Makes you feel sad/angry	Happy
Causes negative self-esteem	Positive self-esteem

Source: Stein, N. & Sjostrom, L. (1994). *Flirting or hurting?* Washington, DC: National Education Association and Wellesley College Center for Research on Women.

To help you make certain that your behaviours in the workplace do not constitute harassment, Bravo and Cassedy (1992) suggest the following:

1. Begin with the assumption that others at work are not interested in your sexual advances, sexual stories and jokes, or sexual gestures.

Can you think of additional
suggestions?

2. Listen and watch for negative reactions to any sex-related discussion. Use the suggestions and techniques discussed throughout this book (for example, perception checking, critical listening) to become aware of such reactions. When in doubt, find out; ask questions, for example.

3. Avoid saying or doing what you think your parent, partner, or child would find offensive in the behaviour of someone with whom she or he worked.

The box on page 326 provides suggestions for what to do and who to speak to in a college setting. Regardless of the setting, it is crucial that you:

1. **Talk to the harasser.** Tell this person assertively that you do not welcome the behaviour and that you find it offensive. Simply informing Tyler that his sexual jokes are not appreciated and are seen as offensive may be sufficient to make him stop his joke telling. In some instances, unfortunately, such criticism goes unheeded, and the offensive behaviour continues.

2. **Collect evidence**—perhaps corroboration from others who have experienced similar harassment at the hands of the same individual; perhaps a log of the offensive behaviours.

3. **Use appropriate channels within the organization.** Most organizations have established channels to deal with such grievances. This step will in most cases eliminate any further harassment. In the event that it doesn't, you may consider going further.

4. **File a complaint** with an organization or governmental agency, or perhaps take legal action.

What would you add to the discussion of harassment presented here?

Don't blame yourself. Like many who are abused, you may tend to blame yourself, feeling that you're responsible for being harassed. You aren't; however, you may need to secure emotional support from friends or perhaps from trained professionals (Petrocelli & Repa, 1992; Bravo & Cassedy, 1992; Rubenstein, 1993).

Power Plays **Power plays** are patterns (not isolated instances) of communication that take unfair advantage of another person (Steiner, 1981). Put in terms of the notion of choice (Chapter 1), power plays aim to rob us of our right to make our own choices, free of harassment or intimidation.

For example, in the power play *nobody upstairs,* the individual refuses to acknowledge your request, regardless of how or how many times you make it. One common form is the refusal to take no for an answer. Sometimes the *nobody upstairs* play takes the form of pleading ignorance of common socially accepted (but unspoken) rules, such as knocking when you enter someone's room or refraining from opening another person's mail or wallet: "I didn't know you didn't want me to look in your wallet" or "Do you want me to knock the next time I come into your room?" Another power play is *you owe me.* Here others do something for you and then demand something in return. They remind you of what they did for you and use this to get you to do what they want.

In *yougottobekidding,* one person attacks the other by saying "yougottobekidding" or some similar phrase: "You can't be serious." "You can't mean that." "You didn't say what I thought you said, did you?" The intention here is to express utter disbelief in the other's statement so as to make the statement and the person seem inadequate or stupid.

These power plays are just examples. There are, of course, many others that you have met on occasion. What do you do when you recognize such a power play? One commonly employed response is to ignore the power play and allow the other person to take control. Another response is to treat the power play as an isolated instance (rather than as a pattern of behaviour) and object to it. For example, you might say quite simply, "Please don't come into my room without knocking first" or "Please don't look in my wallet without permission."

A third response is a cooperative one (Steiner, 1981). In this response, you do the following:

- *Express your feelings.* Tell the person that you're angry, annoyed, or disturbed by his or her behaviour.

- *Describe the behaviour to which you object.* Tell the person—in language that describes rather than evaluates—the specific behaviour you object to: for example, reading your mail, coming into your room without knocking, persisting in trying to hug you.

- *State a cooperative response you both can live with comfortably.* Tell the person—in a cooperative tone—what you want; for example: "I want you to knock before coming into my room." "I want you to stop reading my mail." "I want you to stop trying to hug me when I tell you to stop."

A cooperative response to *nobody upstairs* might go something like this: "I'm angry [*statement of feelings*] that you persist in opening my mail. You have opened my mail four times this past week alone [*description of the behaviour to which you object*]. I want you to allow me to open my own mail. If there is anything in it that concerns you, I will let you know immediately" [*statement of cooperative response*].

Have you witnessed recently any of the power plays discussed here? What is your instinctive response to such power plays? How might you respond more effectively?

The object of power is power.
—**George Orwell**

The purpose of getting power is to be able to give it away.
—**Aneurin Bevan**

Assertive Communication

If you disagree with other people in a group, do you speak your mind? Do you allow others to take advantage of you because you're reluctant to say what you want? Do you feel uncomfortable when you have to state your opinion in a group? Questions such as these revolve around your degree of **assertiveness**. Assertiveness rests upon a foundation of respect for one's own values, rights, and goals as well as for those of others (Dickinson, 1999). Assertive communication is often a learned form of communication, however, and breaking out of passive habits isn't easy (Lynch, as cited in Renner, 1993).

Before reading further about assertive communication, take the self-test on page 331, "How assertive is your communication?"

Nonassertive, Aggressive, and Assertive Communication

In addition to identifying some specific assertive behaviours (as in the self-test), the nature of assertive communication can be further ex-

Listening to Empower

Much as you can empower others by complimenting or constructively criticizing them, you can also empower through your style of listening. Thus, for example, if you manage several workers, an empowering listening style on your part can contribute to these workers' sense of importance and influence in their dealings with you and with the organization in general. So, when you wish to empower through listening, consider these suggestions:

1. Demonstrate that you're listening willingly and eagerly. This makes the other person feel that what he or she is saying is valuable and important. In showing that you're listening, acknowledge your understanding by appropriately nodding or using minimal responses such as "I see" or "I understand"; ask questions if something isn't clear or if you need more information; maintain eye contact; and lean forward as appropriate. Focus on the person as exclusively as possible: Try to block out your focus on anything else. Nothing is worse than speaking with someone who seems focused on what time it is or what others in the room are saying.

2. Avoid interrupting to change the topic or to shift the focus to something or someone else. When you interrupt, you indicate that what the other person is saying is of less importance than what you're saying—a clear way to disempower and to say, in effect, "You don't really count, at least not as much as I do."

3. React supportively. Let the person know that you're listening and that you've heard what he or she said and that you appreciate it. Let the person know what you think of what he or she has said. If you agree, then it's easy; just say so. If you disagree, say so also; but keep your disagreement focused on what was said rather than on the person. And couple any disagreement with positive comments such as "I really appreciate your bringing this to my attention, but I tried out your first suggestion and it didn't work. Is there a way of doing it that might be less costly?"

SUGGESTIONS?

John has been feeling pretty depressed; he lost his job, and his grades have been bad and are getting worse. One day over coffee he decides to tell his friend Sam about what's been bothering him and why things have gotten so out of hand. What suggestions might you offer Sam to help him listen to empower John?

---

plained by distinguishing it from nonassertiveness and aggressiveness (Alberti, 1977).

Nonassertive Communication   The term *nonassertiveness* refers to a lack of assertiveness in certain types of (or even in all) communication situations. People who are nonassertive fail to assert their rights. In many instances, these people do what others tell them to do—parents, employers, and the like—without questioning and without concern for what is best for them. They operate with a "you win, I lose" philosophy; they give others what they want without concern for themselves (Lloyd, 1995). Nonassertive people often ask permission from others to do what is their perfect right. Social situations create anxiety for these individuals, and their self-esteem is generally low.

Aggressive Communication   Aggressiveness is the other extreme. Aggressive people operate with an "I win, you lose" philosophy; they care little for what the other person wants and focus only on their own needs. Some people communicate aggressively only under certain conditions or in certain situations (for example, after being taken advantage of over a long period of time), while others communicate aggressively in

TEST YOURSELF

How Assertive Is Your Communication?

Instructions: Indicate how true each of the following statements is about your own communication. Respond instinctively rather than in the way you feel you should respond. Use the following scale: 5 = always or almost always true, 4 = usually true, 3 = sometimes true, sometimes false, 2 = usually false, 1 = always or almost always false.

_____ 1. I would express my opinion in a group even if it contradicts the opinions of others.

_____ 2. When asked to do something that I really don't want to do, I can say "no" without feeling guilty.

_____ 3. I can express my opinion to my superiors on the job.

_____ 4. I can start up a conversation with a stranger on a bus or at a business gathering without fear.

_____ 5. I voice objection to people's behaviour if I feel it infringes on my rights.

_____ 6. I express my feelings directly, using I-messages (I need you to be more accurate in recording appointments), rather than you-messages (Your work is sloppy and inaccurate) or third-person messages (Everyone says your work is not up to par).

_____ 7. I use factual and descriptive terms when stating what I object to (The last three letters you typed contained too many errors; you complained about the service in the last seven restaurants we ate at) rather than allness or extreme terms (You _never_ do the right thing; you _always_ complain).

_____ 8. I try to understand and accept the behaviours of others rather than criticize them and label them with such expressions as "that's silly" or "that's insane."

_____ 9. I believe that in most interactions, both people should gain something— rather than one win and one lose.

_____ 10. I believe that my desires are as important as those of others—not more important, but not less important either.

HOW DID YOU DO?

All 10 items in this test identified characteristics of assertive communication. So, high scores (say, about 40 and above) would indicate a high level of assertiveness. Low scores (about 20 and below) would indicate a low level of assertiveness.

WHAT WILL YOU DO?

This chapter clarifies the nature of assertive communication and offers guidelines for increasing your own assertiveness. Try following these suggestions to increase your own assertiveness and at the same time to reduce your aggressiveness tendencies.

all or at least most situations. Aggressive communicators think little of the opinions, values, or beliefs of others, and yet are extremely sensitive to others' criticisms of their own behaviour. Consequently, they frequently get into arguments with others.

Assertive Communication

Assertive Communication Assertive behaviour—behaviour that enables you to act in your own best interests *without* denying or infringing upon the rights of others—is the generally desired alternative to nonassertiveness or aggressiveness. Assertive communication enables you to act in your own best interests without denying or infringing upon the rights of others. Assertive people operate with an "I win, you win" philosophy; they assume that both people can gain something from an interpersonal interaction, even from a confrontation. Assertive people are willing to assert their own rights. Unlike their aggressive counterparts, however, they do not hurt others in the process. Assertive people speak their minds and welcome others' doing likewise. Not surprisingly, assertiveness is found to be positively related to flexibility, discussed in Chapter 8 (Martin & Anderson, 1998).

People who are assertive in interpersonal communication display four major characteristics (Norton & Warnick, 1976). Assertive individuals are:

- *Open:* They engage in frank and open expressions of their feelings to people in general as well as to those for whom there may be some romantic interest.

- *Not anxious:* They readily volunteer opinions and beliefs, deal directly with interpersonal communication situations that may be stressful, and question others without fear. Their communications are dominant, frequent, and of high intensity. They have a positive view of their own communication performance, and others with whom they communicate share this positive view.

- *Contentious:* They stand up and argue for their rights, even if this might entail a certain degree of disagreement or conflict with relatives or close friends.

- *Not intimidated* and not easily persuaded: They make up their own minds on the basis of evidence and argument.

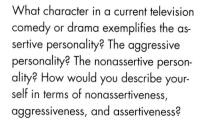

What character in a current television comedy or drama exemplifies the assertive personality? The aggressive personality? The nonassertive personality? How would you describe yourself in terms of nonassertiveness, aggressiveness, and assertiveness?

Make Them Listen When You Speak

Listen up, because Betty K. Cooper's message to would-be communicators is brief.

You win or lose your audience in the first 20 words, or the first two minutes of a longer presentation.

(That last sentence was 20 words.)

"Everybody can talk, but talking isn't going to get your ideas accepted," says Cooper, president of Cooper Communications and consultant to corporate stars. "It's the way you say it that will help your ideas come across."

Most people putting together a presentation decide first what they want to say but that's putting the proverbial cart before the horse, says Cooper, a Calgarian who in 25 years of business has counted among her clients some 75 high-profile Alberta companies.

She urges clients to begin with a goal.

"You have to first look at what you want them (audience members) to do when you stop talking," she says. "I want you to hire me, or increase my budget.

"Then you look at, 'What do I have to say and how do I have to say it to get that action'—remembering always that when you speak to an audience of one or 1,000, business or social, you have to touch the emotions first."

Once people buy in emotionally, it's time to launch into the logic. "You have to remember everyone you talk to is part of an electronic age, and they aren't used to having to wait too long for you to get to the bottom line," she says.

Cooper has shared her skills with senior executives, professional speakers and even image consultants.

TransCanada president George Watson says Cooper has for several years been helping people at the company develop the effective communication skills that are so essential in today's competitive workplace. At TransCanada, she is fondly referred to as the sergeant major.

"Presentations to our board of directors used to be 30 to 40 minutes," Watson says. "She's helped presenters cut them to a maximum of seven minutes, and three to five slides. What we see and hear is clearly focused on the information we need to make decisions."

Bob Baldwin, vice-president of quality and training at Mullen Trucking Inc. where Cooper taught written and oral communication skills, says, "Everybody loved her."

Employees got a tremendous amount out of her classes, learning how to handle themselves in meetings and be more articulate.

When Cooper delivers information in person, she advises that step 1 is to start with your reason for speaking. Maybe it's an opportunity to generate new business.

Step 2 is to tell the audience what happens if the action isn't taken, or a problem solved.

The next step is to state how the opportunity can be developed, outlining two or three main ways without embellishment. The last step is to indicate what's in it for the listener.

Those four steps are covered in the first two minutes.

"And the rest is backfill."

An example: Our south-side vehicle-sales outlet is stalled. And if we don't do anything, the customers will go down the street because there are three new outlets within three blocks.

So here's what we need to do: revisit former customers with a special deal, have a drive for new customers to lease or own. And we need to have a big event that will pull people into our showroom. What's in it for you will be opportunities to increase sales and your income.

"That grabs them," says Cooper.

"At the end of the time, you want them to endorse the three things you need to do. This gives them the road map so you're all travelling in the right direction. You don't have time for side trips."

Most people, she says, speak up to 40 minutes before finally getting to the point of the speech. When Cooper's reviewing a speech, she'll flip to the last slide to find the main point.

The conclusion should be a summing up and a call to action, but the focus so often found at the tail-end should actually be up front, she says.

As well as coaching and giving seminars on organizing a talk, Cooper helps people use their voice to orchestrate delivery of the message.

Last fall, she used her rich, emphatic voice to tell listeners on 40 U.S. talk shows how to deliver their mes-

(continued)

sage through the four Ps—pitch, pace, pause and projection.

Women, more often than men, make the mistakes of finishing their sentences with a rising inflection, a sign that the thought is incomplete, Cooper says.

"I also see an awful lot of grown-up women with little-girl voices because it got them what they wanted when they were little girls."

This fall, she plans to offer small workshops for business women.

"There are," Cooper says, "more and more women moving up the corporate ladder, and the thing that is going to hold them back is (weak) communication skills."

Principles for Increasing Assertive Communication

Most people are nonassertive in certain situations. If you're one of these people and if you wish to modify your behaviour, there are steps you can take to increase your assertiveness. (If you're always and everywhere nonassertive, and are unhappy about this, then you may need training with a therapist to change your behaviour.)

Analyze Assertive Communications   The first step in increasing your assertiveness skills is to understand the nature of these communications. Observe and analyze the messages of others. Learn to distinguish the differences among assertive, aggressive, and nonassertive messages. Focus on what makes one behaviour assertive and another behaviour nonassertive or aggressive. Table 12.3 reviews some of the verbal and nonverbal messages that distinguish assertive from nonassertive or aggressive communication.

After you've gained some skills in observing the behaviours of others, turn your analysis to yourself. Analyze situations in which you're normally assertive and situations in which you're more likely to act nonassertively or aggressively. What characterizes these situations? What do the situations in which you're normally assertive have in common? How do you speak? How do you communicate nonverbally?

Every power is subject to another power.

—Shona proverb

Rehearse Assertive Communications   Select a situation in which you're normally nonassertive. Build a hierarchy that begins with a relatively nonthreatening message and ends with the desired communication. For example, let's say that you have difficulty voicing your opinion to your supervisor at work. The desired behaviour, then, is to tell your supervisor your opinions. You would then construct a hierarchy of situations leading up to this desired behav-

TABLE 12.3 Assertive and Nonassertive or Aggressive Messages

As you read this table, consider your customary ways of interacting. How often do you use assertive messages? How often do you use nonassertive or aggressive messages?

Assertive Messages	Nonassertive or Aggressive Messages
I-messages that accept responsibility for your own feelings (I feel angry when you...")	You-messages that attribute your feelings to others ("You make me angry")
Descriptive and realistic expressions	Allness and extreme expressions
Equality messages that recognize the essential equality between oneself and others	Inequality messages that are overly submissive, polite, subservient or overly aggressive, insulting, condescending
Relaxed and erect body posture	Tense, overly rigid, overly relaxed posture
Focused but nonthreatening eye contact	Intense eye contact or excessive avoidance of eye contact
Expressive and genuine facial expressions	Unexpressive or overly expressive (and often insincere) facial expressions
Normal vocal volume and rhythm pattern	Overly soft or overly loud and accusatory voice

iour. Such a hierarchy might begin with visualizing yourself talking with your boss. Visualize this scenario until you can do it without any anxiety or discomfort. Once you have mastered this visualization, visualize a step closer to your goal, such as walking into your boss's office. Again, do this until your visualization creates no discomfort. Continue with these successive visualizations until you can visualize yourself telling your boss your opinion. As with the other visualizations, do this until you can do it while totally relaxed. This is the mental rehearsal.

You might add a vocal dimension to this by actually acting out (with voice and gesture) your telling your boss your opinion. Again, do this until you experience no difficulty or discomfort. Next, try doing this in front of a trusted and supportive friend or group of friends. Ideally this interaction will provide you with useful feedback. After this rehearsal, you're probably ready for the next step.

The popular view among business professionals is that assertive communication is a valuable tool for advancement. What did your culture teach you about assertive communication? How will these teachings impact on your professional advancement?

Here are three suggestions for increasing your ability to apply the skills learned here to a variety of situations (Sternberg, 1987):

■ Think about the principles flexibly; recognize exceptions to the rule. Note especially that the principles discussed here come largely from research and theory generated in the United States. Ask yourself if they apply to Canadian and other cultures.

■ Compare current situations with those you experienced earlier. What are the similarities and differences? For example, most people repeat relationship problems because they fail to see the similar-ities (or differences) between the old and the new relationship.

■ Look for situations at home, work, and school where you could transfer the skills discussed here. For instance, you might consider how the irreversibility of communication relates to communication problems at home or at work.

EXAMPLES?

Can you give examples of situations outside the classroom in which skills such as assertiveness, active listening, or cooperative response would be useful?

Communicate Assertively This step is naturally the most difficult but obviously the most important. Here's a generally effective pattern to follow in communicating assertively:

■ Describe the problem; don't evaluate or judge it. "We're all working on this assignment together. You're missing half our meetings and you still haven't done your share." Be sure to use I-messages and to avoid messages that accuse or blame the other person.

■ State how this problem affects you. "My grade depends on the success of this project and I don't think it's fair that I have to do extra work to make up for what you're not doing."

■ Propose solutions that are workable and that allow the person to save face. "If you can get your material to the group by Tuesday, we'll still be able to meet our deadline."

■ Confirm understanding. "It's clear that we just can't finish this assignment if you're not going to pull your own weight. Will you have the material to us by Tuesday?"

■ Reflect on your own assertiveness. Think about what you did. How did you express yourself verbally and nonverbally? What would you do differently next time?

Who do you consider to be the three most interpersonally powerful people who ever lived? Why were these people so powerful?

A note of caution should be added. It's easy to visualize a situation in which, for example, people are talking behind you in a movie and, with your newfound enthusiasm for assertiveness, you tell them to be quiet. It's also easy to see yourself getting sworn at as a result. In applying the principles of assertive communication, be careful that you don't go beyond what you can handle effectively.

SUMMARY OF CONCEPTS AND SKILLS

In this chapter we explored interpersonal power from three different points of view. First, we looked at self-esteem and how it might be raised. Second, we looked at how to communicate with power, how to manage power plays, and the strategies for compliance-gaining and compliance-resisting. Third, we looked at assertiveness: what it is and how it can be developed more fully.

1. Self-esteem is the way we see ourselves, the value we place on ourselves. Self-esteem is central to interpersonal power because we are more likely to be effective if we see ourselves as effective people.

2. We can increase self-esteem by replacing self-destructive beliefs with self-affirming ones, seeking out nourishing people, and working on projects that will result in success.

3. Interpersonal power is the ability of one person to control the behaviours of another person. A has power over B if A can control B's behaviours.

4. Six principles govern power in interpersonal relationships: Some people are more powerful than others, all interpersonal messages have a power dimension, some people are more Machiavellian than others, power follows the principle of least interest, power has a cultural dimension, and power is often abused.

5. Sexual harassment consists of sexual advances that are not welcome; such harassment is often based on a need to gain or maintain power.

6. Among the power plays that are used frequently in interpersonal encounters are *nobody upstairs* (in which the power player refuses to hear what we are saying), *you owe me* (in which the power player gains compliance by reminding us that we owe him or her for past favours), and *yougottobekidding* (in which the power player expresses disbelief with your statement and makes both the statement and you seem inadequate).

7. An effective management strategy for dealing with power plays cooperatively consists of three parts: stating our feelings, describing the behaviour we have difficulty with, and stating a cooperative response.

8. Compliance-gaining strategies are the tactics by which we try to get other people to do as we wish. Compliance-resisting strategies are the tactics we use to avoid complying with the requests of others.

9. Assertive people stand up for their rights without denying or infringing upon the rights of others. They are open, not anxious, contentious (argumentative), and not easily intimidated.

Check your ability to apply these skills. Use a rating scale such as the following: 1 = almost always, 2 = often, 3 = sometimes, 4 = rarely, and 5 = almost never.

_____ 1. I challenge self-destructive beliefs.

_____ 2. I seek out nourishing people.

_____ 3. I work on projects that will result in success instead of projects that are doomed to failure.

_____ 4. I engage in self-affirmation.

_____ 5. I manage power through verbal and nonverbal messages.

_____ 6. I avoid behaviours that could be interpreted as sexually harassing.

_____ 7. I respond to power plays with appropriate cooperative strategies.

_____ 8. I communicate social confidence in a wide variety of interpersonal situations.

_____ 9. I use compliance-gaining and compliance-resisting strategies as appropriate.

_____ 10. I communicate assertively when it's appropriate to the situation.

VOCABULARY QUIZ

The Language of Power

Match the terms listed here with their definitions. Record the number of the definition next to the name of the concept.

_5_ self-esteem

_____ power

_____ assertive communication

_____ aggressive communication

_____ nonassertive communication

_4_ power play (as metaphor)

_6_ compliance-gaining strategies

_____ legitimate power

_____ negative altercasting

_____ management strategy for power plays

1. A willingness to speak out for one's rights but with respect for the rights of others.
2. Power held by virtue of one's position or role.
3. Stating your feelings, describing the behaviour you object to, and stating a cooperative response.
4. A pattern of communication that takes unfair advantage of another person.
5. The value we place on ourselves.
6. Tactics that influence people to do what you want them to do.
7. A compliance-gaining strategy in which we put another person into the role of the "bad" person.
8. An unwillingness to speak out for one's rights in certain situations or in all or almost all situations.
9. Expressing yourself without any concern for the rights of others.
10. The ability to control the behaviour of another person.

SKILL BUILDING EXERCISES

12.1 EMPOWERING OTHERS

What would you say, in each of the following situations, to help empower the individuals involved?

1. You're a grade 3 teacher. Most of your students are from the same ethnic–religious group; three, however, are from a very different group. The problem is that these three students are extremely reluctant to participate in class discussions; they stumble when they have to read in front of the class (although they read quite well in private); and they make all sorts of arithmetic mistakes when they do problems at the board. And, not surprisingly with students in grade 3, many of the other students make fun of them and laugh at their mistakes. You want to empower the three students to help them realize their abilities and potential; at the same time, you want to increase all the students' intercultural understanding.

2. You're managing four college interns at a local web design firm, three women and one man. The women all know and are extremely supportive of one another, so they regularly contribute ideas and offer constructive criticism of one another's work. The man, however, seems left out. Although equally competent, he lacks confidence and so doesn't contribute ideas or offer suggestions for improving the work of others. But most of the web visitors for these particular websites are males, and you really need his input.

3. Your partner has been having lots of difficulties: Recently he lost his job, received poor grades in a night class he was taking, and started gaining lots of weight, something he was very careful to avoid in the past. At the same time, you're doing extremely well—just got a promotion, got admitted to a great MBA

program, and are looking your best. You want to give your partner back his confidence and want to empower him.

Thinking Critically About Empowering Others.

What would you stand to gain from your successful empowering of these individuals? How would your relationships with these individuals be different if you were successful in achieving your goal of empowering them? Can you identify any potential problems from successful empowerment?

12.2 MANAGING POWER PLAYS

Here are some examples of power plays. For each one, provide an appropriate three-part management strategy as identified in the text:

State your feelings (remember to use I-messages). Describe the other person's behaviour that you object to.

State a cooperative response.

1. Jason continually interrupts you. Whenever you want to say something he breaks in, finishes what he thinks you were saying, and then says what he wants to say.

2. One of your coworkers responds to your ideas, your plans, and your suggestions with statements like "You can't mean that" and "You can't possibly be serious." So, when you say that you're going to date Harry, she says, "You can't be serious! Harry!" When you say that you're going to apply for a promotion, she says "Promotion! You've got to be kidding! You've only been with the company six months!"

3. Your close friend has helped you get a job in his company. Now, whenever he wants you to do something, he reminds you that he got you the job. Whenever you object that you have your own work to do, he reminds you that you wouldn't have any work to do if it weren't for his getting you the job in the first place.

4. Your supervisor is compulsive about neatness and frequently goes around to the various workers telling them to clean up their work areas. Frequently, this supervisor uses derogatory language that puts down employees' work: "Clean up this crap before you leave tonight" or "Make sure this junk is put away."

5. Your friend Amida sits next to you in class but rarely listens to the instructor. Instead, she waits until you write something down in your notes and then she copies what you've written. In doing this she frequently distracts you and causes you to miss a great deal of what the instructor has said. You've told her repeatedly that you object to this, but she acts as if she doesn't hear you.

Thinking Critically About Power Plays.

Did the cooperative strategies you developed get to feel more comfortable as you worked from the first to the fifth example? If any of these situations or similar ones occurred in your life, would you ignore the power play? Treat it as a one-time event? Use a cooperative strategy?

12.3 ANALYZING AND PRACTISING ASSERTIVENESS

Read each of the following five situations and indicate how an aggressive, a nonassertive, and an assertive person would deal with each one.

1. *Cheating on an examination.* You and another student turn in examination papers whose similarities are too great to be the result of mere coincidence. The instructor accuses you of cheating by allowing the student behind you to copy your answers. You were not aware that anyone saw your paper.

2. *Decorating your apartment.* You have just redecorated your apartment, expending considerable time and money in making it exactly as you want it. A good friend brings you a house gift—the ugliest poster you've ever seen. Your friend insists that you hang it over your fireplace, the focal point of your living room.

3. *Borrowing money.* A friend borrows $30 and promises to pay you back tomorrow. But tomorrow passes, as do 20 other tomorrows, and there's no sign of the money. You know that the person has not forgotten about it, and you also know that the person has more than enough money to pay you back.

4. *Neighbour intrusions.* A neighbour has been playing a stereo at an extremely high volume late into the night. This makes it difficult for you to sleep.

5. *Sexual harassment.* Your supervisor at work has been coming on to you and has asked repeatedly to go out with you. You have refused each time. The supervisor frequently brushes up against you, touches you in passing, and stares at you in a sexual way. You have no romantic interest in your supervisor and simply want to do your job, free from this type of harassment.

Thinking Critically About Assertiveness.

What obstacles might you anticipate in each of these situations if you chose to respond assertively? What suggestions might you offer the person who wants to respond assertively but is having difficulty putting the principles into practice?

12.4 REWRITING UNREALISTIC BELIEFS

Here are five "drivers," unrealistic beliefs that can get you into trouble and can lower your self-esteem: be perfect, hurry up, be strong, please others, and try hard (Butler, 1981). These beliefs are unproductive only when they are extreme and allow no room for being less than perfect. Trying hard or being strong are not themselves unhealthy beliefs; it's only when they become absolute—when you try to be everything to everyone—that they become impossible to attain and create problems. For each belief: (1) explain why these are unrealistic and counterproductive, and (2) identify a more realistic and productive belief to substitute for it.

- The drive to *be perfect* impels you to try to perform at unrealistically high levels in just about everything you do. Whether it's work, school, athletics, or appearance, this drive tells you that anything short of perfection is unacceptable and that you're to blame for any imperfections—imperfections that by any other standard would be considered quite normal.
- The drive to *hurry up* compels you to do things quickly, to do more than can be reasonably expected in any given amount of time.
- The drive to *be strong* tells you that weakness and any of the more vulnerable emotions like sadness, compassion, or loneliness are wrong. This driver is seen in the stereotypical North American man, but is also becoming more prevalent among women as well, who are not permitted to cry or ask for help or have unfulfilled needs.
- The drive to *please others* leads you to seek approval from others. Pleasing yourself is secondary; in fact self-pleasure comes from pleasing others.
- The drive to *try hard* makes you take on more responsibilities than anyone can be expected to handle. This driver leads you to take on tasks that would be impossible for any normal person to handle; yet you take them on without any concern for your own limits (physical or emotional).

Thinking Critically About Unrealistic Beliefs.

Have you internalized any of these beliefs? How do these beliefs influence your thinking and communicating? Might more realistic beliefs prove more productive?

Glossary of Interpersonal Communication Concepts and Skills

Listed here are definitions of the technical terms of interpersonal communication—the words that are peculiar or unique to this discipline—and, where appropriate, the corresponding skills. These definitions and statements of skills should make new or difficult terms a bit easier to understand and should help to place the skill in context. The statements of skills appear in italics. All boldface terms within the definitions appear as separate entries in the glossary.

Acculturation. The process by which a person's culture is modified or changed through contact with or exposure to another culture.

Active listening. A process of putting together into some meaningful whole the listener's understanding of the speaker's total message—the verbal and the nonverbal, the content and the feelings. *Listen actively by paraphrasing the speaker's meanings, expressing an understanding of the speaker's feelings, and asking questions to enable you to check the accuracy of your understanding of the speaker. Express acceptance of the speaker's feelings, and encourage the speaker to explore further his or her feelings and thoughts and thereby increase meaningful sharing.*

Adaptors. Nonverbal behaviours that, when engaged in either in private or in public without being seen, serve some kind of need and occur in their entirety—for example, scratching one's head until the itch is relieved. *Avoid adaptors that interfere with effective communication and reveal your discomfort or anxiety.*

Adjustment (principle of). The principle of verbal interaction that claims that communication may take place only to the extent that the parties communicating share the same system of signals. *Expand the common areas between you and significant others; learn each other's system of communication signals and meanings in order to increase understanding and interpersonal communication effectiveness.*

Affect displays. Nonverbal movements, mostly of the facial area, that convey emotional meaning—for example, anger, fear, and surprise.

Affirmation. The communication of support and approval. *Use affirmation to express your supportiveness and to raise esteem.*

Allness. The assumption that all can be known or is known about a given person, issue, object, or event. *End statements with an implicit "etc." ("et cetera") to indicate that more could be known and said; avoid allness terms and statements.*

Alter-adaptors. Body movements you make in response to your current interactions, such as crossing your arms over your chest when someone unpleasant approaches or moving closer to someone you like.

Altercasting. Placing the listener in a specific role for a specific purpose and asking that the listener approach the question or problem from the perspective of this specific role.

Apprehension. See **communication apprehension.**

Argumentativeness. A willingness to argue for a point of view, to speak one's mind. *Cultivate your argumentativeness, your willingness to argue for what you believe, by, for example, treating disagreements as objectively as possible, reaffirming the other, stressing equality, expressing interest in the other's position, and allowing the other person to save face.* Distinguished from **verbal aggressiveness.**

Assertiveness. A willingness to stand up for one's rights but with respect for the rights of others. *Increase assertiveness (if desired) by analyzing the assertive and nonassertive behaviours of others, analyzing your own behaviors in terms of assertiveness, recording your behaviours, rehearsing assertive behaviours, and acting assertively in appropriate situations. Secure feedback from others for further guidance in increasing assertiveness.*

Attitude. A predisposition to respond for or against an object, person, or position.

Attraction. The state or process by which one individual is drawn to another, by having a highly positive evaluation of that other person.

Attractiveness. The degree to which one is perceived to be physically attractive and to possess a pleasing personality.

Attribution theory. A theory concerned with the processes involved in attributing causation or motivation to a person's behaviour. *In attempting to identify the motivation for behaviours, examine consensus, consistency, distinctiveness, and controllability. Generally, low consensus, high consistency, low distinctiveness, and high controllability identify internally-motivated behaviour; high consensus, low consistency, high distinctiveness, and low controllability identify externally-motivated behaviour.*

Avoidance. An unproductive **conflict** strategy in which a person takes mental or physical flight from the actual conflict.

Barriers to intercultural communication. Those factors (physical or psychological) that prevent or hinder effective communication. *Avoid the major barriers to intercultural communication: ignoring differences between yourself and the culturally different, ignoring differences among the culturally different, ignoring differences in meaning, violating cultural rules and customs, and evaluating differences negatively.*

Belief. Confidence in the existence or truth of something; conviction. *Weigh both verbal and nonverbal messages before making believability judgments; increase your own sensitivity to nonverbal (and verbal) deception cues—for* *example, too little movement, long pauses, slow speech, increased speech errors, mouth guard, nose touching, eye rubbing, or the use of few words, especially monosyllabic answers. Use such cues to formulate hypotheses rather than conclusions concerning deception.*

Beltlining. An unproductive **conflict** strategy in which one hits at the level at which the other person cannot withstand the blow. *Avoid beltlining.*

Blame. An unproductive **conflict** strategy in which we attribute the cause of the conflict to the other person or devote our energies to discovering who is the cause and avoid talking about the issues causing the conflict. *Avoid using blame to win an argument, especially with those with whom you are in close relationships.*

Breadth. The number of topics about which individuals in a relationship communicate.

Certainty. An attitude of closed-mindedness that creates a defensiveness among communication participants; opposed to **provisionalism.**

Channel. The vehicle or medium through which signals are sent.

Cherishing behaviours. Small behaviours we enjoy receiving from others, especially from our relational partner—for example, a kiss before leaving for work.

Chronemics. The study of the communicative nature of time—the way you treat time and use it to communicate. Two general areas of chronemics are cultural and psychological time.

Civil inattention. Polite ignoring of others so as not to invade their privacy.

Closed-mindedness. An unwillingness to receive certain communication messages.

Code. A set of symbols used to translate a message from one form to another.

Cognitive labelling theory. A theory of emotions that holds that your emotional feelings begin with the occurrence or an event; then you respond physiologically; then you interpret the arousal (you in effect decide what it is you're feeling); and then you experience (give a name to) the emotion.

Collectivist culture. A culture in which the group's goals rather than the individual's are given greater importance and where, for example, benevolence, tradition, and conformity are given special emphasis; opposed to **individualistic culture.**

Colour communication. Use of colours (in clothing and in room decor, for example) to convey desired meanings.

Communication. (1) The process or act of communicating; (2) the actual message or messages sent and received; (3) the study of the processes involved in the sending and receiving of messages. (The term **communicology** is suggested for the third definition.)

Communication apprehension. Fear or anxiety over communicating; "trait apprehension" refers to fear of communication generally, regardless of the specific situation; "state apprehension" refers to fear that is specific to a given communication situation. *Manage your own communication apprehension by acquiring the necessary communication skills and experiences, focusing on success, reducing unpredictability by, for example, familiarizing yourself with the communication situations important to you, and putting communication apprehension in perspective. In cases of extreme communication apprehension, seek professional help.*

Competence. "Language competence" is a speaker's ability to use the language; it is a knowledge of the elements and rules of the language. "Communication competence" refers to a knowledge of the elements, principles, and skills of communication and the ability to use these resources for greater communication effectiveness.

Compliance-gaining strategies. Behaviours that are directed toward gaining the agreement of others; behaviours designed to persuade others to do as we wish. *Use the various compliance-gaining strategies to increase your own persuasive power.*

Compliance-resisting strategies. Behaviours directed at resisting the persuasive attempts of others. *Use such strategies as identity management, nonnegotiation, negotiation, and justification as appropriate in resisting compliance.*

Confidence. A quality of interpersonal effectiveness; a comfortable, at-ease feeling in interpersonal communication situations. *Communicate a feeling of being comfortable and at ease with the interaction through appropriate verbal and nonverbal signals.*

Confirmation. A communication pattern that acknow-ledges another person's presence and also indicates an acceptance of this person, this person's definition of self, and the relationship as defined or viewed by this other person; opposed to **disconfirmation.** *Avoid those verbal and nonverbal behaviours that disconfirm another person. Substitute confirming behaviours, behaviours that acknowledge the presence and the contributions of the other person.*

Conflict. An extreme form of competition in which a person attempts to bring a rival to surrender; a situation in which one person's behaviours are directed at preventing something or at interfering with or harming another individual. *See also* **interpersonal conflict.**

Connotation. The feeling or emotional aspect of meaning, generally viewed as consisting of the evaluative (for example, good-bad), potency (strong-weak), and activity (fast-slow) dimensions; the associations of a term. *See also* **denotation.**

Consistency. A perceptual process that influences us to maintain balance among our perceptions; a process that makes us tend to see what we expect to see and to be uncomfortable when our perceptions run contrary to our expectations. *Recognize the human tendency to seek and to see consistency even where it doesn't exist—to see our friends as all positive and our enemies as all negative, for example.*

Contact. The first stage in **relationship development** consisting of "perceptual contact" (you see or hear the person) and "interactional contact" (you talk with the person).

Content and relationship dimensions. A principle of communication that messages refer both to content (the world external to both speaker and listener) and to the relationship existing between the individuals who are interacting.

Context of communication. The physical, psychological, social, and temporal environment in which communication takes place. *Assess the context in which messages are communicated and interpret that communication behaviour accordingly; avoid seeing messages as independent of context.*

Conversation. Two-person communication usually possessing an opening, **feedforward**, a business stage, **feedback**, and a closing.

Conversational management. Responding to conversational turn cues from the other person, and using conversational cues to signal one's own desire to exchange (or maintain) speaker or listener roles.

Conversational maxims. Principles that are followed in conversation to ensure that the goal of the conversation is achieved. *Discover, try not to violate, and, if appropriate, follow the conversational maxims of the culture in which you are communicating.*

Conversational processes. Using the general five-step process in conversation, and avoiding the several barriers that can be created when the normal process is distorted.

Conversational turns. The process of passing the speaker and listener roles during conversation. *Become sensitive to and respond appropriately to conversational turn cues, such as turn-maintaining, turn-yielding, turn-requesting, and turn-denying cues.*

Cooperation. An interpersonal process by which individuals work together for a common end; the pooling of efforts to produce a mutually desired outcome.

Critical thinking. The process of logically evaluating reasons and evidence and reaching a judgment on the basis of this analysis.

Cultural display. Signs that communicate one's cultural identification, such as clothing or religious jewelry.

Cultural display rules. Rules that identify what are and what are not appropriate forms of expression for members of the culture.

Cultural rules. Rules that are specific to a given culture. *Respond to messages according to the cultural rules of the sender; avoid interpreting the messages of others exclusively through the perspective of your own culture in order to prevent misinterpretation of the intended meanings.*

Cultural time. The meanings given to time communication by a particular culture.

Date. An **extensional device** used to emphasize the notion of constant change and symbolized by a subscript: for example, John Smith$_{1986}$ is not John Smith$_{2003}$.

Decoder. Something that takes a message in one form (for example, sound waves) and translates it into another form (for example, nerve impulses) from which meaning can be formulated (for example, in vocal-auditory communication). In human communication, the decoder is the auditory mechanism; in electronic communication, the decoder is, for example, the telephone earpiece. Decoding is the process of extracting a message from a code—for example, translating speech sounds into nerve impulses. *See also* **encoder.**

Defensiveness. An attitude of an individual or an atmosphere in a group characterized by threats, fear, and domination; messages evidencing evaluation, control, strategy, neutrality, superiority, and certainty are assumed to lead to defensiveness; opposed to **supportiveness.**

Denial. One of the obstacles to the expression of emotion; the process by which we deny our emotions to ourselves or to others.

Denotation. Referential meaning; the objective or descriptive meaning of a word. *See also* **connotation.**

Depth. The degree to which the inner personality—the inner core of an individual—is penetrated in interpersonal interaction.

Deterioration. The stage of a relationship during which the connecting bonds between the partners weaken and the partners begin drifting apart.

Direct speech. Speech in which the speaker's intentions are stated clearly and directly. *Use direct requests and responses (1) to encourage compromise, (2) to acknowledge responsibility for your own feelings and desires, and (3) to state your own desires honestly so as to encourage honesty, openness, and supportiveness in others.*

Disclaimer. Statement that asks the listener to receive what the speaker says as intended without its reflecting negatively on the image of the speaker. *Avoid using disclaimers that may not be accepted by your listeners (they may raise the very doubts you wish to put to rest), but do use disclaimers when you think your future messages might offend your listeners.*

Disconfirmation. The process by which one ignores or denies the right of the individual even to define himself or herself; opposed to **confirmation.**

Dissolution. The termination or end of an interpersonal relationship. If the relationship ends: *(1) Break the loneliness–depression cycle; (2) take time out to get to know yourself as an individual; (3) bolster your self-esteem; (4) remove or avoid symbols that may remind you of your past relationship and may make you uncomfortable; (5) seek the support of friends and relatives; and (6) avoid repeating negative patterns.*

Downward communication. Communication sent from the higher levels of a hierarchy to the lower levels—for examples, messages sent by managers to workers, or from deans to faculty members.

Dyadic effect. The tendency for the behaviours of one person to stimulate behaviours in the other interactant; usually used to refer to the tendency of one person's self-disclosures to prompt the other to self-disclose. *Be responsive to the dyadic effect; if it's not operating (when you think it should be), ask yourself why.*

Effect. The outcome or consequence of an action or behaviour; communication is assumed always to have some effect.

Emblems. Nonverbal behaviours that directly translate words or phrases—for example, the signs for "OK" and "peace."

Emotion. The feelings we have, such as guilt, anger, or sorrow.

Emotional communication. The expression of feelings—for example, our feelings of guilt, happiness, or sorrow. *Before expressing your emotions, understand them, decide whether you wish to express them, and assess your communication options. In expressing your emotions, describe your feelings* *as accurately as possible, identify the reasons for them, anchor your feelings and their expression to the present time, and own your feelings.*

Emotional contagion. The transferal of emotions from one person to another, analogous to transmission of a contagious disease from one person to another.

Empathy. The sharing of another person's feeling; feeling or perceiving something as does another person. *Increase empathic understanding for your primary partner by sharing experiences, role-playing, and seeing the world from his or her perspective. Empathize with others, and express this empathic understanding verbally and nonverbally.*

Encoder. Something that takes a message in one form (for example, nerve impulses) and translates it into another form (for example, sound waves). In human communication, the encoder is the speaking mechanism; in electronic communication, the encoder is, for example, the telephone mouthpiece. Encoding is the process of putting a message into a code—for example, translating nerve impulses into speech sounds. *See also* **decoder.**

Enculturation. The process by which culture is transmitted from one generation to another.

Equality. An attitude that recognizes that each individual in a communication interaction is equal, that no one is superior to any other; encourages supportiveness; opposed to **superiority.** *Talk neither down nor up to others but communicate as an equal to increase interpersonal satisfaction and efficiency; share the speaking and the listening; recognize that all parties in communication have something to contribute.*

Etc. (et cetera). An **extensional device** used to emphasize the notion of infinite complexity; because one can never know all about anything, any statement about the world or an event must end with an explicit or implicit "etc." *Use the implicit or explicit etc. to remind yourself and others that there is more to be known, more to be said.*

Ethics. The branch of philosophy that deals with the rightness or wrongness of actions; the study of moral values.

Ethnocentrism. The tendency to see others and their behaviours through our own cultural filters, often as distortions of our own behaviours; the tendency to evaluate the values and beliefs of one's own culture more positively than those of another culture.

Evaluation. A process whereby a value is placed on some person, object, or event. *Avoid premature evaluation; amass evidence before making evaluations, especially of other people.*

Excuse. An explanation designed to lessen the negative consequences of something done or said. *Avoid excessive excuse-making. Too many excuses may backfire and create image problems for the excuse-maker.*

Expressiveness. A quality of interpersonal effectiveness; genuine involvement in speaking and listening, conveyed verbally and nonverbally. *Communicate involvement and interest in the interaction by providing appropriate feedback, by assuming responsibility for your thoughts and feelings and your role as speaker and listener, and by appropriate expressiveness, variety, and flexibility in voice and bodily action.*

Extensional devices. Linguistic devices proposed by Alfred Korzybski to keep language a more accurate means for talking about the world. The extensional devices include **etc., date,** and **index** (the working devices).

Extensional orientation. A point of view in which the primary consideration is given to the world of experience and only secondary consideration is given to labels. *See also* **intensional orientation.**

Facial feedback hypothesis. The hypothesis or theory that your facial expressions can produce physiological and emotional effects.

Facial management techniques. Techniques used to mask certain emotions and to emphasize others—for example, intensifying your expression of happiness to make a friend feel good about a promotion.

Fact–inference confusion. A misevaluation in which one makes an inference, regards it as a fact, and acts upon it as if it were a fact. *Distinguish facts from inferences; respond to inferences as inferences and not as facts.*

Factual statement. A statement made by the observer after observation and limited to what is observed. *See also* **inferential statement.**

Family. A group of people who consider themselves related and connected to one another and where the actions of one have consequences for others.

Feedback. Information that is given back to the source. Feedback may come from the source's own messages (as when we hear what we are saying) or from the receiver(s) in the form of applause, yawning, puzzled looks, questions, letters to the editor of a newspaper, increased or decreased subscriptions to a magazine, and so forth. *Give clear feedback to others, and respond to others' feedback, either through corrective measures or by continuing current performance, to increase communication efficiency and satisfaction. See also* **feedforward.**

Feedforward. Information that is sent prior to the regular messages telling the listener something about what is to follow. *When appropriate, preface your messages in order to open the channels of communication, to preview the messages to be sent, to disclaim, and to altercast. In your use of feedforward, be brief, use feedforward sparingly, and follow through on your feedforward promises. Also, be sure to respond to the feedforward as well as the content messages of others. See also* **feedback**.

Feminine culture. A culture in which both men and women are encouraged to be modest, oriented to maintaining the quality of life, and tender. Feminine cultures emphasize the quality of life and so socialize their people to be modest and to emphasize close interpersonal relationships; opposed to **masculine culture.**

Flexibility. The ability to adjust communication strategies on the basis of the unique situation. *Apply the principles of interpersonal communication with flexibility, realizing that each situation calls for somewhat different skills.*

Force. An unproductive **conflict** strategy in which you try to win an argument by physically overpowering the other person either by threat or by actual behaviour. *Avoid it.*

Friendship. An interpersonal relationship between two persons that is mutually productive, established and maintained through perceived mutual free choice, and characterized by mutual positive regard. *Adjust your verbal and nonverbal communication as appropriate to the stages of your various friendships. Learn the rules that govern your friendships; follow them or risk damaging the relationship.*

Fundamental attribution error. The tendency to overvalue and give too much weight to the contribution of internal factors (i.e., the person's personality) and undervalue and give too little weight to the contribution of external factors (i.e., the situation the person is in or the surrounding events).

Gender display rules. Cultural rules that identify what are and are not appropriate forms of expression for men and for women.

Gossip. Communication about someone not present, some third party, usually about matters that are private to this third party. *Avoid gossip that breaches confidentiality, is known to be false, and is unnecessarily invasive.*

Grapevine messages. Messages that do not follow any format organizational structures; office-related gossip.

Gunnysacking. An unproductive **conflict** strategy of storing up grievances—as if in a gunnysack—and holding them in readiness to dump on the person with whom one is in conflict. *Avoid it.*

Halo effect. The tendency to generalize an individual's virtue or expertise from one area to another.

Haptics. Technical term for the study of touch communication.

Heterosexist language. Language that assumes all people are heterosexual and thereby denigrates lesbians and gay men.

High-context culture. A culture in which much of the information in communication is in the context or in the person rather than explicitly coded in the verbal messages; opposed to **low-context culture. Collectivist cultures** are generally high-context.

I-messages. Messages in which the speaker accepts responsibility for personal thoughts and behaviours; messages in which the speaker's point of view is stated explicitly; opposed to **you-messages.** *Generally, I- messages are more effective than you-messages.*

Identity management. A tactic used to resist a request by trying to manipulate the image of the person making the request.

Illustrators. Nonverbal behaviours that accompany and illustrate verbal messages—for example, upward movements that accompany the verbalization "It's up there."

Immediacy. A quality of interpersonal effectiveness; a sense of contact and togetherness; a feeling of interest and liking for the other person. *Communicate immediacy through appropriate word choice, feedback, eye contact, body posture, and physical closeness.*

Implicit personality theory. A theory of personality that each individual maintains, complete with rules about what characteristics go with what other characteristics, that you maintain and through which you perceive others. *Be conscious of your implicit personality theories; avoid draw-*

ing firm conclusions about other people on the basis of these theories.

Index. An **extensional device** used to emphasize the notion of nonidentity (no two things are the same) and symbolized by a subscript—for example, politician$_{1 \text{[Smith]}}$ is not politician$_{2 \text{[Jones]}}$.

Indirect speech. Speech that hides the speaker's true intentions; speech in which requests and observations are made indirectly. *Use indirect speech (1) to express a desire without insulting or offending anyone, (2) to ask for compliments in a socially acceptable manner, and (3) to disagree without being disagreeable.*

Indiscrimination. A misevaluation caused by categorizing people, events, or objects into a particular class and responding to them only as members of the class; a failure to recognize that each individual is unique; a failure to apply the **index.** *Index your terms and statements to emphasize that each person and event is unique; avoid treating all individuals the same way because they are covered by the same label or term.*

Individualistic culture. A culture in which the individual's rather than the group's goals and preferences are given greater importance; opposed to **collectivist cultures.**

Inevitability. A principle of communication holding that communication cannot be avoided; all behaviour in an interactional setting is communication. *Remember that all behaviour in an interactional situation communicates; seek out nonobvious messages and meanings.*

Inferential statement. A statement that can be made by anyone, is not limited to what is observed, and can be made at any time. See also **factual statement.**

Informal time terms. Terms that are approximate rather than exact, for example, "soon," "early," and "in a while." *Recognize that informal-time terms are often the cause of interpersonal difficulties. When misunderstanding is likely, use more precise terms.*

Intensional orientation. A point of view in which primary consideration is given to the way things are labelled and only secondary consideration (if any) to the world of experience. *See also* **extensional orientation.** *Respond first to things; avoid responding to labels as if they were things; do not let labels distort your perception of the world.*

Interaction management. A quality of interpersonal effectiveness; the control of interaction to the satisfaction of both parties; managing conversational turns, fluency, and message consistency. *Manage the interaction to the satisfaction of both parties by sharing the roles of speaker and listener, avoiding long and awkward silences, and being consistent in your verbal and nonverbal messages.*

Intercultural communication. Communication that takes place between persons of different cultures or persons who have different cultural beliefs, values, or ways of behaving.

Interpersonal communication. Communication between two persons or among a small group of persons and distinguished from public or mass communication; communication of a personal nature and distinguished from impersonal communication; communication between or among connected persons or those involved in a close relationship.

Interpersonal competence. The ability to accomplish one's interpersonal goals; interpersonal communication that is satisfying to both individuals.

Interpersonal conflict. A disagreement between two connected persons. *To engage in more productive interpersonal conflict: (1) state your position directly and honestly; (2) react openly to the messages of your combatant; (3) own your thoughts and feelings; (4) address the real issues causing the conflict; (5) listen with and demonstrate empathic understanding; (6) validate the feelings of your interactant; (7) describe the behaviours causing the conflict; (8) express your feelings spontaneously rather than strategically; (9) state your position tentatively; (10) capitalize on agreements; (11) view conflict in positive terms to the extent possible; (12) express positive feelings for the other person; (13) be positive about the prospects of conflict resolution; (14) treat your combatant as an equal, avoiding ridicule or sarcasm; (15) involve yourself in the conflict; play an active role as both sender and receiver; (16) grant the other person permission to express himself or herself freely; and (17) avoid power tactics that may inhibit freedom of expression.*

Interpersonal effectiveness. The ability to accomplish one's interpersonal goals; interpersonal communication that is satisfying to both individuals.

Interpersonal perception. The **perception** of people; the processes through which we interpret and evaluate people and their behaviour.

Intimacy. The closest interpersonal relationship; usually used to denote a close primary relationship.

Intimacy claims. Obligations incurred by virtue of being in a close and intimate relationship. *Reduce the intensity of intimacy claims when things get rough; give each other space as appropriate.*

Intimate distance. The closest proxemic distance, ranging from touching to 46 centimetres. *See also* **proxemics.**

Involvement. The second stage in **relationship development** in which you further advance the relationship, first testing each other and then intensifying your interaction.

Irreversibility. A principle of communication holding that communication cannot be reversed; once something has been communicated, it cannot be uncommunicated. *Avoid saying things (for example, in anger) or making commitments that you may wish to retract (but will not be able to) in order to prevent resentment and ill feeling.*

Johari window. A diagram of the four selves: **open, blind, hidden,** and **unknown.**

Justification. Justifying a refusal by citing possible consequences of compliance or noncompliance.

Language. The rules of syntax, semantics, and phonology by which sentences are created and understood; the term *a language* refers to the sentences that can be created in any language, such as, English, Bantu, or Italian.

Lateral communication. Communication between equals—manager to manager, worker to worker.

Leave-taking cues. Verbal and nonverbal cues that indicate a desire to terminate a conversation. *Increase your sensitivity to leave-taking cues; pick up on the leave-taking cues*

of others, and communicate such cues tactfully so as not to insult or offend others.

Levelling. A process of message distortion in which a message is repeated but the number of details is reduced, some details are omitted entirely, and some details lose their complexity.

Listening. An active process of receiving aural stimuli; this process consists of five stages: receiving, understanding, remembering, evaluating, and responding. *Adjust your listening perspective, as the situation warrants, between active and passive, judgmental and nonjudgmental, surface and depth, and empathic and objective listening.*

Love. An relationship with another person in which you feel closeness, caring, warmth, and excitement.

Low-context culture. A culture in which most of the information in communication is explicitly stated in the verbal messages; opposed to **high-context culture.** **Individualistic cultures** are usually low-context cultures.

Machiavellianism. The belief that people can be manipulated easily; often used to refer to the techniques or tactics one person uses to control another.

Manipulation. An unproductive **conflict** strategy that avoids open conflict; instead, attempts are made to divert the conflict by being especially charming and getting the other person into a noncombative frame of mind. *Avoid it.*

Manner maxim. A principle of **conversation** that holds that speakers cooperate by being clear and by organizing their thoughts into some meaningful and coherent pattern. *Use it.*

Markers. Devices that signify that a certain territory belongs to a particular person. *Become sensitive to the markers (central, boundary, and ear) of others, and learn to use these markers to define your own territories and to communicate the desired impression.*

Masculine culture. A culture in which men are viewed as assertive, oriented to material success, and strong; women, on the other hand, are viewed as modest, focused on the quality of life, and tender. Masculine cultures emphasize success and so socialize people to be assertive, ambitious, and competitive; opposed to **feminine culture.**

Mentoring relationship. A relationship in which an experienced individual helps to train someone who is less experienced; for example, an accomplished teacher might mentor a younger teacher who is newly arrived or who has never taught before.

Message. Any signal or combination of signals that serves as a **stimulus** for a receiver.

Metacommunication. Communication about communication. *Metacommunicate to ensure understanding of the other person's thoughts and feelings: give clear feedforward, explain feelings as well as thoughts, paraphrase your own complex thoughts, and ask questions.*

Mindfulness and mindlessness. States of relative awareness. In a mindful state, we are aware of the logic and rationality of our behaviours and the logical connections existing among elements. In a mindless state, we are unaware of this logic and rationality. *Apply the principles of interpersonal communication mindfully rather than mindlessly.*

Increase mindfulness by creating and re-creating categories, being open to new information and points of view, and being careful of relying too heavily on first impressions.

Model. A representation of an object or process.

Monochronic time orientation. A view of time in which things are done sequentially; one thing is scheduled at a time. Opposed to **polychronic time orientation**.

Negative feedback. Feedback that serves a corrective function by informing the source that his or her message is not being received in the way intended. Negative feedback serves to redirect the source's behaviour. Looks of boredom, shouts of disagreement, letters critical of newspaper policy, and teachers' instructions on how better to approach a problem would be examples of negative feedback.

Negotiation. Resisting compliance by offering a compromise or by offering to help in another way.

Networking. Connecting with people who can help you accomplish a goal or help you find information related to your goal; for example, to your search for a job.

Neutrality. A response pattern lacking in personal involvement; encourages defensiveness; opposed to **empathy.**

Noise. Anything that interferes with a person's receiving a message as the source intended the message to be received. Noise is present in a communication system to the extent that the message received is not the message sent. *Combat the effects of physical, semantic, and psychological noise by eliminating or lessening the sources of physical noise, securing agreement on meanings, and interacting with an open mind in order to increase communication accuracy.*

Nonnegotiation. An unproductive **conflict** strategy in which the individual refuses to discuss the conflict or to listen to the other person.

Nonverbal communication. Communication without words; communication by means of space, gestures, facial expressions, touching, vocal variation, and silence, for example.

Object-adaptors. Movements that involve your manipulation of some object—for example, punching holes in or drawing on the styrofoam coffee cup, clicking a ballpoint pen, or chewing on a pencil. *Avoid them; they generally communicate discomfort and a lack of control over the communication situation.*

Olfactory communication. Communication by smell.

Openness. A quality of interpersonal effectiveness encompassing (1) a willingness to interact openly with others, to self-disclose as appropriate; (2) a willingness to react honestly to incoming stimuli; and (3) a willingness to own one's feelings and thoughts.

Other-orientation. A quality of interpersonal effectiveness involving attentiveness, interest, and concern for the other person. *Convey concern for and interest in the other person by means of empathic responses, appropriate feedback, and attentive listening responses.*

Outing. The process whereby a person's affectional orientation is made public by another person and without the gay man or lesbian's consent.

Overattribution. The tendency to attribute a great deal or even everything a person does to one or two characteristics.

Owning feelings. The process by which we take responsibility for our own feelings instead of attributing them to others. *To indicate ownership of your feelings: use I-messages; acknowledge responsibility for your own thoughts and feelings.*

Paralanguage. The vocal (but nonverbal) aspect of speech. Paralanguage consists of voice qualities (for example, pitch range, resonance, tempo), vocal characterizers (laughing or crying, yelling or whispering), vocal qualifiers (intensity, pitch height), and vocal segregates ("uh-uh," meaning "no," or "sh" meaning "silence"). *Vary paralinguistic elements, such as rate, volume, and stress, to add variety and emphasis to your communications, and be responsive to the meanings communicated by others' variation of paralanguage features.*

Passive listening. Listening that is attentive and supportive but occurs without talking and without directing the speaker in any nonverbal way; also used negatively to refer to inattentive and uninvolved listening.

Pauses. Silent periods in the normally fluent stream of speech. Pauses are of two major types: filled pauses (interruptions in speech that are filled with such vocalizations as "er" or "um") and unfilled pauses (silences of unusually long duration).

Perception. The process by which you become aware of objects and events through your senses. *Increase your accuracy in interpersonal perception by looking for a variety of cues that point in the same direction, formulating hypotheses (not conclusions), being especially alert to contradictory cues that may refute your initial hypotheses, avoiding the assumption that others will respond as you would, and being careful not to perceive only the positive in those you like and the negative in those you dislike.*

Personal distance. The second-closest proxemic distance, ranging from 46 centimetres to 1.2 metres. *See also* **proxemics.**

Persuasion. The process of influencing attitudes and behaviour.

Phatic communication. Communication that is primarily social; communication designed to open the channels of communication rather than to communicate something about the external world. "Hello" and "How are you?" in everyday interaction are examples.

Pitch. The highness or lowness of the vocal tone.

Polarization. A form of fallacious reasoning by which only two extremes are considered; also referred to as "black-or-white" and "either–or" thinking or two-valued orientation. *Use middle terms and qualifiers when describing the world; avoid talking in terms of polar opposites (black and white, good and bad) in order to describe reality more accurately.*

Polychronic time orientation. A view of time in which several things may be scheduled or engaged in at the same time. Opposed to **monochronic time orientation**.

Positive feedback. Feedback that supports or reinforces the continuation of behaviour along the same lines in which it is already proceeding—for example, applause during a speech encourages the speaker to continue speaking in this way.

Positiveness. A characteristic of effective communication involving positive attitudes toward oneself and toward the interpersonal interaction. Also used to refer to complimenting another and expressing acceptance and approval. *Verbally and nonverbally communicate a positive attitude toward yourself, others, and the situation with smiles, positive facial expressions, attentive gestures, positive verbal expressions, and the elimination or reduction of negative appraisals.*

Power. The ability to influence or control the behaviour of another person; A has power of B when A can influence or control B's behaviour. Power is an inevitable part of interpersonal relationships. *Communicate power through forceful speech; avoidance of weak modifiers and excessive body movement; and demonstration of knowledge, preparation, and organization in the matters at hand.*

Power play. A consistent pattern of behaviour in which one person tries to control the behaviour of another. *Identify the power plays people use on you and respond to these power plays so as to stop them. Use an effective management strategy—for example, express your feelings, describe the behaviour you object to, and state a cooperative response.*

Primacy and recency. Primacy refers to giving more credence to that which occurs first; recency refers to giving more credence to that which occurs last (that is, most recently). *Be aware that first impressions can serve as filters that prevent you from perceiving others, perhaps contradictory behaviours as well as changes in situations and, especially, changes in people. Recognize the normal tendency for first impressions to leave lasting impressions and to colour both what we see later and the conclusions we draw. Be at your very best in first encounters. Also, take the time and effort to revise your impressions of others on the basis of new information.*

Primary relationship. The relationship between two people that they consider their most (or one of their most) important, such as the relationship between husband and wife or domestic partners.

Principle of cooperation. An implicit agreement between speaker and listener to cooperate in trying to understand what each is communicating.

Process. Ongoing activity; **communication** is referred to as a process to emphasize that it is always changing, always in motion.

Provisionalism. An attitude of open-mindedness that leads to the creation of supportiveness; opposed to **certainty.**

Proxemics. The study of the communicative function of space; the study of how people unconsciously structure their space—the distance between people in their interactions, the organization of space in homes and offices, and even the design of cities.

Psychological time. The importance you place on past, present, or future time. *Recognize the significance of your own time orientation to your ultimate success, and make whatever adjustments you think desirable.*

Public distance. The farthest proxemic distance, ranging from 3.7 metres to more than 7.6 metres; see also **proxemics.**

Quality maxim. A principle of **conversation** that holds that speakers cooperate by saying what they know or think is true and by not saying what they know or think is false. *Use it.*

Quantity maxim. A principle of **conversation** that holds that speakers cooperate by being only as informative as necessary to communicate their intended meanings. *Use it.*

Racist language. Language that denigrates a particular race. *Avoid racist language—any language that demeans or is derogatory toward members of a particular race—so as not to offend or alienate others or reinforce stereotypes.*

Rate. The speed with which we speak, generally measured in words per minute. *Use variations in rate to increase communication efficiency and persuasiveness as appropriate.*

Receiver. Any person or thing that takes in messages. Receivers may be individuals listening to or reading a message, a group of persons hearing a speech, a scattered television audience, or machines that store information.

Regulators. Nonverbal behaviours that regulate, monitor, or control the communications of another person.

Rejection. A response to an individual that acknowledges another person but expresses disagreement; opposed to **confirmation** and **disconfirmation**.

Relation maxim. A principle of **conversation** that holds that speakers cooperate by talking about what is relevant to the conversation and by not talking about what is not relevant.

Relationship communication. Communication between or among intimates or those in close relationships; used by some theorists as synonymous with interpersonal communication.

Relationship dialectics theory. A theory that describes relationships along a series of opposites representing competing desires or motivations, such as the desire for autonomy and the desire to belong to someone, for novelty and predictability, and for closedness and openness.

Relationship message. Message that comment on the relationship between the speakers rather than on matters external to them. *Recognize and respond to relationship as well as content messages in order to ensure a more complete understanding of the messages intended.*

Repair. A relationship stage in which one or both parties seek to improve the relationship. *Relationship repair may be accomplished by recognizing the problem, engaging in productive conflict resolution, posing possible solutions, affirming each other, integrating solutions into everyday behavior, and taking relational risks.* See *also* **maintenance.**

Schemata. Ways of organizing perceptions; mental templates or structures that help you organize the millions of items of information that you come into contact with every day as well as those you already have in your memory. Schemata include general ideas about people (Pat and Chris, Japanese, Baptists); yourself (your qualities, abilities, or even liabilities); and social roles (the qualities of police officers, professors, or multimillionaire CEOs). Singular: schema.

Script. A type of schema; an organized body of information about some action, event, or procedure. A script is a general idea of how some event should play out or unfold; the rules governing events and their sequence.

Selective exposure. The tendency of listeners to actively seek out information that supports their opinions and actively avoid information that contradicts their existing opinions, beliefs, attitudes, and values.

Self-acceptance. Being satisfied with ourselves, our virtues and vices, and our abilities and limitations.

Self-adaptors. Movements that usually satisfy a physical need, especially to make you more comfortable—or example, scratching your head to relieve an itch, moistening your lips because they feel dry, or pushing your hair out of your eyes. *Because these often communicate your nervousness or discomfort, they are best avoided.*

Self-awareness. The degree to which you know yourself. *Increase self-awareness by asking yourself about yourself and listening to others; actively seek information about yourself from others by carefully observing their interactions with you and by asking relevant questions. See yourself from different perspectives (see your different selves), and increase your open self.*

Self-concept. Your self-image, the view you have of who you are.

Self-disclosure. The process of revealing something about ourselves to another, usually used to refer to information that would normally be kept hidden. *Self-disclose when the motivation is to improve the relationship, when the context and the relationship are appropriate for the self- disclosure, when there is an opportunity for open and honest responses, when the self-disclosures will be clear and direct, when there are appropriate reciprocal disclosures, and when you have examined and are willing to risk the possible burdens that self-disclosure might entail. Self-disclose selectively; regulate your self-disclosures as appropriate to the context, topic, audience, and potential rewards and risks to secure the maximum advantage and reduce the possibility of negative effects.*

Self-esteem. The value we place on ourselves; our self-evaluations; usually used to refer to the positive value placed on oneself. *Increase your self-esteem by attacking destructive beliefs, engaging in self-affirmation, seeking out nourishing people, and working on projects that will result in success.*

Self-fulfilling prophecy. The situation in which making a prediction tends to cause it to come true. For example, expecting a class to be boring and then fulfilling this expectation by perceiving it as boring, or expecting a person to be hostile, you act in a hostile manner toward this person, and in doing so elicit hostile behaviour from the person—thus confirming your prophecy that the person is hostile. *Avoid fulfilling your own negative prophecies and seeing only what you want to see. Be especially careful to examine your perceptions when they conform too closely to your expectations; check to make sure that you are seeing what exists in real life, not just in your expectations or predictions.*

Self-monitoring. Manipulations of the image you present to others in interpersonal interactions so as to give the most favourable impression of yourself. *Monitor your verbal and nonverbal behaviour as appropriate to communicate the desired impression.*

Self-serving bias. A bias that operates in the self-attribution process and leads us to take credit for the positive consequences and to deny responsibility for the negative consequences of our behaviours. *In examining the causes of your own behaviour, beware of the tendency to attribute negative behaviours to external factors and positive behaviours to internal factors. In self-examinations, ask whether and how the self-serving bias might be operating.*

Sexist language. Language derogatory to one sex, generally women. *Whether man or woman, avoid sexist language—for example, terms that presume maleness as the norm ("policeman" or "mailman").*

Shyness. The condition of discomfort and uneasiness in interpersonal situations.

Signal-to-noise ration. A measure of what is meaningful (signal) to what is interference (noise).

Silence. The absence of vocal communication; often misunderstood to refer to the absence of any and all communication. *Use silence to communicate feelings or to prevent communication about certain topics. Interpret silences of others through their culturally determined rules rather than your own.*

Silencers. A tactic (such as crying) that silences one's opponent—an unproductive **conflict** strategy.

Social comparison. The processes by which you compare aspects of yourself (for example, your abilities, opinions, and values) with those of others and then assess and evaluate yourself on the basis of the comparison; one of the sources of self-concept.

Social distance. The third proxemic distance, ranging from 1.2 metres to 3.7 metres; the distance at which business is usually conducted. *See also* **proxemics.**

Source. Any person or thing that creates messages; for example, an individual speaking, writing, or gesturing, or a computer solving a problem.

Speech. Messages conveyed via a vocal-auditory channel.

Spontaneity. The communication pattern in which one verbalizes what one is thinking without attempting to develop strategies for control; encourages **supportiveness;** opposed to **strategy.**

Static evaluation. An orientation that fails to recognize that the world is characterized by constant change; an attitude that sees people and events as fixed rather than as constantly changing. *Date your statements to emphasize constant change; avoid the tendency to think of and describe things as static and unchanging.*

Status. The relative level one occupies in a hierarchy; status always involves a comparison, and thus one's status is only relative to the status of another. In our culture, occupation, financial position, age, and educational level are significant determinants of status.

Stereotype. In communication, a fixed impression of a group of people through which we then perceive specific individuals; stereotypes are most often negative ("Those people" are stupid, uneducated, and dirty) but may also be positive ("Those people" are scientific, industrious, and helpful). *Avoid stereotyping others; instead, see and respond to each individual as a unique individual.*

Stimulus. Any external or internal change that impinges on or arouses an organism.

Strategy. The use of some plan for control of other members of a communication interaction that guides your own communications; encourages **defensiveness;** opposed to **spontaneity.**

Superiority. A point of view or attitude that assumes that others are not equal to oneself; encourages **defensiveness;** opposed to **equality.**

Supportiveness. An attitude of an individual or an atmosphere in a group that is characterized by openness, absence of fear, and a genuine feeling of equality. *Exhibit supportiveness to others by being descriptive rather than evaluative, spontaneous rather than strategic, and provisional rather than certain; opposed to* **defensiveness**.

Taboo. Forbidden; culturally censored. Taboo language is language that is frowned upon by "polite society." Topics and specific words may be considered taboo—for example, death, sex, certain forms of illness, and various words denoting sexual activities and excretory functions. *Avoid taboo expressions so that others do not make negative evaluations; substitute more socially acceptable expressions or euphemisms where and when appropriate.*

Tactile communication. Communication by touch; communication received by the skin. *Use touch when appropriate to express positive affect, playfulness, control, and ritualistic meanings and to serve task-related functions; but avoid touching that may be unwelcome.*

Temporal communication. The messages conveyed by your time orientation and treatment of time. *Interpret time cues from the point of view of the other's culture rather than your own.*

Territoriality. A possessive or ownership reaction to an area of space or to particular objects. *Establish and maintain territory nonverbally by marking or otherwise indicating temporary or permanent ownership. Become sensitive to the territorial behaviour of others.*

Touch. Use touch when appropriate to express positive effect, playfulness, control, and ritualistic meanings and to serve task-related functions.

Touch avoidance. The tendency to avoid touching and being touched by others. *Recognize that some people may prefer to avoid touching and being touched. Avoid drawing too many conclusions about people from the way they treat interpersonal touching.*

Transactional view. A point of view that sees communication as an ongoing process in which all elements are interdependent and influence one another.

Unproductive conflict strategies. Ways of engaging in conflict that generally prove counterproductive; for example, avoidance, force, blame, silencers, gunnysacking, manipulation, personal rejection, and fighting below the belt.

Upward communication. Communication sent from the lower levels of a hierarchy to the upper levels—for example, line worker to manager, faculty member to dean.

Value. Relative worth of an object; a quality that makes something desirable or undesirable; ideals or customs about which we have emotional responses, whether positive or negative.

Verbal aggressiveness. A method of winning an argument by attacking the other person's **self-concept.** Avoid inflicting psychological pain on the other person to win an argument.

Voice qualities. Aspects of **paralanguage**—specifically, pitch range, vocal lip control, glottis control, pitch control, articulation control, rhythm control, resonance, and tempo.

Volume. The relative loudness of the voice.

You-messages. Messages in which the speaker denies responsibility for his or her own thoughts and behaviours; messages that attribute the speaker's **perception** to another person; messages of **blame**; opposed to **I-messages.**

References

Abrams, Jessica, O'Conner, Joan, & Giles, Howard (2002). Identity and intergroup communication. In William B. Gudykunst, & Bella Mody (Eds.), *Handbook of international and intercultural communication* (2nd ed., pp. 225–240). Thousand Oaks, CA: Sage.

Adams, Dennis M., & Hamm, Mary E. (1991). *Cooperative learning: Critical thinking and collaboration across the curriculum.* Springfield, IL: Charles C. Thomas.

Adria, Marco (2003). Arms to communications: Idealist and pragmatic strains of Canadian thought on technology and nationalism. *Canadian Journal of Communication, 28,* 167–184.

Albas, Daniel C., McCluskey, Ken W., & Albas, Cheryl A. (1976, December). Perception of the emotional content of speech: A comparison of two Canadian groups. *Journal of Cross-Cultural Psychology, 7,* 481–490.

Albert, Rosita, & Nelson, Gayle L. (1993, Winter). Hispanic/Anglo American differences in attributions to paralinguistic behavior. *International Journal of Intercultural Relations, 17,* 19–40.

Alberti, Robert (Ed.). (1977). *Assertiveness: Innovations, applications, issues.* San Luis Obispo, CA: Impact.

Alessandra, Tony. (1986). How to listen effectively. *Speaking of Success* (videotape series). San Diego, CA: Levitz Sommer Productions.

Altman, Irwin, & Taylor, Dalmas. (1973). *Social penetration: The development of interpersonal relationships.* New York: Holt, Rinehart & Winston.

Andersen, Peter. (1991). Explaining intercultural differences in nonverbal communication. In Larry A. Samovar, & Richard E. Porter (Eds.), *Intercultural communication: A reader,* (6th ed., pp. 286–296). Belmont, CA: Wadsworth.

Anderson, Peter A., Hecht, Michael L., Hoobler, Gregory P., & Smallwood, Maya (2002). Nonverbal communication across cultures. In William B. Gundykunst, & Bella Mody (Eds.), *Handbook of international and intercultural communication* (2nd ed., pp. 89–106). Thousand Oaks, CA: Sage.

Andersen, Peter A., & Leibowitz, Ken. (1978). The development and nature of the construct touch avoidance. *Environmental Psychology and Nonverbal Behavior, 3,* 89–106.

Anderson, Claire J., & Fisher, Caroline. (1991, August). Male-female relationships in the workplace: Perceived motivations in office romance. *Sex Roles, 25,* 163–180.

Argyle, M., & Ingham, R. (1972). Gaze, mutual gaze and distance. *Semiotica, 1,* 32–49.

Argyle, Michael. (1988). *Bodily communication* (2nd ed.). New York: Methuen.

Argyle, Michael, & Henderson, Monika. (1985). *The anatomy of relationships: And the rules and skills needed to manage them successfully.* London: Heinemann.

Aronson, Elliot, Wilson, Timothy D., & Akert, Robin M. (1994). *Social psychology: The heart and the mind* (2nd ed.). New York: HarperCollins.

Asch, Solomon. (1946). Forming impressions of personality. *Journal of Abnormal and Social Psychology, 41,* 258–290.

Ashcraft, Mark H. (1998). *Fundamentals of cognition.* New York: Longman.

Atkin, C., Smith, S., Roberto, A., Fediuk, T., & Wagner, T. (2002). Correlates of verbally aggressive communication in adolescents. *Journal of Applied Communication Research, 3,* 251–269.

Aune, Krystyna-Strzyzewski, Buller, David B., & Aune, R. Kelly. (1996, September). Display rule development in romantic relationships: Emotion management and perceived appropriateness of emotions across relationship stages, *Human Communication Research, 23,* 115–145.

Aune, R. Kelly, & Kikuchi, Toshiyuki. (1993, September). Effects of language intensity similarity on perceptions of credibility, relational attributions, and persuasion. *Journal of Language and Social Psychology, 12,* 224–238.

Axtell, Roger. (1993). *Do's and taboos around the world* (3rd ed.). New York: Wiley.

Axtell, Roger E. (1990). *Do's and taboos of hosting international visitors.* New York: Wiley.

Ayres, Joe, & Hopf, Tim. (1993). *Coping with speech anxiety.* Norwood, NJ: Ablex.

Ayres, Joe, & Hopf, Tim. (1995, Fall). An assessment of the role of communication apprehension in communicating with the terminally ill. *Communication Research Reports, 12,* 227–234.

Bach, George R., & Wyden, Peter. (1968). *The intimacy enemy.* New York: Avon.

Bachman, David L., Wagner, Mark T., DePalma, Michael, Spangengberg, Karen B., Hendrix, Shirley, & Perlman, David J. (2000, October). Caregiver attitudes about patients told they have Alzheimer's disease after truth disclosure. *Journal of Clinical Geropsychology, 6,* 309–313.

Balswick, J. O., & Peck, C. (1971). The inexpressive male: A tragedy of American society? *The Family Coordinator, 20,* 363–368.

Barbato, Carole A., & Perse, Elizabeth M. (1992, August). Interpersonal communication motives and the life position of elders. *Communication Research, 19,* 516–531.

Barker, Larry, Edwards, Renee, Gaines, C., Gladney, K., & Holley, F. (1980). An investigation of proportional time spent in various communication activities by college students. *Journal of Applied Communication Research, 8,* 101–109.

Barker, Larry L, & Gaut, Deborah A. (1996). *Communication* (7th ed.). Boston: Allyn & Bacon.

Barna, LaRay M. (1985). Stumbling blocks in intercultural communication. In Larry A. Samovar, & Richard E. Porter (Eds.), *Intercultural Communication: A Reader* (4th ed., pp. 330–338). Belmont, CA: Wadsworth.

Barnlund, Dean C. (1970). A transactional model of communication. In J. Akin, A. Goldberg, G. Myers, & J. Stewart (Eds.), *Language behavior: A book of readings in communication.* The Hague: Mouton.

Barnlund, Dean. (1989). *Communicative styles of Japanese and Americans: Images and realities.* Belmont, CA: Wadsworth.

Barta, Patrick. (1999, December 16). Sex differences in the inferior parietal lobe. *Cerebral Cortex.* www.wired.com/news/technology/0,1282,33033,00.html.

Basso, K. H. (1972). To give up on words: Silence in Apache culture. In Pier Paolo Giglioli (Ed.), *Language and social context.* New York: Penguin.

Baxter, Leslie A. (1988). A dialectical perspective on communication strategies in relationship development. In Steve W. Duck (Ed.), *Handbook of Personal Relationships.* New York: Wiley.

Baxter, Leslie A. (1990, February). Dialectical contradictions in relationship development. *Journal of Social and Personal Relationships, 7,* 69–88.

Baxter, Leslie A., & Simon, Eric P. (1993, May). Relationship maintenance strategies and dialectical contradictions in personal relationships. *Journal of Social and Personal Relationships, 10,* 225–242.

Baxter, Leslie A., & Wilmot, W. W. (1984). "Secret tests": Social strategies for acquiring information about the state of the relationship. *Human Communication Research, 11*, 171–201.

Beach, Wayne A. (1990–1991). Avoiding ownership for alleged wrongdoings. *Research on Language and Social Interaction, 24*, 1–36.

Beatty, Michael J. (1988). Situational and predispositional correlates of public speaking anxiety. *Communication Education, 37*: 28–39.

Beck, A. T. (1988). *Love is never enough*. New York: Harper & Row.

Bedford, Victoria Hilkevitch. (1996). Relationships between adult siblings. In Ann Elisabeth Auhagen, & Maria von Salisch (Eds.), *The diversity of human relationships* (pp. 120–140). New York: Cambridge University Press.

Beebe, Steven A., Beebe, Susan J., Redmond, Vhash V., Geerick, Terri M., & Milstone, Carol (2000). *Interpersonal communication: Relating to others* (2nd Canadian ed.). Scarborough: Allyn & Bacon.

Beebe, Steven A., & Masterson, John T. (2000*). Communicating in small groups: Principles and practices* (6th ed.). New York: Longman.

Behzadi, Kavous G. (1994, September). Interpersonal conflict and emotions in an Iranian cultural practice: *Qahr and Ashti. Culture, Medicine, and Psychiatry, 18*, 321–359.

Beier, Ernst. (1974). How we send emotional messages. *Psychology Today, 8*, 53–56.

Bell, Robert A., & Buerkel-Rothfuss, N. L. (1990). S(he) loves me, s(he) loves me not: Predictors of relational information-seeking in courtship and beyond. *Communication Quarterly, 38*, 64–82.

Berg, John H., & Archer, Richard L. (1983). The disclosure-liking relationship. *Human Communication Research, 10*, 269–281.

Berger, Charles R., & Bradac, James J. (1982). *Language and social knowledge: Uncertainty in interpersonal relations*. London: Edward Arnold.

Berger, Charles R., & Calabrese, Richard J. (1975, Winter). Some explorations in initial interaction and beyond: Toward a theory of interpersonal communication. *Human Communication Research, 1*, 99–112.

Bernstein, W. M., Stephan, W. G., & Davis, M. H. (1979). Explaining attributions for achievement: A path analytic approach. *Journal of Personality and Social Psychology, 37*, 1810–1821.

Bibby, R. (1990). *Mosaic madness: The poverty and potential of life in Canada*. Toronto: Stoddart.

Bierhoff, Hans W., & Klein, Renate. (1991, March). Dimensionen der Liebe: Entwicklung einer Deutschsprachigen Skala zur Erfassung von Liebesstilen. *Zeitschrift für Differentielle und Diagnostische Psychologie, 12*, 53–71.

Birdwhistell, Ray L. (1970). *Kinesics and context: Essays on body motion communication*. New York: Ballantine Books.

Bishop, Jerry E. (1993, April 7). New research suggests that romance begins by falling nose over heels in love. *Wall Street Journal*, B1.

Blieszner, Rosemary, & Adams, Rebecca G. (1992). *Adult friendship*. Thousand Oaks, CA: Sage.

Blood, Robert O., Jr. (1973). Resolving family conflicts. In Fred E. Jandt (Ed.), *Conflict resolution through communication*. New York: Harper & Row.

Blumstein, Philip, & Schwartz, Pepper. (1983). *American couples: Money, work, sex*. New York: Morrow.

Bochner, Arthur. (1978). On taking ourselves seriously: An analysis of some persistent problems and promising directions in interpersonal research. *Human Communication Research, 4*, 179–191.

Bochner, Arthur. (1984). The functions of human communication in interpersonal bonding. In Carroll C. Arnold & John Waite Bowers, (Eds.), *Handbook of rhetorical and communication theory*. Boston: Allyn & Bacon.

Bochner, Arthur, & Kelly, Clifford. (1974). Interpersonal competence: Rationale, philosophy, and implementation of a conceptual framework. *Communication Education, 23*, 279–301.

Bochner, Arthur P., & Yerby, Janet. (1977). Factors affecting instruction in interpersonal competence. *Communication Education, 26*, 91–103.

Bochner, Stephen, & Hesketh, Beryl. (1994, June). Power distance, individualism/collectivism, and job-related attitudes in a culturally diverse work group. *Journal of Cross-Cultural Psychology, 25*, 233–257.

Bok, Sissela. (1978). *Lying: Moral choice in public and private life*. New York: Pantheon.

Bok, Sissela. (1983). *Secrets*. New York: Vintage Books.

Borden, George A. (1991). *Cultural orientation: An approach to understanding intercultural communication*. Englewood Cliffs, NJ: Prentice-Hall.

Bosmajian, Haig. (1974). *The language of oppression*. Washington, DC: Public Affairs Press.

Bourque, Nicole (2001). Eating your words: Communicating with food in the Ecuadorian Andes. In Joy Hendry, & C. W. Watson, *An anthropology of indirect communication*. New York: Routledge.

Bransford, John D., Sherwood, Robert D., & Sturdevant, Tom. (1987). Teaching thinking and problem solving. In Joan Boykoff Baron & Robert J. Sternberg (Eds.), *Teaching thinking skills: Theory and practice*, pp. 162–181. New York: W. H. Freeman.

Bravo, Ellen, & Cassedy, Ellen. (1992). *The 9 to 5 guide to combating sexual harassment*. New York: Wiley.

Bresnahan, Mary I., & Cai, Deborah H. (1996, March/April). Gender and aggression in the recognition of interruption. *Discourse Processes, 21*, 171–189.

Bridges, Carl R. (1996, July). The characteristics of career achievement perceived by African American college administrators. *Journal of Black Studies, 26*, 748–767.

Briton, Nancy J., & Hall, Judith A. (1995, January). Beliefs about female and male nonverbal communication. *Sex Roles, 32*, 79–90.

Brody, Jane E. (1991, April 28). How to foster self-esteem. *New York Times Magazine*, 26–27.

Brody, Jane E. (1994, March 21). Notions of beauty transcend culture, new study suggests. *The New York Times*, p. A14.

Brody, Leslie R. (1985, June). Gender differences in emotional development: A review of theories and research. *Journal of Personality, 53*, 102–149.

Brown, A. (2003). Developing a productive, respectful manager–employee relationship. *Canadian HR Reporter, 7*, 10.

Brown, Penelope, & Levinson, S. C. (1987). *Politeness: Some universals of language usage*. Cambridge, UK: Cambridge University Press.

Brownell, Judi. (1987). Listening: The toughest management skill. *Cornell Hotel and Restaurant Administration Quarterly, 27*, 64–71.

Bruneau, Tom. (1985). The time dimension in intercultural communication. In Larry A. Samovar & Richard E. Porter (Eds.), *Intercultural communication: A reader* (4th ed., pp. 280–289). Belmont, CA: Wadsworth.

Bruneau, Tom. (1990). Chronemics: The study of time in human interaction. In Joseph A. DeVito, & Michael L. Hecht (Eds.), *The nonverbal communication reader* (pp. 301–311). Prospect Heights, IL: Waveland Press.

Buck, Ross, & VanLear, C. Arthur (2002). Verbal and nonverbal communication: Distinguishing symbolic, spontaneous and pseudo-spontaneous nonverbal behavior. *Journal of Communication, 52*, 522–541.

Bull, R., & Ramsey, N. (1988). *The social psychology of facial appearance*. New York: Springer.

Buller, David B., & Aune, R. Kelly. (1992, Winter). The effects of speech rate similarity on compliance: Application of communication accommodation theory. *Western Journal of Communication, 56*, 37–53.

Buller, David B., LePoire, Beth A., Aune, Kelly, & Eloy, Sylvie. (1992, December). Social perceptions as mediators of the effect of speech rate similarity on compliance. *Human communication research, 19*, 286–311.

Burgoon, Judee K., Buller, David B., & Woodall, W. Gill. (1995). *Nonverbal communication: The unspoken dialogue* (2nd ed.). New York: McGraw-Hill.

Burleson, Brant B., & Mortenson, Steven R. (2003). Explaining cultural differences in evaluation of emotional support behavior: Explaining the mediating influence of value system and interaction goals. *Communication Research, 30*, 113–146.

Byers, E. Sandra, & Demmons, Stephanie. (1999, May). Sexual satisfaction and sexual self-disclosure within dating relationships. *Journal of Sex Research, 36*, 180–189.

Canary, D. J., & Hause, K. (1993). Is there any reason to research sex differences in communication? *Communication Quarterly, 41*, 129–144.

Canary, Daniel, Cupach, William R., & Messman, Susan J. (1995). *Relationship conflict*. Thousand Oaks, CA: Sage.

Cappella, Joseph N. (1993, March–June). The facial feedback hypothesis in human interaction: Review and speculation. *Journal of Language and Social Psychology, 12*, 13–29.

Carli, Linda L. (1999, Spring). Gender, interpersonal power, and social influence. *Journal of Social Issues, 55*, 81–99.

Carroll, D. W. (1994). *Psychology of language*. (2nd ed.). Pacific Grove, CA: Brooks/Cole.

Cate, R., Henton, J., Koval, J., Christopher, R., & Lloyd, S. (1982). Premarital abuse: A social psychological perspective. *Journal of Family Issues, 3*, 79–90.

Challenges facing workers in the future. (August, 1999). *Human Relations Focus, 76*, 6.

Chang, Hui-Ching, & Holt, G. Richard. (1996, Winter). The changing Chinese interpersonal world: Popular themes in interpersonal communication books in modern Taiwan. *Communication Quarterly, 44*, 85–106.

Chen, Guo-Ming. (1992). Differences in self-disclosure patterns among Americans versus Chinese: A comparative study. Paper presented at the annual meeting of the Eastern Communication Association, Portland, ME.

Chen, Ling. (1993, Summer). Chinese and North Americans: An epistemological exploration of intercultural communication. *Howard Journal of Communications, 4*, 342–357.

Cherulnik, Paul D. (1979, August). Sex differences in the expression of emotion in a structured social encounter. *Sex Roles, 5*, 413–424.

Chin, Peggy Evan, & Mcconnel, Allen (2003). Do racial minorities respond in the same way to mainstream beauty standards? Social comparison processes in Asian, black and white women. *Self and Identity, 2*, 153–168.

Christie, Richard. (1970). Scale construction. In R. Christie, & F. L. Geis (Eds.), *Studies in Machiavellianism* (pp. 35–52). New York: Academic Press.

Clement, Donald A., & Frandsen, Kenneth D. (1976). On conceptual and empirical treatments of feedback in human communication. *Communication Monographs, 43*, 11–28.

Coates, J., & Cameron, D. (1989). *Women, men, and language: Studies in language and linguistics*. London: Longman.

Coats, Erik J., & Feldman, Robert S. (1996, October). Gender differences in nonverbal correlates of social status. *Personality and Social Psychology Bulletin, 22*, 1014–1022.

Cohen, Joyce. (2001, January 18). On the Internet, love really is blind. *The New York Times*, pp. G1, G9.

Collier, Mary Jane. (1991). Conflict competence within African, Mexican, and Anglo American friendships. In Stella Ting-Toomey, & Felipe Korzenny (Eds.), *Cross-cultural interpersonal communication* (pp. 132–154). Newbury Park, CA: Sage.

Collins, Nancy L., & Miller, Lynn Carol. (1994, November). Self-disclosure and liking: A meta-analytic review. *Psychological Bulletin, 116*, 457–475.

Conference Board of Canada (2003). www.conferenceboard.ca.

Cooley, Charles Horton. (1922). *Human nature and the social order* (rev. ed.). New York: Scribners.

Coon, Christine A., & Schwanenflugel, Paula J. (1996, July/August). Evaluation of interruption behavior by naive encoders. *Discourse Processes, 22*, 1–24.

Crocker, Jennifer (2002). The contingencies of self-worth: Implications for self-regulation and psychological vulnerability. *Self and Identity, 1*, 143–150.

D'Augelli, Anthony R. (1992, September). Lesbian and gay male undergraduates' experiences of harassment and fear on campus. *Journal of Interpersonal Violence, 7*, 383–395.

Davis, Murray S. (1973). *Intimate relations*. New York: Free Press.

Davis, Ossie. (1973). The English language is my enemy. In Joseph A. DeVito (Ed.), *Language: Concepts and processes* (pp. 164–170). Englewood Cliffs, NJ: Prentice-Hall.

Deal, James E., & Wampler, Karen Smith. (1986). Dating violence: The primacy of previous experience. *Journal of Social and Personal Relationships, 3*, 457–471.

Deaux, K., & M. LaFrance. (1998). Gender. In D. Gilbert, S. Fiske, & G. Lindzey (Eds.), *The Handbook of Social Psychology, Vol. 1*. (4th ed., pp. 788–828). New York: Freeman.

de Bono, Edward. (1987). *The six thinking hats*. New York: Penguin.

DeCecco, John. (1988). Obligation versus aspiration. In John DeCecco (Ed.), *Gay relationships*. New York: Harrington Park Press.

DePaulo, Bella M. (1992). Nonverbal behavior and self-presentation. *Psychological Bulletin, 111*, 203–212.

Derlega, Valerian J., Winstead, Barbara A., Wong, Paul T. P., & Greenspan, Michael. (1987). Self-disclosure and relationship development: An attributional analysis. In Michael E. Roloff & Gerald R. Miller (Eds.), *Interpersonal processes: New directions in communication research* (pp. 172–187). Newbury Park, CA: Sage.

Derlega, V. J., Winstead, B. A., Wong, P. T. P., & Hunter, S. (1985). Gender effects in an initial encounter: A case where men exceed women in disclosure. *Journal of Social and Personal Relationships, 2*, 25–44.

Derwig, Tracey, & Munro, Murray J. (2001). What speaking rates do non-native speakers prefer? *Applied Linguistics, 22*, 324–334.

DeTurck, Mark A. (1987). When communication fails: Physical aggression as a compliance-gaining strategy. *Communication Monographs, 54*, 106–112.

DeVito, Joseph A. (1996). *Brainstorms: How to think more creatively about communication (or about anything else)*. New York: Longman.

DeVito, Joseph A., & Hecht, Michael L. (Eds.). (1990). *The nonverbal communication reader*. Prospect Heights, IL: Waveland Press.

Dewey, John. (1910). *How we think*. Boston: Heath.

Dickinson, A. (1999, November 6). Assertiveness creates healthy mentality. *Chatham Daily News*, p. 11.

Dindia, Kathryn (2000). Sex differences in self-disclosure and self-disclosure and liking: Three meta-analyses reviewed. In Sandra Petronio (Ed.), *Balancing the secrets of private disclosures* (pp. 21–36). Mahwah, NJ: Lawrence Erlbaum Associates.

Dindia, Kathryn, & Fitzpatrick, Mary Anne. (1985). Marital communication: Three approaches compared. In Steve Duck & Daniel Perlman (Eds.), *Understanding personal relationships: An interdisciplinary approach* (pp. 137–158). Thousand Oaks, CA: Sage.

Dion, K., Berscheid, E., & Walster, E. (1972). What is beautiful is good. *Journal of Personality and Social Psychology, 24*, 285–290.

Dion, Karen K., & Dion, Kenneth L. (1993a, Fall). Individualistic and collectivist perspectives on gender and the cultural context of love and intimacy. *Journal of Social Issues, 49*, 53–69.

Dion, Kenneth L., & Dion, Karen K. (1993b, December). Gender and ethnocultural comparisons in styles of love. *Psychology of Women Quarterly, 17,* 464–473.

Dittman, David A. (1997, December). Reexamining curriculum. *The Cornell Hotel and Restaurant Administration Quarterly, 38,* 3.

Dolgin, Kim Gale, & Lindsay, Kristen Renee. (1999, September). Disclosure between college students and their siblings. *Journal of Family Psychology, 13,* 393–400.

Dolgin, Kim G., Meyer, Leslie, & Schwartz, Janet. (1991, September). Effects of gender, target's gender, topic, and self-esteem on disclosure to best and middling friends. *Sex Roles, 25,* 311–329.

Donohue, William A., & Kolt, Robert. (1992). *Managing interpersonal conflict.* Thousand Oaks, CA: Sage.

Drass, Kriss A. (1986, December). The effect of gender identity on conversation. *Social Psychology Quarterly, 49,* 294–301.

Dresser, Norine. (1996). *Multicultural manners: New rules of etiquette for a changing society.* New York: Wiley.

Dreyfuss, Henry. (1971). *Symbol sourcebook.* New York: McGraw-Hill.

Duncan, S. D., Jr. (1972). Some signals and rules for taking speaking turns in conversation. *Journal of Personality and Social Psychology, 23,* 283–292.

Eden, Dov. (1992, Winter). Leadership and expectations: Pygmalion effects and other self-fulfilling prophecies in organizations. *Leadership Quarterly, 3,* 271–305.

Eder, D., & Enke, J. L. (1991). The structure of gossip: Opportunities and constraints on collective expression among adolescents. *American Sociological Review, 56,* 494–508.

Edwards, K., & Smith, E. (1996). A disconfirmation bias in the evaluation of arguments. *Journal of Personality and Social Psychology, 71,* 5–24.

Ehrenhaus, Peter. (1988, March). Silence and symbolic expression. *Communication Monographs, 55,* 41–57.

Ehrlich, Larry G. (2000). *Fatal words and friendly faces: Interpersonal communication in the twenty-first century.* New York: University Press of America Inc.

Ekman, Paul. (1985a). Communication through nonverbal behavior: A source of information about an interpersonal relationship. In S. S. Tomkins & C. E. Izard (Eds.), *Affect, cognition and personality.* New York: Springer.

Ekman, Paul. (1985b). *Telling lies: Clues to deceit in the marketplace, politics, and marriage.* New York: Norton.

Ekman, Paul, & Friesen, Wallace V. (1969). The repertoire of nonverbal behavior: Categories, origins, usage, and coding. *Semiotica, 1,* 49–98.

Ekman, Paul, Friesen, Wallace V., & Ellsworth, Phoebe. (1972). *Emotion in the human face: Guidelines for research and an integration of findings.* New York: Pergamon Press.

Ellis, Albert. (1988). *How to stubbornly refuse to make yourself miserable about anything, yes, anything.* Secaucus, NJ: Lyle Stuart.

Ellis, Albert, & Harper, Robert A. (1975). *A new guide to rational living.* Hollywood, CA: Wilshire Books.

Elmes, Michael B., & Gemmill, Gary. (1990, February). The psychodynamics of mindlessness and dissent in small groups. *Small Group Research, 21,* 28–44.

Emanuel, E. J., Fairclough, D. L, Slutsman, J., & Emanuel, L. L. (2000, March 21). Understanding economic and other burdens of terminal illness: The experience of patients and their caregivers. *Annals of Internal Medicine, 132,* 451–459.

Ennis, Robert H. (1987). A taxonomy of critical thinking dispositions and abilities. In Joan Boykoff Baron, & Robert J. Sternberg (Eds.), *Teaching thinking skills: Theory and practice* (pp. 9–26). New York: W. H. Freeman.

Epstein, N., Pretzer, J. L., & Fleming, B. (1987). The role of cognitive appraisal in self-reports of marital communication. *Behavior Therapy, 18,* 51–69.

Eriksen, John, & Lindsay, Jo. (1999). Unmarried cohabitation and family policy: Norway and Australia compared. *Comparative Social Research, 18,* 79–103.

Exline, R. V., Ellyson, S. L., & Long, B. (1975). Visual behavior as an aspect of power role relationships. In P. Pliner, L. Krames, & T. Alloway (Eds.), *Nonverbal communication of aggression.* New York: Plenum.

Feldstein, Stanley, Dohm, Faith-Anne, & Crown, Cynthia L. (2001). Gender and speech rate in the perception of competence and social attractiveness. *Journal of Social Psychology, 141,* 785–806.

Festinger, Leon. (1954). A theory of social comparison processes. *Human Relationships, 7,* 117–140.

Field, R. H. G. (1989, March). The self-fulfilling prophecy leader: Achieving the Metharme effect. *Journal of Management Studies, 26,* 151–175.

Fischer, Agneta H. (1993). Sex differences in emotionality: fact or stereotype? *Feminism and Psychology, 3,* 303–318.

Folger, Joseph P., Poole, Marshall Scott, & Stutman, Randall K. (1997). *Working through conflict: A communication perspective* (3rd ed.). Boston: Allyn & Bacon.

Fraser, Bruce. (1990, April). Perspectives on politeness. *Journal of Pragmatics, 14,* 219–236.

Fratiglioni, L., Wang, H. X., Ericsson, K., Maytan, M., & Winblad, B. (2000, April 15). Influence of social network on occurrence of dementia: A community-based longitudinal study. *Lancet, 355,* 1315–1319.

French, J. R. P., Jr., & Raven, B. (1968). The bases of social power. In Dorwin Cartwright & Alvin Zander (Eds.), *Group dynamics: Research and theory,* (3rd ed., pp. 259–269). New York: Harper & Row.

Friedman, Joel, Boumil, Marcia Mobilia, & Taylor, Barbara Ewert. (1992). *Sexual harassment.* Deerfield Beach, FL: Health Communications.

Fritz, J. (1997). Men's and women's organizational peer relationships: A comparison. *The Journal of Business Communication, 1,* 27–47.

Frost, Catherine (2003). How Prometheus is bound: Applying the Innis Method of communication to the internet. *Canadian Journal of Communication, 28,* 9–24.

Fuller, Linda K. (1995). *Media-mediated relationships: Straight and gay, mainstream and alternative perspectives.* New York: Harrington Park Press.

Furlow, F. Bryant. (1996, March/April). The smell of love. *Psychology Today, 29,* 38–45.

Furnham, Adrian, & Bochner, Stephen. (1986). *Culture shock: Psychological reactions to unfamiliar environments.* New York: Methuen.

Gable, Myron, Hollon, Charles, & Dangello, Frank. (1992). Managerial structuring of work as a moderator of the Machiavellianism and job performance relationship. *Journal of Psychology, 126* (May), 317–325.

Galvin, Kathleen, & Brommel, Bernard J. (2000). *Family communication: Cohesion and change* (5th ed.). Boston: Allyn & Bacon.

Gelles, R., & Cornell, C. (1985). *Intimate violence in families.* Newbury Park, CA: Sage.

Giles, Howard, Mulac, Anthony, Bradac, James J., & Johnson, Patricia. (1987). Speech accommodation theory: The first decade and beyond. In Margaret L. McLaughlin (Ed.), *Communication yearbook 10* (pp. 13–48). Thousand Oaks, CA: Sage.

Glucksberg, Sam, & Danks, Joseph H. (1975). *Experimental psycholinguistics: An introduction.* Hillsdale, NJ: Erlbaum.

Goffman, Erving. (1967). *Interaction ritual: Essays on face-to-face behavior.* New York: Pantheon.

Goldsmith, M. (2003). Feed forward. *Executive Excellence, 2,* 15.

Goleman, Daniel. (1995a). *Emotional intelligence.* New York: Bantam.

Goleman, Daniel. (1995b, February 14). For man and beast, language of love shares many traits. *The New York Times*, pp. C1, C9.

Gonzalez, Alexander, & Zimbardo, Philip G. (1985). Time in perspective. *Psychology Today, 19*, 20–26. Reprinted in DeVito & Hecht, (1990).

Goode, Erica. (2000, August 8). How culture molds habits of thought. *The New York Times*, pp. F1, F8.

Goodwin, Robin, & Lee, Iona. (1994, September). Taboo topics among Chinese and English friends: A cross-cultural comparison. *Journal of Cross-Cultural Psychology, 25*, 325–338.

Gordon, Thomas. (1975). *P.E.T.: Parent effectiveness training*. New York: New American Library.

Gottman, John M., & Carrere, S. (1994). Why can't men and women get along? Developmental roots and marital inequities. In D. J. Canary & Laura Stafford (Eds.), *Communication and relational maintenance* (pp. 203–229). San Diego, CA: Academic Press.

Gould, Stephen Jay. (1995, June 7). No more "wretched refuse." *The New York Times*, p. A27.

Government of Canada (n.d.). The atlas of Canada: Families with children living at home. Retrieved September 21, 2003, from http://atlas.gc.ca/site/english/maps/peopleandsociety.

Graham, E. E. (1994). Interpersonal communication motives scale. In R. B. Rubin, P. Palmgreen, & H. E. Sypher (Eds.), *Communication research measures: A sourcebook* (pp. 211–216). New York: Guilford.

Graham, E. E., Barbato, C. A., & Perse, E. M. (1993). The interpersonal communication motives model. *Communication Quarterly, 41*, 172–186.

Graham, Jean Ann, & Argyle, Michael. (1975, December). The effects of different patterns of gaze, combined with different facial expressions, on impression formation. *Journal of Movement Studies, 1*, 178–182.

Graham, Jean Ann, Bitti, Pio Ricci, & Argyle, Michael. (1975, June). A cross-cultural study of the communication of emotion by facial and gestural cues. *Journal of Human Movement Studies, 1*, 68–77.

Grandey, Alicia A. (2000, January). Emotion regulation in the workplace: A new way to conceptualize emotional labor. *Journal of Occupational Health and Psychology, 5*, 95–110.

Gray, S., & Heatherington, L. (2003). The importance of social context in the facilitation of emotional expression in men. *Journal of Social and Clinical Psychology, 3*, 294.

Greif, Esther Blank. (1980). Sex differences in parent–child conversations. *Women's Studies International Quarterly, 3*, 253–258.

Grice, H. P. (1975). Logic and conversation. In P. Cole, & J. L. Morgan (Eds.), *Syntax and semantics*: Vol. 3. Speech acts (pp. 41–58). New York: Seminar Press.

Griffin, Em, & Sparks, Glenn G. (1990). Friends forever: A longitudinal exploration of intimacy in same-sex friends and platonic pairs. *Journal of Social and Personal Relationships, 7*, 29–46.

Gross, Ronald. (1991). *Peak learning*. Los Angeles: Jeremy P. Tarcher.

Gross, T., Turner, E., & Cederholm, L. (1987, June). Building teams for global operation. *Management Review*, 32–36.

Gu, Yueguo. (1990, April). Polite phenomena in modern Chinese. *Journal of Pragmatics, 14*, 237–257.

Gudykunst, W., & Nishida, T. (1984). Individual and cultural influence on uncertainty reduction. *Communication Monographs, 51*, 23–36.

Gudykunst, W., Yang, S., & Nishida, T. (1985). A cross-cultural test of uncertainty reduction theory: Comparisons of acquaintance, friend, and dating relationships in Japan, Korea, and the United States. *Human Communication Research, 11*, 407–454.

Gudykunst, W. B. (2002). Intercultural communication theories. In William B. Gudykunst & Bella Mody (Eds.), *International and intercultural communication* (2nd ed., pp. 183–206).

Gudykunst, W. B. (1994). *Bridging differences: Effective intergroup communication* (2nd ed.). Thousand Oaks, CA: Sage.

Gudykunst, W. B. (Ed.). (1983). *Intercultural communication theory: Current perspectives*. Newbury Park, CA: Sage.

Haar, Birgit Friederike, & Krahe, Barbara. (1999, November). Strategies for resolving interpersonal conflicts in adolescence: A German-Indonesian comparison. *Journal of Cross Cultural Psychology, 30*, 667–683.

Haddad, T. & Lam, L. (1988). Canadian families: Men's involvement in family work: A case study of immigrant men in Toronto. *International Journal of Comparative Sociology, (XXIX) 3–4*, 269–281.

Haddock, P. (2003). Communicating personal power. *The American Salesman, 6*, 30.

Hall, Edward T. (1959) *The silent language*. Garden City, NY: Doubleday.

Hall, Edward T. (1966). *The hidden dimension*. Garden City, NY: Doubleday.

Hall, Edward T. (1976). *Beyond culture*. Garden City, NY: Doubleday.

Hall, Edward T. (1983). *The dance of life: The other dimension of time*. New York: Doubleday.

Hall, Edward T., & Hall, Mildred Reed. (1971, June). The sounds of silence. *Playboy*, pp. 139–140, 204, 206.

Hall, Edward T., & Hall, Mildred Reed. (1987). *Hidden differences: Doing business with the Japanese*. New York: Doubleday.

Hall, Joan Kelly. (1993). Tengo una bomba: The paralinguistic and linguistic conventions of the oral practice chismeando. *Research on Language and Social Interaction, 26*, 55–83.

Hall, Judith A. (1984). *Nonverbal sex differences*. Baltimore: Johns Hopkins University Press.

Hall, Judith A. (1996, Spring). Touch, status, and gender at professional meetings. *Journal of Nonverbal Behavior, 20*, 23–44.

Harris, Judy. (1995, March). Educational telecomputing projects: Interpersonal exchanges. *Computing Teacher, 22*, 60–64.

Harris, Thomas E. (2002). *Applied organizational communication: Principles and pragmatics for future practice*. Mahwah, NJ: Lawrence Erlbaum Associates.

Hart, Fiona. (1990, September/December). The construction of masculinity in men's friendships: Misogyny, heterosexism and homophobia. *Resources for Feminist Research, 19*, 60–67.

Hatfield, Elaine, & Rapson, Richard L. (1992). Similarity and attraction in close relationships. *Communication Monographs, 59*, 209–212.

Hatfield, Elaine, & Rapson, Richard L. (1996). *Love and sex: Cross-cultural perspectives*. Boston: Allyn & Bacon.

Havlena, William J., Holbrook, Morris B., & Lehmann, Donald R. (1989, Summer). Assessing the validity of emotional typologies. *Psychology and Marketing, 6*, 97–112.

Hayakawa, S. I., & Hayakawa, A. R. (1989) *Language in thought and action* (5th ed.). New York: Harcourt Brace Jovanovich.

Hays, Robert B. (1989). The day-to-day functioning of close versus casual friendships. *Journal of Social and Personal Relationships, 6*, 21–37.

Heasley, John B., Babbitt, Charles E., & Burbach, Harold J. (1995, Fall). Gender differences in college students' perceptions of "fighting words." *Sociological Viewpoints, 11*, 30–40.

Hecht, Michael. (1978a). The conceptualization and measurement of interpersonal communication satisfaction. *Human Communication Research, 4*, 253–264.

Hecht, Michael. (1978b). Toward a conceptualization of communication satisfaction. *Quarterly Journal of Speech, 64*, 47–62.

Hecht, Michael L., Collier, Mary Jane, & Ribeau, Sidney. (1993). *African American communication: Ethnic identity and cultural interpretation*. Thousand Oaks, CA: Sage.

Hendrick, Clyde, & Hendrick, Susan. (1990). A relationship-specific version of the love attitudes scale. In J. W. Heulip (Ed.), *Handbook of replication research in the behavioral and social sciences* [special issue]. *Journal of Social Behavior and Personality, 5*, 239–254.

Hendrick, Clyde, Hendrick, Susan, Foote, Franklin H., & Slapion-Foote, Michelle J. (1984). Do men and women love differently? *Journal of Social and Personal Relationships, 1,* 177–195.

Hess, Eckhard H. (1975). *The tell-tale eye.* New York: Van Nostrand Reinhold.

Hess, Ursula, Kappas, Arvid, McHugo, Gregory J., Lanzetta, John T., et al. (1992, May). The facilitative effect of facial expression on the self-generation of emotion. *International Journal of Psychophysiology, 12,* 251–265.

Hewitt, John, & Stokes, Randall. (1975). Disclaimers. *American Sociological Review, 40,* 1–11.

Hickson, Mark L., & Stacks, Don W. (1993). *NVC: Nonverbal communication: Studies and applications* (3rd ed.). Dubuque, IA: William C. Brown.

Hofstede, Geert. (1997). *Cultures and organizations: Software of the mind.* New York: McGraw-Hill.

Hoft, Nancy L. (1995). *International technical communication: How to export information about high technology.* New York: Wiley.

Hogg, Michael (2002). *Handbook of social psychology.* London: Sage.

Holland, Carol A., & Fletcher, Janet (2000). The effect of speech rate at natural borders on older adults' memory for auditorily presented stories. *Australian Journal of Psychology, 52,* 149–154.

Holmes, Janet. (1986). Compliments and compliment responses in New Zealand English. *Anthropological Linguistic, 28,* 485–508.

Holmes, Janet. (1995). *Women, men and politeness.* New York: Longman.

Horton, Robert S. (2003). Similarity and attractiveness in social perception: Differentiating between biases for the self and the beautiful. *Self and Identity, 2,* 137–153.

Hurston, C., & Wilson, G. (1978). Body talk—The unspoken language. *Management World, 7,* 14.

Ikemi, Akira, & Kubota, Shinya. (1996, Winter). Humanistic psychology in Japanese corporations: Listening and the small steps of change. *Journal of Humanistic Psychology, 36,* 104–121.

Imhof, Margaret (2002). The eye of the beholder: Children's perception of good and poor listening behavior. *International Journal of Listening, 16,* 40–57.

Infante, Dominic A. (1988). *Arguing constructively.* Prospect Heights, IL: Waveland Press.

Infante, Dominic A., & Rancer, Andrew S. (1982). A conceptualization and measure of argumentativeness. *Journal of Personality Assessment, 46,* 72–80.

Infante, Dominic A., Rancer, Andrew S., & Jordan, Felecia F. (1996, March). Affirming and nonaffirming style, dyad sex, and the perception of argumentation and verbal aggression in an interpersonal dispute. *Human Communication Research, 22,* 315–334.

Infante, Dominic A., Sabourin, Teresa Chandler, Rudd, Jill E., & Shannon, Elizabeth A. (1990, Fall). Verbal aggression in violent and nonviolent marital disputes. *Communication Quarterly, 38,* 361–371.

Infante, Dominic A., & Wigley, C. J. (1986). Verbal aggressiveness: An interpersonal model and measure. *Communication Monographs, 53,* 61–69.

Insel, Paul M., & Jacobson, Lenore F. (Eds.) (1975). *What do you expect? An inquiry into self-fulfilling prophecies.* Menlo Park, CA: Cummings.

Jackson, Linda A., & Ervin, Kelly S. (1992, August). Height stereotypes of women and men: The liabilities of shortness for both sexes. *Journal of Social Psychology, 132,* 433–445.

Jacobsen, Thomas (2003). Kandinsky's questionnaire revisited: Fundamental correspondence of basic colors and forms? *Perceptual & Motor Skills, 95,* 903–913.

Jaksa, James A., & Pritchard, Michael S. (1994). *Communication ethics: Methods of analysis* (2nd ed.). Belmont, CA: Wadsworth.

Jandt, Fred E. (2000). *Intercultural communication* (3rd ed.). Thousand Oaks, CA: Sage.

Janusik, Laura (2002). Teaching listening: What do we do? What should we do? *International Journal of Listening, 16,* 5–40.

Jaworski, Adam. (1993). *The power of silence: Social and pragmatic perspectives.* Thousand Oaks, CA: Sage.

Johannesen, Richard L. (1974, Winter). The functions of silence: A plea for communication research. *Western Speech, 38,* 25–35.

Johansson, Warren, & Percy, William A. (1994). *Outing: Shattering the conspiracy of silence.* New York: Harrington Park Press.

Joiner, Tomas E. (1994). Contagious depression: Existence, specificity to depressed symptoms, and the role of reassurance seeking. *Journal of Personality and Social Psychology, 67,* 287–296.

Jones, Edward E., Farina, Amerigo, Hastorf, Albert H., Markus, Hazel, Miller, Dale T., & Scott, Robert A. (1984). *Social stigma: The psychology of marked relationships.* New York: W. H. Freeman.

Jones, Stanley, & Yarbrough, A. Elaine. (1985). A naturalistic study of the meanings of touch. *Communication Monographs, 52,* 19–56. (A version of this paper appears in DeVito & Hecht, 1990.)

Jones, Stanley E. (1999). Contact codes: Proxemics and hepatics. In Laura K. Guerrero, & Joseph A. DeVito (Eds.), *The nonverbal communication reader: Classic and contemporary readings* (2nd ed., pp. 175–123).

Jourard, Sidney M. (1968). *Disclosing man to himself.* New York: Van Nostrand Reinhold.

Jourard, Sidney M. (1971). *Self-disclosure.* New York: Wiley.

Kagan, Jerome (2002). *Surprise, uncertainty and mental structures.* Cambridge, Mass.: Harvard University Press.

Kanner, Bernice. (1989, April 3). Color schemes. *New York,* pp. 22–23.

Kaya, Naz, & Weber, Margaret J. (2003). Territorial behavior in residence halls: A cross-culture study. *Environment & Behavior, 35,* 400–414.

Keenan, Elinor Ochs. (1976, April). The universality of conversational postulates. *Language in Society, 5,* 67–80.

Kennedy, C. W., & Camden, C. T. (1988). A new look at interruptions. *Western Journal of Speech Communication, 47,* 45–58.

Keyes, Ralph. (1980). *The height of your life.* New York: Warner Books.

Kiesler, Sara, & Sproull, Lee. (1992, June). Group decision making and communication technology. [Special issue: Group Decision Making], *Organizational Behavior and Human Decision Processes, 52,* 96–123.

Kim, Heejung S., & Markus, Hazel Rose (2002). Freedom of speech and freedom of silence: An analysis of talking as a cultural practice. In Richard A. Shwede, & Martha Minow (Eds.), *Engaging cultural differences: The multicultural challenge in liberal democracies* (pp. 432–452). New York: Sage.

Kim, Young Yun. (1988). Communication and acculturation. In Larry A. Samovar, & Richard E. Porter (Eds.), *Intercultural communication: A reader* (5th ed., pp. 344–354). Belmont, CA: Wadsworth.

Kim, Young Yun. (1991). Intercultural communication competence. In Stella Ting-Toomey, & Felipe Korzenny (Eds.), *Cross-cultural interpersonal communication* (pp. 259–275). Newbury Park, CA: Sage.

King, Robert, & DiMichael, Eleanor. (1992). *Voice and diction.* Prospect Heights, IL: Waveland Press.

Kleinfield, N. R. (1992, October 25). The smell of money. *The New York Times,* pp. C1, C8.

Kleinke, Chris L. (1986). *Meeting and understanding people.* New York: W. H. Freeman.

Klineberg, O., & Hull, W. F. (1979). *At a foreign university: An international study of adaptation and coping.* New York: Praeger.

Knapp, Mark L., & Hall, Judith. (1996). *Nonverbal behavior in human interaction.* (3rd ed.). New York: Holt, Rinehart, & Winston.

Knapp, Mark, Hart, Roderick P., Friedrich, Gustav W., & Shulman, Gary M. (1973). The rhetoric of goodbye: Verbal and nonverbal correlates of human leave-taking. *Speech Monographs, 40,* 182–198.

Knapp, Mark L., & Vangelisti, Anita. (2000). *Interpersonal communication and human relationships* (4th ed.). Boston: Allyn & Bacon.

Knobloch, Sylvia, Hasall, Matthias, Zillman, Dolf, & Callison, Coy (2003). Imagery effects on the selective reading of internet magazines. *Communication Research, 30,* 3–29.

Koberg, Don, & Bagnall, Jim. (1976a). *The universal traveler.* Los Altos, CA: William Kaufmann.

Koberg, Don, & Bagnall, Jim. (1976b). *Values tech: A portable school for discovering and developing decision-making skills for self-enhancing potentials.* Los Altos, CA: William Kaufmann.

Kochman, Thomas. (1981). *Black and white: Styles in conflict.* Chicago: University of Chicago Press.

Komarovsky, M. (1964). *Blue-collar marriage.* New York: Random House.

Korda, M. (1975). *Power! How to get it, how to use it.* New York: Ballantine.

Korzybski, A. (1933). *Science and sanity.* Lakeville, CT: The International Non-Aristotelian Library.

Kposow, Augustine J. (2000, April). Marital status and suicide in the National Longitudinal Mortality Study. *Journal of Epidemiology and Community Health, 54,* 254–261.

Kramarae, Cheris. (1974a). Folklinguistics. *Psychology Today, 8,* 82–85.

Kramarae, Cheris. (1974b). Stereotypes of women's speech: The word from cartoons. *Journal of Popular Culture 8,* 624–630.

Kramarae, Cheris. (1977). Perceptions of female and male speech. *Language and speech, 20,* 151–161.

Kramarae, Cheris. (1981). *Women and men speaking.* Rowley, MA: Newbury House.

Krivonos, Paul D., & Knapp, Mark L. (1975). Initiating communication: What do you say when you say hello? *Central States Speech Journal, 26,* 115–125.

Kuhn, D., Weinstock, M., & Flaton, R. (1994). How well do jurors reason? Competence dimensions of individual variation in a juror reasoning task. *Psychological Science, 5,* 289–296.

Kurdek, Lawrence A. (1994, November). Areas of conflict for gay, lesbian, and heterosexual couples: What couples argue about influences relationship satisfaction. *Journal of Marriage and the Family, 56,* 923–934.

Labott, Susan M., Martin, Randall B., Eason, Patricia S., & Berkey, Elayne Y. (1991, September/November). Social reactions to the expression of emotion. *Cognition and Emotion, 5,* 397–417.

LaFrance, Marie (2002). Smile boycotts and other body politics. *Feminism and Psychology, 12,* 319–323.

Laing, Milli. (1993, Spring). Gossip: Does it play a role in the socialization of nurses. *Journal of Nursing Scholarship, 25,* 37–43.

Laing, Ronald D., Phillipson, H., & Lee, A. Russell. (1966). *Interpersonal perception.* New York: Springer.

Langer, Ellen J. (1989). *Mindfulness.* Reading, MA: Addison-Wesley.

Lanzetta, J. T., Cartwright-Smith, J., & Kleck, R. E. (1976). Effects of nonverbal dissimulations on emotional experience and autonomic arousal. *Journal of Personality and Social Psychology, 33,* 354–370.

Larsen, Randy J., Kasimatis, Margaret, & Frey, Kurt. (1992, September). Facilitating the furrowed brow: An unobtrusive test of the facial feedback hypothesis applied to unpleasant affect. *Cognition and Emotion, 6,* 321–338.

Larson, Charles U. (1998). *Persuasion: Reception and responsibility* (8th ed.). Belmont, CA: Wadsworth.

Lea, Martin, & Spears, Russell. (1995). Love at first byte? Building personal relationships over computer networks. In Julia T. Wood, & Steve Duck (Eds.), *Under-studied relationships: Off the beaten track* (pp. 197–233). Thousand Oaks, CA: Sage.

Leaper, Campbell, Carson, Mary, Baker, Carilyn, Holliday, Heithre, et al. (1995). Self-disclosure and listener verbal support in same-gender and cross-gender friends' conversations. *Sex Roles, 33,* 387–404.

Leaper, Campbell, & Holliday, Heithre. (1995, September). Gossip in same-gender and cross-gender friends' conversations. *Personal Relationships, 2,* 237–246.

Leathers, Dale G. (1997). *Successful nonverbal communication: Principles and applications* (2nd ed.). New York: Macmillan.

Lee, Fiona. (1993, July). Being polite and keeping Mum: How bad news is communicated in organizational hierarchies. *Journal of Applied Social Psychology, 23,* 1124–1149.

Lee, John Alan. (1976). *The colors of love.* New York: Bantam.

Leon, Joseph J., Philbrick, Joseph L., Parra, Fernando, Escobedo, Emma, et al. (1994, February). Love styles among university students in Mexico. *Psychological Reports, 74,* 307–310.

Leung, Kwok. (1988, March). Some determinants of conflict avoidance. *Journal of Cross-Cultural Psychology, 19,* 125–136.

Lever, Janet. (1995, August 22). The 1995 advocate survey of sexuality and relationships: The women, lesbian sex survey. *The Advocate, 687/688,* 22–30.

LeVine, R., & Bartlett, K. (1984). Pace of life, punctuality, and coronary heart disease in six countries. *Journal of Cross-Cultural Psychology, 15,* 233–255.

Lewin, Catharina, & Herlitz, Agneta (2002). Sex differences in face recognition—women's faces make the difference. *Brain & Cognition, 50,* 121–128.

Lewis, David. (1989). *The secret language of success.* New York: Carroll & Graf.

Lindeman, Marjaana, Harakka, Tuija, & Keltikangas-Jarvinen, Liisa. (1997, June). Age and gender differences in adolescents' reactions to conflict situations: Aggression, prosociality, and withdrawal. *Journal of Youth and Adolescence, 26,* 339–351.

Lister, Larry. (1991, June). Men and grief: A review of research. *Smith College Studies in Social Work, 61,* 220–235.

Lustig, Myron W., & Koester, Jolene. (1999). *Intercultural competence: Interpersonal communication across cultures* (3rd ed.). New York: HarperCollins.

Ma, Karen. (1996). *The modern Madame Butterfly: Fantasy and reality in Japanese cross-cultural relationships.* Rutland, VT: Charles E. Tuttle.

Ma, Ringo. (1992, Summer). The role of unofficial intermediaries in interpersonal conflicts in the Chinese culture. *Communication Quarterly, 40,* 269–278.

Macgeorge, Erina L., Gillihan, Seth J., Samter, Wendy, & Clark, Ruth Anne (2003). Skill deficit or differential motivation? Testing alternative explanations for gender differences in providing emotional support. *Communication Research, 3,* 272–303.

MacLachlan, James. (1979). What people really think of fast talkers. *Psychology Today, 13,* 113–117.

Maggio, Rosalie. (1997). *Talking about people: A guide to fair and accurate language.* Phoenix, AZ: Oryx Press.

Malandro, Loretta A., Barker, Larry, & Barker, Deborah Ann. (1989). *Nonverbal communication* (2nd ed.). New York: Random House.

Manes, Joan, & Wolfson, Nessa. (1981). The compliment formula. In Florian Coulmas (Ed.), *Conversational routine* (pp. 115–132). The Hague: Mouton.

Manniche, Erik. (1991). Marriage and non-marriage cohabitation in Denmark. *Family Reports, 20,* 9–35.

Mao, LuMing Robert. (1994, May). Beyond politeness theory: "Face" revisited and renewed. *Journal of Pragmatics, 21,* 451–486.

Marshall, Evan. (1983). *Eye language: Understanding the eloquent eye.* New York: New Trend.

Marshall, Linda L., & Rose, Patricia. (1987). Gender, stress and violence in the adult relationships of a sample of college students. *Journal of Social and Personal Relationships, 4,* 299–316.

Martin, Matthew M., & Anderson, Carolyn M. (1995, Spring). Roommate similarity: Are roommates who are similar in their communication traits more satisfied? *Communication Research Reports, 12,* 46–52.

Martin, Matthew M., Anderson, Carolyn M., & Mottet, Timothy P. (1999, May). Perceived understanding and self-disclosure in the stepparent-stepchild relationship. *Journal of Psychology, 133,* 281–290.

Marwell, G., & Schmitt, D. R. (1967). Dimensions of compliance-gaining behavior: An empirical analysis. *Sociometry 39,* 350–364.

Mathews, A., & Mackintosh, B. (2000). Induced emotional interpretation bias and anxiety. *Journal of Abnormal Psychology, 4,* 602.

Matsumoto, David. (1991, Winter). Cultural influences on facial expressions of emotion. *Southern Communication Journal, 56,* 128–137.

Matsumoto, David. (1994). *People: Psychology from a cultural perspective.* Pacific Grove, CA: Brooks/Cole.

Matsumoto, David, & Kudoh, T. (1993). American-Japanese cultural differences in attributions of personality based on smiles. *Journal of Nonverbal Behavior, 17,* 231–243.

McBroom, William H., & Reed, Fred W. (1992, June). Toward a reconceptualization of attitude-behavior consistency. *Social Psychology Quarterly, 55* [Special issue. Theoretical Advances in Social Psychology], 205–216.

McCarthy, Michael J. (1991). *Mastering the information age.* Los Angeles: Jeremy P. Tarcher.

McConatha, Jasmin-Tahmaseb, Lightner, Eileen, & Deaner, Stephanie L. (1994, September). Culture, age, and gender as variables in the expression of emotions. *Journal of Social Behavior and Personality, 9,* 481–488.

McCroskey, James C. (1997). *Introduction to rhetorical communication* (7th ed.). Englewood Cliffs, NJ: Prentice-Hall.

McCroskey, James C. (1998). *Why we communicate the ways we do: A communibiological perspective.* Boston, MA: Allyn & Bacon.

McCroskey, James C., Booth-Butterfield, S., & Payne, S. K. (1989). The impact of communication apprehension on college student retention and success. *Communication Quarterly, 37,* 100–107.

McCroskey, James C., & Wheeless, Lawrence. (1976). *Introduction to human communication.* Boston: Allyn & Bacon.

McGill, Michael E. (1985). *The McGill report on male intimacy.* New York: Harper & Row.

McLaughlin, Margaret L. (1984). *Conversation: How talk is organized.* Newbury Park, CA: Sage.

McLoyd, Vonnie, & Wilson, Leon. (1992, August). Telling them like it is: The role of economic and environmental factors in single mothers' discussions with their children. *American Journal of Community Psychology, 20,* 419–444.

McMahan, Elizabeth, & Day, Susan. (1984). *The writer's rhetoric and handbook* (2nd ed.). New York: McGraw-Hill.

Mendoza, Louis. (1995). *Ethos, ethnicity, and the electronic classroom: A study in contrasting educational environments.* Paper presented at the 46th annual meeting of the Conferences on College Composition and Communication, Washington, DC.

Merton, Robert K. (1957). *Social theory and social structure.* New York: Free Press.

Messick, R. M., & Cook, K. S. (Eds.). (1983). *Equity theory: Psychological and sociological perspectives.* New York: Praeger.

Messmer, Max. (1999, August). Skills for a new millennium: Accounting and financial professionals. *Strategic Finance Magazine,* 10ff.

Metts, Sandra. (1989, May). An exploratory investigation of deception in close relationships. *Journal of Social and Personal Relationships, 6,* 159–179.

Meyer, Janet R. (1994, Spring). Effect of situational features on the likelihood of addressing face needs in requests. *Southern Communication Journal, 59,* 240–254.

Michalko, Michael. (1991). *Thinkertoys: A handbook of business creativity for the 90s.* Berkeley, CA: Ten Speed Press.

Midooka, Kiyoski. (1990, October). Characteristics of Japanese-style communication. *Media Culture and Society, 12,* 47–489.

Miller, Gerald R., & Parks, Malcolm R. (1982). Communication in dissolving relationships. In Steve Duck (Ed.), *Personal relationships: Vol. 4. Dissolving personal relationships* (pp. 127–154). New York: Academic Press.

Miller, LaRonda R. (1997, December). Better ways to think and communicate. *Association Management, 49,* 71–73.

Miller, Mark J., & Wilcox, Charles T. (1986). Measuring perceived hassles and uplifts among the elderly. *Journal of Human Behavior and Learning, 3,* 38–46.

Miller, Sally Downham. (1999). *Mourning and dancing: A memoir of grief and recovery.* Deerfield Beach, FL: Health Communications.

Miner, Horace. (1956). Body ritual among the Nacirema. *American Anthropologist, 58,* 503–507.

Mir, Montserrat. (1993). *Direct requests can also be polite.* Paper presented at the annual meeting of the International Conference on Pragmatics and Language Learning, Champaign, IL.

Moghaddam, Fathali M., Taylor, Donald M., & Wright, Stephen C. (1993). *Social psychology in cross-cultural perspective.* New York: W. H. Freeman.

Molloy, John. (1977). *The woman's dress for success book.* Chicago: Follett.

Montagu, Ashley. (1971). *Touching: The human significance of the skin.* New York: Harper & Row.

Moon, Dreama G. (1966, Winter). Concepts of "culture": Implications for intercultural communication research. *Communication Quarterly, 44,* 70–84.

Morris, Desmond. (1977). *Manwatching: A field guide to human behavior.* New York: Abrams.

Morrow, Gregory D., Clark, Eddie M., & Brock, Karla F. (1995, August). Individual and partner love styles: Implications for the quality of romantic involvements. *Journal of Social and Personal Relationships, 12,* 363–387.

Murstein, Bernard I., Merighi, Joseph R., & Vyse, Stuart A. (1991, Spring). Love styles in the United States and France: A cross-cultural comparison. *Journal of Social and Clinical Psychology, 10,* 37–46.

Naifeh, Steven, & Smith, Gregory White. (1984). *Why can't men open up? Overcoming men's fear of intimacy.* New York: Clarkson N. Potter.

Nelson, Adie, & Robinson, Barrie R. (2002). *Gender in Canada.* Toronto: Prentice Hall.

Neugarten, Bernice. (1979). Time, age, and the life cycle. *American Journal of Psychiatry, 136,* 887–894.

Nichols, Michael P. (1995). *The lost art of listening: How learning to listen can improve relationships.* New York: Guilford Press.

Nichols, Ralph. (1961). Do we know how to listen? Practical helps in a modern age. *Communication Education, 10,* 118–124.

Nichols, Ralph, & Stevens, Leonard. (1957). *Are you listening?* New York: McGraw-Hill.

Nickerson, Raymond S. (1987). Why teach thinking? In Joan Boykoff Baron & Robert J. Sternberg (Eds.), *Teaching thinking skills: Theory and practice* (pp. 27–37). New York: W. H. Freeman.

Noble, Barbara Presley. (1994, August 14). The gender wars: Talking peace. *The New York Times,* p. 21.

Noller, Patricia. (1982). Couple communication and marital satisfaction. *Australian Journal of Sex, Marriage, and Family, 3,* 69–75.

Noller, Patricia, & Fitzpatrick, Mary Anne. (1993). *Communication in family relationships.* Englewood Cliffs, NJ: Prentice-Hall.

Nordhaus-Bike, Anne M. (1999, August). Learning to lead. *Hospitals & Health Networks, 73,* 28ff.

Norton, Robert, & Warnick, Barbara. (1976). Assertiveness as a communication construct. *Human Communication Research, 3,* 62–66.

Notarius, Clifford I., & Herrick, Lisa R. (1988). Listener response strategies to a distressed other. *Journal of Social and Personal Relationships, 5,* 97–108.

Oatley, Keith, & Duncan, Elaine. (1994). The experience of emotions in everyday life. *Cognition and Emotion, 8,* 369–381.

Oberg, K. (1960). Cultural shock: Adjustment to new cultural environments. *Practical Anthropology, 7,* 177–182.

O'Hair, D., Cody, M. J., & McLaughlin, M. L. (1981). Prepared lies, spontaneous lies, Machiavellianism, and nonverbal communication. *Human Communication Research, 7,* 325–339.

Olaniran, Bolanle A. (1994, February). Group performance in computer-mediated and face-to-face communication media. *Management Communication Quarterly, 7,* 256–281.

Otaki, Midori, Durrett, Mary Ellen, Richards, Phyllis, Nyquist, Lina, & Pennebaker, James W. (1986). Maternal and infant behavior in Japan and America. *Journal of Cross-Cultural Psychology, 17,* 251–268.

Parker, Rhonda G., & Parrott, Roxanne. (1995). Patterns of self-disclosure across social support networks: Elderly, middle-aged, and young adults. *International Journal of Aging and Human Development, 41,* 281–297.

Patton, Bobby R., Giffin, Kim, & Patton, Eleanor Nyquist. (1989). *Decision-making group interaction* (3rd ed.). New York: HarperCollins.

Pearson, Judy C., West, Richard, & Turner, Lynn H. (1995). *Gender and communication* (3rd ed.). Dubuque, IA: William C. Brown.

Penfield, Joyce (Ed.). (1987). *Women and language in transition.* Albany: State University of New York Press.

Pennebacker, James W. (1991). *Opening up: The healing power of confiding in others.* New York: Avon.

Peterson, Candida C. (1996). The ticking of the social clock: Adults' beliefs about the timing of transition events. *International Journal of Aging and Human Development, 42,* 189–203.

Petrocelli, William, & Repa, Barbara Kate. (1992). *Sexual harassment on the job.* Berkeley, CA: Nolo Press.

Phlegar, Phyllis. (1995). *Love online: A practical guide to digital dating.* Reading, MA: Addison-Wesley.

Pilkington, Neil W., & D'Augelli, Anthony R. (1995, January). Victimization of lesbian, gay, and bisexual youth in community settings. *Journal of Community Psychology, 23,* 34–56.

Piot, Charles D. (1993, June). Secrecy, ambiguity, and the everyday in Kabre culture. *American Anthropologist, 95,* 353–370.

Pittenger, R. E., Hockett, C. F., & Danehy, J. J. (1960). *The first five minutes.* Ithaca, NY: Paul Martineau.

Plant, A., Hyde, J., & Devine, P. (2000). The gender stereotyping of emotions. *Psychology of Women Quarterly, 1,* 81.

Plutchik, Robert. (1980). *Emotion: A psycho-evolutionary synthesis.* New York: Harper & Row.

Porter, R. H., & Moore, J. D. (1981). Human kin recognition by olfactory cues. *Physiology and Behavior, 27,* 493–495.

Proctor, Russell F. (1991). *An exploratory analysis of responses to owned messages in interpersonal communication.* Unpublished doctoral dissertation, Bowling Green State University, Ohio.

Raney, Rebecca Fairley. (2000, May 11). Study finds Internet of social benefit to users. *The New York Times,* p. G7.

Rankin, Paul. (1929). *Listening ability.* Proceedings of the Ohio State Educational Conference's ninth annual session.

Raven, R., Centers, C., & Rodrigues, A. (1975). The bases of conjugal power. In R. E. Cromwell, & D. H. Olson (Eds.), *Power in families* (pp. 217–234). New York: Halsted Press.

Rector, M., & Neiva, E. (1996). Communication and personal relationships in Brazil. In W. B. Gudykunst, S. Ting-Toomey, & T. Nishida (Eds.), *Communication in Personal Relationships Across Cultures* (pp. 156–173). Thousand Oaks, CA: Sage.

Reed, Mark D. (1993, Fall). Sudden death and bereavement outcomes: The impact of resources on grief, symptomatology and detachment. *Suicide and Life-Threatening Behavior, 23,* 204–220.

Reisman, John. (1979). *Anatomy of friendship.* Lexington, MA: Lewis.

Reisman, John M. (1981). Adult friendships. In Steve Duck, & Robin Gilmour (Eds.), *Personal relationships: Vol. 2: Developing personal relationships,* (pp. 205–230). New York: Academic Press.

Renner, M. (1993, May 3). Assert yourself to a more satisfying career. *The Gazetteer,* p. C6.

Rich, Andrea L. (1974). *Interracial communication.* New York: Harper & Row.

Richmond, Virginia P., Davis, L. M., Saylor, K., & McCroskey, J. C. (1984). Power strategies in organizations: Communication techniques and messages. *Human Communication Research, 11,* 85–108.

Richmond, Virginia P., & McCroskey, James C. (1996). *Communication: Apprehension, avoidance, and effectiveness* (4th ed.). Scottsdale, AZ: Gorsuch Scarisbrick.

Riggio, Ronald E. (1987). *The charisma quotient.* New York: Dodd, Mead.

Robbins, Stephen P., & Hunsaker, Phillip L. (2003). *Training in interpersonal skills: Tips for managing people at work* (3rd ed.). New Jersey: Prentice Hall.

Roberts, Carlos A., & Aruguete, Mara S. (2000, February). Task and socioemotional behaviors of physicans: A test of reciprocity and social interaction theories in analogue physican-patient encounters. *Social Science and Medicine, 50,* 309–315.

Roberts, Moss (Ed. and Trans., with the assistance of Tay, C. N.). (1979). *Chinese fairy tales and fantasies.* New York: Pantheon.

Roger, Derek, & Nesshoever, Willfried. (1987, September). Individual differences in dyadic conversational strategies: A further study. *British Journal of Social Psychology, 26,* 247–255.

Rogers, Carl, & Farson, Richard. (1981). Active listening. In Joseph A. DeVito (Ed.), *Communication: Concepts and processes* (3rd ed., pp. 137–147). Englewood Cliffs, NJ: Prentice-Hall.

Rose, Amanda J. & Asher, Steven R. (1999, January). Children's goals and strategies in response to conflicts within a friendship. *Developmental Psychology, 35,* 69–79.

Rosen, Emanuel. (1998, October). Think like a shrink. *Psychology Today,* 54–59.

Rosenfeld, Lawrence. (1979). Self-disclosure avoidance: Why I am afraid to tell you who I am. *Communication Monographs, 46,* 63–74.

Rosenthal, Robert, & Jacobson, L. (1968). *Pygmalion in the classroom.* New York: Holt, Rinehart and Winston.

Rosnow, Ralph L. (1977, Winter). Gossip and marketplace psychology. *Journal of Communication, 27,* 158–163.

Ruben, Brent D. (1985). Human communication and cross-cultural effectiveness. In Larry A. Samovar, & Richard E. Porter (Eds.), *Intercultural communication: A reader* (4th ed., pp. 338–346). Belmont, CA: Wadsworth.

Rubenstein, Carin. (1993, June 10). Fighting sexual harassment in schools. *The New York Times,* p. C8.

Rubenstein, Carin, & Shaver, Philip. (1982). *In search of intimacy.* New York: Delacorte.

Rubin, Donald L., Hanbi, Yang, & Porte, Michael (2000). A comparison of self-reported self-disclosure among Chinese and North Americans. In Sandra Petronio (Ed.), *Balancing the secrets of private disclosures* (pp. 215–234). Mahwah, NJ: Lawrence Erlbaum Associates.

Rubin, Rebecca B., Fernandez-Collado, C., & Hernandez-Sampieri, R. (1992). A cross-cultural examination of interpersonal communication motives in Mexico and the United States. *International Journal of Intercultural Relations, 16*, 145–157.

Rubin, Rebecca B., & Martin, M. M. (1994). Development of a measure of interpersonal communication competence. *Communication Research Reports, 11*, 33–44.

Rubin, Rebecca B., Perse, Elizabeth M., & Barbato, Carole A. (1988). Conceptualization and measurement of interpersonal communication motives. *Human Communication Research, 14*, 602–628.

Rubin, Rebecca B., & Rubin, Alan M. (1992). Antecedents of interpersonal communication motivation. *Communication Quarterly, 40*, 315–317.

Rubin, Zick. (1973). *Liking and loving: An invitation to social psychology*. New York: Holt, Rinehart & Winston.

Rundquist, Suellen. (1992, November). Indirectness: A gender study of flaunting Grice's maxims. *Journal of Pragmatics, 18*, 431–449.

Saboonchi, Fredrik, Lundh, Lars Gunnar, & Oest, Lars Goeran. (1999, September). Perfectionism and self-consciousness in social phobia and panic disorder with agoraphobia. *Behaviour Research and Therapy, 37*, 799–808.

Sadker, Myra Pollac, & Sadker, D. C. (1994). *Failing at fairness: How American schools cheat girls*. New York: Scribner.

Sadr, Javid, Jarudi, Izzat, & Sinha, Pawan (2003). The role of eyebrows in face recognition. *Perception, 32*, 285–293.

Salamensky, S. I. (2001). Dangerous talk: Phenomenology, performativity, cultural crisis. In Author (Ed.), *Talk, talk, talk: The cultural life of everyday conversation* (pp. 16–35). New York: Routledge.

Salekin, Randall T., Ogloff, James R. P., McGarland, Cathy, & Rogers, Richard. (1995, Spring). Influencing jurors' perceptions of guilt: Expression of emotionality during testimony. *Behavioral Sciences and the Law, 13*, 293–305.

Samovar, Larry A., & Porter, Richard E. (Eds.). (1991). *Communication between cultures*. Belmont, CA: Wadsworth.

Sanders, Judith A., Wiseman, Richard L., & Matz, S. Irene. (1991). Uncertainty reduction in acquaintance relationships in Ghana and the United States. In Stella Ting-Toomey & Felipe Korzenny (Eds.), *Cross-cultural interpersonal* (pp. 79–98). Thousand Oaks, CA: Sage.

Sarwer, David B., Kalichman, Seth C., Johnson, Jennifer R., Early, Jamie, et al. (1993, June). Sexual aggression and love styles: An exploratory study. *Archives of Sexual Behavior, 22*, 265–275.

Saunders, Carol S., Robey, Daniel, & Vaverek, Kelly A. (1994, June). The persistence of status differentials in computer conferencing. *Human Communication Research, 20*, 443–472.

Scandura, T. (1992). Mentorship and career mobility: An empirical investigation. *Journal of Organizational Behavior, 13*, 169–174.

Schaap, C., Buunk, B., & Kerkstra, A. (1988). Marital conflict resolution. In Patricia Noller & Mary Anne Fitzpatrick (Eds.), *Perspectives on marital interaction* (pp. 203–244). Philadelphia: Multilingual Matters.

Schachter, Stanley. (1964). The interaction of cognitive and physiological determinants of emotional state. In Leonard Berkowitz (Ed.), *Advances in experimental social psychology* (Vol. 1). New York: Academic Press.

Scheetz, L. Patrick. (1995). *Recruiting trends 1995–1996: A study of 527 businesses, industries, and governmental agencies employing new college graduates*. East Lansing, MI: Collegiate Employment Research Institute, Michigan State University.

Scherer, K. R. (1986). Vocal affect expression. *Psychological Bulletin, 99*, 143–165.

Schmidt, Tracy O., & Cornelius, Randolph R. (1987). Self-disclosure in everyday life. *Journal of Social and Personal Relationships, 4*, 365–373.

Schwartz, Marilyn, & the Task Force on Bias-Free Language of the Association of American University Presses. (1995). *Guidelines for bias-free writing*. Bloomington: Indiana University Press.

Shafer, K. (1993). Talk in the middle: Two conversational skills for friendship. *English Journal, 1*, 53.

Shaffer, David R., Pegalis, Linda J., & Bazzini, Doris G. (1996, May). When boy meets girl (revisited): Gender, gender role orientation, and prospect of future interaction as determinants of self-disclosure among same- and opposite-sex acquaintances. *Personality and Social Psychology Bulletin, 22*, 495–506.

Shuter, Robert. (1990, Spring). The centrality of culture. *Southern Communication Journal, 55*, 237–249.

Siegert, John R., & Stamp, Glen H. (1994, December). "Our first big fight" as a milestone in the development of close relationships. *Communication Monographs, 61*, 345–360.

Signorile, Michelangelo. (1993). *Queer in America: Sex, the media, and the closets of power*. New York: Random House.

Silvia, Paul (2002). Self-awareness and the regulation of emotional intensity. *Self and Identity, 1*, 3–11.

Slade, Margot. (1995, February 19). We forgot to write a headline: But it's not our fault. *The New York Times*, p. 5.

Smyth, J. (2003, June 20). Bullying guidelines to go beyond schoolyard. *National Post*, p. A2.

Snyder, C. R. (1984). Excuses, excuses. *Psychology Today, 18*, 50–55.

Snyder, C. R., Higgins, Raymond L., & Stucky, Rita J. (1983). *Excuses: Masquerades in search of grace*. New York: Wiley.

Sorenson, Paula S., Hawkins, Katherine, & Sorenson, Ritch L. (1995, August). Gender, psychological type and conflict style preferences. *Management Communication Quarterly, 9*, 115–126.

Spangler, Diane L., & Burns, David D. (2000, Winter). Is it true that men are from Mars and women are from Venus? A test of gender differences in dependency and perfectionism. *Journal of Cognitive Psychotherapy, 13*, 339–357.

Spitzberg, Brian H., & Cupach, William R. (1989). *Handbook of interpersonal competence research*. New York: Springer.

Spitzberg, Brian H., & Hecht, Michael L. (1984). A component model of relational competence. *Human Communication Research, 10*, 575–599.

Sprecher, Susan. (1987). The effects of self-disclosure given and received on affection for an intimate partner and stability of the relationship. *Journal of Social and Personal Relationships, 4*, 115–127.

Steil, Lyman K., Barker, Larry L., & Watson, Kittie W. (1983). *Effective listening: Key to your success*. Reading, MA: Addison-Wesley.

Steiner, Claude. (1981). *The other side of power*. New York: Grove.

Steinfatt, Thomas M. (1987). Personality and communication: Classic approaches. In James C. McCroskey & John A. Daly (Eds.), *Personality and interpersonal communication* (pp. 42–126). Thousand Oaks, CA: Sage.

Stephan, Cookie White, & Stephan, Walter G. (1992, Winter). Reducing intercultural anxiety through intercultural contact. *International Journal of Intercultural Relations, 16*, 89–106.

Stephan, W., Stephan, C., & De Vargas, M. (1996). Emotional expression in Costa Rica and the United States. *Journal of Cross-Cultural Psychology, 2*, 147–162.

Stephan, Walter G., & Stephan, Cookie White. (1985). Intergroup anxiety. *Journal of Social Issues, 41*, 157–175.

Sternberg, Robert J. (1987). Questions and answers about the nature and teaching of thinking skills. In Joan Boykoff Baron & Robert J. Sternberg (Eds.), *Teaching thinking skills: Theory and practice* (pp. 251–259). New York: W. H. Freeman.

Strecker, Ivo. (1993). Cultural variations in the concept of "face." *Multilingua, 12*, 119–141.

Szapocznik, Jose. (1995, January). Research on disclosure of HIV status: Cultural evolution finds an ally in science. *Health Psychology, 14*, 4–5.

Tae-Seop, Lim (2002). Language and verbal communication across cultures. In William B. Gudykunst, & Bella Mody (Eds.), *Handbook of international and intercultural communication* (2nd ed., pp. 69–87).

Tannen, Deborah. (1990). *You just don't understand: Women and men in conversation*. New York: Morrow.

Tannen, Deborah. (1994a). *Gender and discourse*. New York: Oxford University Press.

Tannen, Deborah. (1994b). *Talking from 9 to 5*. New York: Morrow.

Tannen, Deborah, & Alatis, James E. (Eds.) (2003). *Language, culture and the real world: Discourse and beyond*. Washington, DC: Georgetown University Press.

Tarnove, Elizabeth J. (1988). *Effects of sexist language on the status and self-concept of women*. Paper presented at the annual meeting of the Association for Education in Journalism and Mass Communication, Portland, OR.

Tate, Marsha, & Allen, Vallerie (2003). Integrating distinctly Canadian elements into television drama: A formula for success or failure? The *Due South* experience. *Canadian Journal of Communication, 28*, 67–83.

Tetley, Deborah, & Seskul, Tony (2003, June 15). Council startled by tale, closed ranks around Dar. *Calgary Herald*.

Ting-Toomey, Stella. (1985). Toward a theory of conflict and culture. *International and Intercultural Communication Annual, 9*, 71–86.

Ting-Toomey, Stella. (1986). Conflict communication styles in black and white subjective cultures. In Young Yun Kim (Ed.), *Interethnic communication: Current research*. (pp. 75–88). Thousand Oaks, CA: Sage.

Titlow, Karen I., Rackoff, Jonathan E., & Emanuel, Ezekiel J. (1999). What will it take to restore patient trust? *Business & Health, 17*, (6A), 61–64.

Torbiorn, I. (1982). *Living abroad*. New York: Wiley.

Trager, George L. (1958). Paralanguage: A first approximation. *Studies in Linguistics, 13*, 1–12.

Trager, George L. (1961). The typology of paralanguage. *Anthropological Linguistics, 3*, 17–21.

Tyler, Patrick E. (1996, July 11). Crime (and punishment) rages anew in China. *The New York Times*, pp. A1, A8.

Tzanne, Angeliki (2000). *Talking at cross-purposes*. Philadelphia: John Benjamins Publishing Company.

VanHyning, Memory. (1993). *Crossed signals: How to say no to sexual harassment*. Los Angeles: Infotrends Press.

Veenendall, Thomas L., & Feinstein, Marjorie C. (1995). *Let's talk about relationships: Cases in study*, (2nd ed.). Prospect Heights, IL: Waveland Press.

Victor, David. (1992). *International business communication*. New York: HarperCollins.

Victor, David A. (2001). A cross-cultural perspective on gender. In Laurie P. Arliss, & Deborah J. Borisoff (Eds.), *Women and men communicating: Challenges and changes* (2nd ed., pp. 65–77). Prospect Heights, Illinois: Waveland Press Inc.

Wade, Carole, & Tavris, Carol. (1998). *Psychology* (5th ed.). New York: Longman.

Wade, Carole, & Tavris, Carol. (1990). *Learning to think critically: The case of close relationships*. New York: HarperCollins.

Walster, E., Walster, G. W., & Berscheid, E. (1978). *Equity: Theory and research*. Boston: Allyn & Bacon.

Watzlawick, Paul. (1977). *How real is real? Confusion, disinformation, communication: An anecdotal introduction to communications theory*. New York: Vintage.

Watzlawick, Paul. (1978). *The Language of change: Elements of therapeutic communication*. New York: Basic Books.

Watzlawick, Paul, Beavin, Janet Helmick, & Jackson, Don D. (1967). *Pragmatics of human communication: A study of interactional patterns, pathologies, and paradoxes*. New York: Norton.

Weinberg, Harry L. (1959). *Levels of knowing and existence*. New York: Harper & Row.

Weiner, Bernard, Russell, Dan, & Lerman, David. (1979). Affective consequences of causal ascriptions. In J. H. Harvey, W. J. Ickes, & R. F. Kidd (Eds.), *New directions in attribution research* (Vol. 2). Hillsdale, NJ: Erlbaum.

Weinstein, Eugene A., & Deutschberger, Paul. (1963). Some dimensions of altercasting. *Sociometry, 26*, 454–466.

Werrbach, Gail B., Grotevant, Harold D., & Cooper, Catherine R. (1990, October). Gender differences in adolescents' identity development in the domain of sex role concepts. *Sex Roles, 23*, 349–362.

West, Candace, & Zimmerman, Don H. (1977, June). Women's place in everyday talk: reflections on parent–child interaction. *Social Problems, 24*, 521–529.

Westwood, R. I., Tang, F. F., & Kirkbride, P. S. (1992, Summer). Chinese conflict behavior: Cultural antecedents and behavioral consequences. *Organizational Development Journal, 10*, 13–19.

Wetzel, Patricia J. (1988). Are "powerless" communication strategies the Japanese norm? *Language in Society, 17*, 555–564.

Whalen-Bell, S. (2003). The strategic power of positive language. *Chartered Accountants Journal of New Zealand, 6*, 69.

Wheeless, Lawrence R., & Grotz, Janis. (1977). The measurement of trust and its relationship to self-disclosure. *Human Communication Research, 3*, 250–257.

Wiederman, Michael W., & Hurd, Catherine. (1999, April). Extradyadic involvement during dating. *Journal of Social and Personal Relationships, 16*, 265–274.

Wilkins, B. M., & Andersen, P. A. (1991). Gender differences and similarities in management communication: A meta-analysis. *Management Communication Quarterly, 5*, 6–35.

Wilmot, William W. (1987). *Dyadic communication* (3rd ed.). New York: Random House.

Winquist, Lynn A., Mohr, Cynthia D., & Kenny, David A. (1998, September). The female positivity effect in the perception of others. *Journal of Research in Personality, 32*, 370–388.

Witcher, S. Karene. (1999, August 9–15). Chief executives in Asia find listening difficult. *Asian Wall Street Journal Weekly, 21*, 11.

Wolfson, Nessa. (1988). The bulge: A theory of speech behaviour and social distance. In J. Fine (Ed.), *Second language discourse: A textbook of current research*. Norwood, NJ: Ablex.

Won-Doornink, Myong-Jin. (1991). Self-disclosure and reciprocity in South Korean and U.S. male dyads. In Stella Ting-Toomey & Felipe Korzenny (Eds.), *Cross-cultural interpersonal communication* (pp. 116–131). Thousand Oaks, CA: Sage.

Wood, Julia T. (1994). *Gendered lives: Communication, gender, and culture*. Belmont, CA: Wadsworth.

Worthington, Deborah, L. (2001). Exploring juror's listening processes: The effect of listening style preference on juror decision making. *International Journal of Listening, 15*, 20–38.

Wright, John W. (1995). *The universal almanac 1995*. Kansas City, MO: Andrews & McMeel.

Wright, Paul H. (1978). Toward a theory of friendship based on a conception of self. *Human Communication Research, 4*, 196–207.

Wright, Paul H. (1984). Self-referent motivation and the intrinsic quality of friendship. *Journal of Social and Personal Relationships, 1*, 115–130.

Wright, Paul H. (1988). Interpreting research on gender differences in friendship: A case for moderation and a plea for caution. *Journal of Social and Personal Relationships, 5*, 367–373.

Wrighter, Carl. (1972). *I can sell you anything*. New York: Ballantine.

Yovetich, Nancy A., & Drigotas, Stephen M. (1999, September). Secret transmission: A relative intimacy hypothesis. *Personality and Social Psychology Bulletin, 25,* 1135–1146.

Yun, Hum. (1976). The Korean personality and treatment considerations. *Social Casework, 57,* 173–178.

Zimmerman, Don H., & West, Candace. (1975). Sex roles, interruptions and silences in conversations. In B. Thorne & N. Henley (Eds.), *Language and sex: Differences and dominance.* Rowley, MA: Newbury House.

Zuckerman, M., Klorman, R., Larrance, D. T., & Spiegel, N. H. (1981). Facial, autonomic, and subjective components of emotion: The facial feedback hypothesis versus the externalizer-internalizer distinction. *Journal of Personality and Social Psychology, 41,* 929–944.

Zunin, Leonard M., & Zunin, Natalie B. (1972). *Contact: The first four minutes.* Los Angeles: Nash.

Zunin, Leonard M., & Zunin, Hilary Stanton. (1991). *The art of condolence: What to write, what to say, what to do at a time of loss.* New York: Harper Perennial.

Photo Credits

1. Mark Richards/Photo Edit.
8. Flash! Light/Stock Boston.
18. Bob Strong/The Image Works.
29. Ilene Perlman/Stock Boston.
32. (left) CP Photo/Fred Chartrand.
32. (right) CP Photo/Jonathan Hayward.
36. Dick Hemingway.
37. © Reuters NewMedia Inc./CORBIS/Magmaphoto.com.
38. Michael Newman/Photo Edit.
43. David Young-Wolff/Photo Edit.
49. Michael Newman/Photo Edit.
55. David Young-Wolff/Photo Edit.
62. Alan Klehr/Stone.
63. (left) CP Photo/Ryan Remiorz.
63. (right) CP Photo/AP Photo/Joe Cavaretta.
66. Michael Newman/Photo Edit.
71. Jeff Greenberg/Photo Edit.
72. Ian Shaw/Stone.
75. Mark Romine/Stone.
84. Bruce Ayres/Stone.
89. David Young-Wolff/Photo Edit.
93. CP Photo/Fred Chartrand.
97. Walter Hodges/Stone.
99. Zigy Kaluzny/Stone.
107. Robert Nickelsberg/Liaison Agency.
109. Michelle D. Birdwell/Photo Edit.
110. Michael Newman/Photo Edit.
115. Photofest.
118. Bob Daemmrich/Stock Boston.
120. © Reuters NewMedia Inc./CORBIS/Magmaphoto.com.
128. Sean Sprague/Stock Boston.
135. Bob Daemmrich/The Image Works.
143. Ann Brown/SuperStock.
147. © Nadia Mackenzie; Elizabeth Whiting & Associates/COR-BIS/Magmaphoto.com.
149. Robert Brenner/Photo Edit.
157. John Moore/The Image Works.
159. © Her Majesty the Queen in Right of Canada. All rights reserved. Source: Let's Talk. 2001. Reproduced with the permission of the Minister of Public Works and Government Services Canada, 2003.

165. Mary Kate Denny /Stone/Getty Images.
167. Dick Hemingway.
174. Al Harvey/The Slide Farm.
177. Steve Jaffee/The Image Works.
183. Paula Lerner/Woodfin Camp & Associates.
188. © John Henley/CORBIS/Magmaphoto.com.
198. Stewart Cohen/Stone/Getty Images.
200. Bill Aron/Photo Edit.
201. Michael Newman/Photo Edit.
211. Photo by Lisa Sakulensky.
225. Walter Hodges/Stone.
232. CP Photo/Paul Chiasson.
233. Michael Newman/Photo Edit.
235. Photo by Peter Thompson/Thompson Sport Images.
238. Robert Brenner/Photo Edit.
239. SIAL Montréal.
244. John Nordell/The Image Works.
249. A. Ramey/Photo Edit.
253. Deborah Davis/Photo Edit.
258. Robert Bremmer/Photo Edit.
263. Mitch Wojnarowicz/The Image Works.
271. James McLoughlin/Stone.
278. Walter Hodges/Stone.
283. Tony Freeman/Photo Edit.
288. Bruce Ayres/Stone.
291. Dorothy Littell Greco/Stock Boston.
301. Owen Franken/Stock Boston.
302. Michael Newman/Photo Edit.
313. AP/World Wide Photos.
315. CP Photo/Tom Hanson.
323. SW Productions/Photodisc.
324. Stephen Simeon Photography/University of Toronto. Reprinted with permission.
332. Everett Collection.
335. Bruce Ayres/Stone.

Index